George Castleden,

Bard of Woburn

Life, Letters and Poems

Edited by

Paul Cox

THE LETERS OF GEORGE CASTLEDEN,
BARD OF WOBURN

Published by Magic Flute Publishing Ltd. 2019
ISBN 978-1-909054-56-1
Copyright © Paul Cox

Magic Flute Publishing Limited

231 Swanwick Lane

Southampton SO31 7GT

www.magicflutepublications.co.uk

A catalogue description of this book is available from the British Library

Contents

List of Illustrations

Cover image: An unidentified gentleman, contemplating his book in Woburn Park, in front of the Abbey. Photographed by W. Daniels, of Tingrith, Woburn. c.1880's.

Foreword

The Duke of Bedford

George Castleden's life in Woburn spanned four of my forebears; John, 6th Duke of Bedford, Francis, the 7th, William, the 8th and Francis, the 9th. He came to work for the Bedford Estates at an early age, and spent his entire career ensuring the records and ledgers of Estate business were accurate and complete. Beyond this, however, he was a loyal supporter of the Russell family, sharing their political affiliations, charitable causes, and support for abolitionism, among other things. He was also an accomplished poet – although the breadth and scope of George's poetry is unusual and sometimes not to modern tastes, but no doubt he had a talent for storytelling through rhyme. It is remarkable that he may receive more of an audience today than he did 140 years ago.

It is always interesting to read of Woburn Abbey's past; not only the major historical events, but the day-to-day activity around the house and gardens. The people that lived and worked on the Estate are fundamentally part of the Woburn story, and it is always wonderful to learn more about life at Woburn through George's work.

I do hope you enjoy reading this well-researched book, as I have done. With George's keen eye for detail and meticulous recording, I think he would have liked it too!

Andrew Bedford.

His Grace The Duke of Bedford
April, 2019

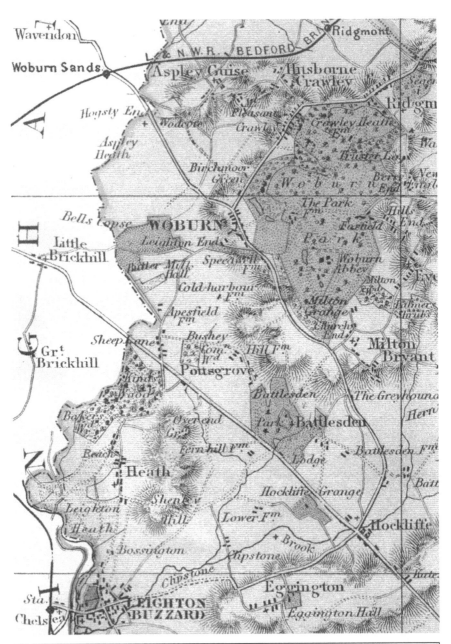

1; *Detail from Bacon's Map of Bedfordshire, c.1901, showing Woburn and Woburn Park, the county border to the west, and the local environs. Hogsty(e) End, Hockliffe, Sheep Lane (Potsgrove), Eggington etc. all marked.*

Introduction

I have been researching the local history of the area around the town of Woburn Sands, near the Bedfordshire and Buckinghamshire border, since 1989. Sometime in the early 1990's, I was browsing the Town Hall Antiques shop in Woburn for local items, and found a little poetry book called "*Woburn Park*". It had been rebound from the original covers, and was a little stained inside, but as I have always had an interest in poetry, and it contained locally-based poems based on the Duke of Bedford's Woburn Park and the local cricket team of the 1840's, it made an interesting addition to my collection. The book was anonymous, but it had been dedicated to the writer's father, Michael Castleden, so it wasn't difficult to discover it was by one George Castleden. As there was no internet available to me then, the next time I was researching at Bedfordshire & Luton Archives and Records Service, (as it was then) I looked him up, but could only find a few dismissive mentions in the Bedfordshire Magazine etc., and so the book was consigned to my shelves. Later, I was fortunate enough to work at the Bedfordshire Archives for year, but still found very little on him.

Now, the internet has become the go-to resource for information, whether local or global. Periodically, I found references to other books by the same author, deposited in the British Library, the major University libraries, or other archives around the country, which I went to see wherever possible. I located two of his other books to purchase, which completed a set of his first trilogy. Yet still, there was scant information available about the author himself.

Then the searchable *British Newspapers Archives* went online, with scanned pages from the unrivalled newspaper collection of the British Library. This provided a treasure trove of articles and information for local and family historians alike, and one day I casually typed in "*Castleden*", expecting to find just a few reviews, but discovered dozens of his letters had been published, mainly in the Northampton Mercury, the Bedford Mercury and the Leighton Buzzard Observer, but also in other provincial newspapers.

However, the scanning process can easily misread and miss-index words, and so even after searching for "*Castledon*", "*Castledan*", "*Castteden*" and countless other misspellings, I decided that the only way to ensure that I had found as many of his letters as possible was to trawl through the Leighton Buzzard Observer newspapers from 1872-1884 in their entirety, transcribing what I found. I also undertook more focussed research on the Bedfordshire Times and Bedfordshire Mercury. Searching for how he generally signed-off his letters, "*Your obedient servant, G. C.*", helped discover more. Sometimes, he had more than one contribution in the same edition, but I am sure there are others still to be found in other publications that I missed, and in those papers not yet available to search.

The letters are mostly from the latter period of his life, after his marriage separation, retirement from the Bedford Estates office, and the commencement of his issuing works of poetry. He was a staunch non-conformist, Liberal, and pacifist, and maintained that a good, free, education for all would be the key to successful future generations of Britons. He returns time and time again to his own impending demise, and the story of his own life. Most interestingly for local historians, he often writes on the local environs of Woburn; the people and buildings, events and tragedies, which create a fascinating glimpse of what Woburn was like in the mid-1800's. He also writes on the local and national political scene, on Britain's wars, and sometimes other international events, and gives us his opinions on the important matters of the day.

He could be repetitive, pompous and somewhat old-fashioned in his language and attitudes, but he was highly principled, loyal and directly honest about the situations that England found itself in, in the middle of the 19$^\text{th}$ century.

A short biography of George Castleden, 'the Bard of Woburn' (a name he adopted for himself after it was used sarcastically by a critic), is followed by chronological transcripts of his letters and poems, exactly as published in the press, interspersed with some background information on the subjects he was writing about. There is also a listing of his published works, and where they may be accessed.

I hope you find it as interesting as I have, to discover what occupied the thoughts and letters of a local scribe of that time.

Paul Cox
May, 2019

George Castleden

A Biography

In the 18th and 19th centuries, Woburn was a bustling, busy market town, on a toll road from London. It was a stopping point for the horses-drawn coach trade, and had shops and services for travellers, as well as being a commercial centre for other nearby villagers. The toll road had opened from Hockliffe to Woburn in 1706, and was the first such road in Bedfordshire. This allowed the appointed trustees to charge a fee for almost all the traffic and travellers who used it, and to use the money so raised to lay a proper surface and keep it in good repair. It was further extended in 1727, through the Hogstye End part of Wavendon, then Broughton, and on to Newport Pagnell. Just north of Woburn, the road went through a ridge of infamously deep sands. Many carriages got stuck, leading to a cartoon by Cruickshank, showing all the passengers dismounted and travelling on foot. Eventually, those treacherous sands provided a more eloquent name for the settlement of Hogstye End, which gradually adopted the name "Woburn Sands", and separated from Wavendon.

In 1836, at the height of the stagecoach era before railways took over, there were 12 regular named services from London passing through Woburn on their way to Leeds, Manchester, Halifax, etc. and another three Royal Mail coach routes through the town. There were also two stage coaches leaving from Woburn itself, one to Bedford and one to Olney. The larger, national coaches usually had four well-to-do passengers inside, and as many as 11 poor souls clinging to the outside, where tickets were cheaper! This would not have been a comfortable trip; the route from London to Leeds took 24 hours to complete. Horses were changed regularly to keep the coach travelling as swiftly (and therefore profitably) as possible, and so it could be turned around to set off again almost as soon as it arrived. A large and commodious inn, known as "The George", was established at Woburn, as well as more than two dozen smaller inns and ale-houses to service the travel-weary. "The George" later became "The Bedford Arms", and is now known as "The Woburn Hotel".

Woburn Abbey itself is just to the south east of the town. Taken from the Cistercian monks in 1547 by Henry VIIIth, (when he decided that being head of his own Church would ease his matrimonial affairs…), it was given to John Russell, the 1st Earl of Bedford, and became the seat of the Russell family and later Dukes of Bedford. It is said the Russell's looked for somewhere safe from the plague sweeping London (and the whole country) around 1665, and so removed from the city to their country seat in rural Woburn, where they have remained ever since.

After the Civil War, and restoration of the British monarchy to the throne in 1660, the Act of Uniformity of 1662 required the Church of England's Book of Common Prayer to be used for all rites and ceremonies by churchmen. However, there were a number of dissenters to that order, for various theological reasons, including Presbyterians, Congregationalists, Baptists and Calvinists who refused to conform to it. Later, other groups, including Methodists, Quakers, the Plymouth Brethren, and the English Moravians were officially labelled as 'Non-conformist' too.

William Croft, who ran a library & bazaar in the High Street, Woburn, wrote in his "Sketch of the Life and Character of the Late John, Duke of Bedford" in 1839, *"The Duke was attached to the Established Church, but extremely tolerant, consequently highly popular, with the Dissenting Body. Clergymen, considered by him deserving, either "orthodox" or "evangelical," were favoured; rather preferring the latter... he held the open opinions...", and* so Woburn became an attractive place to be a non-conformist, as they were openly tolerated, much more so than by some other towns. Whilst attending the regular Woburn Church, the Duke noticed that the other parishioners would not approach the alter-rail until he and his family had received Sacrament and sat back down. He wrote to the clergyman insisting that, at such a time and place, there should be no distinction, and that the townsfolk should join in behind his family. Such liberalism extended to his politics. In the two-party politics of that time, the Russell family were steadfast Whigs, a party who supported non-conformist religions against persecution by the Tory party, who generally supported the Church of England. Thus, Woburn was an ideal place for non-conformist groups to set up and thrive.

As a famous online encyclopaedia succinctly puts it, *"Congregational churches are Protestant churches in the Reformed tradition practicing congregationalist church governance, in which each congregation independently and autonomously runs its own affairs."* This means they have no higher organisation of Diocese or Bishop etc., to report to. The congregation themselves made local decisions of who to admit, and what rules to enforce.

According to the Congregational Church register for Woburn, which survives in the National Archives at Kew, the *"light of the glorious Gospel ... penetrated the dreadful shade and shone light into men's hearts..."* in Woburn in 1781, when Wesleyan ministers from Olney and Newport Pagnell began to visit and preach there every fortnight. By 1789, a private house in West

Street, belonging to Robert Carey, a local surgeon, was being used for worship, with Mr. Samuel Greathead leading services, and Carey eventually became Deacon of the church, and twelve locals banded together to form the first congregation. A Rev. John Croxton also assisted. Whilst at Woburn, Greathead was instrumental in setting up the London Missionary Society and also the Bedford Union of Christians, founded to unify efforts of the various local non-conformist groups. In May 1797, he was offered a post in Kingsland, London, and after spending some months agonising over what he should do, he decided to leave Woburn. After several years without a regular minister, the Woburn Congregationalists were finally able to secure the services of another minister in late 1800, when the Rev. Michael Castleden came to the town.

Michael Castleden was born in King Street, Westminster, in London, in 1769. He was a devoutly religious man, trained at the Hoxton Academy, to which he returned in later life to assist with examinations. He had been preaching at Aylesbury for four years, but word had reached Woburn that he was considering leaving that post, and so they wrote to offer him their vacant position. He agreed, on condition that owing to his health, he would not have to conduct any preaching during the week. The Evangelical Magazine recorded he was officially ordained in "Wooburn, Bedfordshire" [sic] in 1801.

Rev. Michael Castleden had a very successful start to his ministry, and just four years after he arrived, the Woburn Congregationalists were able to cease worshipping in someone's house and erect their own Chapel. This stood in the London End-area of Woburn. His efforts in the neighbourhood also later resulted in new chapels being erected at Hockliffe in 1825, (where they had worshipped in a barn since 1806), at Sheep Lane in Potsgrove in 1839, and at Eggington in 1840, and he was to remain as Congregational Minister at Woburn for the next 40 years. The Woburn Congregationalists Chapel is sometimes referred to as the 'Independent Chapel'. The other chapel nearby, which still stands, was a Methodist Chapel.

The local publisher, Stephen Dodd, issued a guide book 'The Town of Woburn, its Abbey and Vicinity', in 1818, which recorded: *"There is a meeting house in this town which belongs to the Independents."* The Congregational Magazine, of the same year, (obviously slightly more bias in opinion) recorded that it was a *"neat and commodious place of worship, erected in 1804"*. There is also a description in J. D. Parry's 'Woburn and its Abbey' from 1831. By this time, Woburn had grown from 283 houses and 1563 inhabitants in 1801, to 305 houses and 1827 people thirty years later. The Established Church gets several pages of detailed description, yet the Congregationalist Chapel has just a dismissive line under the heading of 'Miscellaneous': *"In Duck Lane is a large and neat Meeting-house for the Dissenters of the Independent persuasion, which also has a Sunday school."* Parry, obviously, was not of the *independent persuasion* himself.

Before coming to Woburn, Michael Castleden had married a Mary Horsley, in Deal, Kent, in October 1797, and soon after arriving here, they had two sons; Samuel, on 4th September, 1801, and then George, on 8th November, 1804, when his wife was 40 years old.

The elder child, Samuel Castleden, grew up and moved to London, where he became a Registrar, although he returned to Woburn to baptise his own sons, Michael John Castleden, in November 1824 and George Tyndale Castleden in September 1826. On both of these occasions, he gave his address as Bencroft Place, Mile End Road, Stepney. There was also a daughter, Mary Horsley Castleden, whom he brought to Woburn for baptising in September 1830, when he gave his address as Limehouse. Sadly, his daughter passed away at just 13 months old, and was buried in the vaults of Brunswick Chapel, Limehouse. The rest of this book will deal with Rev. Michael's younger son, George Castleden, and his writings.

By the age of about 15, George was already working as a trainee clerk in the Duke of Bedford's Estate Office, as in May 1820, a letter between two other employees, Robert Salmon and a Mr. Adam, recorded: *"George Castleden, a boy, has taken the place of the late Butcher, his business being to enter the Farming account copy and examine Bills, Abstracts of Day accounts and assist Mr. Hirdle, for this he will shortly be superior to Butcher, he being ready at Finance and a fair penman."* Later that year, Mr. Salmon left the Park Farm office, and Mr. Hirdle made arrangements for business to continue: *"Mr. Castleden will continue in the same situation, this now full."*

George was not the only member of his family to correspond in the press. The Rev. Michael had several letters printed in the mid 1820's, in the Monthly Magazine, regarding the successful tarmacking of Woburn's roads, and how London should follow suit. (*See Appendix 1*) George was used as a witness on some of the Woburn Congregational Chapel deeds in 1823, when it was enlarged.

According to a Hastings & St. Leonards Observer article on the Congregational history of that town, published in 1887, they had asked the Rev. Castleden to come and take on their chapel in about 1817, but he refused, owing to the ill health of his wife. She eventually died 17th July, 1828, aged 64. Although Rev. Michael completed the Registry Book for her burial in the Chapel grounds himself, her funeral service was conducted by Rev. Bull of Newport Pagnell. Her death occasioned a small reference in the Evangelical Magazine of that year.

All through this time, George continued as a clerk in the Bedford

Estates office, as part of a letter from Mr. Adam to Mr. Crocker at Park Farm, Woburn, in January 1830 shows: *"Mr. Castleden's salary will be £130 a year from 1 January last. Have the goodness therefore to pay him at that rate and to change in your account with the Duke of Bedford."* But George obviously did not consider this to be enough, and wrote requesting a raise, which was flatly refused. Mr. Adam to Mr. Crocker, in February 1830: *"I am sorry I cannot accede to Mr. Castleden's request. Will you have the goodness to let him know that, while I am sensible of his utility, I am aware of the length of his service, but he must recollect the age that service began. 'Tis always to wish to remunerate everybody liberally, but I think he is so. 'Tis not a correct way of setting such a price to refer to other cases... Mr. C. was raised in 1829."*

George was a keen cricketer, playing for the Woburn team in many matches, and seems to have been quite successful as both bowler and batsman, playing on until he was over 40 years old. Cricket had the support of the Duke and his family, and various members of the Russell family even played for the team. There was a fierce rivalry with Aspley Guise, and their contests were keenly fought. A Mr. Fane was another successful Woburn player, although he lived in Aspley Guise. This caused much upset, which spilled over into the local press in August 1834, with an unnamed Aspley player saying they were not prepared to play Woburn again while Mr. Fane played for them! Yet by 1840, the teams seem to have been reconciled and had united to play under the name "Woburn and Aspley".

In December 1834, the Northampton Mercury reported George Castleden's marriage to Fanny Hall, who, at 18-years old, was twelve years his junior, and after they had had just a four-month courtship. Soon after, he was asking for better accommodation from his employers. Part of a letter from Mr. Adam to Mr. Crocker in February, 1836: *"Castleden writes to me to have Mr. Bachelors home rent free or a lower rent and says that I have possession of a note I see for an advance of his salary! I don't know what note he means and I think £140 a year enough. What does he refer to? It was raised in 1829."* ...so he had worked seven years without a raise it would seem.

For four years, Castleden and Fanny lived together, seemingly happy, as man and wife. She worked for the family of the local solicitor, Mr. Green, as a governess. However, when Fanny's parents were visiting Woburn in 1838, she let it slip to them that the marriage had never actually been fully consummated, and it had been ten months after the wedding before she even realised exactly what 'consummation' was. Horrified, her parents immediately challenged Castleden about this state of affairs. Castleden abruptly left the house and then wrote to say that he and Fanny should never meet again, and she should leave his house immediately. Heartbroken, I imagine, she went to live in Holloway with her parents, although she

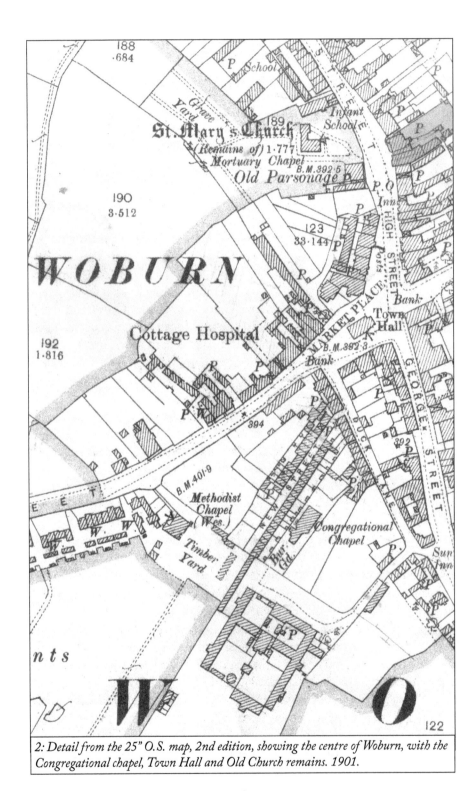

2: *Detail from the 25" O.S. map, 2nd edition, showing the centre of Woburn, with the Congregational chapel, Town Hall and Old Church remains. 1901.*

made at least one attempt to return to Castleden, but his father intervened and sent her back to London, promising he would try to get his son to transfer his employment to the Dukes' offices in London, so he could join her there, and thereby avoid any unnecessary scandal in Woburn, but it never happened.

Now living alone again, Castleden asked for another rise from the Estate Office, but it came with extra responsibilities. Part of a letter from Mr. Heady to Mr. Bennett in October, 1839: *"I have considered the applications made by Mr. Castleden & Price for an increase of salary on the grounds of length of service. £20 a year may be added to Mr. Castleden's salary, and it may be considered as having commenced from Christmas last, when his application was made. But it must be a condition that he is to take upon himself such parts of the work of the Park Farm office, as, on rearranging the work of keeping the accounts &c. you shall think it proper to allot to him."*

It was at this time that he started publishing his poetry, with his first book, "Woburn Park", which was moderately successful enough to encourage him to issue further books. It was dedicated to his well-respected father, the Rev. Michael Castleden, who had recently caught a chill from preaching in damp clothes at the Sheep Lane chapel. Extra help was sought to assist him in his duties at Woburn and Rev. James Spong came to their aid, but he did not wish to stay permanently as a co-pastor, so Rev. Castleden eventually resigned his position on 1st January, 1841, although he continued to preach at other local Congregational chapels.

By happy coincidence, later the same year as his book on Woburn Park was published, Queen Victoria and Prince Albert visited Woburn Abbey, to stay with the Duke of Bedford. The Duchess of Bedford had been a "Lady of the Bedchamber" for Victoria, a trusted personal servant, and they had become close friends. Although the stay was for just three days, the Woburn townsfolk celebrated day and night, with festivities, fireworks, feasts and 'rustic sports'. After dinner on the first night of her stay, a choir from the town paraded to the Abbey and sang to her from below the dining room window at the Abbey. The tune was 'God Save the Queen', but it had been specially rewritten with additional lyrics by Castleden, which were published afterwards in many newspapers. We are fortunate that a first-hand account of the dinner at the Abbey survives, in a letter by Lucy How, writing to a relative a week later. It was reprinted in "The Journal of the Friends Historical Society" in 1914:

"There were to be 26 of the party - it was a long table oval at each end - from nearly one end of the table to the other stood a magnificent plateau of silver, most richly chased, on which stood vases of alabaster filled with the most exquisite artificial flowers, between which were interspersed figures of

the Graces & Heroes, animals, etc all in alabaster – with small lamps of a most delicate description throwing a pale light over the whole. This plateau occupied so much of the table that only room enough was left round the sides for the plates, glasses &c to stand with one dish at each end. All the plates, dishes and covers were that night of silver – the evening previous everything was gold – thou mayest form some idea of the quantity when I tell thee that it occupied the waiters two hours & a half to carry the plate for dinner from the butler's pantry to the dining room – and when I saw the room all this was arranged on side tables. There were a great many splendid massive salvers placed round the room, I suppose chiefly for show. Altogether it was far too gorgeous for description. As it was near 8 o'clk we went down to the hall to be out of the way, and when the clock struck, the Band played "God save the Queen" and the party immediately entered the dining room.

When the first course was removing we were allowed to go up, and by standing in the adjoining room we could peep thro' without being perceived. The Queen & Prince sat at the centre of the table on the right hand side, the Duke of Bedford on the left of the Queen and the Duchess by the Prince. The Duke of Wellington exactly opposite the Queen. Many others we could easily distinguish. The Queen was the most simply attired of all the ladies, she wore a black satin dress made very plain – nothing over her shoulders, and round her neck a plain black necklace united by a small black heart– her hair combed quite straight and a wreath of small white roses round her head; she looked very sweet – tho' she is certainly a very plain person. The Prince looked really beautiful I think I never saw a young man look so interesting and handsome…

…After we had staid as long as we thought prudent we were allowed to see the dessert all ready to be carried up. It was most beautiful, everything, plates, dishes, &c, rich cut glass. The dishes contained pine apples, grapes, melons, peaches, nectarines, preserved fruits and many things we could not tell anything about. There were sweetmeats of the most fantastic description – standing a foot high, of divers colours and as thin as bonnet wire but quite stiff and indeed more like wire than anything else; the fruit knives & forks of gold with jasper handles of the most exquisite beauty. I certainly never imagined anything could be so splendid as the whole set out was, it is quite beyond my power of description…"

It was a great honour for him to have his work performed in front of Her Majesty, and became a fond memory he returned to in his letters time and time again.

The 1841 census shows that Castleden was living with a 25-year-old servant, Eliza Cockerill, for company. Court papers from 1860 describe him as leaving the employ of the Duke of Bedford in 1842. I doubt he thought he could make a living from his poetry. He is described in the censuses as "Annuitant" or "Pensioner and Fund Holder", so a reasonable income must have been coming from somewhere. It seems he was in the habit of writing in to the Estate Office, asking his ex-employer for various pieces of equipment, as a letter in December, 1841, from Mr. Bennett to Mr. Heady, shows: *"Dear Sir, I am not the least surprised at Castleden's application, from my knowledge & experience of him; nothing just now appears too heavy or too light for his wants, he has not yet asked for the stool he has sat on, and the inkstand he has dipped his pen in, for so many years but I expect that he will. He is the best beggar I ever met with, and he has so many tender reminiscences (poetical no doubt) of certain things which he finds it hard to part from, however your negative may probably stop any further requests here. I suppose the origin of his being the pay clerk was as he states, but I thought he considered it a high honour, and I did not like to ask him to give it up lest I offended him...."* Thus his poetical effusions were well known to his former employers. I wonder if any of his office time had been spent writing poetry at his desk when he should have been attending to the Woburn Park accounts? Perhaps he had even regaled them with his *"Farewell – To an old Office Desk"* from his poetry book "Retribution", which had been issued the previous year.

Against the Rev. Castleden's 40-year tenure at the chapel, the Rev. Spong lasted just 2½ years before resigning, so the Woburn Congregationalists had recruited the Rev. James Andrews in 1844. Although retired since 1845, the Rev. Michael Castleden still took a very active part in the local Congregationalism, visiting the local chapels he had helped to build up. His Temperance beliefs too, were not neglected. He was well connected to the Woburn Sands and Aspley Guise Total Abstinence Society, and spoke at the National Temperance Society Annual Meeting in 1847, and in the same year, was quoted in The Teetotallers Companion: *"Never at 77 did man enjoy so good health and spirits at that age, as I do at this moment; and all this I attribute to aqua pura, and to aqua pura alone. Thank God, from my youth up, I have been a temperance man; but thought, as thousands do, that ale and wine were necessary for labor and toil, and so took them. Then, when I rose on the Monday morning, weariness was my companion, with restless nights. Now, after three services on the Lord's day, I rest well, rise refreshed, and am cheerful all the day. Sadly, sadly mistaken have we all been on the necessity of stimulating drinks! How singular it is that man is the only animal that seeks them; and hence man by them lives not out half his days, and that half by their use rendered miserable."*

Despite this teetotalism, cheerfulness and 'rising refreshed' with his predilection for pure water, the Rev. Michael Castleden passed away the next year, in 1848. He was on a visit to his other son, Samuel, at Cottage Grove, in London's Mile End. His passing was reported in the

Congregational Year Book, which noted he had preached at Canterbury the weekend before. He died at midnight, and was heard to cry out, "*Behold the Bridegroom cometh!*" and "*Oh, I am dying, this is death!*". His last words were "*The Lord have mercy on my soul*", and he passed away. He had been due to preach at Coverdale Chapel, Limehouse, later that day. An inquest was held at the Plough Inn, Stepney, as he had been in good health until that day, and the coroner recorded the death as due to a diseased heart. His body was brought back to Woburn, for burial at the Chapel, beside the body of his late wife. Their grave inscription ran:

> "*Beneath rest the remains of Mrs. Mary Castleden, who departed this life the 17th of July, 1828, aged 64 years. "Kind designs to serve and please, Through all her actions ran." Also of the Rev. Michael Castleden, forty years minister of the adjoining chapel who departed this life the 5th day of November, 1848, aged 79 years. "He, being dead, yet speaketh."*.

Lord C. J. F. Russell asked that he be allowed to lead the procession to the grave, and was accompanied by Rev. J. Andrews, and Rev. Henry Hutton. Many other ecclesiastical men then followed, with the deacons of the church coming next. There were many mourners, so much so that "*... but for the services of the police, the chapel and grounds would have been most inconveniently thronged.*" The Duke of Bedford and Lord and Lady Charles Russell were also among the subscribers to his memorial plaque, which was erected inside the Woburn Congregational chapel. Rev. James Andrews went on to serve as pastor at Woburn for 52 years, meaning three ministers had run the Woburn chapel for almost 96 years between them.

In his will, the Rev. Castleden divided all his cash at the bank equally between his two sons, but to George, he also gave the whole of his freehold property, consisting of two cottages with land in Ridgmont, along with all his "*household furniture, plate & cork, watches, wearing apparel, linen, boots and effects found in the house at the time of my death for his sole use and benefit absolutely*". Both sons were named as executors.

George Castleden's second trilogy of books, "Lays of Home" (issued 1850-51), were further volumes of poetry on Woburn, the Abbey grounds and the environs. The first of these looked at the declining coach trade and therefore dwindling numbers of coaching inns in Woburn, the second on Woburn tradesmen and the town market, and the third on the Woburn churchyard. In the 1850 *Slater's Royal, National and Commercial Directory of Bedfordshire*, George was listed under 'Nobility, Gentry and Clergy', a step up from the general tradesmen, and living in George Street. At the census of 1851, he was living with a different servant, Lucy Sear, who was 59. He was also very fond of his '*fine cat*', which he asked one of the Bedford Estates employees to sketch for him!

No doubt inspired by the 1851 British Exhibition, the town of Woburn decided to stage their own version of the Great Exhibition. From the Northampton Mercury, 3rd September, 1853:

"EXHIBITION - WOBURN, BEDS. An Exhibition of Models of Machinery, Objects of Natural History, Mineralogical and Geological Specimens, Paintings, Engravings, Photographes, Natural and Artificial Curiosities &c. &c. &c., kindly lent for the occasion by the Society of the Arts and the Nobility, Gentry and Clergy of this and neighbouring counties, will be opened in the Town Hall, Woburn, on Wednesday, the 14th of September, 1853, and following days under the immediate patronage of Her Grace the Duchess of Bedford and Lady C. J. F. Russell. Further particulars will be given in future advertisements. The Exhibition Catalogue will be a valuable medium for local advertisements, which may be sent to Messrs. Dodd and Peeling, Woburn, not later than the 8th inst."

…and Northampton Mercury again, from 24th September:

"Woburn Exhibition - The Committee beg to announce that, at the earliest solicitation of many friends, they have decided to keep the exhibition open until Tuesday the 4th of October, and His Grace the Duke of Bedford has been kindly pleased to continue the privilege of visiting the Sculpture Gallery to the same time. National and other Parochial Schools admitted to the Exhibition, from four to six in the afternoon, at 1½d. each, on giving notice to the Secretary the previous day."

The exhibition was a great success. Some 8000 visitors raised £170. A static electricity generator was exhibited, which young ladies were encouraged to touch. Apparently, the electric jolt it inflicted made some of them jump back in alarm, exclaiming *"It bites!"*.

Sadly, the copy of the official exhibition catalogue, which had been lodged at the British Library, was lost in the bombing in the Second World War, but Castleden wrote and published his own work about this Exhibition in 1854. The Bedfordshire Mercury: *"Just Published, Price 6d., Dedicated, by permission to Her Grace the Duchess of Bedford, and the Right Honourable Lady Charles Russell; a Memorial of THE WOBURN EXHIBITION, by George Castleden. Dodd and Peeling, Booksellers, &c., Bedford Street."*

Thanks to the descriptions in his book, we know that among the many wonders on show from around the world were the barrow and spade used by the Duchess of Bedford in turning the first soil for the new Bedford to Bletchley Railway line in 1846, which passed through nearby Woburn Sands. Of this, Castleden wrote: *"We imagined the incredulous stare of some of our "market-house ancients" if, standing at our elbow, we had called their spectacled orbs to this barrow and spade and said The Duchess of Bedford had used them in the formation of a London Road to which we are obliged to go down to "Hogstyend!", that this road is made of iron, that passengers wide awake, travel upon sleepers, and are whisked by steam to London in as short a time as in slow days and dark hours, it took, with breakfast and the encasement of overalls, top coat and kerchief to prepare for the same important journey by The Wellingboro Bold, Northampton Light or Heavy Leeds."*

After more than 25 years apart, Castleden's estranged wife, Fanny, got back in contact in 1854. She had become unwell and unable to work, and so wanted Castleden to pay for her medicines. An arrangement was made for him to give her £80 per year, which he continued to do for the next four years, after which his solicitor sent her a letter stating that in consequence of his own reduced income, he could no longer afford the arrangement and would only send her £45 a year from now on. Although several local people, who knew her and her family well, beseeched him to take her back, Castleden *"...expressed a distaste for the revival of the scandal which would arise in so small a place as Woburn."* After much failed negotiation, by 1858, she felt she had no alternative but to petition for a decree to nullify the marriage, claiming "frigidity, impotency, or malformation," and citing that they had never consummated the marriage. Whether this was to obtain a lump sum of his assets, or just shame him into paying her medical expenses, I do not know, but Castleden did not respond to the petition. The case made it into the columns of The Times in 1859, after the solicitor acting for Fanny asked that their case be heard in private. The judges decided there were no grounds to hear it under such conditions, and said they did not have the power to hear it thus anyway. Nevertheless, the Court was then cleared of ladies and children, although the evidence was not actually presented due to a procedural error in the case papers.

When the case was eventually heard, even the evidence from Castleden's meeting with Fanny's solicitor seemed to condemn him, as Mr. Ford recollected he had said to Castleden some years before, *"You ought to assist your wife, because you have inflicted on her the greatest injury a man can on a woman; you know you ought never to have married her"*. Ford said that Castleden had not denied this, and in fact, did not say much at all, *"...but his demeanour was mournful and shamefaced."* Castleden had only met with Fanny twice after she left Woburn, once when she returned to attempt a reconciliation with him, and once when he had to sign some papers, as her husband, in order for her to claim an inheritance she was due in about 1844. Mr. Green, the Woburn solicitor for whom Fanny had worked, was called as a witness, and told how he had met Castleden after their marriage break-up, and as Fanny was employed looking after his children, he had asked

12

Castleden on what grounds she had left him? Green said Castleden had *"...stated two or three absurd, frivolous things that he charged her with."* Green said these reasons were absurd and tried to get Castleden to take her back, suggesting that any difficulty might be removed, to which Castleden had answered, *"Oh no! It is impossible."*

After much legal argument, and opinions of various Doctors, who had examined both parties over the years, eventually the bench decided her case would not be allowed. The judges commented on the fact that it had taken her 20 years to bring the action after leaving him, and that in the meantime, she had expected him to pay the debts she had incurred. Fanny took her case to appeal, but the case was finally refused in 1860, without Castleden having ever personally appeared in court to give any evidence whatsoever. A copy of the court proceedings has found its way to the U.S. Supreme Court Library, in Washington.

From the mid-1840's, Castleden had begun writing regularly to the Northampton Mercury. He submitted letters on local, national or international themes and the debates of the day. Religion, politics, the wars that Britain was involved in, or even the death of local tradesmen he had known for years were all covered. In the early 1850's, he switched to the Bedford Mercury, and poems were added to his submissions. In the spring of 1867, something happened to stop his writing to the Mercury, and I can find no submissions to any papers between April 1867 and September 1869. A prolonged bout of illness perhaps, as he was now in his 60's? Then they restart, and after a few submissions to the Bedfordshire Times, from 1872, he settled on the Leighton Buzzard Observer to receive his regular missives. Scattered throughout these are a few letters and poems in other local papers, as far away as Hertford, Cambridge, and even Chelmsford.

In 1855, seven years after his father's death, he submitted a *"Biographical Notice of the Late Rev. Michael Castleden, Woburn, Beds."* to the Evangelical Magazine and Missionary Chronicle, in which he details some of the history of the Chapel at Woburn, which had been rebuilt in 1854.

The 1861 census showed him as a 56-year old *"Pensioner and Fundholder"*, still with Lucy Sear, who was now 69, as his servant. Ten more years of poetry books and newspaper letters filled a decade of his time until the census of 1871, where he is described as an *"Annuitant"*, with Lucy Sear, now 79 years old and still looking after him! She had also been one of the witnesses to his fathers will.

Despite his advancing age, his letters to the local papers actually began to increase in frequency. Many local events are commented on, such as the opening of the John Bunyan statue in Bedford in 1874, the storm which felled some of the great trees in Woburn Park in 1879, and many letters

WOBURN ABBEY,
Bedfordshire.

3: *Woburn Abbey, from an 1801 print by J. Britton and J. Powell, as published in The Beauties of England & Wales.*
4: *Woburn Abbey, from an 1802 print by Nash & Angus, also as published in The Beauties of England & Wales.*

WOBURN ABBEY.
Bedfordshire.

about the local school system. In August 1875, he wrote a poem suggesting that, as the power of electricity had now been harnessed for use in the telegraph, and steam harnessed for engines, perhaps the sun's rays should be caught and bottled too, so that they could be released during the winter. He followed the poem with a mock prospectus for investing in the "Woburn Solar Rays Bottling Company". He faced some ridicule afterwards, but pointed out that the sun's rays could be used in warming houses and lighting dark streets. Thus it appears he was way ahead of his time in thinking about the possibilities of solar energy.

He got into several protracted arguments with other local writers through the newspaper letter pages, most notably with Mr. Edward Franklin of Eversholt, with whom he crossed literary swords on many occasions. A couple of times, the newspaper editor even had to bring a long running argument to a close with a note of *"No further correspondence on this subject"*, yet at least once it appears that they simply adopted nicknames and continued.

The Bedfordshire Mercury of 1st February 1873, reported that his brother, Samuel Castleden, had died aged 71, on 23rd January, at 4 Bancroft Road, Mile End. London. Samuel had worked as the registrar of Mile End for 35 years. His son, Michael John Castleden, followed in his father's footsteps and worked in the General Register Office at Somerset House.

From 1875, George Castleden assisted with the blossoming relationship between the town of Woburn and their namesake in Massachusetts, America. In 1879, Edward Francis Johnson came from Woburn, Mass. to visit Europe, and had just one free day on which to visit Woburn, Bedfordshire. Thus, on 26th September. Johnson and his companion, William B. Doyle, amused themselves by telling the "barge driver" who took them from Woburn Sands station to Woburn, that they were both natives of "Woburn", which very much confused the poor man. They were very impressed by the local countryside and the Park grounds, but less impressed by the Duke's *"... silk and satined lackeys"*. They were shown around the town and Abbey by Castleden, and Johnson wrote up his experiences once back in America. He noted, *"Mr. George Castleden, in addition to frequent contributions to the newspapers, was the author of a large number of tracts and small pamphlets, several of which he gave to me as souvenirs of my visit. His composition is peculiar and, for want of clearness, very difficult to appreciate. Being a man at that time 75 years of age, his thoughts seemed to dwell somewhat on the glories of the past as compared to the degeneracy of the present age. Seeing a bicycle go by, he said to me in all seriousness: "I don't believe in those things. If I had my way, they would not be allowed on our streets."*

Johnson went on to become the first Mayor of Woburn, Mass., and in

1889 gave a lecture to the Rumford Historical Society about his visit to Woburn a decade before. His one day-long trip and meeting with Castleden had had quite a profound effect on his attitude to the English as a whole, *"Previous to my visit to Woburn, my impressions of the English were not of the best. The supercilious and almost sneering tone in which they are prone to speak of America, and Americans, had disgusted me; and the ignorance they display when talking of our country and its institutions, is sufficient to stir up the blood of even the most phlegmatic. But I left Woburn feeling that I had grievously misjudged our cousins over the water and that I had either been unfortunate in my previous acquaintances, or had too hastily formed my opinion of certain English traits of character. We left the country very shortly after our Woburn visit, so that it is not strange that my present recollection of England and its peoples are of the pleasantest; and I'm sure they will always remain so whenever I call to mind the incidents of the day..."*

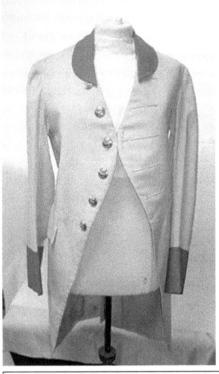

5: *An undated example of a Woburn Abbey servant's livery. Material unknown, but possibly "silk and satin"...!*

Castleden contributed a small verse to a handwritten notebook on bellringing, compiled by Charles Herbert of Woburn in 1878, now stored at Bedfordshire Archives & Records Service. It appears Castleden had been a bell-ringer in his youth:

"This Book if seen in times of yore
Had suited me, perchance, much more
When RCS, JP, GC
Were Frater ringers, one, two, three."

Lucy Sear, Castleden's long-serving domestic servant, died in Solihull in 1878, and the 1881 Census records Castleden living at 10 George Street, Woburn, now with Mary Reynolds, aged 30, as a servant. In 1882, he was one of the local gentry who signed a Memorial Scroll presented by the inhabitants of Woburn, Aspley Guise, Woburn Sands, Wavendon and

Husborne Crawley to Major General Drury Curson Drury Lowe, C.B., Commander of the Cavalry Division of the Expeditionary Force, to offer their "*…most cordial and respectful congratulations on your return from active service in Egypt.*", on his return, as the Major lived nearby in Aspley Guise.

Castleden's letters and poems to the Leighton Buzzard Observer continued very frequently, sometimes two or even three in a single edition, on many topics. This reached a peak in 1881, with no less than 50 letters and poems appearing, either from him or about him, and then 42 more in 1882. In July 1883, his last correspondence appeared, on the continuing problems in Ireland. Yet he continued to write, and published another small collection of poetry in the spring of 1884. After a more than a year's silence in the press, it was reported that he had passed away on 1st September, 1884, aged 79. His nephew, Michael John Castleden, was present at time of death, presumably called to his dying uncle's bedside, and acted as informant for the death certificate. Castleden's occupation is given as "Gentleman" and cause of death as "*Morbus Cordis*", a catch-all phrase used at the time for heart disease and death by natural causes when the exact cause was not evident, just as his father's death had been before him. He was buried in the small graveyard at the Woburn Congregational Chapel that he had known and loved.

As well as his nephew and a few distant relatives, Lord Charles Russell and Mr. George Russell, M.P., and the principle tradesmen of Woburn attended his funeral, a sign of the high esteem in which he was held. The household of the Duke was also well represented, with current and former members of the staff from the Abbey and gardens. His obituary recalls he was "*an inveterate cricketer*" in early life, playing alongside Lord Charles Russell, and that "*…he was the author of many little volumes of local poetry*".

Given his verbose letter-writing, his Last Will and Testament was unusually succinct:

"George Castleden. My Last Will and Testament made this 13th day of December 1879. I leave to Fanny Castleden now living near Liverpool one hundred pounds to be paid to her alone in quarterly payments of £5 till the £100 is exhausted. Michael John Castleden my nephew I appoint my sole executor. To him I leave my freehold at Ridgmont Beds. Let him realize my personally, pay my few just debts and the remainder to my funded property and then for five years receive the interest then equally divide the principle among his four now children. And may God bless to each this residue small but honest of our long Woburn residence Amen. George Castleden. Signed and declared by the Testator George Castleden in the presence of us together present at the same time, who in his presence at his request and in the presence of each other have hereunto subscribed our names as witnesses - W. H. Smith,

Clerk to Guardians, Woburn, Beds. – J. F. Smith, Woburn, Beds."

All that remained of his worldly goods, including his library of 800 books, his pianoforte, and *"a miscellaneous assortment of useful and curious items..."* were sold by auction, and the whole of his estate was valued at £1230 17s. 3d.

The four freehold cottages in Ridgmont had been bought by the Rev. Michael Castleden in 1826. and he supplied one to George, who had inherited the rest on his father's death. This arrangement had given George not only an income, but as a freeholder, also an all-important right to vote. They stood in Ridgmont between Church Street and where Mount Pleasant now is, on the south side of the High Street, and were obtaining £14 6s. annually in rent. George's nephew Michael (by now of 1 Campden Villas, Marlborough Road, Ealing) offered them to the Duke of Bedford in 1887, as he knew it was his uncle's wish for the Duke to have first refusal, as the ducal estate surrounded the cottages. The Duke agreed, and purchased them for £200, although his agent wrote on the correspondence that the four low-roofed cottages would be better suited if knocked into two houses.

The £100 left to Fanny by her husband would equate to about £10,000 now. However, the fact that it was only to be given £5 (£500 now) three-monthly instalments seems particularly harsh, as all the blame for their failed marriage seems to be squarely George's shoulders. She moved around quite a bit after their separation in 1838. In 1851, aged 36, she was in a house in Westminster, and described as a *Matron of the Servants Royal Provident & Benevolent Society.* I cannot locate her in the 1861, but by the 1871 census, she had moved to Birkenhead, where she worked as a *Guardian and Teacher* and lived at no.2 Alfred Road. By 1881, she was a housekeeper at a school in West End Park, Knaresborough. It appears she had retired by the 1891 census, aged 76. She was back in Birkenhead, now at 7 Alvanley Place, described as a Widow, with no profession given. She eventually died on 14th March, 1899, aged 85, by which time she had moved again, to 17 Mount Pleasant Road, Lewisham.

The Chapel at Sheep Lane, Potsgrove, had become disused by this time, and was sold to a local business man for £20 to be used as a warehouse, with receipts said to have gone into a restoration fund for the Woburn Chapel.

As for the Woburn Congregational Chapel in London End, Sarah Ann Castleden, the third wife of George's brother Samuel, who was buried there in 1896. It underwent another renovation in 1898, when the vestry was enlarged, the pews replaced, and the organ moved to a raised platform, as well as a complete redecoration. Student-pastors were now in charge of the chapel, and one, Mr. W. M. Barwell, wrote a history of the Woburn chapel in 1899. There was some resurgence of interest in Congregationalism around that time, but it slowly declined again over the next 40 years.

The last public worship services were held there in 1943, although there was a funeral in 1946, and a wedding as late as 1948. It had lost its iron railings for the war effort in 1943, which led to a long correspondence with the Ministry of Works, arguing over the £2 2s. 2d. compensation they offered. In February 1949, the dwindling congregation could no longer be ignored, and the boiler had been inoperative for two years, so at the annual meeting, the minutes recorded: *"...after considerable and earnest discussion it was proposed by Mr. James Bell and seconded by Miss Broughton that we accept the situation as it now stands, i.e. the Church shall be closed down and friends continue to worship with the Methodists. Carried unanimously by Woburn members present (although with considerable regret)".*

The arrangements for closing and removing the fixtures and fittings took some time. The pews and clock were sold to the Long Buckby Congregational Church for £12 10s., the organ, (by A. E. Pease) was advertised in several religious magazines and attracted great interest, even from as far away as Jamaica. Some offers were in the region of £200, and Mr. Crute of Aspley Guise simply offered *"£5 more than any other bid you receive"*, yet in the end it went to the Drayton Parslow Baptist Chapel for £175. The piano was given free of charge to the Methodist Chapel in Woburn, and the crockery to the Dunstable Congregational Church. The large memorial tablet to Rev. Michael Castleden inside the chapel was removed and transferred to the Hockliffe Chapel, where it still resides, although that chapel is now a private residence. All the proceeds collected were given over to the Congregational Section Fund of the Bedford Union of Christians. The Blunham Baptists wrote to enquire if there were any hymn boards for sale? Woburn chapel replied that they had looked all over, but the only board they could find was a 'push-halfpenny' board and wryly added *"...perhaps this is what sowed the original seeds of decay at Woburn".*

The building itself was put up for auction in 1951, and advertised in the Beds Times and also the Northampton Mercury:

> *"Woburn, Beds. In a secluded position but near the centre of the town. The Substantially built brick and slated premises formerly used as the CONGREGATIONAL CHURCH, comprising Chapel, 56ft. by 27ft. by 19ft. high, Schoolroom 26ft. by 14ft. 6in. Wash-house, Offices, and Graveyard. Suitable for use as a social centre or for conversion to dwellings. Total area nearly ¼ acre. Freehold, main services available. Will be offered by Auction, on the premises (unless previously sold by private treaty) on Wednesday, 1ˢᵗ August, 1951, at 6 o'clock, by Foll & Parker from whom full particulars can be obtained."*

The auction was successful, and the chapel buildings were sold to

Mr. Aubrey Boutwood of Toddington, for £110, but after solicitors and auctioneers fees, they were left with just £49 3s. There had been a great deal of legal wrangling about locating the executors of previous trustees to obtain the correct legal documentation.

The sale report mentions that the graveyard at the rear of the premises was entirely full, and the front one was partially full, and that some graves were still being tended. It is not known what happened to the other original memorials from inside the chapel or headstones from the graveyards outside.

Despite expectations that some entrepreneur would convert it to residential use, it sat empty and abandoned for nearly 10 years until it was sold again, to be used as a studio by the artist Derek Greaves. He recalls, *"I bought the chapel in 1959-1960 and used it as a studio until 1983 when it was sold. When I bought it, it was a wreck and everything had already been taken out, except the gallery. I replaced the glass in the windows and some of the larger windows with plastic corrugated sheeting. The gallery floor was levelled to create a flat space. The subsequent people demolished it and houses were put up on that site."*

6: *Woburn chapel, when derelict, from the Beds. Times, 1948. (Courtesy of Ampthil-limages.com)*

Indeed, the Woburn chapel was demolished in 1988. The English Heritage description for it reads: *"Woburn – Former Congregational, Duck Lane. Red brick with yellow brick dressing to tall round arch windows, rendered pilasters and slated roof. Gabled NE front with two round arched doorways apsidal SW end. Built 1854 to replace chapel of 1804 (demolition proposed 1986)"*. Congregationalism as a whole had changed. In 1972, most English Congregationalists had merged with the Presbyterian Church of England to form the United Reformed Church, but a few still chose to continue in their historic independent tradition.

George Castleden's books had been published in such small numbers, and he achieved so little success outside the immediate vicinity of Woburn during his lifetime, that he was soon forgotten. With no direct descendants or wider family residing in the area, there was no one to look after his legacy of work. The American visitor's description of his peculiar composition and *"want of clearness"* making his poems difficult to appreciate seems very apt. His writing is not to modern taste, and indeed, his copious notes, frequent tangents and obscure classical references make it had to follow and appreciate. Yet I have found glimpses of otherwise forgotten lives and local scenes brought vividly to life by his writing. One or two mentions are made of his 'Woburn Park' book as a footnote in the history of rural poetry, but George Castleden and his writings were otherwise consigned to history.

I have transcribed in full the letters and poems he sent to newspapers, and précised the text of longer news reports where he was only mentioned incidentally, and also some of the replies about his letters from others. Some of his spelling is old-fashioned, but spelling and punctuation have been left as originally published. Whether any errors should be attributed to Castleden or the newspaper type-setter, I leave to the reader to decide…

I

Letters: 1840 - 1855

Cricket – *"Woburn Park"* published – Woburn Church – Potato Famine – Education – The Woburn Book Society – The Eastern Question – A séance – The Woburn Exhibition – Cholera – Russia – Bedford Reform School – Biography of Rev. Castleden.

I have not transcribed the numerous reports of the Woburn & Aspley cricket matches in which Castleden played, but as the following report of a game was unusual, and he referred to it many years later, (see 9th August 1858) I have made an exception. (I also think this may be the only game of cricket played by an English Lord with four Popes on the same pitch!)

19th July 1840 Bell's Life in London & Sporting Chronicle

Woburn and Aspley v. Biggleswade and Sandy

The return match between the above parties was played in his Grace the Duke of Bedford's park, at Woburn, on Thursday and Friday, the 9th and 10th inst. It excited a great deal of interest in Bedfordshire, the Woburn gents challenging any two adjoining parishes in the county of Bedford. The Biggleswade and Sandy gents accepted the challenge, and in the first game beat their opponents on their own ground at Biggleswade, and were freely backed against them in this game. At the close of the first innings of each party, the odds were 2 to 1 on Biggleswade, which continued to increase, and at the 5th wicket down of the Woburn second innings, 10 to 1 was offered and some takers. Messrs. Castleden and Price took their places as 6th and 7th wicket, and by some steady batting caused the odds to fall to even betting, and, at the close of day, each brought out his bat. The parties then adjourned to the Goat Inn, where the evening was spent in the most social manner. The game resumed on the following day, when the Woburn gents becoming the favourites, and were freely backed at 2 to 1. Messrs. Castleden and Price again took their bats, and kept their wickets another half hour, nearly ninety runs having been marked between them. The two others that followed made the score of the second innings 200 runs, thus leaving the Biggleswade gents 149 runs to go in again. They commenced batting very steadily, but at the close of the game they were left in a minority of 98 runs. The score: -

Woburn and Aspley   1st inn.

G. Wilson, caught by Roberts   2
J. Hutton, bowled by Moseley   1
W. Pope, bowled by Moseley   22
W. Bacchus, caught by Moseley   8
Rev. J. More, stumped by Roberts   1
Lord C. Russell, bowled by C. Pope   3
J. Phillimore, caught by Burton   0
W. Hensman, bowled by Moseley   0
G. Castleden, not out   5
J. Price, hit wicket   2
G. Circuitt, caught by Burton   2
Bye 1, wide balls, 2   3
Total   49

Biggleswade and Sandy   1st inn.

A. Burton, caught by Hutton   1
W. Roberts, bowled by Phillimore   1
C. Pope (Sandy), bowled by Phillimore   35
W. Carrington, caught by Pope   6
L. Moseley, leg before wicket   0
F. Sale, caught by Hutton   8
C. Pope, stumped by Hutton   4
J. Pope, caught by Castleden   6
R. Moseley, bowled by Castleden   0
R. Bird, caught by Hutton   1
- Beauford, Esq., not out   10
Byes 9, wide balls 19   28
Total   100

Woburn and Aspley   2nd inn.

G. Wilson,   bowled by Moseley   11
J. Hutton,   caught by Moseley   18
W. Pope,   bowled by Bird   15
W. Bacchus,   caught by Moseley   4
Rev. J. More, caught by Moseley   0

Lord C. Russell, caught by Carrington	12
J. Phillimore, bowled by Moseley	2
W. Hensman, bowled by C. Pope	10
G. Castleden, caught by J. Pope	36
J. Price, caught by J. Pope	50
G. Circuitt, not out	18
Bye 7, wide balls 16	24
Total	200

Biggleswade and Sandy	2nd Inn
A. Burton, run out	1
W. Roberts, caught by Wilson	5
C. Pope (Sandy), bowled by Phillimore	10
W. Carrington, bowled by Phillimore	5
L. Moseley, bowled by Pope	2
F. Sale, caught by Circuitt	0
C. Pope, caught by Price	0
J. Pope, caught by Lord C. Russell	2
R. Moseley, not out	1
R. Bird, bowled by Pope	4
- Beauford, Esq., bowled by Pope	0
Byes 8, wide balls 13	21
Total	51

Perhaps Lord Charles Russell would have been expected to do a bit better, as he played for Marylebone Cricket Club between 1833 and 1846. He was a third son of the Duke, by a second marriage. After a career in the military and politics, he was appointed as Sergeant-at-Arms for the House of Commons in 1848, only retiring in 1875.

In 1841, Queen Victoria paid a visit to Woburn Abbey, as the Duchess of Bedford had been her "Lady of the Bedchamber" since her accession in 1837, and they had become great friends. The visit only lasted a couple of days, but Woburn went into a frenzy of Royal celebration, amongst which, the Northampton Mercury reported the:

"Rustic Sports, in commemoration of the visit of her Most Gracious Majesty Queen Victoria, to Woburn, on Tuesday, July 27, - Donkey Race: The several donkeys entered for this prize will not be ridden by the owners, but will be contended for after the manner the feats adopted by the Ancients - each donkey must be rode by opposite party, not being the rider of the same donkey in the last race, and the last donkey to be declared the winner. The winner to receive 7s. 6d., second, 2s. 6d. The colour of the riders to be named before starting. - Climbing the pole for a leg of mutton, value 5s. - Sack jumping, for 6s.: 100 yards, the first to receive 3s.; second, 2s.; third, 1s.; six to start. - Wheelbarrow race, by men blindfolded; the winner to receive 5s.; second, 2s.; not less than five to start. - Biscuit bolting: Ten boys to eat pennyworth of biscuits each; the first shall have a new white beaver tile, the second a regular out-and-out wide-awake, warranted to fit. - Gown piece, value 4s.: sweepstake, open to all ages, to be run for by the ladies; from the park gate to Mr. Devey's corner; not less than four to start. - Half a pound of best Scotch snuff will be given to the old lady who shall take half an ounce (clean snifting) in the shortest time. - Half a pound tobacco, 2s 6d. to be given to him who can smoke half an ounce of prime shag in the shortest time; a damper of one pint of heavy (Morris's Entire) to be allowed to each man whilst smoking. - Rolls and treacle, for a prize of 2s., for boys. With a variety of other sports. To commence at six o'clock. - God save the Queen!"

Bizarrely, these 'Rustic Sports' are described almost exactly the same as similar events which took place at Midsummer Green, in Cambridge for Queen Victoria's Coronation in 1838. Perhaps Buckingham Palace made standard suggestions to Committees who enquired about how Victoria liked to be celebrated! Castleden took the opportunity of the visit to expand on the National Anthem lyrics:

31st July 1841 Stamford Mercury (amongst others)

The Queen and Prince Albert, attended by the Dowager Lady Lyttleton, the Hon. Miss Sarah Cavendish, the Marquis of Headfort, Mr George Edward Anson, Colonel Buckley, and Colonel Bouverie, arrived at Woburn Abbey, Beds, on Monday evening, having experienced a most gratifying and enthusiastic reception throughout the whole of the route from Windsor. The Royal party occupied three carriages and four. The Duke of Wellington, the Duke of Devonshire, the Duchess of Sutherland, the Duke and Duchess of Leinster, Earl de Grey, Viscount Melville, Viscount Palmerston, and other visitors who had been honoured with invitations to meet her Majesty, arrived at the Abbey in the course of the day on a visit to the Duke and Duchess of Bedford. After dinner, the following loyal ode, in honour of her Majesty's arrival, was sung in the west front of Woburn Abbey, to the tune of "God Save the Queen:" -

God bless the Royal pair
This is our midnight prayer
God save the Queen
Now stars their vigils keep
Now night winds round us sweep
And now the worlds asleep
God bless our Queen

Day's pageant now's away,
Yet loyal hearts will stay,
Prolong the strain;
Guard, Lord our Royal pair,
Thy mercies let them share,
From every harm and care
God save the twain!

The Royal parents bless,
Their child - our young Princess
Do thou defend;
And when life's day is done-
Its course in glory run-
O may their mortal sun
In brightness end.

Now let the welkin ring,
While Woburn minstrels sing
Their loyal theme;
May Britain's sons prolong
Our Woburn park night song,
And shout the anthem strong,
God save the Queen!

Although the author of the lyrics was not named, it was confirmed to be Castleden by a piece the same day in another article:

31st July 1841 Bedford Mercury

.. A little after ten o'clock a respectable group of the inhabitants assembled at the west front of the Abbey, and sang the following National Ode, which does much credit to the author, the same who wrote a beautiful poem entitled "Woburn Park," which may be had of any of the booksellers in Woburn, and is well worth inspection.

...and so got himself some free publicity for his book too! The Loyal Ode lyrics were also printed onto silk handkerchiefs, presumably as souvenirs for sale to mark the event, and one survives in the archives at Woburn Abbey. But not everyone liked his poems...

31st July 1841 The Spectator

Woburn Minstrels. In the Tenpenny-Post-Bag is a letter from an eminent bibliophile to an unlucky author, informing him that Scott,

"Having quitted the Borders to seek more renown,

Is coming by long quarto stages to town;

And, beginning with Rokeby – the job's sure to pay –

Means to do every gentleman's seat by the way."

The object of the communication was to hint that the gentleman to whom the letter was addressed may find it not a bad speculation to allow himself to be started as "a fresh poet through Highgate to meet him," in order that he

"By dint of short proofs, no revises, long coaches,

May do a few villas before Scott approaches;

Indeed, if his Pegasus be n't cursed shabby,

He'll reach without stumbling at least Woburn Abbey."

Woburn Abbey seems to have been, in the estimation of the ingenious writer, not particularly propitious to spontaneous inspiration – a dull locality, where a poet might be apt to feel exhaustion and draw bridle. There is something calculated to corroborate his opinion in the "loyal ode," which the Court Circular informs us was sung, "after dinner," in honour of her Majesty's arrival "in the west front of Woburn Abbey," on Monday last. It is the effusion not of one Woburn minstrel, but all of the clan –

"Now let the welkin ring

While Woburn's minstrels sing

Their loyal theme."

And like enough to a schoolboy's "theme" it is. But the urchin who in our school-days should have inflicted such a finale upon his preceptor as the following, would have incurred some risk of having his head' antipodes crowned with the antipodes of laurel –

"May Britain's sons prolong
Our Woburn Park night-song,
And shout the anthem strong,
God save the Queen."

All the strength of the minstrels' lungs seems, however, to have proved inadequate to keep attention awake; for though the ode was performed after dinner, the luckless performers are obliged to confess -

"And now the world's asleep."

A consummation not to be wondered at, seeing that these soporific lines were taken upon a full stomach -

"The Royal parents bless,
Their child - our young Princess -
Do thou defend."

Some attempts have been made by the Court scribes to run a parallel between the visit to Woburn and the visit to Kenilworth; we may, however, say with Mercutio, of ELIZABETH - "Marry! She had a better poet to be-rhyme her."

The local press were not kinder:

21st August 1841 Northampton Herald

Woburn Park, A Fragment of Rural Rhyme.

We had not intended to have taken any notice of this contemptible publication, but the pertinacity of its unfortunate author in dragging himself before public notice (witness his loyal ode) makes it incumbent on us to put a stop to any further nuisances of the present nature.

We do not propose to criticise the Author's preface very minutely; but for the amusement of our readers we will point out one or two of the numerous absurdities it contains. He commences with informing us that his motives for publishing this poem was, to satisfy himself, and then proceeds to observe that most probably the former edition of this Work, or, to use his own language, "the obtrusion in a smaller way" had been consigned to the "tomb of all Capulets," for which reception he thanks his readers, "we doubt whether they ever existed in the plural number), and hopes for the same fate for his larger "obtrusion," which hope, we venture to say, has not been a vain one. He next tells us, and coming from such experienced authority this information will be entirely credited, "The more some persons do indite, Folly increases as they write;" that this essay is irregular in its construction, and rugged in its rhyme, and therefore called a fragment. By the way, he does not explain the origin of the term 'rural rhyme,' which we never heard of before: and taking this work as a specimen, hope most fervently that we never shall again. Then follows some mawkish twaddle about "Elysian fields," "Sublunary Paradise," "Mortal wrong and mortal woe," the meaning of all which is not very clear either to the "outward vision," or the "mind's eye."

A fear is next expressed that either the second section of the lay must be skipped, or the book be thrown away: of the two alternatives, we strongly recommend the latter.

The Preface concludes by stating that "if there be but one line of local or historical worth in the Poem, the Author will be very well satisfied;" whether the purchasers of his book will be equally contented with such a result is what he never thinks of, though we assure him that, looking for a needle in a bottle of hay is an easy task compared to that of wading through upwards of a thousand lines in search of a single one worth reading.

We have actually, with a view to do justice to the Author, gone entirely through his poem, and though we have not found "the single line of local or historical worth," we will quote some of the most remarkable passages. Take the two following as speciments of his very refined and original vein of humour:-

"We guilty plead, yea, pardon beg,
That we sometimes are short a *leg*.-
Foot this should be; each rhymester knows
All Poet's feet have not ten toes:
I limp sometimes on eight, - excuse the pun –
If you are very cross, I'll cut and run."
"Intellectually I hope to write,
Though not correct by grammar light;
Ditto as to orthography.
Now we'll jog on Ge-o-graphy
Unto another local spot, &c., &c."

To keep this precious morsel in countenance, we will quote a specimen from his account of the Romans:-

"They then possess'd this northern clime,
From eighty three A.C. to 329
A.D. the emperor then was Constantine."
Turn to page 141 and you will find the following lines:-
"Struck down by Gaul's proud eagle's fearful swoop,
Abject they lie, beneath his iron hoof."

It is not so much as a specimen of rural rhyme, that we point out this passage, though of that it is a remarkable example, and only to be paralleled by the following couplet at p.36:-

"Now to make my rhyme close even,
The bowler makes up the eleven."

It is not so much for that purpose, as for the sake of indicating a slight want of clearness in the manner in which the passage is expressed. The "iron hoof" must belong, either to the "proud eagle," or to Napoleon; which of the two we cannot say, as this peculiarity in the formation of the foot, is not mentioned in any account of the eagle, nor in any biography of the Emperor.

Had we leisure, we could point out many other passages far more obscure, a circumstance the more extraordinary, as the merit of writing intelligibly, is that which, by the author's own confession, is to atone for all the offences against grammar, good taste and common sense, with which the poem abounds. At page 139 the Author steps out of his way, to make a most unfeeling and uncalled for allusion, to the misfortune of a gentleman, formerly member for the county of Bedford; he then enumerates the evil consequences of ambition, omitting, however, the effects of a poetical ambition, which has succeeded in the present instance in turning a private and obscure individual, into a public, but we trust only temporary nuisance.

Our readers must by this time be heartily sick of this absurd work, and we will therefore only give the sublime concluding lines, of which, we think, the dullest schoolboy would be ashamed,

"And now - what now? Once more adieu
Sweet Woburn Park, I say to you."

In conclusion, we would point out to our readers the only passage we can mention with praise. It is an address to the subscribers:

"However, to the most noble and very distinguished individuals, to the Clergy and Gentry, who have patronised it, the Author's very humble and grateful thanks are here presented."

So infinitely superior is this passage to any other throughout the whole work, that we were led to doubt its originality, and after a diligent search, we found the idea and nearly the whole of the language, in a handbill of Messrs. Smith and Co., Linen Drapers, Holborn, issued by them on the reopening of their shop in the spring of 1840.

We must apologise to our readers for detaining them so long over such a production. We should not have noticed it at such length, but for the threat it contains of a still larger obtrusion, in the shape of an essay in blank verse, on Conscience.

This harsh criticism of Castleden's work did not go unrebuked.

CONSCIENCE:

An Essay in Blank Verse;

BEING A SEQUEL TO

"WOBURN PARK."

To man of every colour, clime, and class,
My theme applies; where'er the vault of heaven
Extends its boundless arch, "the still small voice,"
In whispers, though unheard by other ears,
Can shake or soothe, convulse or calm the soul.

LONDON:

THOMAS WARD AND CO., PATERNOSTER-ROW.

1842.

7: *Frontispiece from Castleden's "Conscience – An Essay in Blank Verse", published 1842.*

28th August 1841 Bedford Mercury

To the Editor of the Bedford Mercury.

Sir, The disgraceful attack in last Saturday's Northampton Herald, on the unassuming author of a little work called "Woburn Park," caused here a strong feeling of disgust. The writer being well known, and who not quite relishing some lines in "Rural Rhymes," may dread the appearance of the work on "Conscience." Lost, indeed, must that man be to all feelings of honour who could go out of his way to insult one he had before so grievously wronged; surely he might be satisfied with the wreck he has already made.

Yours truly, Q, but not in the corner. Woburn, August 26, 1841.

28th August 1841 Hertford Mercury and Reformer

Woburn. – Mr. Dodd, of this town, has lately published some lines, by the author of "Woburn Park," commemorative of the late visit of her Majesty to the princely seat of the Duke of Bedford. We have been much pleased by a perusal of the little poem, which is in an easy measure; it contains two very happy allusions to the royal visits of Elizabeth and Charles to the Abbey; and, unlike many "Odes on Royalty," possesses no mawkish and affecting specimens of sentimental loyalty.

Queen Elizabeth I had visited Woburn Abbey in 1572, and Charles I in 1647. Adverts for his books are few and far between in the newspapers he wrote to. Probably unwilling to pay the advertising rate, he relied on his publishers to advertise it if they wanted to increase their sales. However, his second book was advertised:

9th April 1842 Northampton Mercury

Just published, 200pp. 18mo, Gilt Edges, Price 4s. Conscience. An Essay in blank verse, by the Author of "Woburn Park."

"To men of every colour, clime and class
My theme applies; where 'er the vault of heaven
Extends its boundless arch, 'the still small voice'
In whispers though unheard by other ears
Can shake or soothe, convulse or calm the soul"

Ward & Co. Paternoster Row: Dodd, Woburn, Beds.

The Temperance movement was gaining popularity, as the effects of cheap alcohol on the working classes, with the social and economic problems it caused, began to be recognised. Medical and religious campaigners organised meetings where the audience were encouraged to "Take the

Pledge" to give up the demon drink. His father had been very much involved in the local campaign, and now Castleden took up the baton too.

1st June 1844 Northampton Mercury

The 'celebrated' Dr. Lees of Leeds, a 'great gun' of the Temperance movement, came to Woburn to give lectures in the Town Hall. Advance notices were distributed, challenging any local minister or Doctor, who disagreed with his assertation that teetotalism is in accordance with the word and works of God, to come to the meeting. The sparse audience was in agreement with his lecture, until he stated, "In a point of Religion what do you do? You do not ask the opinion of your neighbour – you do not perhaps even refer to your Minister, but you go to the highest authority. Do so with regard to teetotalism. Do not go to your village Doctors, your parish surgeons, your town apothecaries, your petty luminaries, farthing rushlights, but be guided by those who are able to give an opinion on the subject." At this point, the Woburn surgeon, Mr. Parker, interrupted and asked if Dr. Lees distinguished between 'farthing rushlights' and brighter stars of the medical profession. After some short, terse, comments about his profession being criticised, Mr. Parker left the hall with two other members of the audience. Dr. Lees then continued to allude to the local surgeon after he had left, to which Castleden and two other remaining members of the audience objected, as Mr. Parker was not there to defend himself. The lecture continued, but the paper noted that a second planned lecture was even more thinly attended than the first.

*The Northampton Mercury had been publishing a series of descriptions on Bedfordshire churches, and on **7th February 1846**, it was the turn of Woburn. It was a very disparaging piece, claiming the church at Woburn contained Christian and Pagan architecture "jumbled together", and that some parishioners had to sit with their backs to the Altar, which whilst alright for dissenting meeting houses, should not be tolerated in a church. The writer, [W.A.], also thought that it was dark and dingy, as the lamps had blackened the walls, and, apparently, the floor was strewn with nutshells! It was the off-hand reference to 'dissenting meeting houses' that riled Castleden enough to make him respond.*

14th February 1846 Northampton Mercury

"Bedfordshire Churches". To the Editor of the Northampton Mercury.

Sir, - As under the above title an ungracious reference to "a dissenting meeting house" appeared in your last paper, I feel assured I have only to appeal to your many years impartiality for the admission of a few lines at this ungenerous remark.

Whether "W.A." be one mild enough to teach, patient and humble enough to learn, I know not; but in hands more competent to argue upon the properties of Church Architecture and the fillings up, I must leave him. My intention is merely to caution against unfair comparisons. To lug into "Woburn Church" "a dissenting meeting house," "W.A." will excuse the remark, betrays a want of good taste, and peradventure may endanger his own Orthodoxy.

Surely with "sheep nibbling without," and "nutshells" within, not to say a word about "Auctioneer's decks -fonts misplaced – miserable galleries – theatrical appearance – stopped up windows – walls defaced by tablets – naves, aisles, chancels, &c, &c. &c. Surely "W.A." has, in all these matters, 'ample scope and verge enough,' without letting imagination rove into" a dissenting meeting house."

If only an itinerant, my next few words may not avail, but should "W.A." be a Bedfordshire resident, it may be of use to inform him that the genius of toleration has had its gentle reign in our county for many a long year, and Woburn was the last parish in it that should have afforded, even by inference, the bigot sneer, relative to "a dissenting meeting house."

"W.A." ought to be told when power *commands*, bigotry is willing to play the Tiger – when policy suggests, it can creep into the coils of the snake.

Ere "W.A." sneers again, I would have him search the records of some of the Bedfordshire meeting houses – Dr. Johnson - the late poet laureate, Dr. Southey – and that learned man and estimable Christian, the late Dr. Arnold, have paid strange homage to one of the occupants. Whether the "pulpit" be adorned was fixed with Apostolical accuracy I know not, but most certainly it was in "a dissenting meeting house," and when the churches in our county town are visited by "W.A." it might vary his ecclesiastical topography if he looked into the "Old Meeting." If he found a pulpit out of place, John Bunyan's chair he would find in its place; and, dare he, with Dr. Pusey in his head, trust his head's antipodes with a rest in that said chair, if he dreamt not of Popes, W.A.'s excursive fancy would at once revert to those halcyon days of Prerogative and High Church Supremacy-

When Bedford's dungeon scorn, abuse, and shame,

A strange baptism was, of John's enduring name!

I remain Sir, Your obedient servant, G.C. Woburn, Beds, 9th Feb, 1846.

Castleden was obviously unaware that the writer who signed himself off as "W.A.", was actually John Martin, the librarian to the Duke at Woburn Abbey (hence "W.A."). I can't believe Martin had written what he did on his own accord, and it is interesting to think that this might be an early move by the Duke in starting to sow the seeds for the idea of getting a new church built for Woburn.

The next issue to exercise his mind was the humble potato. Potato blight had ravaged crops across Europe during the 1840's, decimating whole communities in Ireland, who relied on the crop as their staple food. Someone, signed as "J.P." of Woburn, had written into the Northampton Mercury to say his own crop was affected, and he was looking for any remedy for the blight.

22nd August 1846 Northampton Mercury

The Potato Disease. To the Editor of the Northampton Mercury.

Sir, - If the inquiry in your last week's Paper by "J.P." shall elicit even a germ of a thought calculated to stay or provide some remedy for the plague which is now destroying this food plant all over our island, you will rejoice in allowing your columns to subserve so useful a purpose.

I remember, when very young, seeing potatoes come out of the ground much larger than they do now, and from inquiries, I find *sorts* have been lost and *sizes* lessoned; if this be a fact, have we not been doing the potato wrong in its culture? Have we been right in continually slicing from the root, instead of raising from the seed, or of sending for a fresh supply from Virginia? - the country from which Sir Walter Raleigh brought them in 1623.

These questions I submit to you, Sir, and whilst my slender experience can offer no remedy for present desolation, I would earnestly ask those, of whom it may be said it is their "vocation, Hal," to apply their practical knowledge, and horticultural advantages to their examination. If the stamina of the potato be exhausting - and dwindling size bespeaks this - disease naturally follows, and while we lament present destruction, perchance worse may follow. By still planting the infected root the ground may become poisoned, and perhaps, be rendered pestilential to any other succulent crop.

I could, were it not trespassing, give a quotation to the point from the Quarterly Review, December, 1839, by Mr. Aiken. One extract will suffice - "By this means (cutting) the plant becomes old in constitution, and decays. It is profitable to the cultivator but destructive to the plant."

I remain, Sir, your very obedient servant, G.C., Woburn, Beds, 13th August, 1846.

A basic free education, available to all, was one of his main interests. He wrote often on the education system, and those who tried to change it.

5th December 1846 Northampton Mercury

"The People's Education". To the Editor of the Northampton Mercury.

Sir, - A letter in a recent number of your paper induces me to ask the privilege of a corner on this all-important subject.

On the side of the establishment, the Rev. Dr. Hook has written much, in non-conforming zeal Mr. Baines has, perhaps, written more on "popular education;" without presuming to arraign either method. I recur with pleasure to the simple plan laid down by John Lancaster, and it does appear this plan came nearest to the only true National School. For in the nation, where we must, ay, will agree to differ, the secular dominancy of a particular class, has been and will be the blight of an otherwise People's Education.

When will the time arrive, both in education and religion, when the following lines shall have full realization: -

When shall this axiom reign beneath the sun,
All tolerate but tax not all for one:
People shall hail the change with grateful voice,
And statesmen, then untrammelled, will rejoice,
Priestcraft and persecution far be hurled,
And bigotry shall flee the emancipated world.

When this all glorious morn shall rise, the clouds of doubts and the mist of fears which now darken and obstruct the sunbeams of popular education, will flee away – no more shall the gives of creed, nor the shackles of catechisms fetter or appal, but in the full liberty of conscience each unit of the mighty whole shall find as his birthright an education untainted by sectarian interference – unawed by Episcopal domination.

This, Sir, I trow, is 'a consummation devoutly to be wished,' both to governors and governed. Hoping I have not *presumed* in this day of railway press and speed.

In the New Year, he had a series of three letters printed, on consecutive weeks, on the famine in Ireland.

13th February 1847 Northampton Mercury

Ireland. To the Editor of the Northampton Mercury.

Sir, - Perhaps upon this all-absorbing topic you will allow me to ask, was the Right Hon. John Philpot Curran correct when, at Newry, on the 17th October, 1812, he made the following statement? –

"Let me rapidly sketch the first dawn of dissension in Ireland, and the relations of the conqueror and conquered. That conquest was obtained, like all victories over Ireland, by the triumph of guilt over innocence. This dissension was followed up by the natural hate of the spoiler and despoiled; followed up further by the absurd antipathies of religious sects; and still further by the rivalries of trade, the cruel tyrants of Ireland dreading that, if Irish industry had not had her hands tied behind her back, she might have become impatient of servitude, and those hands might work for her deliverance.

"To this growing accumulation of Irish dissension, the miserable James II., his heart trotted by the depravity of that France which had given him an interested shelter from the just indignation of his betrayed subjects, put the last hand; and an additional dissension, calling itself political as well as religious, was superadded.

"Under this sad coalition of confederating dissensions, nursed and fomented by the policy of England, this devoted country has continued to languish, with small fluctuations of national destiny, from the invasion of the second Henry to the present time."

Taking this language to be true, we have the cause why Ireland, instead of being a healthy appendage to England, has ever been a cancerous excrescence. "But," says Mr. Bull, "with famine staring me in the face, and millions rolling out of my exchequer, I don't want to know so much about the cause as the remedy." True, old gentleman, but this has puzzled good men and true for generations, and is puzzling good men and true now. As I perused Curran's ominous sentences, it did flash across the mind, would that we could in this national disease apply the ether and perform painless separation; this might save both. Together, as we are, involves ruinous catastrophe. Whether in the history of nations we are working out the eternal truth "that wrong never was yet right," the future historians may tell; but it will be a singular item to record, that after 700 years conquest, the conqueror had done so little for the conquered, a failure of a potato crop entailed a penalty, in money value, of seven millions sterling!

That we seized Ireland was our first sin; our punishment has been the poverty of the most fertile spot on the globe. But as if the "sin original" involved not enough of punitive consequences we have, under the despotism of a governing minority, been adding to wrongs, and so increasing retribution. In addition to making the Irish civil bondsmen, this minority, for many years, insultingly hung around and before them religious fetters, and now that we are feeling in our purse for these outrages on principle we are inclined to say hard things of poor Pat, and having destroyed energy by burking hope, we further wrong by accusing him of indolence and improvidence; and thus we lay a flattering unction to our own souls by making him accountable for our misdeeds.

Alas, when will the unit as well as the nation believe this truth. "As ye sow, so shall ye reap." Annex a colony by the principle of mutual welfare, sow among the people the seeds of justice, mercy, peace, and good will, and your colony shall return to you sevenfold. Conquer a country, and, in addition to sowing it with military combustibles, sow also the explosive materials of a Church Militant, with igniting influences, and behold, on the soil of fertility desolation and death remain!

May I not say Europe is waiting to see how Ireland is to be governed. How she has been is now plain. Poverty reigns where plenty, by all the laws of nature, should have abounded, and if anything could, as a nation, hold us up to the extremest ridicule for our abuse of a 700 years' tenure, it is the fact that the failure of an esculent root, yet the subsistence of a people, is giving John Bull a very sensible premonition of national paralysis.

But how is Ireland to be governed? Wrong has been done, No repair can heal that wrong, but if this be impossible, and if for the past we are paying present penalties, let us be careful we store not up aggravated woe by future aggression. A bold statesman must be he who, against the combinations of self-interest, which have preyed, which are preying upon Ireland, will say "This wrong, at any rate, shall cease; the minority must abdicate, and the majority shall rule, for it be evil or for good; here we recognise it from the parish vestry up to St. Stephen's, and Ireland shall no longer smart under this offence."

But as I write for the moral side of the question, I venture not here further into its political bearings, but beg to subscribe myself, Sir, Your obedient servant, G.C.

N.B. – The above was written ere my attention was called to the first article in Chambers' Journal, 23rd January, "Historical Tableaux; Conquests." The whole is so confirmatory, and the diction is so brilliant, that to any reader disposed to follow out what I have written, its perusal will edify. Allow the closing climax.

"Whatever be the actual methods of operation, it comes to this – Nations dishonestly taken possession of, like ill-got wealth, seldom thrive. 'We may read our sin in our punishment;' so says Scripture. 'Our pleasant vices make us whips to scourge us;" so says Shakespear. 'Every immoral act contains the seeds of its own dissolution;' so says philosophy."

Woburn, Beds, 8th February, 1847.

20ᵗʰ February 1847 Northampton Mercury

Ireland. – No.2. To the Editor of The Northampton Mercury.

Sir, - The cry of famine is now sounding through the length and breadth of England, and the philanthropist, priest, and politician are employed in saving a people from starvation. Not one word would I utter to cool this charitable fervour, but as you have obliged by the admission of some thoughts issuing from a text by a great bygone Irishman relating to the cause of Ireland's misery, allow me still further to offer for consideration some remarks on present politics, and also point to the hope which may prevent the reoccurrence of this calamity – a reoccurrence which, with an increasing people, will have an increased power, and, like an enlarging tumour, will burden national vigour, absorb political strength, and finally, prostrate us into united helplessness. Do I dream? Is not Legislature at this time exhibiting an untoward spectacle? Instead of letting the Prime Minister's plan have a fair trial, a railway party springs up in the senate house, and asks, with the assumption of honest, well-meaning men, for sixteen millions to make railways in a country where its peasantry are still satisfied with their pig as a sleeping companion, and their dunghill for their resting place. Can mockery be more supreme than this? Foster, civilize, and advance, then add arts and sciences. But as if to carry out national blundering even in legislatorial proceedings, a party asks for sixteen millions to make railways in a country where native energies are so depressed as to be satisfied with potato growing; whose national wealth is abstracted from the soil that pays it, and by absentees lavished upon the frivolities of foreign climes. This scheme surely must be relinquished; and when the cravings of the people are allayed, I fancy a poor-law will find support where it met with former opposition. It is with regret I come to this alternative, but what other legislative measure will coerce permanently the absentee? Such a law may have the tendency to degrade still further the peasantry of Ireland. Perchance satisfied now with potato growing, then they may say idleness is better still. But this would soon bring on a crisis, whereas the absence of the landed proprietors entails prolonged misery and pining distress without a remedy. This law would compel residence among, or relief to the poor; and when I read of such a reclamation as in that caper in Chambers's Journal, entitled "Facts from Gweedore," I could honestly, with every courtesy, say to all Absentees, go ye and do likewise, and don't, because the ground is exhausted by growing an exhausting root, lay to Providence the result of your own inattention, or ask us to make up what your own cupidity and injustice have lost. "Put your own shoulders to the wheel." I have a hope, founded on these "Facts," that were the proprietors to reside on their estates, the peasantry must advance in manners and in customs. This rise would act upon the next class, and renovation might commence; but as it is you might as well expect the body natural to flourish under daily depletion as that the body social of Ireland should be healthy, drained as she is by agents and absentees. Let the Minister have fair play. To a staving people food ought to and must be sent; but when the lull comes, when the dangers of starvation have a pause, then let a poor-law as any rate be introduced to meet a famine emergency. John Bull, I believe all will admit, shows no lack of generosity now; perhaps would not again and again, but a time may come when it will be different, yea, impossible. Then for some sure support, let there be a law which shall touch the Absentee. This seems indispensable, and it may prevent deeper ruin. One word on railways. I fancy it will be time enough to ask John Bull for a loan of his millions when some hundreds of thousands lent of previous speculations have been refunded. To ask seriously for this seems such a monstrous presumption on his gullibility that I don't know which to admire most, the modesty with which the sum is asked, or the value of the security offered. I remain, Sir, your obedient and obliged servant, G.C. Woburn, Beds, Feb. 16, 1847.

27th February 1847 Northampton Mercury

Ireland No.3. To the Editor of the Northampton Mercury.

"But I have heard that the smaller tenants were saying not only that they could not cultivate their land, but that they did not intend to do so, because they did not believe they would derive any benefit from the best harvest that might occur." – Lord John Russell, 20th February.

Sir, - The melancholy truth contained in the above sentence impels me to trouble you with this sequel relative to unhappy Ireland. In my first letter I spoke of our "sin original;" in the second I touched upon present perplexities; and now, taking the Prime Minister's information as indicative of very, very gloomy prospects, would I, amidst apparent hopelessness, extract counsel and afford warning.

Had the calamity which is now engaging public attention, and summoning the best energies of the country to its relief, have followed the mandate of Omnipotence, or had Pestilence been winged by the breath of His power – had the whirlwind devastated; the lightning blasted; the hot thunder bolts smitten; the hoar frost laid waste; the mildew withered, and the caterpillar consumed - Man had submitted, would have hoped, and when these judgements had been overpast, mercy would still have smiled; but *now* where is hope, with a soil *not* desolated by the vengeance of Heaven, but which has been poisoned by the cupidity of man.

I remember reading, in the last illness of John Howard, a friend rallied him by saying the attack would soon give way to medical treatment. "No," said the great philanthropist, "my mode of life has rendered it impossible that I should recover from this fever. * * * I have been accustomed for years to exist upon vegetables and water, a little bread and a little tea. I have no method of lowering my nourishment, and consequently I must die. It is such jolly fellows as you, Priestman, who get over these fevers." Now if the reference be not far fetched, may we not say Pat has been reduced to this condition, socially, by his vegetable diet, the cultivation of which induces idleness and produces vitiation of moral stamina, and now the national pulse has become so feeble, the faculty are at a loss to invigorate and retone. Distress from the scarcity of wheat, the blight of the olive, or the destruction of the grape, Statesmen may grapple with, and seek supplies in meaner foods; but when a people have learnt to live upon seaweed and potatoes, *and they fail*, then famine stalks in its most inveterate form, and while "jolly fellows" may bear deprivation when corn, oil and wine, refuse their increase, and on short commons, pass tolerably a season of destitution, what is to become of a nation looking for it's life blood from the potato root?

The prospect here is dark, but darker 'tis yet to come, if the Prime Minister's information be correct. If the tenantry are coming to the direful conclusion not to cultivate the land, what next? In this interrogatory is involved the awful why of such a dislocation of landlord and tenant interest. Into this question I cannot go at length without trespassing on your columns. It will be enough for our purpose to say the same harsh treatment and the same neglect Ireland has experienced would have turned our fertile fields into waste places; and had the same uncertainties of tenure been the scourge of our sons of the soil, where would have been our past substantial yeomen, and our present wealthy men? Here the character of the landlord is pledged to do his duty while he enjoys his privilege; and that character is an effectual shield against many a pitiful act of tyranny which otherwise would be enacted. Here, from oppression we have an appeal to character-esteeming peers, and a character-supporting press. But in Ireland how stands the matter? Evictions of the most ruthless nature take place, not by the order often of the landlord, but perchance by come subordinate adventurer, who, without one particle of compunctions, feeling, levels the crazy cabin, yet the Irishman's home, turns husband, wife, and babes adrift to the howling storm without, with a wilder storm raging within; and then, when no hope of appeal, no kindly-hearted landlord to stand between him and the oppressor, if goaded to madness by such inhumanity he puts a bullet in the tyrant's breast, we, at our very comfortable firesides, are to lift up our hands and exclaim, "What blood thirsty villains those Irishmen are; nobody is safe!" Rather, when all the truth is told, shall we wonder that native buoyancy and a simple-hearted reliance upon religious truths have kept in check so long those resentments common to us all, and which have an additional fervour in our sister isle, and which, unhappily, have been there the more wantonly and outrageously provoked.

Fifty years ago the nation was alarmed by a mutiny at sea. Now, by the non-cultivation of the soil, we are threatened by a land mutiny. As that one subdued, earnestly do I hope this one will be allayed – allayed by legislative enactments which shall, as far as man's prescience can, prevent poverty becoming starvation; which shall give an Irishman hope on his natal will, and, though but a mud-built cabin, security in his home.

I beg to subscribe myself, Sir, You obedient and obliged servant, G.C. Woburn, Beds, Feb 23, 1847.

It took a brave writer of that time to infer that the problems in Ireland had their roots with England. Many English voices were loudly proclaiming the problems in Ireland were all their own doing, and Castleden's stance would not have been popular, however, it is generally considered to be correct now. Then he returns to education. The new Factories Act of 1847 required all children to attend school, and many hands were stirring the pot about how they should be taught, and who should be doing the teaching.

13ᵗʰ **March 1847** Northampton Mercury

"The Government Education Scheme." To the Editor of the Northampton Mercury.

Sir, - Last November you favoured me with a corner on "The People's Education;" on the faith of that indulgence, and also venturing to make a passing remark on your last week's leader, I offer the following communication.

Your own words, 'regret' and 'disapprobation,' on the course pursued by Protestant Dissenter have powerful support in "The Times" of the *same day*, and had I nothing to offer in opposition but the sentiments of Dissenting Journals, however just I might think them, I should hesitate on account of the charge of partiality; but in the Morning Chronicle of March 1ˢᵗ there is also a leader on this Education Scheme, and surely three extracts which I now give, will prove that Dissenters have some reason to be alarmed.

1. - "The minutes could scarcely make less of the civil power if they dated from the Vatican, and perhaps we should add – in the twelfth century."

2. - "But then, why is the action of this plan clogged, and the ascent of superior minds restrained by religious tests and disabilities, as bad and intolerant as any that the present century has seen abolished?"

3. - "The clergyman may at times withhold this testimonial, and thereby blast the fortunes of the youth for ever, without any one having the power to ask him for a reason."

Now, Sir, while you and *The Times* take one view and *The Chronicle* another on so important a subject, unbiased and unprejudiced as we believe you are, grant a little indulgence to those intimately concerned who see in this measure germs of disastrous consequences.

The Protestant Dissenters have ever been the firm supporters of Civil and Religious Liberty - they have ever opposed restrictive measures, whether proceeding from Church or State. Of course with the *bigot* churchman, and the *exclusive* politician, they are marked individually and collectively. This scheme, with the present government, might proceed harmlessly, but have we so far advanced in liberality – have we so forgotten the past – as to leave such a piece of political machinery to be worked by our sworn enemies? Is it politic of Whig statesmen – is it just to Dissenters – thus to endanger their own principles by strengthening the hands of their sturdiest opponents, and also by arming men who, "believing they are doing God service, may breathe out threatening," if not slaughter, against fellow citizens whose sin will be in the resistance to a catechism and the rejection of a creed?

I would hastily conclude on this matter; if the unfolding of the scheme proves your view of the subject to be correct, well; but if the discussion of the question, both in and out of Parliament, should substantiate the views of the Morning Chronicle, I leave it then to your long adherence to a liberal policy whether you will not *then* "regret" such a consummation, although "great disapprobation" is the lot of those *now* who are conscientiously striving to prevent injury to future liberal governments, and to ward off "a heavy blow and a sad discouragement" on the rights and liberties of Protestant Dissenters.

I hope to remain, Sir, your obliged servant, G.C., Woburn, Beds, March 9th, 1847.

[Our correspondent's letter confirms our impression that the opposition has been taken up hastily and with imperfect information. The Clerical testimonial is only required in the case of those who are training for Masters in Church Schools.]

10th April 1847 Northampton Mercury

To the Editor of The Northampton Mercury.

Sir, - Amidst the conflict of opinion on the government scheme, I feel a pleasure that in the columns of your paper last November, I referred to Joseph Lancaster's simple plan as *neutral ground* on which all contending parties might meet, in order that "each unit of the mighty whole might find, as his birth right, an education untainted by sectarian influence – unawed by episcopal domination."

With a trust still in the politicians whose principles I have imbibed from my earliest days, surely in this measure there are grounds for fear; and if a paper, unrivalled for Whig consistency, is to be credited, this fear cannot be without foundation. From the Morning Chronicle, I gave three extracts, and now I add a fourth, of the 2d April: -

"The obvious and common-sense method of avoiding all these inducements is, to confine inspection strictly to secular education, and to allow no ecclesiastical authority to have any control over it. The Clergy, of all denominations, will be themselves inspectors in their localities, as far as religious instruction is concerned; but the inspection of the methods in which reading, writing, ciphering, and so forth, are taught, will be the same kind of thing as in all schools, and should be entrusted to laymen, responsible only to the State. We have not seen any reason offered against this arrangement; and we are convinced that it is the only one which the Cabinet can adopt with any assurance of receiving support from the great bulk of the intelligent community."

Though this suggestion may not obviate all objection, and satisfy all objectors, yet, admitting the State ought to, or may, educate, it will denude the measure of ecclesiastical supremacy, and, as a consequence, infuse trust by dissipating fear.

In this question, I frankly say, if it is to be a State measure, and laymen are solely employed, as a Dissenter, I dare not object to its benefits being available for all sects. *Admit all, exclude none.* This maxim I hold to be in accordance with the great principle laid down by Philip Nye, who, before the Assembly of Divines, as Westminster, in 1644, in maintaining the rights of the Independents, uttered these words – "the right of every man to maintain and teach his religious opinions, be they what they may, without the interference of the magistrate, so long as they contain nothing hostile to the civil government."

To exclude any one differing from me in matters of conscience from his privileges as a citizen is the germ of Popedom, and the earnest of persecution.

Believing your object is the establishment of truth, I ask for your columns to subserve the circulation of sentiments calculated, I hope, to serve this great object.

I remain, Sir, Your obedient and obliged servant, G.C., Woburn, Beds, April 5, 1847.

Not all his letters were published, and here, the Northampton Mercury Editor address a letter Castleden had sent in, but was left unprinted, in which it seems he had taken issue with a recently printed obituary.

13th **November 1847** Northampton Mercury

To Correspondents. Our Woburn Correspondent, G.C., is mistaken to suppose the "tribute" to which he alludes to be ours. We thought it was well understood that such notices, except in extraordinary and easily distinguished cases, proceed from the friends of the deceased, and that the Editor is no more answerable for any eulogy they may express than for statements made in advertisements. In the great majority of cases it must be obvious to our Correspondent that an Editor can know nothing about the matter, and that if he were really to be held responsible, he would, for his own credit sake, strike out everything but the simple statement of fact. In other respects it is impossible not to admit the force of G.C.'s remarks.

Castleden was always keen to correct mistakes in the press, especially if they involved him or his father.

3rd June 1848 Northampton Mercury

Woburn Chartists Meeting. To the Editor of The Northampton Mercury.

Sir – "Fair play's a jewel." In a report of a Chartist meeting held here, your correspondent writes, "The leading members of the Woburn Teetotal Society * * have the credit of calling the meeting." Sir, partial truth, as well as truth suppressed, often leads to wrong conclusions; therefore, as my father at the Woburn Temperance Meetings has often taken the chair in the "Town Hall" I have to state in his absence, his utter ignorance of such a meeting; and my avowal that his views of Chartism are quite in accordance with sentiments I troubled you with last week, but for which you had no spare corner.

I remain Sir, your Obedient servant, George Castleden, 27th May 1848

Sadly, before the end of the year, his father, Rev. Michael Castleden, fell dead at this other son's house in London. His body was returned to Woburn for burial.

25th November 1848 Cambridge Independent Press

Woburn. – On the 11th inst., the interment of the Rev. Michael Castleden of Woburn, took place in the Burial Ground connected with the Independent Chapel of that place. The procession left the house as about 20 minutes past noon. Lord C. J. F. Russell, out of respect for the deceased, having intimated a wish to be allowed to accompany the remains to the grave, walked first, supported by the Rev. J. Andrews on the right, and the Rev. Henry Hutton, A.M., rector of St. Pauls, Covent Garden, London, on the left; the Rev. T. P. Bull, of Newport Pagnell, and the Rev. John Jukes, of Bedford, next. After these, the three deacons of the church, Messrs. Hill, Joseph Osborn and Wright, and Mr. George Gascoyen, of Birchmore. Then came the corpse, carried by six members of the church, the pall being supported by the Revs. Edward Adey, of Leighton Buzzard; J. H. Brooks, of Ridgmount; Josiah Bull, A.M., of Newport; W. C. Robinson, of Ampthill; J. Sleigh, of Hockliffe; and Charles Mears, Esq., of London. The two sons, grandson, and three nephews of the departed were chief mourners, followed by many members of the church and congregation, over whom he had presided for forty-eight years; also, by many of the respectable inhabitants of the town and neighbourhood, and by representatives of the Woburn and Ashley [sic] Guise Temperance Society, with which the departed had long been connected, and by whose members he was greatly beloved. As soon as the cortege arrived at the chapel, the remains were carried within. After singing the hymn, "Hear what the voice form heaven proclaims," &c., the Rev. T. P. Bull read part of I Cor. XV., and offered up prayer. The Rev. J. Andrews of Woburn, successor to the deceased, pronounced the funeral oration and gave out a hymn. The remains were then carried to the grave, and, having been deposited, the Rev. John Jukes made a few remarks to the spectators, and concluded with prayer. A large concourse of people attended; and, but for the services of the police, the chapel and grounds would have been inconveniently thronged.

It was several months before Castleden felt able to write to the papers again.

3rd February 1849 Northampton Mercury

The Woburn Book Society. To the Editor of the Northampton Mercury.

Sir, - A brief sketch of this local society may be interesting in some of the district where the Mercury is read.

October 17th, 1796, a small band, residents of Leighton, Woburn, Ampthill, &c., met at the Coach and Horses Inn, Woburn; a book society was formed, which, through all the vicissitudes of time, has continued to the present hour. Its commencement seems to have been a very modest and economical; two or three periodicals and a sprinkling of current cheap books, principally pamphlets of the day. For some time after its rise meetings were held every two months alternately at Leighton and Woburn at which were discussed curious and learned questions; this debating adjunct continued for some few years and then fell into disuse. To give a by-gone association to our long unobtrusive society I believe an aged inhabitant, long a member, still survives, who remembers in the day of Mr. Pitt's supremacy, a letter being received intimating if certain books then circulating, were not discontinued, the Government would be obliged to notice them; however, whether this was so or not, those harsher days have passed, and pursuing the even tenor of its way the Woburn Book Society has, in neighbourly union combining individual independency, continued of for the long run of fifty-three years.

Its fluctuations have been singular; I have a "Monthly Magazine," dated 1805, exhibiting on its cover only five names; thirty members have been on the list, - now it numbers about twenty. Its plan of procedure is so simple that half a dozen lines will explain. Early in December the meeting is called, the periodicals for the coming year are ordered, - the opposing quarterlies; Blackwood and Tait, and lighter literature in abundance. In addition, each member, as the year rolls on, is allowed to order any book he chooses, not exceeding 10s. 6d.; or two or more may join for some expensive work; the books of the past year are sold, the proceeds of the sale are deducted from the bill, and, share and share alike, settles it. Perhaps the average of the last fifteen years has been 15s. In olden times, I see 8s. to 10s. covered the year's expense for each. At the annual meeting members enter or retire.

Sir, age has ever a claim on our regard, and as an aged literary association, perhaps the oldest in the provinces, and being restricted by "no invidious limits of class in society, religious persuasion, nor party feeling," I hope I ask not too much when I solicit the insertion of this notice of "the Woburn Book Society."

I am, Sir, Your very obedient servant, G.C., Woburn, Beds, 29th Jan., 1849.

The membership names, minutes and accounts for the Woburn Book Society were entered into a ledger, which Castleden must have had in front of him to write his letter. The 304-page ledger, which covers 1796 to 1856, now resides at the UCLA archives in California, USA. (MSS no: 170/19). Books may have been on his mind as the next month saw the release of his next published work, on the coaching inns of Woburn, which had rapidly fallen out of favour with the coming of the railway to nearby Woburn Sands.

23rd March 1850 Northampton Mercury

JUST PUBLISHED, in small octavo, in coloured wrapper, gilt edges LAYS OF HOME: OUR "INNS" NOW "OUT." By GEORGE CASTLEDEN, author of "Woburn Park," etc., etc. Part 1. London: Paternoster and Oakley, Paternoster Row. [Price Ninepence.] Sold by all Booksellers, and at the Office of this paper.

The second part of "Lays of Home", subtitled "Woburn Long Past and Present", was reviewed in the "Christian Witness and Church Members Magazine" of 1850. "In his own sphere, Mr. Castleden has been taking a leaf out of the book of Crabbe, the poet of the multitude. There are many passages in the present piece which Crabbe would have read with pleasure, especially 'The Town Hall's Opening Day'."

The Great Exhibition of 1851 drew crowds from all over England and even abroad, and Woburnites were keen to go and see the attractions for themselves.

16th November 1850 Northampton Mercury

Woburn. The Grand Exhibition, 1851. A Public Meeting of the Inhabitants of Woburn and its Vicinity was held in the Town Hall, Woburn, on Monday, November 11th, at seven o'clock in the evening; for the purpose of taking into consideration the best mode of affording the Inhabitants the opportunity of visiting the Grand Exhibition of the Industry of all Nations in 1851. Lord C. J. F. Russell in the chair. There was a large number of mechanics present. Short addresses were delivered by Messrs. Pearson, Castleden, Farrow, and the Rev. J. Andrews, after which a Society was formed, and a Secretary, Treasurer, and Committee of six appointed to carry out the object of the meeting. A vote of thanks to the noble chairman was carried with great enthusiasm.

"M." had written into the Bedford Mercury to complain that new legislation had made cottagers liable to pay Poor and Highways rates, as if they weren't poor enough already. Unscrupulous landlords had simply increased rents to cover their costs.

26th April 1851 Bedford Mercury

Cottage Property. To the Editor of the Bedford Mercury.

Sir, - By allowing me a corner for a word or two on a communication signed "M." Another view may be gained of Cottage owners, and *"jobbers."*

It will be in your recollection, in by-gone election strifes it was almost indispensable to acquire a bit of freehold property in order that the balance of County representation should be maintained. The acquisition of a forty-shilling freehold was considered then a privilege and a duty. Hence "a vote for the County" was the common entice; went on bill sales, and hence a number of voters consisted of cottage owners. As it regards being "selfish speculators," I would advise an application for some of the depreciated properties, and then see how self will be served by the acquisition. Of these owners, all I can say, from experience, is, that the Act passed last Session causes a loss of more than 5 per cent., and I presume this extra income tax is, generally speaking, paid by the owners.

The exception referred to by your correspondent may be justly noticed. No one can more heartily respond to the latter part of his letter than myself. A cheering sight it is to see rising round us convenient habitations, attached to garden plots, for the peasant sons of the soil; may the "noble example" be followed, and permit me to add, may the wishes I have heard expressed from my boyhood be realised, and may the wholesome sub-division of the land give a chance to the industrious man with his *hundreds*, instead of all being reserved for the capitalist with his *thousands*.

Let but the great landed proprietors follow the noble example, and 'Cottage jobbers' or 'dealers' must become extinct, and let there be but a return to the industrial occupation of small holdings, and we may see restored a healthy peasant population linked with a yeoman occupancy.

More might be written on this regenerative process, but your correspondent having an instance of extortion, consumed in language rather ambiguous, I finish by asking for the insertion of this to qualify impressions relative to a class occasioned by the high colouring bestowed on a *particular* delinquency.

I am, Sir, your obedient servant, G.C. Woburn, 21ˢᵗ April, 1851.

The London Nonconformist of **12ᵗʰ November 1851**, *ran a small advert for "Lays of Home", the latest booklet by Castleden. "Lays No.3 contains Our Church, a Nightstroll in the Churchyard; Our Chapel & c. Price 6d. London Partridge and Oakley, Paternoster-row". The Northampton Mercury of* **15ᵗʰ November 1851**, *reported that Castleden had attended a lecture on John Howard of Bedford, given at the Woburn Independent Chapel, by the Rev. William Charles Robinson of Ampthill. There was a description of "…the life and labours of this noble-minded, benevolent, and extraordinary man. His sacrifices of time, health and property, to reclaim the erring, and to elevate the poor, degraded and despised outcasts of society…", to which Castleden seconded the vote of thanks from the Rev. James Sleigh of Hockliffe. Not all Castleden's submissions to the papers were letters. He very obviously penned the following news report:*

8: The Woburn Parsonage and Bedford Street, on a postcard published c.1910.

21st August 1852 Cambridge Independent Press

Potsgrove. – Sheep-lane Chapel. – In this Bedfordshire nook, in 1838, a small place of worship was built in connection with the Independent Chapel, then under the pastorate of the late Rev. Michael Castleden. Through the last fourteen years it has been supplied with preachers and teachers from Woburn, and their hearts have been cheered both by the attendance of the congregation and the school. On the 3rd instant the children and the friends were invited to take tea in the chapel, and after enjoying themselves, they adjoined to a piece of enclosed ground, kindly granted for the occasion, where the children, and children of larger growth, spent a grateful hour in rustic festivity. The party afterwards returned to the chapel; thanks by praise and prayer were offered to the Giver of all good. Short addresses were delivered by the Revds. J. Andrews (pastor), and J. Sleigh (Hockliffe). Two or three friends added their "five words" of eloquence, and then "Praise God from whom all blessings flow" finished an evening which may be recorded, not on account of the attractions which favoured localities can boast, but because in so arid a spot the rite of Christian philanthropy did cheer; and while for generations, in this wild spot,

"Knowledge to their eyes her ample page,
Rich with the spoils of time, did ne'er unfold."

Yet the believer in the Bible, in looking upon such a rising group, with here and there the sturdy peasant and hoary hind, hopes, under the blessing of that Bible, to see a better knowledge realised; and in their attendance on "the word of truth and love," to see verified, even in Sheep-lane, one of our good Doctor's verses:-

"Lions and beast of savage name
Put on the nature of the lamb –
While the wild world esteems it strange,
Gaze and admire, and hate the change."

Whilst sometimes happy to append his name to his letters, he seemed shyer with his poetry, usually just signing as "G.C., Woburn".

29th October 1853 Bedford Mercury

A Thought on the Grasp after Human Knowledge

Why should we crave a larger share
Of intellects broad orb,
To shine o'er disappointment, care;
Or kindliest light absorb?

51

Look at yon hind whose glow-worm ray,
Just twinkles in life's night;
It sheds along obscurest way
Unenvied, saving light:

It cheers its mortal sojourn through,
Nor apes ambition's glare;
It gilds his home, nor opes to view
The prospect false as fair.

"Know all," and, lo, Change has said,
"'Tis nothing that you burn?"
The margin of expanse we [dread?]
Time's titles only turn?

Beyond, an ocean vast flows on,
Unshadowed by a sail;
And life's a volume scarcely known,
And endless is its tale.
G.C. Woburn, Oct.

19ᵗʰ November 1853 Bedford Mercury

To the Editor of the Bedford Mercury.

Sir, - Some phrases acquire a world-renown in a short time. The one I choose for this communication has acquired this celebrity. Till of late, with many, knowledge relative to the East was summed up in the infant's couplet –

When from the chambers of the East
The sun its rise begins

Or, peeping on "rosy-fingered morn;" or in Hudibrastic verse,

"When, like a lobster boiled, the morn
From black to red begins to turn;"

we say, with multitudes, the rising sun was the boundary of their knowledge relative to the East. But soon as ever the rising leaf appeared on the table, tongues at once became vocal on "the Eastern Question;" and really, Sir, when amidst other articles which have "riz" alarmingly, tallow rose also, we thought it possible the old lady's fear in the late war was coming to pass, and that "the Eastern Question" was about to be settled by candle light, and after all the diplomacy exhibited that "At set of sun" these Orientals were going to "Cry havoc, And let slip the dogs of war." Then we have had the strife of pens, and many a splendid "leader" for and against has been written on the Eastern Question. Statesmen have differed upon it, and the chief harmony at present elicited is between those directly opposite citizens, the Protectionist and Free-trader. What senates struggled for seems now accomplishing; the one is satisfied with present markets, and the other has no corn law to be discontented with. Thanks to the Eastern Question for this balsam to lull awhile local irritations.

Then we have had the Edinburgh pacificators. All honour to their endeavours for the extinction of war, and the introduction of universal peace; but while they think I must be permitted to think too. They think discharging our soldiers and the dismantling of our navy the best way of settling the Eastern Question; I cannot think so, nor see a hope for the *peace* of nations, while I find bitter strife among kinfolk, friends, and neighbours. No, when the agent of all wars shall be renovated, in fact, when the human heart *is not* "deceitful above all thigs and desperately wicked," then, philanthropic dreamers, dream of universal peace – but not till then!

Now we hear war has actually commenced; the Cross and the Crescent are flaunting challenges to each other. The onslaught cries for "God and right," for "Allah and his Prophet," are echoing under the Eastern cape. The clash of steel is ringing; and the roar of artillery is appalling the peaceful dwellers of the Danubian plains. The very lines of Lord Byron are being literally fulfilled;

"The night is dark, and the thick mist allowed
Nought to be seen save the artillery's flame,
Which arched the horizon like a fiery cloud,
And in the Danube's waters shone the same –
A mirrored hell! The volleying roar, and loud
Long booming at each peal on peal, o'ercame
The ear far more than thunder; for Heaven's flashes
Spare, or smite rarely – man's make millions ashes!
And one enormous shout of "Allah" rose
In the same moment, loud as even the roar
Of War's most mortal engines, to their foes
Hurling defiance: city, stream, and shore,
Resounded 'Allah'! "

Shakespear speaks of "plucking safety out of the nettle, danger" – also of "the jewel in the toad's head." Well, let us see whether out of this Eastern war stinging and hideous, we may not pluck safety, and extract worth which may serve humanity, whether a dweller in the inclement North, the sunny South, in Western climes, or oriental realms.

This shall be in the shape of an anecdote lately published. As I quote from memory verbal inaccuracy must be pardoned.

The four brothers, on the death of the Emperor Paul, were – Alexander, Constantine, Nicholas, and Michael. On the succession of the first, Constantine became heir presumptive to the Russian throne. Of a Sythian disposition, he was possessed of a most impractical temper; and so self-convinced of its tyranny, and the awful risk an empire would be in by his ungovernable passion, that in a time of calm decision he formed this truly heroic resolution: he knelt at the knee of his mother, the Russian household divinity, and solemnly vowed he would not reign. Years elapsed; another incident occurred; Constantine became enamoured of a beautiful young Polonese. To marry it was necessary to have the consent of the Emperor Alexander, and the mother. It was given, on the condition that Constantine pledged himself never to seat the Polish wife on the throne of the Romanoff's. This was done; under her happy influence, the Sythian was tamed; and as the viceroy of his brother at Warsaw, he became quite popular. A few years later, death struck Alexander. Nicholas hastened, as the first subject, to proclaim Constantine Emperor of all the Russians. The messenger arrived in Warsaw; consternation prevailed in the palace. Constantine retired to an innermost chamber; and there alone, refusing entrance even to his wife, he waged a fearful war with his own spirit; every article in the room was broken and trampled to atoms; but he conquered self. At eventide he came out, threw himself at the feet of his wife, and the strong man, in broken accents, uttered – "They shall not part us." The messenger returned with the older brothers abdication; and when Nicholas was crowned at Warsaw, he elder brother, Constantine, stood amid the assembly as the colonel of his regiment, and was the first to cry 'all hail' to the new crowned monarch. A short time after, the attached pair retired into Lithuania. Happy in their retirement, time passed, till death struck him, and then she, still in the bloom of life, in a few months joined in the grave the husband who, for her sake, sacrificed empire and said to ambition – "avaunt!"

Respectfully, we say, ponder this anecdote. If all are not born princes, yet 'one touch of nature makes the whole world kin;" so this illustration of a man ruling his own spirit – this exhibition of fraternal affection and devoted love – may, in some portion, prevail with all.

If these vagrant thoughts catch but one eye, and incline but one heart to emulate, then they will not have been prescribed in vain: and once more smiling over the association of the rising sun and the rising loaf, we commit to the candour of the reader this our view of "the Eastern Question."

I am, Sir, Your very obedient servant, A Hater of War, Woburn, 12th Nov.

The story above relates to Grand Duke Konstantin Pavlovich of Russia, and Castleden's retelling of it would seem to be pretty much accurate. The "Eastern Question" mentioned was the uncertainty of what would happen to the collapsing Ottoman Empire, and whether Russia would gain territory and influence at the expense of the rest of the western European powers. In the following letter, he relates a story obviously passed down to him by his father, who had attended Hoxton Academy.

24th December 1853 Bedford Mercury

The Spirit Rapping Question. To the Editor of the Bedford Mercury.

Sir, - May I be allowed a part of your columns on this mystery of our day. For when I find Christian folk, grave divines, and men of intellect vouching to its verity, I must call it a mystery, or I am in danger of impeaching the sanity of its advocates, or of questioning the veracity of its believers.

The Sacred Book says – "There is nothing new under the sun." If I give an anecdote of the last century, it may afford thought to the Mahogany Thumpers of our day.

Before Academies became Colleges, among dissenters, were gathered a happy and a time-honoured group of young men preparing for the ministry, under the well-known and highly esteemed tutor, the Rev. Robert Simpson. On the like of one of these winter evenings, round the common room fire, a mysterious conversation was entered into on supernatural appearances, second sight, &c. A gaunt son of Lancashire gave out ominous words, and announced his belief that he could CALL spirits, and that they would COME at his bidding. His auditors, excited, challenged to the proof. He agreed. The incantation was to proceed in a dark room, he, alone, while in one adjoining the group were, unknown to him, to agree on whom he should call from the slumbers of the tomb. Retiring to his room, he returned with a visage solemn and mystical, bearing a staff of ancient appearance, and then in sepulchral tones, rendered more effective by his dialect, enjoined profound silence during the mystical process. Into the dark room he went; singular tones were heard, then the scrape as of a circle forming, and then followed at intervals – thump – thump – thump. This was continued, till all of a sudden a rustling sound was heard, then a mystical stamp of the foot, and wildly rushed out the weird-brother shouting "Chatham, Chatham." Had a bomb-shell fallen among the listeners the effect could not have been more complete on hearing the very name shouted which they, in secret, had agreed upon. Self preservation being the first law of nature, out of the room they rushed, persuaded the veritable Lord Chatham was after them; some went down the stairs at a bound; head over heels rolled Buck, Castleden, and Slatterie, and found themselves pitched upon an unfortunate brother, who, much against his inclination, had become the ottoman to these retreating Christians. After listening to the tutors "What's all that noise about?" and then congratulating each other on the escape from accident, and still peering into the dark, and wondering whether the ghost would still walk in. Curiosity, at length, was satisfied. The ghost-raiser had had his double among the students; the thump of the staff answered to letters of the alphabet; a concerted signal informed of each letter, and thus at Hoxton Academy the spirit of "the great Lord Chatham" was rapped up in 1793-4.

The anecdote, here repeated, has caused the boisterous laugh in the room where I am inscribing it; and it seems somewhat akin to the rapping mania of our day. Then, men who have filled worthy stations in life were beguiled, for a time, out of their sober senses, and given evidence of credulity incompatible almost with sanity, and inconsistent with a belief in Divine inspiration.

Excess of light, they say, is darkness. We live in a very light, and a very fast age. If, from seizing the sunbeam and bidding it o inscribe the human face divine – if, from putting in irons the very lightnings of the clouds, holding them to our behests – if, from sending the Bible all over the world, we are to turn and grope our way into the darkest things of the dark ages, plunge the gospel lamp into mephitic gloom of divination and magic, - let us at any rate be consistent; cut Christianity, laugh at immortality, dismiss our divines, and drop the Bible; patronize the wizard, and cry "all hail" to the necromancer, and say, "these are our gods."

Let us ALTER Prospero's words, and honestly appropriate them (See "Tempest, a.5 s.1"

> "But this *true* magic
> I *seal* and *sign*; and with it will call *down*
> Some heavenly music, or spirits will call *up*
> To work mine end upon the senses, that
> This potent charm may cozen; I'll *wave* my staff,
> New resurrections work, and spirits call
> From deeps where plummet never sounded;
> I'll *read* this book."

I am, Sir, your obedient servant, G.C., Woburn, Dec. 19th.

His next submission was a graphic description of the efforts of some amateur Woburn Carol singers, which seem to have been in vain...

31ˢᵗ December 1853 Bedford Mercury

Christmas Waits of Olden Time. To the Editor of the Bedford Mercury.

Sir, - At the season of festivity, an incident from the past may move the merry vein in some of your present readers, while perchance it will recall to the few left their time of carols, mistletoe, and fun.

Thirty years ago, the provincials entered but slightly into the axiom, "knowledge is power." Of literary societies, scientific associations, and arts mysteries, they were comparatively ignorant.

Knowledge was thinly scattered; nevertheless, rich in hospitalities and scenes of boisterous humour, our fathers made their halls and house ring with festive mirth; and, at that day, or rather night, the Christmas singers, perambulating our streets, were invested with an importance unknown to our enlightened day.

It was one of these bye-gone Christmas-eves the incident occurred which we will attempt to depict. In a very small room were gathered a group of musicians and vocalists, waiting to perform their several parts in the "waits." Imbibition and the fragrant weed were the preparatives to a rehearsal; the face of the venerable conductor was seen every now and then looming through the narcotic mist – at intervals it disappeared; then, like a sun, beamed bright again.

After a while a significant clear-up took place, and it was announced, as two tunes were to be sung, on the catholic principles of pleasing all, that while the ancient strain, "Christians awake," was to be the principle piece, yet to gratify some Christians, "Suffolk New" was to be performed, with the additional attraction of a new young singer volunteering at the PIANO. "And now, gentlemen," said the conductor, "let us just try it over before we start, and let Mr. ___ sing the PIANO solo."

This went off well as could be expected, considering the company and compounds. After the coughing congratulations, the party emerged; and under scudding, sleety clouds, and upon snow, ankle deep, they gave to the night winds notes more loud than sweet – the leader of many years, grey in the service, zestfully discoursing eloquent music through the reedy pipe. Time and also dimmed, if not darkened the larboard peeper; this casualty rendered it necessary for an attendant to throw the lantern's glimmering light upon the notes of "Suffolk New." His companions in melody gathered round him; and, to use his own words, "the tune went off capitabal."

But it hath been said by some sage – Fortune seldom smiles without having a frown in store; so the course of true melody was no to run smooth. At a corner of the town, whose angle stands E. by S. Suffolk New was to be again warbled; the young warbler, under the wing of the amply-coated conductor, had just reached the PIANO pitch – the accompanying clarinet

THE

"HOPE OF RIGHTEOUSNESS."

A Sermon,

BY THE

REV. J. ANDREWS,

PREACHED IN THE

INDEPENDENT CHAPEL, WOBURN, BEDS,

ON LORD'S DAY, SEPTEMBER 18TH, 1853.

LONDON:

JACKSON AND WALFORD,

18, ST. PAUL'S CHURCHYARD.

Price Threepence.

9: Frontispiece to "Hope of Righteousness", by Rev. James Andrews, 1853.

was indulging in a brilliant shake, - when lo, like a bullet from a gun, a ball of snow struck the convalescent orb, and suddenly dousing it, caused a staccato movement from the performer altogether interruptive of the choral harmony.

Alas for the uncertainty of human joy. The instant before it might be said of this ancient –

"As he caught the measure wild,
The old man raised his head and smiled;
And lighted up his faded eye
With all a poet's extacy:"

Then, as in an instant, complacency was disturbed – confusion fell around – key and tune were lost; and the couplet of the Scottish minstrel well describes the FINALE of these "waits," all of the olden time –

"Among the stops his fingers played,
And an uncertain warbling made."

I send this scrap of the retiring past – when Christmas coaches loaded with turkeys, fish, and game, rattled through our streets; when at the rail we did not wail; and life's strange tale, in our snug vale, was, if a dream, a different scene.

I am, Sir, your obedient servant, G.C., Woburn, Dec. 28th, 1853.

The good people of Woburn had obviously had quite enough of the late-night warbling, festive as it may have been, and decided to put a stop to it. At least they had only pelted the lamp with snowballs and not the carol-singers themselves!

The Cambridge Independent Press of **28th January 1854** *ran a piece that the accounts of the Woburn Independent Chapel had been audited, and found to be in a "flourishing condition". William Perkin, one of the deacons, chaired the meeting, which also presented the Rev. J. Andrew with a purse containing £20, as a token of their esteem and affection. Castleden then took the floor, and gave "one of his most happy and witty speeches", although sadly this was not copied into print. Castleden now had competition for Christian literary work emanating from Woburn. The Bedford Mercury of the same date as above carried an advert for a new book by the Rev. Andrews of Woburn Independent Chapel. His book-sermon, "The Hope of Righteousness", (3d.) was, according to the Evangelical magazine, "a solid faithful scriptural discourse... a vast deal of sound Christian instruction..."*

1st April 1854 Bedford Mercury

The Turkey-Partition Sure. To the Editor of the Bedford Mercury.

Sir, - I am proud of my country: and, need I disguise the honest expression I am proud of the two statesmen whose names are attached to the "Secret Correspondence" which has enlightened us on the Eastern question. In reading it I felt a glow of satisfaction akin to one who boasted that he "lived in Chatham's day."

Far from me to enter into the vocation of the statesman, or to venture criticism on state affairs, or meddle, wantonly, with diplomatic machinery; but, perchance, a single-minded Englishman, although obscure and unknown, may afford in his own locality thought for thought upon this *now* world-talked question; and, as one of the people, his utterances may find response in some as *peaceably* inclined as ever Henry Pease or Joseph Sturge were when shaking hands with the Emperor, or *are* now while avowing that "the Czar is kind and temperate!"

First and foremost, we eulogize the prudence of the Government, even to the risk of its own popularity, in withholding, till challenged from Petersburg, such exculpatory and damnatory documents. In a letter published in your columns we asked, what is to be done when all forbearance has no weight, and indulgence prevents not hostility? Months ago, speaking to a sailor, now in the Baltic, relative to the possibility of war, with the frankness of his class he said, "There will be no war, England won't strike till she is struck, and the Czar will not be such a fool as to do that." But who ever thought, at that time, he was daring to *cajole* her; that he was looking upon the high-minded honour-esteeming Englishman as one willing first to be hugged, and then to be pilloried for European scorn: ay, with 800 years' independence, character, and progress on his brow, that he was willing to fall *self*-degraded, far in the rear of a Russian animal serf, and to be sunk infinitely lower than a shackled Siberian slave. Thanks that Lord John Russell and the Earl of Clarendon, of Queen Victoria's day, have so worthily anticipated the nation's voice, and, like to the great statesman of Queen Elizabeth's reign, have shewn that England can afford to lose all but her honour; and now, like the Drakes and the Howards, our Napiers and Dundancs, with their French brethren, have sailed in order to teach this European traitor that the "ultimate partition of Turkey and the exclusion of France from the arrangement," *must not be* consummated. Verily, attempting this on the religious plea is uncommonly like a celebrated pickpocket, whose tactics were to visit fashionable congregation, mark down some autumnal dame, and, while piously presenting the psalm-book, was performing the character of conveyance of any unguarded property. No, no, great Emperor! in such hypercritical despoliation don't quote the Psalms against a people who, whatever may be their sins or errors, individually or nationally, have ever paid allegiance to their divinity, and who publicly avow their belief of those words of a paraphrase of the 103rd Psalm,

"He sees the *oppressor* and the *oppressed*,
And often gives the sufferers rest."

Surely we may add if ever a nation's oppression was attempted, it was when, with the bait thrown to Sir G. H. Seymour, the tempter implied "all these things will I give you;" or, in his own language, "I beg you to convey these words to Lord John Russell. When we are agreed, I am quite without anxiety as to the west of Europe; it is immaterial what the others may think or do."

Now, to put the case closely. Suppose England had been as needy or mercenary as he thought her mean, yet with a maritime force sufficient to support his purposes; then this atrocious suggestion might have prevailed, and as a nation we had been blasted with well-deserved and ever-enduring infamy. Now the proud contrast is, we have scorned the temptation and have defied the tempter; and, looking upon the map of Europe the other day, surveyor Russia's almost boundless possessions, and then resting the eye upon our own "sea-girt" isle, and associating the lines,

"He bade the waters round thee flow,
No walls of brass could guard thee so,"

I had an indefinable joy that in such Russian criminality, Britain stood stainless, and finding forbearance had reached its limit, from her waters had sailed those "wooden walls," inclosing munitions for the "oppressed," and bearing avenging thunder for the "oppressor."

"Long may she hold the awful right,
In her restless hour
Hurl her swift vengeance in the fight,
On each oppressive power."

And as on the same evening I was looking into a periodical, and saw the once European antagonists, Wellington and Napoleon, arm in arm, looking down from the clouds on the combat below, and saying "United they will conquer the world," thought started, and we said,

See the Frank and the Briton in battle unite,
Apart may they never more ruthless fight.
But, shoulder to shoulder, arrayed in the field,
Teach the despot to tremble, the tyrant to yield.

Here we might stay: we might not presume to throw light on the future! To "the God of battles," in the language of olden chivalry, has been committed this European quarrel. If among our peacemakers any remain pertinaciously attached to the idea that all has not been done that England could do to prevent war, we emphatically say, read the "secret Correspondence," and then the last scathing words in the Times of the 29th, "But it is not the least singular part of this transaction that Russia herself should have called for the production of evidence which establishes to demonstration the enormity of her bad faith;" and then while we will not severely criticise philanthropic credulity, we dare not assent to that pacific policy which waits for seizure to confirm, and partition to convince. This seems akin to the humanity of the man who, having an opportunity of dealing a *saving* blow upon the head of the stricken traveller, yet tries *first* expostulation, affording by his measured sentences ample time for the ruffian to pull the trigger of his second pistol.

If, ever on a grand scale, illustration of our schoolboy fable, "the wolf and the lamb," was afforded, it is in the reasoning of Russia towards Turkey. "Turkey is on the verge of ruin" - "the sick man is dying" those, and such like reasons, are given for seizure. "Keep France away; I hold in check the other powers; let your Government aid, and with me divide the spoil, and all will be well." *These* were the lures, the wily arrangements with which the wolf of the North was to make a savoury snap of the lamb of the East.

Whether war rages with devastating fury or no, the warning to Russia's Emperor against "unprovoked conquest and ephemeral glory" by Lord John Russell, and the confidence expressed by the Earl of Clarendon "in the rectitude of his Imperial Majesty," leave these statesmen in a proud position; while, in our humble estimation, the Ministry occupy this very high ground: for a *still lingering hope of peace*, they have submitted to an imperilment of their public character, and, with confounding documents to all questioners, have risked an impeachment of their political fidelity.

I am, Sir, your obedient servant, G. C. Woburn, 25th March.

The Crimean War had plunged Europe into crisis again, pitching the British, French, and Turkish Ottoman Empires against Russia.

15th April 1854 Bedford Mercury

The Russian Policy - "Divide and Devour". To the Editor of the Bedford Mercury.

Sir, - This is the policy of the destroyer. It has been so from Edenic days. Satan watched for the temporary separation of Adam and Eve; and then, assuming the shape of the serpent, beguiling her with flattering words:

"Wonder not, sovereign mistress, if perhaps

Thou can'st, who art sole wonder, much less arm

Thy looks, the Heav'n of mildness, with distain."

He divided, and sin and death devour.

The same policy the modern Nicholas has tried on the statesmen of

Europe: he stooped to flatter the Englishmen in order to sow division between neighbouring nations, and give him the easier task to devour peoples.

Let us look at this satanic axiom as it bears upon nations, friends, relatives, and *self*; and suggest the foil to its destructions.

Divide nations, say France and England; devour Turkey; hold Constantinople, and wait to ravage Western Europe.

The Foil: Unite England and France, prevent the seizure of Turkey, and hope, by a restoration of Poland, a bulwark against northern ambition may be reared.

Divide friends for some sinister design; and then, weakened, devour in detail.

The foil: Unite on principle; hold fast to things that are right; let truth link with truth.

Divide a family, devour its prosperity, happiness, peace.

The foil: Unite: if the suggestion comes from *without*, say whatever is wrong *within* our home, your advice must widen the breach.

It is written, *an offended brother is harder to be won than a strong city*; and lamentable it is when offence comes and divides and devours from *within*; this may be one of Time's keenest afflictions; but when the agent from without consummates this desolation, merely to gratify selfish purpose, or fiendish propensities, we should suppose no punishment, out of hell, more bitter than the consciousness of having "privily plotted" a division ending in a family's ruin. Well will it be if, having gone to such a depth, the evil-doer finds not "a lower deep," and, selling his whole soul to the arch fiend, says, callous to all the humanities of our nature, "Henceforth, *evil* be thou my good."

Divide self from self-respect, depravity must t hen *devour*. Oh, on you go on a downward course, and, separated from self-esteem, step by step you near perdition so faithfully portrayed by Shakespear,

> "My conscious has a thousand several tongues,
> And every tongue brings a several tale,
> And every tale condemns me for a villain.
> I shall despair – there is no creature loves me,
> And if I die, no soul shall pity me:
> Nay, wherefore should they? since that I myself
> Find in myself no pity to myself."

The foil: Defy the tempter; say I will *smite* with self-respect, whatever else will go. With this you would walk into the Union-house with a prouder step than if, by wrong, you took possession of a palace. Your road may be rough, and your skies dark, but you will always have a mystical light and help if you don't *hate yourself*. Let this salvatory selfish alliance never be broken, and, stricken with sorrow, but unscarred by crime, as sure as to-morrow's sun must rise so shall the orb, self-respect, ascend.

It may be the lot of some undeservedly to find the happy "Night Thought" of the late Thomas Moore illustrated in their experience:

"How oft a cloud, with envious veil,
Obscures your bashful light
Which seems so modestly to steal
Along the waste of night:
'Tis thus the world's obtrusive wrongs
Obscure with malice keen
Some timid heart which only longs
To live and die unseen."

But to use a bolder figure, we say, as well attempt to hide the mounting sun with a few fluttering rags as to hide the shining of *true* character by the tatters of opinion or the flimsies of falsehood. Aspersion may cloud; prejudice may shroud; misfortune may darken; but a sense of an inward self-rectitude must ultimately surmount all that is outwardly adverse, aye, even if in the least extremity he sinks, dividing not from self-respect, he nails character to the mast-head and finds a glorious grave. Here, to return to Eastern affairs, is England's enviable position. She has been tempted to *divide* in order to *devour*. She has united to succour the weak against the strong. Our statesmen have nobly sustained national *self*-respect. If, to carry out inscrutable purpose, the Czar's millions were to overwhelm, the "Albion" would go down with this high distinction among the nations of the earth, at her mast-head, flying proudly to the last, would be seen CHARECTER, or, in the words of unpolished and uneducated integrity, HONOUR BRIGHT.

We close with the words of one of our weekly prints, because they truly develop the malignant cause of division and destruction; and because they very ably defend our agency in this Eastern war: "The Queen of England preaches no crusade, and declares no conviction that she shall not be "eternally confounded," but if ever there was a holy war, it is the war of Right against Wrong. One of its forms, and the one on which the attention of Europe is just now turned, is that of physical struggle; but this is to be but a part of the grand campaign ever conducted by enlightenment against barbarism; and this mortal strife, for which our fleets and armies are now moving on, is ennobled by the consideration that it is but one of the operations of the age against the common enemies, tyranny and imposture.

I am, Sir, your very obedient servant, G. C., Woburn, 6th April.

Juxtaposing his warnings of a dire European war, his next letter recounted a carefree walk through the local villages to Ampthill.

27th May 1854 Bedford Mercury

To the Editor of the Bedford Mercury.

Sir, - On the Crawley road we passed, and gazed on as pretty view as any in this neighbourhood. The morning sun fell upon the new cottages; and the red tiles, glistening among the trees, gave a cheerful contrast to the thatched cottages, something of regret lingered about the 'chimney corners' of olden style. Memory would dwell on the fire-lit faces around the 'wooden blizzy,' and the rosy-faced comfort of the 'ingle nook.'

Ridgmount we passed, and looked on the rising walls of the new church, whose foundation-stone, in solemn service, was laid by Her Grace the Duchess of Bedford on the 25th of April.

A mile on the road we spied a lad, snug under the hedge, just finishing his morning nap. 'What are you doing?' 'Shepherding,' was the prompt reply of this precocious youth. Thinks I, this is coming it as strong as the 'juvenile' who, at one of his first essays at rubbing down a horse, gave great significance to his task by that peculiar emission of breath indulged in by the stable fraternity. On being asked why he made such a blowing noise, the younker replied, 'It's a way us grooms has got.' Smiling over our 'shepherding' acquaintance and grooming serap, we walked on, cheered by the rival melodies of the piping nightingale and the blithesome carol of the soaring lark. We passed the 'Ossory Arms,' and saw in this heraldic sign a memento of glory passed away!

Turning from this beautiful road, we entered an enclosure, and trod the turf of former cricket glee, where more than twenty years ago the Woburn *old eleven* won the victory, with 130 runs to spare. Stopping to tell some of the incidents of this match to an aged companion, we had a hearty laugh over one of its anecdotes; and then, with the *gay* mingled with the *grave* conclusion that a cricket-field is but a type of life's expansive plain on which men and women are players, or shadows following shades, till fleeting time its shadowy race is done. This brought us to ascending ground; and here we threw mind three centuries back, and from the historic page contemplated the mighty reformation originating in Henry's qualms of conscience relative to his marriage with Catherine of Arragen. On the very ground we were treading, this injured Queen, the wife of Henry's youth, and the mother of his child, mused over her wrongs.

> "Ampthill's romantic spot asylum gave
> To broken-hearted Kate
> Its former towers, its sylvan solitudes,

Proud Henry's wife inhabited; and 'neath
Its oaks, then in the autumn of their sap,
She strolled; and making Heaven her only judge,
Nobly she scorned acknowledgement to men."

Here, summoned to appear before the Commissioners sitting at Dunstable Monastery, with righteous scorn the queen refused to appear; and being then pronounced 'contemacious,' then did these 'just judges' of the Tudor King 'Denounce, degrade, and then divorce.' As a local voucher, we copy the inscription on a monument erected by the Earl of Ossory in 1773.

"In days of yore, here Ampthill's towers were seen,
The mournful refuge of an injured Queen;
Here flowed her pure, but unavailing tears;
Here blinded zeal sustained her sinking yers
Yet Freedom hence the radiant banner wav'd,
And love aveng'd a realm by priests enslav';
From Catherine's wrongs a nation's bliss was spread,
And Luther's light from lawless Henry's bed."

On the steps of this "Cross" lounged the herd-boy, who little dreamed of the historical divorce, deaths, and destructions, we memorialised by his resting place –

"If ignorance is bliss
'Tis folly to be wise."

From this elevated mound the landscape was exquisitely fine. On the foreground, hill and dale, spring-tide verdant beauty, intermingled with ancestral oaks hollow and crumbling, yet from ruins throwing out green garlands still. Over the vale hung luminous masses of clouds, from out of whose skinks woodland fields and villages were lighted as intervals, giving to the darker portions of the same shades as deep as Indita black, while southward the Chiltern hills piled the horizon's verge and the full shining of the sun on them distinctly pencilled their peaks and wavy lines upon the distant sky. Descending we come to the patriarch of the forest. Under its time-mangled members we stood, and looked upon the garden in front of the Mansion, and then recited to our companion the inscription –

"Majestic tree, whose wrinkled form have stood
Age after age the patriarch of the wood;
Thou who hast seen a thousand springs unfold
Their ravell'd buds and dipt their flowers in gold;
Ten thousand times you moon re-light her horn,
And that bright star of evening gild the morn.
Gigantic Oak! Thy hoary head sublime

Erewhile must perish in the wreck of time.
Should round thy head innumerous lightning shoot,
And no fierce whirlwind shake thy steadfast root,
Yet shalt thou fall, thy leafy tresses fade,
And those bars shatter'd antlers strew the glade:
Arm after arm shall leave the mouldering bust,
And thy firm fibres crumble into dust.
The muse alone shall consecrate thy name,
And by her powerful art prolong thy fame;
Green shall thy leaves expand, thy branches play,
And bloom for ever in th'immortal lay."

A trite remark say, "Nothing is certain in this uncertain world." Our May morning had been breezy and fine; we had finished "copy," and were congratulating each other on the proposed stroll when darkness overspread; a few drops sounded warning; the flood descended, and, sheltered in one of the out-houses, while musing upon regal misfortune and patrician mutabilities, we were obliged to call to aid the plebian philosophy contained in Kirks White's line – "Come, disappointment, come." And in the drops of this desponding shower dropped this truth -

"Man's life is like an April day;
A little sun, a flood of rain,
Anon night hurries o'er the plain
And we are soon no more!"

Our purpose being broken, with a look at the front of the house we trudged homeward. If we say we dropped short at "Dropshorts," dried ourselves, and fared better than some of our brethren at Gallipoli, we may be but noting truth. We then around the fields, and at the brow of Broomhill, Lidlington, we watched one of the grandest junctions of clouds we ever saw; then the ebon mass hung above the whole of the valley, and palled the distant hills; then up and across played vividly surmountive? lightning, and reverberating rolled the thunder from west to north. Again taking refuge, as creatures of association, while heaven's artillery was sounding over our home plains, we heard the booming of our ?? over the waters of the east; and while we know – "Heaven's flashes, Smite rarely, men a make millions ashes," we did, relative to the bombardment of Odman, congratulate ourselves on the fact, that mercy mingled with the chastisement May it be so in the future; and then as Britain entered this quarrel only as the helper of the oppressed, she may retire from it with a glory eclipsing the meretricious glitter of conquest, with a pride untarnished by territorial aggrandisement. But we have rambled from the pastoral scenes and find ourselves mentally looking

10: A plan of the Woburn chapel, drawn in the 1950-60's, by Foll & Parker estate agents, of Woburn Sands.

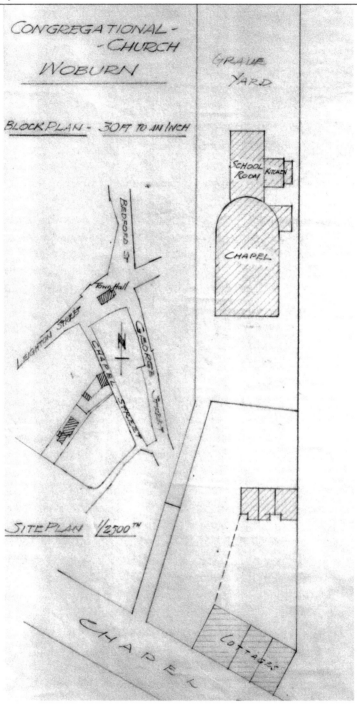

CONGREGATIONAL -
- CHURCH
WOBURN

BLOCK PLAN - 30 FT TO AN INCH

GRAVE YARD

SCHOOL ROOM

KITCHEN

CHAPEL

BEDFORD ST

Town Hall

LEIGHTON STREET

CHAPEL STREET

GEORGE STREET

N

SITE PLAN 1/2500TH

CHAPEL

COTTAGES

from one of our verdant towns upon the frowning cannon bristling fortress of the Black or Baltic Sea, or watching on the Turkish plains the gathering of Europe's armies eager for the fight. Then, around the walnut-tree table with the refreshing laden, all their warlike thoughts have vanished under the genial humour of our hostess, and the inspiration of the passing jobs.

This remark we may finish another day.

G. C., Woburn, May, 1854.

The Woburn Exhibition had now occurred, and Castleden was moved to write a description of it, not for the papers, but for sale.

22ⁿᵈ July 1854 Bedford Mercury

Just published, Price 6d., Dedicated, by permission, to Her Grace the Duchess of Bedford, and the Right Honourable Lady Charles Russell; a Memorial of The Woburn Exhibition, by George Castleden. Dodd and Peeling, Booksellers, &c., Bedford Street.

A long article in the Cambridge Independent Press of 5ᵗʰ August 1854 describes an important event in the history of the Woburn Independent Chapel, when the Rev. T. P. Bull of Newport Pagnell, laid a memorial stone in connection with the rebuilding. The Rev. Bull's father had been a visitor to Woburn 80 years previously, and had also preached at the opening of the old Chapel, in 1804, when Castleden's father was Minister. Castleden is not mentioned by name, but I am sure he would have been there to see this event, if indeed it was not him writing the report. The Rev. Bull was presented with a silver trowel, inscribed: "Presented to the Rev. T. P. Bull, on laying the foundation stone of Woburn Independent Chapel, July 20th 1854." Over £345 had been promised to the building fund, with subscriptions including donations from Their Graces the Duke and Duchess of Bedford, and the Right Hon. Lord and Lady Charles Russell.

On 26ᵗʰ October 1854, the Woburn Chapel work was completed. It had been lengthened by 32ft., the old galleries removed, and new ones installed which would hold the organ, the choir and 120 children. The work had been put out to tender in June by Lander & Bedells, architects, of London. However, it was to be December before the services that were being conducted temporarily in the Town Hall would cease.

Whilst war still raged abroad, it was disease that struck at home. More than 600 people died in the Soho area of London alone, but the outbreak led to John Snow discovering that it was transmitted by infected water supplies, and therefore led to the disease being tackled more successfully afterwards.

28th October 1854 Bedford Mercury

The Cholera. To the Editor of the Bedford Mercury.

Sir, - While the pestilential cloud, we trust, is thinning, the poisoned air, we hope, is becoming purified, and, for this season, alarm is subsiding, still we may profitably employ an hour in gaining instruction from the *past*, and by it offer counsel from the future. I, therefore, venture a few lines for our county on the present escape of this town from the past which has filled streets with mourning, and houses with lamentations.

If ewe revert to the times when, even mildly smitten, the voice cracked, the eyes dimmed, the throat thickened, and strength failed, we say where these sudden premonitory symptoms alarmed, a grateful attention may be enlisted, and while acknowledging Providential preservation from the *last remove*, let us improve the extension of our inch of time by adverting to the probable cause of our escape from the severity of this scourge.

Believing in the judgements of the Most High, yet facts are too palpable and proofs too positive that the *means* are our's, while the *end* belongs to Inscrutable Wisdom.

Now for a fact: more than fifty years ago, our town was traversed with "capital common shores" (our fathers were not so polite in their pronunciation as their sons; and they used to add, gratefully, "a rare good job for the town was that by the Duke Francis.") So complete and effectual is the drainage, that with very few exceptions, a connection with the common sewer can easily be made available for the removal of all filth *underground*. In our streets the sense of smelling is rarely offended by kennel exhalations: and as it regards their general state of cleanliness, let others testify. A friend sitting in a public room far away, heard this reference to Woburn - "Aye, that is the cleanest town I know in my travels; why, you may walk from one end to the other in silk stockings and hardly get them soiled." And I have heard of an itinerary which puts us down as the second clean town in England. If, then, cleanliness has shielded in choleric visitations, we offer a good local illustration for its observance. We have much woodland round us - our waters are artificial, and so often stagnant - heavy fogs hang over us - yet, with these probable helps to this epidemic, we have escaped. We say, not presumptuously, that cleanliness has contributed to our salvation: we do refer to the words of strangers to the *fact*; and we do offer this, our exemption from this pestilence, as worthy the consideration of those now searching into the sanitary state of towns.

We have stated what was done in our fathers' day, let us gratefully record of the many pleasant homes lately erected by His Grace the Duke of Bedford. Great precautionary measures have been made against the pestilential smite; and if the cottages themselves will but be cleanly, I hope still this parish will exhibit the example, that while the fire of pestilence may pervade the atmosphere, the ignitable refuse shall not be found on our premises, nor inflammable vapours rise in our streets.

On the provinces of the Faculty we intrude not; yet while with them the cause of disease and the precise remedy is still in debate, we leave the fact of home cleanliness to stimulate to a continuance of this healing virtue, and by a strict observance it may mitigate the visitations of other epidemics. If so, this hour's thought, published through your columns, may serve the cause of suffering humanity.

I am, Sir, your obedient servant, G. C., Woburn, 23rd October.

Death was still on his mind when an acquaintance passed away.

18th November 1854 Bedford Mercury
Woburn – A Dark November Day's Thought.

Dark was the day, and thought was dark,
As on earth's shadowed scene
A dreaming bard in lonely hour
Would on earth's trouble dream.

For neighbour dead he heard the bell;
Saw 'dust' and 'ashes' go
Adown the street to that last bourne,
The home of human woe.

His neighbours, too, avouched the tale
Pertaining to the tomb;
And if a moment broke joy's gleam,
It mocked the thickening gloom.

These home-thoughts passed: *abroad*, the gun
Has boomed out many a knell;
Darkened, 'ere noon, their mounting sun
In bloody darkness fell.

There they sleep well; *here* mourners wake,
And sorrow 'murders sleep;'
In many a home poor orphans sigh,
And wretched widows weep.

And shall we spare the burning curse
On him whose despots will
Withers broad Europe's fairest plains,
And speaks command to kill?

Can we withhold the astonished *why*
Such atom-wrath should sweep;
That one should scatter blood-steeped seeds;
Bid Slaughter's sons to reap?

That one lose despot, in his rage,
Should raise this murderous gale;
And where it sweeps in scathing wrath
Red ruin should prevail?

And coward, too. He speaks the storm,
Secure *himself* from harm;
And while his pride bids peoples bleed
Enjoys his palace-calm.

Compunctionless his death-word flies;
Immortals fall as prey;
As food for powder they become,
To appease Ambition's sway.

Can this be right? Can ordered *good*
From Slaughter's *evil* rise?
Can light be sown in such dark deeds
To enlighten future skies?

Enough! strifes, woes, and fightings come,
Some purpose to fulfil;
And man, all curious, must be dumb,
Nor doubt the ETERNAL WILL.
G. C., Woburn, Beds, November, 1854.

When Castleden uses the term 'neighbour', it could apply to someone as far as a neighbouring village, so sadly we have no idea who it was who had passed "…adown the street to that last bourne".

2nd December 1854 Northampton Mercury

Woburn – Independent Chapel – On Sunday evening last, the congregation of this chapel worshipped for the last time in the Town-hall, where for six months, by the kind permission of his Grace the Duke of Bedford, they had been most pleasantly accommodated during the rebuilding of their own place of worship. The hall was full. The service had reference to the death of a young townsman; the text was, Job 14, chapter 1, and 2d verse. A solemn admonition on the frailty of life and the certainty of death, with the hope of the righteous in death; these formed the subject matter of this last discourse. After the majority had left, a few remained to offer prayer. The long familiar words were last sung –

"When I can read my title clear
To mansions in the skies,"

And at the close the minister added a sentence of grateful acknowledgement; and then half a dozen lingered, and in their farewell responded a tribute of thanks for the ducal favour in their time of need, and then this remnant of Protestant Dissenters left the hall; and how upon this; another of its scenes, may memory dwell, and the children of our Sunday-school may, in the future, tell the year they said their lessons and sung their little hymns beneath the arches of Woburn's hall. From a Correspondent.

...a correspondent who, judging by the language and content, was no doubt George Castleden.

13th January 1855 Bedford Mercury

Mechanics' Institutions. Woburn Literary, Scientific and Mechanics' Institution.

To the Editor of the Bedford Mercury

Sir, - In all probability you have a detailed report of a very pleasing meeting held in the Town Hall on the 10th inst., under the patronage of Her Grace the Duchess of Bedford and Lady Charles Russell.

At this soiree the social beverage was kindly attended to by the ladies; the tea was highly commended, and looking forward to the evening's exhibition of wisdom, profound discussion was avoided while in our cups. After the removal of the uninebriating machinery, the Chair was taken by Colonel Gilpin, M.P., who, in his opening speech, after regretting the absence of Lord Charles Russell, gave the key to the speeches of the evening. With every mark of respect to the several speakers, even to name them may be unnecessary in this scrap, and to select were invidious, when all so ably and kindly contributed to the evening's amusement and instruction. Rather as one gratified with the whole, we analize not the parts, but for this scene humbly tender thanks to each who contributed of his stock to inform and gratify.

On looking round the hall we saw a very happy association of the orders of English society, and we could not but come to the conclusion that the cause of such a combination was good; and the purpose which brought us together was calculate to harmonize some of those necessary differences which ever exist in separated orders.

Here was one common object having the suffrages of all, and in the advocacy of this 'School' the poor, clergyman, gentleman, professional, and artisan, could unite. While it was well observed by Colonel Gilpin "the education of these institutions is not that which fits for the world, yet it may assist," and methinks many a thought may be gathered from the libraries, lectures, and other privileges of these institutions. But is there not this charm, this utility, which may be considered peculiar to Mechanic's Institutions? May nit rank, talent, learning, give of their polished stores with grace and dignity, and may not nature's master-sons, though under the peasant's garb, utter oracular truths fervently and independently? If so, this mental communism must serve, and form suchlike schools may issue knowledge which shall leave past wisdom far behind. It may be from these platforms shall drop the stone into the sea of thought, which shall cause a circle comprehending length and breadth "undreamt of in our philosophy."

These were some of the thoughts of an auditor in the Town Hall, sitting nigh in the spot where in 1807-8 Joseph Lancaster, under the auspices of the late Duke of Bedford, first lectured on his simple elements of education, and having one of his Borough school-boys at my elbow, this coincidence may be registered, if only to compare the primitive times when our fathers listened to the unpolished sentences of the Quaker schoolmaster, enlightened only by the flicker of the tallowed cotton, while we, in January 1855, beneath the blaze of gas, making a mimic day, were enjoying a feast of reason and a flow of soul in aid of the Woburn Literary, Scientific, and Mechanics' Institution.

I am, Sir, your obedient servant, G. C.

A column and a half on the meeting had indeed appeared under the 'Woburn' column that week, in which Castleden is mentioned once, as proposing a toast to Maj. Gilpin for acting as Chair. These Mechanics' Institutes were popping up all over the country, to provide adult education to working men. National events were the subject of his next letter. A coalition Government of the Whigs and Peelites, which had ruled since 1852, collapsed in February 1855, after a large parliamentary majority voted for a select committee to enquire into the incompetent management of

74

the Crimean War. Castleden's father, the Rev. Michael, had assisted in the 1831 election, accepting contributions from subscribers towards conveying prospective freehold voters for the Marquis of Tavistock and Sir Peter Payne to Bedford, as a poster for the arrangements survives in the Bedford Heritage Library. Now his son began to write on politics.

17ᵗʰ **February 1855** Bedford Mercury

What of Politics? To the Editor of the Bedford Mercury.

Sir, - But for the despotism of circumstances, we had not ventured upon this paper: and when we say – What of Politics? we may answer in a way otherwise than political. However, What of Politics? A Ministry has fallen: another has been re-constructed. Will that stand? Its conditional commencement is ominous. If it falls, WHO then shall build up? Answer Time.

Our purpose is to work out a thought or two acquired while trudging the frozen snowy streets of London during the ministerial crisis. We tarried a moment to catch the "latest news," and as we read or heard the censures against the statesman of his day, as a unit of the mighty whole we could not but retire on the past, and then say, - suppose an error of judgement has been made, is that to nullify a whole life of political fidelity? If so, who is safe? Truly treacherous is any statesman's renown if, with half a century's labour for the good of the Commonwealth on his brow, an error, not an offence, is made a political crime and visited with penalties severe. In all exalted principle, whether cherished by the patrician or plebeian, the suffering is the more acute when the character is assailed, speciously and successfully, while a self-consciousness of rectitude remains. Sometimes, I presume, among political friend-foes, Lord Byron's words have an acute realisation –

"But keener far to feel,
He nursed the pinion that impelled the steel."

These thoughts started as we hurried the crowded streets, and glanced at placards penned by political rancour, and for the nonce condemning a once popular statesman.

It is written of a great Roman general, that in adverse days "He begged the realm his valour saved." While this line would be romantic applied here, yet an obscure individual who has travelled more than 40 years along the political road, and who has always looked upon Lord John Russell as a representative of Liberty and Progress, to hear such a 40 years lightly spoken of because of a passing error of judgement, involves the interrogatory – who is safe, if such service is to be cancelled by the mistake of a moment?

We know alike the courtier's goblet may be poisoned by the hand of jewelled malice, and murderous hate can distil the henbane into the cottage cup. An ephemeral combination may destroy in an hour the honest servant grown grey in the service of his master, and much as we value the liberty of the Press, let it turn vicious, and the "all hail" of a country's statesman is forgotten, if it be not changed to the yell!

"Public favour is a public cheat," so says the poet. "Now we go up, now we go down," so said the boy in the village-wake swing. He began wide awake, let us seize his philosophy to illustrate the mutations of man, - the orbs of empire or a country's stars, - favourites of a Court and favourites of a people. Essex was beloved and then beheaded! Burns was petted and then starved! Canning was flattered and the worried to death! And William Carleton writes, self-exiled, to his native land,

"I fling you back my curse of fame."

THE MORAL "Now we go up, now we go down!" In all like mutations, were it not for the self-supporting consciousness of right which sustains alike the man who has honestly held the staff of empire, and him who has laboured to leave some thought imperial in Mind's vast realm, each might sink into the atrophy of despair. But they not KNOW, TRUTH uttered politically, morally, socially, spiritually, SHALL LIVE – shall have an influence in the HEALING of NATIONS irrespective of blunders, sins, or reverses, while Truth lives to guide and save. This sustaining thought even fructifies the dust of their own crumbling humanity, while it uses the anomalies of their enemies as the DUNG from which shall spring a more luxuriant crop.

I am, Sir, your obedient servant, G.C.

P.S. – Our nation is in a great crisis. Wherever these few lines on "Politics" may be read, let the counsels of a Lord Lansdowne and the devotion of a Lord John Russell prevail to hush present recrimination strife. May we not as a people, at this conjuncture, add strength to the outward foe by intestine disputes: and for our country's sake, and for our beloved monarch's peace, may we study the things which are for peace WITHIN our own borders: and may the pilot now holding the helm of the state vessel 'neath darkening cloud, so steer that it may escape the sands of democratic destruction on one side, and the no les fatal rock of oligarchic perdition on the other. Thus writes a politician of an olden time, who, in venturing his "word" within his own country, inculcates the patriotism, in each and all, of quenching the coals of internal political resentment. Woburn, Beds, 13th February.

The situation was drastic enough to warrant Castleden wandering the Woburn churchyard at night to reminisce…

24th February 1855 Bedford Mercury

A Night Thought – On Woburn Park Cricket Ground, by one of the "Old Eleven."

I strolled our Park 'neath winter's sleet,
The stars were glittering high,
The hoar-frost glistened round my feet
And stinging was the sky.

Upon our cricket-ground I paused,
Invisible its green,
And busy thought called visions up
From out of past's day-dream.

Yes, treading over crispy snow,
Its carpet smooth and white;
By memory's magic, joy and woe
Arise on mental sight.

Upon the emerald plain I see
Our cricket's smart array;
Below is fun; above the sun
Pours down a dancing day

I see *him* on the low rail now
Observant of the game;
His hearty voice and *beaming* brow
Recall that day of fame.

And as I peer, full may a farm
Stands forth in star-lit gloom;
Neighbours who did our town adorn,
Who moulder in the tomb!

Beneath you beechan shade I see
A Woburn Bacchic lot;
Night's arch re-echoes revelry
Of men almost forgot.

I see the many circle round,
I hear the Stentor shout
Hurra the skill of clever bat,
Or praise the catch of scout.

This sunny slide now fades away
Across cold winter's night;
From mind's reflex swift speeds the day
Of cricket, warm and bright.

Well! Cricket-forms who crossed our plain
Have melted into air!
Some growing "ancient," soon must pass
Into the unknown – *where!*

We won and prize a cricket name,
Though fleeting as the day;
No "curse" remains, nor that of "fame"
We "fling" it not way:
Though with our cricket feres, who now are not,
We soon may mingle, may be soon forgot!

MORAL
"A shadowy race! Shade follows shade!"
So songs grave Doctor Young.
Scout follows *scout*, and *bats* go out!
And *sides* no more are sung!
In Spring man *springs*, in Summer *runs*,
In Autumn *toddles*, and then Winter comes!
G.C., 13th February

Whilst on the subject of graveyards, the latest news from Europe was that Czar Nicolas 1 of Russia had died on 2nd March 1855, at his Winter Palace in St. Petersburg. Having caught a chill, he refused medical treatment and died of pneumonia, although there were also rumours that he had committed suicide. His expansion plans for the Russian Empire had worried England, and his death was roundly rejoiced here.

10th March 1855 Bedford Mercury

To the Editor of the Bedford Mercury.

DEATH!

"Death! great proprietor of all, 'tis thine
To tread out empire, and to quench the stars."

Sir, - I have heard my father say, in March 1802 he stood at the west porch of Woburn Abbey, amid a large concourse of mourning tenantry and retainers, and as beneath the cape of night he saw the coffin holding all that was mortal of Francis Fifth Duke of Bedford brought out, and then heard the hearse door graze as it shut up in darkness the illustrious dust, he lifted his eyes from the light of the torches, and fixing them on the starry heavens, Young's lines received a potency which ever recurred on the recall of this Woburn Park mournful scene.

Now, after 52 years, on a March evening we quote them not in connection with the removal of a local benefactor, and a country's patriot, but we use them over a departed "empire" of Russia's Czar.

Death has conquered. Death may be the great peacemaker. The war-maker has been struck by the Power to whom he was offering the sacrifice of climes! Remorselessly was he consigning hecatombs to the grave, when, behold, his warrant was signed, and ere his own signet ink was scarcely dry, Death said unto the Emperor "Thou shalt die and not live." And suddenly the Autocrat over a seventh portion of the globe, and the owner of 60,000,000 serfs, succumbs to the worm and claims kinship with corruption. And he, to-day almost took precedence before Omnipotent, becomes on the morrow of less importance than the dog that drew his sledge.

But we say Death is the great peacemaker. May he be so in this case; and while we search not into Inscrutable, and before the King of Kings we must be dumb, yet, with our limited vision we may look forward to a resumption of peace by this triumph won by death! And it may be seen by the nations of the earth that the circle of God's providence involved the benignant removal of a despot who, as the impersonation of autocratic tyranny, was meditating for self-aggrandisement the murder of millions and the subjugation of Europe. "Hitherto" is the merciful limit of all tyranny, whether of dwarf dimensions,

"Or like some huge Colossus,
Aside this lower world, while men like mice
Peep fearful out atween his legs."
"Man's inhumanity to man
Makes countless thousands mourn."

Let European testimony for the last six months evidence to the truth of

Burns's truth; and while the mysterious doctrine of retribution no man may safely apply, yet we nevertheless extol the doctrine. "it will come home to you" has been the heaviest curse to many a plausible villain, and the fear of this has scared many a dubitating sinner. "How or when," it has been well observed, "has been a greater deterrer from crime than all the penal statutes put together." And then, in the eloquent language of the *Times*, we find in one of earth's mightiest men, full bent on iniquity, broken - and at full flight in oppression, falling, - at any rate solemn attention must be bestowed on such a singular frustration of tyrannical intentions.

After reading these "leaders" we found ourselves by the bedside of a dying girl. The labouring lungs were giving their last heavings; the lustrous eyes were fixed; the hand, powerless and chill; and the cherub spirit seemed only waiting the expiring breath to wing its way beyond the stars. Four hours after death struck; and looking on the pallid copse from her chamber, we could not help a thought speeding to the palace of the "Emperor of all the Russias." Made common prey by the common enemy, she departed with seraphs singing "Come, come away!" and left in the small circle of her home the fragrance of the cherished flower; he, the military despot, grasping at Empire to the last, died haunted by gibbering ghosts; and while War's red arm waved madness over the dying king, his last sigh sounded hope and peace to a conflicting world.

> Hail, tyrant Death! thy dart may speed to save!
> Wrong's shackles and Woe's fetters thou can'st snap:
> Affliction's friend, crime's foe, the tear, the curse,
> Confess thee as Earth's great conservative!
> The despot's despot thou! Thy bony clutch
> Seiges Ambition's madmen – holds them fast –
> While nations hail the invincibility of DEATH.

I am, Sir, your obedient Servant, G. C. Woburn, 5th March.

P.S. - When in the Mercury of February, 1854 we wrote - "This is mysterious to us who believe 'By Him kings reign and prices decree justice.' We are puzzled that inscrutable purposes are to be consummated by this decision of an obdurate despot who cogitates a war manifesto calculated to echo death throughout the world, manure Russia's soil with human flesh, and to the waters of the Danube gave a sanguinary pulsion by the flow of human gore." How little, affiantly, did we enter into the truth - *By Him kings reign*. We cannot use words more humiliating to human pride than by quoting part of that brilliant "leader" which, informing all Europe of Nicholas's death, should teach all Europe too.

"The touch of the omnipotent will reduces the fabric of all earthly power to dust and ashes, and vindicates the course of eternal justice by means infinitely above our knowledge. Such an event silences the discord of the world as it were by the stoke of heaven, and must suggest even to the most indifferent minds thoughts which cannot find their place among the petty interests of daily life." – The Times, 3rd March.

While many imagine that spying on the internal civilian population by a department of secret police to be a post–World War One invention, here it is, alive and well, in the 1850's.

17th March 1855 Bedford Mercury

Russia. Her Spy System. To the Editor of the Bedford Mercury.

Sir, - On the evening of the 28th February, we were listening to an instructive lecture on Russia, by the Rev. W. R. Freemantle. How little did we think the references to the Czar's character were as the soundings of his knell, and as the prefatory words to the grave's obsequies: that this "herculean" Emperor was then under the grip of Death's bony clutch! On Wednesday we listened with some terror as the description of the present cruelties, and the prospective desolations of this despotic demigod! On Saturday, in the same hall, we drew our breathe more freely on reading that this Northern Colossus had fallen from his pedestal; and, on account of suffering and oppressed humanity, we could not but be gratified. "One mental world of evil and machination was quenched in our firmament."

In the course of the lecture to which we refer, a just reprehension was expressed against the spy system organised in Russia. Among Englishmen any reference to this despicable policy is received with the indignant "shame." It is so un-English, so unnatural to the true-born Briton, that give him his choice, he would rather fraternize with the law's last officer than hold communion with a spy: and in our own time it required every care by a very unpopular Government to protect a Castles and an Oliver from Lynch law; at last, they were sent out of the country, and we believe these were the last specimens of political spies which were dared to be patronized.

Now see how the system works. A French writer has said, "In all Russia there is but one man." "The secret police have formed in Russia a terrible inquisition; its agents bland and smiling were everywhere." "A father not long ago denounced his son; it was regarded as heroism." "It is exceedingly rare to find in a Russian city a man who can look you straight in the face." "Generous and ennobling literature was systematically discouraged." Take these as illustrative, and they bespeak at once the despotism of the ruler and the degradation of the ruled.

Now for one deduction from this system, and rejoice O Englishmen, while to your very nature this treacherous sin is apparent, and with your

Constitutional Government in cannot agree, that with a free press a "drop of ink," acts as caustically on the spy fraternity as salt is anguishingly destructive to the snail family. Therefore, as we are all, more or less, talking about Russia, let this national mask be held up to reprobation in a country where men are ashamed to "look and smile and be a villain," – who do not follow these honourable vocations – Brave, Thug, and Spy, for their portions from the flesh-pots. No, fellow countrymen, whatever may be our national sins, England stands proudly here; and whatever humiliation may be in store, this blot will be saved us as long as a free press exists. On this point hear the eloquent words of Robert Hall, written in the dark days of our forefathers: - "Calumniating its friends, and smiling only on its flatterers. Should it encourage informers, and hold out rewards to treachery, turning every man into a spy, and every neighbourhood into the seat of inquisition, let it not hope it can long conceal its tyranny under the mask of freedom. These are the avenues through which despotism must enter: these are the arts in which integrity sickens and freedom grows pale."

Think of a father, for fee and reward, playing the spy on his son! Why, our vocabularies want a word to abominate such paternal infamy. We have read of the Roman ruler who, for a state offence committed by his son, the penalty of which was two eyes, submitting to the loss of one that his boy should not be totally blind. This deed of love deserves classical immortality. Let the Russian inhuman have deathless execration, and in the volume of despotism let this black page ever warn against the like monster-creating system.

"The life of nation never dies." Individuals perish. What is written remains. The historian ransacks the past, works in the present, and bequeaths to posterity. May he record of our tight little island that, having within he the repellent power to resist the influence of such like political putridities as the spy system, she became renovated amid the decay of empires founded in despotism, and existing under the auspices of the assassin and the spy.

In 1820 a son of Woburn wrote the following. It is an aspiration we gratefully quote relative to the brighter and better mission for Britain:-

On! glorious, on!
Far as the day hath dawn'd, the light hath shone.
The Christian glories o'er the earth to bear,
Than gems more precious, and than gold more fair;
To free th' unhappy captive, and to bring
Peace to the slave; beneath thy fostering wing
To rear th' uncultivated savage: every cline
Shall hail the brightness of thy path sublime,
T' abase the mighty wrong, to aid th' opprest,
"For ever blessing, and for ever blest.

I am, Sir, your obedient servant, G. C., Woburn, March 11th.

Between letter and poem writing, Castleden also made trips to London, perhaps to see his brother, and took the opportunity to see some of the sights of the capital.

19th May 1855 Bedford Mercury

To the Editor of the Bedford Mercury

Sir, - On the death of an European Emperor we troubled you with a few weeks ago. May we ask a small space for a few tributary words on a great man fallen in our locality.

On the 7th, entering a friend's home in London, we were told of the decease of one of Bedfordshire's gentlemen. I had not heard of previous illness: not a great while had elapsed since he trod our street. Then it appeared time had not very heavily laid his hand upon him: and a continence beaming with kindness seemed to shed autumnal sunshine on the gathering cloud of age. On the 8th I was at the Royal Academy, and amid all the creations of genius which adorned those walls the picture my eye dwelt upon was the life-likeness of the deceased Baronet. Won by the law of association I lingered, mused; home incidents arose, early events travelled up the dimming arches of the past, and though unknown yet standing before the canvases pulsed and tinted with life, I could not help reverting to a parental reminiscence which might appear intrusive to narrate; but in honour of the dead I may mention an early service Mr Robert Inglis rendered the Woburn Bible Society when, at one of its early anniversaries, disappointed of a chairman, he shopped his carriage at the church gates, and, on that sunny day, presided over a group of Bedfordshire worthies – now no more! And to link this spring-time of life with life's decline, in 1854 Sir Robert Harry Inglis rendered his last services as a patron and chairman at Dunstable. In 1853, the same kind office he filled at Woburn, and who was not delighted with the catholicity of his utterances, and charmed by the courtesy of his manners?

I may also mention a fact told me years ago by the worthy secretary of one of London's noble institutions: - "In the applications made the heart of Sir Robert Inglis was open to all, he knows no distinction here between Churchman and Dissenter: and in the distribution of the fund you lose sight entirely of the Member for Oxford University in beholding the catholic philanthropist." I refer to the Royal Literary Fund.

To return to the full length portrait, - which the catalogue informs us was "painted by subscriptions of friends and former constituents for the picture gallery of the University, as commemorative of the nine Parliaments for which Sir Robert Inglis was member," – we looked upon the life lineaments fresh from the easel, as the memorial of death! We looked upon artistic immortality while mortality was returning to dust! While the scarlet robes were novel, the well-known features identified a part of life's tale! and as we cast a last lingering look through the arches of the gallery for a moment we forgot the hum and beauty of intellectual humanity surrounding, and as the eye fell upon the floral effigy in the button-hole, how did that pencilled flower associate a Woburn bygone, when on the platform of its Town-hall, in 1853, Sir Robert Inglis read the prefatory psalm to the evening's engagement. We say we looked upon the life-canvas, and knowing, not too far from that spot, the lifeless form of the original reposed in the calm sleep of death, we did with that tinted bud link corruption with incorruption! mortality with immortality! A clime of change and chill and dark decay with the plains of Heaven lit by the sun that shall no more go down.

"There everlasting spring abides
And never-withering flowers."

These household words toned the mind as we descended the steps of the Royal Academy and plunged into the surging human tide of London's crowded street.

In no rush or obtrusive spirit have we penned these sentences. A good man has fallen among us: a voice from a father's grave stimulates: and in reverential fidelity we offer on the tomb tributary homage. Let Dr Young's apposite lines close the obitual reference to the late Right Hon. Sir Robert Harry Inglis, Baronet:-

"The chamber where the good man meets his fate
Is privileged beyond the common walk
Of virtuous life, quite in the verge of heaven.
You see the man: you see his hold on heaven:
If sound his virtue: as *Philander's* sound,
Heaven waits not the last moment; owns her friends
On this side death: and points them out to men,
A lecture, silent, but of sovereign power!
To vice, confusion; and to virtue, peace."

I am, Sir, your obedient servant, G. C., Woburn, 15th May.

30ᵗʰ June 1855 Bedford Mercury

The Reformatory School. To the Editor of the Bedford Mercury.

Sir, - The following lyric on the philanthropic object in our county was prompted by the following words in the opening speech delivered by Lord C. J. F. Russell: "Voluntary effort, God willing, shall prevent any boy of Bedfordshire perishing eternally through the lack of home!"

1.

HOME! 'Tis the keynote of time's song,
It sounds through every stage:
It tones life's journey all along,
And cheers man's latest age.

2.

It is the home of infant years;
The hoary headed stay;
Midst deaths, vicissitudes, dark fears,
Home's early sun-beams play.

3.

If as a vagrant he shall roam,
Home must forsaken be;
Beneath the shade, above the green
Sounds home's first melody.

4.

'The heart untravelled' seeks a rest
In home's warm ingle nook;
Fend memory finds sweet childhood's nest,
Forgets life's blotted book.

5.

If these remembrances of *home*,
Its joys, its counsels, bless,
O think upon those homeless ones
Born on want's wilderness.

6.

O hear the dictates of thee good:
Give them a home in time,
As surging on the treacherous flood,
To avoid the abyss of crime.

7.

A home to shelter and reform,
To win from error's way;
Reformed by kindness, led to learn
'To enjoy is to obey'.

8.

And let this school a nursery be
For brambles from the wild;
Here grafted, blooming may we see
The desert Christian child.

9.

Our homeborn strain hails homeborn love.
Sings mercy's kind emprize,
Which builds a lodge on earth below
For Home above the skies.

A Bedfordshire Boy, Woburn, June 25th.

No doubt a Castleden poem, but the only one I have seen in which the verses are numbered. The Reformatory opened in 1857, in what is now Carlton. Boys who had been convicted at Court would be sent there, so I am not sure any boy would want to view it as 'home'! It is now the site of the Emmaus Village, a homelessness charity. The subject brought him back to education again.

14th July 1855 Bedford Mercury

The Education Questions. To the Editor of the Bedford Mercury.

Sir, - More than forty years ago I received, to use parental words, "the best portion" of my education at the Woburn Free School. If limited, so much my loss and regret; but as these elemental rules have served so far on life's road, I, with others, have to be grateful to the prescience of the late Duke of Bedford, who saw, in the simple plan laid down by Joseph Lancaster, a foundation which, but for the strife of sects, had borne the structure of a people's education. But bigotry has much marred this scheme. Religious envyings and emulations have rendered it, comparatively speaking, ineffective.

To cram the child with creeds offends conscience and mocks the God of conscience. To exclude the Bible is Christian heathenism. A purely secular education may be polished Paganism.

Now, did not Joseph Lancaster's plan, which gave us portions of scripture to read, and put the Bible into our hands, meet the difficulty? And while in the advance of education you may give all its modern advantages to the present trace, recollect on precepts and moralities you can never advance on the Bible.

"This is the judge that ends strife where wit and reason fail." Its guiding and saving rules project safety to time's latest futurity, and as well send the sailor to sea without the compass as embark the child upon the uncertain waves of human life without those Biblical precepts, which, as beacons and soundings, must lessen the dangers of the mortal voyage.

"Woburn," named in your leader, has incited these few remarks on the much-vexed question of education. Whether, as a nation, we shall ever harmoniously agree to pay for it the future must tell, but include the Bible; exclude creeds and catechisms, and we may start a fair as citizens in the institution of a national education. This ought to be inoffensive to man.

I ask no pardon when I boldly say that I look suspiciously on all systems where the Bible is systematically excluded. It should not be sect taught, but as a Christian nation, taking it as the standard of eternal knowledge, I say it is very inconsistency to exalt any scheme excluding this great everlasting "guide book" from the youth of England. If one of our immortals, in hoary days, said, when asked "have you a guide book?" on his going his last continental journey – "Yes, and the very best," showing a pocket-bible; then we say, perish any scheme that would filch from the child this "guide," and bid them rove this wilderness of moral sweets and sours without even the head knowledge of precept and injunction to prevent preposterous and ruinous conclusions.

Can a nation's education become truly national in merrie England if spiritual ascendancy plays the Pope, or a secular domination enforces practical Atheism? Good and great men are puzzled with this interrogatory. Perhaps, in this matter, a better time coming may show the ground of Christian neutrality: then:-

Strifes that vex would vanish from the land;
Long educational disputes would close,
And tired statesmen find a blessed repose.

This is a consummation which a Lancasterian boy of olden time would be glad to see.

I am, Sir, your obedient servant, G. C., Woburn, 9th July.

4th August 1855 Bedford Mercury

Poet's Corner. The Martyrs' Monument in Nunhead Cemetery, Surrey.

"Individuals may perish; but Truth is eternal" – Part of Gerald Massey's defence. Written on an obelisk raised in memory of the Scotch [sic] martyrs. These men were transported in 1793 – four for advocating Parliamentary Reform Truth.

These sowed the light, and garnered night –
The night of penal doom:
Arraigned, condemned, as culprits then,
They perished in the gloom.

A principle this granite bears
Time ne'er can wear away;
The name oblivion may inter,
Memorials may decay.

But Truth ne'er dies – it even must
Survive the death of Death.
The tongue that utters turns to dust,
And lost is fleeting breath.

But truth is on the hills secure;
Uprooted they may fall;
Yet truth eternal shall endure –
It echoes from Heaven's hall.

Truth long may wrestle, long may thole,
'Neath stormy, darksome skies;
Yet still divine, a part of soul,
It shall enlightening rise.

A people, or a man, shall see
The triumph of the day.
Corruptions hide, and liars flee
The searchings of its ray.

These vagrant thoughts a rambler had,
Musing on death's domain,
And pondering this memorial stone,
Its words he links again

With truth – a new accomplished fact.
They sowed in darkness, shame,
"Reform;" we shouted harvest home,
And sang the ripened grain.*

These northmen perished; truth survives;
Their ashes silent lie;
Their truth, eternal, vocal lives
Till truth itself shall die.

G. C., Woburn, 31st July.

* "11th June 1832. A public vestry meeting was held at Woburn to arrange for a general illumination and a regalement of the poor, to celebrate the passing of the Reform Bill."

I doubt Castleden had been to see the monument, perhaps he was working from a report of it in the press.

3rd November 1855 Bedford Mercury

"The Lower Orders." To the Editor of the Bedford Mercury.

Shepherd, - "Yet think ye, Sir, that thousans and ten thousans o' millions since the time when God's wrath smote the earth's soil with the curse of barrenness, and human creatures had to earn their bread with sweat and dust.

"If there be no agonies that wring the hearts of men and women lowly born, why should they read the bible?

"If there be no heavy griefs, making oftentimes the burden of life hard to bear, what means that sweet voice calling on them to "Come unto me, for I will give them rest?

"If love strong as death adhere not to the auld widow's heart, while fairly bowed down, till her dim een canna see the lift, but only the grass aneath her feet, how else could she totter every Sabbath to kirk, and wi' her broken, feeble, and quiverin voice, and withered hands clasped together on her breast, join, a happy and a holy thing, in the holy psalm?"

Bedford Mercury, October 27.

Sir, let this extract preface a Bedfordshire anecdote.

In 1854, in one of our rambles, which you have kindly published, climbing the heights of Bedfordshire's Switzerland, it was my fortune to fall in with one of these "lower orders;" and what he then said will echo through time.

I had viewed from the stile a very pretty landscape; I had repeated lines from Mr. Roger's "Pleasures of Memory;" I had crossed the churchyard, looked upon the sculptured lineaments of the world's "great," pondered some of the memorials of the village forefathers, and, descending the path, on the road just below the rectory, I met with one stooping with years; he was patching up the bank. I stopped, and said, "Well neighbour, you are bending to your origin: I suppose you have pretty well completed your tease. With a quickness which surprised me, the old man at once said – "Ay, sir, I have; I have nothing to look for down here; I am only hoping now, through mercy, for the crown above."

I was amazingly struck with the reply, and after a little more chat I passed on, this musing – Here is one, perhaps a Lazarus on earth, stretching out the hand of faith to the regalia of heaven!

Well, the year rolled on; on a different errand I found myself near the same spot. Another labourer was there. I said to him, "Nigh this place I had an answer from an old man I shall not forget." "Oh," he said, "I know who you mean. He is gone. He died of the cholera. His grandchild was first taken, the old man took him to the churchyard, another relative died, and then himself. Ah." Added the villager, "Our minister was very kind in this time of trouble; he was with the old man in his affliction, and I was pleased with his state of mind." Perhaps, like a mortal Hopeful, he encouraged the aged Christian amid the billowy strife and death.

On reading your scrap from the "Noctes," this personal fact struck me, and it will support the shepherd's divine philosophy, and it may establish the reply to this aged man's great words, "With that hope, poor as you are, you are richer than the richest without it."

When, in "Blackwood," years ago, I dwelt upon these northern lights, I little thought of adding a home reflection of one "under the burden of life," stricken and bowed, having "nothing to look for down here, yet hoping, through mercy, for the crown above."

Here was one deep in the vale of human misery anticipating the tumult of everlasting joy – one whose days were "dwindled to their shortest span," realising the boundlessness of an eternal NOW ' – one in the winter of age's gloom looking with the eye of faith for the sunburst of never-withering spring and an immortal youth."

And this hope the sceptic would destroy! One question to such an one should this weal fact fall under his eye. Where this hope even fallacious, how much better with it stands the peasant here, and if realised hereafter, where is the sceptic philosopher? If false, the peasant still moulders with him into annihilation; if true, where is he?

Perhaps after the crushing words of Baron Alderson to the three great criminals in the metropolis, the above village illustration that "Poverty's no sin" may, among the annals of the poor, be instructive. Deeply lamenting the plunge of the rich man from the heights of station and rank into the abyss of characterless perdition, we cannot but be pleased that one of our "lower orders" in the obscure of penury, evidences to the worth of religion; and while just now heavy and well deserved censure falls from many on the praying rich man, yet none will dare to question the divinity of prayer which gives to the peasant-worm an angel's wing, and which, even uttered in the union house, becomes his title deeds to mansions in the skies, allies him with seraphs, and seals his patent for the crown above. Thanks, mouldering peasant!

I am, Sir, your obedient servant, G. C., Woburn, October 30.

His next submission is a biography of his father, who had died in 1848.

90

November 1855 Evangelical Magazine & Missionary Chronicle, Vol. 33.

Biographical Notice of the Late Rev. Michael Castleden, Woburn, Beds. To the Editor of the Evangelical Magazine.

Rev. Sir, Last October appeared in your pages "An Address, by the Rev. T. P. Bull, of Newport Pagnell, at the laying of the memorial stone in connexion with the rebuilding and enlargement of the above chapel, July 20th. 1854:" perhaps a few supplemental lines at its completion may be permitted to this chronological and biographical reference to the rise and progress of this interest.

Mr. Bull's own words shall preface the subjoined narrative: "Having paid this tribute of respect to these good men, I return to the history of this cause. In the year 1800 the Rev. Mr. Castleden was chosen pastor, and under his zealous ministry much good was done."

Why no memoir of the worthy Mr. Greathead has been published is still regretted; so of his successor, why the long life and pastorate of Mr. Castleden should not have supplied some pages of biographical and Christian instruction may also cause regret. Materials remain, and time may tell a more lengthened tale.

Michael Castleden was born in Kingstreet, City of Westminster, 22nd February, 1769, "The great year." His childhood was tended by a "most affectionate mother," and by her solicitude early impressions of revealed truth were watched and fostered. From his youth he was taught to keep the Sabbath-day holy, often a worshipper at St. Martin's Church, and at Westminster Abbey, or with his father at a neighbouring Episcopal chapel. While a youth, a wandering visit to Tottenham-court-road Chapel gave to religious views those convictions which led to the solemn consideration of entering the Christian ministry. In an upper room, in an obscure alley leading out of St. Martin's lane, he first associated with a few friends who met in secret to pray. Then followed the happy Hoxton hours. "Good Dr. Simpson, Buck, Slatterie, Gunn, Marlow," *c, were household words for half-a-century; and academic scenes and student days ever rose on his mortal gaze, and on to the evening of life would memory's orb shed "the mild magic of their reflected light." And while, with many of his contemporaries, he was there forgot, never did he forget that time of Christian fellowship and student happiness.

His first hope of settlement was at Deal, Kent: but disappointment here caused keen regret. Then Faversham invited; but being made uncomfortable, he was hoping for a change, when one morning two letters arrived, one from the Rev. Joseph Brooksbank, and the other from the Rev. Rowland Hill; the first pointed to Aylesbury, the second to Gloucestershire. Puzzled, he conscientiously chose the first he opened, and in 1797 was settled and ordained at Aylesbury; and then, to use his own words, "having married a church, I married a wife." One tributary line to this peaceful, devoted mother: as "wife, companion, and the best of mortal friends," she pursued her unostentatious path for thirty two years, and then suddenly entered her rest, 17th July, 1828.

In Aylesbury discomfort came from part of his people. Sound in the great doctrines of the gospel, any acrid ebullitions of high sentiment painfully affected the geniality of his nature. When they persecute you in one city, flee ye into another: this he adopted, and, in 1800, turning his back on Aylesbury, found home within these "pleasant lines."

The incidents of a provincial pastor's life are rarely of that nature to obtrude themselves on the public notice. Much must be done without reward or renown. In the Evangelical, Magazine of 1804, page 334, 335, there is an account of the church and congregation under Mr. Castleden's pastorate. Up to that time a thatched barn had been their meetinghouse, but its inconvenience was so great, that efforts were made, a piece of ground was conveyed by Miss Susan Rock, and on it a new structure was raised. On June 14th, 1804, it was opened by "Mr. Bull, sen., of Newport Pagnell, who had laid the foundation of the present interest, by preaching once a fortnight, for several years I and Mr. Greathead, under whose ministry a church was formed in 1789, preached in the evening." The edifice became too small; galleries were added, additions were made; and over a goodly, long attached

11: The plaque to honour Rev. Michael Castleden, originally erected in Woburn chapel, 1847.

congregation, enjoying much peace, Mr. Castleden laboured on till the close of 1840; then a severe attack gave thoughts of retirement. "I have buried my congregation," he would oft mournfully say, on reviewing the past, and placidly using the words: "I cheerfully say, God speed to another that can be more useful to the rising congregation;" the reins were given up, and an annuity to the retiring pastor sealed the separation.

It ought to be stated, in the early days of Woburn residence, district preaching was so regulated that at weekly periods most of the villages in the county were visited by Bedfordshire fathers, who trudged many a miry mile beneath winter's sky, its dunnest cloud, pelting rain, or blinding snow, cheered only by their "errand," and helped on by a warm heart within. And when I name a Hillyard, Hobson, Wake, Ramsay, Castleden, Morris, &c, now sleeping under our skies, I pay but a just tribute to men in the past who, as local preachers, were prompt at every call, And watched, and wept, and prayed, and felt for all."

Hence my father first preached at Hockliffe, and from those labours the present chapel dates; also the one at Eggington, and partially the one at Toddington. "Union Chapel," at Sheeplane, is another local voucher linking the latter days of his pastorate. One of his life - attached Christian brethren, the Rev. George Clayton, of London, came down and opened it in 1838.

Of his home services many a bygone parochial scene would witness, and though old Time is a great burker, yet relics may remind of bygone neighbourly amity and ever ready service. With the charities and institutions of the town this pastor and his chapel are associated, and to its societies he was both friend and servant to the day of death.

His occasional labours after retirement were acceptable, and with renovated health, almost too good for his years, he preached near and wide, finishing on the last Sunday in October, 1848, at the Guildhall Chapel, Canterbury. On the 5th of November he was to have preached and administered the Lord's Supper at Coverdale Chapel, Limehouse, London; his text was chosen, Galatians v. 1; the heads of discourse were written, but his work was done! Seized suddenly, on the Sabbath-morning, with heart-spasms, his grandchildren were summoned, the brief struggle was severe, and with the penitential prayer, "Lord, have mercy on my soul," he passed the gulf of death.

Thus, within three months of eighty, fell this Christian warrior; one of the pioneers of the past, clearing the way for after operations and achievements. The honour paid to his remains, as they were carried along the familiar streets, afforded evidence to the worth of one loving mercy and pursuing peace; and the esteem he was held in as a neighbour and as a Christian minister, his marble tablet now testifies.

To this memorial His Grace the Duke of Bedford, the Lord and Lady Charles Russell, the Rev. Henry Hutton, of St. Paul's, Covent Garden, London, with many neighbours, kindly sent their donations. Further we would not intrude: the dead might rebuke, and, writing truth, it might appear we wished to laud the ashes of the dead.

But here three rare facts in a Dissenting minister's life may be recorded. March, 1802, my father stood among the tenantry and retainers at the "West Front of Woburn Abbey, under the Starry sky, when the coffin of Francis, fifth Duke of Bedford, was brought out, and by torchlight shut up in the hearse; and in his thatched meeting-house he preached a funeral sermon to his little flock, on the death of that lamented nobleman, whose premature close filled the heart of the great Charles Fox with mourning, and caused the tongue to give utterance, in the senate-house, to words of pathetic eloquence. Nigh forty years after, with his locks silver, he stood among a large concourse of mourners in the Chenies mausoleum, and saw go down into the chambers of the dead all that was mortal of John, sixth Duke of Bedford; - in this first and last visit to this tomb he laid his hand upon the coffin of the civil martyr, Lord William Russell. On the following Sunday he preached the tributary sermon on the local and personal loss of this benefactor; and the quiet of his own home witnessed unfeigned sorrow at the loss of this noble "friend."

Not long before death he was cheered by an appointment for his grandson, a Her Majesty's Customs, and among his last letters were those of gratitude to His Grace the Duke of Bedford and the members of the ducal family, for kindness rendered in this relative boon.

Perhaps the inscription on the tablet will be a grateful close to this tributary relic:-

In Memory of the Reverend Michael Castleden, Born February 22nd, 1769; died November 5th, 1848; Forty years Minister of this Chapel. He retired from the Pastorate January 1st, 1841; But occasionally To the last Sabbath of his mortal life, At home, in London, and at Canterbury, He preached "Christ crucified." This Tablet Is not Adulatory, but Tributary To his Piety, Peacefulness, and Catholicity; And is the last Token Of Neighbourly respect, Christian affection, And Filial gratitude. "He being dead yet speaketh."— Heb. xi. 4.

"We now subjoin a brief account of the Independent chapel at Woburn, Beds, in which Mr. Castleden laboured for so many years, with so many tokens of the Divine presence.

In 1804, the then "new chapel" was opened. In 1864, it was thought advisable to reconstruct; and while there were lingering partialities to the long-familiar oval chapel, on the plans for the newer structure being submitted, these partialities were kept in abeyance. After due consideration they were agreed to, and it is but fair to the committee, architect, and builder to say, the work proceeded in peace, and has been done well; and in. its completion, convenience, neatness, adornments, and economy have combined. We may add, the building was not commenced without counting the cost, and no debt remains.

"Praise God, from whom all blessings flow," was gratefully quoted by the old pastor, at the conclusion of his collecting work, and its repetition may key the thanksgiving of the present pastor and people.

After six months worshipping in the Town-Hall, which was kindly granted by His Grace the Duke of Bedford, the congregation finally entered their newbuilt chapel on the first Sunday in December; the services under their minister, the Rev. J. Andrews, were impressive, and the wish for prosperity to the new walls was in the hearts of many.

The conclusion of the whole matter may be best expressed in a Statement read on the anniversary eve, 26th October, 1855, in the vestry, before the Rev. J. Andrews, pastor, and friends.

"Christian Friends, - As one of the Treasurers of the Building Fund, I beg to lay before you a statement of accounts. It may introduce the service of this evening gratefully, inasmuch as it will inform you, that before your anniversary came round you owed no man anything for the 'house' in which our fathers worshipped, and to which you have added the newer structure, forming now the whole. May the union be symbolical of growing strength: may the peace of the past continue to a far generation: may the prosperity of these walls be established on the great gospel truths, long uttered and faithfully preached on this spot; and may the lyric prayer of 'our good doctor' tune all our hearts in their best wishes for the welfare of this sanctuary-

"Thus we begin the lasting long;
And when we close our eyes,
Let the next age thy praise prolong,
Till time and nature diet."

This statement referred to the expenditure for the building of the 1804 chapel, amounting from first to last to £750, and the present erection costing nearly £500.

I am, Rev. Sir,

Your very obedient servant, George Castleden. Woburn, Beds, 31st October, 1855.

29th December 1855 Bedford Mercury

Woburn "Tyndal and the English Bible". To the Editor of the Bedford Mercury.

Sir, - A lecture on "Tyndal and the English Bible" was delivered on Wednesday evening in the Town Hall, by the Rev. E. Carr, of Millbrook. The audience was few but fit. The matter deserved to be heard by many. Much chronological, historical and biographical information was afforded. With a fragment, showing the potency of a single mind, I was struck. Here was an obscure man who had fled to Antwerp printing a single copy of the New Testament, and from this one seed of Gospel truth behold the great harvest sowing of the British and Foreign, and other Bible Societies. What a glow-worm twinkle was this commencement to the now sun-blaze of revealed light.

When the reverend lecturer said King Henry, Wolsey, More, Tunstall - Monarch, Prime Minister, Lord High Chancellor, and London's Bishop were dead set against the introductions of the printed book, looking at this mighty opposition to the unit, with man's agency, we linked the mystical truth involved in Cowper's lines –

Deep in unfathomable mines
Of never failing skill,
He treasures up His bright designs
And works His Sovereign will.

In such a result human wisdom is at a loss to account for an exile being the sole pioneer to cut through forests worse than those, the growth of pagan darkness. For recollect Christian prejudices hold keener destructions and more cruel darknesses than the gloom of paganism, the mists of philosophy, or even the midnight of heathendom.

William Tyndal sowed the seed; he watered it with his blood, and now a mighty tree. Under its healing leaves the nations should remember the solitary Englishman who at Augsburg in 1536, fell victim to prelatcial persecution, and Christian demonism, whose last words were –

"Lord, open the King of England's eyes."

While listening to the lecture the recent death of Memory's bard came to the mind. Millbrook's romantic hills he had trod, and though the associations may appear somewhat fanciful, yet the martyr of 1536 and the minstrel of 1855 may, released from life's vicissitudes, mocking fashions and fleeting good, realize that eternal substance dimly shadowed in these musical lines from Memory's song –

There thy bright train, immortal Friendship soar
No more to part, to mingle tears no more!

And, as the softening hand of Time endears
The joys and sorrows of our infant years,
So there the soul, releas'd from human strife
Smiles at the little cares and ills of life,
Its lights and shades, its sunshine and its showers,
As at a dream that charm'd her vacant hours
I am, Sir, your obedient Servant, G. C., Woburn, December 25, 1855.

William Tyndale, (c.1494 – c.1536), had translated the Bible into English for ordinary people to access the scriptures. This was seen as wildly dangerous by the Church authorities, and a direct challenge to both the Catholic Church and the Church of England, which Henry VIII had just set up. Tyndale was arrested for heresy, convicted, and then strangled at the stake and his body burned.

II

Letters: 1856 - 1869

Jury Duty – Financial Speculation and Ruin – Gambling on Trials – Peace – Elections & The Ballot – The Wreck of The Dunbar – South Sea Bubble – Rev. Spurgeon – Sheep Lane Chapel, Potsgrove – Eggington Sunday School – The American Civil War – Penny Readings – Bedford Cemetery – London City Mission

12th January 1856 Bedford Mercury

Poet's Corner – An Anecdote. (From an unpublished M.S.)

Now tell a generous deed in home-born verse;
Relate an act of one which known, may teach;-
On who in her day thrilled many a heart,
And bade the pulses pause or quicker throb.

At Moscow Catalini poured forth song:
Twas melody delicious, charming sense:
She ceased, and bosoms heaved the bent-up breath.
By chance or else design, a gipsey girl
Step't on the stage and fearless gazed around
And where the southern songstress had entranced
The rover of the Eastern forests stood.
Light kindling flashed from out her ebon orb
Then from her swarthy throat ethereal tones
Poured forth in mystic harmony. It rung
Unearthly on astonished ears, and filled
With sound the amplitude of that vast dome.
Tis said the Queen of Song enchanted heard;
The wondrous strain was hushed: Imperial Fame.
Thus spake and generous homage paid the girl.
"His Holiness the Pope designed this shawl
For her whose song should second be to none;
Thus from mine own, they shoulders let it grace;

99

I give to merit merit's due reward."
Then on the Egyptian girl she cast the scarf,
While Moscow's throngs appausive greet the scene,
Here honour due, at sight, was promptly paid.
Lustre the Italian gave and love received:
Her dise expanded as it warmth diffused:
Meridian brightness sparkled from her orb
While its rich beams played o'er the gipsy girl
And cheered her heart with glowing gratitude.
G. C., Woburn, January 7, 1856.

There are several versions of this story about Angelica Catalani, an Italian soprano (1780-1849). They all feature her hearing a Russian gypsy singer and, being so impressed, presenting her with a gift, but other details seem somewhat flexible. His next letter was on 'Get-rich-quick' schemes, which it seems are nothing new, and nor is losing everything to 'delinquent bankers'.

22ⁿᵈ March 1856 Bedford Mercury

Ruin! To the Editor of the Bedford Mercury.

Sir, - Sometime ago in your columns I said "the philosophy of pace" might be a good title for an instructive essay for the present race. Now a few sympathising words may be permitted on the dark cloud over some of our neighbours, and a conservative moral may be extracted from an unexpected tale of local woe.

But of "Pace." The delinquent bankers were fast. The Rugeley celebrity was fast. The Sadliers were fast. What was the first spur to the pace is not yet told in all these cases; possibly all have been lured on to the stream which may engulf many more who have embarked upon the rapids of our commercial Niagara.

On the turbulent, ceaseless tide of speculation in our own Metropolis or great cites barks are constantly going down. The seductions for the ventures are great; the perils are madly risked, and the bitter penalty of destruction and poverty is paid! But the surge sweeps over the mariners - they have sunk -

"Unknelled, uncoffined, and unknown."

Not so with those who go down in our home streams; with the heart pulpy, many local laments and neighbour recollections hang long about these melancholy ruins!

Well, may not some of these be attributed to the heedless pace we are going. For when I find sous, as in a moment plunged into ruin, and, by children, parental economy in an instant confiscated, I ask what fascination has prevailed over the preserving examples of the past? "Pace" gives the answer. Fast prosperity, or fast adversity is the rule now! Extravagancies overrides economy, and splendid Misery takes the lead of substantial Hospitality. Ten and thirteen per cent have lured from the bank and the farm; and, smiled into ruin by the "gentleman" who kept hunters, all recollection of the truth that "he that maketh haste to be rich shall not be innocent, and often falls into a snare, is forgotten!"

Now for this "haste" of our day. Here "Pace" must be our expositor again. Steam, rail, and telegraph have become the swift agents of speculation. Hurry, whirl, and flash confuse, excite, and ignite; they may involve demon mockings, and 'neath the inspiration of their haste the corn or share market is sought, and remediless ruin ensues.

Speculation is a trap. Sometimes an old bird flies safely off with a scrap of the bait; he chirps, and down come dozens of silly birds; the chaff lures, the peck is made, the spring flies, the iron teeth close, and – what then?

Sir, these are trial-times. A public calamity has fallen; neighbour misery is all around us. May the victims have patience, and may none among us "fly from present ill to ills they know not of," but from this calamity may the future learn; and while the very utterances of "Tipperary" is striking terror over many a hearthstone, let it also warn,

May some interposition still save from utter destruction.

Some think these heavy drops betoken a coming storm. We hope it may be averted, but should it roll, at a distance, die away, or desolate, still one of the maxims of the slow pace age may be quoted. To some listener it may scout the wheel of helter-skelter pace on the drawn hill of present ruin. "Don't be tempted at every provocation to confide your conscience to another's keeping, and don't let the lure of usury tempt you to put your cash into another's hand."

May some Bedfordshire boy read, mark, learn and be saved from future wreck on speculation's treacherous waters is the sincere wish of Your obedient servant, G. C., Woburn, March 17.

Castleden served on Jury duty at least twice. The first term was reported in the Bedfordshire Times (and also the Cambridge Independent Press), of **12th April 1856**. *Castleden attended at Bedford Court, with 21 others, among whom were Mr. H. Durrant of Aspley, and Mr. H. T. Wolfe of Woburn. The Chairman spoke of the recent outlay at Bedford Prison for the provision of an association room, for juvenile prisoners, but now the Government had decided to house juveniles separately, and so 50 cells were* *left empty at Bedford. Castleden assisted in deciding the following trials:*

Percy Kendell, for theft of two shovels, a draining tool, two planes, one auger and a spoke shave. Pleaded Guilty. Four months.

Samuel Field, for receiving stolen beans, knowing them to be stolen. Twelve months.

Joseph Field, for stealing the above beans, yet he only received two months!

Enoch Peacock, stealing two draining hoes. One month.

Thomas Adams, stole two cruet glasses. Three months

Priscilla Brown, stealing money at Luton. Acquitted.

Joseph Wiggins, stole two wheelbarrows, and took three planks, and eight sleepers, which he had found floating down the river. Guilty, but recommended to mercy, he received just one month.

Perhaps fresh from his jury experience, Castleden wrote to a paper at some distance to complain about the current vogue for gambling on the outcome of criminal trials.

6ᵗʰ June 1856 Chelmsford Chronicle

Gambling – Palmer's Trial. To the Editor of the Chelmsford Chronicle.

Sir – Your excellent article on this trial fell under the eye of a stranger in one of our obscure villages, and if you think the following may assist in saving even one Essex youth from a fatal path of gambling, I should be gratified for its insertion.

It is stated that not less than £200,000 was depending in the "sporting world" in bets on the acquittal or conviction of Palmer. This fact may partly explain why there is an inexplicable impression in some that the verdict is erroneous. I was surprised as I read, publicly exposed, the odds on this issue! I said to myself, this must be wrong. It is an offence against morality of the country; it is an affront to the judicature of the land. And it seemed a crushing fact, proving the revolting insensibility attaching to the gambling mania. The solemnities of one of the most awful trials ever known were to contribute to the gratification of the destructive passion – the majesty of the law was to be subpoenaed to settle the "odds!" – and death was to play confederate with the gambler! O young men BEWARE, beware in time.

I am, sir, your very obedient servant. George Castleden, Woburn, Beds June 3.

Palmer, known as the "The Rugeley Poisoner", had poisoned his own brother, his mother-in-law, four of his own children and a close friend, in order to obtain their insurance monies to cover his gambling debts. The vogue for betting on court cases whilst they were active, and therefore encouraging people to root for an outcome based on the prospect of winning their bet, was abhorrent to the fervently anti-gambling Castleden.

12th July 1856 Bedford Mercury

Palmer's Last Words. To the Editor of the Bedford Mercury.

Sir, - We enclose a thought, thought over while strolling castle heights of historical celebrity. As we looked seaward, and then inland, the details were everywhere beautiful, while, in combination, nature presented a picture of the grandest dimensions. Looking upon such a scene, how sad the contrast while contemplating the moral gloom occasioned by the Rugeley tale of horrors; and yet, when re read the anguished exclamation of "pray for my boy," we said, here on this shrine of humanity, though all besides had been quenched, was one spark left to prove divinity. Here the soul threw out its last beam to vindicate its immortality.

A perfect monster of wickedness was not William Palmer. Gambling of the most heart-hardening kind, robbery subtle and successful, murder, inexpressibly cowardly and atrocious, with vile vice selfish and impure, had all assailed this "Mansoul," had made it a ruin hideous and repulsive, yet, yet, the father's love threw the last gleam over it, and "pray my poor boy may be kept away from my wicked life" seems the only chink of light in that pall of hall which shrouded the mortal sunset of this stupendous criminal.

This tale may afford startling and fascinating materials for many days to come; may its moral be the beacon to warn many a heedless voyager against such horrible shipwreck.

I am, Sir, your obedient servant, George Castleden, Woburn July.

The end of the Crimean War had finally come, officially ending on 30th March. Much of the ground taken and claimed by both sides was returned to the original owners. Despite inflicting some serious defeats on the Allies, (such as the Battle of Balaclava, which saw the ill-fated Charge of the Light Brigade) Russia had been forced to the negotiating table, and had lost over twice the number of men than the Allies. The most shocking figures are those of soldiers lost to disease, rather than the fighting. England lost fewer than 3000 troops in fighting, but c.17500 to disease. The terrible conditions led Florence Nightingale to set up the first training school for Nurses when she returned to England. Castleden's poem to the war dead reads very much like the First World War poets, who were to experience the same emotions 60 years later.

12th July 1856 Bedford Mercury

The Peace Rejoicings. To the editor of the Bedford Mercury.

Sir, - Perhaps, after all the blaze of illuminations, the enchantment of fireworks, and the madness of mirth, which have played over the ashes of the brave, to them a few lines may be dedicated. This thought struck us as we viewed the memorial tablet and window erected to the brave Viscount Chewton in the church at Hastings; and we enclose them to the Mercury as tributary to Englishmen who won the victory on Alma's hill, on the sod of Inkermann and Balaklava, by the banks of the Tchernaya, and who now sleep around Sebastopol.

Life may rejoice; I'll mourn the dead,
A dirge shall be my strain;
Life, jubilant, in sunshine shouts;
I'll mourn the dark "red rain!"

Let Peace men hail; I'll not forget
The memories of the brave;
For home they paid the mortal debt,
From home they found their grave.

On Alma's steep they won the fight,
'Tis scorched on Europe's sky;
Bright Inkermann, in War's red night,
A planet blazes high.

'Twas morn, and Balaklava's sod
Shook 'neath victorious breath;
'Twas noon, and see those doomed men
Charge hot sulphurous death.

And many a deed in many a trench
Has died without a name;
While heroes nameless mouldering sleep
Unchronicled by fame.

Sebastopol and Kars shall live
While war the earth shall curse;
That grand retreat, that stern defence,
Deserves heroic verse.

Adieu, immortals, you have found
In Russia's soil a grave;
And many a mourner's heart now sighs
Peace, peace to heroes brave.

George Castleden, Woburn, July.

16th August 1856 Bedford Mercury

Woburn. Sudden Death. – An inquest was held on Thursday, before John Green, Esq., coroner for the Honour of Ampthill, on the body of Mrs. Turney, a lady who had been for some time past a visitor in this town. It appeared that deceased was suffering from Spasmodic Asthma, and that, even as lately as Sunday evening, she had had a very severe attack. The body was found in a field on the Leighton Road. The probability is that she died from angina pectoris. The verdict was, "Died from natural causes." [We feel that it is just, alike to the public and ourselves to state that on application for permission to see the depositions (as is our practice in all cases where sufficient notice has not been given to us of an intended inquest), that permission was refused. There must be surely some very urgent reason for thus, I effect, closing a public court.]

Sunday School Annual Festival. – The annual piente of the Sabbath School connected with the Independent chapel was held in the usual place, the beautiful nook in the park, which for many years past kindness of the Duke of Bedford has appropriated for the interesting occasion. More than 150 children partook of the customary refreshments and spent a very pleasant evening in the sports suitable to their age and character as Sunday School children. The friends mustered in large numbers to witness and take part in the festivity of the young. Two hundred sat down for tea. In the course of the evening, addresses were delivered in the tent by the Revs. J. Andrews (the pastor), T. Baker of Ridgmount, W. C. Robinson of Maulden, and the proceedings were brought to a close by praise and prayer.

Mind-strugglers have many depressing incidents to contend with, and perhaps no one more cools mental fervour than the discovery that their "original" is not an original idea. I was struck by this as I read your scrap "Cowper forestalled by Bishop Berkley" – relative to the "cup which cheers, but not inebriates."

Bookworms may disenchant of many cherished delusions, perhaps rob some dead immortal of long awarded, and *deserved* fame, for we take it as provable continually in the world of letters –

That on two minds the self same thought may strike,
Though far as northern from the southern pole
Have been the impulses which have moved each soul.

The experience, and, I trow, testimony of all expansive intellect must be – "The new beneath the sun hath never been." The charm of thought seems that it *is* original to the thinker, and then with a worthy purpose he clothes it in local costume, or a world-accepted dress which, if it be flimsy, flaunts a summer day, or, if, like Olney's bard, it be manufactured of "good broad cloth" it will last – "While a warm heart may beat within."

Bishops Berkley's words had, to multitudes, lain among the unknown relics of the Literary Republic. Cowper threw the charm of song around the same idea, he touched the *heart* string, and in every home the melody now sounds.

Perhaps you will favour me with a corner for this thought on this extract from "Notes and Queries."

G. Castleden.

The example above shows Castleden was also occasionally contributing the news column for Woburn, yet he couldn't resist slipping into verse here and there. The usual Woburn report-writer was far more sober and factual! The annual Woburn agricultural meeting was a highlight of the local calendar. Prize-stock was shown, the latest innovations in farming methods discussed, and the villages all around turned out to see the great and the good. There is a famous illustration of the meeting in 1811, by George Garrard, with an extensive key of those present.

11ᵗʰ October 1856 Cambridge Independent Press

Woburn Agricultural Meeting.

Sir, Perhaps a contribution from one who can, by memory, just link this scene with the Park gathering of 1811, may not encroach on your regular report, while it may add a moral to this Show. As with our friends we entered Woburn Park, on the way to this Meeting, our mind was toned by the expressive Iine:

This life's dream, passing show. And when we arrived at this pastoral scene, we thought - where ate the fathers? The present generation were full of vigour and bustle, while the remnants of the last, with furrowed cheeks, whitened heads, and stiffened limbs, gave evidence their activities were o'er! Contemplating the prosperities of some, and the adversities of others, these words struck us - "His sons come to honour, and he knoweth it not; and they are brought low, but he perceiveth it not of them." Job xiv. 21.

Among the gazers we stood, looking at one of the wonders of the age-the steam plough. Of its capabilities, we must leave the practical man to decide; and of its economy we can be judge. On returning from it, the appearance of the field attracted attention, grouped as it was with bulky farming sons; and as we viewed the accession of the ladies, it was one of the novelties of the scene; - as the shower came down, how umbrellas went up! And we did think if some of the primitive shades had seen us, this, part of the Show, had been one of their chief wonders.

The ploughing, machinery, stock, I handle not, neither the dinner do I presume to discuss - of the latter, those may tell who did enjoy-

The feast, the flow, the prises of the day;
Drank wisdom in, and gave to humour play.

To return to the Show: Again the skies darkened, and the rain pelted down. Fortunately for some of us, the chesnut's broad leaves, a vegetable umbrella, aided the cotton ones materially during a shower which extinguished much of the fervency of amateur agriculturists, and sent them, at a quick pace, in search of shelter and a change of garments. One Woburn poet, of bygone day, hath written -

'Tis said the Spanish maid most loves
The gentle gloom of chesnut groves.

But, most certainly, looking at some fair specimens of Nature's handiest work, under our chesnut groves, in "gentle gloom," it was not at all suggestive of the pleasant incidents of Spain's sunny hours, and only hope cold and the "awful tic" may not refresh our memories of this untoward contribution to the Show. However, under this chesnut grove some of us, past the fiftieth milestone of life's journey, did recur times when "Woburn Sheepshearing" was one of the celebrities of the Isle; giving an impulse to farming operations which have issued in improvements astonishing, and which may result in discoveries which may leave present novelties the fragments of antiquated age.

In the evening, looking the familiar picture by Garrard, Memory did waken up to the times when as a boy we mingled with the burly, stalwart forms of that day and looked at Prince, Peer, and Plebian, all in kindly association. Again Memory played this magic slide across the mental vision, and then we asked— Where are they now? Few of us remain to tell the tale. All honour be to the memory of these fathers! and let it never be forgotten in the modern gatherings, and in the flush of present improvements, that first, under the auspices of the great Francis, Duke of Bedford, began that pastoral revolution which has made many a sand tract fruitful plain, and covered local sterility with waving corn. While congratulating present patrons and enterprising farmers, yet, as all substantial good has a gradual growth, so we may date from the May scenes of olden time to these Michaelmas festivals;

and, as we saw his Grace the Duke of Bedford ride through the assemblage, now and then were linked by the thought, that the past noble landlords and their tenants were as the pioneers in that agricultural movement which, under their sons, has resulted in such success. Of that time, some of the heir-loom "cups," treasured among few of the old tenants' descendants, still testify of "Woburn sheepshearing," and join that slow pace and substantial past with the fast speed of the present—

Time's play proceeds: this is its fresher scene,
And present actors dress for life's el naive dream.

I am, Sir, your obedient servant, George Castleden, Woburn, 6th October.

Elections arrangements were another important part of his life. As a staunch Liberal supporter, he had campaigned on their behalf, and the aspiration of a fair election, contested in a Gentlemanly-fashion, was one he felt moved to write on.

11th April 1857 Bedford Mercury

Sir, - As the organ of the Liberals in our county, I ask the privilege of a space for this letter. I would first refer to the past.

In the election of 1826, from the 15th to 27th June, I was actively engaged. Perhaps nigh 3000 voters then polled. This was the stern contest in which the Tory headed the poll; but much earlier was I introduced to these county strifes. A personal anecdote may interest juvenile politicians, as well as prove the heedless prodigality then in play. As a lad I visited a friend in Bedford: it was one of Sir John Osborn's contests: three of us strolled into an "open house," and immediately was placed before us, three boys, a black bottle of wine! This fact, to the reflective mind, will account for some of the sad election ruins which our county has known, and for the stoppage of which it was first indebted to the noble resolve of the Marquis of Tavistock, no longer to sanction such election profligacy. In 1830 the Marquis of Tavistock and William Stuart, Esq., were returned; in 1831, the Marquis of Tavistock and Sir Peter Payne; in 1832, Lord Charles J. F. Russell and William Stuart, Esq.; in 1835, Lord Charles J. F. Russell and Lord Alford. Further record I have not, but I think once since two Tories were sitting for the county; then Hasting Russell, Esq., and Col. Gilpin, and this brings us up to the present time.

On the day of nomination, in the Swan square, I did remark, "Let us take care; three to one is great odds; and besides, in this day of free trade, a monopoly of the representation may be used as a reproach," and to more than one gentleman I used words similar to these, "If the Conservatives are a minority, they are a powerful one, and there may be a question whether it would be right to ignore them altogether. However, the gauntlet was thrown down, it was taken up, and the battle has been fought. Let me add of the nomination day, standing at the hustings, I felt proud of that English fair-play scene, and amid personal excitement of the gentlemanly and manful utterances I then heard, I did admire the men, though to some

Of their principles I was opposed. It has been, I presume, a fair trial struggle. I am exceedingly pleased our Liberal member, Hastings Russell, Esq., heads the poll, and I use a veteran Whig's sentiment, when I say, if a Conservative is to be returned we cannot have a better, or one who is identified more with county interests, than Colonel Gilpin.

And now one general hint I venture for the future. Having canvassed, I am warranted in saying the registration should be looked after better. This done it might save needless contests, and as a consequence, neighbourly alienations and trade injuries would not be risked. Ignorance, on either side, with fervency of zeal, may precipitate a county into wanton strife, which, in its results, pass harmless as summer's clouds over the privileged portion of any constituency, but which often fall with crushing severity on the little tradesman and fortyshilling freeholder. These men are not answerable for this contest, therefore, gentlemen of Bedfordshire, let all reprisal hostilities to the weak be honourably avoided. I would pour them as oil on the troubled waters. In the great principles of civil and religious liberty I was initiated when a child, and I shall hold them to the grave; nevertheless, while claiming for myself the right of private judgement in those matters, I dare not turn traitor to this right by denying it to another.

I am, Sir, Your very obedient servant, George Castleden, Woburn, 7th April.

On the 2nd May, the Bedfordshire Mercury ran a leader on the proposed changes to elections and the introduction of a ballot.

16th May 1857 Bedford Mercury
The Ballot

"It must be, there is no doubt: it is a great disgrace, little doubt about that. It will somehow or other involve a stern retribution on those who have, by their unscrupulous use of power, rendered it necessary – and it may even work out in the characters and fortunes of the electors themselves some small measure of that punishment which sooner or later befalls every man who is untrue to himself, a coward at heart." – Bedford Mercury, May 2.

Sir, - Thoughts from solitary thinkers may be the germs of politics, - ay, resolutions seized by master minds they become levers which move the social, moral, political world. I claim no such importance for the following thoughts, but to strengthen the above extract I venture them, backed by the catholic axiom – "Think, let think."

In 1838, to the "Bedford Beacon," on this question I wrote on a decision in the House of Commons, giving a majority of 200 supporters, "each member of this 200 having some instance of cruelty, oppression, and injustice to support his vote: what a startling sum total of slavery shall we arrive at in this free country?" Then, fervent for the trial of this expedient, we thus wrote, – "If, now, in advanced years, we pause, hear our reasoning; and if any solution of the difficulty should be offered, gladly would I concede, ay, confess to error."

The two evils are – Oppression and hypocrisy

Oppression is another's wrongful act done to me; hypocrisy is self wronging self. The first may be borne by a man; the latter will assuredly make a man hate himself.

The word hypocrisy is limited often in its application. Let some religionist make a stumble, how open-mouthed are men to dub him "hypocrite." To a double share of scorn on him I have no objection; but "fair play, Hal;" are there no hypocrites elsewhere? But for hypocrisy of the darkest kind, that silky scoundrel at Rugeley had not given the criminal page its hideous stain. But for hypocrisy of the most subtle guile, our professional rascalities would not give us an unenvied notoriety in Christendom. But for cruel hypocrisy our commercial delinquency had not arrived as such colossal dimensions, hurling thousands into ruin, and filling with fear the hearts of myriads, – not to say a word about social hypocrisy, the snug covert for the snakes of our localities. No, no; give the devil his due; and while, no doubt, he exults heartily over the fall of the "saint," he has his most Sardonic grin at that plausible "sinner," who, callous, blushless, and repudiating all saintship, blinds his fellow-creatures by taking the sacrament on Sunday in order the more safely to slay on a Monday! This we read of in a kept diary; and surely in the late public revelations we have affecting proof that hypocrisy is not altogether monopolized by the "saint." This is defensive of some who may play hypocrites as the exception, and then bitterly mourn the sin; whereas, to the demon hypocrite, continuous hypocrisy is his selfish glory, and its success is his rule of faith.

Now for its application, nationally. Can we have the ballot without making political hypocrites? Is it not a people's question? and by adopting it, do we not openly proclaim our principle? our want of faith in the press to expose and punish? and do we not humiliatingly post ourselves – "Cowards at heart?"

The experience of years gives me pause in the advocacy of the ballot to be applied generally. In many cases it will be the lure for the "living lie," or give an Englishman a hangdog look, of which he ever ought to be ashamed. If a way were opened by which the ballot might honestly serve, then let all canvassing be made penal. We ought not to inflict this task on those who serve us.

Still with all precautionary conditions might not the representative principle be weakened in attempting to meet unenglish oppression by an unenglish expedient? Might it not be laying down the element of a machinery which, ere long, would mould our three estates into one "organised hypocrisy?" Our great dramatist has it – Man, to thyself be true!

Will not this method be a temptation for man, political, to play false to himself? And by asking this secrecy for this hypocrisy, may we not be degrading ourselves below Russia's serfs? or may we not be taunted by our ballot brother in America, that we are about to adopt means he thinks or resigning as inutile and false in working out the desired results – political integrity?

Here we stop. These thoughts are put on the stream of letters; they may float under the eye of some far-seeing statesmen, who, while lamenting one evil may regretfully pause at a remedy worse than the disease.

With your ominous words, "a stern retribution for unscrupulous wrong," my thoughts have often associated. But while the tyranny of man may be hard to bear, that is lighter far than the crushing self-imposed despicability which allows –

> The man to smile, and smile,
> And play the hypocrite by law.

I remain, Sir, Your obedient servant, George Castleden, Woburn, May 6.

23<u>rd</u> **May 1857** <u>Bedford Mercury</u>

The Ballot. "It must be, there is no doubt." – Bedford Mercury, 2nd May.

Sir, - I quake fearfully at encountering one who has had the experience of years to give him pause in the advocacy of the ballot to be applied generally," I am unable to produce any experience of any kind to make me pause in the advocacy of the ballot." I have seen much showing the necessity of it; I have read more against it; I have met with no single argument that can induce me to "pause in the advocacy of the ballot." The more I see, hear read, think, the less weighty do I deem what is said against it. I read Mr. Castleden's letter and rise from its perusal convinced that his objections are nugacious.

But I will follow Mr. Castleden through his letter. And, first, for the heading of his letter. My heading agrees with his in the best part about it; what follows I cannot accept, and regret to have seen it in the leading article of the Bedford Mercury. For the letter itself, I think that "thoughts from solitary thinkers" are the germs of policies; "resolutions seized by master minds" is a phrase put in apposition to "thoughts from solitary thinkers"; now "thoughts" and "resolutions" are two different things: "thought" differs from "resolution" in that it has no necessary connection with the will to act. What then is meant when one speaks of "resolutions seized by master minds," &c., I have not yet made out. "Think and let think."

Singularly stupid as I am, Mr. Castleden will forgive me for not understanding the next paragraph; I therefore pass on to his definition of oppression and hypocrisy. "Oppression," says Mr. Castleden, "is another man's wrong done to me; it may be borne by man." Is not it a truer account to say, "oppression is wrong done or suffered, being the offspring of the devil; to true man will practise, no free man will submit thereto." "Hypocrisy," says Mr. C., "is self wronging self; it makes a man hate himself." Rather, as it seems to me, "hypocrisy is the obtaining goods under false pretences; it makes a man hate the upright." So there are hypocrites where men get or try to get what they wish for, under false pretences. Are there no hypocrites at an election with the so called open voting? I have known several who have voted for a candidate without protest, when his heart was for the opposing candidate. And why? Because his living depended upon the canvasser that he must play the hypocrite to get his living from so vile a source. The same would vote as his conscience dictated, were canvassing rendered illegal by the introduction of the ballot. The same would conceal his real convictions or vote from anyone, if his bread depended upon him. He would be as much a hypocrite with as without the ballot. On the contrary, the honest man who snaps his fingers now in his employers face, would, with the ballot, say to him, "you have no right to ask me for my vote, but I don't mind telling you that you won't get it." But he would not be asked for his vote.

The ballot will not alter a man's nature; it will increase the number of voters and there will be less hypocrisy.

I can conceive nothing more likely to give a man "a hangdog look" than his speaking among his friends, for seven years, against principles which he must vote for (if coward at heart) at the end of that term, to "keep in" with the landlord. Are not those "coward at heart," pray, who now abstain from voting at all, because they must either suffer in their livelihood, or violate their conscience? How many were there, last election, who did not vote for these motives?

What infidelity to principle is it to say – the Englishman's right of private judgement is as much a right as his home? The law, at present, allows the former to be violated and rudely trampled upon by an oligarchy.

That the ballot should be "applied generally," if by that expression Mr. Castleden meant to include members of parliament when voting, no sensible man would deem requisite or otherwise than pernicious; but if it merely mean that the ballot should be used in electing the representative of every body of men, I think this as desirable as that every member of a club should use it.

Has Mr. Castleden's years of experience not yet taught him that such an idea as "making canvassing penal" must be impracticable; such a law would be evaded. His suggesting it shows the need we have of the ballot. We did not inflict canvassing upon those who serve us; they take it up of themselves.

Unenglish oppression! Good heavens! Would that it were so. To make oppression unenglish, we must make the ballot English. America is not so near as Belgium; in Belgium the ballot works well. America is not as English as Australia; in Australia the ballot has begun to work well. A man's heart beats unseen; the English heart suffers from constant bareing. The voters of England stand in the same relation to her representative in the body politic as the heart to the head in the natural body. Baring in mind the simple fact that the face is part of the head, that smiles belong to the face, I will conclude with Mr. Castleden's apt quotation, introducing it by saying, that we now, through lack of the ballot, are suffering

The man to smile and smile

And play the hypocrite by law.

Most truly yours, Audi Alteram Partem

Unlike Castleden, most other writers to the newspapers at this time were anonymous, like the above, which was another of Castleden's bugbears. If a man was not prepared to sign his name to his opinion, what was the point of his opinion? Many times, he simply ignored any anonymous criticism, but sometimes he engaged them in argument for several weeks.

30th May 1857 Bedford Mercury

The Ballot.

Sir, - "Audi alteram partem," with your permission, shall have a few sentences in reply.

"Hear the other side." Honestly attended to, would save erring man from many a scrape. It would be as the bull's-eye flash of truth, discovering many a dark job; it would preserve short-sighted humanity from committing irreparable wrong, and as a consequence prevent self inflicting life's fiercest barb, when true remorse finds itself powerless to repair.

1. I either wrote the word obscurely, or it was printed wrongly. "Revolutions," not "resolutions," was the word. This mistake creates a pardonable confusion in your correspondent's mind.

2. "Oppression" may have a meaning according to the many shapes it takes. In my letter I limit to injury returned for open voting.

3. "The Englishman's right of private judgement is as much a right as his home" is endorsed with pleasure; and as I would not be ashamed of my name or home, so let me not be ashamed of publicly expressing as a citizen any private judgement.

4. What I meant by the ballot "applied generally" was – might not some special act be framed to be as a just terror ever proven election oppression?

5. If, as constituents, we are the obliged, ought our representatives to be put to any expense, or to the trouble of canvassing? With the ballot, these, with conveyance to the poll, &c., should be done away with.

6. The last paragraph, quoting *where* the ballot serves, would open a wide field of discussion. In all great changes we must remember Britain is an eight hundred years' monarchy; and if *within* we have not renovating and conserving remedies from *without* we can hardly expect to find them. To adventure a little humour – John Bull is rather obese, and age has too much complicated causalities and infirmities to expect the recipes applied to juvenile monarchies and boyish colonies to touch this case. Time-hallowed gout and long-revered rheumatism may not yield to simple treatment. Elemental principles may apply to elemental states of the body, physical or political, but these may only mock or torture when the combinations of time alter either, or the chemistry of events fashion and years accelerate the progress of decay.

These explanations I offer, believing the intent of your correspondent is to search out and establish the truth. I know full well "the other side;" have much to say in favour of the ballot. With no intention to dictate did I moot my views; and I merely add – my argument rests on the fear that the remedy may be worse than the disease. In a sentence – I hesitate at a measure involving legalised hypocrisy. Hypocrisy in open voting is *simple* treachery; legalise it, you make it *compound*. And, as thought for thought, I ask, - should we not pause ere we post ourselves "cowards at heat" because some - Little tyrant of his fields - plays the oppressor? And shall some petty tyranny frighten the Lion of England into this covert to hide himself? Surely your correspondent would rather hear the honest roar of "no" to such possible national poltroonery.

I remain, Sir, your obedient servant, George Castleden, Woburn, 26th May.

6th June 1857 Bedford Mercury

Protection for the Voter.

Sir, - I thank Mr. Castleden for believing that I wish to "search out and establish the truth," and therefore express my conviction that Mr. Castleden has not found it out so far as the ballot is concerned. I will only say that he will find what I believe to be true in the ballot argument from the leader which appears in the same page of the *Bedford Mercury* as his letter. Mr. Castleden will, I doubt not, come to see that the ballot is a very easy and honourable method of voting.

Let me, however, run through Mr. Castleden's six sentences, if you can spare me so much of your paper.

1. What is the meaning of the corrected sentence – "thoughts from solitary thinkers may be germs of policies – age, revolutions seized by master minds they become the levers which move the social, moral, political world?"

2. What are the shapes according to which oppression changes its meaning? Mr. Castleden does not limit his definition of hypocrisy to open voting.

3. Mr. Castleden shows some respect for the right of private judgement, he allows it to be as much a right of the Englishman as his home; he is not ashamed of publicly expressing as a citizen his private judgement; the ballot will not make him ashamed of his vote, but of expressing his private judgement publicly. The ballot will make these become *safe* rights protected from the only influence exerted by agents &c.

4. Surely Mr. Castleden was not happy in his making the expression "the ballot applied generally" equivalent to "some act framed so as to be a just terror over proven election oppression." Some acts have been tried and found of no use.

5. Canvassing, electioneering agents &c., will become illegal with the ballot made legal. Why leave the question of members paying for their seat to those who uphold the present state of things?

6. I can see no signs of decay in my country; I think that England is young, though she be 800 years old. I see no truth in the picture of John Bull as hobbies, &c. I do not like metaphors; Mr. Castleden knows that we find remedies for disease in obtaining them from foreign lands and applying them with good effect both to old and young. I was in favour of the ballot before I knew it worked well in any land.

But, indeed, all Mr. Castleden's reasons against the ballot are based on a lemma which is untrue, namely – that the introduction of the ballot will increase hypocrites and legalise hypocrisy. This has nowhere been proved, only *assumed*. The ballot is not designed to shut the mouth of the voter, and it will surely not do so; nay, the ballot will, I am confident, make many a man who now keeps his politics within his burning breast, speak them out so his friends will think of him as Saul who is also among the prophets.

No! The ballot will give freedom of thought and action in harmony with this freedom of thought; it will untie tongs and release the tenantry from such hypocrisy as that which a Marquis of Waterford shamefully causes. Let the British Lion roar loudly against iniquity such as this, and may she speedily get rid of all these thorns.

I am not ashamed of my name, but I do not wish that to become personal which concerns the nation.

Audi Alteram Partem

13th June 1857 Bedford Mercury

The Ballot.

Sir, - Allow this brief reply to "Audi Alteram Partem."

"Cowards at heart" first struck a responsive chord, and I ventured a few accordant sentences.

I know in all explanatory writing is a risk of making that darker that was dark enough before, and so increase misapprehension, but if the conviction rules that the main object is to "search out and establish truth;" this mutual guide will ensure manly courtesy and banish malevolent criticism.

The name given is to me proof in support of the argument that a special act might meet, like proven tyrannous acts, without branding a whole proprietary as oppressors, or subjecting a whole people to a legalised secrecy, involving the temptation of hypocrisy. Tell me this is "assumption;" I reply - seeing what we see in open voting would it not, by secret voting, hold out greater facilities for citizen delinquency?

But your correspondent is a stern Ballot advocate. Here we retire upon our motto - "Think, let think." We differ on the two evils, oppression or hypocrisy - which? Secrecy of voting will encourage the latter, and I think vititate as essential element in an Englishman's character. Institute it in the body politic it would imply tyranny, which neither trial by jury - free press - nor the courage of a great nation, could put down. Let us come to this sneaking conclusion, and say there is no remedy but secret voting, then how are we fallen.

"Shame! where is then thy blush?"

And, supposing such a result, the sooner some more of us were off to Australia, or even the East, the better.

Ever recollect in all public affairs secrecy is dangerous to Englishmen. This is a constitutional dogma which might be enlarged upon. Ventilation is our safety, and closed doors, hole and corner meetings, one-sided statements are abhorrent to honest Englishmen. Let the people beware of setting any example of walking in dark paths, for it may, as it regards the liberties of our common country, be very pernicious now, and lead to the most disastrous conclusions. As a nation, let us rather "suffer and be strong."

With one personal reference on the last sentence I close. These views might have been given, also, under a veiled signature, but as, in the past, I have had attributed to my pen the honour of another's composition, I would protect self and serve truth by the unmistakeable name. And, now, perfectly satisfied with the amicable course this discussion has taken, and leaving it as thought for thought, I remain, sir, your obedient servant, George Castleden, Woburn, June 9th.

The Bedfordshire Mercury of 15th August 1857 reported that Castleden addressed a meeting at Hockliffe, to say farewell to the Rev. Sleigh, as he left for Australia to join the Colonial Missionary Society after 11 years of ministry locally. He was presented with a purse of gold, and an inkstand from the female Bible Class, along with a mat they had made for him. In May, the Indian Rebellion had begun. Ultimately unsuccessful, the uprising against the rule of the British East India Company, started in the form of a mutiny of sepoys of the Company's army in the garrison town of Meerut. Exceptional cruelty was inflicted by both sides. At Cawnpore, 120 British women and children captured by the Sepoy forces were killed in what came to be known as the Bibighar Massacre, and their remains were thrown down a well in an attempt to hide the evidence. Following the recapture of Cawnpore and the discovery of the massacre, the angry India Company forces engaged in widespread retaliation against captured rebel soldiers and local civilians.

26th September 1857 Bedford Mercury

India – "British Vengeance."

Sir, - On the 1st August I copied from the Times this ominous sentence – "The storm is terrible, but the darkness is even more awful than the lightning." Since then I have added passages from other leaders on this Mutiny. With the views first impressed, and which views have been strengthened, I cannot but consider words, now toning the public mind, as brilliant sophistries, and I regret that public writers generally are spurring on to British vengeance.

This time I will not intrude on your columns more than to say, it seems to me there is a side to this question which as a moral and religious people we avoid too much. Put us in the position of Pagan Rome, our course would be very clear; if big enough for the job, reconquer, slay all mutineers, sack and devastate till full-gorged Revenge might say "Enough." But as Christian England, it should be a different process. If with one century's occupation we have done so little to humanise or moralise India, then the question arises, What sort of schoolmasters we have been, and how practice has harmonised with precept?

I am not a student in history, yet I have read much, but surely on no page, ancient or modern, barbarian or civilised, can you find such a blot as our

English history will now retain; and if there be not a cause, then the East, the cradle of knowledge, sinks into abysmal infamy, compared with cannibal islands; the crudité Brahmin is infinitely below the wildest savage in cruelty; and the educated Mussulman sleeps himself in ignominy from which the benighted Laplander would shrink in horror.

Pondering in the lonely hour on the dark cloud hanging over so many English homes, I am forced to ask, is there not a cause? Say no, then I am on the dark sea of fatalism, without pole-star or compass; but believing God will vindicate truth, and knowing also "He sees the oppressor and the oppressed," so I am afraid the chronicles of our Indian occupation will prove, as a Christian nation we used the Cross as our emblem, and the sword as our sceptre! Then, if it be true that those who trust to the sword shall perish by the sword, this problem may be solved, and while the brilliant sophist derides the solution, the warrior feels the "enjoying half-pay for life makes mankind worth destroying;" and even the statesman, buried by "glory" and studying the "honour" of his country; yet after all, as a Christian people, we ought to be in dust and ashes in the contemplation of ill-gotten gold and prospective massacre.

One of our old poets seems to have put our Indian conquests, with the present appalling repayment, in a single couplet. I leave it, paradoxical as it is, and leave it as thought for the future –

"Thus, in our gain become we gainful losers,
And what's enclosed, encloses the enclosers."

The millions to be spent, the blood to be spilled, will prove the first line, and a melancholy home annotation on the second will remain in the immortal barbarities of Cawnpore.

I remain, Sir, Your obedient Servant, Geo. Castleden. Woburn, 20th September.

Before the coming of the industrial transport age, the greatest losses of life in single events were usually down to sinking ships. Without radios, and at the mercy of the weather, boats could be days overdue before an alarm was even raised that they had disappeared, often with no trace. But when the calamities were within sight of shore, and the devastation plain for all to see, the horror and helplessness was all the more brutal.

7th December 1857 Bedford Mercury

The Wreck of the Dunbar. (In sight of home, - the night of 20th August.)

Note. – Summer time in England – winter-time in Australia. Night falling the gladsome look on the light of home – the last turn into the berths – the dreamy sleep – the bump! the shrieks. Wails, and groans under the dark, dark sky – and broadside crash – 'And the sea yawed around her like a bell' a few short minutes – all was still of human kind 'except the bubbling cry of some strong swimmer in his agony,' – and then the wild breakers whirled around and danced above their prey. (In this awful wreck one incident struck, on reading the particulars in the "Empire," Sydney paper. The master of the lighthouse having occasion to go out about the fatal time observed his dog run to the edge of the cliff, and, an unusual thing, over the abyss kept up a loud barking howl! Our dirge merely notes the main fact, leaving imagination to supply the horrors of this home engulfment of 120 souls.)

'Twas Summer time, the harvest fair
Gladdened our land, perfumed our air,
And England's homes were light:
The seasons, rolling, brought their food,
And Ceres with her sickle stood.
And smiled our prospects bright.

'Twas winter time; 'neath murky cloud,
The haze enwrapping like a shroud,
A ship ploughed on her way;
And, peering through the stormy night,
The Captain viewed the harbour light
Which shone o'er Sydney's bay.

Home, home, – the dangers are all past;
'To bed, sweet babes, you'll sleep your last,'
Fond mothers said with glee:
'Good night,' the kissed adieu once more,
'To-morrow we shall be on shore,
Our dear home heights to see.'

The babes, unconscious slumber blest,
The mothers, in a transient rest,
Half dozing, dreamed of woe –
It was a vision – no, no, no –
Another bump! it must be so!
Upon the rocks they go.

O! who can tell the fearful tale?
Over its horrors drop the veil –
An utter wreck she lay:
As wild beasts roaring o'er their prey
The tiger-billows crashed away,
And, growling, leaped to slay.

In shelfy caves, in depths beneath
Encompassed in the arms of death,
Babes, mothers, fathers, sleep!
United in one dark, dark doom,
Their home is found in Ocean's tomb,
While risen hearts aye weep.

Upon the cliff, storm lashed behold
A pair who brave the stormy cold;
They walk the lighthouse steep!
They stand and listen, but no sound
Told him of nature's wrecking wound,
How death had 'Murdered sleep.'

But hear the howling dog, - ay, list,
He hears from out the thunderous mist
Of breakers far below,
Some woman's shriek, some strong man's cry,
Or the wild roar of agony;
And Instinct utters woe.

Poor brute: - immortal be this line
If but to tell this grief of thine
O'er Dunbar's yawning grave:
On that lone rock, 'neath that wild sky,
Sole mourner, hark, - I hear thy cry,
Remediless to save!

'He rides upon the stormy sky,'
He speaks, and atoms, nations die;
His mysteries, who can tell?
Proud man resists, he asks the why,

While humble souls will trust and die
Assured it shall be well

Thus wrecks on land, and wrecks on sea
If view'd aright may lessons be
To teach the christian this: -
A feeble, faithless, fickle world,
Shall to destruction all be hurled,
And sink in death's abyss.
G. C., Woburn, November 26th.

One crewman actually survived the wreck; he was thrown onto the rocks, and climbed up a cliff, where he lay injured for two days before being found and treated for his injuries.

Tea meetings seem to have been the 19th century equivalent of the charity jumble sale for raising money for good causes. It was an excuse to see and be seen, hear some speeches, and raise some much-needed funds to support those less fortunate than you. Although each town and most villages had a correspondent who supplied the newspaper with a few inches of column news about such local events, sometimes Castleden took it upon himself to supply reports of the meeting he had attended. These are usually signed off as "Communicated", but sometimes you can easily tell by the language used that it was him.

9th **January 1858** Dunstable Chronicle

Tabernacle Social Tea Meeting – This meeting was held on Tuesday evening in the School-room adjoining the chapel. After the "cup which warms and cheers but not inebriates" had been partaken of, and the "hissing urn" had been dismissed, the chair was taken by the Rev. Stephen E. Dodge, the minister, and the meeting was addressed by the Chairman, Rev. Daniel Gould, Mr Webster, of Luton, and Mr. G. Castleden, of Woburn. The addresses breathed a wish for the prosperity of the new chapel; they were toned by a catholicity of spirit which was very grateful – they were keyed by the lines

"Let names, and sects, and parties fall,

"And Jesus Christ be all in all:"-

And they were stimulating to the performance of those good works which at once serve man, and show man's desire to honour God. This meeting was much enlivened by the harmony of friends: two or three anthems were tastefully performed and added much to the pleasure of this pleasant evening.

12: *Three young Woburn lads have spotted the camera on the High Street, and stop playing for a moment to pose, with the Market Hall behind. An undated postcard.*

18th January 1858 Bedfordshire Mercury

Our Monster Age

Sir, - In the Christmas week I trod London's streets - heard of monster sights, and saw some monster things. Conversation keyed thought, and in the quiet of home we cogitate old year's reflections which may be expository and instructive for the New Year. A Patrician Poet in his "Age of Bronze," has written on the comparison of the past with the present.

"The 'good old times' – all times when old are good –

Are gone, the present might be if they would;

Great things have been, and are, and greater still

Want little of mere mortals but their will:

A wider space, a greater field is given

To those who play their 'tricks before high heaven.'

I know not if the angels weep, but men

Have wept enough – for what? – to weep again."

If it be the certain lot 'to weep again' surely any sentence that may distinguish the future's tears will not be penned in vain.

But to our little record - On the 18th, with a friend, I paddled round the Leviathan, a monster beauty of naval architecture. I register not her dimensions, tons, horse-power, or capacities; my wonder was, gazing on this iron-built Citidel whether, after she was launched, she would – 'Walk the waters like a thing of life.' Or whether, so huge, so heavy, she would ever walk at all; however future progress may be reported.

On the 19th, I read the monster list of smashes in the last two months. Perusing the admonitory sentences for the future we thought on some of our 'fast pace' sentiments, and somewhat oracular, we came to this conclusion; - if the immoral system of trading is persisted in the commercial pestilence will spread far and wide.

If the 'good old times' are ever past still we may stick to the good old principles. They will do for all revolving years. Forsake them for the mushroom opinions of the hour, and wonder not at catastrophe. The going down of the late fleet of City Merchantmen indicates departure from them, and proves monster credulity which has inflated them, and consigned cash to the safe keeping of vessels built of rags!

Two great things were strictly attended to in the 'good old times' Cash and Conscience were considered always the safest at home. Some who dwell upon these 'old times' think conscience now is let out to opinion; and cash is given up in order to permit the disburthened citizen to fly his paper kite with the greater freedom. Looking at the amount, fifty millions, of this monster crash, what a symptom of commercial delinquency. Conversing with some on these wrecks, some who have proved the "good old times," and meditating the repetitions of such disasters, we agreed that the light of the dark ages was the best beacon, and the polestar of Truth the only safe guide. To try to understand the late monetary crash we put it thus: The contributions of the many to joint-stock banks and bubble companies, and the appropriation of the few bespeak the association of flats and sharps, which, however conducive to harmony in the notes, are generally discordant in the ring of pure metal: add to this the expansions of modern pride, and then wonder not when dire collapse ensues at home, desolation, and mercantile ruin.

We may touch another item – monster crimes. If we say they have been rapid in succession, horrible in nature, and ruinous in their efforts, we strain not the truth. Commence at the delinquent bankers, swindling senators, railway criminals, friend poisoning friend, Haidees consigning their Juans to a self-murderer's grave, and ending with the before unheard of combination of matricide, fratricide, and suicide in one: these, with the slaughterers of the "one flesh," are a simple in one short year of monster criminality, which makes hell to rejoice, earth to tremble, and heaven to mourn.

Monster machinery, monster monetary crashes, and monster social and home criminalities, we have touched. On the first, not endowed with the mechanical bump, we dare not enlarge; from the mystical skirt to the stupendous ship expansion is the order of the day. How far enormity shall proceed ere deformity commences I suppose must be left to the taste of our emulative age.

On monster monetary credulity, &c., and delinquency, I use the words of a public print, dated 19th, on the "Deplorable effects of the Bank Failures in Scotland": - "Crowds of excellent ladies have not a crust remaining, and every day the dark horizon round that cruel bank grows blacker, &c. It is believed that about £2,500,000 have melted away, and how is poor old Scotland to meet such a loss. In what terms shall the criminality of the men sustaining the characters of directors be held up to public indignation. The hulks and Norfolk Island are crowded with criminals who, in a social and moral point of view, are not one tenth part so guilty as they."

Let these extracts prove our case on monster commercial delinquency. Here credulity has been entrapped - cunning has triumphed, and treachery has slain.

As it regards monster home criminality, this recipe will ever ensure its continuance. Deal treacherously, smile the lie, ignore the truth, gild with sophistry and glaze by fashion; deceit works surely on to dark crime, and then, when the climax of atrocity is reached, and the criminal becomes a world-name we take refuge in execration while we often convict ourselves. Yes - for if men would but frown upon that which they themselves would be ashamed to enact, many a monster crime might be nipped in the bud and many a dubitating sinner be saved - monster criminality plunging him into irretrievable perdition.

We would here introduce the fact that on the morning of the 20th we found ourselves among the monster congregation in the Surrey Gardens. As the preacher discoursed on "Peace, good will towards men," we heard many a salutary truth which would aid the suppression of those moral monstrosities which are an awful sign of the times, and which every lover of his country deplores. Sinking this monster congregation with preceding passages we would take up the burden of Mr. Spurgeon's theme, and say - "Stay, stay sinner, on the gospel plains.'

We might write more, but these thoughts will suffice for the thoughtful. Cast on the tide of intellect, if they should reach some commanding mind, let him try whether he cannot stay that general wreck of principle among the middle classes of which our monster items are significant. If so the vagrant thoughts of a wandering provincial in London's dirty streets will not have been stored in vain.

I am, Sir, Your obedient servant, George Castleden, Woburn, December 31st.

The "Leviathan" that Castleden had been paddled around in London was the S.S. Great Eastern, an iron sailing steam ship designed by Isambard Kingdom Brunel. It was the largest ship built at the time of the January 31ˢᵗ launch, and could carry 4,000 passengers from England to Australia without refuelling. The Scottish banking crisis was fuelled by the Western Bank of Scotland (Glasgow) collapsing in November 1857, and taking with it several million pounds of investors' money.

8ᵗʰ February 1858 Bedfordshire Mercury

Deaths Doings.

"O man! Thy kingdom is departing from thee;

And, while it lasts, is emptier than my shade."

Let these lines preface a few words on the doings of the grim despot – Death. Personal reminiscences may give an interest to the following local illustrations; and viewing alike the fall of the poor and the peasant let me, on such a theme, sow a word of warning and instruction.

On reading of the death of the late Earl Spencer, K.G., thought woke up. We mused on boyish time. One winter's day curiosity led us to follow a large party of sportsmen from Woburn Abbey. Entering the covert and thinking all was safe in one of the ridings I strolled behind; a hare crossed at my feet; a gentleman in advance, on a shooting pony, threw himself back for a shot, a loud exclamation followed, and directly a kindly-hearted keeper came up, pointed out the risk, and for the rest of the day I was a beater, much to my delight. The nobleman who saw the danger and stayed the shot was the then Earl Spencer; and when I recur to that forty-years-ago-scene, with the remembrance of that patrician-group, how do the lines apply –

"Shades of the Great! Departed shades, ye live.

On memory still a part of life's strange dream."

Time rolled on, and in one of the Bedford County Elections I was much engaged. The Marquis of Tavistock was prevented by indisposition from meeting the electors, and on one day Lord Althorp came to address us. The assemblage was very turbulent, and gave his lordship a noisy reception. The late Mr. Astell then attempted to speak, and it was our turn to noise, and doing it effectually the wrath of our opponents was so roused that, but for the intervention of a friend, the writer would have had a toss from the hustings, while he was vociferating "You would not hear Lord Althrop, and you sharn't hear Mr. Anstall;" and among a knot of olden neighbours I was playfully called "Lord Althrop's friend." Of this amicable nobleman, knowing something of the bitterness of bygone politics, it is but tributary justice to record the exultation of our passed away neighbour politicians at the good-humoured tactics with which Lord Althorp met and foiled many an attack; and if not an inspiration of the Reform Bill, yet no combatant aided more successfully the winning of that civil victory. Then as Earl Spencer, after a few years, he passed to his ancestors. Then his brother, and then Captain Spencer, succeeded to the Earldom; and now, suddenly, this Earl has passed away.

"Should not each warning give a strong alarm?"

The above are tributary sentences on the politician dead; now for a few on the peasant dead.

"How jocund did they drive their team afield,
How bowed the woods beneath their study stroke?"

The last line expressly applies to the subject of this scrap. For nigh forty years he was a woodman on the adjoining ducal estate. As we stood over his remains with his daughters and a grand-daughter (deaf and dumb), a brief review of "destiny obscure" told us of honest servitude, a sober economy which kept his little house over his head to 71, enabled him as a conscientious duty to owe no man anything; and pleased we were to hear in that death-room that on the question from a kindly neighbour "Is Christ precious now, Thomas?" he gently answered "He is;" and shortly after this peasant son of Ridgmount ended his struggling life. The evening of age, cloudy by reason of trouble and fear of "owing anybody anything," was mercifully lightening by the glorious beams of the gospel, and as we looked upon the peasant's countenance cold in death, the placid smile of hope seemed to rest as preclusive to the joy of sight. To such a class in their mortal career, how true is Gray –

"Far from the madding crowd's ignoble strife,
Their sober wishes never learned to stray;
Along the cool sequestered vale of life,
They kept the noiseless tenor of their way."

And as the "wayfaring man" looking to a "better inheritance" through the merits of a crucified Redeemer, how far above while here below, "Those transitory joys, Which mock pursuit, or wither as we grasp!"

G. C., Woburn, 30th January.

8th February 1858 Bedfordshire Mercury

India.

Sir, - To-day I signed a memorial to the Imperial Parliament relating to the future of India.

How this question will progress it is not of me to say, - whether in the conveyance of such a mass of patronage political strife will so rage as to upset Administrations time will determine. But for the present it may be allowable to ask - Is India to be governed according to Pagan Rome or Christian

Britain? The first may be attained if strong enough for the job; and as long as we can hold it we may boast a clime of gems, jungles, tigers, human and bestial, - but if the genius of Christianity is to rule, let it have *fair play*. Don't let the Bible be ignored while you elevate the Shaster and Koran. Don't make the decree that Christian men shall bow down to the "image" set up by the depraved Hindoo on India's plains, and don't let us any longer be the scoff of a sceptical world, that for Oriental wealth we play the veriest hypocrites that ever affronted the sun. As a nation of "Mawworns" and "Simon Pures" we have reaped ignominious retribution, a retribution that has filled many an English home with lamentation and woe of the most poignant and humiliating kind. Now, let hypocrisy at any rate be banished, and let us stand boldly out either as Pagan Rome for *conquest*, or as Christian Britain for the *conversion* of India's tribes. If the first, the sword is all that is necessary; if the latter, the Bible is indispensable. For this, with others, I signed today, and I do sincerely hope national contrition will be so followed up, that while bitterly lamenting the storm which has blown, we shall not by contumacy provoke the whirlwind of utter desolation.

I am, sir, your obedient servant, G. C., Woburn, Feb. 1.

Like his thoughts on the Irish famine, these ideas about the British Empire rule in India would not be popular with most people of the time.

22ⁿᵈ **March 1858** Bedfordshire Mercury

Woburn. The South Sea Company – Bubble. "Earth hath its bubbles as the ocean hath."

Sir, - An unexpected incident may interest some of your readers, recall a byegone bubble, and prove to our day the truth of the man's words – "There is nothing new under the sun."

In the late winter's week I paced London streets; white at eve, the next day the snow, churned into cream, made butter, I presume, for the shoe-black brigade. Through this composition, with a friend, I surged along the human tide and found harbour in a nook where stands a large brick house, built in olden time for the great British Company of the last century.

This Company was established by act of parliament 1711, under the title of "The Company of Merchants of Great Britain, trading to the South Seas, and other parts of America, and for the encouraging the Fishery."

Well, this bubble rose; all classes clustered round it; it was clutched at by the peer, philosopher, poet, politician and priest: commoners of all grades shouldered each other in its chase; crowds, immortalised by the painter and the poet, gasped for, and grasped at, this bubble; they found it a tinted cheat, and then ruin, broken hearts, madness and death ensued. We give two or three extracts.

"The promoters of the scheme are said to have exaggerated the profits; rumours were at the same time circulated that the Company, by monopolizing the whole of the national funds would reduce government to the necessity of taking loans.

The public, intoxicated with these ideas, purchased with avidity; and the stock, which at Christmas, 1719, was only 126, rose at the opening of the first subscription, on the 14th of April, to above 326... As the frenzy spread, and the desire of making rapid fortunes became contagious, the stock successfully rose to above 1000 per cent., at which price the books were opened for the fourth subscription on the 24th of August; and this subscription, notwithstanding the market price of the established stock was 800, was sold the same day at a premium of 30 or 40 per cent."

Though prospects were promising some were sceptical, and in a ballad of the day satire had its laugh at the utopian dreams of the spectators.

"What need have we of Indian wealth,
Or commerce with our neighbours?
Our constitution is in health,
And riches crown our labours

Our South Sea ships have golden shrouds,
They bring us wealth, 'tis granted;
But lodge their treasure in the clouds,
To hide it till it's wanted."

Whether the directors had deliberately palmed the delusion on the public, or only profited by it when they saw the opportunity, there is no doubt they resorted to desperate means to keep it up. South Sea stock fell as rapidly as ever it rose, and in a few weeks sunk from 1,100, which it had reached, to 135. The distress occasioned by such fluctuation was dreadful. Estates were confiscated to the amount of £2,014,000.

"Numerous are the anecdotes connected with this fatal speculation. The story of the poor maniac – 'Tom of Ten Thousand,' who lost his whole fortune, and his reason too, is well known, as is that of Eustace Budgell. Others, though less melancholy, are worth recording. A tradesman at Bath, who had invested his only remaining fortune in this stock, finding it had fallen from 1000 to 900, left Bath with an intention to sell out. On reaching town it had fallen to 250; he thought the price was too low, would not sell, and lost his all. The Duke of Chandos, who had £300,000 in this stock, was advised by the Duke of Newcastle to sell all, or at least a part, but he anticipated it would bring him half a million; he delayed, and lost every shilling. Gay, the poet, had £1000 stock given him by the elder Scraggs, Postmaster General, which, added to the stock he had before purchased, amounted to £20,000. He consulted his friends, and Dr. Arbuthnot advised him to sell out, but he hesitated and lost every shilling. Others were however more fortunate. The guardians of Sir Gregory Page Turner, then a miner, had purchased stock for him very low, and sold it out when at its maximum, to the amount of £20,000. With this sum Sir Gregory built his fine mansion at Blackheath, and purchased 300 acres of land for a park. Two maiden sisters, whose stock had accumulated to £90,000, sold out when the South Sea stock was at 970... Thousands of persons were, however, totally ruined by this speculation."

Thus we conjure back this bubble of 1719-20. As in March, 1858, we entered the Muniment-room and saw, covered in the dust of a century, the title-deeds of many an estate, and on the shelves the volume vouchers of many a ruined home, how did the truth of Scripture strike – "He that maketh haste to be rich shall not be unpunished." And then we thought of the line.

"As Croesus, rich, then poor as poet Gay."

Yes, we thought, here was the golden calf set up, and here the victims danced around, themselves the sacrifice! In this visit we were allowed to look upon an autograph pf Queen Anne's authorizing the traffic in slaves, and were also shown sundry branding-irons such as our farmers mark sheep with, with this small difference, they hardly singe the senseless wool, whereas these were used on "human cattle," hot, to scar the shrinking flesh

There lay the parchments; their owners had long melted into undistinguished dust. Still new bubbles rise, and crowds of full-grown children run, gape, and grasp, - and though they win not the historical renown of this City-house, many, to their cost, in clutching, find them "airy nothings."

Now, in this remembrance of a first and last stroll among the archives of this defunct Company, let the moral be the warning. As the rule, hasty gotten wealth stinks or curses. It is valueless, or, worse. In the seizure of it peace of mind is often sold, and when gotten, often comes with it the gnome – More, more, more; and then the richest man is wretched-poor.

Walk the streets, bubbles are constantly advertised. Sharps and flats are in close contiguity. The rail

Conveys the provincials into the circle of the professors, and to make use of a familiar figure, the sieve is up, the string is hid, the chaff of cupidity is lavishly strewn, ten per cent. Dividends id the luring bait, hop, hop, hop, so the sparrows, finches, and blackbirds, they are in the charmed circle, under they are, the string is drawn, they are for life enclosed, while the worthy directors of such a ruin-scheme, at a small cost of personal convenience, and, perchance, a large transfer of their dupe's property, may retire with even sympathy, affording a waiting batch great encouragement to blow another bubble of legalized plunder.

Still, we hope a pause will come, and bronzed scounderalism will be checked; but significant sighs are abroad startling things appal; ominous words are spoken; and if half be true, as it regards commercial delinquency, we have cause to tremble.

To close, recollect that in earth's ages there is a despicable age. This may curse a locality, or a nation. A time may arise when the common principles of honour are so forsaken that even honest vice will cut, with unutterable scorn, the companionship of sneaking knaves, who, forsaking Nature's noblest instincts, systematically smile themselves into the graces of others to trap, delude, destroy. A knavery so contemptible, Nature abhors it. Civilization in its language has never found a word degrading enough to denounce it; and perhaps only the Bible shows both the keen peril to the victim and the dark ignominy of the dissembling knave. See Prov. 26, 20-28.

I remain, Sir, your obedient servant, George Castleden, Woburn, March 11.

Charles Spurgeon, (1834-1892) was a Baptist preacher who rose to fame for the quality of his oratory skill from a young age. He was appointed to the New Park Street Chapel, in Southwark, then the largest Baptist congregation in London. His audiences quickly out-grew that building, and he was regularly preaching to 10,000 people at a time. He toured the country, and had visited Cranfield in Bedfordshire in April. "A Reading Reformer" had written into the Bedfordshire Mercury to complain that parts of the sermon preached at Cranfield were scripturally incorrect.

17th May 1858 Bedfordshire Mercury

Mr. Spurgeon and the "Reformer."

Sir, - I seem to regret the learning of your correspondent is arraying against this very useful preacher of our day. I have no knowledge of the "original Greek," therefore I leave the criticism open; but having been a witness to the broad casting of the true seed of the kingdom over soil but little cared for, I regret any classical recluse should hinder the efforts of such a day labourer, and, possibly, without any such intention, be the "enemy" to sow a few "tares" of scepticism after the good man had sown his spring crop in Cranfield open field.

To venture an illustration on the criticism I would suppose "Reformer" and myself fully agreed that the motive of Mr Spurgeon is to save sinners from the everlasting burning. Now I have looked on the finished fire-escapes at corners of the streets in London; suppose my home was on fire and a kindly hearted neighbour put up his ladder to my window and I were to meet such kindness by saying – fetch me the very finished fire-escape from Algate pump. Even the critic would say I deserved a singe; and to apply the illustration, the finished scholar may find other work to do than knocking rounds out of plain ladders *put up to save.*

There is no need for disputable passages to be brought to bear on the ministrations of one who seems to be doing a work among the "fools" and "wayfaring men," which some of our highest dignitaries seem anxious to emulate. *Go ye and do likewise* will be a much more laudable occupation than the obstructing, by objections on exceptional translations, - objections which may chill faith, darken hope, and ultimately lead mind into the abyss of infidelity. "Hear the other side" will plead for the admission of this rejoinder, should you chance to differ from the sentiments.

I am, sir, your obedient servant, George Castleden, Woburn, May 11.

24th May 1858 Bedfordshire Mercury

Mr. Spurgeon and his Bible.

Sir, - Mr. Castleden is angry, or at least, somewhat vituperative in his remarks upon my former letter (see *Mercury,* 10th May). What does Mr. Castleden find in that letter to induce in him the surmise, that I may "possibly, without any such intention, be the 'enemy' to sow a few tares of scepticism after the good man had sown his spring crop in Cranfield open field?" Or, in other words, Mr. Spurgeon is – I tremble at the seeming blasphemy – the sower; whereas poor I am the devil, or, *hodiabolos,* as the original hath it, which means, in plain English, "the calumniator!" Pray, Mr. Castleden, do look before you leap. (See Luke viii., v.11,12.)

Where do I say that Mr. Spurgeon is *not* a "very useful preacher of our day? It is true that I think a more accurate study of even the authorised version of Holy Scripture would not impair his usefulness. This is what I intimated in my letter; but I have nowhere said that he, "the good man," is not useful. By putting "original Greek" in inverted commas Mr. Castleden intimates that those words are in my letter. They are *not.* Does not Mr. Castleden know that the Old Testament was originally – for the most part – written in Hebrew? Again, who told Mr. Castleden that I am a "classical recluse?" If I were, it would not prove me wrong, nor Mr. Spurgeon right, would it?

I know how frightfully near to us all "scepticism" may be; yet I am indeed puzzled to see any single word of mine that can justify so, at all times, unjustifiable an accusation as that of scepticism is. I should feel obliged to Mr. Castleden if he were to point out any such words in my letter. But, perhaps, Mr. Castleden alludes to my wish, that "The Westminster Review" for January last should be retained in our Bedford Library. If so, then I can only state my belief, - the light shineth in darkness and the darkness does not hold it down. I do not understand Mr. Castleden's "illustration on the criticism, as he is pleased to call my parallelism of that which Mr. Spurgeon is reported to have called the Bible's "own words," with the words themselves. Do I "deserve a singe" for this? I only hope that *really* finished scholars will have set to work and knock the rounds of all "ladders put up to save," if they be of man's fashioning. There is but on ladder from earth to heaven, Mr. Castleden, and that ladder it is not in man to move, nor for the gates of hell to prevail against. May all other ladders be broken to bits and be speedily put up for sale.

Our authorized English version is so far from being either "a disputable passage," or "an exceptional translation," that it was my surprise at seeing Mr. Spurgeon's reputed version, which caused me to consult the original, and to plead for our own authorized version, which is so utterly as variance with his. Why should this "lead (? Load with lead) any mind into the abyss of infidelity?" So far am I from sympathyzing with those who omit a single passage from the Word, that I would have *every word* read in our daily services, and let *none* fall to the ground.

Mr. Castleden will excuse me if any words in this letter seem personal; but I feel with Socrates of old, that it is better and even necessary for the conservation of the truth to annul the nearest ties: for where truth and friendship are both dear, it is a duty we owe to heaven to prefer the former.

Yours respectfully, A Reading Reformer.

P.S. - Mr. Castleden says "Go ye and do likewise" will be a more laudable object than the obstructing-," he does not tell me what. I go all lengths in willingness to "hear the other side." I hope Mr. Castleden does not array himself on the side of those who misquote and thereby falsify, I do not say the Hebrew, but the English authorized version. Mr. Castleden should have observed that I did not dwell on Mr. Spurgeon particularly, he served me as an illustration of what *we* do, including myself: for I wrote - "When shall WE give over maltreating the Word?"

31ˢᵗ May 1858 Bedfordshire Mercury

Mr. Spurgeon and his Bible

Sir, - I meant neither to be angry nor vituperative: in the search or advocacy of truth neither are necessary.

Controversy I dislike, but as "Reformer" refers me to Luke VIII., 11 and 12 verses, and from this passage founds a specious argument against me, I feel necessitated, with some diffidence, to destroy the conclusion by dismissing the premises altogether. I used the word "enemy". "an enemy hath done this" - also "tares." And now I must refer "Reformer" not to Luke, but to Matthew

XIII., 24-28 verses, and feel assured he will be obliged by this light on his misapprehension, that I made "a leap without looking."

I used "original Greek" not as "Reformer's" words, but playfully, to signify I was not alive to the dead languages. One word here. Learning I respect: I regret my want of it, but I see it is perilous. When learning teaches us how little we know, then the more we get the safer we go; when it stilts us, then "a little knowledge is a dangerous thing."

"Classical recluse" was only a designation significant of any learned man who, assuming the censorship of common or popular phraseology, thinks he does the republic of letters service.

I have a partiality to a pun when it either flashes truth or lightens argument, but the turning my "lead" into *lead* puzzles my punning predilections, and I confess I am not leaden-headed enough to extract the sunbeam from such weighty wisdom.

Now relative to "Bedford Library and the Westminster Review" I am in the dark. To proceed, as the great bard says, "may lead to most preposterous conclusions." I took up my pen, as I hope some one would in my behalf in like circumstances: I had heard Mr. Spurgeon in town and country; I read your reports from Sandy and Cranfield, and as far as a local objector ventured his circulation, I offered my rejoinder in perfect ignorance of your correspondent.

"Reformer's" self-confession seems so genuine and the important "we" is so important, that I quote the passage entire – "Mr. Castleden should have observed that I did not dwell on Mr. Spurgeon particularly, he served me as an illustration of what we do, including myself: for I wrote – "When shall WE give over maltreating the Word?"

I say this confession as once justifies reply, and ends controversy. "Reformer" knows this replier, and with every courtesy I beg him to follow out his own precepts and this drop of ink may have its use.

Now one word on Mr. Spurgeon and his Bible. "I endeavoured to command the gospel earnestly and with power, and with a plain, outspoken, earnest, and honest ministry." This sentence may be the endorsement of hundreds of sermons this young preacher has delivered, and to his own Master he must stand or fall if he treats as the Holy Scriptures unfairly and against his own conviction; if not, "his Bible," Reformers phrase, is incorrect. As general admonitions, I would warn of "Envy, child of hell"; and, moreover, as in this fast day learning rather rides over the old version of the Scriptures, I would say to the wise, there are multitudes of "fools and wayfaring men" who inherit them as the best legacy of their fathers, - who find in them "the pearl of price is unknown." And who say of the Bible as it is

"This is the *judge* that ends the strife
Where wit and reason fail.
And who *believe* it is
Their *guide* to everlasting life
Through Time's dark stormy vale"
I am, Sir, Your obedient servant, George Castleden, Woburn, 24th May.

7th June 1858 Bedfordshire Mercury

Misuse of the Bible

Sir, - Allow me to thank Mr. Castleden for his kind explanations of what he did mean when he intimated that I "may possibly, without any such intention, be the 'enemy' to sow a few 'tares' of scepticism after the good man had sown his spring crop in Cranfield open field." Why Mr. Castleden should see in my plea for the very words of Scripture, as it is, against Mr. Spurgeon's careless pervasion of them; why he should see in this anything to remind him of an enemy sowing tares among the good corn is, indeed, more than I can comprehend. My motive in writing the letter which drew upon me Mr. Castleden's censure, was, I do sincerely believe, a most pure one. I wished by this most striking instance to impress upon myself and others the necessity there is of taking heed how we quote the sacred Scriptures, lest, like tavernkeepers with their wine, we adulterate the Word. For, in the language of a true man, "the more I read in the Bible, and believe it, the deeper is my sense of the fearful sin of sacrificing truth in the slightest degree for the sake of making out a case in favour of it. God has confounded many such tricks which have been resorted to in support of His cause. May He confound mine if I have committed what I know must be a more grievous offence in His eyes than many open professions of doubt or unbelief."

A Spelling Reformer.

P.S. - Allow me to add a few remarks on certain points in Mr. Castleden's letter. At first I did not intend to do so, and, indeed, had not time to do so. Since I wrote the above an unexpected opportunity hath arisen. First of all let me assure Mr. Castleden his explanations are so satisfactory that to me they are final. Mr. Castleden should not have abused quotation marks in his "playful" use of "original Greek." A little knowledge is not a dangerous thing, - it is the abuse of knowledge, whether little or great, that is dangerous. Mr. Castleden's definition of "classical recluse" does not apply to me, for I am not a "learned man." About my "turning" Mr. Castleden's "lead into *lead*," it is to be noted that the phrase employed by this gentleman – "objections which my chill faith, darken hope, and ultimately *lead mind* into the abyss of infidelity," is ambiguous, owing to our bad spelling, miscalled orthography. I was mis*led* through the outward resemblance between "lead mind" and "lead mine."

I thank Mr. Castleden for his courteous monitions about following my own precepts. I will endeavour to avoid "Envy, chill of hell." I can assure him that I do not envy Mr. Spurgeon. It is mainly through fear of teaching what is not true that he has prevented me engaging in what I should love above all things. I so value the Bible that I would have our version revised and made more Saxon, and more in accordance with "common or popular-phraseology." For example, I would have "taxgatherer," instead of "publican;" "Jehovah," instead of "Lord," in the Old Testament; remove all that modern criticism proves to be interpolation; revise such translations as are faulty: thus, "Avoid every kind of evil," instead of "Avoid all appearance of evil;" or, again, "The Spirit breathes where he willeth," and not "The wind bloweth where it listeth," for the wind has no will of its own. Finally, I am assured Mr. Castleden doesn't mean any harm; on the contrary, I hope to see many more letters from his amusing pen, and that he may hear many more sermons from Mr. Spurgeon. Only let him verify Mr. Spurgeon's quotations and compare parallel passages.

Castleden decided he had had enough now, and did not rely on the topic further.

19ᵗʰ July 1858 Bedfordshire Mercury

Woburn. City Mission Society. – An interesting meeting in behalf of this society was held in the Town Hall on Wednesday evening. The chair was taken by Lord Charles Russell. The meeting was opened with prayer by Rev. F. Cumberlege and a speech from the noble chairman; then the financial statement from the Rev. G. Whitlock. Addresses supporting the claims of the society were delivered by the Rev. H. Hutton (of St. Paul's, Covent Garden), Rev. J. Andrews, and the Rev. and Lord Wriothesly Russell (the deputation). Rev. Mr. Tyrrel followed with startling facts; Rev. F. Cox touched on the principal points of the previous speakers, and then with a parting word from Lord Charles Russell, this very catholic and pleasant meeting closed with the doxology, in which all Christians unite and harmonize, and which is a type on earth of the great anthem of praise, power, and glory, to Him that sitteth on the throne for ever and ever. So ends this hasty scrap of a well-spent hour.

A "well–spent hour" was another of Castleden's favourite phrases.

19th July 1858 Bedfordshire Mercury

To a Starling. On Woburn Park Cricket-ground one July morning in 1858.

Old Homer sang the starling crew,
Then, starling, I may sing of you,
Hopping about "our ground."
Familiar words! On this green spot,
With July sultry, June all hot,
Our cricket fame we found.

Some birds will talk, and you lone bird,
If bashful, may by me be heard,
And I'll repeat its story: -
It tells of sunshine ever fled,
Of sons now sleeping with the dead, -
Decline of cricket glory;

It tells the oft repeated tale
Of many a scene in Woburn's vale,
For ever hid from sight –
The merry group beneath yon beech,
The circle which around would reach,
All vanishing in night!

It tells of that bright summer day
When dukes, and lords, and ladies gay,
All gazed upon "our ground";
When Queen Victoria's gracious eye
Beamed gratefully on passing by,
And shed delight's light round.

It tells of time's on winged flight
Of friends and neighbours lost to sight –
These were life's shadows then.
It tells too now of life's shadowy dust,
Like morning flowers, in ruins must
Mingle with mouldering men.

So from yon bird, 'neath July skies,
I learn and teach the rude, the wise:
Its tale applies to all.
A few more years of change and strife,
And then death's dart shall end this life.
- Oblivion be our pall!
G.C., Woburn

…and having been bird-watching at the cricket ground, his thoughts turned to the game again:

9th August 1858 Bedfordshire Mercury

Woburn. The Game of Cricket.

Note. – As a continuation to the cricket season I enclose two scraps testifying to bygone sunny hours, and to encourage the rising youth of Bedfordshire to carry on, in all its integrity and zest, this king of summer games.

Two Bygone Cricket Matches (part of an unpublished lay)

Seven notches for one hit we scored – a fact
Established by our toes, and cricket tact.
'A sweet point hit' 'Bill' made; in merry cue
We tripped the turf, and twice we toddled two:
A puffing race it was to make four,
And straining muscles had not strained for more,
But, as an arrow from a stringed bow,
The ball flew by – it was an overthrow.
'Come, come along,' I cried in heated glee,
'We've made a fourer, try another three.'
'Midst shouts we ran, then triumph crowned the game,
And Luton added laurels to our fame.*
We our grand match with Biggleswade include,
Ere these rude fragments on the past conclude.
This sunny, merry day, receding fast
Adown time's stream, towards the engulfing past,
We now recall, to prove in life's stern game
Till all is lost the fight we should maintain,
Philosophy, oracular and pat:
Nil desperandum, speaks our cricket bat.

Shun dark despair; if hopeless block and wait,
If slow you score repine not as its state,
Play careful, honest, steady, and beat Fate!
*　　*　　*

Our side from home met with a keen defeat,
And in our Park 'return' were nearly beat:
Our second innings on, the sixth hat dropped,
And still our score their first had not o'ertopped.
Then we, old bat, went in, and lingering yet
Over this noontide we may ne'er forget.
Again we run the turf, quaff balmy air,
While penning rhymes within, "the Old Arm Chair;"
And join our springing and declining day,
The 'shades' remaining and the 'shades' away
Yes, we went in, old bat, and 'steady' play
Restored the fortune of our nigh lost day.
My batting partner boldly swished away,
While points, slips, legs told up a 'tottle' gay;
Fifty and forty, byes, wides, round-arm throws,
Astonished friends and discomposed our foes.
Old *Sol* grew winky, nodded off to rest
The cloud his nightcap, and his coach the West;
Eve's softest zephyrs wooed him to repose
As down he sank in somnolescent doze;
Night drew the curtains, and our stumps were drawn,
While the old gentleman snoozed of till morn.
Tired nature slept, and tired players too,
Till *Sol*, refreshed, flashed forth his beams anew,
And bade earth's tribes both work and play anew.
Hail, rosy day! let cricketers cry hail!
We on the morn resumed our winning tale;
Their field arranged, the remnant of our side
Played well their parts, and showed good batting pride.
While our opponents viewed the forward pace,
And Biggleswade, like Botheram, saw the race.
So life's good start links not to closing fame –
A moral taught from our old cricket game:
For like our Biggleswade and Potton friends
Man finds morn's gain in evening's loss oft ends;

And mocking hope with such a winning score
Then bid defeat to darken loss the more.

* Note. – Season 1836. In the first match played in Woburn Park we were soundly drubbed. With a weaker side, we went to Luton, and there won. To show the glorious uncertainty of cricket I give the total scores of this singular game: - Luton, first innings, 54 – second, 19: total 73 runs; Woburn first innings 84 runs.

Note. – These games exhibited the great features of cricket as the open field, manly, honest pastime of Englishmen. From them we extract a lasting moral, put into playful rhyme.

George Castleden, August 3rd.

A report of the second match, alluded to above, appeared in the Bell's Life in London & Sporting Chronicle of **19th July 1840***, and appears under that date. He obviously enjoyed the minor celebrity-status this victory had accorded him. His next, slightly rambling, letter takes a swing at science, progress, greed and profit.*

13th **September 1858** Bedfordshire Mercury

Confusion.

"The world itself has its limits, as it also has its unbending laws; and we know certainly that with all our discoveries and most prodigious efforts we shall never be able to abrogate the conditions of humanity, or render of no effect the restrictions by which we have been wisely – yes, wisely – though we are so inpatient of them, girded about by the union of soul and mind with that "maddy vesture of decay which grossly shuts them in." We may set ourselves to build towers by which we shall reach to heaven, but the end of all such understandings will, as in the beginning so new, and ever will be, confusion" – Patriot.

Sir, - Thoughts following this quotation may be a sequel to a letter on "our monster age," published last year.

All truth is generally unheeded in its first utterance. To give caution, or to reprove amid the profligacies of Pagan Rome, or to exhibit the simple emblems of Christ's religion amid the pomps and ceremonies of Papal Rome – the first would have consigned the utterer to the wild beasts of the arena, and the last to the dungeon and the stake. So the truth-seeker amid the conflicts and prejudices of the times he lives in, finds reason rules not against the rage of fashion, and all argument bow to the despotism of opinion. In every age of the world, folly has built its tower of Babel, till the workers aiming at the sky have been whelmed in the ruin of their own Luciferian pride.

While the ruins of empires would afford illustrations of this result, in our own land we supposed there was an element which would prevent Britain falling into perdition through this blunder. With the pure light of the gospel beaming upon us, it might have been supposed that the madness of wisdom had been restrained, and that we should not have known the lunacy of wealth, exhibiting in golden fetters our idiocy, and in deep degradation dancing to their sorry jungle. On these two points let us have a word or two.

The madness of wisdom. Mortal man, holding also his immortality, can only be safe in the search after any wisdom as he makes it subservient to the ultimate destinies of the soul. If the "wisdom of the gods" leads only to make man the more refined brute, then all his discoveries, mechanical, philosophical, or scientifical, will be but the building of a tower to become the stupendous ruin of his shame. As an immortal, if wisdom be not drawn from the fountain of all true wisdom, bitter indeed may be the waters; and if man, in homage, reflects not light from the eternal sun, they may follow that blindness of intellect stated in Matthew - "If the light in you be darkness, how great is that darkness."

As a Christian nation, in the great exhibition of our wisdom by the accomplishment of achievements which will immortalize even disgrace, have we given honour to whom honour is due? Have not our great feats of architecture and locomotive power subserved more the kingdom of Satan than to the glory of that God we profess to worship? Here we presume not; we argue by comparison. A purely heathern nation, a land of deists and philosophers, would not be judged by our law; but if it will be more tolerable for the cities of the plains than for Jerusalem, then by the like reasoning we ask, may not the rites of Vishnu or the moralities of Confucius have the precedency of the wisdom of a Christian nation, using that wisdom to dishonour the God they profess to adore, and to degrade the religion they profess to observe. This is the madness of Wisdom with a vengeance - a madness which will not only involve a Babel-tongued confusion, but also impel the groping at mid-day.

Now a word or two on the lunacy of wealth. Mammon worship is said to be England's bane. Gold delusion is hurrying on to perdition; pace and speculation feed this "fever of the mind." Considering the age we live in, when even the navvy may with his pick acquire a fortune in a nugget, if alone, gold is to command homage, then "Deify the dirt matured to gold", and let our mammon devotees cancel our Christian duplicity.

This lunacy exhibits us either as senseless hypocrites or as grinning, chattering apes. If this be severe I speak of it thus, only, when wealth is the sole aim and distinction. Bless it by charity, sanctify it by some good, consecrate it to virtuous and religious ends, - it will use sweet as well-got hay, and refresh like the limpid brook; hoard, spend upon self selfishly, parade it, or tyrannize with it, - then, like mouldy hay, or foul water, gain is loss, and moral poison fills with death. Now has the haste to get rich in this fast day been conducive to men's own peace and true prosperity - the county's virtue and integrity - or to the honour and glory of God?

This is the great question to try, and if the verdict goes against each of these clauses wonder not that many of the community look on with something like the awe of the gazer who, viewing the lurid cloud gathering, wonders where the hoarded stores of wrath may fall and desolate.

Some may call this silly talk, and some critic may say this is an ill-timed grumbling letter just now whom we have laid down the Atlantic tell-tale, and are going to play Mr. Gulliver over the myriads of China. These are two great facts. In sober seriousness, I would say, turn my countrymen, from the madness of wisdom; run not into the lunacy of wealth; let the Cable's inaugural message, "Glory to God in the highest, and on earth peace, and good will toward men", be flashed into the far future; let China have to bless the Gospel, and not to curse a "Church"; then an epoch will commence with Britain which may leave all previous renown as but the dawning of a perfect day. Still, ominous sighs are about: Sabbath desecration is rife, and may be legalised; profuse extravagances are around; commercial defalcations startle; a reputable vagrancy is spreading; home honesties are being sapped by specious foes; conscience and cash and being transferred from a man's own keeping; and all this looks significant of an adjusting the balance in order to conform the Divine government over the moral machinery, which, paradoxical as it may be to write it, God eternally establishes, but which man for a time can derange.

In proof of the confusion of the day failing dividends alarm; commercial crashes and smashes appal; a railway collision, with a slaughter exceeding an Indian battle, is filling a locality with mourning; but, as the leading journal has it, "We must go on, on, on. We have proved we can annihilate space and time, and, having divulged the secret of our capacity, the inexorable necessities of *competition* seize upon us, and insist upon working up to the full pressure of our power" - 25th August.

I might extend, but, closing this extract, ask, Are we not realizing the mythic fable by the manufacture of a monster which, ultimately, is to destroy its maker? We have found out power - have we controlled it? can we use it safely? May it not be said of Christian Britain, at any rate, knowledge trending only earthwards must end in the madness of wisdom which, allied to the lunacy of gold, may cause confusion most confounded. May Heaven preserve our native land from such terrific national insanity.

I am, Sir, your obedient servant, George Castleden. Woburn, September.

A news item on the Woburn chapel expenditure has all the hallmarks of being penned by Castleden.

30th **October 1858** Dunstable Chronicle

Woburn. Independent Chapel. - To "be just before we are generous" applies alike to a community and an individual. Upon this maxim the minister and congregation of the above chapel have acted. Involved in an extra expenditure, by the rebuilding part of the chapel, the erecting of a wall &c., to nearly £600, they have thought it prudent to forgo the annual missionary collections. But "out of debt and in pocket" they have resumed their connections with the Society to which, from its earliest day by their old pastor, they were allied, and through him contributed annually to its funds. On Sunday the broken link was joined, and after services morning and evening at Woburn, and in the afternoon at Sheep-lane, and then Monday evening meeting, the pleasing sum of between £11 and £12 was contributed in aid of the London Missionary Society. The Rev. J. O. Whitehouse, from India, preached on the Sabbath; and the meeting was addressed by Revd' J. Andrews: S. E. Dodge, Dunstable: W. Baker, Ridgmount: and the Missionary Deputation; and it is pleasing to record the satisfaction of a large attendance as the claims of all missionary society were enforced, and the duty of all Christians to support them was urged. May kindred institutions prosper; and may all come "to the help of the Lord against the mighty" was the keynote that tuned the evening's catholic harmony.

22nd **November 1858** Bedfordshire Mercury

The correspondence on Mr. White's lecture on "The Morality of Secret Voting".

Sir, - Relative to the lecture I touch it not. Of the correspondence between Lord Charles J. F. Russell and Mr. Whitehurst, I venture to say, if any gravity attaches to the fact of his lordship taking the chair on this occasion, I may vouch that it was quite an incidental matter. One of the Vice-Presidents failed in his engagement, and on the emergency the writer of this note promised, if neither of the other vice-presidents entered in time, to preside.

This evidence is perhaps unnecessary, but it may qualify the impression that this little gathering had either "the pride, pomp, or circumstance" of a meeting worthy the criticism which has been bestowed upon it by the earnest Vice-Chairman of the London Ballot Society.

What is in print may be for controversy, but the fact here stated I think by all fair play rules ought to be known.

I am, Sir, your obedient Servant, Geo. Castleden, Woburn, 15th November.

The Woburn chapel having already been refurbished, it was now the turn of Hockliffe.

29ᵗʰ **November 1858** Luton Times (and also in Dunstable Chronicle)

Hockliffe. Independent Chapel. – "And the people had a mind to work." – This village, on Thursday the 18ᵗʰ instant was a scene of animation and cheerfulness. Six months since when the present Pastor settled here he found the chapel in a dilapidated condition, and the friends resolved to repair, paint, and cleanse the building. With a considerable zeal, the ladies, assisted by friends produced fancy and useful articles sufficient to make a Bazaar, which realised £34. The entire renovation of the fabric cost above £52, and Thursday was the day set apart, if possible, for the extinction of the debt. At half-past two, p.m. (the day being fine), a numerous congregation assembled to assist and co-operate. There were present Rev. E. Adey & Mr. Purser, Leighton – Rev J. Andrews, and Mr. Castleden, Woburn – Rev. S. E. Dodge, J. Osborn, Esq., and L. Moinier, Esq., Dunstable, and Rev. J. Lawton, of Berkhampstead. The service commenced by the Rev. J. Andrews and S. E. Dodge offering praise and prayer. The sermon, founded on Acts iv.33, "And great grace was upon them all," was delivered by the Rev. J. Lawton, with an apparent unction from the Holy One. The chasteness of language employed – the propriety of arrangement observed, the fervour displayed, and the practical tendency of the discourse, gladdened many hearts. A public tea followed, the ladies gratuitously supplying the provisions, and many enjoyed the social meal. At half-past six, a public meeting was held in the chapel, and friends from Tebworth, Toddington, Dunstable, Woburn and Leighton came to help. Rev. E. Adey conducted devotional exercises, and Rev. J. R Smith presided. Mr. G. Castleden delivered an interesting speech, in which he graphically sketched the introduction of the Gospel into this village, by his sainted father, fifty-six years since, who first preached in a cottage. The Rev. E. Adey was the next speaker, and with unusual strength of memory he recalled the talents and virtues of each minister, as he filled the pastorate, particularly alluding to the holy life and character of Rev. J. Sleigh. Rev. S. E. Dodge in the methodical arrangement for which he is celebrated, delivered a speech characterised by instruction, encouragement and hopefulness. Rev. J. Andrews followed, and now came the season of trial, £8 0s 11½d were the proceeds of tea and collections but £6 and upwards were required to liquidate the amount. The appeal to the liberality of friends was responded to by minister, deacons, and friends, and the sum required was more than realised. Now Mr. Smith thought it was time to retire and praise the Lord. Votes of thanks to Rev. J. Lawton for his suitable discourse – to the Brethren for their valuable services, to the ladies for the provisions supplied, and the friends for their liberality, brought the meeting to a close. It is worthy notice that the friend shave nearly completed a Parsonage House. Will not wealthy friends assist this worthy people? From £200 to £300 are required. Rev J. R. Smith will gratefully receive and acknowledge donations. Help for Jesus' sake!

29th November 1858 Bedfordshire Mercury

The Secrecy of the Press. "We have the freest in Europe, but I say that every man who writes as article in a newspaper ought to do it under a solemn sense of responsibility."

Sir, - I use this quotation to offer a few observations on a gigantic system of anonymous writing. I think our newspaper leaders would be more valued, while many of them would be very different, if the signature was attached. This certainly would be done where persons are attacked. Lately I read a very keen leader on the popular preacher at the Surrey Hall. Much intellect was exhibited, but I could not help regretting it should rake up and record an opinion of an eminent minister for the multitude, whim, perhaps, that minister would hesitate to repeat a word said in haste.

For an unknown hidden scribe to take advantage of the editor's room and concoct an article foreign to his paper, is not only by all fair play rules impertinent, but it may be grossly cowardly. As a scribe by education he may be as much at fault in a spiritual critique as the fool and wayfaring man would be in an essay on the architecture of Nature, or at a lecture on the science of the stars, not to say a word about his solution of Euclid's problems. Each one to his vocation; and don't let an open browed-mouthed minister be struck in the dark by one who might be ashamed of his own antecedents, and if he gave his name it might give to the lucubration the value of waste paper.

This introduces your leader on the *Morning Star*. Now our meeting might as a public matter be subject to a passing criticism, but the open scribe would have hesitated ere he had endorsed such unjust conclusions. To make of such grave importance our little evening party, to elevate an ethical lecture into such political importance, and to make of it an occasion to most unfairly hit a patrician house to whose liberality their political foes bear witness – these "preposterous conclusion" from such flimsy premises no scribe having a regard to reputation would have openly published. With these two illustrations, and a third I might publish, of secret writing, I can't find it in them very ample encouragement to trust to secret voting.

With Mr. Sidney Herbert's opinion and a few words, I close this; - "at the present time newspaper writer are anonymous. My belief is, that for the mission of public instruction it is a great disadvantage. It puts on a par in point of weight and authority the most scrupulous and the most unscrupulous writer."

That check should be the name: till this is giv'n.

The gentleman may with the ungentle herd;

The scholar with the stilted needle class;

The man of courage with the coward join,

And all be critics, 'worse than ten Munroes.'*

I am, Sir, your obedient servant, George Castleden, Woburn, 23rd November, 1858.

* Munroe was the great surgeon in poor Burn's day, and smarting under the critic's lash, Scotland's bard immortalizes him – "Worse than ten Munroes, He hacks to teach, they mangle to expose."

18th December 1858 Dunstable Chronicle & 20th December 1858 Bedfordshire Mercury

Sheep Lane, Potsgrove

This locality has been in the shade, now for a sunny memory. Thirty years ago one of "destiny obscure" gathered around him the children of the lane; steadily has he continued his work of love, and to this small beginning may be traced present results. In 1838, the chapel was built: the school increased, Sabbath services became regular, and in the last seven years prospects have brightened, and we hope the future has good in store. The chapel is sometimes filled, and the week-night services are very cheering. On Wednesday evening a social tea meeting took place; forty children and nearly two hundred adults sat down: it was a real festive treat –

"The glad circle round them yield their souls

To festive mirth and cheer that know no gall."

After the clearance of crockery and tables, the chapel was filled to an overflow: praise and prayer opened the meeting; then Mr. G. Castleden being called upon to preside briefly addressed the assembly. He expressed his general surprise at such a meeting; impressed upon all the worth of gratitude for temporal mercies, and linking the honoured dead with the living in such a happy scene he closed by quoting Roger's suitable lines –

"But can the wiles of Art, the grasp of Power

Snatch the rich relics of a well-spent hour?

These, when the trembling spirit wings her flight

Pour round her path a stream of living light;

And gild those pure and perfect realms of rest

Where virtue triumphs, and her sons are blest!"

The Rev. J. Andrews then read from Miss March's "English Hearts and Hands" several well selected extracts: these, with some well time dexpository remarks won complete attention from the village throng, and sustained the interest of the meeting till nine o'clock. Other friends were to have spoken but at this hour it was thought best to close, and with singing the grateful Doxology,

Praise God from whom all blessing flow –

And then the Benediction, thus ended this "well-spent hour" in Sheep-lane "Union Chapel."

Note. – We drink not health on these occasions but it be recorded, ere we drank our tea the Pastor loyally called the attention of the Sheeplaners to our gracious and beloved Sovereign; and then the kindness of His Grace the Duke of Bedford in providing that blessed boon, the Well, was noted with gratitude, and from many a humble cottager was given the tribute of dutiful respect and heartfelt thanks.

G. C., Woburn, Dec 16th.

This letter was typical of others to come; a mixture of news report, some history, expressed in prose and poetry, (either his or someone else's) yet still full of his favourite expressions. Occasionally, he sent the same news or poem to two local papers, and both were published. It gives some idea of the standard of work of the poor news typesetter, trying to decipher handwriting, when you can see differences between what they thought he had written at different newspaper offices! In the following ode to Burns, the main text is from the 5th February 1859 Dunstable Chronicle, and anything bracketed BM is from the 7th February 1859 Bedfordshire Mercury.

Original Poetry – Burns (A Festival Scrap)

Pelted, then crushed behold the heart's aln bard; [BM - "heart's sin bard"]

- He sang the "daisy glinting forth alane" – [BM - "for thalane'"]

His life a tale of WON and LOST regard!

Inspired, then wronged, self-struck, this son of Fame

Climbed Helicon, and, DYING, carved his name.

Burns was a man, and man 'grows up to moan'!

Life's daybook proved the entries to his shame;

The DEBIT of his sins were largely shown

While Time's short day forbade the CREDIT side t'atone.

Death cancelled life's insolvency – Enough!

When tombs and tokens mock Time's blighted way

Years flee, then crowds of Scotia's sterling stuff, -
Peer, Poet, Cotter willing homage pay,
And hail the minstral's jubilate day. –
A STARVED bard gauger dies: this FACT must stand
With THIS – when fifty years had rolled away
His Country rushed to FEAST[?] his final hand [BM - "filial band"]
Re-christen Bruce's soil and name it "Burns' Land"
The MORAL of his tale we would improve;
Dwell on it penmen, privilege to write;
Let, let the wish to save your passions move. –
The pen then dipped in Truth's deep sea of light
Shall flash rich rays on Time's sad murky night.
Burns wrote insanely, and he lived to tell
That he repented but could not recal!
Vice, SPOKE, may linger, hardly say – farewell –
Vice, WRIT, may sound, to some through Time, as Virtue's knell
G. Castleden, Woburn, Feb 1st, 1859.

5th March 1859 Dunstable Chronicle (and 7th March 1859 Bedfordshire Mercury)

To the Editor of the Dunstable Chronicle. "The State of Europe."

Sir, - On the *eve* on which we are to be told the great secret of the future's representation, permit me to have a few words on the late very satisfactory result of present legislation.

To express pleasure at the tone, tact, and transparency of Lord Palmerston's speech is but to give the general assent to an achievement of statesmanship under great risks. A Continental war might explode from a word: a party move might have precipitated Europe into confusion. Instead we have just seen how the ambitions of the hour are to be subjugated, and a grave question may receive the most conclusive answer, irrespective of the glitter of oratory and the dazzle of sophistry.

The Chancellor of the Exchequer's reply was not only frank and lucid, but apparently, catching the sprit for the nonce of the noble veteran, it was free from every particle of acidity so natural, and even he forebore to sprinkle it with the Attic salt for which the right honourable gentleman is so famed. May we not say, perhaps this talented chief never made a speech in which there was *less* to criticise and *more* to commend.

And to clinch the whole, a few calm, dignified and distinct sentences from Lord John Russell gave to the reflective mind tranquillity, seeing that the destinies of this great country were still under the eye of Minds wise enough to weigh, and prudent to advise and decide. – Of Statesmen who showed they knew when, what, and how to speak. If a great man of our own day right be right that true eloquence is the saying "apt words in apt places, and at apt times," methinks these speeches may stand as apt illustration of the rule.

Of the future we know not. A remnant of us remain who fought in the 1831 Civic battle. Now another generation will enlist for newer conflicts. We had a hard fight of it, and looking back from the present stand-point, surely the country in 1859, on such an important question as "the state of Europe," may congratulate itself on this senate exhibition of statesmanship, as worthy to be a model for all such future emergencies.

Honour to whom honour; tribute to whom tribute prompts the pen to give a local circulation to what may be the grateful response of climes and nations. May Britain long be a peace making and a peace preserving land.

I am, sir, Your Obedient Servant, George Castleden, Woburn, March 1st.

Lord Palmerston had already served as Prime Minister from February 1855 to February 1858, and was then leader of the Opposition. Castleden's next letter is far more local. Eggington, near Leighton Buzzard, was another village where he was involved with the chapel and school. The Independent Chapel was built in 1840, and Rev. William Lewis of Hockliffe ran it for the first five years, before the Rev. James Sleigh took over. Castleden's own father, Michael, preached here too, after he had retired from Woburn. The chapel survived until the early 1960's, when it was demolished and Tudor House now stands on the site. This report is almost certainly by Castleden himself:

4th April 1859 Bedfordshire Mercury

Eggington – British Schools

A meeting was held in this village on the 24th, on behalf of the British School, now completing its tenth year. The examination of the children, more than fifty, was pleasing and satisfactory. After this a large party of friends sat down to a social tea; and in the evening was held the public meeting, opened by singing and prayer. – The Rev. Mr. Hureell [Hurnall] took the chair, and in a frank and feeling manner expressed his gratification at the existence of such a school; impressed its importance on the audience, and hoped for its continued prosperity. – Mr. Castleden said a few words, and gave two or three anecdotes to the children on the items of their examination; and begged them in after life to remember gratefully their present friends and instructors. Then with friendship's remembrance of the founder of the school, Rev. James Sleigh, now in Australia, he finished by wishing the school might long continue a rill of local fertility. – Mr. Thomas Southam read a statement of receipts and expenditure, leaving a small balance against the treasurer. – Rev. G. Barker, Leighton, mingled the humourous with graver matters very happily, and pressing home the advantages of education, hoped this village school would be supported and its usefulness extended. – Rev. J. Andrews stated some of the difficulties in the commencing of this school, and as they were conquered rejoiced in the present meeting, as a proof that the day of small things was not to be despised. Great results often had insignificant beginnings, to wit, the bubble of a tea kettle and the fall of an apple; so he hoped the rill would swell to a stream, and, like rivers speeding to the sea, it might flow on widening and deepening to the ocean of eternity. – A few genial words from the Rev. Chairman concluded the proceedings. The Doxology and benediction then closed this Christian and catholic association, to aid the instruction of the young in one of England's long neglected spots.

...but then it was back to politics.

11th April 1859 Bedfordshire Mercury

The Reform Match.

Sir, - Having passed the fiftieth mile-stone man looks back and realizes the line, "He gazes on the overthrow of Time"; and of course he is not so fervent in politics as when in early days, "with marrow-flaming bones" he fought and won the victory. Hence some of us have gazed upon the late Senate strife, not with indifference, but with an absence of which belongs to early contests. Perhaps a present locomotive figure may explain: we have seen the steam getting, and if it please the newer generations to hear advice about the speed, we would so regulate it that the triune train – Queens, Lords, and Commons, might make a long journey in safety.

But of the great fight let me attempt an illustration from a bygone sunny pastime. I would say, looking back to 1831, of the remnant of the "Old Eleven" on life's cricket plain, like Goldsmith's broken soldier, while observant of the newer game, we 'Shoulder'd our *bat* and show'd how fields were won.' And uncommonly pleased some of us were to see our veteran bowler strip, and from the first batter his opponents; some of the fielding and batting among the newer players somewhat surprised us, and some we thought, more showy and safe; yet we admired often the clean *point hit*, *neat slip*, quick *leg swipe*, and there was often some capital *hard hitting*. If we particularize, for the encouragement of the juniors, it is to notice a splendid innings by a stripling who went in and met with troublesome balls at once, and made some fine runs, retiring from the wicket with the cheers of the whole assemblage; if we venture to predict, we should say he will be the noble Felix of this part of life's cricket field.*

While praise is given where it is due, we saw a dodge or two we did not like, not among the young players. Putting your wicket down behind your back, by a trick gave us the glumps when we played, and we were sorry to see the oldest player try it on in such a grand match, and when at its close the score stood 39 majority, in favour of the straight forward bowling, we were certainly pleased that the round armed twisters received so signal a defeat.

Fair play is the pride of Englishmen, and however cunning we run for the laurels, cricketers and Commoners should know that "all round my hat" is not the road to win them honestly.

This is written on the decision – what next is not known. As nobody is named, and nobody blamed in our cricket illustration, I shall adopt a characteristic signature, and remain, Sir,

Your obedient servant, One of Woburn's Old Eleven.

...and some anonymously-issued election posters and leaflets, known as Squibs, had annoyed him greatly:

25th April 1859 Bedfordshire Mercury

Electioneering Tactics. - Cowardly!

Sir, - "Fair play is a jewel." In our locality bills have been *stealing* about, bearing no authentic signature, nor any printer's name. My use for these unfair things would be either the fire or the dirt-hole.

In the various contests of human life it may be hard fighting with the open foe, but, falling or conquering, it is then fair play. But, whether it be a private individual or a public man, to be nibbled to death by vermin below contempt is ingloriously falling under attacks as despicable as may be safe!

Years ago our fathers were worried by some insect crawler or skipper, and, while we hoped it had been *cracked*, it seemed the breed is not extinct. While we revere the man who acts the manly part of open hostility, let me say to the electors of Bedfordshire what I need not say - don't be influenced by any masked assassin who, using the glorious privilege of the Press, strikes and then slinks away, and under the refuge of

"Thou canst not *say* I did it,"

Consummates cowardice as refined as it may be destructive.

I am, Sir, your obedient servant, George Castleden, Woburn, April 19th.

The new Liberal Party swept to success in the election, but Castleden was more concerned with how the election had been run, than who had won it.

150

23rd May 1859 Bedfordshire Mercury

Bedfordshire Election. Canvassing – The Ballot – Coercion.

Sir, - The fight has been fought; the victory has been won. Englishmen knowing how to win know how to bear defeat. We enter not into the policy of the late contest, our purpose is to touch on two or three items springing out of it.

Relative to canvassing: a partial canvas by candidates should be avoided; ask all or none. Agent canvassing is often unsatisfactory, and may end in delusion. A word on canvassing manoeuvres. They may depreciate the standard of the man. To wit, first to ask the voter to plump; next to split and neutralise himself; and, these failing to beguile him, to vote for the sure Liberal. This may be good election tactics, but the gain of the candidate is the loss of the voter's self-respect.

Can canvassing be avoided? Might not every district have its public meeting where the candidate's exposition, heard of all men, should precede the poll? To simplify elections thus might we not avoid the use of the ballot.

Adopt the ballot and continue canvassing, and with the increase of the constituency insincerity will increase, and among the crafty class *gammon* to the last will be the more extensively practised.

Englishmen ought not to want the ballot, but if they insist on it then relieve the candidate from the irksomeness of asking without security for the promise. If the constituents feel fear, don't impose on the representative a task which may be humiliating and futile.

Relative to secrecy we say, face to face, and the calumnly-monger shows not, and the whisperer finds his vocation gone! But if the ballot be the voice of the people, as a last roar John Ball, say – "Fair play, no canvas, boxes in every town, and do as you like." But one hint and I have done on the ballot. If we, the people, are 'a feared' how with the member? Should he not have the immunity of secret voting? Recollect I don't speak without my card when I say that the ruin of one of our county members was completed by an honest, but an adverse vote to the then misery. And I pay but honest tribute to a late amiable man, though opposed in politics, when I say Thomas Potton Macqueen was cruelly sacrificed by the heads of the party whose cause he espoused. Secret voting might have saved this M.P. from the wrath of the minister, as it might of late some being sent right-about by the fickle multitude.

One home word. I was hurt to hear of the utterance to one of the Duke of Bedford's tenants – "You have had the screw put on tightly." A more unfounded allegation was never made. If to canvass constituents was the charge defence cannot be offered, but, if the fact of staunch Tories living for generations under the tolerant House of Bedford, increasing in property and rising in position, be fair evidence, we at any rate may say the ballot is not wanted here. I merely say such a charge is "too bad." I would avoid personality in giving an indignant refutation to such an expression, and telling not the whole truth, I leave to those who have calumnly to the winds by – quoting themselves.

Some who have pursued an extra political animosity and anonymous sourility may be left with their coin and – conscience.

To close as we begun. The battle has been fought, the victory won, and in this good bye to county strife we may say according to recognised tactics fairness has been observed, and while from the open, manly foe the loud and honest tones – "We shall beat you to-day" did not grate, yet some painful reflections last relative to traitors in the camp –

"Who keep the promise to the ear,

And break it in the heart."

Class may be let alone in their glory, contemplating a political, perhaps a lucrative insincerity.

I am, sir, Yours obedient servant, George Castleden, Woburn, May.

The comments provoked a stinging reply in another (more right-leaning) local paper.

28ᵗʰ May 1859 Beds Times

Shooting with a Long Bow, At Woburn. To the Editor of the Bedford Times

Sir, - The Woburn "great gun" (castellated) of your contemporary, the *Mercury*, fired a "long" shot last week in honour of the Bedford family. Those who merely hear that this gentleman is a *pensioner* of the Duke of Bedford, without hearing of his profound *erudition*, surprising *modesty*, and oracular respect in the town, might think that a more *independent* advocate would have been better, - thus avoiding the slightest suspicion of "lickspittleism" or "eating" those really disagreeable creatures "toads." His communication would not, however, have been noticed by me had it not been for his attack on others.

Perhaps he will name to us, as "*news*" the "staunch tories" who do as they please under the Russell family; refute that voters around Woburn told Col. Gilpin *he had their best wishes* - that they could not vote for but would not vote against him; and that Lord Charles Russell afterwards, by personal canvas. Got their second vote for Col. Higgins, and also took one gentleman to task for supposed canvassing for Col. Gilpin. As it is understood that Lord Charles moves but little in any important county business without first consulting his elder brother and "his ever-active and intelligent steward," the acts must be held identified.

Had Mr. Castleden told us at the same time of the unknown popularity the steward's amiability and generosity command, it would have been the last touch to his wonderful work of art. Possibly he will next tell us that Woburn is as prosperous and happy in the present "reign" as the last, in short, as he shoots with such a "long" weapon there is no telling what astounding things he may offer for our reflection.

Faithfully yours, A Conservative. May 24th 1859.

... but Castleden seems not to have replied. Instead, he reported on a recent trip to Dunstable.

25th June 1859 Dunstable Chronicle

A Day at Dunstable. On a sunny June morning we travelled through the chalky gorge, and entered this world-esteemed locality –

Where lassies smile, and BONNETS win renown

You there will hear of Dunstable's old town:

The morning market was ending, the plait -buyers were leaving, and the streets were filling with persons flocking to the Bazaar, opened by an address from Lord Charles Russell, in aid of Wesleyan funds. – We strolled the town, and when we reached the ancient church we rather wished for "old antiquary" to tell us more about Normans and Gothic style; however we mused on mouldering stone and mutilated images, and supposing six or seven centuries had rolled since its erection, and thinking of the generations which had fled since then, Watts came to our help in this musing –

"Time like an ever rolling stream

Bears all its sons away;

They fly forgotten as a dream

Dies at the opening day."

From the Church we turned into the Priory grounds, we strolled the tents, looked upon some of Nature's best workmanship, and Art's very pretty manufacture; and the we found ourselves kindly asked to look into the Priory, and there we were told, we were standing in the very chamber where Cranmer and the Commissioners signed and sealed the divorce between Henry and Katherine of Aragorn: History tells the swift retribution on this delinquent deed. – Looking up at the grained arches, Shakspeare vitalized them –

"The Archbishop

Of Canterbury, accompanied with other

Learned and revered fathers of his order

Held a Court at Dunstable, six miles off

From Ampthill, where the princess lay; to which

She oft was cited by them, but appeared not":

Bye the bye, sometime since we heard a noodle say Bedfordshire had no historical renown: I suppose he meant warlike renown. – What relics other parts of the County may turn up I know not, but when I think of *Woburn* being immortal in history while Patriotism is valued, and Affection is hallowed – of *Dunstable* and *Ampthill* from which, as the mysterious result of a very sad deed, first flashed the Luther light," and first sprang our Protestant liberty – of *Toddington*, where royal Tudor and Stuart progresses were often known: where the lord Stafford oft has trod, and later down we read in Macauley's brilliant page, the melancholy tale of Monmouth and the Baroness of Wentworth; add to which the "Roun House in *Ridgmount* parish where the last "regicide" was killed: and then if *Bedford* boasts a Bunyan lauded by sages, poets and divines; and a Howard eulogised by Burke, I think these scraps, alone, will rescue our native country from something like the ignorant assertion that it has not historical interest. But to our 2little day." After musing the days of Rufus, Henry 1st., and 8th, Mind leaped the gulf of Time, and alighted on the plain of 35 years ago! *Then* and *there* we fought our first great battle in Cricket war: we attempted to explore what was then called "Crow Field.

There, on the turf in July's hottest day

We faced the foe, and bade him fire away:

Smote with our bat the balls till set of sun

And, bloodless, SANG the victory lost and won –

But Crow Field had flown quite away, as if it had been a Dunstable lark, and settled down in streets, houses and gardens; and verily I began to think myself "venerable" when, upon some enquiries, a native opened his eyes, seemingly in wonder at my antiquarian researches relative to this scene in Dunstable's bygone scenery! and as I met one of the ancient brethren of the bat, I could not help laughingly telling the anecdote of one of our late Judges, who, after an absence of forty years went on the Assize of his native county, at its bar stood a criminal, recognised as one of his village green companions: the man his lordship sentenced, but as in the evening memory fondly dwelt on early days, throwing on a loose coat he entered the prison, and going into the condemned man's cell he began to ask after several of their companions. – "Ay, my lord, they are all transported, or hung, besides you and I," was the poor prisoners reply. – Well, I said, we have to be thankful it is not so bad with us, the remnant of the old Eleven." Making our way to the "Wagon and Horses," we did find a portion of the *turf*, and we looked upon the dell where we sent the *Leg scout*, at a slapping pace, to catch the spinning ball, but on looking for the *sign* it was a sign we *could not* see! Our eyes have become dim and that sign belonged to the dark ages, and we suppose with other wrecks of matter it has been boiled down and turned to steam, and is aiding in our slap dash, flash and crash Age! Well, we mused upon this modern melting down of the old properties of "Life's stage," as friend Shakespeare has it; the passing away of scenes; the exit of actors, and then, on the 'veteran' list, we wave the playful with the serious, thus –

You sun which now in its meridian height
Sheds o'er Time's ruins its warm summer light;
Gilds too the dust of many a well-known form
Who shared our sunshine, braved the passing storm;
Their INNINGS finished, ours must soon be done,
While o'er our graves shall shine yon Summer's sun!

In the Priory courtesy was shown to us, and looking at the picture of the Battle of Bassano, we were pleased by the great moral it taught. – A faithful dog on the dead body of the slain soldier is deeply mourning his loss: Napoleon I. is pointing to it, and turning to his Marshals is saying –

"That dog, gentlemen, should teach us humanity."

We were struck with this more, as we heard a capital sermon from the Rev. F. Tucker, at the Baptist Chapel on the subject of War. I merely refer to it to say there were passages of deep eloquence, with often a pathetic description which absorbed and moved best feelings –

War's murders tone our European sky.
The shout, groan, shriek, the sob, the wail, the sigh
Commingle, and affront to Heaven's high gate,
While Hell, delighted, quaffs the blood of hate!
Blasted is earth: a proof what ruin can
Attend the pride or lust of moth-dust man!

So, strange to say, Mind picks up the seeds of mirth and grief in the same hour, and dropping them on this summer morn as seedlings, on more fruitful soil they may germinate afresh. – I hope these jottings of a Dunstable day may instruct some, please all, and offend none.

G. C., Woburn, June, 1859.

6th August 1859 Dunstable Chronicle

Woburn – Independent Chapel Sunday School. The annual holiday was held at the usual beautiful locality, kindly granted by the late, and present, Duke of Bedford. Nigh forty-five years have run since first a very few gathered on the same spot: this year above 160 children were regaled with tea and cake, and then as many visitors sat down. This anniversary was favoured by the company of the Lady Charles Russell and the Miss Russells': with

13: An aerial view of Woburn from 1938. The Methodist chapel is centre top, and Congregational chapel just left of centre.

this kindness it was a pleasure to some to link kindly words spoken many years ago, on a similar, by the late Duke of Bedford. After tea recreation and juvenile fun was the order of the turf, and after a stroll up the pleasant path we went down the tent; a familiar hymn was sung: prayer and a short address was offered by the Rev. J. Andrews. Mr. Henry Gee, an old scholar, and an intended missionary to the South Seas, said a few words on union, and of encouragement to the teachers. Mr. G. Castleden spoke of the holiday spot, its bygone memories, and of hands and hearts which gladdened once! and thanking the visitors for their presence and liberality the parting lyric

"O that will be joyful, joyful,

When we meet to part no more," –

Rung under the tent, and with the Benediction ended this well-spent hour – and another anniversary became entombed in the past.

G.C., August 2nd.

A week later, and another school tea at Hockliffe, with this report probably by Castleden.

13th August 1859 Dunstable Chronicle

Hockliffe. Sabbath School Anniversary. On Lord's day last, the anniversary of the above school was held. The sermons were to have been preached by Joseph Maitland, Esq., of London, but that gentleman being taken ill during the night of Saturday, Mr. Symington of Hockliffe, and the Rev. S. Cowdy of Leighton supplied his lack of service. The children sang suitable hymns, and the collections exceeded the former year. On Monday afternoon, a tea party and public meeting took place, Rev. J. R. Smith, pastor, presiding. Effective and excellent addresses were delivered by Joseph Maitland, Esq., of London, Messrs. Philpot, Toddington; Sell, Leighton; Castleden, Woburn; Rev. S. E. Dodge, Dunstable, and Mr. Symington. The tea was numerously attended by friends from Eggington, Tebworth, Toddington, Houghton Regis, Dunstable and Leighton.

"Delightful task, to lead the youthful mind
To happiness and God."

The funeral of the late Mrs. John Adams of this place was numerously attended on Thursday. The interment took place at the parish church. Mrs. Adams died deeply lamented by a large circle of friends.

17th September 1859 Dunstable Chronicle

Woburn. Missionary Meetings. – Amid its gloom this town has been cheered by some friendly gatherings to aid Missionary operations. Last week the Ordination of Mr. Henry Gee was recorded. After sermons on Sunday in the Church, on Monday a good meeting was presided over by Lord Charles Russell in aid of the Church Missionary Society. His Lordship opened the meeting by a speech toned in a true missionary spirit, and in reviewing the operations of the different societies paid tribute to each. This speech was enlivened by two or three anecdotes; one of which – relative to the wit and his ridicule of the "Clapham set" and the "Consecrated Cobbler," and then his living to see and own the injustice of the sarcasm, - told as a severe rebuke on all decriers of Missions. The Rev. J. F. Cumberledge gave a statement of accounts and earnestly appealed to the humbler classes to attend and support such like societies. The Rev. E. W. Cook spoke feelingly in behalf of Missions, and then the Deputation, Rev. M. Jonson, opened with a graphic sketch of India, as a Continent; spoke of its Caste, its Heathen superstitions; sketched Missionary operations; told a pathetic tale of the Missionary's death, and then finished with some home facts humorous and instructive. Prayer commenced, and the Benediction closed another pleasant anniversary.

On Tuesday evening, and interesting and affecting meeting was held in the Independent Chapel to say "good-bye," and to present "a good will offering" to Rev. Henry Gee. One hundred and fifty sat down to tea, and at

Seven the meeting was opened by singing –

"Jesus shall reign where'er the sun, &c.

Prayer was the offered by Rev. J. Andrews; and then, as the pastor, he addressed the young missionary; reviewing his early Sunday school days; spoke a word of encouragement to Sunday school teachers; then impressed the greatness of the work about to be embarked in, and invoking the blessing from on high, he affectionately committed the young couple to the care of God. – The purse was then given containing £17 13s 3½d, the kind contributions of all classes and denominations, from the mansion of the noble and the cot of the peasant: the gift was feelingly and gratefully acknowledged by Mr. Gee. After which Mr. G. Castleden read an extract from some remains of his father relative to the commencement of the South Sea Mission. – "In this year, 1796, I had the pleasure of accompanying the first band of Missionaries in the ship "Duff" to Gravesend. This was a great treat. There were the venerable Hawies, Eyre, Wilks, and a host of London and Country ministers. As soon as we had gotten down the Pool, Dr. Hawies in the middle of the ship gave out –

"Jesus, at thy command

I launch into the deep," –

And a deep impression the singing of it made. I have the placid countenance of the missionary Jefferson before me at this moment, enthusiasm apart he really looked – *Strong in the Lord and in the power of his might*. It was a most interesting scene and not a heart I believe on board but ejaculated – *Now Lord send prosperity*." This long by-gone links this congregation with the earliest efforts of the London Missionary Society, and now, after 63 years, from its church, proceeds a Woburn boy to this very group of Islands in the great pacific, in order to preach the gospel. – *May God send him prosperity* will be the response of every heart. A collar worked by a little invalid Sunday school scholar was then feelingly presented by Mr. Andrews to Mrs. Gee, and tears spoke thanks. A parting hymn was read and sung; the Benediction closed the service, hearty farewells were taken, and then, with a lingering good-bye under a full-orbed moon, this young Missionary couple passed from us –

Now as they speed to distant Isles
We pray, O heaven, that 'neath Thy smiles
Their voyage of life shall still be blest,-
Their port at last – Eternal Rest!

The above was written, no doubt, by Castleden. The Rev. Gee went to be a Missionary in Samoa.

5th **November 1859** Dunstable Chronicle

Original Poetry – Over the Grave of a "Labouring Man" in Potsgrove Churchyard.

The day of life for aye is ended,
Its toil and sorrow done;
No MORE offending, or offended
The home of rest is won:
No more the labour-weary feet;
No groaning heart – the sleep is sweet.

The storms of life shall smile no more,
Life's tumults all are still!
Its shade and sunshine now are o'er,
No more shall wound, the will!
The body fits the narrow cell,
The struggle's done, and he sleeps well.

'Tis well in death if all is right!
O man, let this endure,
Let not black Sin chain down to Night!
But seek salvation sure:
Then the grave's rest rejoicing great, -
Then, labouring man – THE SLEEP IS SWEET.
G. C.

What a shame the labourer isn't named! It would have been interesting to know who it was. Castleden then made the jump from provincial to national newspapers, but it was not in a way he would have appreciated. The Times ran a story on the divorce proceedings brought by his wife, whom he had separated from in 1838. Entitled "Hall, falsely called Castleden v. Castleden, Hearing Causes in Private", the 15th November article mainly focusses on the legal implications of whether the Judges could grant an application made to have the causes discussed in private. Ladies and children present were asked to withdraw, but a technical error in the court papers meant the case was not heard further. Castleden was not present himself, and was suspiciously quiet in the local papers for six weeks. Then he had local social event arrangements for a tea-meeting at Eggington to help with:

24th December 1859 Dunstable Chronicle

Eggington Sunday School. In connection with the Independent Interest, will hold their annual Tea-meeting next Monday, the 26th inst., at 4 o'clock p.m.

At 6 o'clock a Public Meeting will be held, presided over by Rev. J. R. Smith. Revds. S. E. Dodge, Dunstable, G. V. Barker, Leighton, J. Andrews, Woburn, G. Castleden, Esq., and other gentlemen, are expected to address the meeting. – Tickets 6d.

When the prospect of changing the arrangements for local Coroners Inquests was raised, Castleden was keen to keep the tradition as it was...

16th January 1860 Bedfordshire Mercury

Coroners' Inquests.

Sir, - In the "presentment by the Grand Jury" at the late Sessions we supposed the memorialists came to the conclusion that an "anomaly" existed which we hoped would be met, so that Englishmen paying should have some part in saying. As it regards Coroner' Inquests permit a few words written on the same evening.

This matter, from the shortness of time, we hastily considered, but our united opinion was that this ancient household institution should be maintained unimpaired, and that we hoped, on the score of economy, a perilous secrecy in suspicious deaths might not ensue.

If I add, personally, from what I heard on the only inquest on which I have sat, that I fear enough irresponsibility exists without further weakening this home protection, I state but truth. Surely the probability of the enquiry and publication of it may warn, and words uttered by our respected foreman we all concurred in, "I would rather six unnecessary inquests were held that one necessary be omitted."

The economy of inquests may be a question; the policy of them is for Englishmen to determine who, in this day of swiftness, science, and secrecy, fear more the poison than the pistol or the bludgeon. Show us a motive, is sometimes said. Some of us think, with the Palmer assassins of the land, our popular institutions may offer a strong motive and a present temptation. But, at any rate, let us beware of lessoning a salutary fear, and while we use the inquest now to deter the incendiary let us be careful of a perilous economy which may shield the murderer.

On this subject I was pleased to read your leader, and I hope other influential pens may aid in a matter of great importance.

I remain, Sir, your obedient servant, George Castleden, Woburn, January.

On the **3rd February 1860**, *The Times newspaper and The Globe ran articles about Castleden's continuing divorce proceedings, but none of the local press around Woburn chose to report it. Again, Castleden did not attend any of the court proceedings.*

31st March 1860 Dunstable Chronicle

Eggington. British School. On Wednesday the 28th was held the twelve Anniversary. The Examination was pleasing to friends and encouraging to the worthy schoolmistress. The children were then regaled and afterwards fifty or sixty friends took tea and spent a pleasant hour. In the evening the public meeting was held, the accounts were read by Mr. Batchelor, and the committee proposed by Mr. T. Southam. The Rev. W. Hurnall addressed the meeting, impressing on parents a greater attention to the school; inculcating obedience on the part of the children, and then enforcing the value of this school, he hoped for a steady continuance of support. Mr. G. Castleden congratulated the meeting on the fact that these institutions afforded ground for all to stand on. Missions, Bible Societies, the cause of Education were the legacy of our fathers, and in them, on the same platform, the Christian's "unite and conquer" might frustrate the satanic motto "Divide and devour." In reviewing the twelve years, he linked the school with its originator, the Rev. J. Sleigh, now in Australia, with a Kentish anecdote on the "watching eye and listening ear," and then a scrap of humour for the children. He was followed by the Rev. J. Andrews, who spoke of the process of training flowers, plants and trees, and then applying the imagery to the training of the tender mind, by argument and illustration, he enforced the worth of Education as the great trainer for the duties of secular life. The Rev. Mr. Smith, minister of the chapel presided, and after a short address, the Doxology and Benediction closed another grateful anniversary.

An evening of entertainment by people from outside of Woburn was an exciting event, although there were travelling shows and circuses occasionally. So a concert by musicians not usually heard in Woburn would have been a popular concert.

9th June 1860 Dunstable Chronicle

The members of the Dunstable Choral Society paid a visit to Woburn on Monday last to give a concert of sacred music in the Town Hall, under the patronage of Lord Chas. J. F. Russell. Permission being obtained, the whole of the Society took a stroll in the Abbey Gardens and pleasure grounds, after which they returned to the Bedford Arms, where tea was provided in the highest style, to which the members nearly forty in number sat down. Thanks are due to Mr. & Mrs. Barr for the great exertions put forth for the comfort of the company. In the evening the concert commenced, consisting of Choruses, Solos & Duets, from Handel, Mozart, and various other composers. Miss S. A. Barber with her clear voice and the pathetic manner of her singing thrilled the audience with feeling. The sacred air - "Meek and Lowly," sung by Miss Potter with great exactness, gained the admiration of the audience, and was loudly cheered. The Misses Potter, Miss Goode and the Misses Buswell also enlivened Duets, &c. Mrs. E. B. Donne sung the favourite song - "Consider the Lillies how they grow." The words of this piece combined with the effective manner in which it was performed caused a deep feeling to pervade the whole assembly. The whole of the Pieces were loudly cheered and many of the encored. The thanks of the society were tendered to the meeting for their kindness in patronising them, after which G. Castleden, Esq. rose and presented the thanks of the assembly. The performers were all of the Society, no help being obtained from other places. It is wished by many that they again visit Woburn, to give a second concert.

26th January 1861 Bedfordshire Mercury

Castleden was present at a presentation to the minister for the new Chapel in Queen Street, Hockliffe, a Rev. W. Griffiths, who was given fifty sovereigns and a bound copy of an address signed by 332 members of his church and congregation, in recognition of his "pastoral devotedness and energy".

The American Civil War was now raging, and in March there was a naval engagement between two 'iron-clad' warships for the first time. Both unable to decisively beat the other, the ships eventually retired to a draw. The European powers watched with great interest, as this development effectively made their traditional wooden navies redundant at a stroke. Castleden regretted most scientific advancement, and advancements in modern warfare even more so.

19th April 1862 Bedfordshire Mercury

The Merrimac and Monitor: Peace.

Sir, - We have passed some hours lately in a playful essay on some local bygones – such as inns now out, lamps which were the lights of other nights, watchmen now lost, singers who belonged to 'Auld Land Syne,' – with other incidentals of our fathers' days, and of which their sons will soon be as ignorant as the present Chinese race are of their ancestors first relish for roast pork. But in marking down these home oblivions, and tracing some of them till they turned into steam, we never dreamt of a marine wonder which in an instant has darkened the fame of former years, and has left the 'wooden walls of Old England' as material for an old song! – and has consigned the honoured names of Duncan, Howe, and Jervis to the care of some septuagenarian chorister who remembers his father telling him on certain days, marked in the calendar, glorious naval battles were fought by those gallant admirals, at once drubbing the foe, winning for their country renown, and for themselves fame and coronets. All this, and

"'Twas in Trafalgar's bay
We saw the Frenchmen lay"

Must remain only as history's photographs of brilliant bygones, or be a little while longer cherished by Neptune's sons laid up in Greenwich tier, who may use their eyes and limbs, and pertinaciously insist that when these naval notorieties braved the battle and the breeze *that* was England's meridian day! and that in no future time can there be such sailor-supremacy and such hero-tars. Well, we must not attempt to argue against such a foregone conclusion; the delusion will sweeten life, and flavour the quid. And to tell them they navigated tubs – that deck and quarter-deck firing was human target-shooting, and the whole system was a splendid mistake – all this would only make Jack irate and say something very much hotter than it might be polite.

But we come to the fact. If the thunder of the press has rolled over the world that England's war-navy is reduced to two or four iron ships, it is either true or false. When we read the Illustrated News, and just scanned the pictures, it looked very much like the truth. And as we read this evening its endorsement by our Prime Minister, surely it must now take its place among the "inexorable logic of facts."

As on some morning a billow breaks on a distant shore, leaving behind the deposit of gold, at once exciting curiosity and rousing energy among the inhabitants, so this billow of the sea of mind has broken upon the shore of Time, leaving knowledge which excites astonishment and is causing grave commotion over all the civilised world.

Perhaps one thought for profounder minds and more influential pens may have a force given to it by the press, and then we wait Time's development.

The men of science will be at work. What may the men of peace say? They may hope this wonder is one of God's strange methods to banish national war. From evil, good may evolve. This terrific discovery must arrest all Europe, as it may be horrific to all. National affront prompting the spirit of revenge, what seaboard would be safe? Even round our "tight little island," and up our Thames to Greenwich, these machines, propelled for infernal designs, might shell, shot, and devastate with impunity, while our army and volunteers would stand helpless to hinder, and the only hope would be in destructive reprisals! Therefore, will it not be the way of meeting this surprising thing by a wise sinking of "national honour" in the ships which now must go down, and then elevate national arbitration on the rock of truth?

Should the Merrimac and Monitor bring Earth's potentates to such a conclusion – should such a revolution have been worked for all the world by our brethren in their own waters, let all the world be grateful if such an experiment has been as confounding to the demon of bloodshed as it may be comforting to the sons of peace. And let such a fact be hailed by every lover of his kind as one of the most conclusive arguments against the "pride, pomp, and circumstance of glorious war" the world ever knew; while in a monetary view it would afford a most cheering reference in any future speech on the Finances, for while America is charged for the retention of some taxes our Chancellor may yet eloquently descant upon a discovery which may frighten the nations from war, and enable him to propound to "wondering senates" and to John Bull the beneficial appropriation of such a surplus as the most sanguine Chancellor never could have imagined. Young say "Our waking dreams most startle and appal"; and waking up to such a sudden fact, we jot down these thoughts for further thought, and remain, Sir, your obedient servant, A peacemaker, Woburn, Beds, April 8.

17ᵗʰ May 1862 Bedfordshire Mercury
A Hymn for the Opening of the Exhibition.

Praise earth and heaven's eternal Lord,
Inventions, treasures, here are stored;
Nature and knowledge both compete
To lay their tribute at His feet.

First, mourn the father of our kings,
No more to wake on earth-born kings;
No more that placid bow will bend
To assist the wise, to serve the friend.

Memorial link this structure stands
Of his kind heart and generous hands;
"Albert the good" in light shall rise,
His peaceful fame tone Europe's skies.

And while stern death can proudly scoff
At purpose all broken off,
The tyrant foiled, owns in this hour,

There is rich fame above his power.

Peace bids his trophies here to stand
As peaceful spoil from every land;
Here nations mingle, feuds will cease,
An earnest of the world-wide peace.

And while our hymn this mournful May
Inaugerates a peaceful day,
Heart-strains ascend to close the scene
God save and bless our mourning Queen

The Royal children Heaven protect;
At home, abroad, uphold, direct;
This may be our prayer for each, for all –
May hope arise when woe may fall.

G.C., Woburn, Beds, May 1st.

Note. – These lines sprung from other lines. Perhaps the Laureate bard will not frown on a country minstrel in giving currency to one of his thoughts by the notes of the grand household melody. It may be a memory of the International Exhibition which may please *home* circles, where the magnificent music roll of the "wide hall" may never reach.

The Great London Exposition of 1862 covered 21 acres of South Kensington. Exhibitors numbered c.28,000 and came from 36 countries. These included Charles Babbage's analytical engine (considered to be an early forerunner of the modern computer), the electric telegraph, submarine cables, and Parkesine, the first plastic.

21st June 1862 Bedfordshire Mercury

"The Murder of the Innocents."

Sir, - Homes are being horrified by the repetition of these terrible murders. Manchester and London, just now, have awful celebrity - two fathers and two mothers have imbrued their hands in innocent blood; and this, too, with so much method that had it not been murder no one would have thought of calling it madness. How juries may decide may been seen; but a thought on prevention may, through the press, stir thought on these increasingly alarming and appalling crimes.

Years ago, reading a portion of Roman history, I came across a fact: Suicide by the women had become so frequent that the senate decreed for the future, and woman destroying herself should be dragged by a car, naked, through the streets of Rome. The mania was abated by this severe, yet salutary law.

Now, sir, might not a law that all children murdered by their parents should be handed over to the surgeons, to be at their sole disposal, give a check to this infant destruction? Might it not give pause to the wretched parent, inasmuch as seeing himself the butcher of a child he would know he was consigning it to strangers for a sort of ignominious dissection?

Call this harsh to the dead? I reply, any remedy that might save the living should be tried. This is my sole reason for asking a small space in the Mercury.

I am, sir, your obedient servant, An Englishman, Woburn, June 14th.

The Manchester case appears to relate to William Taylor, who, driven mad by having had one of his children killed by a faulty boiler exploding in a house he had rented, killed his landlord's agent and then the other three of his own children. The London case was probably that of the two children of Mr. & Mrs. Valentine Vyse, who were allegedly poisoned by their mother after she became mentally unstable when another of her children had died. After two trials, she was found Not Guilty of Murder, but was detained at Her Majesty's pleasure.

19th July 1862 Bedfordshire Mercury

Woburn. Independent Chapel Sunday School Holiday. – Another anniversary was held last Thursday, at the spot where for 45 years this festival has been held. Change and absence marked humanity, but nature remained the same. This beautiful eminence has always a charm. The peep at the Abbey, portions of Woburn Park, a view of Ridgmount village, these, some of nature's pictures, original, hang in the distance; while, on these occasions, the frolics of the children give near life to this country Greenwich-hill, without the drawbacks of its dissipations. And now a word on the purpose of these holidays. It is to please, stimulate, and encourage Sunday School children and teachers. Sunday Schools may be subjects of criticism in their future results relative to the scholars, but the present propriety of teaching children the keeping of the Sabbath, and giving them counsel for the battle of life cannot be questioned. Their abuse of this must fall on their own heads. Well, then, these holidays bring minister, parents, friends, children and teachers together, and under the charm of tea, cake and smiles, and a summer sun they all unite heart, hand or feet in mutual happiness.

'Neath memory's magic charm
Age for awhile forgets the "frosty pow,
Time-rusted limb, and springs to catch the ball,

Or toddles round the ring, obliviates all

Of rheumatic, lumbago, or the cramp.

Forty-five years in one spot! This involves a solemn thought, and musing on this verdant height we thought of the fathers, mothers, friends, children and teachers who had run up and down this hill, and then we thought of how few remained! In this space of time two Ducal owners of the domain have passed to the mausoleum, and of former participants in this holiday where are they? The fact established locally, by this annual festival –

"Time like an ever flowing stream

Bears all its sons away"

for the exception of the few of the past, the present generation were inheritors of a scene bequeathed by our fathers and mothers, and which linking to an institution to save youth, and to warn them of the paths of folly, sin and shame, we hope may continue one of Britain's institutions while she remains eminent among nations of the earth, for her charities, societies and missions to better this sin stricken, death-smitten world.

In the continuing American Civil War, Castleden was firmly behind the northern States and their action to end slavery, but he also pointed out the England was benefitting from the produce of slave-owning firms, which he naturally believed it to be un-Christian.

22ⁿᵈ **November 1862** Bedfordshire Mercury

The American Civil War.

"No war which we have ourselves been engaged in has ever caused such intense, such concentrated misery amongst our population as the one now raging in America, and which is now so hopelessly beyond our control or interference." *Beds. Mercury, 15ᵗʰ November.*

Sir, - These words shall key a few others on this brother war. The present emergency must be attended to; the rivulets of charity should mingle, and one broad stream must flow to the North. God grant it may avail to stay fever and pestilence; but the prospect is very gloomy.

A question: What has this brother war sprung from? Cruel iniquity. In working out this answer we hope for words few and apt.

America, by profession, stands A 1 among the nations for civil liberty. America, by profession, stands No. 1 among Christians for pure and undefiled religion. America, practically, stands a monster lie to the world, inasmuch as she limits civil liberty to the colour of the skin; and in her religious worship we wonder whether she ever uses the line: -

"He sees the oppressor and the oppressed?"

But a more gigantic organised system of *oppression* the world never knew; and when we think of Christians, differing in skin, joining in the same church, yet in the *field* "the drunkenness of unrestricted power" changes one into the *tyrant*, and makes the other the *victim*; then we wonder such arrant hypocrisy has had prolongation, and a course of such apparent success. But we see through a glass darkly. The ulcer has long been gathering; hands have joined together to bandage it; long has it been hidden; but it was working. It has at last burst, and terrible is its slough and stench.

Are our hands clean? Would that they were. After our own sacrifice to destroy the accursed thing; after doing this, then, by mind and machinery, we cause such a demand for the growth of cotton that the slave *breeding* States, supported by English custom, go to lengths in the acquisition and retention of slaves which at one time was never contemplated; and each of these nations, professing to "serve God," for a league with mammon, and under that idol's inspiration, in this the 19th century of the Christian era, they have winked at and fostered a system of slavery at which heathen world would cry, and Pagan Rome would blush.

Is the punishment just? Stop – "What have the innocent operatives to do with your premises?" My friend, this is a mystery; but if we take not the doctrine of retribution for the standplace we are upon bog, sinking deeper and deeper into perplexity. Retribution is the only doctrine that checks selfish man. "It will come home," whether it sounds in a cot, a hamlet, or over a clime, prevents the perpetration of crime more than all the penal statutes ever framed.

"Let God be true, but every man a liar;" and what God says – "For the oppression of the poor, for the sighings of the needy, now I will arise, saith the Lord." In that arising the judgement falls, and while the North is bleeding and exhausting, the South is being desolated, England, as the receiver of slave produce, putting money into her purse by American working of human cattle! England, we say, is startled with the cry of famine after an abundant harvest, and many thoughtful minds are looking to the terrific sequel of slow consuming fares, or the pestilential fire which may devastate far and near. These thoughts may move deeper thoughts, and we finish by saying, let charity flow to those who among us are the present sufferers; still we avail ourselves of this opportunity of impressing on individuals, as well as nations, one great consecutive statute from the BOOK which America and England, professedly, make their own – "Though hand join hand in iniquity, the wicked shall not go unpunished."

I remain, Sir, your obedient servant, G. C. Woburn, 17th November.

The **10th January 1863** *Bedfordshire Mercury & also the Bedfordshire Times reported that Castleden had served on the Grand Jury for the Bedfordshire Epiphany Quarter Sessions, along with, among others, Mr. J. A. Harbutt of Woburn. They decided on the following cases:*

Anne Foskett, stealing £3 6s and a purse, from Charles Tysoe, shoemaker, at Turvey. Not guilty.

Amos Burgess and James Mann, labourers of Caddington, stealing a pig. Guilty. One year and six months hard labour respectively.

Ebenezer Northwood, stealing a donkey at Luton. Hearing it was done whilst drunk, the jury decided he was Not Guilty, and discharged, but cautioned him to refrain from drunkenness in the future!

Amos Roberts, who assaulted Joseph Osborne with a fence rail, at Heath and Reach. Guilty, four months hard labour.

Charles Devereux, theft of various objects at Campton. Guilty, 12 months.

Robert Elston, stealing five game fowls from the Star and Garter public house in Luton. Guilty, three months hard labour.

James Bradshaw, stealing firewood from Rev. E. Searle at Odell. Guilty, six months hard labour.

David Beard, stealing a shirt left out to dry at Houghton Conquest. Guilty. The Governor of the prison was called, who explained Beard had a long history of pilfering, back to 1850, and since that year he had spent eight years in prison. Sentenced to ten years penal servitude.

James Webster, receiving stolen potatoes at Leighton Buzzard. Not guilty.

John Wright, a pick-pocket of Luton, Guilty, four years.

John Neale, stole a silver watch from the Fox beerhouse in Keysoe, Guilty, four years.

James Price, another Luton pick-pocket, Guilty. With no previous convictions, three months hard labour.

William Clark and John Neale, burgled a house in Knotting. Guilty, 12 months hard labour.

Joseph Theobalds, maliciously wounding a mare at Potton, Not guilty, as he proved it was an accident.

William Paternoster, stealing six bushels of potatoes at Henlow. Pleaded Guilty, and as he had convictions going back to 1834, but was now 69 years of age, he was given only(!) 12 months.

10ᵗʰ January 1863 Bedfordshire Mercury

Woburn. – Two Stuart Poets. (Milton – Butler)

Note. – From a "Portfolio" still closed we select two poets. One has been the theme of many writers; the other gave the subject for the lecture in our Town hall. These stanzas were composed years ago. They may suitably follow this lecture, and the truly excellent tribute paid by Lord Charles Russell to one of our Bedfordshire worthies

"Mewling and puking in his nurse's arms,"
Behold the babe of vast poetic life:
A moment look on his rare infant charms;
Spake not the coming scars of Time's stern strife.
View the boy's budding bloom, whose beauty rife
The enduring fragrance of maternal art
Shed mystic sweetness through life's afternight;
The father's nature toned the manly part,
The mother's gentle love like music sheered the heart.
London's Paul's School the poet ne'er forgot;
There masters furnished rudimental lore;
Christ's College, Cambridge, next the honoured spot,
Which added classic, mythological store:
The Church *they* chose; the Muses pleased *him* more:
He took the tour through Italy to Rome,
There had he lingered but from Britain's shore,
Across the sea, winds bore a nation's groan,
And Liberty's life-cry recalled the rambler home.
Let cavaliers defame, and courtiers sneer,
The civil war emblazons honest fame;
His giant heart beat high and knew not fear;
His *pen*, and not his *sword*, inscribed his name
'Mongst patriots born the Rule of Wrong to tame.
Cromwell he served, for he *believed* him great
With all his faults; this won him loss and blame;
The lees of life ran out in bitter fate,
Harsh venal scribes would scoff, Court sycophants did hate.
His outward vision quenched, Sol's lucent ray
Bathed not his orbs; but blindness, most profound,
Made out ward night, yet bright the inner day:
His Heaven-lit soul beamed radiation around,
And still it warms and fruits poetic ground.
Behold yon girl, and see the sightless sire
Tuning his hidden harp to mystic sound;
On Oreb's top, enthroned in rapt desire

He wakes the wondrous chords of his angelic lyre.
"Of man's first disobedience and the fruit,"
Who quotes not now? Of Eden lost, his theme,
Where is the Englishman who does not bruit
Kinship with him whose pencil drew each scene,
And threw on Eden's blight this Heaven-song beam?
Yet hear and wonder, with this priceless lay,
The minstrel abject, indignant, is seen;
And while 'tis mean to talk of lucre-pay,
Yet *ten* pounds was the dole for twelve years *mused* away.
Three score and six, and life's sad tale was done!
Nothing could further harm the imperial man:
Tell now the truth – all adulation shun;
And as this Puritan we fairly scan,
His aim was truth – for truth he suffered ban.
Enigma strange! He left a world-bequest!
He, Mind's great noble, styled republican;
And, while proud titles, all obscurely rest,
His patent Climes endorse, and Peoples boast his crest.
Thus sinking bright, 'twere impious to regret
The darkling clouds which shrouded life's decline:
His sun, at eve, in full-orbed splendour set:
Upward it beamed upon the clouds of time,
Majestic, sinking, found a nightless clime.
So have I seen Sol pour his tinted rays, Dropping to rest beneath the
horizon-line;
A type – how soul, long clouded, still may daze;
It's evening beams preclude Fame's aye-meridian blaze.
'Mongst Milton's fellows Samuel Butler sings:
Diverse the music and distinct the style:
With song divine one soared on seraph's wings,
But Butler's hoofs trod dirt, which left the soil,
And tipsy hiccups oft his numbers spoil.
Angels might list the diapason play
As Milton rolled it over Eden's spoil!
Then, wondrous change, he struck Salvation's lay –
Told Christ regained, restored, what Adam flung away.
Not so the bard whose pipe and tabret sue
The satellites of Charles's sunny hour;

To Butler, for his song is tribute due.
He wrote to tickle sons of pomp and power,
And please voluptuous dames in Hampton bower.
Cople, in Bedfordshire, yet shews his "hole" –
If such rude words incense, restrain the sour
Reproof, good critics: bid no thunders roll.
Nor charge your *magazines* to blast my poet-scroll.
His life obscure, a warfare to the grave;
Where he learnt lore is left in learned doubt.
At manhood poor and stricken, see him crave
To earn his bread a Roundhead's serving lout;
His master "Hudibras," in dress, deeds, rout.
The merry monarch quoted Butler's rhymes;
Nobles applaud; his unique couplets shout;
Fair ladies smiled on the immortal lines.
The bard the while unsought; unhelped, depressed, he pines!
'Tis told, "proud Villiers, Duke of Buckingham,
Allowed the imploring bard an interview;
And as he listened to the moon-struck man
A brace of beauties caught His Grace's view;
The bard was cut, and to the dames he flew."
Now Grandeur's gone, and nought remains but lead!
Now Beauty's vanished like morn's pearled dew;
Now Princes are unknown, his lines are read,
As mental food remain, while once he sued for bread.
Yes, Butler reaped in full the "Genius curse!"
An ill-starred son of Fame he suffered ban;
A struggler all his life, and low in purse,
He died at sixty-eight an obscure man.
"a man whose name will last while language can."
In Westminster's hoar fane his bust has place,
And as the eye along the inscription ran,
It left a *moral* we would not erase,
And told a warning tale we care not here to trace.
G. C., Woburn, 1st January, 1863.

Royal marriages, births and birthdays were always a cause for celebration. The hard work of the agricultural labourer could be forgotten for a day, and it was an excuse for the entire town to come together and organise festivities, and also for Castleden to pen some more "expressive lines" at this marriage of the then Prince of Wales (the future Edward VII) to Princess Alexandra of Denmark.

16ᵗʰ March 1863 Bedfordshire Mercury

Woburn. Marriage Festivities. "The Feast to the Labouring Classes and Tea, Cake, and Buns to the Schools" – This the foundation of Woburn's celebration of the marriage of Her Royal Highness the Princess Alexandra, was well laid as a public meeting presided over by Lord Charles Russell. Messrs. Freeman and Castleden were requested to wait on the inhabitants for subscriptions; they liberally responded, and this, with the kindness of His Grace the Duke of Bedford, in adding £58, placed the committee in a safe position relative to finances.

Early in the morning the merry peal woke to day and duty. Members of the committee were at the Town Hall by seven, to see to the cutting up of the beef and the reception of plum pudding and ale; at nine, the distribution began, and a very pleasing process it was, giving provisions and pleasure to upwards of 500 adults and 300 or 400 children; this being finished, superintendence was transferred to the tea, cake and bun department. Her the ladies were busy, some on the creature comforts and others in the decorative department; each seemed to vie in the art of pleasing; mottos were many; mock roses almost rivalled real ones, and happy smiles shed continual sunshine in rather a shady nook. A hasty meal for some, and then on the Markey Hill assembled a godly number of the lieges, and all the schools of the town mustered, "God save the Queen" was sung, then the procession was formed, and it passed along the streets till it finally settled, a hum and swarm, humming musically, under tarpaulings and tents kindly lent and sent for the occasion. Here expressive lines suit: -

"sweet is the hum of children's tones,
All busy bees in the world's hive;"

And amid these tones as we looked down the dim tent festooned with evergreens, and adorned only as women's tastes can adorn, what with attendants and visitors, it was a memorial scene not to be forgotten. The lady Charles Russell and Miss. I. Russell, with a number of ladies having taken their seats, grace was sung by the children, and then tea and cake, under pressure of steam and appetite, vanished with great celerity: the hum changed to a liquid music, and though the tune was not – "Polly put the kettle on": there were many smiling Pollies who kept good time tripping up and down to the boilers in which tea was made, by the gallon, at a saving of time and expense which had associated all tea makers of the last Prince of Wale's time. The consumption of cake and flow of tea came to a close, and then "Praise God" expressed the gratitude of the children for their feast. Then neighbours 'high and low,' sat down together, and the fervency of the tea was companioned by the fluency of the tongue. Then night fell, and after China tea and cups, Chinese lanterns, prettily hung, gave a dim and social light, enabling groups to chat over the events of the day; then came a rush to the school room told of magical delights, superintended by Mr. Farrow. Children of all ages hailed the delusive and illusive toy, and cheered lustily some of the humourous slides; we hope the moral of "Whittington and his Cat" may remain - "that kindness even to a dumb animal may lead to fame and fortune."

'Tired nature' then sought its 'restorer,' and coming out under the "V.R. and Crown" in illuminated lamps on the gable end, also the Prince of Wale's feathers in tinted light, and then passing the "A.E.A" flashing in gas, on the front of the Hall, we joined present hours with the light of other nights! And a "night thought" came up but as I had just left the magic lantern slide of Burn's Cottage," a thought from Scotland's bard may best fit. Looking on the day spent; the happy occasion of a nation's joy, and thinking of the neighbour agencies which. For a week, had been so kindly engaged to promote the joy and comfort of others, and feeling the conviction, these 'well-spent hours' would light, cheer, and refresh in present and future gloom, Burns came to our aid, and we may briefly close of brief report of loyal Woburn's festivities, on a royal wedding day, with the verse

Alas! Life's path may be unsmooth!
The way may be though rough distress!
But they who pains and ills will sooth,
Balm their own wounds and make woe less.

Having been made by the chairman, the assembly adjourned to the cross, where a display of fireworks was provided; and thence to the west end, where the evening of this ever memorable and very happy day was cheerily wound up around a huge and brilliant bonfire. The general comment was that Stevington* had never seen a day like this before. One sad circumstance we sincerely regret to add - the occurrence of an accident, which marred the pleasure of many an inhabitant of the parish. Mr. Pike's youngest son - by whose father's kindness and exertions the day's joys had been so much enhanced - himself a fine young fellow almost four years old, was mounting a waggon, when the horse made a sudden start, the ladder fell, and the hapless youth with it, fracturing his right arm in two places.

*Quite how the Stevington reference crept in, I do not know. Perhaps the newsprint typesetter had other places on his mind that day!

14: A view of the Woburn Independent (Congregational) chapel, from the 1899 book-let on the same by W. M. Barwell. (Courtesy of Dr Williams's Library, London)

14th April 1863 Leighton Buzzard Observer

Woburn. Tea Drinking – On Good Friday, April 3rd, a public tea meeting was held in the Independent Chapel, at half-past four o'clock. About 160 sat down to tea; and, if their faces were an index to their feelings, everyone thoroughly enjoyed this social gathering. At half-past six a public meeting was held in the same place, when addresses were delivered by the Rev. J. Andrews, and Mr. Castleden, of Woburn. At intervals of music, given by members of the Woburn Singing Class, some of which were executed in a manner very creditable to the performers.

I note the report says only 'some' of the singers were creditable! Russia, fresh from defeat in the Crimean War, now faced an uprising in its western provinces of Poland and Lithuania. Known as the January Uprising, some sources say as many as 70,000 people were detained or transported to labour camps, and after the collapse of the uprising 18 months later, many harsh reprisals swiftly followed. Britain and her allies decided not to get involved in what it considered to be a Russian affair. Castleden was never shy at referencing his own published works. The book he mentions here was the third volume of poetry he had published in 1843:

1st August 1863 Bedfordshire Mercury

Poland - Retribution.

"The question of Poland has intrinsic difficulties which I fear are enormous. Those difficulties are the *consequences of former misdeeds* - not only of those who have inflicted wrong, but of those who allowed it to be inflicted. To undo political crimes, especially after they have been so long subsisted, is almost in many cases beyond the power of man." - The Chancellor of the Exchequer.

Sir, - Twenty years ago appeared a little volume entitled "Retribution, &c.". Among the future "curiosities of literature" it may turn up as one voucher of our past, and when "nothing can harm further" it may be evidence to a part of life's tale. In that book are these lines: -

"O Tyranny! thou hydra-headed fiend!

What hecatombs of victims stain thy path!

Thy murd'rous wants are not confined

To a clime's spoils, but individual wrong,

The widow's tear, the orphan's sigh, attest

The potency of thine insatiate reign!

Whether a Russian autocrat, by slaves, Or though arts of congregated lords

O'er Poland's patriot plains the ploughshare drives,

And blots her name from out the world's wide map."

And now, in July, 1863, we have a great orator of our day confirming the wrong done, and deploring "consequences," which in the king-plotted destruction of Poland seem inevitable.

When, as a boy, I sat among some of the fathers of Bedfordshire, and heard these words - "Brother Hillyard, the partition of Poland will be England's curse," - how little did we dream of endorsing these oracular words from one of England's illustrious obscure by the brilliant amplification of a Horsman, and the conclusive eloquence of a Gladstone; and that in the decline of life I might have to record the responsive cheers of Britain's senate-house over the execration of tyranny which was denounced in this home, half a century ago, as a cowardly and detestable sacrifice of a brave people.

Now the question is, what can be done for "that gallant, unhappy, and long-suffering people"? While democracy pauses, France may answer by the sword. What then? Will the mysterious process of retribution go on in fire, sack, and blood? Where will the flames end? If the passive policy rules, are the Poles to be exterminated; or the remnant to live the branded, oppressed white slaves of Russia?

"O what a tangled web we weave

When first we practice to deceive";

- and whether this be the craft of crowned heads to destroy an empire, or it be the plotting to crush an individual, alike shall retribution, sooner or later, restore the balance, defeat the oppressor, and "vindicate the ways of God to man."

"He sees the oppressor and the oppressed."

I quote the Congress of 1814 Lord Castlereagh's words. It was a "discordant intrigue and a lawless scramble for power"; and of this national oppression he then wrote – "It has only excited sentiments of discontent and self-degradation, and can never do otherwise than promote commotions, and awaken in them (the Poles) recollections of their past misfortunes."

Here we combine the *now* and *then*. *Then* the oppression was denounced; then the oppressor was strong, and scorned and scoffed: *now* another generation are reaping the dragon's teeth sown in the past. This is mysterious, but the doctrine of retribution, less mysterious, would not be so awing. It has been well observed, it preserves more by its uncertain-certain secret and open punishment than do penal statutes made and provided. Many a scoundrel evades them, but when the King said "Richard hates himself," he pointed the inexorable penalty of selfish sin, not from man, but from an eternal law which God has mercifully implanted in every breast, and the breach of which either hardens the heart into marble obduracy or melts it into penitential grief. That law – "As I would have another to do unto me, so I should do unto him," sinned against, must have *reparation*. It is nature's law, confirmed by God. Yet despite of it, man would depose nature, dethrone God, and make the fair fields of humanity an Aceldama by his selfish lusts and tyrannous passions.

Here retribution punishes and rectifies! and we only hope that in the wrong inflicted by Russia and those who stood by and permitted that wrong may not be made to feel severely the "consequences" of past delinquency; but may the cloud now gathering, if it overspread Europe, alike teach mighty monarchs who spoil nations, and miserable atoms who spoil their neighbours, one great truth from that grand old law book, the Bible – "Though hand join in hand, the wicked shall not go unpunished." Confederacy, secrecy, security, and here combined: add the power of the despot, and we establish the Polish difficulty as an Imperial crime, which has darkened Europe for nearly a century – which is perplexing the profoundest minds; and while the superficial are looking to the chapter of accidents for results, those who take the higher ground of justice and moral right hope for a solution which, sounding over the sunny plains of the South and the snowy deserts of the North, may teach Tyranny another warning lesson wherever "the oppressor's

RETRIBUTION,

𝕷𝖔𝖞𝖆𝖑 𝕷𝖞𝖗𝖎𝖈𝖘, 𝖆𝖓𝖉 𝕱𝖚𝖌𝖎𝖙𝖎𝖛𝖊 𝕻𝖎𝖊𝖈𝖊𝖘.

COMPLETING THE SERIES OF

"WOBURN PARK," AND "CONSCIENCE."

" Go, little book,"—as "bread on waters" flung—
As harp once tuneful now once more unstrung,
Go forth, my song, upon thy dubious way,
Establish truth whate'er the sceptics say.
Should fruit "return" though "after many days,"
The minstrel's harp may wake in future lays.

LONDON:

THOMAS WARD AND CO., PATERNOSTER-ROW.

1843.

15: *Frontispiece to Castleden's "Retribution - Loyal Lyrics and Fugitive Pieces", published 1843.*

wrong" would crush, and the despot's sword would enslave.

These thoughts have followed reading the debate, and by their admission into your columns you will oblige, Sir, your obedient servant, George Castleden, Woburn, 26th July.

He next reported on a visit to James Lucas, also known as the Hermit of Hertfordshire, or Mad Lucas, of Elmwood House, near Redcoats Green. Having inherited a family fortune, Lucas had barricaded himself inside his house, and lived solely in the kitchen, sleeping on a bed of ashes and soot. He never washed, and it is said he lived on bread, cheese, eggs, red herrings and gin brought to him. The Victorians loved an eccentric, and would visit him to converse through an iron grille. Castleden's report of their conversation makes one of his more surreal reports...

29th August 1863 Bedfordshire Mercury

A Rambler's Prose. A Hertfordshire Celebrity.

When little Watts wrote the couplet – "I write not for your farthing, but to try; How I your farthing-writers can outvie" – he little thought a Bedfordshire rambler might use it as a sort of an apology for writing on a subject which has moved the pen of Charles Dickens, and others. This subject is the tenant of one of Hertfordshire's homes, now noted for decay and desolation.

Starting with the mother and her juvenile group in a primitive conveyance, drawn by a quadruped famed for patience and persistence since the days of Balam, after a time we found ourselves at "Titmill Green," Great Wymonday; giving our steed full liberty, to crop his thistly food, we made our way up to a barricaded house, and then through a dilapidated entrance found ourselves before an iron-barred window; one look told dirty desolation. The voice of my young companion – "How do you do to-day Mr. Lucas" caused a sudden apparition, which, had I not been prepared for something of the sort, would have been startling. – No Indian, in his forest haunts, ever appeared dirty and dishevelled as did this occupant of the Parents home! And most certainly on this, the first appearance, I might have uttered with Hamlet – 'Angels and ministers of grace defend us.' Thou comest in such a questionable shape?

From soot and ashes this form arose; and standing in his dingy blanket, but for his dark eye resting on the lassie, and the tone of his voice, I had still wondered whether to humanity this form belonged. After some enquiries of my companions he turned to me asked my name, whereabouts, and then a local chat followed; Toddington started a remark on Wentworth, the great Earl Strafford; looking at me full he said – "Ay, you don't like Earl Strafford" – "Why say so," I replied. "He was no friend to dissenters." – "Well, Mr.

Lucas, all I can say is, I wish Charles had had a better counsellor; it might have saved them both their heads, and our history a bloody blot which I should like to see erased." Taken aback a bit on this point we next tried Italy and Garibaldi. "He was factious and he served right" – "Yes," I said upon the grounds that "Treason never prospers" – as quick as thought he finished the quotation – What's the reason? When it does, none dare call it treason.

"But supposing he had won Rome" – "I wish he had, the crisis would have come, the factious would have been dispersed, and Italy would have righted herself." – "What, would you not wish to see Italy a nation?" "No, no, Italy never was a nation, and never can be, that's all bosh." Touching the Exhibition as a peace promoter among the nations, this he would not allow, and spoke scornfully of it, but having through his bars handed a sketch of a day's visit, I was then asked to take a glass of wine. All I can say is the glass was clean and the wine was good; as I retuned it I found it served the extra purpose of a bottle stopper. Resuming our chat, happening to say – "Well sir, struck as I am with this singular interview and with your strange seclusion, yet I find you have great knowledge of what is going on" – "Oh! I have all the news of the world brought me for I see all classes." And as I finished by saying – "I have no reason to complain of any want of courtesy in this visit of curiosity on my part." I shall not forget the flash of that dark eye as he instantly rejoined – "Oh, Sir, if I am treated properly I know how to use the *suaciter in mode*, but if otherwise I can give the hard word as well as anyone."

Wishing him 'Good day' and saying gently – This will be a memorial visit, indeed, and may God have mercy on you" – as these words fell the look of that eye, if it spoke surprise flashed no resentment at what might have been called a liberty towards one in his own home. The farewell was impulsive, and a bend of the brow intimated he was not displeased, and thus this singular visit closed. As we retired other visitors drove up, but we had interested him for on looking back, through the final barricades we saw the unearthly visage gazing after us.

Over this visit we have often grave thoughts, and we trust nothing impertinent or unjust may proceed from our pen.

The appellation of "Hermit" we dismiss; the leaf-strewn call, the wholesome root and the crystal fount, belonging to this poetical fraternity, are all wanting at 'Titmill Green'; and we dare not say Misanthrope; the ready response, the sweetmeats in store for children; the wine for visitors; the coppers for beggers, intimate no hatred to women, man, or child. Then is he a lunatic? The man who keeps his money at a banker's and can draw cheques cannot be said to be incapable of taking care of his own affairs. Then what is the reason for this maceration of soul, this high scar of all decencies and goods of social life? Homes, lands, education, wealth, appreciation of knowledge, sympathies, all sacrificed! and the degradation or penance, is so complete that he recreates in ashes; mocks himself in the dispensation of his charity, and hospitality, and inflicts *self* torture as he gratifies the taste of children. Now shall we venture a solution to this mystery? Is it true that "the fear of relative persecution" has led to this self-imposed ignomy? Something like this we were told slipped out in one conversation. If so a clue is given to this misery. If wounded by relatives the true man cannot resent; revengeful reprisals only store up future woe; as a man he conquers agony; perhaps suffers and is strong.

Thought has been stirred on this Hertfordshire celebrity into the mystery we have no business to dive; only we may say if persecution has impelled such resentment against himself, still, while soot and ashes, as a resting place, under some stern motive, is a very dirty bed if in it are not the thorns of injury and wrong to others, even then it may afford the victim that sweet sleep which flees the assassin's couch although of softest down.

We repeat we pry not into the mystery; our only aim is to encourage the amenities of our social relations by a painful exception, unexplainable, unexpectedly brought before us. - We know "our lives through various scenes are drawn," and as one day in 1862 this scene presented, and as we stood before this *living soul*, we were forcibly struck by a thought from John Foster: - The great essayist says - "There is an inner apartment in every man's breast where none but God and the soul can enter: where the passions mingle and fluctuate unseen, and deep mysteries are hidden utterly from the eye of man, and where it would be useless, while the attempt would be impertinent and presumptuous in any mortal to penetrate."

G. C., Woburn, August, 1863.

10th October 1863 Bedfordshire Mercury

Woburn Bygones! - Cricket.

"It is much to be regretted that the inhabitants of a town formerly so conspicuous for the zeal with which they supported and the dexterity with which they practised this noble English game can only play one match on their own ground during a season, and that a single wicket match with experienced players from a secluded village." - *Bedfordshire Mercury*, 25th of September, 1863.

Sir, - As an old cricket player I was pained as I read the above; turning to some old papers I found the following relative to the "noble game" when played in Woburn Park. Inserted in your columns it may afford local information, and in a future season it may aid a resumption of the honest game of cricket.

Cricket Bygones: Again I may say of this bygone 'read my book', 'Woburn

Park'; and as a supplement when 'our old bat' is published it will tell its tale of *field*, if not of *flood*.

Woburn Park is historic hallowed ground, and writing these words in one of the loveliest of our Mays, after having rambled it with an artist, how have we paused at different points of the landscape, and have contemplated the far and the near objects of sylvan and verdant beauty. The *eye* has been delighted, gazing on the pictures of animal and still life, painted and framed by nature's sunny skilful hand, and while the mind has been pondering many bygones which, to the present generation are as legendary tales.

Two or three remain who may remember our early trap-balls. Forty-five years have flown since two of us chose our sides on the West Front-place, and still we remember how our town mates beat tilled side; and now, 'duct to dust'! and silenced heads admonish the few left!

Another event in our juvenile experience was, stripping on the same plain in a celebrated match between a Dunstable eleven and twenty-two of the Woburn and Abbey; ere the second or third over the last player made his appearance. This game was one of Woburn's great days. Then, under the trenches we played our threepenny match against the Farm and Abbey boys, though we had not read Butter, we realised two of his lines – 'He that fights and runs away, May live to fight another day.' – for, displeased, on losing, we did cut and run and had to meet the street taunt – "here are the runaway cricketers."

Well, we bridge time with our old bat, and come to 1824. Our Dunstable meets for three successive seasons were study fights; some stratagems still cause the laugh, but home and home we were beaten, and then for three seasons's cricket lapsed, then the sun of Woburn Park, not Austerlitz, shone again! In 1829 we played the Shefford, and then, up to 1847 it was – cricket.

Thirteen summers, and I tell this with gratitude, it was that continuity of pastoral fellowship, and happy association which is even the charm of a well-conducted local cricket club; and while some of our mates toddle on, and some sleep under the turf(!) sunny memories travel with the thought that it was by acting in harmony with the truthful spirit of cricket, this pleasure, in life's decline, is still fragrant. Let us record a scrap of philosophy gathered from the "noble game."

A real cricketer cannot be a cowardly foe. A hard-up cricketer may be tempted to steal for bread, but he won't stab in the dark. These assassin tactics are so contrary to the manly game that we hold it as one of the national pastimes, proclaiming our open fair play code, and evidencing to the Englishman's love of honest emulation, and his native hatred of envy's dark-night deeds.

This much for the spirit of the game; its present prospects call for a cautionary word. This applies to county fields, and it may be of some little service in the debates of the cricket parliament which we are told must revise, and re-enact old and new laws for the bat and ball portion of Her Majesty's loyal subjects.

Then we say beware lest cricket play degenerates into cricket dissipation. Be careful the mercenary and the made-up match do not subvert home muscularity, and destroy that home interest in a match which is at once the charm and stimulus of a local game. This distinction in county places, and then instead of an anxious concourse of neighbour friends, free in their censure of anything wrong, while hearty in their applause, you will have only betters and special spectators; and, perchance, if the sides are arranged to "bowl time down, every indulgence is to be given for the cigar, and other pic-nic accomplishments, unknown in sterner times, when the preliminaries of older matches were closed by the toast – "A fine day, a smooth turf, no favour and may the best men win."

This was country cricket when it was parish against parish, county against county. And the question is whether innovations will not damage, if not destroy it as a local, healthy, honest pastime, altogether.

But as a Woburn player I linger over our beautiful ground, and by memory's magic power we photograph many a pastoral scene of cricket chivalry and neighbour revelry. Now let me leave a few forget-me-nots on this spot, we ne'er forget, and then, as what is written, is written, it may tell a plain of local, and again may people this portion of Woburn Park, when penman, player, and brother "bats" shall all have "melted into thin air."

G. C.

What neither the original report, nor Castleden's lament mentions is that the match had been between just three players from Milton (whether Bryan, Ernest or Keynes is not made clear) against Woburn. Mr. Assbee bowled all three of Milton team (W. Bailey, Osborne and J. Bailey) out in the first innings, and caught all three out in the second! They had made just 4, and one of those was a Wide. Woburn managed a score of 6 to win.

12th October 1863 Bedfordshire Mercury

A Cemetery Visit (Bedford). 30th September.

An autumn summer day found us ascending the steep of this last home of the Bedford folk.

A luminous haze hung over the living town, and around and beyond the changing foliage gave to the landscape the first signs of the declining year. Alone we mused on the memorials of several of our early acquaintances, and thinking of our associations with them in some of the sturdy political conflicts, how did their fervent countenances, stalwart forms, and shouting lungs again appear and sound as we paced this last place of rest! - while their silent tongues seemed to say "A few more setting suns at most, and you, rambler, shall be as we are."

I had just left the new grave of the young minister with whom, some months ago, apparently in health for years, we had the morning stroll in Woburn's beautiful park; and, contemplating such youth and prospects blighted, I found myself attracted by a most beautiful moth. It flitted before me, settled at my feet, and gazing on it thought flew into rhyme, which may revive a Bedford memory in life's later hours: -

Tinted moth, why here to-day,
Here, the home of man's decay?
Things of life, ye mock the dead!
Tinted life, their bloom is fled!
Fragile dust, thou pretty thing,
Thy colours gaily glistening,
A moment wins the stroller's eye,
Suspends the tributary sigh: -
Yet, tinted dust, we see in thee
Fit emblem of mortality,
For fragile is life's longest span,
And *crushed before the moth* the strongest man.

As we jotted down from contiguous graves the dates Oct. 21, 1769 (April, 1804) we little thought it might bear on an after incident. Leaving the cemetery, and strolling round the Green of bygone stentor stouts and civic rows, and then looking on other familiar spots we got to the Station, and under the power of steam reached Ridgmount, and there we were struck as a party came on to the platform. The "Good day" was so impressive that when a fellow-traveller said "Depend upon it, he is somebody 'nobby,'" thought struck it might be some personage of note on a visit to Woburn Abbey. Another glance at the "Sands" Station left its memory, and then at home it told us the Prince Napoleon and suite were the party with whom we had so unexpectedly journeyed! Now for the date 1769. In that "great year" we are told "The man who scourged or feasted kings" was born, and also his great conqueror, Wellington, not to mention others, now historical celebrities, born in that year. Now for a thought on this travelling incident in 1863. As we throw back mind, and by history and personal knowledge revert to the babe of 1769 as the founder of a dynasty, think of his life of sunshine and shade, ending in darkness, desertion, and the cancer's pang on the lone rocks; then the restoration of the Bourbons – they, like the Stuarts, learning nothing by adversity, losing again the throne of France, and then its occupation by another Buoneparte: we say, reverting to our childish terrors at the very name, and the arming of our island home to repel the threatened invasion by the Napoleon-uncle, what would our fathers have thought – especially the 1769 men – of the fact, beating all fiction, that their sons would welcome the nephew Napoleon, who on a peaceful errand would enjoy our beautiful scenery, and then by a noble scion of the ducal house have the farewell homage as he took his seat with first, second, and third class passengers, loyal lieges of Her Majesty Queen Victoria!!

Talk of the "Romance of the Peerage," I fancy the romance of royalty would make a most fascinating addition to our book shelves: at any rate this railroad "meet" we put upon paper, and it may remain as evidence of the romance of travelling that, on the same day, the jotting down a date among Bedford's graves should mystically link a noon incident with a birth which pulsed Europe's bygone history, and, by calling up "the desolator, desolate," give to the thoughtful mind an epitaph on the vanity of empire, and for the tomb of kings!

G. C., Woburn, 2nd October.

This Napoleon had a much better relationship with Great Britain than his forebears had had, and his visit to Woburn is confirmed by a small report in the New York Times, saying he had visited Woburn to see John Russell, 1st Earl Russell, who was then Britain's Foreign Secretary.

7th November 1863 Bedfordshire Mercury

The American Civil War. To the Editor of the "Bedfordshire Mercury".

Sir, - Early in the strife you inserted a letter: in it I ventured upon the high, and, I still think, the *only* safe ground for Christian Europe to view this sad brother war. The accursed thing, slavery, was the *crime*, how far my country has clean hands the future historian may tell, but, surely the *butchery there*, and the *famine here* ask of Christians – 'Is there not a cause?' The answer involves the doctrines of retribution.

With this thought I attended the lecture delivered by Mr. Washington Wilks, at Dunstable. On the stern eloquence of the advocate, the irrefutable logic he employed to bring out the conclusion that slavery, and slavery alone was the *cause* of the war, but one option could be entertained. His premises he laid down as firm as the giants' causeway, and he trod it with a Titan's tread to the one result that slavery, and nothing but slavery had produced this bitter war; and that no hope of its cessation could be entertained except by a mutual extinction of slavery, or y revengeful reprisals, on the part of the oppressed, too horrible almost to contemplate. Still, throughout this attractive and instructive lecture, Mr. Wilks kept on political ground, and as the resolution was put, proclaiming the meeting's approval of the Federal Clause, and their hope that the utter extinction of slavery would be the result of this contest, I could not help thinking some sentences I had repeated in a different assembly, might have supplemented such a vote, as expressive of our detestation of the crime, and our Christian sympathy and hope that out of such a fiery punishment our American brethren should come chastened, humiliated, penitent and *saved*.

Here let us remember our kindred in America; both North and South. It was a blasting sin they nurtured, and they have sinned against light and knowledge, hence the aggravated intensity of their punishment. It appears almost as if the fearful things recited in the chapter read (21 Luke) were to be literally realised in this bitter brother war; and yet we know, convulsed as America is, reeling as she is in this intoxication of intestine desperation, and bleeding at every pore, she has a goodly band of praying people, and amid the din and carnage of the battle-field, the continuous roar of Artillery, the sack of towns and villages, and the cries of the helpless; with all Hell glorying over a people's ruin and such butchery – in the midst of this horrible tempest stand the servants of God, some deeply humiliated, some like Moses and the patriarchs, they wrestle in prayer; amid blood, smoke, and repine, they *look up*, and cry – "In deserved wrath, O God, do thou remember mercy?" – What mitigation the prayer of the righteous may produce it were impious for us to attempt to search out. Enough for us to know, whether for a home, a locality, or a nation, that *true* prayer breath was never spent in vain; therefore dark and dolesome as is this war we hope still for our brethren across the Atlantic, because we know there are many there who *look up*, and on Heaven the eye of faith is fixed!

Thinking this excellent lecture still left the question open to a remark we did say to a friend after its delivery – impossible as it would be to refute the arguments advanced, what chance would they have against the prejudices, prides and lists enlisted in this brother-conflict: if it be as scripture has it – "the offended brother is harder to be won than the strong city," what shall be said of a people arrayed against a people who are the lineal descendants of the *same* parents; whose language is the *same*; and whose faith is *one*; and whose hostilities are embittered by fraternal recrimination and hatred so maddening and burning that fratricidal blood, in torrents is the Niagara libation which must be poured forth in order to distinguish this stupendous was, and to propagate the remorseless fiend who gloats over this unparalleled exhibition of brethren-animosity.

If you will give insertion to these further remarks, you will oblige, Sir, your obedient servant, G. C., Woburn, Oct. 31.

186

Yet the American War would rage for another 18 months. Having been instrumental in the setting up and chairing Penny Readings, where the locals could come to hear literary extracts and poems read to them for a penny, Castleden was disappointed that not many Woburnites were taking advantage of the offer:

26th December 1863 Bedfordshire Mercury

Woburn - Penny Readings. On Friday, the 18th, the second of the fortnightly penny readings came off. They consisted of an account of a visit to Stratford-on-Avon, the birth place of Shakespeare, by the Rev. Southey. Some original verses on Woburn past and present by Mr. Castleden, and a history of ecclesiastical music in Britain, to the 17th century, by Mr. Gilby. We had no difficulty in hearing and understanding the former and the latter, but some of the portions of the poem were lost to a part of the audience. We heard several quaint and rather humorous verses however, which speak well for the *perceptive* faculties and several moral ones, which drew forth the *preceptive* qualities of the composer. We are very sorry to have to report a less favourable audience in point of numbers than on the previous occasion. It is much regretted that any movement of this kind, which has for its object the cultivation of literary tastes, and the improvement of the townspeople generally, and which is within the reach of all classes, should be allowed to subside though the indifference manifested by the very persons one might reasonably suppose to take most interest in its progress. Surely an apathetic disregard of any means of improvement, in these, days, when mental superiority is the chief passport to individual success in life, and general advancement, as well as key to national prosperity, is a proof that we are behind the age. The next reading is on Friday, January 7th, when we hope the stamp of permanency will be given to this movement by an increased audience, and abundance of talented volunteer readers.

28th December 1863 Bedfordshire Mercury

A Christmas Strain.

Old Time speeds on. Lo, many years
Have vanished with their hopes and fears
Into the ever past!
Still impulse prompts this Christmas time
A short memorial, homeborn, line –
A line which yet may last.

Where home is valued, and where love
Glows, cheers below, and points above;
Where this warm love is found,
To those who meet as kindred dear,
Who cluster round the Christmas cheer,
That home is hallowed ground.

It is not deathless; no, death's woe
Will wither, desolate below –
Will cause the heart's deep sigh.
Still, left ones, loving, yet may smile:
The darkest sorrow may beguile
By looking upon high.

Yes, while sackcloth sign may tell
The last fond look, the last farewell,
And cause grief's sad unrest,
Yet, soothing calm, *above* all fears,
Above this vale, its waste of years,
The loved ones eye are blest.

Christians alone know lasting love,
It blooms below to fruit above:
And Faith, this Christmas time,
Views Home where through the love of Him
Whose *birth* we sing, whose death slow sin.
Reunion is divine.

The Christian's Christmas *merry* is,
His years as *happy* run;
United, *now, past*, and to come,
With *home* above the sun!
There neither change, sin, sorrow, death,
Distress, divide, destroy;
Here, Sabbaths, ending, mingle *there*
In ONE of endless joy.

This unit, this eternal One!

What ken can grasp or scale, -
What art can calculate the sum,
The product of the Tale?
'Tis measureless – 'tis infinite,
To solve no figures tell,
It is GOD'S LIFE – Here mind finds night
In this ineffable! –

Then "merry" be this Christmas time
In every Christian's home;
He loves its boons but in earth's home
He views Heaven's home to come!
To him 'tis happy each new year,
It hears his heart's desire –
'Excelsior' – home, home, I view,
My home is higher – higher.
G. C. Woburn, Beds, December, 1864

Penning an annual Christmas poem had become a tradition that he carried on for many years. The Bedfordshire Times reported on **5th November 1864** *that some time ago, it had been decided to enlarge Woburn Church, and eventually plans had been drawn up for a new church completely. The old church was quickly demolished, but then it was discovered that the plan for the new one was not suitable for the site, as other buildings over-looked it, graves would be disturbed, and the Duke did not like the fact that the chancel would be so overshadowed and dark.*

On the Duke's instruction, a meeting was held to consider a change of site, but only 24 persons attended, and this disappointing number included the Duke's agents, the Churchwardens and clergy, and the architect himself.

Those present were very upset by the destruction of the old church, made worse when the architect refused to show them the plan for the new one. The Duke had arranged for temporary accommodation be provided for church services, but, the general view was "..had the Duke of Bedford commanded his agents to do all in their power to make it as uncomfortable as possible, they could not have carried out his Grace's views more successfully."!

Castleden is listed as being one of the people present at this meeting, and the report concludes, "There was certainly some plain speaking at this meeting on truths untold to absent chiefs, and comments on what had been styled egregious blunders by officials, and a general feeling seemed to prevail that the Duke had been misled, and that a liberal purpose was blemished by lack of fair dealing. It was however, resolved that the Duke's letter should be met with assent, and Woburn waits beneath the gloom of her present desolation for a further step in this remarkable course of Radical Church Reform." The piece is signed off as "From a correspondent", which was almost certainly Castleden.

In the end, the tower of the old church was kept, and a mortuary chapel added to it, and the new church built in Park Street. As a dissenter, it is perhaps surprising that he had chosen to involve himself in the arrangements for the mainstream church in Woburn, seeing as he always so quick to defend dissenting rights…

16: (Inset) *Woburn Old Church, in a print by Grieg, published 1818.*
17: *Woburn New Church. Originally built with a spire on top of the tower, it was found to be unsafe in 1890 and removed. An undated postcard.*

8th April 1865 Bedfordshire Mercury

Illiberality

Sir, - A coincidence prompts me to write a few lines. I learn from your columns that as a vestry meeting at St. Paul's, Bedford, a parishioner was constrained to deliver an admonition on a discourtesy observed towards the dissenters: at our parish meeting I was constrained to do the same. I said, "I must either protest or play false to principles, and I was very sorry that where dissenters had so long been treated with respect I should have to complain." When I was told it was legal, I replied, "I came not to fence words, - was it liberal?" &c.

One sentence more. It is "too bad" in a county town, immortalised by the religious martyr, and at the spot where the memory of the civil martyr is hallowed, for sneaking intolerance to be trying on its hand, and while, nationally, we fight against unjust imposts and uncharitable exclusions, locally we are to be subjected to neglect, not to say insults which sometimes are the more irritating by reason of their contemptibility. Surely, when our pockets are to be visited courtesy should be observed, and not that sharp practice which might be in unison with Stuart times: which might be advised by a Laud, and carried out by a Strafford; but which in the year of grace, 1865, and in the reign of our beloved Queen seems so out of place that I can hardly credit myself in complaining of such a petty annoyance in the town of Bedford and Woburn! and which I trust, most sincerely, the press of this free country will aid to prevent repetition and aggravation.

I remain, Sir, a hater of all bigotry, yours obediently, George Castleden, George Street, Woburn, 5th April.

There were a large number of chapels and faiths in the area, all competing for not only members, but also the money to run them.

6ᵗʰ January 1866 Bedfordshire Mercury

Woburn – Independent Chapel. A debt of about £10 having accrued in the incidental expenses, the committee joined head, hearts, and hands, and the result was a very pleasant tea party in the above chapel on New Year's Day. The chair was taken by the worthy Mayor of Dunstable, who for many years held the office of deacon to this church; the meeting was then energetically and pleasantly addressed by the Revs. W. Cuff, of Ridgmount, J. Dixon, of Dunstable, H. Gee, and J. Andrews, of Woburn. A vote of thanks to Jos. Osborne, Esq., by the latter, seconded by Mr. G. Castleden, brought this "well spent hour" to a close. A suitable hymn and the benediction gave to this evening a good finish. Perhaps the pleasure was enhanced by the minister announcing that so liberally had friends responded that the debt was cleared off; and not only were the committee out of debt, but about £2 in pocket.

A mistake in the name of a notable Woburn Estate employee that Castleden had worked alongside as a boy elicited a correction.

24ᵗʰ November 1866 Bedfordshire Mercury

"Things in America."

Sir, - On "Things in America," by Mr. Howard, there is a misprinted name, "Gannon." Robert Salmon was first employed under Francis, fifth Duke of Bedford; but under the patronage of John, the sixth Duke of Bedford, he perfected his inventions, and in after years, meeting with a thoughtful young man by the name of Hensman, in the Park Farm shops, "scantlings" of some other inventions were first cut which now, in form and use, win a world renown. At Mr. Salmon's death in 1821, a friend wrote a brief memoir, enumerating his useful discoveries, and in the Mortuary Chapel in this town a plain marble slab is affixed, the inscription – a noble tribute by his ducal master – closing with the line, "An honest man's the noblest work of God!"

Mr Salmon was not born in Bedfordshire, though well known in Bedford's street for a quarter of a century. Here his name was a household word for thirty years, and, mouldering under our sky, I give this tributary emendation relative to one local benefaction, and a pioneer in the science of agriculture, which gives England peaceful celebrity among the nations of the earth.

As the dead cannot speak for themselves, permit this voice to rectify a typal error, leaving in the gloom a long acknowledged name, linked with works of past utility and present renown.

I am, Sir, your obedient servant, George Castleden. Woburn, 15th November.

Robert Salmon was an inventor, engineer and architect. Among the seed-drills, ploughs, cultivators and reaping machines he designed or refined, he also found time to design a canal lock, a weighing machine, and a humane mantrap for poachers! Possibly through the Duke's London connections, Woburn had become a supporter of the London City Mission, set up in May 1835, by David Nasmith. This charity sought to support the destitute of London, and encourage them to attend Protestant Christian ministry. They set up Ragged Schools, to give children of the poor some basic free education. Meetings were held in Woburn Town Hall describing their work and appealing for more funds. Castleden was also the secretary of the local branch.

8th December 1866 Bedfordshire Mercury

Woburn – The London City Mission. – In the Town Hall, on the evening of the 29th ult., a public meeting was held under the presidency of Lord Charles J. F. Russell. The meeting was opened by singing; the Rev. S. F. Cumberlege offered prayer. Mr. G. Castleden, the secretary, was then called upon to read the financial statement of this auxiliary, which, helped materially from a Christmas sale by the Lady Charles Russell, amounted to £54. The Rev. T. Scott, Chaplain of the London Hospital, gave a very interesting speech; his lighter anecdotes were appreciated, and as he dwelt on some of the darker chapter of crime, disease, and death, there was some pathos which held the meeting in attention, and through the speech the urgency of supporting such a catholic institution was ably sustained. The Rev. D. Waters, of Hockliffe, followed with some proofs of the working of the society from his own personal knowledge, and then the Rev. J. Patterson, rector of Spitalfields, closed with details illustrative of the work to do; the men who have to do it; and some of the results; and then lamenting a reduction of the missionary staff, the urging was "if possible prevent this," and while heathendom is dark within the sound of Bow bells, throughout these addresses it was – "Come to the help of the Lord," in relation to perishing sinners at home. This was impressed by the noble Chairman in a few feeling words, stimulating to a steady and continued support of a society which, helped by Christians, has a stern battle to fight, and which requires for success a forgetfulness of all "names" and a union of all "sects" to achieve the victory. May such like catholic societies prosper, and be at once the glory and bulwark of our native land. The meeting closed with singing and the benediction. The collection amounted to £5 6s 11d. We were pleased to see from the villages several friends in a full hall. Contributions will be thankfully received for this mission at Bedford, Toddington, Aspley, Biggleswade, Dunstable, Leighton, and Woburn

2ⁿᵈ February 1867 Bedfordshire Mercury

Woburn. New Year's Gift. – On Monday evening, January 28ᵗʰ, and interesting public meeting was held at the Independent Chapel, for the purpose of presenting a purse, containing upwards of £21, to the Rev. J. Andrews, as a New Year's gift from members of the Church, and congregation, and friends in the town and neighbourhood; James Louden, Esq., in the chair. The following resolutions were proposed and seconded in interesting and effective speeches. The Rev. W. Cuff, Ridgmount, proposed, and Mr. G. Castleden seconded, "That this meeting expresses its sympathy with the Rev. J. Andrews as the pastor of this church and congregation and acknowledges with thankfulness to God the measure of success attending his labours amongst them." The Rev. G. Walker, Fenny Stratford, then proposed, and the Rev. J. Inglis, Wootton, seconded, "That this meeting acknowledges with gratitude to God the sound and evangelical preaching of its pastor, the stern defence of truth he has been enabled to make, his catholicity of spirit, and his readiness to assist other ministers and Christians in every good word and work." The Rev. H. Gee then presented a purse to the minister, and in doing so stated that the gift was no act of charity, but the giving back in another form what the givers had received from him, viz., sympathy, help, and affection. The Rev. J. Andrews then replied stating with what surprise and delight he received the gift, and that he accepted it as proof of the sympathy of the givers with him, and their affection for him.

27th April 1867 Bedfordshire Mercury

Tea Meeting. – A well attended and most interesting tea and a public meeting were held in the Independent Chapel, on Good Friday, April 19. About 200 persons sat down to tea. At a public meeting the pastor, the Rev. J. Andrews, took the chair. In the course of his remarks, the chairman spoke of cultivating independent and vigorous thought, of studiously guarding against superstitious reverence of times, persons, and places, and of so employing these holidays as to render them subservient to bodily relaxation and to mental and spiritual improvement. He argued that seasons like the present should furnish opportunities for combating prevalent erroneous views of social life and of religious responsibilities. Such work, devoutly performed, is worship. Large hearted and strong but liberal minded men of past ages, who have trodden similar paths to that which the present generation is now treading, so acted and felt assured that religiously and politically they were honouring God and serving their day and generation; and to them, under God's divine blessing, are largely owing our privileges enjoyed in the present day. Brilliant exploits, observed the speaker, are not expected of all men; but, as the present advanced state of the world in science, commerce, and literature are owing to a devoted, right use of principles existing in the past, so the truth and goodness, by the lowliest as well as the most exalted, must and will, through divine mercy prayerfully obtained, accelerate the oft-vaunted "Good times coming," and ensure to no far distant generations the realisation of the highest good. The Rev. Henry Gee, and the Rev. D. Waters, of Hockliffe, addressed the meeting in a similar strain; the latter, in a very marked manner, expressing his deep regret that many avowedly evangelical men should sanction and maintain rites and formulas of faith, not only of doubtful import, but which, alas! are being only too vigorously worked by many to inculcate Papal rites and dogmas directly antagonistic to the written Word of God, the sacred rights of conscience, and contrary to the faith and practice of the avowedly Protestant Church of Christ throughout the world. Mr. Castleden, after a few remarks, concluded by proposing a hearty vote of thanks to the ladies and other friends who had so admirably contributed to the enjoyment of such a happy and well spent evening.

…and that was the last report by Castleden that I can find for almost two and a half years. Why he stopped is not known. Ill-health perhaps, or a disagreement with the editors? Reports about the events at the chapel at Woburn certainly continued, but it was definitely in another hand, without any recourse to poetry at all. When Castleden did return to the papers, it was to another title, and it was the reminiscing of earlier local times which prompted it:

11th September 1869 Bedfordshire Times

To the Editor of the Bedford Times & Independent

Sir, I would thank your Olney Correspondent for this relique out of the "breeches Bible." Perhaps you will permit another relique from a Testament of olden time; the writing is my father's. Nigh fifty years he was one of Bedfordshire's "illustrious obscure."

"Woburn and Dunstable Branch of The Bible Society May 1812

"Collected at the doors of Woburn Church after a sermon by Legh Richmond, of Turvey, for the British and Foreign Bible Society, July 1812

	£	s.	d.
3 Half-guineas	1	11	6
10 Dollars	2	15	0
39 three-shilling pieces	5	17	0
1 Half-crown	0	2	6
22 Eighteen penny pieces	1	13	0
205 Shillings	10	5	0
112 Sixpences	2	16	0
8 £1 Notes	8	0	0
Copper	1	1	0
	34	1	0

We need a little of this past union in our days, and surely your Olney Correspondent will not object if I close the Woburn bygone with words which were at once the guide, bond, and charm of the local worthies given in your last – "Behold how good and how pleasant it is for brethren to dwell together in unity."

I remain, Sir, your obedient servant, George Castleden, Woburn, 9th September.

III

Letters: 1870 - 1875

Woburn Liberals – Papacy – Bunyan Statue in Bedford – The Wigan Rail Crash – Streets (and fog) of London – The West Haddon Tragedy – Education – Poetry criticism – Gas supply at Woburn – Leighton Buzzard Exhibition – The Sun Ray's Bottling Company – OXY

There is another long wait of over a year until the next 'communicated' news piece which is undoubtedly from him:

13th December 1870 Bedfordshire Times

Woburn - The Bible Society. - The annual meeting of one of our oldest institutions was held on Thursday evening under the presidency of Lord C. J. F. Russell. Though winterly a good audience met in the Town Hall. We could have wished to have seen more of our townsfolk, but from the time and weather we could hardly expect attendance from the villages. The meeting was opened by praise and prayer, and then the financial statement was read by the Rev. S. Cumberlege, and we were pleased to hear, by the great help of the Ladies Association, the figures continue as good as former years. Lord Charles Russell then made an effective speech, toning it with remarks on the "Book of books" and the "Word of God," which may be thought for thought in some minds when the elder advocates of this society sleep. Having ably urged the claims of the Bible, his lordship called upon the Rev. W. Baker, rector of Eversholt, who in a feeling and impressive speech supported this noble society. Mr. G. Castleden on being called upon, used the lines: -

"This is the Judge that ends the strife
Where wit and reason fail,
Our guide to everlasting life
Through Time's dark stormy vale."

And by them keyed a few sentences on the various controversies in the religious world, and referring to this as "a well-spent hour," closed. A cheerful hymn was sung, and then Major Fawkes, the deputation, in personal anecdotal, narrative, and pathetic words held the attention of the audience for nearly an hour; then the Rev. J. Andrews, one of the local secretaries, gave a few sound supportive sentences, and impressing the value of the Word of God, was followed by the Rev. Mr. Dennys, who gave us two or three good catholic sentences, and then the Doxology and Benediction closed these winged pleasant hours of Christian fraternity in this good cause. – Communicated.

In the Spring of the next year, local boards and committees fell under his gaze, and finally his name appeared again:

25th April 1871 Leighton Buzzard Observer

Home Rocks Ahead. To the Editor of the Leighton Buzzard Observer.

Sir, - Our Lady-day storm having sunk in calm, I would ask, through you, two or three questions; and, if some of our authorities will heed them, it may serve truth and save in future neighbours' brawls, which, to some of us, have more the appearance of cunning running than the open fair-play tactics of Englishmen.

Have not our vestries become a mockery, a delusion, and a snare? Have not our Board of Guardians become a centralisation power, which may be dangerous by secrecy and personal permanency? Are there not grounds for grave suspicion in the persistent retention of local offices may there not be pay, patronage, or power? Should the ratepayers abdicate their duties of supervising their monthly bills, directing rates to be collected, and attending to their own business? If it be woe to a house where a servant rules, may it not be perdition to a parish or locality where servant officials bear sole rule?

A neighbour wish for right prompts these questions. I could quote facts in this parish, but, if fair play and open dealing are sought, then these few words may be stimulative; if the opposite policy rule, things may go on from worse to "worser," and, when they come to the worst, the consolation is, 'tis said, "They sometimes mend," May good counsel prevail, and, while we are eagle-eyed relative to Imperial taxation, don't let us be owl-eyed relative to our local rates and expenditure.

Our walls are being used for anonymous writing. Will this mend matters in our injured town? Are we to avoid strife in our county elections, and encourage neighbour ill-blood and treachery in our homes? Open your vestries, and let Englishmen be at liberty to speak, argue, and manfully assert their rights and wrongs; then we shall have a wholesale remedy against secret writing, and an appeal against secret stabbing.

You have aided the ventilation of local matters, and perhaps by the insertion of this it may be thought for thought.

I am, sir, your obedient servant, Geo. Castleden, George Street, Woburn.

30th December 1871 Luton Times

Woburn. Penny Readings. – The fourth of the present season was given on Wednesday evening, the 20th inst., to a very respectable audience, which, however, was not quite as large as on the former occasions. The chair was taken by Mr. G. Castleden, and he introduced the Misses Hall and Brown, who played a duet on the pianoforte, "The great Globe" Quadrilles. This was an excellent performance and was warmly applauded. Mr. John Gilby then read some selections from the earlier volumes of "Chambers," now almost forgotten, but which are of exceeding interest, and were fully appreciated. This was followed by Miss Brown, who sung "Far Away" (Miss Lindsey), which was rapturously encored. W. E. Russell, Esq. then recited "The Execution of Montrose (Dibden) in capital style, and received a deserved encore. Mr. John Gilby then read "Humorous Sketches," which were humorous enough, for they kept the audience in a broad grim from the beginning to end; after which Miss Brown sung "The Winter Night" with charming effect. Then followed a reading by W. E. Russell, Esq., "Miggs," which excited some considerable merriment. Mr. Apps then sung "The Bloom is on the Rye" (Bishop), which was uproariously encored; indeed the juveniles behind seemed in ecstasies. It would be well if some of the committee were to devote a little attention to the repression of the exuberant demonstrations of delight which these occasionally indulge in. Some of the members of the Woburn Harmonic Society, led by Mr. Gilby, then sung "God bless the Prince of Wales" with thrilling effect, the whole audience upstanding and uncovered. At the conclusion of this song the audience thought the entertainment was finished, and about half had left the room before "Erin-go-bragh" Quadrilles (D'Albert), was played; these were received with general applause. "God save the Queen" brought the entertainment to a close. Miss Hall accompanied the songs very cleverly on one of Burling & Burling's grand double-action pianofortes, hired for the occasion from Mr. Sergeant, Woburn, a fine powerful instrument. It is rumoured that the Woburn Harmonic Society are preparing for another concert soon after Christmas.

"...Miss Brown sung 'Far Away'..." reminds me of an old music hall joke. Given that he had already complained about the lack of attendance, the fact that this one had even less than former occasions must have been a disappointment. It would also appear that bored children have misbehaved at performances they don't want to be at for many years, and Mr. Sergeant's harmonium seems to be an early example of what we know as 'product placement'.

There were letters in the January and February Leighton Buzzard Observer, regarding the treatment of the inmates at Woburn Union Workhouse. A Woburn correspondent had given an account of the Christmas Festivities that were enjoyed by the inmates, but an un-named letter writer objected to some of the details. It rumbled on until the beginning of March, when the Editor stepped in and stopped further correspondence. I don't think either party was Castleden, as the language and style are not his, but it is possible that one of the protagonists it could have been him. In the Spring, Francis Russell, the 9th Duke of Bedford, had achieved a peerage, and therefore stood down from being the local MP. A by-election was called, and Francis Bassett stood in his place.

18th June 1872 Bedfordshire Times

The Liberals have opened a Committee Room at The Bedford Arms Hotel, and have formed a committee consisting of Mr. George Castleden (chairman), Mr. E. Sanders (vice-chairman) Messrs. E. Jones, E. Kinns, G. B. Clark, W. A Horton, J. McKay, Jessie Lewis and G. Turney, who have divided the town into districts in order thoroughly canvas the electors on behalf of F. Bassett, Esq., the Liberal Candidate.

The campaign was successful, and Bassett was elected.

BEDFORD ARMS HOTEL, WOBURN, BEDS.
Proprietor: JAS. C. WALKER.

18: The Bedford Arms Hotel, on old postcard stock produced for James Walker (landlord 1901-1909), cunningly re-utilised by a later landlord, Mr. F. Hart, in 1911.

22ⁿᵈ June 1872 Bedfordshire Times

Woburn. A Town meeting was held at Woburn Town Hall on Friday the 14th inst. At 7p.m., convened by public notice, the Rev. S. F. Cumberlege in the chair, to take into consideration, the best means of giving a public reception to their Graces the Duke and Duchess of Bedford on their entry into the town. The Rev. Chairman said he had received a very kind letter from His Grace, who had received notice of the intended meeting from some source, and although he appreciated the kindly feeling of the townspeople yet he wished that there should be no public demonstration. Mr. Sargeant then moved and Mr. G. B. Clarke seconded the following resolution: That this meeting, after hearing the statement of the Rev S. F. Cumberlege, feel much obliged by the expression of good wishes of His Grace the Duke of Bedford for the town of Woburn, and although they feel much regret at the decision of His Grace, yet they feel compelled in accordance with his express wish to relinquish the proposed public reception on the entry of their Graces into Woburn." This resolution was carried unanimously, and after a few words from Mr. Castleden the meeting broke up.

25th June 1872 Leighton Buzzard Observer

Bedfordshire Election

To the Editor of the Leighton Buzzard Observer

Sir, - Permit a line on your Town Hall report. The "few words from Mr. Castleden" consisted, first, of the preliminary words which I thought essential, and, when inserted by the rev. Chairman, the resolution was carried unanimously. Secondly, I had to call for a committee to aid in the forthcoming election of Mr. Bassett. My few words were – "I hope this will be done, and I feel assured the good old cause of civil and religious liberty will ever find, in Woburn, supporters and helpers." My name being in print, please to insert this, and any unintentional ambiguity will be explained.

I remain, sir your obedient servant, George Castleden

29th June 1872 Bedfordshire Mercury

Our Woburn friends have requested us to publish the following letter: To The Rev. John Brown.

Rev. Sir, - Permit an old Noncon. To offer a very short criticism on yours, dated Bunyan Meeting, 19th.

Just now to pen a letter, and publish it through Tory organs is, I venture to say, a feat that our Bedford Noncon. fathers would not have endorsed. In support of this mark two facts, - Mr. Bassett's antecedents have been Liberal enough through life: will he falsify them? Col. Stuart's have been Tory all his days: will he falsify them?

Thin in weighing these merits, as John Bunyan once said, "I hope I know the difference betwixt Christmas and -pie," so I hope to distinguish between the lifelong friend and the consistent foe.

Your education item may be for another day. Mr. Bassett, methinks, is not happy in that paragraph; neither I fancy are some of our great Noncons. who have signed the Round Robin. Our Tory friends have gladly seized it as an election cry. Some of your reasoning I have utters, but, just now, to use this blot to help our hereditary foes is, in my esteem, to play false to our fathers' faith; to wound friends, to aid foes. Ina sentence, in such a struggle I scorn to ignore myself, and I dare not help *principles* which I believe inimical to civil and religious liberty, and which I have fought against all the days of my life.

Your letter may demand a more lengthy reference; time is short; hastily but truly I have written this. You may make what use you please of it; but; to still strife and to state the truth, as an old Nonconformist of the county of Bedford, I leave it for what it is worth, and remain, Rev. Sir,

Yours sincerely, George Castleden, George-street, Woburn, 20th June.

As someone obviously well involved in the local arrangements for the Liberal party campaign for the election, he took very personally some remarks which had criticised their work:

2nd July 1872 Leighton Buzzard Observer

Bedfordshire Election – Woburn. To the Editor of the Leighton Buzzard Observer.

Sir, As Chairman of the committee who at once responded to the appeal made in our Town Hall, permit another line. How we could be "dull" yet "brisk" in our canvass I must leave. Whether our "squibs" were "tame" or not, I must also leave, but we are vain enough to think "Purity and Freedom of Election!!" has done much service, and as Lord Chas. Russell, in a good and telling speech at Ampthill said, "Don't trust the Tories," so we, the Woburn committee, hope in throwing this "squib" into the Tory camp it helped a little in the victory. This cheers the hearts of all who rejoice in this county triumph. If I were to retort upon our Tory friends of whom perchance the reporter is one, I might regret so much talent is hidden, and that they did not, as a committee, give us a *brisk* exhibition of their canvassing abilities; and that our "dull tame squibs" were most enlightened by some of their brilliant fireworks, or other works. Secret criticism may be foul. Open competition is fair and manly. I send one of these same squibs for your inspection and, heartily congratulating my native county on the return of Mr Bassett, in conclusion say of my colleagues they were *brisk* enough not only to poll *every* returned vote, but we also added two or three doubtful, which gave, from our little town, a bumper majority in favour of your worthy neighbour, friend, and now honourable representative.

With thanks, I remain, sir, your obedient servant, George Castleden, George Street, 26th June

Election 'squibs' were the leaflets and poster put up around town, soliciting votes. Some promoted their own party, others ran down the opposition. They usually had the name of the printer and the person who had paid to have it made attached, but some anonymous ones were appearing, which contained claims which could not be tracked back to the issuer.

3rd December 1872 Leighton Buzzard Observer

Local Papacy. To the Editor of the Leighton Buzzard Observer.

Sir, Reading your report of the "Farewell to the Rev. H. Wilkins," I was struck by the thought – surely this proves that Papistical presumption and Papistical persecution may be among us Nonconformists. Let a home fact of long ago tell what I mean. In this room, more than fifty years ago, a stranger sat down to breakfast. His errand was what used to be called "begging for a Chapel." My father had given him names of persons whom he thought would aid, but, as they were parting – "By the bye," my father said, "I take it for granted you are at open Communion." The stranger humblingly replied, "Really we are not," I shall not forget the somewhat righteous stern utterances of "Had I known this, in my conscience I could not have asked you to have breakfasted with me. With the light of Robert Hall's book beaming over you, and still to nurse such darkness verily it is Protestant Dissenters Papacy, and nothing else." It was one of the few occasions in which I saw the geniality of his nature disturbed, and the catholicity of his soul roused to resentment, and, as a son, I deeply lament to find so near to us a fossil relic or specimen of Papacy, cloaked and veiled in high Protestant costume." While bigotry rejoices, Christianity sighs and mourns. Please to serve truth by giving this a space.

I remain, sir, your obedient servant, George Castleden, Nov. 27th 1872.

Castleden's memory of his father's treatment of the man led to swift rebukes by two unidentified writers, one signed as by "A Former Resident", and the other by 'Ryland', which in turn led on a long religious argument in the press.

10th December 1872 Leighton Buzzard Observer

To the Editor of the Leighton Buzzard Observer

Sir, - There appears to exist a considerable amount of misunderstanding concerning the Hockliffe Road Baptist Church, and the resignation of Mr Wilkins, for Mr. Castleden charges the strict Communionists with Papistical presumption, Papistical persecution, bigotry, &c. Allow me to state the principles and practices of strict communion, which have called forth such strong assertions from the Woburn scribe. They believe that Christ, who is the sole lawgiver of His church requires His disciples to be baptised before they partake of the Lord's Supper, and this they profess to learn from the teachings and practices of the Apostles, who were under the direct and special guidance of the Holy Spirit. They also believe that this order cannot be lawfully set aside, and therefore, out of love and reverence for what they consider to be the will and law of Christ, they practice what is called strict communion, and when they are charged with bigotry, & c. The answer is – "While we are anxious to cultivate Christian charity, and to have a hand and heart for all true lovers of the Lord Jesus, yet, in matters pertaining to Christ's Church, we must be governed by what we believe to be His will. Surely Mr. Castleden has mistaken his calling when he comes forth as the champion of Christian charity and advocate of brotherly love, for the manner in which he speaks of those who differ from him will lead most quiet thinking Christian men to fear he has forgotten the nature thereof, and neglected to practice the same. Mr. Castleden speaks of his father as a man of genial and Catholic spirit, and yet tells us he could not have eaten a meal with one of strict Communion views. Evidently his open views did not lead to the practice of Christian benevolence. Your correspondent speaks of strict communion as a fossil relic of the Papacy. Allow me to say that nearly all denominations of Christians have acted on the principle that baptism should precede the Lord's Supper – and among those who have taught this may be named Justin Martyr (who wrote about fifty years after the death of St. John), Baxter, Wall, Marston, Dwight, Doddridge, Fuller and Carey; and among living divines may be mentioned Hugh Stowell Brown, one of the most eloquent of preachers and large-hearted of men; so that the very frequent practice of representing strict communion as being held by only a few narrow-minded, bigoted people is far from the truth. Let me inform your Baptist readers that, taking the Baptist among English-speaking people, the strict communionists are a very large majority. Now, in regard to the second communion service which the Rev. H. Wilkins has established, and to which he stated that it is the rule of the Church over which he was pastor that no alteration shall be made in the practice of the Church, unless *three-fourths* of the members shall vote for such alteration, and , as there were not two-thirds who voted for the course taken by the minister, there was some opposition, for many felt that the rule of the Church had been violated, and some who had strongly advocated open communion thought it should not be done while the rule of three-fourths, which was passed with especial reference to the communion question, stood unrepealed. Surely, however, much as others may differ from us in matters of judgement, it becomes us to treat them in that spirit of charity which thinketh no evil, reminding Mr. Castleden that while strict communionists claim the right of acting according to the dictates of conscience, they cheerfully accord to others the same liberty, unfettered by external control.

Yours truly, Ryland.

Next was a rare admonishment from an Editor:

14ᵗʰ December 1872 Bedfordshire Times

To Correspondents.

G. C., Woburn. – The lines are not suitable for our columns.

We will never know for certain what those lines were, but it is possible they were along the same lines as he had sent to the Leighton Buzzard Observer at almost the same time:

17ᵗʰ December 1872 Leighton Buzzard Observer

Sir, - My notice had been fuller, but I demur to masked writers. I fancy it is only the *secrecy* of writing that would tempt any fair-play scribe to use a legal twist, in order to turn a home fact of laudable wroth against bigotry into a lapse of charity. While I leave your correspondent "Ryland" to square "the spirit of charity" by the dogma of this very straight sect, I refer to "A Former Resident," merely to say- when he solves Pilate's question, "What is truth?" I may try "What sayeth the Scriptures?" relative to this sad chilling separating dispute in the Christian Church, from the times of Justin Martyr, through the ages down to Hugh Stowell Brown. Till then I leave this water feud, and say farewell to all disputants who assume, assert, but who are shrewd enough not to endorse by name. For the coming wishing season I say – may the morn of emancipation soon come, and charity in peace and good will rule from pole to pole.

I remain, sir, your obedient and obliged servant,

George Castleden, George Street, Woburn. December 11ᵗʰ 1872.

24ᵗʰ December 1872 Leighton Buzzard Observer

To the Editor of the Leighton Buzzard Observer

Sir, - In my former letter I had no intention of putting your correspondent, George Castleden, out of temper; but, judging from his last effusion, I fear I have done so. Your correspondent says "I fear it is only *secrecy* of writing that would tempt any fair-play scribe to use a legal twist, &c." Now, I have an impression, though of course it may be a mistaken one, that it was not by the "twist" of my remarks, whether legal or otherwise, but by their *truth* that your correspondent was stung. Certainly, I am not conscience of having at all used any "legal twist," nor does your correspondent afford any proof that I have done so. His "fancy," therefore, as to *secrecy* of writing tempting me to any such thing is, like many other fancies, without foundation in fact. The truth is, no "legal twist" was necessary to turn your correspondents "home fact," into a "lapse of charity," for the simple reason that there was no charity in it. Nor do I think, Mr. Editor, that your correspondent, by his second communication, has made the first any better. I rather think that he has made it worse. He again refers to his unfortunate "home fact" as "laudable wroth" against bigotry." If this language mean anything, it means, without any "legal twist," that strict communionism is bigotry. And if your correspondent intended such an insinuation, *in the interest of charity*, I unhesitatingly tell him not only that he is lamentably deficient in the charity for wh9och he professedly pleads, but also that he has thrown himself into perilous antagonism with an old command, in very Old Book, which saith, "Thou shalt not bear false witness against thy "neighbour." Like your correspondent, "I leave 'Ryland,'" and, perhaps, "Ryland" will be thankful to the pair of us. But I must not "leave" Mr. C. Without reminding him that the first thing to be done with any dogma is not that of squaring it "with the spirit of charity," but with the word of truth. "To the law and the testimony." The wisdom that cometh from above is first pure. Christian charity cannot be promoted by the violation of revealed truth, nor can the belief or practice of anything which revealed truth demands involve the violation of Christian charity. Your correspondent wishes me to solve Pilate's question – what is truth? From my former letter he may gather that I am not at all disposed to go even to Robert Hall for an answer to that inquiry; he may be quite sure, therefore, that I shall not go to Pilate. And if he waits for this question to be solved at Pilate's bar before he *tries* "What sayeth the Scriptures?" the great probability is that the solution to which he attains will be altogether erroneous. He must ask in regard even to "this chilling dispute &c.," first of all – what saith the Scriptures. Only thus can he either know or tell – "what is truth?" Your correspondent seems riled that I write under what he calls a mask. Will he allow me to assure him that he knows as much of me under the designation I have chosen as I know of him under the great name of "George Castleden." No doubt that name represents a person of great importance and power. But even important and powerful persons are not always known to everybody, and among others in the world who have possibly no personal importance will be George Castleden.

Your obedient servant, A Former Resident.

31ˢᵗ **December 1872** Leighton Buzzard Observer

A Correction. To the Editor of the Leighton Buzzard Observer.

Sir, - In the last letter which you did me the kindness to insert, you made me say "among others in the world who have possibly no personal importance will be George Castleden." What I intended to say was, "Among others in the world who have possibly no personal *acquaintance with* George Castleden is" Your obedient servant, A Former Resident.

[The concluding portion of the letter above referred to, in which the mistake occurred, was so illegibly written and crowded together that it would be impossible for anyone but the author to decipher it. If our correspondents desire to avoid the possibility of errors creeping into their productions, it is only reasonable to expect them to write that which can be read. – Ed. L.B.O.]

...and that seemed to end the argument.

The New Year saw an election for the Woburn School Board, and one of the few times that Castleden put his name forward for a vote. However, there were so many names in the hat; he seems to have withdrawn before the voters even had the option to vote for him.

15ᵗʰ **February 1873** Bedfordshire Times

Woburn. School Board. – A meeting of the townspeople – The Rev. R. G. Bulkeley in the chair – was held at the Town Hall, on Tuesday, the 4ᵗʰ inst., to hear the result of the nominations made at the meeting held last week, when the following names were nominated: - The Rev. S. F. Cumberlege, Rev. J. Andrews, Lord C. J. F. Russell, Messrs J. Gilby, Z. Philips, G. Castleden, J. Sargeant, C. Stephenson, and G. B. Clarke. Of this number Lord C. Russell, Mr. C. Stephenson, and Mr. G. Castleden resigned or withdrew their names. The meeting now unanimously agreed upon the nomination of the Rev. S. F. Cumberlege, and the Rev. J. Andrews as representing the two sides of the religious part of the question, and Mr. Z. Philips as representing the acres. In voting for the others, Mr. Gilby received 27 votes, Mr. Sargeant 23, Mr.

G. B. Clarke 13; so that the question may be considered as settled, and the following will form the School Board without the necessity of an election, viz.: - Rev. S. F. Cumberlege, Rev. J. Andrews, Mr. Z. Philips, Mr J. Gilby, Mr. J. Sargeant.

18th March 1873 Leighton Buzzard Observer

PENNY READINGS - MR. PLIMSOLL, M.P. To the Editor of the Leighton Buzzard Observer.

SIR, - Among many, in our Town Hall, I was startled by the revelations from "Our Merchant Seamen" by Mr Plimsoll, M.P., read impressively by Lord Charles Russell. His lordship has done good service by such a reading to the very stamina of our mercantile life; and as the grandson of one who used to "go down to the sea in ships," allow me to ask your service in spreading locally the name of this book, which, dealing in facts stranger than fiction, ought to be known world-wide. A thought struck me while listening to this reading – See the worth of ventilation. Whether in a home, parish, board, company, or Parliament, open discussion is safety. Ventilate, ventilate, ventilate. Dry rot flees. Slander shuts up. Columny cuts away to more congenial shades and lairs. The characteristic of Englishmen is fair play. See their open field pastimes. Secrecy is suspicious; and where *self-interest* is to be served, and cunning secures the evil-minded, be he the peasant, or merchant prince, they are in the way of temptation, and seeming security increases danger.

I hope Mr Plimsoll's book may be read in every market town and village. May Englishmen everywhere learn that to deal treacherously, while it gives *present pay* its righteous penalty, is *ever* ignominious pang. It makes a man "hate himself."

I remain, sir, your obliged servant, George Castleden. Woburn, 14th March.

Over-laden ships were the cause of many sad losses at sea, but the ship-owners had been slow to adopt safer working practices. A social reformer and politician, Samuel Plimsoll, introduced a Bill to get ship-owners to take more responsibility, and to set a maximum load-weight for ships. This was defeated at first, as many M.P.'s were also ship owners, but eventually the Board of Trade was given powers to inspect ships, and the mark on a ship's hull that gives the safe limit to which it can be loaded became known as the 'Plimsoll Line'.

13th May 1873 Leighton Buzzard Observer

Original Poetry. Two Verses on reading Bunyan's Statue, presented by the Duke of Bedford, to be erected on St. Peter's Green

St. Peter's Green, the site where John must stand-
I mean the John of Stuart's bigot day,
The tinker known in every Christian Land!
When John through Bedford trod his tinker way,
Strange dreamer as he was, we dare to say
He never dreamt that, in the future town,
With steam to improve and gas to light it gay,
He, pedestalled by Bedford's Duke, renown
Would be his lot, and immortality his crown.

St. Peter and our John, a worthy pair,
Both sinners once, now safe above earth's strife;
Both left rich love for *Christians all* to share.
Now on the Green, where, in our early life,
We met to settle stern electorial strife,
There John shall sit or stand, and *pilgrims* may
Visit the shrine and think of John's rare wife;
As offerings they may bring, heart tribute pay,
Let bigotry be shamed by Bunyan's Bedford day.

G.C., Woburn, May 10

Here was a subject that would have delighted him on more than one front: a statue celebrating local history, John Bunyan, the world-famous nonconformist Baptist preacher and writer of "Pilgrims Progress", and it was being funded by the Duke of Bedford, all subjects that he would gladly have described in verse on their own, let alone in threes! He chooses to mix the modern innovations of steam and gas into his pen picture of St. Peter's Green, in Bedford, an area he says he knew from earlier election campaigns. He would revisit the statue as a theme when he attended the unveiling of it in June 1874.

Next, he returns to the Woburn School Board, which he had recently resigned from:

27th May 1873 Leighton Buzzard Observer

The Education Question. To the Editor of the Leighton Buzzard Observer.

Sir, - I was pleased to read your report of Earl Russell's speech. Perhaps personal experience may testify to some of the truth. In 1807-08 my father was appointed inspector of our school. He served in that office till he died in 1848. Well do I remember, in that day of the respected John Grant and that generation, the gig coming to fetch him and J. H. Wilton to some of the early annual meetings of the Leighton School. The reading of Bible lessons was part of the system; expounding it was omitted; and, as it regards the "worship of the Book," I suppose this was an invention of some who, seeing in this system the elements of a *true* nation's education, became afraid of their "craft," and, adopting the paralising motto, "divide," they set up Dr. Bell, and then education faction feuds commenced.*   In this town, under the wisdom and liberality of John, sixth Duke of Bedford, this unsectarian system was established; it has had generous aid from the succeeding Dukes, till, as I said as a public meeting, "the voluntary system had failed," and then this old Woburn Institution, pronounced not according to the law, adopted the later code, and by a School Board has passed into newer management. As once its scholar, and filing various offices, my parting wishes are may it be as economical, catholic, and useful as our school of sixty-five years. As a committee, we said our good-bye on the 5th. As the senior member I moved a tributary and respectful resolution, but not seconded, it was dropped. I may trouble you with it at another time, but having travelled the old paths for above three score years, I look at words of the veteran Earl Russell as expository of the past, as advising for the present; and, perhaps, predictive for the future. And as our two towns evidence to its truth, I hope the future may not disappoint the hopes of all for a truly national unsectarian education. If you can spare a space this may tell a local tale; it may prove, if "deep sleep reigned around" in the past, the towns of Leighton and Woburn were awake to the call of education when George the Third said of Joseph Lancaster's system "Here is a good man who is going to teach all the poor boys in my kingdom to read the Bible. Charlotte, you must subscribe." Surely my Tory friends will not object to this authority and approval.

I remain, sir, your obedient and obliged servant, George Castleden, Woburn, 21st May.

*Note – Earl Russell says – "But, unhappily, instead of adopting the principles of the British and Foreign School Society, which comprehended all Protestants, it was thought wise to narrow the subjects of education and the practice of worship."

Another poetical entry appeared for Queen Victoria's birthday:

3rd June 1873 Leighton Buzzard Observer

Original Poetry – The Birthday Peal. Early Morn, 24th May, 1873

Within my parent's room I dream
I hear the morning peal;
Another birthday for our Queen
Those merry sounds reveal.

Cloudless the sun comes o'er yon hill,
I hail the pearly light;
Sol ushers in the newer year
Robed in spring's dresses bright.

Hands, hearts, which gladdened mine, are gone!
I stroll Time's shore alone;
Across the waves oft echoes come
From *friends* who loved the throne.

God bless the Queen in Scotland's home;
Death's cloud still mars the scene;
But, thanks to God, the mother's fame
Shines bright above our Queen.

Health aided in the now past year;
Its months are ever fled!
The Palace home scarce grief has known,
Bright joy has smiled instead.

May coming years still tell the tale
Of Palace happiness;
To the far future, God of love,
The Palace home still bless.

Guard, bless the Queen; her children bless;
Each Royal household bless;
Crown good Prince Albert's kindred all
With lifelong happiness.

While bells now tone the morning air,
These wishes sound sincere;
Three score and more, I pen this prayer,
And hail another year.

If death has struck, and homes must weep
Over life's closing scene
If still I sigh, I, loyal, shout
God save Old England's Queen.

G.C., George Street, Woburn.

If Castleden had been unable to show his wife, Fanny, any affection during their short marriage, he certainly didn't hold back when writing about Queen Victoria. Having had his lyrics sung the Queen outside Woburn Abbey in 1841, he still appears smitten with her 30 years later. This is one of a number of Birthday poems he wrote for her, and he always followed Royal family news, whether it be happy congratulations, or heartfelt commiserations, as the following poem was:

10th June 1873 Leighton Buzzard Observer

Original Poetry. The Death Toll. Prompted by the Accident to the Second Son of the Prince and Princess (Alice) of Hesse.

Most birthday gratulations see
Death's causes night;
A bud of lost humanity
Is crushed and lost from sight

The palace mourns an infant grave!
Homes weep 'neath Death's sad gloom!
Disease and danger carry down
Their myriads to the tomb

Life is a mystery; Death supplies
A mystery dark and lone!
The atom breathes, it lives, it dies
At fourscore, and is gone!

Like to some beauteous tiny thing
On Time's fresh billows lost
This infant price sinks suddenly-
A moment he is lost.

"Those the gods love die young;"* accept
This line, ye parents all;
Secure they wing their cherub home,
No more to fear or *fall*

So Life and Death go hand in hand
Morn's *post* bright joy may tell
Then eve's slow toll sounds o'er the land
A last, a sad farewell.

So different grades of mortals pass;
So generations flee;
While Life exhaustless scorn for death,
And feeds Eternity.

* "Those the gods love die young was said of yore,
And many death do they escape by this;
Youth, hope and love; and as the silent shore
Awaits e'en those who longest miss
The Archer's shaft, perhaps the early grave
Which men weep over may be meant to save."
G.C. George Street, Woburn, 5 June.

Prince Friedrich, of Hesse and by Rhine, was a grandson of Queen Victoria, the son of her daughter, Princess Alice, who had married Louis IV, Grand Duke of Hesse. At the age of two, he had been diagnosed as a haemophiliac, and one day, while playing with his brother, he fell from a bedroom window onto a balustrade 20 feet below. Although he survived the fall, the bleeding could not be stopped and he died some hours later. Death and dying were on Castleden's mind often. He was now 69, and about to reach his 'three score years and ten', which Psalm 90 describes as the usual span of life. For that time, it would have been considered unusually old. Most labourers of the period would have had a far shorter expectation,

but Castleden's fairly sedate life as a clerk, and possibly his regular walks in
the fresh air, seems to have preserved him well. No doubt many of his walks
would have been around Woburn Park.

24th June 1873 Leighton Buzzard Observer

Original Poetry – Lines on the Woburn Park Evergreens and Flowers
- June

"Elysian fields!" my father cries,
Full seventy years and more;
And now his aging son supplies
An echo, nearing to that shore
Where clouds ne'er darken, storms shall wreck no more.

"Elysian fields!" I still will cry,
Now brilliant in their bloom;
But the chill wind and stormy sky
May scatter beauty, soon
This tainted show will deck the floral tomb.

Again these garden evergreens
I stroll, enchanted still;
And as I pace the vernal scene
Or saunter on the hill.
Past memories, sad and glad, the present fill.

A painted bird these tinted hours
Struts round me in my stroll,
And as I scan deer, birds, and flowers,
On this pictorial knoll
I pay park friends now gone the tribute toll!

Yet while we sigh we grateful sing
'Neath Time's sun-setting hours;
And hope for everlasting spring-
The land of deathless flowers,
Unpanged by woe, untouched by earth's wild stours

After another ramble among the aisles of this floral temple, while admiring the forest of flowers, we adored the Hand which had scattered this tinted beauty round, and under the summer blue, the air toned by singing birds – not forgetting the painted peacock – we impressively realised the grand lines –

"To Thee whose Temple is all space,
Whose alter, earth, seas, skies;
One chorus let all beings raise
All Nature's incense rise."

G. C., George Street, Woburn, 19th June

Castleden is mentioned as a mourner at the funeral of Mr. George Rock, aged 60, as he was laid to rest in Woburn churchyard, in the **5th July 1873** *Bedfordshire Times. In national news, while the Bishop of Winchester was out riding with Lord Granville, on route to see Gladstone, his horse stumbled and threw him. He landed on his head, the horse rolled over him, and broke his neck, death being instantaneous. This tragic accident brought forth another poem from Castleden:*

29th July 1873 Leighton Buzzard Observer

Lines on the Death of the Bishop of Winchester – July 19th

Beneath that balmy July noon,
How little did he dream of doom!
A moment, life *in* death!
One instant life with him was high,
Then, in the twinkling of an eye,
Rushed out the vital breath.

The Premier nobles met that day;
The social band, in converse gay,
Prepare their friend to hail:
The messenger of death flew by,
Proclaimed to life its vanity-
That he had told its tale!

"How many sudden fall," so young
In his "night thoughts," has aptly sung,
"but few may fall more sure."
Improve this accident of time:

215

Life is a vapour, yet sublime
Life ever shall endure!

An instant, and he passed from men;
A moment, lo! Where was he then?
This question ushers *night*,
Unless God's Word shall show the way
From murky earth to Heaven's own day,
The Lord of cloudless light.

This solemn close tells a stern truth
To agile age who rival youth:
Press not on life's last power.
At threescore, mark, life's lease is run;
'Tis grace if still your sinking sun
Beams out in rosy hours.

This sudden death in life's strange dream
Shall give a moral to my theme;
To mortals let it teach
The truth – *Prepare to meet your God!*
Soon, late, *all* bow beneath His rod,
This Wilberforce would preach.

A Memory
Once ushered to you Golden Senate Hall
I saw him ride; his figure, portly, tall;
I heard his splendid voice of trumpet tone;
I sat within that gallery alone,
And heard the son of Wilberforce proclaim
His charming eloquence, and with a fame!
He sleeps all lone within the coffin's space;
How silent Death may soon the past erase.
G. C., George Street, Woburn

*Still sometimes not confident enough to add his full name to poetry,
there were also more news pieces from him anonymously:*

12th August 1873 Leighton Buzzard Observer

Woburn. Woburn Independent Chapel Sunday School Holiday. – This holiday came off on Thursday, at the long-frequented and beautiful spot. Nigh fifty years ago, I remember, our then noble John, Duke of Bedford, shaking my father's hand and congratulating him on the happy group around; and to the succeeding dukes we are still indebted for this kindly privilege, in one of the prettiest spots on the domain. While the past has fled, hands and hearts which gladdened ours are gone; yet friends came down in troops, and, had not a painful accident occurred to one of the boys, who falling, broke his leg, this recurrent holiday in the brightness of this weather, the beauty of the scenery, and the happiness of the party, would have been a success. Among our friends we were glad to see a few from Leighton, and we hope, in memory of long past associations, this holiday, all of the olden time, may still receive kindly assistance, and while the busy tribes of men are ever on the wing, the time is ever flying, still may these anniversaries please youth and cheer age; and, as generations flow on, may the instructions of mind and the activity of body combined, add worth and strength to the commonwealth. I ought to add that the liberality of our visitors was increased by a tent collection to help the poor Sheep Lane boy under his heavy misfortune; near upon £2 was promptly and kindly contributed, and any little sum will gratefully serve. – *Communicated.*

A broken leg in those days could mean using crutches for the rest of your life, if the bone was set incorrectly, and with no NHS available, a Doctor had to be paid for his services. The Wigan Rail crash was an early rail disaster, where 13 passengers were killed and 30 injured as a "Tourist Express" derailed and collided with station buildings. It was on the way from London to Scotland, and consisted of 25 coaches. The 16th coach, and all those behind, derailed over some points, and demolished some station buildings. Amazingly, the front portion of the train, which was unaffected, continued on the journey just 90 minutes later! Several of the coaches were private family ones, and there was speculation afterwards that it could have been one of these badly maintained old carriages which contributed the accident, but Castleden blamed progress and science for the accident...

12th August 1873 Leighton Buzzard Observer

Original Poetry – A Railway Rhyme on the late Terrible accident

Mad, science mad, we're lunatic,
Without the waistcoat strait;
The laws of safety found, dismiss,
Trust scientific fate!

Slap, dash, we fly on wings of fire,
The steam is up, we go.
Wild power we drive without the rein,
And oft we plunge in woe.

If day or night, 'tis furious pace,
But, madness, most supreme
In midnight gloom to whirl along
And still of safety dream.

The Wigan waking surely may
Arouse a safer speed;
Or else demented is our day
And steam deaths will succeed.

Awake, or if intoxicate
You will presumptuous sleep,
On danger's line you rush express,
Homes, friends are brought to grief.

This caution, then will close our rhyme,
On this wild pace we warn;
If for this gain you madly sow
You'll reap destruction's storm.

Note – Surely there are *conditions* and *limits* to this wild-fire pace which may lessen the chances of these appalling catastrophes. I see the public are moving relative to this insane speed.

G. C., George Street, Woburn. August 6th

Castleden hated the steam-driven industrial revolution, and always harked back to days in Woburn when the stage-coach was king, but as Queen Victoria had been happy to use the train, her peoples flocked to copy her. The benefits of mobility enabled even the working classes to travel by train (albeit third class) but this seems to have escaped him. Land-based travel accidents before the invention of steam were limited to how many people you could fit into a stage-coach, and even with run-away horses, this was unlikely to incur any great loss of life if it turned over. Castleden did not believe the new powers of steam, gas and later, electricity, could be trusted when harnessed for man's use. He visited his brother in London in August, and found time to pen another poem on a police chase he witnessed:

26th August 1873 Leighton Buzzard Observer

A London Street Scene

'Twas noon; the tide of vast humanity
Came surging on; its billowy roll I heard,
While at the window high I saw its flow.
But now to leave poetic imagery,
I heard a row; irate and angry men
Appeared, and Cabby looked at them perplexed.
"Stop him! Stop him!" sounded down the street;
Blows were exchanged; the crowd increased, and then
Across the road they hurried, vanished – where?
Anon, I saw an energetic man
Who to a "Bobby" in the Bancroft Road
Beckoned all wildly; then the official man
In ruminating mood smelt Mile End prey
Fat, full, and forty, he began to run,
But after dinner this was perilous;
Short, stertuous were his strides; methinks he felt
In jeopardy: perchance he reasoned thus –
"This haste will never do; efficient now,
Her Majesty in me a servant has;
Portly and sound, not to be idly lost
Or periled in a Mile End brawl." He passed,
Erect he passed, each button with himself
On duty stern. His garb was blue, his face
Was red, his body fat, his step was firm;
While as he passed, this vagrant thought was mine –
To caution 'gainst rapidity, and warn
Of dire collapse and sudden doom!
He passed, "a shadow hunting shades!" and then,
"Dressed in a little brief authority,"
He, mingling in life's surging tide, I lost
This man of blue, and with him Humour's cue;
And here I end this fragment tale.
G.C., 21st August 1873.

Although no longer on the Woburn School Board, Castleden was still keen to involve himself in the current education question.

9th September 1873 Leighton Buzzard Observer

19: *A view of London Road, looking north towards the centre of Woburn, from a postcard c.1910.*

Education – Voluntary v. Compulsory. To the Editor of the Leighton Buzzard Observer.

Sir, - A letter from Leighton reached me in London. In it was the following: - Can we settle the great question of the age – 'What are the best means to employ, in order that the people may be universally and efficiently educated?' – and yet the education of the people ought to be free, perfectly unfettered, no ecclesiastical trammels thrown in the way, no dictation, no despotism. Can Bright square up all this, and out of our discords bring forth harmony? I venture a short answer to your enquiring, thoughtful townsmen, and perhaps you may serve this question locally, by giving us a space in the Observer. Methinks all these items were met by Joseph Lancaster's system. I give as my proofs Woburn, Tavistock, Leighton Buzzard, and I venture to assert this system, founded on the Catholic motto – "Think, let think." might have served the Isle, might have been *truly* national; but Party v. Bigotry frowned, and said no; and, perchance, the present mess arises from an unwise attempt to propitiate these incorrigibles, and slighting the *proven facts* of our fathers' wisdom and justice, a retributive process seems to punish. May it convince. In the present jeopardy in which our persons, consciences, and pockets are placed, we have a pertinent proof that the forsaking of the beaten path of truth and right, I order to "make things pleasant," often leads to lamentable conclusions. Could our yielding statesmen have said (ay, followed the noble example of that patriot, John, Duke of Bedford), the Columbus of education we support, methinks, honour would have been paid to the lone Englishman, and most certainly it would have prevented the forsaking of the plain path, and the plunging into a labyrinth which, me-thinks neither the eloquent Prime Minister, Mr Forster, nor the great Tribune will be able to find the extricating clue for the puzzled, demoralised ranks of Liberals. I hope the clue may soon be found.

I remain, sir, your obliged servant, George Castleden. George Street, Woburn, 3rd Sept.

Note – A Woburn fact may add interest and touch to this one of my last on education. A late worthy townsman, Henry T. Wolfe, told me, "Well do I remember one morning seeing the Duke of Bedford and Earl --- in their white coats come into our dingy coal shed in St. George's Fields, and after a talk with the master they come amongst us boys, said some kind words, then leaving some coin for our gratification, they left a life memory to us, the first school boys of Sir Joseph Lancaster." And when both of us sat as aged men in our School Committee we have thought of

"The school-boy spot

We ne'er forget, tho' often there forgot"-

And with departed neighbours have gratefully called back this almost forgotten pioneer in the field of education. After writing this I read "Mr Gladstone on School Boards;" in the *Times*, 18th Aug. Here the Prime Minister leans to the voluntary system. Why then the compulsory, with the irritating addition of denominational teaching, and the aggravation that all are to pay for the promulgation of what conscience in many objects to.

"Let Caesar's due be ever paid

To Caesar and his throne;

But conscience and souls were made

To be the Lord's alone."

The 'Bright' mentioned was John Bright, M.P. for Manchester. A Liberal and Radical, he was a famous orator, he campaigned for better schools, and is said to have coined the phrase "flogging a dead horse", over the apathy of the Government in reforming democratic representation. Not every answer to Castleden's letters was a disagreement...

16th September 1873 Leighton Buzzard Observer

Education – Voluntary and Compulsory. To the Editor of the Leighton Buzzard Observer.

Sir, - I believe your correspondent, G. Castleden, is quite correct in his high opinion of the British School system. The object of that system ever has been that all should be instructed, irrespective of age, condition, creed, or party; and, if the Government had acted according to *its principles*, as well as taken it for its *model*, a really national education could have been obtained, with the help of School Boards, *where needed*, and the people would have had no ecclesiastical trammels thrown in their way. It is the *Shibboleth* of first one party and then another which has been the bane of so many districts throughout the land. The education of the people, to be popular, must be free. Mrs. Grimshawe, in her excellent address on Friday, the 5th inst. At Aspley, says, "I believe the present confusion will never cease until education is free and the legal inheritance of the whole nation." We are aware that, by maintaining the free and perfectly unshackled education of the people, we are giving offence to many, but I will not occupy your space by writing upon a subject which is now continually discussed by the greatest men of the age. Just allow me to say, in answer to the last question in Mr. Castleden's letter – "Can Bright square up all this, and out of our discord bring forth harmony?" that I believe if Mr. John Bright's health will enable him to enter into the subject with that solidarity of thought, sagacity of judgement, and firmness of purpose which has always characterised him, aided by effectual help from Liberals, he will accomplish the arduous work of harmonising the extreme opinions of different parties.

I remain, sir, yours obediently, C.B.S.

23rd September 1873 Leighton Buzzard Observer

Education – Voluntary and Compulsory. To the Editor of the Leighton Buzzard Observer.

Sir, - Your correspondent "C.B.S." and myself so well agree upon a truly national education that I will not intrude upon your columns further than by saying, may his hopeful predictive answer have a full and satisfactory accomplishment. But in looking over the *Bedford Times* I found a letter from the Rev. George Maule, on the Ampthill meeting. I copy part of it to enforce our argument.

"Why should I, as a clergyman of the Church of England, be compelled to put aside her Prayer Book when I enter my schools? Why should I no longer be permitted to instruct the children in the catechism which (whatever others may think) all intelligent churchmen regard as an admirable summary of the principles of the doctrines of Christ."

I ask, does not this explain the controversy, and does not the rev. Gentlemen give us a conclusive answer when he writes, "my schools?"

Surely in this divided country on religious matters no truly national education can be organised if such like conditions rule. How would Churchmen like our catechisms? Our fathers struggled for an open, unsectarian school. Methinks the Lancasterian, afterwards called the British, came highest to the true model, but "my schools" mar this useful, catholic, and just system.

"If you tax all for a certain object all should have a voice" is a rule just, and empathically applicable in this education tax. Persons, pockets, and consciences suffer by this rate. If not a sad blunder by the Liberals, I would have thought it was the craftiest and the most successful invasion bigotry ever made at the pockets of an Englishman and the rights of an Englishman's conscience.

It is a retrograde move by which our mental nurseries are put under denominational training, and, whether it is high Romanism or high Ritualism, *Protestation is obliged to pay*!! This, surely, to use an oft-quoted saying, "is too bad."

I remain, sir, your obliged servant, George Castleden, Woburn, Sept. 17th, 1873.

18th October 1873 Bedfordshire Mercury

Ridgmount. Baptist Chapel. – On Sunday last the anniversary sermons in connection with the settlement of the present minister, the Rev. W. Hillier, Mus. Doc., were held in this place. The Rev. D. Mace, of Stotfold, preached two excellent sermons to good congregations. On Monday evening a public tea was provided, to which a goodly number did ample justice, after which a public meeting was held the pastor in the chair. The chairman opened the business by giving a pleasant review of the work of the year, including the ordinary church work and the duties entailed by the social and secular lectures on every day subject; the latter embracing allusions to the able lecture by Dr. Burns on his trip across the American Continent, which was fully reported in these columns, the minister's own addresses on Music, and his still more recent but not less attractive one on Love, Courtship, and Marriage, all of which the people held in lively remembrance. The Rev. George Walker followed with an address on the Spiritual life of the church, and the Rev. J. H. Readman, with one on the Bible, in the course of which he invited his young hearers to attend the Bible Class which Mr. Hillier presided over; they were now studying the life of Christ in a systematic way, on the principle of Mimpriss, the additional attraction of a large and beautiful map rendering the classes very instructive and entertaining. Mr.

George Castleden of Woburn, gave a history of the church connected with which they were then meeting; he saw the old chapel pulled down, and the present one erected in 1811, and in it he heard the voice of Robert Hall, the veteran orator, and in later days the familiar voice of Mr. Spurgeon, and many others, but never before had he heard of a pastor who was a Director of Music, and who could play on twenty different instruments: surely such an one would live in perfect harmony with his people, and he was glad to hear that such was so. Other speakers followed, all referring to the ability and earnestness of the pastor. The choir added much to the enjoyment of the meeting, which was brought to a close by the doxology and benediction.

It is interesting to note that some Woburnites travelled all the way to London to visit a cattle show. Not that they saw very much when they got there...

23rd December 1873 Leighton Buzzard Observer
London's Fog! A Memory of the Cattle Show (1873).

From Bedfordshire and other shires
The farmers went to see
Fat oxen, sheep, pigs, cattle, all
Of London's rivalry.

East, west, north, south, they travelled up,
They found a fog in town
Which darkened all the country folk
And bade them hasten down.

The fog was here, the fog was there,
The fog was everywhere;
Bucolic men coughed, sneezed and wheezed,
While some did really – dare

To go to merry Islington
To see what couldn't be seen;
This was a sight which o'en repaired
Now optic powers, I ween

But still they dined, and many wined,

In fog obscurity;
They told on rail the funny tale,
Of what they didn't see

At home, on farm, or village green,
This fog of seventy-three,
May, chronologic, mark this show,
And be a memory.

Our Christmas wish, when next to town
They go to see the show,
The sun may shine, and all may dine,
Without the foggy woe

So country rhyme this Christmas time,
May bid our friends remember
Prize cattle slain, the show so vain
In London's fog, December.
G.C.

This unusually thick and persistent coal-smoke-saturated fog, which enveloped the city for days, caused at least 268 deaths from bronchitis. The annual cattle show at Smithfield market was ruined, with the "fat cattle... panting and coughing", so much that many of the animals collapsed and died. Later the term 'smog' was coined for it. Castleden ended the year with another of his Christmas poems, which sadly lacks some of the local characters and locations that his previous seasonal work had included.

30ᵗʰ **December 1873** Leighton Buzzard Observer

A Christmas Song.

'Tis Christmas morn, the carol girls
Are singing at my door;
Now let me join a note and tell
The flight of one year more.

'Tis gone! inexorably gone,
With all its joy and pain;
Its births and deaths in register
Eternally remain.

225

'Tis past! Past memories fill the brain –
Forms, faces ever gone!
Along the valley, dark, I stroll
And feel almost alone.

Yet pleasant tokens fall around,
To illumine darkening years;
Kind words and deeds in truth abound
To cheer this vale of tears.

And so another year we view,
Joined to the one now fled;
We say to *this* a long farewell,
And welcome *that* instead.

For neighbours all our wish to come,
Be home, goodwill, and peace;
If Death should strike, may Home be found
Where sin and sorrow cease.

May Bethl'am's birthday gild our land
With Heaven's own summer light;
The Sun of Righteousness shine forth,
And chase all heathen night.
Woburn, G.C.

20th January 1874 Leighton Buzzard Observer

The West Haddon Tragedy. To the Editor of the Leighton Buzzard Observer.

Sir, - One of my last public citizen duties was as grand juryman, at Bedford. Our foreman was your late worthy townsman, Joseph Procter. Part of our business was a presentment relative to an altercation from fees for a stipulated sum to the county coroners. We had a long day's work, and at the close of this came on. Rising, Mr. Procter said – "Gentlemen, my opinion is we should do nothing to weaken this protective law. I would rather have six useless inquests held than omit one which should be held." This opinion we at once endorsed. What an illustration of this wise remark is the home tragedy in Northamptonshire. A gentlemen breaking his neck in the hunting field, or Pat slipping off the ladder, or the plunge, shot, or knife, and over these deaths, which are patent, the inquest, is held but our house crimes may be made "snug as murder." "all honour to gossip," this foul murder did "out." The victim, under the doctor's certificate, had been buried a month; the grave, apparently, sealed secrecy. Gossip was the Nemesis. I trust such a *fact* may not be lost on our authorities, that our homes may be saved from these perils, and in these temptations may the facilities for chamber murder be lessened. Medical men may be timid when placed in the very trying position of detectives in these home murders, and I would relieve them of the terrible responsibility of certifying deaths which may be, by medical rule, suspicious. At any rate in these *bed deaths* that responsibility ought to be shared by a plurality of certifiers. Our fathers were not so daft as some of us imagine, and, when they insisted on a strict "Crownersquest," they did it because they knew "the heart of man is deceitful above all things and desperately wicked." Since writing this I have read your leader. That takes the indulgent view of the suicide. If so, might not that have been prevented by a prompt inquest? *But if* the torture of conscience drove to this self murder, surely the *moral* of such swift retribution should *save* and *warn*. Please to give this a local circulation.

I remain, sir, your obliged servant,

George Castleden, Woburn, 14th January, 1874.

The West Haddon Tragedy that Castleden referred to in the title of his letter, was a case that caused much sensation at the time. A 78-year old lady, Mrs. Gulliver, who had been unwell for some time, passed away after a few days of severe illness. One of the doctors at her inquest suggested that he believed a noxious substance could have been administered to her just before her death, but that he could find no trace of it in her system. This caused enough controversy for her body to be exhumed a month after her burial, and another autopsy to be performed. Her niece, a Mrs. Waters, who had visited her stricken aunt, had made her some tea, containing the medicine which had been left for the patient by her doctor. She also put some eau de Cologne on the woman, who asked for some to be put in her mouth. After checking with the doctor, who was present, that it would be alright, she did so. There were also tiny traces of Morphia in Mrs. Gulliver's system, but not enough to have killed her. The new inquest decided that a poison had been administered, and applied for a warrant for the arrest of Mrs. Waters, who was present in the building where the inquest was taking place. Even before the end of the inquest, Mr. Waters rushed into the room, and said that his wife was dying. Despite receiving medical assistance, she passed away, and her inquest decided she had poisoned herself. As a suicide, she was buried without clergy, within three hours. The British Medical Journal then examined the case, and pronounced that there had been no poisoning of Mrs. Gulliver, and the death of Mrs. Waters had been brought on by the false accusation of murder. "Two more monstrous verdicts never were delivered", they believed. Hence Castleden's request that bed-deaths be examined by more than one certifier, to avoid such mistakes in the future.

The Duke of Edinburgh in 1874 was Alfred, the second son of Queen Victoria. He had been chosen in a referendum to succeed King Otto of Greece in 1862, but Queen Victoria blocked the move, as they had plans for him to succeed in the Duchy of Saxe-Coberg. He was a naval officer, and commanded his own ship, The Galatea, and made the first visit of a royal family member to Australia in 1867. He was welcomed warmly, although on his second visit, a year later, there was an attempt on his life! His marriage to Grand Duchess Maria Alexandrovna of Russia caused problems with Royal protocol, as Queen Victoria's daughter had married into the Danish Royal family, which the Tsar consider beneath his own, leading to difficulties in the Royal pecking order of who should yield to who!

3ʳᵈ February 1874 Leighton Buzzard Observer

Loyal Verses. On the Marriage of H.R.H. The Duke of Edinburgh to the Grand Duchess Marie of Russia.

Right Royal match. Predictive sight may scan
The future prospects of this plighted pair;
While present hope predicts good will to man,
A union happy, may it well prepair
Each realm for peace no discord may impare.
A joyful wedding, may its bliss remain
A long repeated tale on Europe's air;
And on this morn of Queen Victoria's reign
May health, love, joy, attend, bedeck the bridal train.

To all obscure, an Englishman may sing
Upon this English-Russian marriage day;
His note truth-toned, if drooping is his wing.
Court-bards may soar and sound the faultless lay,
And on the harp's gold strings the scene essay;
Mine be a memory-note along home's way,

Which, musical, may sound in Spenser's verse
Of good Prince Albert's Alfred's marriage day –
One wish, the cup of joy a bumper cup may stay.

A day of boon, a day of memory's gloom
Is now this January happy day;
It joins the alter to the darksome tomb –
A brother's tribute to the dead I pay!
Still while I sigh smiles sun the bridal way;
So, chequered are th' events beneath the sun;
'Tis light and shade! The mournful and the gay!
God bless the Royal pair, our prayer shall run,
A life of love be their's till time with them is done.

Queen of our Isle! May this new happiness
Exhilarate thy heart and balm it too;
May God's best blessing all thy children bless.
This was our early wish 'neath summer's blue,
Again we hymn this prayer in winter's hue.
Good bye to loyal themes, age perhaps may say;
* On "forty-one" I cast a backward view,
Though nigh forgot that July Woburn day,
And prince, dukes, sieges, friends have melted all away!

Note – With a felicitous passage from Dean Stanley's Petersburgh sermon, coincident with our first thought, I may close my rhyme,

"We are on the eve of a nuptial alliance, such as has not taken place for more than eight hundred years in European history. The last marriage between the Royal Families of England and Russia was far away in the dim twilight of the twelve century, when the ablest and best of the earliest princes of Muscovy, Vladimir wooed and won the hand of the Princess Gytha, the daughter of Harold, the last of the Saxon kings. Could either monarch then have foreseen the world-wide progress which each people would make before another prince and another princess of either realm should cement by a sacred family union the amity of the two countries!"

Then Russia wooed and won; eight hundred years
Comprise infinitude of smiles and tears;
These all have vanished, died away!
Now England's – Scotland's Duke reverses fame,

He woos and wins the Royal Russian Dame.
All hail to life's long happy day.
G.C. George Street, Woburn, Beds, 23rd January.
*This refers to the Royal visit paid to Woburn Abbey.

He then switched back to more local affairs, and the recent election.

17th **February 1874** Leighton Buzzard Observer
A Last Election Rhyme 1874.

If reminiscent now I sing,
And o'er the past awhile I wing –
I mean, on mind, to soar –
Election conflicts of the past
Upon mind's vision lingering last
As I approach the shore

Of that dark, silent, depthless tide
Which rolls o'er poverty and pride,
Where prince and peasant hide –
On, sweeping on, from Adam's day
Till at last son the debt shall pay
In its remorseless tide.

Yet ere we sink – are swept away,
How chequered oft the mortal way,
We many parts essay;
As actors, 'neath time's varied skies,
New characters, new scenes arise,
Ere "exit" calls life's play.

Now aging in my natal town,
Which erst stood high in Whig renown
I fought 'neath men of might.
They cast religious gives aside,
They curbed despotic Tory pride,
And gave us day for night.

'Twas "twenty-six," the battle keen
Between Lord Tavistock, Macqueen;
We fought it to the close.
Since then, in our election fame,
Russell and Pym, Sir Peter Payne,
Have led against our foes.

And now I work with newer men;
This novel age I don't condemn,
I only, filial, say,
Be grateful that our fathers fought –
Won victories which blessing brought
Down to our modern day.

The "test" they broke, they won "Reform,"
They forced from foes free trade in corn,
And many measures more;
Then Tories tried their *mystic* hand,
They "dished the Whigs," surprised the land,
And now, in seventy-four,

A last election I may see;
The Whigs and Tories both agree
It is an English fight;
Fair play, we hope, on either side
The quarrel now may well decide –
Establish what is right.

And if the Tories further will
But educate, perhaps measures still
All Liberals may surprise;
And the Lowe surplus still may tell
Disraeli's friends, if they look well
It yet may higher rise.

Be this or not the future case,
I hope in this election race
For Britain's future weal;
Of Bedfordshire, I passing say,

While Gilpin, Bassett, serve the day
Each man his faith will seal.

Now, perhaps, upon the edge of life
I say goodbye to party strife,
I've know it dark, severe;
And yet from controversy may
Break out beams of brighter day
To light point, save and cheer

Thanks, thanks for this Ashantee "win;"
If Whigs are out and Tories in
We march with colours flying.
"Trust not the Tories," still we must
To them the money surplus trust,
And this is rather trying.

Still may the Tories live and learn
From bygone errors to return
And govern right and pure;
"Shine, mighty God, on Briton shine,"
This prayer shall close election rhyme,
May truth and peace endure.

A solemn verse shall *key* my theme;
Friends, foes, pass on in life's strange dream;
Friends, foes, fall in the tomb!
A little day time's noise is done,
Friends, foes, beneath the circling sun
Must sink in death's *still gloom.*

Notes –While writing this rhyme Baron Rothschild dies! And I hear of the sudden death of a fellow worker in the last election, and with whom in the street, we had a passing word on the present not a week ago. Of this election may it not be written the *secrecy* of the Ballot, the libellous cry of the Bible, and the potency of beer have combined and won a victory which *all* Liberals will regret, and which may be rendered keener by the thought that revenge and ingratitude have aided to stab a Government which deserved a better fate. Who was it that wrote – "Beware – public favour often is a public cheat."

G.C., George Street, Woburn, February.

Woburn continues their fundraising for the London City Mission.

10ᵗʰ March 1874 Leighton Buzzard Observer

Woburn – London City Mission. A public meeting under the presidency of Lord C. J. F. Russell, in aid of this home mission, was held in the Town Hall on Tuesday evening last. The meeting was opened by praise and prayer, after which Mr. G. Castleden was called upon to read the financial statement of the past year. Lord Charles Russell then gave an explanatory speech relative to the mission and to the extent and object. His lordship interspersed some personal reminiscences, graphic and interesting, and after urging its importance, closed his address by reading "Come and help," written by a friend:-

> Oh come and help – 'tis London's cry,
> Come, help its sin and woe;
> 'Tis mercy's call; your aid supply,
> And mercy you shall know.
>
> Yes, come and help; the misses lie
> Unseen, unsaved, unknown;
> Oh, aid this London Mission cry,
> To hush dark misery's groan.
>
> Or else, perchance, this fester may
> Envenomed grow and spread;
> Rank, properties, and homes some day
> In Crime's vile slough be led.
>
> Ay, come and help while sorrows last,
> Or sin's dark billows roll;
> "Well done" shall be the benison
> To clear and light your soul.

Then the Rev. H. Southey spoke a few words in support of the society, and, finishing with a humorous anecdote, another hymn, commencing - "He who with generous pity glows," was gratefully sung by the audience of a crowded room; and then the Deputation, Mr Grimmett, commenced a speech which kept his hearers in pleasing thrall for an hour and a half. As the missionary to the cabmen, he told some London day and night tales with great pathos, mingled with humour. Explanatory of the mission, exhortive of its support, this appeal became energetic at times, and truly eloquent, inasmuch as coming from the heart it went to the heart of many, and, when the noble chairman said he would not weaken its effect by any further observations, due tribute was given. And so a well-spent hour was closed by singing the Doxology, after which the Benediction was pronounced by the worthy incumbent.

The collection amounted to £4 11s 9d.

Lord Russell's closing poem "by a friend" has all the hallmarks of being penned by Castleden. The new Royal couple had returned from their honeymoon, which gave Castleden an excuse to write a poem:

17th March 1874 Leighton Buzzard Observer

A Countryman's Welcome – To the Home-Coming of their Royal Highnesses The Duke and Duchess of Edinburgh. March 7th, 1874.

Fair lady from the North, we shout
A welcome to our Isle;
And if the skies be cloudy, clear,
Thy sunshine be our smile.

Fair bride of Sailor Alfred's day,
For thee this prayer shall rise –
O may thy British home be blessed,
And long, 'neath England's skies.

May joys increase and love abound,
Nor happiness decay
Till long, long years have rolled their round,
And love must pass away!

Yes, Princely Pair, our loyal shout
Speaks a heart welcome pure;
And may God's blessing on both rest,
Then blessings shall endure.

Now, while far off your land of birth,
Fair lady, may you find

Sweet compensation on our Isle,
For home-joys left behind.

On the Queen mother's heart may long
Affection's sunshine fall,
And in her children's happiness
Time's happier hours recall.

And, mystic, smiling o'er the scene
In Windsor's Royal towers,
The sainted father still may bless
Prince Alfred's happy hours.

Again I sing, obscure, unknown
I pen this loyal theme –
God bless good Albert's children, all;
God save our worthy Queen.

Note. All the congratulations and public rejoicings will be recorded in the chronicles relative to this Royal home-coming. Court bards will courtly sing. But as in our park these thoughts, as spring's first shoots, burst into words, I leave them, and if fruit from an aged tree, then may I say in the witchery of song I have been beguiled, and if I please others then for friendly officers in the shape of material fruit, gratitude's return shall be a present of mental fruit, which, "such as it is" – the words of a native wit – pray, good readers, accept.

G.C., George Street, Woburn, March 12.

Next, he took up the pen to reply to a letter writer from the week before, who had signed themselves as "Liberal".

24<u>th</u> **March 1874** Leighton Buzzard Observer

The General Election – The Ballot. To the Editor of the Leighton Buzzard Observer.

Sir,- Permit a few words on the letter by your correspondent, "Liberal." Never over fond of the Ballot, that being adopted, it appears to me the whole expensive machinery of agents, committees, and canvassers should be consigned to the past. I illustrate what I mean by a personal reference. From 1826 I have been engaged in our elections. Open in my politics, they have been patent. Now, were a friend to come and ask me how I intend to vote I should smile; if a foe, I might tell him to mind his own business. Surely for candidates and voters it was a mistake to do away with solicitation. The views of candidates, publicly given, should be sufficient. Paid agencies should be abrogated, canvassing should be dismissed, or, with the Ballot, it may conduce and double distilled hypocrisy. It may be seen while open voting has slain its tens of thousands, I, for one, shall think the sun of England is on the decline when Englishmen dare no longer look each other in the face and openly avow their opinions. Gag free speech, it may be detrimental to a locality; to a nation ominous of ruin. We want the moral sanitary officer to tell us, while *ventilation* may expose as to peril- which all can see and remedy, *secrecy* initiates the dryrot which, unseen, works insidiously, treacherously ruinously. "The Ballot has introduced new conditions," as your correspondent states. I venture to meet those conditions in a way by which Englishmen should neither be degraded by the opportunity offered to play traitor, and at the same time, affording this selfish security – "Thou canst not say I did it!"

I remain, Sir, your obliged servant, George Castleden, Woburn, 18 March.

The Licensing Act of 1872, brought forward by the then Home Secretary, Henry Bruce, had sought to curb drinking and the resultant drunkards, The system of licensing was to be overhauled, and it attempted to give some control given back to local courts, but with little support from the powerful brewery lobbyists, it was brought in, but much watered down (if you'll excuse the pun...) from the original ideas put forward. However, it set opening hours, banned sales to children, addressed adulteration of beer and enshrined fines for drunkenness.

31st March 1874 Leighton Buzzard Observer

The General Election – Beer. To the Editor of the Leighton Buzzard Observer.

Sir,- Beer was potential in the last election. Whether beer should be so strong may be a question for Parliament to determine. From publicans I have heard praise of Mr. Bruce's bill. It limits nocturnal profligacy, and gives the "public" the features of home. In that bill there were defects; perhaps it trenched on the liberty of the subject; hence affront was taken, animosity was shown, and, under the Ballot, beer had a sweet revenge. As a portion of the common weal, the licensed victuallers are a united body; their influence is great; add agency, canvassing, and, to use a sporting phrase, the odds are against any candidate they do not favour. Whether this influence may keep the balance *rightly* adjusted, the future may tell. I have been led into this train of thought after reading in your paper the letter signed "Liberal" on the late election. That it was a *surprising* defeat all admit. If the Liberal party accept it as final, all inquiry relative to this rout is idle; but, while I might tell the former "fields were won," I feel inclined to show how, perchance, this has been lost by the Ballot beer, and, charge not irreverence when I add, the election cry of "kicking the bible out of school." These B's may have been very influential against the party who won for us the vantage ground on which they were attacked and beaten. Hence, as an old Liberal, I sigh, and, while thankful for good measures from fees, say truly –

"I greatly venerate all recent glories,

But wish they were not owing to the Tories."

I remain, sir, your obedient servant, George Castleden, Woburn, 27ᵗʰ March.

In the campaigning of John Bright, Castleden could see a kindred spirit to his thoughts on a free education, unencumbered by religious funding.

19ᵗʰ May 1874 Leighton Buzzard Observer

Education. To the Editor of the Leighton Buzzard Observer

Sir,- Mr Bright writes – "The time may come, thought I can scarcely hope to live to see it, when there will be less grasping for power on the part of the professed ministers of Christ," &c. This I read in London; may I trouble you with two or three questions on this sad dispute? Did not a lone man propound and establish a system of education which might have served the Isle if "professed ministers of Christ" had not been jealous and bigoted? Did not the Duke of Bedford and others nobly support and munificently promote this education? Did not my father serve it as an inspector for forty years? And did not this model school continue, prosper, and meet every need of a people's education, and *no* religious difficulty haunted it? These questions, by truth, are answered in the affirmative; then, I say, as a nation, we had the secret of a just education. If we play false to it, are we to feel surprised at a punishment which plunges into perplexity, and taxes with a pecuniary penalty, and which is weighted by an invasion of the rights of conscience. Verily, if this be not acting out nationally the fable of the dog and the shadow, I know not what it is, and it serves us right.

I could sign this, "A Lancasterian School-boy, all of the olden time," but I verify it, sir, by remaining your obedient servant, George Castleden.

The Lancastrian education system was named after Joseph Lancaster. He developed a "mutual instruction" method where brighter pupils were engaged to assist in teaching the less able ones. This reduced costs, and enabled class sizes to be larger. He went as far as to design ideal classroom layouts to be used, itemising how high the master's desk should be, and how wide the gaps between desks should be. This conformed to the Victorian view that everything could be distilled down to an ideal version, in a replicateable system, and then rolled out across the world. After the marriage of Russian Grand Duchess Maria Alexandrovna to the English Duke of Edinburgh, the Tsar had come to visit England in May 1874 to alleviate his daughter's homesickness. Castleden felt moved to write a poem on his return home again. This came 19 years after Castleden had written a poem to the paper celebrating the death of a Russian Tsar!

<u>26th May 1874</u> Leighton Buzzard Observer

A May Rhyme.

O, chilly May; O, chilly May,
Turn, turn your frowning face away;
O give us smiling weather;
For now 'tis teasing, rather freezing;
In colds, catarrhs, coughing, sneezing,
Friends recreate together.

Perhaps, Springtide lassie, 'tis the Czar,
Who comes from polar scenes afar
To scent our flowery air;
Perhaps, to win the Imperial smile,
You coldly frown, and o'er the Isle
Scatter spring-winter fair.

To-day he leaves our Gravesend shore;
Speed, speed his ship, return once more,
Miss May, with winsome smile;
Let balmy sunbeams warm the day
And he not glittering, icy May,
But, flower crowned, cheer our Isle.

Then when the Czar has sped away
We'll hail thee, England's Queen of May;
And, for the coming year,
May fruitfulness and peace increase,
Taxes, and rates, and colds decrease,

Coals, gas, be not so dear.
G.C., Woburn 21st May.

This year, the birthday of Queen Victoria fell on the Whitsun and a Sabbath, a rare combination that Castleden pointed out in print.

2nd June 1874 Leighton Buzzard Observer

A Whitsun Sabbath – Birthday Memory, 1874.

The morning peal again reveals
How time steals on; while life it steals
It leaves us memories yet;
Memories dark, and memories bright,
Friends cold and gone; scenes dark and light,
Rejoicing and regret.

Ye bells, now chase this chilly May;
Ye tell another natal day
Of England's monarch Queen;
And while obscure the bard may be
It may record, still loyally,
While dwelling in home's scene.

His fervent wishes by his pen:
And leaving them to sons of men
This Whitsun Sabbath day,
May future birthdays come and go
Undarkened long by Death's dark woe;
And as this merry May

Tells days and scenes of Royal lore,
May God's best blessing from above
Upon the Union rest:
May the Czar's visit in this May
Hold mystic peace for Empire's day,
Then friendship shall be blest.

Then ring away ye chattering bells,
Your peals we welcome, while your knells
May start the parting tear;

Still for our Queen we loyal say,
God bless and save on this birthday,
Preserve for many a year.

We tone our Sabbath morning song
With one last wish; this can't be wrong;
We bid this prayer to rise –
Time's birthdays o'er; may life's far close
Bring sweet re-union, blessed repose,
The birthday of the Skies!

Note. – Three questions put to a Sunday school –
When will the birthday again be on a Sabbath day?
When will it again be on a Whitsun Sabbath day?
Where may we all be before that occurs?
G. Castleden, 25th May, Woburn, Beds.

The statue of John Bunyan, Bedfordshire's most famous son, had been now been erected in Bedford at the expense of the Duke of Bedford, and Castleden was there to see it unveiled. This was quite an occasion in Bedford, part of the Bunyan Celebrations, and a sketch of the crowd at the unveiling was published in the Illustrated London News ten days later.

20: The unveiling of the Bunyan Statue at Bedford, from the Illustrated London News, 1874.

16th June 1874 Leighton Buzzard Observer

The Unveiling of the Statue, 10th June. To the Editor of the Leighton Buzzard Observer.

Sir, - On this ducal gift to the town of Bedford I beg to send a fragment of a part of the day's proceedings. It arises from Dean Stanley's Exchange address. I borrow the Dean's three thoughts – local, ecclesiastical, and national. The filling up must be my own, for "while distance lends enchantment to the view" it does not help afar off a dunny ear, and I wait the reports to see what the Dean did say.

But for a local view I may say the person place, and pilgrims were in harmony. Such a concourse I fancy Bedford rarely saw, and as a surging crowd gathered by the river to see thousands of children go in procession to the tea, this was a local sight which will make 1874 a year of note for Ouse's Bedford town.

Ecclesiastical – I expect the Dean's remarks on this head impressed Catholicity of sentiment. It struck me, looking around, the poet's lines might be apposite:-

"Let names and sects and parties fall,

And Jesus Christ be all in all."

Surely, seeing all professing Christians assembled, the familiar lyric, "No sect in heaven" might key such harmony. O that this union were realised on earth more and more. Another thought, ecclesiastical, struck, and gathering it from Pagan Rome, it may be a *hint* to save "religious difficulties" in the world of Christendom.

In a little book I published in 1843 is this pertinent note:- "Yes, rather than see the Christian, whatever his denomination, *magisterially* 'dealing the curse,' I would, for the *brotherhood* of the State, invoke that genius of toleration which presided over Pagan Rome, and which saved for centuries that mighty republic its area of religious gore. Nero commenced the persecution of the Christians. Constantine, by his headship, established man's domination over his fellow man in religious beliefs, and succeeding popes have fulminated their bulls, edicts, and degrees. The various modes of worship which prevailed in the Roman world were all considered by the people as equally true; by the philosopher as equally false; and by the magistrate as equally useful. And this toleration produced not only unusual indulgence, but even religious concord. - Gibbon"

National – Men like John Milton and John Bunyan pulse a people's tongue with life. They strike tones which never die. The bold blasphemy of Shelley I quote for its point only: - "He has written an epic poem which

will last and be cherished when its theme shall be an exploded myth."
"Paradise Lost" is for the learned, while Elstow's John, for *all*, wrote his
matchless dream; and alike the child and old man, the learned and the rude
are amused, fascinated and instructed, and to myriads over the river, they, by
mercy led, see the shining ones and find eternal rest.

A thought may be allowed on this head, and Goldsmith, a little altered,
may well express it:-

"But England's language, now a world's wide pride,

If these, *John's* words, were *lost*, could never be supplied."

Then surely universal authors are national property. As national mind
– minds they deserve homage, for they *retone* a nation's tongue; *refresh* a
nation's taste; and *repeat*, in ever living sounds, a nation's household words.

Other thoughts are in store relative to this red letter day in an aged
pilgrim's experience. Through the crowds I made my way to the station, met
with an unexpected friend of olden times, held Christian pleasant converse
till at Woburn Sands he sped on the wings of fire and steam homewards,
while I, as a slow pace, trod amid our verdancy, and, at a neighbour's home,
"rest and be thankful," was the motto of our weary man; while "the cup which
cheers but not inebriates" refreshed, and gratefully closed my pilgrimage to
John Bunyan's shrine on St. Peter's Green.

"Thanks I pay for this John Bunyan's day,

Thanks which I leave when life shall pass away."

I remain, sir, your obedient servant, George Castleden, Woburn, 11th
June.

For someone who had regularly criticised the steam trains, for their
speed, danger, and modern-ness, he obviously didn't mind using the train
to get home quickly!

30th June 1874 Leighton Buzzard Observer

Local Boards – A Word to Rate-Payers

To the Editor of the Leighton Buzzard Observer

Sir,- In this short note I do not intend to tread upon anyone's corns,
but in ventilating a public question it is hard to escape a personal twinge.
Boards are increasing; Boards are local powers; Boards are arbiters of our
"ways and means." Taxation without representation is tyranny. We say this
of an Imperial Parliament; how does this truth stand with our Local Board
Parliament? Ratepayers ought to answer the question. But "it is law," What!
Is it *just* law to collect monies under the guise of "poor-rates," and find,
like the merry knight's tavern bill, that items chiefly are for "sack" in the

shape of different charges, and for the "three-halfpence" is for the poors' bread? Well might Sir John cry, "O, fie! O, fie!" My sole object is now to call ratepayers to the question of facts and figures. An abdication of this duty, an absence of vestry supervision, indolence, and indifference on the part of the payers, and a corresponding activity in officials to collect and lay out, is rather an alarming climax for John Bull to contemplate; and while he, with a knowledge aforesaid, pays all demands with a little commendable grumbling, it is hard upon the old gent to pay in the dark what the light might show to be a queer item. Let our "poor rate" be detailed. Let our "Boards" be under public inspection, and wholesome ventilation may serve and save the dry rot of suspicion and disaster.

This warning is the counsel of years, and most certainly I cannot recommend to juvenile ratepayers a moral more to the point than the old fable of "the waggoner and Jupiter," which, when I first read, I should have been a dreamer indeed to think I might use in 1874.

I remain, sir, your obliged servant, George Castleden.

Castleden was never happier than relating the Royal visit to Woburn of 1841.

21st July 1874 Leighton Buzzard Observer

A Woburn Park Scene, 13th July.

"Life is a dream, a passing show." So says the poet, and so our "Cherry fair" and all its shows have passed away. Well, the fair day came round, while, pondering bygones, we heard that Royal personages were coming from the Agricultural Show to Woburn Abbey. Thought struck I might see another Royal Show. Speculating upon the chance, we trod the sun-scorched turf, and then, taking shelter 'neath the sylvan shade, we reclined by the bason pond till the Abbey clock sounded five, and then three carriages came down the hill. In the first sat the Crown Prince and Princess of Germany, and their graces the Duke and Duchess of Bedford; the others we presume, were occupied by their suite. Driving by the passing homage of a few spectators was paid and returned, and on through part of the ducal domains the Royal party were conducted, and then, as we turned homewards, mind was busy with 1841; Then our beloved Queen and her Princely Consort travelled the same road enjoyed the then July scene, and with dukes, duchesses, lords, ladies, and lieges, mingled in the same pastoral pageant, and made that last summer day renowned in Woburn annals. Now this newer scene we put in print, and leave it as an aged man's record of one last Abbey Park event in which Royal and Ducal party we glanced at are the present actors, and while, amid our beautiful scenery, we mentally wished for them a long, bright, and useful career, yet with our own years, the reminiscences of time, and "the inexorable logic of facts" our solemn closing thought on this summer day Royal scene was toned by the poet –

Princes, this clay must be your bed
In spite of all your towers;
The high, the proud, the reverend head,
Must lie as low as ours.

Yes, death despotically strikes in the palace, mansion, home, and cot; he levels all distinctions in time, and pure democracy is realised in the grave.

Here rank and fashion, beauty, all
Must in communion sleep!
Princes in dust with peasants fall,
And mourners vainly weep.

Yes, in life's tale the ever moral tells -
Man lives to die! Alike the royal throne
The peasant's home, avouch death's potent power.
Yes, as I looked upon our Park's day scene,
Methought of July's groups in Forty-one!
Then Queen Victoria smiled, as by her side
The good Prince Albert sat; now death has smote!
"He gave his honours to the world again,
His blessed part to heaven, and slept in peace."
The fathers sleep, the prophets are unknown!
And in this newer scene a newer race
Look on; another generation lives.
The aged man may sigh as o'er times past
He cats his eye – views "vanity" o'er dust
Inscribed, and in life's present pageantries
He see fresh fodder for death's hungry mow.
Mine be the solemn line to infex this show
In Woburn's Ducal park; a line which may
Immortalise a sunny royal scene
And bid the day imperishably live!
Beneath the sylvan shade three lay, and now
I flash thought's photograph of life and death;
Which, falling 'neath the eye of memory
May be a picture of a sun-lit scene,
And may recall this glance on Prussia's pair;

May link, with this noon vision, transient, bright,
Wide Germany and Home's Elysian fields.
And if this line should sound along Time's waste
To tell to Woburn's sons this Royal scene,
A memory and a joy it may remain
And be a light to shine along this vale,
To vouch for truth when falsehoods fail and fall;
To be a record of this hot July
When now, as actors we our exit make,
And like our fathers, walk earth's stage no more.
G. Castleden

His next poem celebrated a far less regal individual.

18th **August 1874** Leighton Buzzard Observer

Betsy Leatherland
"Nothing like leather," fables say;
The why, it wears so well;
Now "Leatherland," an ancient dame,
Our local records tell
Long in the land has dwelt, and still may dwell.

As she may tell the news, long past,
A lengthened tale will be;
And in the harvest field it links
A century's history
Of chequered life and human mystery.

May this Tring dame yet live in fame,
And when her reaping's past,
"Like a full shock," t
hen gathered in,
Sing harvest home at last,
Where storms ne'er roll, now clouds their shadows cast.
G.C., August, 1874.

Betsy Leatherland was a figure who came to national attention. Supposedly born in Chinnor in 1763, she had moved to Tring by 1830, and spent the next 40 years selling her wares around local villages. Thus, it was believed she was 111 years old. She was still reaping corn at that age, although crowds would form to watch, and each wanted an ear of corn cut by Betsy to take home as a memento. She achieved some fame, and had been featured in Pictorial World.

25th August 1874 Leighton Buzzard Observer

Endowed Schools Bill. To the Editor of the Leighton Buzzard Observer.

Sir, - On reading in the *Nonconformist* the tribute paid to two youths at Birmingham, Messrs. Dale and Vince, the thought struck – how the curse of sectarian domination might have withered these lads, and have robbed the State of future services of, perchance, two master minds. How many, able and willing to serve, have been estopped, locally and nationally, by the ban of priestly power, and on account of a conscientious regard to their religious faith, who can tell? As it regards our many grammar schools and our British and foreign schools, I did think *progress* had been made, that darkness had been kindled into light; and, as a Lancasterian school-boy, I little dreamed that in aged years I should witness the attempt at a re-actionary policy, plunging us into the darkness and cruelty of denominational supremacy and exclusion. And, while I deeply regret our departure from the light our fathers left us, most certainly the effort of the present Government to foist such an unjust, retrogressive scheme on the country is to be watched, and should make us more and more vigilant in taking heed of the Russell warning – "Don't trust the Tories."

I remain, sir, your obedient servant, George Castleden, Woburn Aug. 20th.

8th September 1874 Leighton Buzzard Observer

Town Rhymes of our Time – A Ballard of old Back Lane

> So this vast world, and all who it inhabit
> Shall, like the baseless fabric of a dream,
> Vanish and pass away, like our old Back Lane,
> Leave not a "Court" behind.
> [Shakespeare - altered]

> As I do take my walks abroad
> How many scenes I see;
> I in life's play may still record
> Time's ever changery.

This cornet year, midst change, death, fear,
I stroll my natal town;
Familiar spot, 'tis very hot,
Life's hill, I'm going down.

Names, neighbours flee, how many fled!
No more they joy or sigh;
No more they mingle in our street;
No more fret 'neath our sky

They sleep! No more perplexed with care,
No more feel woe and pain;
Life's dream is done, and 'neath the sun
They'll never wake again!

Among the sleepers in your yard
A sleeper long remains;
And as I wander parish graves,
O'er dust midst newer strains –

I think of Dick, his wit was quick,
And stingless was his joke;
I muse his dingy Back Lane home,
His smithy and his smoke.

Poor Gorick! poverty with thee
Darken'd not into sin;
Beneath its shade a sunny mind
Illumed the prospect dim.

This ruling passion, strong in death,
Lit up life's darkening hours;
In chimney nook the lingering flash
Played o'er decaying powers

"Queen's Court," a royal nook here known,
Sometimes a fragrant spot;
And here still wells the Packhorse well,
The "Queen Court's" pump's forgot.

And now I see this ancient way
Enclosed by post and rail;
So in times new, new scenes arise
To illustrate home's tale.

The old Back Lane, a legend soon,
Past generations knew;
There parsons lived, their tinkers died,
Cried welcome and adieu!

A precinct long now in my song
Its name yet may remain,
With Abbey, Duck, and Castle lane,
May live in local fame

As in this July morning's stroll
Adown my native town,
I saw upon its pitching men
Fence in this up and down;

Me thought while over buries Rome
The classic pen may write,
A rustic bard may point Back Lane
When it is lost to sight.

And while the public on this way
No more a path may claim;
Yet homes, accommodated, may
Still tell this ancient lane.

If Volney's ruins certify
Of many a classic tomb,
My busy mind may scribe a line
O'er Woburn's deepening gloom;

And prove the ever-proving tale,
Life's vanity and dust!
Alike 'neath stars the mutable,

The trustlessness of trust.

If then a line of fleeing rhyme
Should bid home sports endure,
When vanished, our familiar names
Drop into Times obscure;

My epitaph may speak farewell
To bygone local fame;
Thebes, Rome, and Babylon, all fall
Now falls our old Back Lane.

"For poverty's no sin" still lingers on life's road, though more than half a century has fled since we heard it trolled; and, amid smoke, cough, and shortness of breath, "I have oft the bellows blown, but soon my bellows will be blown," are bits of humour a man as ever cheered poverty with a joke, and who in Back Lane was born and died in the same home. "Queen's Court" was, in ancient days, the Packhorse Inn, a reference to these hostelries may be found in Shakespeare's Henry 4th, Act 2, sec. 1. Locke also writes – "A packhorse is driven constantly in a narrow lane." And now these rhymes may remain to tell former worth, importance, and *stable* renown. While Woburn's surroundings will ever make it beautiful, may its future, if wealth flies away on steam, know the compensation of pastoral happiness and neighbourly confidence, esteem, and security. And now for a last verse –

While others roam I at my home,
Muse on the olden times;
Dwell on the tale of Woburn's vale,
And talk in prose and rhyme,
Oft rustical, but not sublime!
G.C., George Street, Woburn.

N.B. – Having, in parish vestry, aided in stopping up this ancient way, let me say no private rights are injured, tenants conveniences are increased, and the public pathway in front remains.

Personally, I like his work best where he describes the people and environs of Woburn. Back Lane ran behind the shops that lead from the Market Place along the High Street, and came out roughly where the bus shelter now is. Duck Lane is still there, running southwards from the back of the Market Place, to come out on London Road. I do not know the location of Abbey Lane, but Castle Lane could have been off Park Street as that was where the Castle Works, the home of William Hensman & Son, engineers, and manufacturers of agricultural implements were based. A completely different poem on Back Lane had appeared in his book 'Lays of Home', in 1850.

21: Woburn market place and High Street, from a postcard c.1910.

<u>29th September 1874</u> Leighton Buzzard Observer

An 1874 Good-bye to the Swallows.

Good-bye, my Swallow friends, good-bye!
Once more a circling in our sky,
Before you take your flight
I say good-bye! Where you may go,
With neighbours, wond'ring, I don't know;
Once more I say good-night.

My "Swallow song" was sent to one
Who now with earthly things has done!
This twitter pleased my friend;
And now a note, date seventy-four,
May tell a swallow tale once more,
As down time I descend.

To swallows, as I say farewell,
A boyish memory I may tell
Of my sole brother, gone!
"Do swallows, as in days of yore,
Flock on the roof before our door,
As when I lived at home?"

So youth's dim days and early things
Come floating up on memory's wings;
Now aged and alone
I watch the swallows' circling flight
And, as the skim their airy height,
I bid these friends again good-night,
In our old house at home.
G.C. Woburn, September.

6th October 1874 Leighton Buzzard Observer

Lines on Lord Charles Russell's Speech, in the Town Hall, 21st Sept.

An apt quotation from Dr. Chalmers on the magnitudes scanned by the telescope, and the atomic wonders developed by the microscope, enforced and moved thought.

With telescope I sweep night's spangled sky,
Orbs infinite its magic lens supply,
It fills with most profound amaze!
Then, with the microscope, I scan the earth,
And, dwelling on its wonderous atom birth,
Infinitude my optics daze. *

Puzzled, I pass Dame Nature's problems by,
Infinity in earth and in the sky,
They light and live beneath His nod,
But what is man? A twin-born atom he,
Breath-living, and a spirit mystery!
This image after Nature's God.

Science may soar; philosophy may swell;
Chance impious dare; solution neither tell;
God's Word can only harmonise.

Faith lifts the man above atomic dust,
Bids soul immortal fix his lasting trust
On Him who built the earth and skies
So faith supports the simple and confounds the wise.
G.C., George Street, Woburn, 28th September.

*Turning to animal life, the microscope in the hands of Ehrenberg disclosed animalcules so infinitesimal in size that a single drop of water was computed to contain 500,000,000 of them. Here was not only a picture of a universe of atoms, but the living proof of a universe of organic beings equal in number to the entire human population on the surface of the globe. – (John Dalton).

This was a time of great advancements in scientific knowledge, which often led to conflict with the traditional religious explanation for the world around us. Castleden seems quite amazed at the world discovered at the end of a microscope, but seems to cope with the discoveries by retreating to his faith. Next, he took up pen again on Woburn's own history.

20th October 1874 Leighton Buzzard Observer

Original Poetry – Rhymes of our Times – Reminiscences of our Old Town

"Behind my office bell" – who now
Recalls that Woburn row?
Long time the combatants have fled,
Then noisy, stilly now!

And yet it was an open row,
As Englishmen they fought;
Disguised, they never struck as foes,
In masks they were not caught.

These burly men, in honest wrath
Would wage a stand-up fight,
But, when they grounded arms and fled
Unto the grave's cold night,

No residue of malice stayed
To harm a coming age;

No, no, the quarrel closed by death,
Left not a future page

On which is writ the doom of hate,
Extending on to years;
"The past is" now, and that is fate,
Fate causing sighs and fears!

But let this pass; another thought,
Who "Camps's Corner" know?
Our hosier then of town renown,
A Quaker home also.

The passage ran betwixt the homes,
It was a parish way;
And neighbours passed beneath its arch
By night, and eke by day.

We boys at "hare and hounds" would run
Adown the snug retreat;
And by the "Rose and Crown" we sped,
And turned into Park Street.

Where are my merry mates? Nigh all
Have passed into thin air;
Their active limbs melt in the grave.
And I must slumber there.

This passage led on to a yard,
A cooper plied his trade;
His bull-dog growled and prowled the streets –
Commotion sometimes made.

And now the office and the bell,
The lawyer, and the *friend*,
Once "properties," are now unknown,
Forgotten all descend!

Yes, now 'tis past, old scenes are gone,
Old actors in the dust
Inform life's play is finishing;
They sleep – we also must.

Yet I still linger on Time's stage,
Life's prologue long is past;
Its epilogue may soon engage,
Then "exist" ends the *cast*.
Like Walter Scott's "Mortality,"
I linger on the spot,
I freshen up the fading lines –
They should not be forgot.

I leave an epitaph of truth,
Not scribed on brass or stone –
"We could have better spared some men;"
Not faultless, now unknown,
They, honest, loved this verdant home,
And in our graveyards rest, no more to roam!

Note – This public passage-way, perchance a portion of a spot once named "Abbey Lane," having become private property, its bygone may only last in this town rhyme.

"Guard then these ancient trees, beneath whose shade
Our fathers have sat down, and of whose fruits
They ate, and went upon their way in peace -
Part not with these old names.

Say not our age is wiser; if it be,
It is the wisdom which the past has given
That makes it so; for in these names is writ
That wondrous wisdom that has made us wise."
G.C., George Street, Woburn, October.

There are many clues here to Woburn's ancient history. The row about the office bell, I do not know, but "Camps Corner", which was a Quaker hosier home, was probably the building originally adjoining the George Inn, for many years The Bedford Arms, and now The Woburn Hotel.

This was the home of Elizabeth Pattinson, a dressmaker who married a travelling salesman, John Wiffen. They were both Quakers, and John set up as his ironmongery shop here. The shop was demolished over 100 years ago, and is now the site of the Woburn War Memorial. Much of Woburn has always been owned by the Duke of Bedford, but The Rose and Crown in Park Street spent many years in private hands, before being sold to the Duke in 1872. It is thought he closed it immediately, and it had been demolished by the time of the first 25-inch Ordnance Survey map of 1882. Despite the usefulness of Castleden's memories to local historians today, not everyone was a fan at the time...

27th October 1874 Leighton Buzzard Observer

A Word upon "Original Poetry." To the Editor of the Leighton Buzzard Observer.

Sir, - Will you allow me to say a word of commendation upon the composition of your Woburn poet, who signs himself "G.C." If it is rhyme, I am so obtuse that I cannot find any valuable sense or valid reason in it. His "office bell," "merry mates," "parish way," "snug retreat," "bull dogs," "hare and hounds," "verdant home," "ancient trees," "sighs and fears," "sylvan shades," "old actors," "fading lines," and "wondrous wisdom," to my mind, present a strange conglomeration of heterogeneous funny things, like –

A Pretty, Witty, Ditty, What a Pity!

Censor

As ever, anonymous criticism was easily brushed aside.

10th November 1874 Leighton Buzzard Observer

Original Poetry. Tinted Leaves.

As tinted leaves around us fall,
They unto mortal, mystic call –
Ye dying men, come see
In us an emblem of your end;
Green, bright, and strong, you must descend
To dust and vanity.

Sun-lighted giant flowers hang gay,
They please the rambler on his way;
All beautiful the scene;

In fancy still I rove the spot
And think on what is ne'er forgot,
And muse on Woburn's dream!

A whirling wind o'er our Park gay
May beauty blast into decay:
Death's tinted leaves may tell.
In springtide green, in summer light,
'Neath autumn's suns we coloured bright,
Then fading, withering, fell!

Now seventy years of flowery spring,
Blue summer skies, on mystic wing,
I lose in Time's obscure,
Autumn and winter seem to say,
Again we come, then haste away,
While seasons shall endure.

Se Thompson on "The Seasons" round,
And, treading his poetic ground,
I find a charm, in time,
Which elevates above this clod –
From Nature leads to Nature's God,
By jewelled thoughts divine.

Again our leafless woods may preach
And "Redall's trees" again may teach,
A home bard this to say –
Man green, proud, and strong, lives out his day,
But death will claim, and then, his prey,
Man, like the leaf, must find decay!

Note. – I have a word for "Censor," but on principle I pause relative
to recognition of the anonymous, whether written or spoken. For his
"commendation" I suppose I should be grateful; for other "funny things" I
may be in a funny mood some day, and reply.

George Castleden, Woburn, 5th November, 1874.

17<u>th</u> **November 1874** <u>Leighton Buzzard Observer</u>

Matter and Spirit

Science may soar, rush by the stars,
Or dive to either pole,
In *Matter* find birth and grave
Of Nature's varied whole;

But what of Spirit? tell me, sage,
Where does Spirit dwell?
Whence its beginning and its end
Ye Matter-mongers tell.

Will thoughts, *your own*, for ever die?
And do you wish they may?
Then, decide and suicide, *
You darken hope's bright day.

Repent, believe beyond your ken
There lives a life to *come*;
This warns and cheers the Spirit here,
And *there* it points to *home*.

I dare not, sages, list to you,
Seek light in Matter's night!
I dare not say to Hope adieu,
Or quench my parents' light;

But rather, holding it aloft,
A beacon, may it save
Some traveller or mariner
From Matter's gloomy grave.

A Pharo's torch, O may it rise
On some lone sailor's sight;
Warn off of Matter's whelming sands,
And guide to Spirit light.

Let Nature ever keep her place,

O'er Matter hold her sway;

But Spirit, mystic, God's own breath,

By grace will God obey

G. Castleden, Woburn, 11th Nov.

Note – Mr. Hewells, a celebrated preacher, once said, "Man is naturally so rebellious that he could be at once deicide, homicide and suicide."

24th November 1874 Leighton Buzzard Observer

Popedom. To the Editor of the Leighton Buzzard Observer.

Sir, - May not the controversy now raging be epitomised thus – does not the Pope claim infallibility – power uncontrolled? Power uncontrolled, is it not perilous? With priestly pride dangerous and cruel results follow. Does not Protestantism check Rome's Popedom? Where Popedom rules, whether in the Vatican, cathedral, church, chapel, or barn, the rights of conscience are invaded; civil liberties may be abridged, and *the will of one*, uncontrolled, may initiate a despotism ending in tyranny and persecution, hateful and detestable. My protest us against Popedom in its germ and growth. If *simper idem* be the motto of Rome – *through all time ever the same* – we know her antecedents have been pride, despotism, cruelty, and death. I speak of her here in her impartial rule. Whether the Emancipation Bill did "unchain the beast," to use an expressive simile of the fathers, I leave, but it may be a problem for a Bismark, a Gladstone, or a Disraeli, of the future to solve how European secular freedom and rights of conscience can progress and exist, with a religious power dominating and supreme, which, in its infallibility is arbitrary and antagonistic to all who dissent or protest against its decrees. This is my motto against all Popedom –

"Let Caesar's due be ever paid,

To Caesar and his throne;

But conscience and souls were made

To be the Lord's alone."

This controversy is world-wide. Governments watch it. The Papacy may be shaken by it; while I trust true Protestant principles will firmer stand. I close this brief reference to it by saying, "Down with all Popedom!" and to this end let John Milton's words rule – "Liberty to think, liberty to speak; liberty to print."

I remain, sir, your obedient servant

George Castleden, Woburn, November 20th.

Hot on the heels of Censor's complaint in October, the following appeared. Could they have been from the same sarcastic critic?

1<u>st</u> **December 1874** Leighton Buzzard Observer

Our Modern Poets

It is really so amazing,
What some folks will be choosing,
To gain in this world of ours a fame.
Some are found delighting
In poetry, and writing
Lines to which they do not even add their name.

I do not know "G.C.,"
But, whoever he may be,
In your paper, sir, I often read his rhymes;
You'll excuse my being bold,
But I think he's growing old,
By the way he writes of Woburn's bygone times.

Not only, does it seem,
Does his wondrous "Woburn's dream,"
Incite his ever-ready pen to write;
But his brain a poem weaves
Even on "Tinted Leaves,"
And he them compares to men "green, strong, and bright."

On "Matter," once again,
He seizes ready pen,
And the "Home Bard," unto "matter-mongers" writes;
And grave old sages heed,
And in these columns read
The poetry in which "G.C." delights.

Another poem, too,
I in your columns view;
Another lettered poet tries to rise.
But not of "office bells"

Or of "Tinted Leaves" he tells.
No; "He aims too low who aims beneath the skies!"

He bends his ardent gaze
On the stars. And he obeys
The promptings of his genius, and sings
Of one that is so bright
That 'tis seen in the day light;
And of also many other funny things.

He says, We call thee Venus!"
What knowledge! And between us
And the sun this beauteous goddess is to come.
"They'll watch her going forth
"In the south and in the north."
Dear me! such wisdom almost strikes me dumb.

Hail "H!" We'll honour thee,
Not as a deity,
But as a man who really makes us smile.
Twinkle, literary star!
How I wonder who you are,
And where you got your metre and your style!
An Awe-struck Admirer

...was closely followed by another:

5ᵗʰ January 1875 Leighton Buzzard Observer

A Recovered Poem. To the Editor of the Leighton Buzzard Observer.

Sir, - I venture to think you will be gratified to be the means of giving publicity to the following poem, recovered from oblivion by the thoughtful care of our charwoman, who was about to light the fire with the paper on which it was written. The woman, being of an inquisitive turn of mind (unlike charwomen generally), fortunately endeavoured to make herself acquainted with the contents of the paper and the meaning; but failing to understand (doubtless for want of a School Board education), she, in her perplexity, brought it to me for explanation. It is evidently a prospective elegy, written by some enthusiastic admirer of our local poet, and in humble imitation of the great master's style:

"Stupendous shade! Ah, why do I evoke
Thy name so glorious? Time has giv'n the stroke,
And thou hast pass'd away from Albion's Isle;
Calmly serene, thou glid'st from out our view.
Through other rushing, to the realms so true
Of happiness, with a perpetual smile.

We track thy path aloft; this mortal clay
Thou shufflest off, and intellect sheds a ray
Resplendent as a mid-day sun;
Orator, historian, essayist, first rate poet,
And where's the Briton, pray, who doesn't know it,
And make his boast while endless cycles run?

But thou art gone, thy page behind is left;
And, losing thee, we're not of all bereft;
And though to-day we gaze upon thy tomb,
Amid the great ones of the earth, thy head
Softly reposes, covered o'er with lead;
Ah! who can gaze on this and not feel gloom.

Great shade, adieu – of local poets long
The chief; so mightily sublime in song;
Accept this tribute of a poet's mind,
But little known to fame – although in Woburn town
He modestly can say he's met renown,
And his name floats on many a wavy wind.

Man struggles with his fate – death waits on age,
The young, the beautiful, the dull, the sage;
Each champion we cheer on; while hoary time
Points to the goal where many a gallant breast
Confronts the tide dear Liberty has blest;
Which brings me to the bottom of my rhyme.

Montigopeligo Shandrigodos, Woburn, January, 1875.

12th January 1875 Leighton Buzzard Observer

"Three Single Gentlemen Rolled up into One." To the Editor of the Leighton Buzzard Observer.

Sir, - I fancy "Censor," "Awe-struck Admirer," and the unpronounceable of to-day's Observer, make up a compound which may fit Tommy Hood's line; and, as co-workers or helpers, these correspondents and "charwomen" are both used to dirty jobs. If they belong to that modest class who do good by *stealth*, I would not wrong them; but, as I have remarked, surely they should show the *shirt* if they don't mean secret stabbing. To please others who do think, one, who as "orator, historian, essayist &c.," he would be ashamed to own, or one to wound; but who in behalf of truth, peace, and good will has ever *openly* written, I, retortive, say it is rather too bad in such a laudable courses to be stopped by some clerkly coward who, masked, is

"Willing to wound, yet afraid to strike."

I wish you could have inserted my last, but a verse written to "Awe-struck Admirer" at the time may suit the "Stupendous Shade!" I thank thee, scribe, for teaching me this word; it may also be a salutary hint that the detective may be useful among neighbours as the police officer is among crime-seeking knaves –

It really is amusing,
Tho' a bit confusing,
When a bard, in musing,
Dubs himself a –
"I do not know G.C.,"
This may do, perse,
But tell it honest folk,
If not a lying joke,
A crammer they may smoke
From "Awe-struck Admirer."

Castleden ignored these critics and their barbs, and concentrated on his Christmas poem for 1874, which centred on the Woburn Post Office.

12th January 1875 Leighton Buzzard Observer

Original Poetry. The Woburn Postman's Carol. Christmas, 1874.

My Carol reminiscent sings
How men and things on Time's swift wings

All flee, have flown away!
Tyers, Walker, subs, have closed life's days –
Their shadows gone for aye!

And now again cold Christmas comes,
The time of boxing, sweets, and plums;
First heave the tribute sigh
O'er friends departed! this their due;
To neighbours fled we say adieu
With lingering heart and eye.

Ye busy folk who come and go,
Who have no cause to think of woe
This season, may it be
Unmixed with unexpected ills,
And may no bills, draughts, squills, or pills,
Vex your festivity.

Still, in your fun remember woe;
In the *fast* joy pray also know
Slow sorrow creeps along;
With cakes and wine the bitters fall,
Now mask and dance, then drops the pall –
The dirge concludes the song.

Neighbours, this merry berry time
*New*berry calls with Christmas chime,
And asks a plum from you:
And still as postmen come and go
May rhyme and coin to cheer them flow
When I shall say adieu.

Hark to you bell; one neighbour more
Dwells now among the dead;
Ere one short month six home-known names
Have from us ever fled.
G.C.

22: *Woburn Town Hall and Market Place, from a postcard c.1910.*

<u>26th</u> **January 1875** Leighton Buzzard Observer

Original Poetry. We are Three.

Attend, all ye who last week read our noble poet's praise;
He long hath sung the famous deeds of Woburn's ancient days;
And it seems our fleet of "three is one" against him bears in vain
The longest words in lexicon or coinage of our brain.
For some one witty – that's to say, he'd be witty if he could –
Has taken "G.C.'s" cudgels up, and mentioned "Tommy Hood."
Who's *Tommy*? I should like to know; I always read him "Tom;"
And I wonder where our cudgel-bearer gets his knowledge from.
Knowledge! I correct myself, I mean nothing of the kind;
For this valorous no-named man, I think, is a little bit behind
In answer to the poetry he dedicates to me,
The offensive line I must repeat – "I do not know 'G.C.' "

But one more verse, and then, i think, for this time I have done
With him who says three single men can be rolled into one.
I'm more awe-struck than ever, and congratulate "G.C."
On having such a clever man to take his part 'gainst three
But one more thought before I let "G.C.'s" defender pass,

And that is, don't throw pebbles while you live in homes of glass

Don't sneer at "Censor," "Funny-name," or the "Awe-struck One" – that's me;

But please to sign your own name are you fault with us three.

Awe-struck Admirer, Birmingham, January 16th, 1875.

As well as critics, Castleden also had his supporters, although I'm unsure if this one was just being sarcastic...

26th January 1875 Leighton Buzzard Observer

Our Woburn Poet and his Critics. To the Editor of the Leighton Buzzard Observer.

Sir, - In what a masterly, pleasing style does Mr. "G.C.," the Woburn poet, *roll three gentlemen into one!!!* But why call anonymous critics gentlemen? Their names are most insignificant - "censor," "Awe-struck Admirer," and "Unpronounceable." Let such crickets remain and chirp in their crevices so long as our Woburn bard "G.C." is willing to charm us with his innocent rhymes. I would humbly suggest that he publishes a book with the title –

"Song of the leaves

From Woburn Park Trees;"

I shall be happy to become a subscriber.

I remain, yours truly, A Delighted One.

The other poets who occasionally had their work published in the LBO also became embroiled, with the discovery that one of the critics had plagiarised another's poetry:

2nd February 1875 Leighton Buzzard Observer

Original Poetry. The Birmingham "Awe-struck Admirer."

I would not, Sir, have interposed in other folk's affairs,

For that imposes on the party numerous toils and cares;

Besides our poet gay has his fables thus declared –

With those who've interposed in quarrels often hard it's fared

But, Sir, a friend of mine to me some lines has just now shown

Which prove the first liners of our poet's rhymes are not his own;

They're taken from Macaulay, who upon th' Armada wrote

And palmed on us as if they came from some great man of note.

Now, he has had a shy at me, and used some lines of mine,

And tried with them, at what I wrote, some sneer to intertwine;

He criticised my thoughts and words, with a view to write me down,
Affirming that in what I penned my object was renown.
I therefore now advise him to lay down his witty pen,
And not attempt t'impose his rhymes on other folks again;
To cultivate his mind with care, ere he attempts to write,
To study English grammar well, and keep its rules in sight.
And if some one should me demand whose poetry I prefer
Than his, I say the Woburn poet's lines more please my ear;
I may be wrong in judgement, but, I certainly opine,
Though sometimes wrong in grammar, in him sparkling thoughts oft shine.
Now let him criticise these lines, and other people's too;
I'll let him have his way this time – this I detest to do,
To answer one whose disposition is disposed to carp,
Rather than lyric odes compose for music and the harp.
H., Leighton Buzzard, January 26

Castleden went back to more local topics: the question of the gas lighting (or lack thereof), collecting for charity and the Woburn Workhouse.

2<u>nd</u> **February 1875** Leighton Buzzard Observer

The Gas Question at Woburn. To the Editor of the Leighton Buzzard Observer.

Sir, - I pray you to lighten our darkness. At the *first* I paused relative to the policy of lighting up our *town* by gas, on account of its traffic decline. I remember we were promised a wonderful light, wonderfully cheap. On the decision I stayed further criticism. The light in the street is not to be found fault with, but, as to the wonderful economy, I think that was rather imaginative. Nor, sir, isn't it too bad going out ignorantly to find ourselves in danger of breaking our shins against a neighbour's step, or plunging headlong on a passenger, or risking some other peril because, forsooth, two or three in public meeting moved, seconded, and carried nem. con., that there was to be an extinction of the gas in our streets. While I hold the original objection that it was the wrong time for this levy, let that pass, but, surely, feeling a respect towards the poor old town, I may ask, through your columns, who put on the extinguisher? how long it is to remain? and whether we ratepayers are to pay the same? These questions might be put in vestry, but this is prohibited; therefore be so good as to strike a light – I don't want a Lucifer – and lighten our thickening gloom, and you will oblige others with your obedient servant, George Castleden

10th April 1875 Bedfordshire Mercury

Woburn. London City Mission. – An interesting meeting was held in the Town hall on Easter Tuesday evening. The chair was occupied by Mr. F. A. Bevan. The meeting was opened by singing and prayer. Mr. Castleden then read the statement of receipts for the district, showing a total of £57 paid in the last year 1873-1874 to the funds of this excellent Home Mission. The chairman gave an address on the society, and, urged its claims on the provinces. Another hymn was sung, and then Lord Charles Russell gave a speech emphatically pressing home the duty of the country to aid London in this great enlightening work among its teeming, seething, masses. Mr Clark, a missionary among public houses, also spoke, and, in giving personal experience, and many details graphic, humorous, and pathetic, he held the audience in attention for an hour, and then solemnly finished by pointing to the eternal nature of this mission in its one great object to save the souls of London's neglected, erring, and poverty stricken people. The meeting was closed with the Doxology and benediction by the Rev. H. Southey. The collection at the doors amounted to £4 4s 6d.

18th May 1875 Leighton Buzzard Observer

Woburn Union House.

To the Editor of the Leighton Buzzard Observer.

Sir,- Permit me a brief note on your last week's report relative to the doing away with the union. At a previous vestry I called attention to a paragraph in the Observer, and now I ask another word. Mr. Gilby is strong when he says "no notice has been given to parishioners that the question was to be discussed in vestry." I believe a bagged fox is not highly approved of by open, fair riding sportsmen. But in this move there is a higher consideration. It is a "flesh and blood" question, and this raises it above a monetary view. Experience has shown that while you may repair the loss of money or offend against mercy by any assault on the laws of humanity, you invoke a retribution, certain, mystic, and severe. Hence I should like this *home* question relative to our poor to be discussed from a philanthropic more than a rate-paying point of view. My intent is to say, in a cautionary spirit, let what is done be done openly; let the for and against appear, and, if justice and mercy approve, objection ceases. "Do unto another as ye would another should do unto you." In regard to his home, person, and purse. 'Tis the best remunerative policy; it pays in the pocket, and in peace of mind.

I remain, sir, your obedient servant, George Castleden. Woburn 12th May.

Leighton Buzzard staged two Working Men's Industrial & Arts Exhibitions, in 1868 and 1875. The second, open for nearly a month, from May 12th, was considerably larger, with about 600 exhibitors and over 10,000 exhibits, and Castleden went to see it.

1st June 1875 Leighton Buzzard Observer

Original Poetry. A short rhyme on a visit to the Leighton Exhibition 26th of May.

'Twas a May day, in one-horse chay
We trotted by the hedgerows gay,
Along to Leighton town;
And many a scene in life's long dream,
Came up amid the white and green -
Scenes once of some renown.

And actors, too, who once we knew,
By magic memory came to view;
These shadows passed as fast!
Sheep Lane, Stone Lane, and Heath & Reach,
Did unto me grave sermons preach,
All of the buried past.

Then the "North End" we hardly knew;
So much of old appeared now new,
I hardly knew this place;
Still, as we trotted o'er the ground,
By signs and specimens around,
We traced the olden race.

Then by the Cross I was set down,
And in the heart of Leighton town
I met my father's friend
Then to th' Exchange I paced my way,
And gazed on relics rich and gay,
Which may in time descend.

What there I saw, what then I thought,

May be of value or of nought;
Enough, this newer scene
Gives to "Beaudesert" modern fame,
Gives Leighton town a local name,
In Time's all-changing dream.

In this short rhyme I've only time,
In numbers rustic, not sublime,
To say in this rare show -
An hour well spent, you'll not repent
The time or money in it spent
Then, all to see it, go.
George Castleden, Woburn, 27th May.

8th June 1875 Leighton Buzzard Observer
Original Poetry – Another Birthday Rhyme, 24th May 1875

'Twas Early morn – the sounding peal
Roused me this sunny May;
Sol climbs over old Stump Cross Hill,
Laughs over flowery May,
A welcome smiling on the Queen's birthday.

Another twenty-fourth I see,
The twenty-fourth of May,
Nor will I pass it by this year,
I hail this natal day;
God bless our Queen I sing on this birthday.

Grateful I raise on this birthday
My rustic tones, unheard;
Still singing in our verdant May,
Like night's sweet toning bird
I sing for love, and not for fame's reward.

Again I sing we love our Queen
Fir loving deeds long done;
The nuptial love, the mother's love
Lives lustrous 'neath the sun,
And will be loved while Time's oncycles run.*

Thus heart-felt homage I may pay
At threescore years and ten;
God save our Queen once more I sing;
May blessing cheer, and when
The Cloud may fall! O peaceful be it then.

While thus we see another year
And hail this flowery May,
Yet singing still, the tribute tear
Heart-feelingly, we pay
To Auld Langsyne, friends all awa';
They sleep! And hail no more our gracious Queen's birthday.
G. Castleden

* Note – I might not have ventures these lines, but having, this year, been favoured by a lady with a perusal of "The Life of H.R.H. the Price Consort," a loyal impulse prompts an obscure liegeman to leave memory of this triune tale of love, friendship, and history, on returning birthday of her Majesty Queen Victoria.

Woburn, 29th May.

Then, he returned to the Leighton Exhibition again. Other poems had been printed after a prize was offered, although Castleden intimates he did not wish to enter.

22nd June 1875 Leighton Buzzard Observer

Lines on the coming Exhibition at Leighton Buzzard. By an Aged Bard.

What Leighton Was.
What Leighton *was*, when in my boyish time,
Before I dreamt, in age, once to rhyme,
I may recount. I was a market town
Of neighbour, social, pastoral renown.
A rustic independence its chief pride
The fathers, mothers lived, and then they died.
Substantial some, and some were very poor;
Round the old Cross they gathered long obscure
Then in the graveyard found their final home,
These ancients, now forgot, are now unknown.

What Leighton is.
What Leighton *is*, some local bard may tell;
I rhyme on it in Age's long farewell.
Its station is important unto all,
Here peasants tarry, and here princes call;
Perhaps progressing it may still go on,
See brighter days, find doughtier deeds are done:
The past in shade may hide its shrinking head,
The present-future win renown instead;
Pyne's team forgot in Time's past-coaching tale
While all speed now along by steam and rail,
And smoke and screech curls, sounds o'er hill and dale.

What Leighton will be.
What Leighton *will be*, prophet bards may tell,
My rhyme is dark, but as I say farewell,
I muse the past, and think of olden time –
Of men and things which, drawn in modern line
Would look antique in this pictorial age,
And be odd relics for a funny page.
Enough to write of Leighton's ancient town
Its fairs, feasts, markets, won a long renown;
How farmers, commerce, fly on wings of steam,
And *what will be* is in the future's dream!

A Moral.
A moral stern may close my Leighton verse,
But first a local tribute I rehearse:
Thanks in our county strait a Bassett's son
Came to our rescue, and his "M.P." won.
Life's rolling stream bears all its sons away,
Fame, homes and wealth and whelmed in Time's decay
Towns rise, progress, decline, and fathers sleep!
Sons from their ashes oft rich harvests reap.
I leave this truthful moral unto those
Who must, as sons, with fathers soon repose!

P.S.

I write not for your book or books; I try *

My hand your local poets to outvie,

Accept my wish sincere that Leighton may

On Monday's coming Exhibition day

In useful art, and ornamental sheen,

Have much to boast; may crowds enjoy the scene;

"Beaudesert," may it flourish in renown,

And add a glory to old Leighton town;

This the good wish, among the rhyming men,

Of one who signs himself, George Castleden

*Note – This has reference to the prize offered. It was not my intent to compete; mine was a lone impulse to link Leighton of the past with its present. The Exhibition formed that link, in London I welded rhyme, and if, as a chain of thought, it has strength and gives pleasure to anyone, I shall be gratified.

23: *Bedford Street, looking back towards the main crossroads. The Magpie Inn stands on the left. Postcard used 1916.*

29th June 1875 Leighton Buzzard Observer

A Woburn Week. June 5th to 12th.

Obscure, quiet – shall we say sleepy? – still a week of varieties, has wakened up and occupied different sections of inhabitants.

Monday. – A stroll among the flowers in the evergreens was a rich treat.

Looking on these original pictures, man's copies were dwarfed and become dim, and then to admiration adoration joined as we thought of the Hand which tints the flower and bowls the fiery orb through boundless space. At eventide a meeting for good occupied a few; while the many contemplated a monetary depletion on the coming day.

Tuesday. – A town-day, inasmuch as it was the return of his Grace the Duke of Bedford's audit. As one of the oldest payers, the walk through the park, over new scenes, was strewn with many reflections, and, ruminating on successive reigns, mind fruitful, and memory teeming, we found, in familiar lines, solution for things changing, time fleeing, and death clearing; and, as among the newer generations I stood, reminiscences of the olden Park Farm Office flashed vividly up, men and manners fell on memory's gaze, and we repeated –

"Man is but vanity and dust
In all his flower and prime."

And, as a senior name on the rent-roll, might I not, in the extinction of Woburn's past tenantry, realise the truth of the lines –

"See the vain race of mortals move
Like shadows o'er the plain."

For as shadows have not our then familiar shades of port, wealth, and local fame vanished? Then the thought on creatures bids us sighingly say –

"They make man's expectations vain;
Death disappoints our trust."

Wednesday. – A lecture on "England – Past and Present," in the Town Hall, by the Rev. W. Gooderiche (Lord Chas. Russell presiding), deserves notice. After a happy lecturer gave a very fervent – some portions humorous and dramatic – address on our own native land. To attempt to collate the portions of it I do not; to criticise or censure I dare not. Energetic in the delivery, fervent in telling truth, interesting in historic facts, and very audible in tone, the lecture was a success; and the two hours, well spent, flew rapidly on. After deserved thanks had been paid to the worthy lecturer and the noble chairman, the crowed hall emptied itself of an audience satisfied and gratified.

Thursday. – Seventy years ago kind men and women, seeing the perpetuity of sickness and sorrow, sowed the seeds of balm and relief; and "Woburn's Sick Man's Friend" flourished amid the decays and declines of time, and still ministers to "ills to which flesh is heir;" and in committee we sat to pass the monthly accounts; and this thought did strike – if ratepayers personally looked after their pounds as carefully as we do our shillings, local taxation might not be so grinding, and spigot-hole economy might give way to bung-hole contraction. I must leave this thought for the heavy laden to think over. Only, me thinks, imperial taxation is light, compared to local imposts, which are mysterious and heavy, and aggravated by the wrong of non-representation.

Friday. – "Wombwell," of ancient fame and of modern renown, occupied our Pitching. On it the newer generations gathered to look at lions and beasts of savage name. Livingstone I had read in the morning, and this collection at eventide gave life to the morning's tale; and again upon the caged denizens of the desert and jungle I looked; and while the *roar* and *bulk* told of power and ferocity, yet the child played around the asp, and rode the camel without being afraid. Once again we viewed a scene to which the father took us as boys, when Wombwell used to enter our town, and, as "Harry's Beef-eaters," dressed in Tudor costume, peal out the grand notes of the Old Hundreth Psalm. Life and death go hand in hand. While animal life was rampant, and was engaging our townspeople, the light of one of our homes was being quenched by the cold hand of death; and amid the hurly-burly of our pitching-occupants sounded solemn tones of the passing bell.

> Remorseless tyrant! beauty, youth, and bloom
> Become thy prey, and feed the yawning tomb;
> All matter claiming motion, pulse, and breath,
> Fall 'neath his sceptre – are the prey of death.

Saturday. – Morn. – The fourth Duke of Bedford we have known, and from whom we have received kindness, rode by his home. Noon. – I looked on a cricket match in his Grace's Park. It afforded a beautiful picture; and, viewing the muscular activity of the present, I thought of the *past*, when our day and celebrity was local and known by many. And again came back forms and name familiar then, but now lost. *One, this week*, levelled by death's ground-hopper, and now waiting in the grave, prompts our closing tributary lines –

> Now, waiting for the grave, a cricket friend
> Unto his kindred dust will soon descend.
> Memory brings back the sunny Aspley scene,
> Now fading in our cricket-playing dream.
> Two Georges bowled; the elder wields the pen,
> The younger, bowled, has left the sons of men.
> The score was short; the bowling told so well
> That, when on "Pawage" the ten wickets fell,
> A baker's dozen marked the Aspley score.
> Then cricket was a game, and something more.
> Here memory sighs above companions fled!
> And, as we number *Circuitt* with the dead,

We think of *Moore, Smith, Bacchus, Assbee,*
Our worthy *Rock, Stears,* others hid from view,
While thirty years and more have flown away
Since Woburn, Aspley struggled for *that day*
This "Auld Langsyne" a few still ne'er forget;
The old eleven now pays Nature's debt;
As *scout* and *bat* may fall, as *bowlers* cease,
And on earth's *field* their *wickets* fall in peace,
Their memories, while I last, will call back time
When life was young, and hope was in its prime;
And we ne'er guessed that life might ever be
The sepulchres of youth, love, probity.
Now, as we wander back in life's strange game,
The *score* nigh finished, closing now its fame,
We seem to woo the *hush*, the wakeless sleep
When hearts shall ache no more, no more eyes weep;
Wrong rob no more, hate may no more infest;
"The wicked cease from troubling, and the weary are at rest."
George Castleden, George Street, Woburn.

"Wombwell's World Renowned Menagerie – The Oldest, Largest and Best travelling Exhibition ever organised" must have been a sight to behold for Woburnites at that time. In a change to his usual letters and poems, Castleden had now tried his hand at a news diary, quite a strange column for the time, it is almost Blog-like in style. Part diary, part poem, part news. Whether this was requested by the LBO, or he did it on impulse, we shall never know, but it seems it did not go down too well with some of their readership...

6th July 1875 Leighton Buzzard Observer

"The Woburn Week, From June 5th to 12th" To The Editor of the Leighton Buzzard Observer.

Sir, - In your last week's issue your Woburn correspondent kindly favoured us with a report of how he spent his time during a week, which may be briefly stated as follows: - Monday – strolled into a shrubbery; Tuesday – walked through Woburn Park to pay rent; Wednesday – heard a lecture on "England – Past and Present;" Thursday – sat upon a committee, to audit some accounts; Friday - had a peep at "Wombwell's menagerie; Saturday – saw a cricket match played in Woburn Park. All the aforesaid important transactions and events were chronicled with many sage reflections, interspersed with original lines of poetry, and must have been, without doubt, very interesting and edifying to your readers. For my own part, I heartily thank him for his poetical effusions, and am glad that we have a real native poet in the county of Bedford, and hope some day to have an edition of his poetical works, which will be highly prized by

Yours obediently, A Bookman.

I'm sure any local person would have been well aware that Castleden had published a couple of dozen small poetical works by now. Sarcasm was often used in the letters pages, to appear to remain perfectly polite, while issuing a stinging attack.

6ᵗʰ July 1875 Leighton Buzzard Observer
A Peasant's Death – 22ⁿᵈ June

No more he'll drive his team afield,
No more he'll welcome morn;
No more he'll stubborn soil will yield
Unto his plough – low, lorn!
No more he'll sow, nor reap the ripened corn

A peasant, nigh on forty years
He worked on Speedwell Farm;
Age brought its shadows and its fears,
Yet on kind Mercy's arm
This peasant passed to death and closed life's harm

The Master's words we read; * he spoke
Of comfort they had given.
His cottage home is vacant now!
The mansion up in heaven
By mercy is prepared for souls forgiven.

"A weak and helpless worm I fall,"
Were some of his last words;
"Across the river" he has gone;
Mercy these words *records* –
Toil, pain, all o'er; peace, joy, she aye awards.

Together on the Sabbath-day
We mused on Calvary's scene;
That tragedy of saving love
We mourned, yet blessed the theme:
Now by this death we prove life is a dream.

Yet, if "in Jesus they are blessed,
How kind their slumbers are;
From sufferings and from sins released,
And freed from every snare."
May ploughman Cox, in death, bid all prepare!

Note – At *noon* I read the first fourteen verses of the 14th chap. St John's Gospel, and he spoke of the comfort the scriptures had given him in the past. After shaking hands, I left him poorly. An increase of malady came on, and at *morn* Death struck in this peasant's home; so sudden, that before our charity could aid he fell!

George Castleden. 30th June

A William Freeman was the farmer at Speedwell Farm in the 1871 Census, but immediately next door lived William Cox, with his wife and two sons. He would have been 67 by 1875, a good age for a hard life of agricultural labouring.

20th July 1875 Leighton Buzzard Observer

The "Woburn Week" Again. To the Editor of the Leighton Buzzard Observer

Sir, - May I say a word in reference to "A Bookman's" satirical remarks upon our respected friend, Mr. George Castleden, of Woburn, which appeared in your issue of the 6th last? Some persons are shrewd enough in observing others' failings, but not as penetrating in regard to their own. Surely it becomes every man on earth to exercise charity and forbearance –

"To gaze with pity on the throng,
To failings somewhat blind;
To praise the right, forgive the strong,
And feel for all mankind."

Such were the sentiments of Old Humphrey, and I cannot help comparing our Woburn friend to Old Humphrey, for in the preface of one of his books the latter writes: - "I want you, readers, to accept my *Observations* as the remarks of a friendly old man who has some affection in his heart for every human being under the canopy of the skies. While perusing the following pages, they may possibly remind you that age has its infirmities; sad that among them may be reckoned the disposition to talk faster, and dwell longer on past occurrences than is agreeable to some hearers; but, when you put my errors into one scale, forget not to put my friendly intentions into the other." Will "A Bookman" read, mark, learn, and inwardly digest?

Yours, in charity, Eye-Bright.

"..read, mark, learn and inwardly digest.." is a phrase which appears frequently in Castleden's own letters. I wonder if Eye-Bright was actually him? A few scattered lines of poetry in the midst of a letter is certainly his style.

20th July 1875 Leighton Buzzard Observer

"Look at 'That' Picture, then on 'This.' "

That picture is one dated 1811 – "Woburn Sheep-shearing." On it I have often looked. Among the group – a little boy I stood; and now, as I look, I see the seven sons around John, Duke of Bedford, three of whom have departed. The aged earl, and three younger scions in silvered years, remain to testify of time past, and record the fact that that Woburn Park assembling of royal, patrician, plebeian, and pastoral life have nearly "all melted into thin air." What a moral might be taught from this tale of olden time. And, linking my day with the four Dukes of Bedford, and associating with the grandchildren of my father's "sheep-shearing" farmer friends, I find in the picture a local chronology of three score years and ten, also a pictorial voucher of death.

> Men of degrees and class I see,
> Where are they now? Death's mystery
> Hides equally the ducal lord
> And shepherd John; his grim reward
> Has taken life which, as life, *then*
> Comprised our local famous men
> *Now* lost are they, forgot they lie,
> Yet this they speak to moderns –
> "You must die."

5th July

Sixty years and more have flown away since that picture told of the first impulses given to agricultural operations by the Duke Francis, and fostered by his ducal brother John. The Park Farm crowds gave life and activity which pulsetive was felt over the isle, and which may be considered as the initiative of present great results. Now, under the auspices of the grandson, ninth Duke of Bedford, a picture is to be seen in the Elm Avenue. Preliminary, I may say, while time is repeating itself, new scenes and new actors established the ever-living truth – "Vanity of vanities, all is vanity." A walk home under an evening sun, gazing at our park pictures, I found myself at the Avenue, looking upon canvas, and the fragile booths erecting. Job's words fell impressively as in age I trod the path of youth – "He buildeth his hope as a moth, and as a booth the keeper maketh"

6-7th July

The Show – 6th.

It was an agricultural show, which, for magnitude, value and numbers, has not been seen in Woburn Park for a generation. I recount not detail; I relate not the tent speeches; I review not the judgements of the judge; all these and sundry other items of the day, reporters will amply give; but in such a scene, having played a humble part, I link the past, present, and to some, by Lord Chas. Russell's happy reminiscent points, when, referring to the olden Woburn sheep-shearing – "In it you see the child in arms, which, as the patriarch, is now addressing you." And again, as we repeated to a friend in such a show, we prove the flight of time, the vanity of mortality, and the inexorability of death. This newer scene was a theme for a poet's dream; but when a lady kindly suggested a composition, fear of failure prevailed, and, methinks, my Georgina may be left alone. I just record a few facts of this 5th July, to remain documentary of another summer day of bodily health and mental vigour, for which I am grateful. To have looked upon the present ducal family; to have received a passing recognition from the fourth chief; to have sat and listened to the third Marquis of Tavistock; to have heard some of the first utterances of a mind which we fervently hope may long link the house of the past and present in serving the commonwealth; I say, standing "on historic ground," to quote Mr. Howard, these results on this show day was some of the prize giving value to the saying – "Fact is stronger than fiction;" and also, again, enstamping the truth of Young's line-

"Man is immortal till his work is done."

Thus, to be an actor in this scene seemed destiny. Arrangements by relatives were kindly made for me. Again I dined under canvas in Woburn Park; and there, roving down times, ruminating on the past, as I missed many, once contemporary; as I chatted with feebler but younger men; as I gazed upon the blooming lassies and the rising sons of the soil, my musings on the scenes of this sunny July noon, mingled with the mourning contemplation that, recording these reminiscent thoughts, I was adding a last item to the "finis" which as the older actors may soon fall; and, as at eventide I win from this material show this mental *stuff*, I would close with a solemn couplet or two, and as bid a home adieu to this Avenue concourse, representing agriculture in all its ranks, branches and utilities: -

If life's a show – an empty one,
This newer one beneath our sun
Follows still on with shows before,
Till safe upon the silent shore
Where waves ne'er whelm, storms wreck no more.
Yes, as the actors *then* have passed away,
A large crowd my eye now rests upon;
Peer, farmer, peasant, then will be unknown!
Alike forgotten, sinking into the doom,
Rank, riches, rags, all hidden in the tomb.
As empire's pageant and the village fair
Pass on life's way, and melt in vacant air.
And so with *that* "sheep-shearing," long ago,
We join this present agricultural show;
This record offer to the sons of men,
Endorsed and signed as truth, George Castleden.

P.S. – In these home lines I have encroached on no one's path, nor, with intrusive wish, have gone beyond my last.

Local reports are full and fair. Of what I saw and heard I believe this to be true; the reflections I venture are thoughts my own; while a verse learnt by my mother's chair will join the child to the old man, and link Time's shows fleeing, vain and void, with the home eternal on high.

This life's a dream, an empty show,
But the bright world to which we go
Hath joys substantial and sincere;
When shall I wake and find me there?
George Street, Woburn, 13th July – Cherry Fair.

"That picture..." is the "Wobourn Sheepshearing" by George Garrard, a famous detailed agricultural print. The Russell's were pioneers of new agricultural methods and stock breeding, and their Woburn Fairs were the place to be see new inventions and techniques. Garrard captured the annual fair at Woburn in 1811, and the people gathered are nearly all named under it in a key. This shows that amongst many of the Russell family, and other Dukes, Lords and M.P.'s, are an envoy from Russia, Henry Hoare of Wavendon, Samuel Whitbread of Southill, Sir Humphry Davy, the chemist, Robert Salmon, the local inventor, and members of the Board of Agriculture.

27th July 1875 Leighton Buzzard Observer

Lady Russell's Bazaar. To the Editor of the Leighton Buzzard Observer.

Sir, - On the 14th many a child was made to mourn by reason of the ceaseless rain; and on the 15th two valuable societies had their energies damped, though we are glad to state that the Lady Charles Russell's annual missionary sale, including the proceeds from the missionary basket, amounted to the highest sum yet - £68. This satisfactory figure we record with gratitude under the stress of unkind weather, and only add to your last week's report the hope that such-like laudable intentions and kind liberality may, on another annual sale, be welcomed with more auspicious skies.

G.C. 22nd July.

"The Woburn Week". To the Editor of the Leighton Buzzard Observer.

Sir, - I feel obliged to "Eye-bright" for his kind note. More pleasant, apter words could not have been quoted than the sentence from "Old Humphrey." A most truthful exposition of my wish, by the pen, to serve, to please, *not* to pain. "Eye-bright's" note and a kindly word uttered in our Town Hall on my now somewhat famed "week," if they make not "the old man eloquent," they bid him still go on to serve, to please, and grateful be; and for this expression, if you can spare me a space, you will, sir, further oblige your obedient servant,

George Castleden, 21st July.

If "Eye-bright" was Castleden, as I believe, he had just replied to himself!

17th August 1875 Leighton Buzzard Observer

Original Poetry – Rhyme

In Woburn's home I ponder still,
Progressive, dying time;
And in an idle hour I will
Record some thoughts in rhyme.

No classic lore, no learned stuff
I seek this summer day,
My fabric homely 'tis and rough,
But 'tis an honest lay.

Upon my father's pulpit seat
I trace this lyric line,
And if the inspiration hit,
It may hit coming time.

"All flesh is grass;" grass newly mown
Will wither in a day;
Men, fresh as grass, I've seen cut down
And pass to dull decay.

Where are the mates of youthful hour,
Of manhood's later time?
They sleep and wither in grave-yards,
No more to walk, joy, pine.

Where are the Dukes who once have reigned?
Their stewards, tenants, too;
Life's stewardship is closed, and all
To earth have bade adieu.

Life's tale goes on, and newer men
New manners rise to view;
New policies now occupy;
Old times we see are new.

Steam, telegraphic wonders tell,
Science now reigns in power;
Photography, the sun's own art,
Is at its zenith hour.

What wonders next I cannot guess;
A lunar railway may
Bridge partial space, and fling its arch
Across our night and day.

Some wizard-king may bid the stars
Run up to premium height,
And to this moonshine scheme lure dupes
And make their pockets *light*.

Greed, pride, and hope fill many a breast;
Fast wealth is still a snare:
In vain the moralist cries, "Hold!"
In vain he shouts "Beware!"

Some merchant scamp, some gilded name,
Dazzles with future gold;
Dupes, Hudson led, dance on to fame,
In buying shares are sold.

And so my morning song is done:
I sow thoughts oft in rhyme;
And, if it grow in print, why, then
Pray reap this harvest time.
George Castleden
10th August.

24th August 1875 Leighton Buzzard Observer

Local Flower Show. To the Editor of the Leighton Buzzard Observer.

Sir,- Lord Bacon declares "Gardening to be the innocentest, happiest, and most profitable of all employment for mind and body." Not possessing a garden, I copy these words without practically feeling their truth. Yet, as I stroll our Eden nooks, and look upon the tinted flower stars of earth, I feel a mystic delight; and as I read in your columns of the prizes given to our peasants for vegetables, fruits, and flowers, we may say Bacon is right. And now I write a word of commendation on our local shows, and hope such pastoral rivalry may still be stimulated by kindly patronage, be honestly rewarded, and gratefully received. If I hear aright, the shows of Woburn, Fenny, Aspley &c., have been successes and we trust they may herald future comfort, pleasure and profit to many a cottage home.

Perhaps a few lines after a stroll in one of these shows may point part of the tale of 1875, and in its passing from spring to summer on to autumn, may onstamp the ever-living moral – "We all do fade as the flower."

This life's a dream, a flowery show,
We wake to weep, feel blight and woe!
Full many a lovely flower we see
Is struck by death and misery.
The loveliest flower inherits blight:

Oft sheds sweet scent in noisome night.
The prettiest flower may fade ere noon,
And if there tarries aged bloom,
Tint mock the *strength*, and soon decay
Sweeps Beauty's flower show all away.
Alike Imperial tints enchant and fade,
And home's sweet roses, prized, are soon decayed;
Alike the Empress and village belle
May o'er love's wanderings weep a fond farewell!
Alike the pyramid and hamlet tomb,
Hide mortal flowers in mouldering silent gloom!
We read the epitaph, and, mournful, sigh
The sweetest oft the fleetest fade and die,
Like flower shows vanished – vanity
Is scribed on all beneath the summer sky!
George Castleden, August

A New Rhyme for a Novel Company

To the Editor of the Leighton Buzzard Observer

Sir,- By granting admission to this rhyme you may set the stone of thought rolling, and, as wondrous things have been done, greater wonders still may come. There may be something in this home philosophy the world dreams not of; and if, at seventy, I waken up another, as Longfellow has it –

"Age yet may do or date
The oldest tree some fruit may bear."

A little fun amid this sun
May wile an hour away;
Amid men's schemes and vagrant dreams
We'll start one now on day.

Sol's rays now fall upon our ball,
Are lost in depths profound;
I moot a scheme, a useful dream,
Lost sunbeams may be found.

A company in harmony
Might a world blessing be:
Bottle these rays, in Christmas days

Uncork felicity.

Share buyers come and bless each home,
Lay in a present store;
While now we sweat with summer heat,
In winter we'll adore.

And bless the hand, that Britain's land
Can boast of such a boon;
That, bottled nigh, December's sky
A world celebrity.

All ranks, all grades, professions, trades,
May in this venture vie;
Come; purchase shares, leave to your heirs
The *gold* of summer's sky.

No south sea bubble causes trouble,
'Tis wealth in view of home;
Unite, shares buy, let science try
To make a boon our own.

My natal vale may tell a tale
Of wonder and delight;
Aladdin may make summer's day
In winter's Arctic night.

Call not this vain, nor truth distain,
Tho' tis a mystic dream.
This thought, if fraught with might and light,
May rival giant steam.

A Possible Prospectus
Woburn Solar Rays Bottling Company:
An Eligible and Benevolent Investment
Dividends secure, and kept up
So long as Sunbeams fall down.

Principle Office: Woburn, Beds.

Agents may aid and be well paid in all parts of her Majesty's dominions.

The only bar – no agent need apply holding commissions in any moonshine concern. Lastly, as Woburn is gloomed to darkness by the extinction of the gas, it seems the very time of utility and success, insamuch as this company may lighten out streets and warm our homes.

George Castleden, 17th August

N.B. – Directors, bankers, officials, & c. will be published as soon as the company floats.

Comedy is seldom seen in Castleden's writings. Whether he intended to be funny, or purely sarcastic, to mock the advancements of steam and telegraph, I am not sure, but if he only knew how prophetic his words were on capturing and storing solar power!

7th September 1875 Leighton Buzzard Observer

Original Poetry. A Bedford Day. 25th August, 1875.

Through fields all white, brown, black, and green,
I steamed into town
Where Bunyan's statue shining stands,
And tells his world renown.

My thoughts, mine own, which I must hide,
Rose up as on I sped;
Winged by the vapour, on we flew,
Nor met with crash or dread.

From Woburn Sands to Bedford town
Thoughts flashed upon the mind
And many a bygone scene came back
With men and things behind.

Familiar things will haunt and dwell
Within this heart of mine;
Like music's echoes sound and swell,
And key all future time.

I need not tell, men cannot now
Reciprocate past scenes;
And idle 'twere to seek regard
For cherished, vanished dreams.

And yet no miser e'er can be
More dwelling on his gold
Than the heart-miser of past joys
When all those joys are cold.

Enough to scribe, this harvest morn
I trod and mused alone,
Paced the old streets, and thought of days,
Familiar faces flown.

My father's friends, I passed each door;
There he found welcomes, warm.
Upon the bridge I viewed the site
Of past election storm.

I strolled, and looked on Hillyard's tomb –
The pastor, brother, friend;
Through many years of sunshine, gloom,
That friendship did descend.

In realms celestial, ever pure,
The brethren happy dwell;
The ashes mingling, o'er their graves
I heave a fond farewell.

I called upon a Woburn friend;
I saw the brother, gone!
Kindness conferred may never die,
Though kind friends all have flown.

A chat with one of Howard's firm
Links a world-honoured name;
John Howard lives! Now Howards win
An agricultural fame.

One other call enforced the truth –
Friends wither, change, and die!
The moral may serve age and youth;
Time's tale is vanity.

And then along home's fruitful vale
I sang the harvest song;
With it I close this visit-tale;
This surely can't be wrong.

"To praise the ever-bounteous Lord
My soul wake all thy powers;
He calls, and as his voice comes forth
The smiling harvest hours

Well pleased the toiling swains behold
The waving yellow crop;
With joy they bear the sheaves away,*
And now again in hope."
George Castleden, 30th August.

* This was being realised on this day, and now the notes of gratitude around in many a homestead for such a glorious disappointment of fears, and such a sunny garnering of harvest fruits. Let lines form a national hymn close this Bedfordshire day –
"Earth shall obey her Maker's will,
And yield a full increase;
Our God will crown his chosen isle
With fruitfulness and peace."

14th September 1875 Leighton Buzzard Observer
Original Poetry – A Loyal Temperance Rhyme

Thanks, worthy Queen! A letter, worth
The gold of Ind, I read;
The temperance cause may sound its worth,
It suits its urgent need,
'Tis catholic, inclusive, good indeed.

Had like advice but influenced then,
When temperance became
A principle to govern men,
Its charitable fame
Had won from north to south a saving name.

But rigour reigned, extremists vowed
No medium they'd obey;
The pledge or nothing was the cry;
And so in early day
The tongue vowed scorn, and blight and sad decay.
I've known its worth, but still I ne'er
By fetters felt the ban;
Free, grateful that I broke the snare,
I hail this liberal plan
And shout, God save our Queen, who seals it now for man.

The following extract of a letter from Sir Thomas Biddulph to the Temperance Society impelled my rhyme:-"I am commanded by her Majesty, in reply to the prayers of it that her Majesty should become the patron of the society, to say that her Majesty has already expressed her opinion in favour of the objects which the society desires to promote, and consents to become patron of it, organised, as it appears to be, on the basis which includes all who advocates temperance, without insisting necessarily on total abstinence – Balmoral, August 28th.

George Castleden, Woburn 8th Sept.

14th September 1875 Leighton Buzzard Observer

Woburn Solar Rays Bottling Company. To the Editor of the Leighton Buzzard Observer.

Sir,- I use "fun" in my rhyme; it has been dubbed "nonsense," and the scheme or dream has been laughed at in the streets. Now I am not displeased at this. The first stop has been attained. My Rhyme has fallen upon thought. Criticism, ridicule, and incredulity have been the pioneers of notable discoveries, and the sneer of the sceptic has been the harbinger of truth in all ages. I occupied your columns by playful verse, permit a space for graver prose. In reply to "nonsense" I say – how long was steam, as a locomotive power, considered nonsense? Suppose years ago some dreamer had said the lightning would be collared, and become man's errand boy, don't you think that had been called nonsense! If electricity may be cabined, cribbed, confined, by logical inference, I see no reason, mind and machinery meeting, why the manipulation of the solar rays may be long a mystery, and when solution *is*, the sceptic may safely adopt, and incredulity, which may now scorn, may then hail a beneficent discovery, which may light warm, and bless a world.

There may be a *sense* in nonsense. It may tell mystic truth of which this world dreams not of in its philosophy, and which, sleeping in mental depths, profound, may waken up in some poetical "ariel," to the utter surprise of a present mole-eyed vision, while it may be a keen rebuke to the obstructive audacity of a very limited self-sufficiency relative to knowledge that is to be. From the *Rock* of Sept. 3rd, I support what was written in August. I quote words confirmatory of the "nonsense|" ventured, and I might add its weight to the oft-quoted truth – "It is not *what* is said, but *who* says it that the world pays heed to: -

"At present we are engaged in studying the sun with new instruments of wondrous precision, but we cannot yet tell any more than the patriarch of old 'where light dwelleth.' Nor can we explain a hundredth part of the ordinances of Heaven,' although one of the Bristol illuminati would have us believe that corn averages sympathise with the solar spots. We may have dropped the lead 'deeper than ever plummet sounded' into the dark unfathomed caves of ocean; but there remains a lower deep, into which vain man shall never penetrate until he have shuffled off his present mortal coil. We may have gained some insight into the law of storms, but we cannot 'bind the sweet influence of the Pleiades' or 'stay the bottles of Heaven.' "

May these words and extracts teach and warn. Peradventure in fun, nonsense, doubt, there may be hid truth and love, which is now fathomless to science, and to present philosophy is past finding out; but which, as facts, may be as veritable as the return of

"The illustrious stranger

After the long travel of a thousand years"

In the British Museum is a rare book – "The First Scantlings of a Hundred Inventions." How much nonsense is in it I must leave, but perchance, in it have been found the first cuts into hidden, valuable, and serviceable truth.

I am, sir, your obedient servant, George Castleden.

P.S. – One of Humour's last remarks I append. A neighbour said, what a capital consignment for our Arctic explorers your bottled sunbeams would have been. In reply I would say, had the discovery been made, in that eternal ice and snow it might have comforted and saved a repetition of Polar tragedies.

Another regular poetry contributor had started sending poems to the LBO. Unlike Castleden, O.X.Y. preferred to remain anonymous, but Castleden appreciated their efforts.

21ˢᵗ **September 1875** Leighton Buzzard Observer

Original Poetry. To "O.X.Y."

I like your rhyme-bard, "O.X.Y;"
The Daisy tells of *home:*
A trivial thing, yet on mind's sigh
To far lands it has flown

And while the emigrant may tell,
Across the water's foam,
Of dear delights left far awa'
In his loved native home,

Let those who stay in England's day
Hail ever her wild flowers;
Like "O.X.Y." repeat in song
The Daisy's spring-time hours.

And if from home still forced to roam,
The Daisy, lowly flower,
May rise and blow where'er we go
By mind's mysterious power.

While autumn's fringe flies fast to join
Dear winter's frowning wing,
The Daisy, named as the "Day's eye,"
Shuts up till laughing spring.

A brother bard thus pays regard,
And in his winter time
Welcomes the spring-time, "O.X.Y.,"
And hails his genial rhyme.

So poetry may join all time,
And kink life's flying hours;
And kindred poets sing and praise
Home's fields, flocks, fruits, and flowers.
G.C.

Then it was time for what had become an annual farewell to the Swallows.

28th **September 1875** Leighton Buzzard Observer

Original Poetry. Good-bye to the Swallows.

Farewell, my birdie friends;
In glorious sunshine now you close
Your summer visit here:
To what fair clime your speed away
And follows up the orb of day –
With it return next year –

Is all unknown; your twittering tone
And ebon wing will soon be gone
To some far distant shore
Your circling flight, your breast of white,
Your chimney home at morn and night,
My eyes may watch no more.

And should it be another year
You come again, if I'm not here
To hail the summer, new,
Still on this sunny Sabbath-day,
As friends you wing your mystic way,
I wave a home adieu.

Our fathers watched the swallows too,
They hailed the summer birdie crew;
They in our grave-yards sleep!
Sons, ere the swallows come again,
May leave this mortal scene of pain
Where man grows up to weep.*
G.C.

* Four in our homes waiting the grave when these lines were written

The LBO was never shy of printing letters from critics of his style and content.

5<u>th</u> **October 1875** Leighton Buzzard Observer

To the Bard of Woburn
Your effusions I've read, but, oh! With such pain;
Their meaning I've tried to elicit;
Common sense must be precious – pray try once again,
I implore you to be more explicit.
Your "Loyal Temperance Rhyme"* I've once or twice scann'd,
To it's meaning I am mentally blind;
Oh! deep are your thoughts when none other understand
The essays of your poetical mind.

This "Loyal Temperance Rhyme" in words seems to me
To cast doubt on the score of your sanity:
Your brain from disease can't be entirely free
Or you possess unmeasured vanity.
If septic I am, it is not without cause,
Every week egotism is more o'er you stealing;
Your mind must be wandering, pray give it a pause,
Or, like Burns, we shall hear of you "reeling."

Your "soda-water" rays have been bottled and bunged,
Your "Loyal Temperance Rhyme" is no better,
Such nonsense from print should be straightway expunged –
Pray pardon this rhythmical letter!
When you swim the Hellespont, some one's equal you'll be,
To your career it will be a sure coup de main;
But whatever you do, whether by land or by sea,
You cannot keep from us *your name.*
J. H.
   * Respectfully dedicated to the author of "Loyal Temperance Rhyme," published in your issue of 14th September.

Of course, Castleden took the tongue-in-cheek reference to being a Bard as a great honour!

12th October 1875 Leighton Buzzard Observer

Woburn Darkness. To the Editor of the Leighton Buzzard Observer.

Sir, - I like to be grateful. "J.H." has given me the distinction of "the bard" of my native town; for this thanks are due. Still I cannot help thinking my "effusions" "elicit" things which are too "explicit" for "J.H" and gentlemen of his kidney. Light and darkness never did agree, and Woburn's night just now is peculiar. I know learned critics are privileged, and, too old now for critical contention, while ever grateful for kind words, unkind, or unjust ones, anonymously said, sung, or written, I have neither time, will, nor wit to battle with. A corner for this once, and you, sir, will oblige "the bard,"

George Castleden, Woburn, Michaelmas Fair.

26th October 1875 Leighton Buzzard Observer

Woburn Darkness. To the Editor of the Leighton Buzzard Observer.

Sir, - The report in the Observer of our School Board puzzled us. "Rumour" may say anything. Why should not "Truth" speak? Is a neighbour row wanted? Are we to have the disgraceful doings of a late election repented? Are secret consultations and foregone conclusions to override open debate and honest intentions? The puzzle is increased by being informed of the 1s. in the pound added to the very premature move for new school buildings. The ratepayers are quite in the dark relative to this vote of two and two and the "tie!" Surely, on such important moves constituents might consult with, and, perhaps, beneficially check their representatives. Light is wanted. We are kept in the dark. The night of Woburn is more lonesome and "inked" than was ever known by that worthy resident the oldest inhabitant; and if the wink, nod, and *silence* are to rule, and no ventilation is allowed, while Shakespeare talks of something being rotten in the state of Denmark, it strikes me a moral sanitary inspector might find putrescence nearer home. Woburn is now without a watchman, its night policeman is removed, and its lights are extinguished. These three guards have been taken away. Insecurity is; accident or urgency may be, and yet the inhabitants grope, and hope some one may lighten our darkness. A corner may serve humanity, save calamity, and preserve persona and properties.

I am, sir, your obedient servant. George Castleden, October 20.

26th October 1875 Leighton Buzzard Observer

An October Rhyme.
The fading leaves around us falling
Tell the summer fast is dying;
The seasons changing, neighbours falling,
Inform that Time is swiftly flying:
All nature living still is dying.

And so we sing in our home tale
Amid a last October;
How many more within this vale
May find me yet a rover
I cannot tell in this a last October.

But, as we take the wonted stroll
With one in weakness smitten,
Each tinted leaf may tell the soul
That Death is on it written,
And man, sin-blighted, by Death will soon be hidden.

Yet, still the hope may point us on,
As leaves are round us falling.
To Eden's blightness, vernal land;
These withered leaves are calling
Where winter's rains and snows no more are falling –
Sin, grief, pain, death no more life's joys are palling.
"The Bard of Woburn."

Having been given the title Bard, he obviously felt free now to use it.

2nd November 1875 Leighton Buzzard Observer

Impromptu Lines to "O.X.Y."

Thanks for your fitting "cranky" word
About the friendly singing bird,
Whoever it may be.
But for the notes which you disown

I might surmise the pleasing tone
Resembles often thee.

But let this pass, the singing bird
May thank you for the friendly word,
Whoever you may be;
And let us hope that birdie may
Around the cottage lingering stay,
Please with its melody.

And should some envious "cranky" scribe
Pick up another stone to drive
The bridle from his home,
May O.X.Y." again defend,
And friends like him each bird befriend,
Who sings in friendly tone.

Sing *peace* to shame the sons of strife,
Sing *truth* to heal the ills of life,
Sing *home*, and leave the rest;
Sing hymns and songs our fathers proved,
Sing melodies our mothers loved,
And then we sing the best.
G.C., Woburn, 26th October.

30th November 1875 Leighton Buzzard Observer

Sunbeams and Raindrops. To the Editor of the Leighton Buzzard Observer.

Sir, - If the axiom be correct, "Nothing is right if anything be wrong," methinks there is still much to put to rights, naturally and morally. Some time ago I was twitted relative to a project for bottling off summer's surplus sunshine. An anecdote may serve. George Stephenson, asking one to define the power that propelled the train, illuminated his perplexed and cloudy friend by saying – "Bottled sunbeams deposited in bygone centuries, and which is called coal." This nature achieved; and may not art, the pupil of Nature, copy? and, as she finds all her models in Nature, surely, with the aid of chemistry, some day she may be seize the sunbeam, and deposit in some organism the solar rays to warm in future days, and give a next generation a pleasant and profitable boon. And then that which is now occult, and which present minds call "nonsense," may blaze out as a most benignant discovery, cheering and lighting our winter, and conferring immortality on the discoverer while summer shines. Just now we are perplexed what to do with these redundant rains. All receptacles are at fault; and desolation, disease, and death are the consequences of these wild floods. And yet another year the heavens may be brass, and the earth iron by reason of the drought. Not long ago a writer in the Times descanted on this topic, and I thought, as I read, a critic might call this article brilliant nonsense, and yet who dare say there is not hidden truth in it, and something of value not dreamed of in present philosophy? To finish with a reference to my first sentence, as an observer of Nature, may I not write that we are wrong relative to economising the sunbeams, and the proper utilisation of the raindrops, and, should any philosophic or chemical Columbus arise and discover a way to secure the one and confine the other, two wrongs, naturally, which we suffer and groan under may be put to rights; and, should it be that, out of this floody disorder, order springs, the, in further "nonsense" a damp hour on a dark November eve may have been usefully spent, and you, sir, may set the ball of thought rolling, by kindly giving this a place in your columns.

I remain your obedient servant, George Castleden, Woburn, Beds.

21st December 1875 Leighton Buzzard Observer

Woburn – Home and Foreign Missions.

An incident in this quiet little town may class among the charitable events of the coming Christmas. Instead of Lady Charles Russell's usual "winter basket," a sale of useful and fancy articles was held in the Town Hall on Wednesday, in aid of missions at home and abroad. The stalls were amply filled, and kindly attended by Mrs. Southey, Mrs. Windham, and Miss Runciman. One kind lady was missed, but absence may be happily accounted for. Between three and four o'clock her Grace the Duchess of Bedford arrived, and, with several of the local clergy and gentry, and some of the townspeople, kindly helped the receipts of a satisfactory sale, and we hope the results may be a good augury in this town of the season's benison – peace and goodwill. "Light and hade attend our path," and, while this scene was pleasant light, shadow fell across by reason of affliction, and the absence of Lady Charles Russell, to whom kind care these societies have been much indebted for many years, was much to be regretted. But, in Time's incertitudes, we urge –

"While neighbours go, and changes come,
Support the missions still of home."

In the **28th December 1875** Leighton Buzzard Observer, a writer, who had written into the paper a letter covering many subjects, ended their letter:

"…The approaching New Year, which we hope will be a "happy one" to all your readers, we expect to be hailed with some "glad stanzas of rhymes" by our Woburn bard, G. C., who is always on the qui vive.

On earth be peace, to men good will;

Now it becomes me to be still,

And sign myself a Goose's Quill.

IV

Letters: 1876 - 1880

Woburn School Board – Death of Abdul Aziz – Turkish Atrocities – War in the East – Gladstone – The Zulu War – 74th Birthday Party – Bonaparte – Storm at Woburn – Woburn, Mass. – Afghan War – Election Corruption.

11th January 1876 Leighton Buzzard Observer

Woburn School Board Election. To the Editor of the Leighton Buzzard Observer.

Sir, - You may do service by granting a space for a few cautionary words. Fellow ratepayers, avoid a contest. This may be done by adopting the wise suggestion of a *representative* board. Five interests in this parish should be represented. Let the public good rule, and methinks you will have a peaceful and economical solution of a question which may have imported into it wanton neighbour strife and needless expense. Peace, truth, and economy all vote for this plan, and it is for you, ratepayers, to do your duty; in these cautionary words I have done mine.

I remain, sir, your obliged servant, George Castleden, Woburn, 6th January.

18th January 1876 Leighton Buzzard Observer

Woburn – An Annual Tea Meeting was held in the Independent Chapel, on Monday last, and a goodly group met, and, though cold without, what with gas, tea, tattle, and wool, it was warm within. After tea a Christian hour was spent, Major Windham presiding. Praise and prayer opened the service; a kindly address from the chairman was followed by others from the Rev. W. Attack, Messrs. Davis, Horton, Castleden, and the Rev. J. Andrews; and we may say of all that they were keyed in practical Christianity, and that it was a well-spent hour, and, as we spoke of the passing away of the old generation, and of the aged feeling, nature's decay, in such a scene, while age might sigh farewell, it could wish many happy new years to youth, and so in this spirit closed one more new year's tea meeting.

And so these annual days run round;

They measure out the mortal ground,
While travellers in each past year
Fall from our ranks and disappear!
So we must follow who remain,
Must quit this scene of joy and pain;
As fathers, prophets fell, so must we fall,
And death, in time, will strike and bury all.
- Communicated

...but with the "well spent hour" reference, it can only be Castleden. Then it was back to the education question again.

15th February 1876 Leighton Buzzard Observer

Woburn School Board Election. To the Editor of the Leighton Buzzard Observer.

Sir,- Some of us will be obliged by the insertion of this brief note. Practically, it is now a representative Board. By casting the lot at last, this proves to me it might have been so decided at the first, and by it strife and cash been saved. But experience is the only school some will dance in. I only regret the ratepayers have to pay the piper. Now the question is settled, let the forced lot-casting in our town be adopted as the voluntary method in other places; it will save unkind and unjust speaking, angry acting, neighbourly animosity, and unnecessary expense. And surely this recipe is worth something in this strifeful world. As a son of peace, I commend it, and, as an aged Woburn son, I say, avoid neighbourly treachery and strife, which are the certain agents of destruction, whether it be a home, town, city or land.

A word to the wise is sufficient; and prey serve peace by the insertion, and you will oblige, among others, your obedient servant, George Castleden, February 9th.

22nd February 1876 Leighton Buzzard Observer

The School Board Question. To the Editor of the Leighton Buzzard Observer.

Sir,- As I am but a small ratepayer, the question of a rate would not be much to me. I think, however, that Mr. G. Castleden's letter in your paper last week is a warning worth notice. Depend upon it the voluntary scheme will pay in peace and economy, whereas the compulsory system creates discord and animosity amongst neighbours; and few people like coercion. A remark made by Mr. Forster at Edinburgh is worth notice. He said – "I expect, first or last, we shall have School Boards pretty well over England, and for these two reasons – first, that every year Englishman and every English ratepayer is getting more and more to feel the duty; and moreover it will become more difficult to obtain voluntary subscriptions when the subscriber feels he is doing one of two things – one which he fully approves of, namely helping education, and another, saving the pocket of his more stingy neighbour, which he does not so much wish to do." These words of Mr. Forster's are true, but we hope Leighton Buzzard will prove to all the neighbouring towns that there is vitality in the voluntary principle amongst its residents yet.

Sir, yours, A Small Ratepayer.

29th February 1876 Leighton Buzzard Observer

School Boards. Voluntary v. Compulsory – Which! To the Editor of the Leighton Buzzard Observer.

Sir,- To "A Small Ratepayer" I would say I hope Leighton may prove that there is vitality in the voluntary system. Briefly compare the two. The voluntary says "I will;" the compulsory says you shall. The first suits Englishmen, the last is more for Orientals; first is liberty, the last akin to despotism. Neighbour strife never was known while the voluntary system ruled. From the seed lately sown I fancy a harvest of animosity, and perhaps secret treachery, will produce bitter fruit in years to come. Sixty years, and no coercive tax was known. Economy and utility ruled. Monthly inspection and personal supervision kept things right. Now coercion produces contortion of the face by the money twinge; and, devolving their duties on a Board, ratepayers must pay with some pardonable ejaculations. Part with the voluntary for the compulsory, and you may find, in the loss of money and temper, an aggravating realisation of the old fable of the silly dog who lost the solid beef by snapping at the shadow. May Leighton still remain as an example of what the voluntary system can do in serving education, and in saving the pockets of the ratepayers, if it be fairly and liberally supported.

I remain, sir, your obedient servant. George Castleden, February 23.

2nd May 1876 Leighton Buzzard Observer

Woburn Almshouses. To the Editor of the Leighton Buzzard Observer.

Sir,- In the "Observer" I read – "It was remarkable that as much relief went to the Almshouses at Woburn as was distributed to the whole of the two parishes of Brickhill – no less than £120 a year."

On this fact a question starts – Are these almshouses occupied by destitute Woburnites? For I read on, and find "Destitution, not pauperism," is to be the rule. If destitute, then, we say take care that the practical mercy of England's poor's provision be not set aside by theoretical experiments or local legislation. This will never pay.

The question is put in print – why? With the exception of a cold Easter meet, no public meetings are held; questions can neither be asked nor counsel given. So, right or wrong, perpetuity is the motto. To help the honest poor; to hint to ratepayers, once more, their duty; and to gently warn our guardians on taking a step, which, legally right, may be morally and loudly wrong, I ask the admission of this, on Mr Gilby's statement, and remain, sir, your obedient servant, George Castleden, 27th April

In 1635, Sir Francis Staunton of Birchmoor made his will and arranged to leave funds for the erection of houses for the poor of Woburn. The original buildings were replaced by Staunton House in 1851, and the number increased to 20. They were listed by English Heritage in March 1987 as Grade II, of special interest.

23rd May 1876 Leighton Buzzard Observer

Tributary. To the Editor of the Leighton Buzzard Observer.

Sir,- I hear one of your contributors has gone the way of all bards. In the Observer he did me a great kindness; over his ashes let the aged bard tone requiem note; and *now*, knowing who "O.X.Y." was, gratitude asks this favour as a mark of respect to one who "did good by stealth," and who, having usefully served his generation, amid Nature's new life, fell asleep to waken on the resurrection of the just.

The Funeral of Mr Inwood, Woburn Sands: -

A tributary line I send
Upon a modest bygone friend;
I knew him in our verdant vale,
I knew him *not* in my rhyme tale,
When signing "O.X.Y."

No "cranky scribe" was "O.X.Y.,"
His friendly verses ever lie
In memory's casket cell.
I thanked him as a friend unknown,
And now I hear of his last groan–
Of "O.X.Y.'s" farewell!

Long silent notes may still sound fame;
A kind word needs no sounding name;
It, mystic, keys the heart!
I know his name, but speak it not,
His kindness shall not be forgot
Till Time and memory part.

Like to the nightingale's sweet strain,
Unseen, it fills the wood and plain,
And cheers a wanderer, lone;
So, "O.X.Y.," they friendly line
May echo o'er the path of time,
Recall a music tone.

Which bids heart gratitudes to rise;
Now, in this scene of tears and sighs,
Peace to thy memory, peace!
Then, "O.X.Y.," *now* in the sky,
Thy seraph song sounds – Victory!
There jars and sorrows cease,
From sins and woes he finds a blest release.
G. Castleden

So, only upon his death, was the local poet O.X.Y. unmasked. Charles Inwood ran a tailor business in Woburn Sands, and later his sons ran a branch in Fenny Stratford. His eldest son, another Charles, became a Methodist missionary minister and toured the world for many years, his reminiscences being published.

23rd May 1876 Leighton Buzzard Observer
To the East Wind

Charles Kingsley lauded thy *sword* breath,
Gave thee poetic praise;
And thou didst stab the bard to death,
Cut short his useful days.

In this May month, 'neath sun and shade,
Thy breath has cut most keen;

The rich and poor before it fade,
And vanish from Time's scene!

The statesman Frenchman whose rich mind
Was stored to save a State,
Fell 'neath thy stab; a parent, kind
He met a cruel fate. *

And others who I name not here
As victims fade and fall;
I laud not thee, assassin East,
I shrink, and to thee call –

Depart! depart! Thy stinging breath
Bids flowers to wither, die;
Birds hush their song, and chilling cold
With silent death are nigh.

He stays his rough wind when the East
Spits forth its poison-breath;
'Tis neither good for man nor beast,
'Tis springtide's lingering death.

Yet sages say that things unkind
Are still in kindness given;
They flee from earth, and bid us find
Substantial joy in Heaven.
G.C., George Street, 17ᵗʰ May.

*Note. – I had written part of this, and then read the sudden death of
M. Ricard – a master mind, and a mind to which France may be indebted,
and perhaps Europe may own its supremacy. In an act of fatherly kindness
extinguished. How mysterious! In a moment darkness falls on mental light
which had politically lit France; and, if good, which may illumine lands.

*This reference to the East was the first signs in his writings of the coming
conflict in Eastern Europe. Serbia and Montenegro declared independence
from the Ottoman (Turkish) Empire, at the same time as Bulgaria rose up.
Within a year or so, the Ottomans were also fighting against the Russians,
and the combined situation became known as the "Great Eastern Crisis".*

Atrocities were committed on all fronts, and reported freely in the press here. All that was to come though, and in the meantime, the Queen's birthday had come around again.

6th June 1876 Leighton Buzzard Observer

A Royal Memory - The Birthday, 24th May, 1876

"This, the Monarch's birthday, prompts a last loyal lyric. As a year of Royal travel on the sea, and some regal deeds on land – to wit, your London Hospital day, it may be sung by favoured bards, but I am grateful, on another natal day, I can pipe my rustic reed and sing at home, "God save our worthy Queen."

> Another May brings forth the day,
> The birthday of our Queen;
> Again I say, on this birthday,
> While all these days I've seen,
> God save and bless old England's noble Queen.
>
> In going out and coming home (1)
> Health, safety, both were found;
> In Windsor's keep a royal group
> Have circled, happy, round,
> While cheers have rung o'er deeds on Britain's ground. (2)
>
> O, may the Prince, as India's friend
> Be known in coming time;
> When England's kingly crown descends
> May the far Eastern clime
> Feel in his rule peace, joy, and justice shine.
>
> So with the mother Queen I join
> Prince Albert's princely son;
> This year their mutual travels shine,
> And each good-will has won,
> From the uprising to the setting sun.
>
> A year of light and shade has fled!
> How swift the years fly away!
> The Queen has mourned her kindred dead,

New life has cheered the day;
Then death swift struck and gloom'd the parent's way. (3)

Our bells now ring "God save the Queen;"
May Time's still-winged flight
Bear blessings to each Royal scene.
Till through death's parting night
All re-unite in ever-spring delight

Our bells now tone my natal town;
How mocking are those bells;
Their changes tell life's up and down,
Its welcomes and farewells!
They sound joy-grief o'er Woburn's hills and dells

Once more I hear the birthday peal,
Once more I hail its tone;
Once more in Woburn flowery vale
We join the prayer alone –
"God save our gracious Queen – God bless the throne"
George Castleden, George Street, Woburn 25th May
Notes.

1. I may refer to Dean Stanley's warm hearted sermon from the 122nd Psalm, 1v., in Westminster Abbey, on the safe coming home of the Prince of Wales.

2. Here I refer to the hearty greetings at Her Majesty's kind visit to open the "Grocers' Wing" of that noble institution – The London Hospital.

3. In this natal month a prince was born, and, as a tiny bud, it was conveyed to yon Eden-house where blights whither not, nor Easterlies kill. This may be a cloud in any home, but, with faith in the silver lining, surely *it is right* whene'er the babe may die,

"Heaven's angel kind enfolds the bud,
And bide it blossom *there*."

27th June 1876 Leighton Buzzard Observer
On the Death of Abdul Aziz, Sultan of Turkey

One Sardanapalus, in ancient time,
Within his palace home, Assyria's clime,

Died in the fiery flame; self-crushed he died,
The pile funereal of stupendous pride!
All lost in Time's dense thickening, hiding gloom,
Grand Ninevah tells this obvious tomb. *

Another land sends forth a present sound,
Which jars on Europe's nations all around:
The Sultan of the East, dethroned today,
With his own hand draws the red blood away!
In his own palace, midst his wives and gold,
He sighs and dies! His days are ever told.
Now Eastern waters flow round Abdul's tomb,
And Moslem skies mock suicidal gloom.

Moral
So potentates of greed, pride, pomp, and power,
Unstable, vanish in the mortal hour;
Crowns fall in dust! Inevitable doom,
The peasant, prince, all feed the hungry tomb.
G. Castleden, London 8th June
*See Lord Byron's drama of "Sardanapalus."

On the Newer Assassinations
These startling murders, 'neath the Eastern sky,
An added pang to Europe do supply;
They prove where'er man's heart, sin-cursed, is found,
'Neath every sky 'tis murder's haunted ground.
Revenge, lust, greed exist, incite, enslave;
They suit the coward and seduce the brave,
Make man the fiend, and bid him in his hate
To shoot a girl, and men of Moslem State.
They sadly rage to spoil or blast a home,
They thunder round the world and startle Rome!
A simple sin may cause home's lasting smart,
While compound crime to madness stings the heart:
Men are sin's serfs, and men its victims too,
And so 'twill be till Time shall say adieu
G.C, 17th June.

The Sultan had just been deposed from power, and at the time, it was thought he had committed suicide. It is now believed other hands may have been on the scissors that used to cut his wrists.

4th July 1876 Leighton Buzzard Observer

A Woburn Park Thought. The "Marlboro' Oak" and the Plain Scenery.

In balmy nooks of solitude
I mock the rough and miss the rude,
Win pleasure e'en from out keen pain,
And tune the sigh with this park strain –

Majestic tree,
I've seen my neighbours flee
Since I round thee
Have strolled in boyish glee.

Three dukes from yon grand gall
I've seen in ashes fall!
Have seen them covered by the pall –
Deaths pall – which covers all.

Stewards and tenants, where are they?
Once active men of mark;
They know not now this sunny day –
They stroll not Woburn Park!

And so our fathers, friends, and foes,
Have withered, fled from sight!
The present links the grave's repose,
Our day, its noiseless night!

See, all around is parkly, gay,
'Tis smiling, staging June;
Yet as we gaze, this flower-crowned scene
Is garnished for the tomb!

Again this June's returning noon
I joy, and yet I mourn;

The living live, the dead in gloom
Are hidden in the bourn,
From whence no traveller shall e'er return.

P.S. - 28th June.
Thou mighty tree, thou mighty tree
Now laughing in midsummer glee,
When whelmed in yon dark sea
The present will the future be;
Then in renowned verdancy
On death may live this tree.

A moral and a monk I see
As I survey this sturdy tree;
Man sows the acorn – dies!
Within this vale of hopes and fears
This oak survives a thousand years,
A native of home skies.

This rhyming record it may be
An epitaph on this oak tree;
All matter must decay;
While soul, immortal, surely must
Rise o'er the ruins of man's dust
And lives an ever day.

Note. – Sitting on the stumps of this oak, surveying the Park's pretty scene – the summer sky, the emerald carpet, the costly herds, the silvery Bason, and the Abbey pile, all make a picture dwarfing into insignificance man's copies. But, gazing on such a scene, reminiscent thought conjures back life's bygones! Then we think and sigh! Perhaps on these Elysian fields, oft sown by death, impressive and solemn lines may best fit and close this little home-rhyme legend.
    "A span is all that man can boast,
    An inch or two of time;
    Man is but vanity and dust
    In all his flower and prime.

See the vain race of mortals move
Like shadows o'er the plain,
They rage and strive, desire and love,
But all the noise is vain.

Some walk in honour's courtly show
Some dig for golden ore;
They toil for heirs, they know not who;
They dig, are soon no more!"
George Castleden

The Eastern Crisis was becoming more pressing, and became a precursor to the Russo-Turkish War. Newspapers ran lurid descriptions of the various atrocities committed by both sides.

19ᵗʰ September 1876 Leighton Buzzard Observer

Turkish Atrocities in Bulgaria. To the Editor of the Leighton Buzzard Observer.

Sir,- On things tingling the ears of Christendom, and which are mantling the cheek of humanity all over the world, I would ask a corner of your paper. Predictive and nervous words from the *Daily News*, to which all honour be given, prompted a few lines on barbarities which cannibals would not perpetrate, and which fiends in hell might execrate. And you say, oh, statesmen of Europe, that the *status quo* must be maintained; that this must last. I tell you it will not last. You must find another solution for the Eastern Question, or civilisation is a delusion, justice a mockery, and Christianity a farce and a failure.

What falsehoods in thy name will men repeat,
O Policy! Delusive, cruel cheat;
Truth slain by thee, when lust, pride, hate combine
And tongue and sword ally in hell's delight,
Pen, pulpit, platform, all may convert men,
And strike at right by lies which all condemn.
Bulgaria bids cry of shame to rise;
It echoes under Europe's Christian skies.
Wrongs deepest groan, mercy's beseeching cry
Are both ignored by party policy.
Outrage and murder revel in the plea,
We must preserve the East's integrity;
Turk tyranny may triumph by a lie,

310

And statesmen jest, while victims shrieking die.

Methinks this is not a question for politicians; it is not a question of civil and religious liberty all over the world; it is a question of universal humanity to record its protest on such unutterable deeds. If "One touch of nature makes the whole world kin," this unnatural touch has caused a shriek and shudder which has pulsed the heart of humanity wherever it beats, and has made kin of all nations, in their cry of horror over such detestable infamies, such novel cruelties, such wanton desolations.

May I ask the favour of an insertion for this local protest, echoed by neighbours who to the Press pay homage, and who had it as the vindicator of right, and the scourger of wrong; for its service relative to the exposure of these Satanic deeds all Englishmen are thankful.

I remain, sir, your obedient servant, George Castleden, September 8th

There had been reports of the apparent massacre of thousands of Bulgarian civilians by Ottoman forces at Batak. News of the refusal to take prisoners, the barbaric killing of civilians, and the desecration of churches was reported world-wide.

30th September 1876 Bedfordshire Times & 3rd October 1876 Leighton Buzzard Observer

Ridgmount. Turkish Atrocities – A large and influential meeting of Nonconformists was held at the Baptist School, on Wednesday last. The Rev. A. Knell, chairman, and the following ministers were present: Revs. R. Speed, of Bedford; J. H. Blake and J. Tuckwell, of Luton; D. Attack, of Hockliffe; J. Andrews, of Woburn; S. McAlister, of Cranfield; G. Ducred, of Leighton; and J. Readman of Wootton. It was moved by Mr. Castleden, of Woburn, and unanimously carried: - 1. That the hearty thanks of this meeting be given to the press, and special thanks to the *Daily News* for the open and truthful reports of the abominable atrocities perpetrated in Bulgaria and other provinces of Christian Europe by that human fiend, the brutal Turk. 2. That this meeting in behalf of the principles of our common humanity, beseeches of the Government that they immediately urge the cessation of these abominable crimes and cruelties. 3. To their beloved and gracious Queen this meeting ventures to approach and say – Known to all is her Majesty's kindness of heart therefore this meeting very humbly suggests that, then the nation shudders in horror, and all its members are giving utterance by groan and execration, and the flowing tears of sympathy, that, for the honour of England, the lords spiritual and temporal and the honourable Commons should be assembled soon to solemnly endorse the voice of an outraged people, and to confirm the verdict of civilisation,

Christianity, and universal humanity, of crimes and cruelties which stain the glory of this land, unsettle the peace of Europe, make hell to blush, and heaven to crimson with holy indignation.

10th October 1876 Leighton Buzzard Observer

Turkish Atrocities – The Leighton Meeting. To the Editor of the Leighton Buzzard Observer.

Sir, - I would first copy terse and truthful words uttered in London's City Guildhall – "Logical diplomacy might still be working out its problem, but the generous heart of the nation had leaped to the right conclusion." – The Rev. Newman Hall. – May we not say, if the statesman sticks to policy and befriends human fiends, then in such company will he not deservedly win the groan of humanity, the hiss of civilisation, and the sigh of Christianity all over the world? To strengthen this I copy sentences spoken in your town, and in which, as a local meeting, many absentees were much interested and pleased. In a well arranged speech by the Marquis of Tavistock these sound words occur – "He readily acquitted Lord Beaconsfield's Government of wilful complicity with the crimes which the Turks had committed, but we must be careful that we did not occupy the position of accessories after the fact." From Sir Richard Gilpen's speech I copy the last words – "Lord Charles Russell, at a gathering in this town for a different purpose, had said, "I hope that our party for political purposes will be turned to the politics of humanity and civilisation." That was a sentiment worthy of the noble lord. A patriotic course would be to strengthen the hands of those now in office, and if they could not, then, backed by that strength, settle the question, let somebody else try their hand at it. Above all, we must uphold the honour and interests of Great Britain." Now, if I close by a cogent extract, given by Lord Charles Russell, I offer a threefold argument which may not easily be broken:- "Instead of looking at those atrocities, he would ask them to listen to the words of a great English divine. Richard Hooker said, "Of law there can be nothing less allowed than that her seat is in the bosom of God, her voice the harmony of the world; all with universal consent admiring her as the mother of joy." What law or joy had those provinces to lose or retain?" Many such like utterances have weight and prevail; and if you can allow a space for this, some of your local subscribers and readers will be pleased, while I shall remain, sir, your obedient servant, George Castleden

6th March 1877 Leighton Buzzard Observer

Woburn – Obitual Respect.

As a town we regretfully notice the premature death of the daughter of Lord and Lady Charles Russell, whose household name, Miss Russell, told of one who, in our streets and cottages, went about doing good. A sister of mercy in kind words and deeds, this lady passed several years amongst us with a loving and willing spirit in the Master's service. We might multiply Woburn home reminiscences of bygone happy, useful hours, but we only say that in our peasant homes will linger a long regret on the departure of one as kind, so good; and many a friend will shed the tributary tear over this kindly-hearted lady, while the deepest sympathy is felt for the sorrowing homes now darkened by death. About a year ago this estimable lady became the beloved wife of Theodore Harris, Esq. and the bright happiness of the union was only interrupted by the dark bitterness of death.

"Safe in the arms of Jesus,

Safe on his gentle breast" –

Speaks at once the eternal security and happiness of the departed, while it is the life consolation of those near and dear mourning the mystery of such a separating stroke. Dr. Young says –

"Death each moment plays

His little weapon in the narrow sphere

Of sweet domestic comfort, and cuts down

The fairest bloom of sublumary bliss."

"Life makes the soul dependant on the dust,

Death gives her wings to mount above the spheres!"

And now, the bell sounding, on this burial day, we close this brief, heartfelt tribute to one deeply remembered, locally respected, and mournfully regretted.

Communicated.

A death in the Russell family would have been felt keenly by Castleden. Lord Charles Russell was the third son of the 6th Duke of Bedford, and had been M.P. for Bedford. A "L.R.S." had been sending in poems to the paper too, and had one published on June 19th on Leighton Buzzard Cemetery.

26th June 1877 Leighton Buzzard Observer

Tributary Lines. Addressed to "L.R.S." (See Observer, June 19)

Ye Leighton sleepers, Woburn sleepers, too,

I often think of you, and our adieu,

As in this noisy town I transient dwell,

And hear from Leighton spire this passing knell

It moves fond memory's reminiscent sigh

OLD GRAMMAR SCHOOL AND CHURCH, WOBURN.

24: The Old Grammar School and old Church, Woburn. Undated postcard.

O'er dust respected, mouldering 'neath home's sky:
Age views the stream which bears unto the grave
The youthful, useful, happy, bright, and brave;
Forms, faces, gestures we shall see no more!
Kind words and deeds are now for ever o'er,
And, only may this tributary strain
Point to loved shades we ne'er shall see again
These sleepers, known and loved in waking hours,
With them we soon may rest 'neath grave-born flowers;
Life's fret and fever all shall pass away,
The sting of heat and cold no more shall stay;
With "silent sleepers" all earth's woes shall cease,
And with them we shall find the ever peace.
G. Castleden, London, 20th of June.

17th July 1877 Leighton Buzzard Observer

Education. To the Editor of the Leighton Buzzard Observer.

Sir, - An article in a London paper, on "Over-taxing the young brain," may weigh with all who would save the rising race from premature death. Give the true elements of education, the sound brain will assert its healthy supremacy. Drug it with educational nostrums, and wonder not at the witherings of humanity. By undue pressure, force mind to express speed, and wonder not at the "fine fabric of the brain" collapsing, physical strength giving way, or worse. A father and son inspectorship, more than 60 years, of an original Lancasterian school may excuse this tributary lone to one of England's illustrious obscure; and a comparative criticism may be permitted on the pride, circumstance, and cash payments of the compulsory system, and which is a problem to be solved whether, having parted with voluntary economy and utility, policy, patronage, and pay are not more likely to prevail than the proper healthy instruction which may fit the bone and muscle of Britain's future sons and daughters. I might write more, but I won't intrude. If this may serve, I shall be obliged, and remain, sir, your obedient servant, George Castleden.

11th September 1877 Leighton Buzzard Observer

Lines on the Death of a Leightonian. ("A Cricketer of the old School.")

Foe of the bat, in bygone hours
I do remember thee;

That day of such sun, health, hope, and flowers,
That day of cricket glee;
That day, not faultless, still returns to me,
With foes who friendly strolled beneath the beechen tree!

When Loke, Webb, Franklin, Walker played,
Upon our parky green,
And Woburn 'gainst them was arrayed –
It was a cricket scene
Of olden time, no more to see, I ween.

But, after bat departs, and scouts
Are gathered to the grave –
Alike the victor, vanquished fall,
Alike the coward, brave,
Alike good, bad, the tyrant and the slave –

A cricketer now keys my rhyme;
He lived in Leighton town;
We fought it out in bygone time,
Our game had then renown
Which modern tactics weaken, dwindle down.

And when I read the latest death,
I think how busy men
Have vanished from the plain of earth,
No more to play again!
A tribute sigh I heave for them;
Their frater cricketer, George Castleden.
Woburn, 29th of August.

Castleden was lamenting the death of John Loke, late proprietor of the Ewe and Lamb Inn on Canal Street, Leighton Buzzard.

In the **20th November 1877** *edition of the Leighton Buzzard Observer, under the Woburn news column, there appeared an extract from an article which had come from The Echo. It detailed the leases and rents at which the Russell family had obtained land from the Crown in the late 1700's, and in some instances, had not had to repay, leaving them with real estate* *worth tens of thousands in the local area, and some of the best real estate in central London, described as "comfortable little transactions". The implied accusation of improperness could not go unchallenged...*

27th November 1877 Leighton Buzzard Observer

Hear the Other Side. To the Editor of the Leighton Buzzard Observer.

Sir, - The Press may unwittingly slur and injure. Let me ask a space in the Observer to qualify a one-sided extract under the head of "Woburn." We are in the shade enough without the intervention of scribes whose pen concealed spite on a noble house, which in its rise, more than 300 years ago, if amenable to the critics pen, surely should have the *whole* truth told, and then methinks a higher position for patriotism, citizen and State service, and a worthier appropriation of wealth, might not be shown in all the patrician rolls of Europe. This opinion I believe all unprejudiced, intelligent Englishmen would endorse, and, as *audi alteram partem* should rule in all ranks, I beg an insertion of this as an impulsive act of justice to the ducal descendants of the historic House of Russell, who have proved themselves for generations to have been the right men in the right place.

I remain, sir, a lover of fair play, and also your obedient servant, George Castleden, Woburn, 20th of November.

1st January 1878 Leighton Buzzard Observer

Hear the Other Side. To the Editor of the Leighton Buzzard Observer.

Sir, - Your last leader, echoing the note of the war party, impels a word which I hope may serve truth, peace and humanity. When some blackguard, with bullying propensities, gets, as his desserts, a good hiding, good men smile and bad men frown; at any rate, no humane or honest man would care to rescue the oppressing bully till he showed signs of contrition. Apply this illustration to Turkey, and the Eastern problem, I fancy, may be solved without England, on the veriest sophism ever started, plunging into the maddest and wickedest war which ever cursed a Christian nation. Pray oblige by a small space for this "other side" view, and you will, methinks, serve fair play, and also, with other local readers, your obedient and obliged servant, George Castleden, 28th Dec.

8th January 1878 Leighton Buzzard Observer

The Eastern Question. To the Editor of the Leighton Buzzard Observer.

Sir, - Setting side by side your leader of the 1st inst., and the statement of the Eastern Question Association, one cannot but be surprised at the contrast. Addressing itself, as your Observer does, to wise men, they judge for themselves of the principles advocated. That there is a diversity of opinion about this Eastern Question is evident. One thing, however, is certain – namely, that unnecessary wars have always been among the world's greatest curses. This fact all history, ancient and modern, proves. If therefore, Russia is unnecessarily waging war with Turkey, she will be no exception to the Divine law of retribution. If Turkey is in fault, she must submit to the same law. It will be impossible to convince enlightened Englishmen that to go to war for Turkey *before* it becomes necessary would not be *sinful*, and consequently disastrous. Christians have the consolation of knowing that, however the war-dogs may delight to bark and bite, the universal King will, when it pleases him, shut their mouths, abate their thirst for blood, and convert them into peacemakers. While so many are throwing firebrands for the setting of England in a blaze of war, it is pleasing to see, sir, that you allow correspondents to speak in your valuable paper a word on the other side.

Yours respectfully, J. Summerford, Salford, Woburn.

8th January 1878 Leighton Buzzard Observer

Hear the Other Side. To the Editor of the Leighton Buzzard Observer.

Sir, - Your leader does me wrong. "Insinuation" I never meant, nor to change "traversity of truth." No, no. "Agree to differ" – "think, let think," have been mottoes in this home for many a year. But believing in the "Bulgarian atrocities," and in the "two voices" at the Conference, I see in the retribution falling on Turkey a just punishment for its barbarities, and in the perplexity and disunion of our country a just reward for doubleness which may have encouraged and deceived. I believe it was Talleyrand who, with a sneer, said "Diplomacy and truth never could be companions;" and, to use Mr Elliston's quotation, "Righteousness exalteth a nation," let this Christian nation look at this scripture truth, and ask itself – is its blood and treasure to be poured out of a people who, leaving out their unutterable criminalities and cruelties, find in their creed a receipt in full for Christian massacre, and who, to show loyalty to Mahomed, may mercilessly destroy their vey deliverer because he is a Christian dog? Russia may have motives and designs hidden. Who are we that judge? Is she not right now, standing between the oppressor and the oppressed? Her future history will declare, and then it may be seen that indecision, if not a leaning towards the oppressor, has given to Russia the position she had never else obtained, while it has placed England in this fix – a divided people, and, I am afraid it may be, the scorn and scoff of the opposing hosts. Pilate's question still remains. To class Englishmen as Russians and Turks is ominous and perilous; and, to barter our island security and honest fame for some oriental myth, or Eastern sophism, may, leaving out all the horrors and insolvencies of wear, put Great Britain in as foolish a plight as the dog was when he snapped at the shadow and lost the beef. Does England stand in this war pure? I wish it may be so, and sure no one will more rejoice than, sir, your obedient servant, George Castleden. Woburn, 3rd January.

15th January 1878 Leighton Buzzard Observer

The Russo-Turkish War. To the Editor of the Leighton Buzzard Observer.

Sir, - As a believer in the "Bulgarian Atrocities," and in "Russian atrocities" too, allow me a few remarks on Mr. Castleden's last letter, just to remind him that, whilst the Turks properly deserve condemnation for those Bulgarian atrocities, I my opinion the Russians deserve it far more for having instigated the Turks to the commission of them. Mr Edwards, the member for Weymouth (of the same side in politics as your correspondent), who has been to the locality where the cruelties were committed, says he is convinced that the whole affair was the outcome of the artful and deceptive work of Russian agents, who bribed, intrigued, and then allured the unwary Bulgarians into the first acts of violence and insurrection. This, however, only confirms the evidence as our own Blue Books on the subject. I cannot help wondering also how the same persons who, when Lord Salisbury so ably executed the mission of our Government at Constantinople, could first lavish all their praises and confidence on him, can now, by believing in the "two voices" at the Conference, forget that by so doing they refuse to give him credit and keenness enough to have seen and known that his efforts were being foiled by the action of his colleagues at the Conference Board, whilst, if he did seen and known it, the praise of three radicals was undeserved, and their confidence greatly misplaced. If Talleyrand did say with a sneer that "diplomacy and truth could never be companions," I can only say that the remark is quite deserved as far as concerns the diplomacy of Russia, whom Mr. Castleden seems not unwilling to be an apologist for, whilst he does just perforce admit that she may have designs and motives hidden. If she has not, why was it necessary for her to flaunt that lie in the face of Lord Derby when she said, just before the signature of the Protocol, that she had mobilised an army of 500,000 men, when, from the actual facts since well known, it now appears that nothing like half that number were ready to go into an immediate war. But Russia has suffered enough already for having thus under-rated the Turks by the severe reverses they have inflicted upon her army. Then, it is asked – "who are we to judge?" thus insinuating that England has done wickedly; to which I would answer that to pick holes in our own coat is but a poor way of mending the rents in the clothes of other people; and, if that is the only way that Russia can get her clothes repaired by the Radicals of England, I dare to venture to say that they are likely to remain, as they now are and deserve to be, a small though noisy minority of the people of England – sufficiently noisy enough perhaps for mischief, as they doubtless last year misled Russia into the present cruel and inhumanely-waged war, and are again attempting the detestable work, while our Government is manfully and eagerly doing their upmost to bring peace to Europe once again. The Bulgarians have now learned to regard those who professedly came, in your correspondents own words, "to stand between the oppressors and the oppressed" as their worst oppressors, as the correspondent of the Daily News of January 4th states (and whose opinion even Mr. Castleden will be willing, no doubt, to listen to.) I hope we shall not actually realise the position of the dog who snapped at the shadow and lost the beef, but I should be very much afraid we should have done so had we not such a very deep-sighted Premier, who will pursue an eminently wise course, notwithstanding what either raving fanatics, prancing historians, or fuming philosophers may say or do.

I am, yours &c., Edward Franklin, Eversholt, Woburn. Jan 11, 1878.

That was the first direct communication from Edward Franklin aimed at Castleden, but certainly would not be the last. Franklin was a committed Tory, putting him at odds with nearly all Castleden's principles.

22nd January 1878 Leighton Buzzard Observer

Hear the Other Side. To the Editor of the Leighton Buzzard Observer.

Sir, - I shun controversy - I would not promote division, but, having been an early denouncer of "Turkish atrocities," I demur to Mr Franklin or any other balancing them by "Russian atrocities," The first were wanton and fiendish, the last, war's revenge. Will not history vouch to this? And, if my words be not wrested, did not Russia in this quarrel stand well at first as the helper of the oppressed? In any future arbitrament I hope policy, humanity, and religion may unite to chain the creed-cruel Turk, and restrict despotism having selfish ambition as the motive, and tyrannous subjugation as its aim. Whether "the pride, pomp, and circumstances of glorious war" will allow such a peaceful solution time will prove. I fancy the aged will "sleep well" before a happy realisation; still it is "a consummation devoutly to be wished" by all and, instead of dividing Turks and Russians, may we as Englishmen unite for peace, and rejoice, amid the religious prides and secular despotisms of the world, that of our tight little island it is truly said - "He bids ocean round us flow; not walls of brass would guard us so." I trust to-morrow may tell of counsels placing England high among the nations, and may these counsels unite Englishmen in "the cause of civil and religious liberty all over the world."

I am, sir, your obedient servant, George Castleden, 16th January

29th January 1878 Leighton Buzzard Observer

"Hear the Other Side". To the Editor of the Leighton Buzzard Observer.

Sir, - Whilst shunning controversy, and professing to avoid promoting division, Mr. Castleden still continues to "demur" to my balancing the "Turkish atrocities" with the "Russian atrocities." Therefore, whilst submitting to his "demurrer," I must ask any impartial or patriotic Englishman who has read the accounts of the heartrending sufferings and miserable deaths of the innocent refugees, flying from the advance of the merciless hosts of that "divine figure" who is carrying out the "holy crusade," to the immense satisfaction of those Russian partisans who style themselves as Liberals (amongst whom I suppose we can, without "wresting his words," class our "local poet," who claims to have been an early denouncer of "Turkish atrocities") – I ask, whether those "cruelties" are not only balanced but very greatly and unnecessarily over balanced? Again, not to "wrest" Mr. Castleden's words – "Will not history vouch to the fact that it is a wanton and fiendish action – and, above all things, in the name "Christianity" – revealing an utter and wilful disregard of its first principles and plain teaching? Meanwhile the action of Russia in delaying the announcement of her proposed terms o9f peace has compelled our Government to select that moment for measures of precaution which you intimated in your leading article of last week it was their duty to do. That measure, though an act of caution, is not necessarily warlike, but is more likely to maintain the peace, and I hope and firmly believe your widely-circulated journal will wisely and unflinchingly support such a policy, and thus continue to show that you are patriotic enough in this time of grave danger to our English Empire to place the honour and interests of your country before the interests of any party, whether Radical or Liberal, who would sit meekly at the feet of a despotic Russia whilst she sapped and undermined the just and beneficent influence of England; and, not only sit still, and allow such disastrous work to be done, but would hamper and weaken the hands of those who would wisely and justly prevent the success of such dastardly schemes from taking effect, to the great injury of old "tight little island," whose cause Mr. Castleden rightly says is that of "civil and religious liberty," the very mention of which, by the side of Russia, the blood-stained oppressor of the Poles, is an anachronism too great for your courage, no less than that of Your humble servant, Edward Franklin, Eversholt, Jan 25th 1876

But now the Editor had had enough…

5th February 1878 Leighton Buzzard Observer

"The Other Side" – A further letter from Mr. Castleden under this title, is omitted. We lack space, and the controversy has gone on long enough. Besides, the "other side" of public feeling on the Eastern Question is now too manifest to leave room for local dispute.

Yet the argument continued, albeit under assumed names. I assume this was Franklin:

16th April 1878 Leighton Buzzard Observer

Russia and the Powers. To the Editor of the Leighton Buzzard Observer.

Sir, - I would just take the liberty of asking those readers of your widely-circulating journal who may be "Russophiles" to "read, mark, and inwardly digest" that correspondence which is published in the daily papers of Friday, the 4th inst., on the Bessarabian question. Their feelings after doing so I certainly should not envy, as it only proves what dupes such persons have been, and how cruelly that crafty diplomatist Gortchakoff has befooled his agents in this country. How Mr. Gladstone got caught in such a net is as inexplicable to many Liberals as it is to Your humble servant, An Englishman & then a Conservative. Eversholt, April 6th, 1878.

…and this was Castleden still:

23rd April 1878 Leighton Buzzard Observer

Is it to be War or not? To the Editor of the Leighton Buzzard Observer.

Sir, - A respected Leightonian puts it to us, "Philip is drunk; we must wait Philip sober." Should a national fit of delirium tremens plunge into war, History, after wealth has been squandered and mankind have been sadly butchered, may write it was a causeless, cruel, and a crimeful war. Methinks, success too us would be loss and disgrace, defeat, lasting and burning ignominy. The words I quote have been approved, and by an Observer circulation they may remain to show that all in Leighton do not bow down to the Baal of war.

Your obedient servant, An Englishman and War Hater. Woburn, 19th April.

Edward Franklin had another letter printed under his own name in the 7th May 1878 Leighton Buzzard Observer, in which he continued to put across the Conservative view of Europe's current woes regarding Russia and Romania, but a postscript received later was described by the Editor as "couched in language too strong for publication, and omitted to print." Castleden, meanwhile, stuck to his newly adopted pen-name.

21ˢᵗ **May 1878** Leighton Buzzard Observer

Shall it be War or Not? To the Editor of the Leighton Buzzard Observer.

Sir, - Since men spoke in 1876 on the Bulgarian atrocities, England has been divided, and, whether we escape or plunge into war, tongue and pen strife has raged to an extent which I hope may not increase I bitterness. Three ways are open by which Englishmen may oppose an indefensible and uncalled-for war – by petition, by vote, by protest. In the last a free press is palladium. Surely every village, town borough, and county will petition. Surely the vote of England would be against it; and surely the free press will denounce a causeless war, involving perilous, and, perchance, disastrous and ignominious conclusions. If these appeals fail, and war is willed, then let us no more boast of Constitutional government. But surely no Minister would resist such a triune power, applied constitutionally. If the people say "arbitration, war will flee, and peace will smile." In behalf of peace, please give this insertion.

I remain, sir, your obedient servant, An Englishman and a War-Hater. Woburn, May 10th.

13ᵗʰ **August 1878** Leighton Buzzard Observer

To the Editor of the Leighton Buzzard Observer

Sir, - I thank you very much for your patriotic conduct during the Eastern struggle. But I am puzzled to understand why Nonconformist preachers arrogate to themselves all knowledge on foreign policy. Can you riddle me a riddle? It is really amusing to see the way in which these ministers of Jesus(?) meddle with things outside themselves; and this is what they should put to themselves – do they not stultify in the most solemn manner the profession of their so-called call to minister in things holy? Whenever I see a political parson, of whatever denomination, I put him down as a renegade to his Master Jesus. It seems to me that piety in Nonconformist congregations has given place to politics, and I think even the recluse in the Woburn Castle-Den, having regard to the daily news which we have all round, can hardly controvert this.

Minnie.

25th January 1879 Bedfordshire Mercury

Woburn. The Late Mrs Buckett. – The remains of this lady, who died at Eversholt, were interred at Woburn on Wednesday last, the Rev. H. W. Southey officiating. Among the mourners were the following, - Rev. E. N. Coles, Mr. James Buckett, Mrs. Hill (Cold Harbour), Miss Buckett, Mr. W. Hill, Mr. G. Castleden, and Mr. J. F. Smith. The funeral arrangements were carried out by Mr. J. Gilby, of Woburn.

29th April 1879 Leighton Buzzard Observer

Mr. Gladstone at Leighton. An Acrostic.

G reat was the day for Leighton Buzzard town;
L et verse tell its untrumpeted renown –
A mind supreme surveyed the market street,
D welt on the Cross, and did its antiques greet.
S o in the ages master men arise,
T o battle for the right beneath our skies;
O h may they win, their foes be made to flee:
N ow may the vote of those who would be free
E xalt the worth of Gladstone's chivalry.
G. Castleden

With poetry, Castleden felt secure enough to begin using his own name again. But his acrostic was not universally popular…

13th May 1879 Leighton Buzzard Observer

Mr Gladstone at Leighton. Another Acrostic.

E mpty the honour for Leighton Buzzard Town!
N ow can G. Castleden deny it!
O h, look at the once great statesman passing down
T he Leighton street, and talk of public merit!
S trike anywhere! E'en help our deadliest foes!
D estroy, at whate'er cost, my rival's fame!
A h! This is the "chivalry" that caused our country's woes
L ove of power before an Englishman's good name.
G ladstone must certainly be upside down.
W., Leighton Buzzard, May 7th, 1879.

The Eastern Crisis had come to an end, but Russia had immediately turned attention to Afghanistan, and sent an uninvited diplomatic mission to Kabul. Britain objected, and launched a military force from India, and so began the Second Anglo-Afghan War. By the end of the year, Britain was also engaged in the Anglo-Zulu War, which led to the famous defence of Rorke's Drift.

20th May 1879 Leighton Buzzard Observer

Mr. Gladstone at Leighton. To the Editor of the Leighton Buzzard Observer.

Sir, - Agreeing to differ, pray admit with this a short rhyme in reply to the challenge of my name in the Observer by "W." And then let Time prove who is right – those who denounce invasion or those who slaughter the owners and are consigning England's chivalry to Afric's burning sands.

Cui Bono? The Zulu War!
To play the classic may be vain
In one of rustic mind,
And yet "cui bono" suits my vein,
And truth in it I find.

The Press I ask to speed this strain
Upon its wafting wings,
It may add caution on earth's plain,
Save war's sad stabs and stings

Win Africa, and what reknown
Will grace old history's page?
Lose Africa – lost men and coin
Will deepen hate and rage.

Win Africa, a burning sand
May be the white man's tomb!
Lose Africa, in Britain's land
Homes will be palled in gloom.

Win Africa, "cui bono" still
May be the victor's sigh!
Lose Africa – shame, blood, and ill,
May stamp delinquency.

So, winning, losing, we may learn
What wise men said in yore –
Might, if not right, no fame will earn,
Annexing shore to shore:
The more that's seized the cures will be the more.
George Castleden, Woburn. May 14th, 1879.

Note – May not this be recorded as one of the most untoward, inconsistent wars a Christian nation was ever engaged in? Surely, if ever a blunder was worse than a crime, it is when a Christian people massacre heathens because a first mistake must be made compound by an exterminating decree conducted under the "pride, pomp, and circumstance of glorious war!" This is a conclusion, indeed, to make angels weep – "Hear the other side."

7th June 1879 Bedfordshire Mercury

Woburn. Children's Holiday. – On Monday about 130 members of the Band of Hope met at the Wesleyan Chapel, where they received a card inviting them to a tea later in the day, principally provided by Mr. Castleden as a thank-offering on his 74th birthday. A procession formed, the children carrying flags and banners with suitable mottoes inscribed thereon, and the town was paraded; the destination of the young people was a pleasant meadow lent by Mr. J McKay. Tea was here provided under Mr. Lilley's tent, but rain prohibited open air amusements. In the evening "Bart's Joy" was given in the chapel, the readings by the chairman, Mr. E. Blundell, of Birchmoor, and the music by an efficient choir, Miss Lilley taking the harmonium. At the close of an agreeable entertainment several young people gave in their adhesion to the temperance movement.

1st July 1879 Leighton Buzzard Observer

Historic Lines of Our Times. *[Sic transit Gloria mundi!]*
"Bonaparty!" the boy's first scare;
We saw him melt into thin air,
In St. Helena's cell!
His Austrian son obscurely died;
Louisa sank in rank and pride;
To Time all sighed farewell!

Napoleon the Third found fame
A juggling cheat, an empty name;
An exile his last lot!
And now his son 'neath Afric's sky

Is slain, and may forsaken lie;
He was, and now is not!

"Imperial" gods, ye die as men;
I see the *now*, I've seen the *then*;
Life's grandeur ends in smoke!
These sons of Empire pass away;
Napoleon pets, O where are they –
Proud fame's historic joke?
A blaze, once bright, these "Naps" are lost in smoke!
G. Castleden

The spectre of Napoleon Bonaparte lived long in the psyche of the British. His name had even been used in place of the Boogieman by parents to frighten their children into behaving.

8<u>th</u> July 1879 <u>Leighton Buzzard Observer</u>
Historic Lines of Our Times No.2

This Zulu war methinks just men
In future records will condemn;
Denounce its dingy fame;
In it the young Napoleon fell,
Our guest, forsook, on his farewell,
While men may praise or blame.

He, as a victim may enshrine
This raid-invasion, and our rhyme
May point his soldier grave;
If comfort may the Mother cheer,
This be her solace on his bier –
He sleeps among the brave.

He sleeps, she weeps, and each true heart
Pulses in sympathising part,
At her material grief;
She finds Fame's breath is but a joke,
That Grandeur's blaze ends in vain smoke –
That dearest joys are brief.

In this wid storm all good men pray
Strength may be given for her day,
May mercy anguish calm;
While vanity marks all below,
Yet, on this keen and crushing woe,
O Heaven, drop sacred balm!

George Castleden

Note. – These lines were written, then the eye fell on the Prince's prayer. Such words may be as balm on the regal Mother's anguished heart. To all who value practical Christianity let this extract teach:-

"The only satisfaction I seek is that which lasts forever, that which is given by a tranquil conscience. O, say God! Show me ever where my duty lies, and give me strength to accomplish it always. Arrived at the term of my life I shall turn my looks fearlessly on the past. Remembrance will not be a long remorse. Then I shall be happy."

Yet his latest lines confused and annoyed some readers.

15th July 1879 Leighton Buzzard Observer

The Poet's Corner. To the Editor of the Leighton Buzzard Observer.

Sir, - May I, as one of your many readers, ask you to have more pity on us, and less upon your mistaken poetical contributors? Exact from these last, for their own sake, some little literary decency in their effusions. Genius, we know, must not be too restricted; but let us find it first. The rhymester who took shelter in your poet's corner last week does not show it to us. What does he mean by these lines?

"He sleeps, she weeps, and each true heart
Pulses in sympathising part,
At her material grief;
She finds Fame's breath is but a joke,
That Grandeur's blaze ends in vain smoke –
That dearest joys are brief."

What does he mean by a "wid storm?" Your rhymester - if he reaches even that point in his ambitious ascent - has in these lines no "reason." I am sure that, whatever the Empress (of whom I suppose he writes) finds "Fame's breath" to be, *he* will certainly find his poetical fame something worse than "a joke." And, since he so well knows where "Grandeur's blaze ends," I strongly advise him for the future to commit his poetic efforts to the "smoke" also. He had better consign them to the "wid storm," even whatever that terrible thing may be, than to your columns; and, if he does not, I, and I am sure your readers also, devoutly hope that you yourself will in pity preform these kind offices for him. I have said nothing of the longs and shorts" in these lines, and the less said the better.

Yours & c., A Constant Reader.

Not that it seemed to put him off…

22ⁿᵈ July 1879 Leighton Buzzard Observer

Historic Lines of Our Times No.3. The Napoleons. "Sic Transit".

Our fathers fought, and conquered "Nap,"
Ambition's chiefest son;
The man whose footfall was earth's shock
Was captured, and on yonder rock
Sank down his mortal sun.

His Nephew ruled fair, fickle France,
A rule of glittering fame!
That rule, its wrong and eke its right
Is sinking fast in History's night –
Pomp, pride, and potent name!

His chequered life he closed in Kent;
Once in Imperial light
Meridian glory sunned the twain;
High, bright it blazed, and then their reign
Was tombed in German night.

Napoleon the Fourth, the last,
Will sleep in Kentish ground,
Fate's irony may point his grave!
He, butchered, fell, but 'mongst the brave
His name will aye be found.

We mourn that birth, wit, fame, and might
Were lost in their grand tale;
The World not bettered, Wrong's sad blight
Gave to their rule War's lurid light,
And blasted Earth's fair vale.

The Father, son, in death now lie,
Peace to their memories be!
Their tale is told, the moral may
Still rise, instruct all Europe's day,
We in Eternity!
G. Castleden, 12th July

If "Constant Reader" will read "maternal" for "material," and add an "l" to "wid" (both typal errors), I fancy he will find his blaze of criticism end in smoke! I hope not in the more offensive stench of some snuffed-out glim. – G. Castleden.

Despite the history between Britain and the Bonaparte family, by the 1870's, surviving descendants had moved to England. Napoleon, the Prince Imperial, had trained with the British Army, and had begged unsuccessfully to be allowed to go on active service. Queen Victoria had to intervene before he was finally allowed to go to South Africa, to the Zulu War, albeit officially only as an 'Observer'. Thought by many to be the last serious dynastic hope for the restoration of the Bonapartes to the throne of France, he was allowed to go forward with an escort into an area thought to be clear of Zulus. However, they were attacked and Bonaparte was killed. Some of his escort survived, and were later blamed for not protecting him well enough. Many of his supporters thought Britain had engineered the whole thing. His body was returned to England and buried in Kent, and Queen Victoria attended the funeral.

19th August 1879 Leighton Buzzard Observer
The Storm of Storms, 2nd and 3rd of August

The tempest fire is passed, the morn is calm,
Yet clouds tell gloomy hours;
The summer flees, the harvest crude and late,
The hay still drenched by deluge showers,
The land still mourning, waiting other storms.

Methought, as on the pillow this night's storm
Flashed, roared its mystic way!
How helpless man, and how forlorn –

How, in God's wrath man, gay,
Might be engulfed, and find the Judgement Day.

This relic verse may tell a storm
Unknown in local lines,
With thanks we of escape inform:
Now closing stormy times,
Let age look on to ever calm and cloudless climes

Note. – Monday – "The thunder of his power who can understand!" has special illustration in the shattered ancestral oak near Woburn Abbey. As I look upon this park ruin, by elemental conflict, I say, designate by what scientific term you like, or expound by what natural law you will, solution only is in the sublime words of Job, and before me stands an irrefutable evidence of "The thunder of his power."

The thunder of his power – this tree
Is proof of Nature's fame!
It stands a blasted mystery!
A twinkling and a Hand divine,
Left this old oak a monument for time.

Who may it understand? Not man;
He finds all knowledge vain.
Almighty power no power can ban,
Power infinite, no wit can scan,
Is seen upon this plain.

Then bow, behold this blasted tree,
An oracle in light!
Omnipotence in it I see,
And this its true theology - *
It speaks Jehovah's might!

George Castleden
*"The science of God and of divine things."

This storm was a very large one, and caused much damage. More than 3500 panes of glass at Kew Gardens were smashed by hail.

9th September 1879 Leighton Buzzard Observer

On Mr. Gladstone's Speech at St. Pancras – August

The Senate, hall, and green have known
Your tones of potent power,
But in St. Pancras' poor man's home
You had a triumph hour.

Age spoke to age – told solemn truth;
Pointed to "Christ the Way;"
From Time's old age to ever youth
From earth to Heaven's bright day.

My bardic thanks, nigh seventy-five,
To threescore years and ten,
For such a ring of eloquence
O'er London's pauper men.

This wish accept; 'tis truthful, sound –
May years still find you hale;
With heart, tongue, hand, may you be found
To serve in Time's strange tale.

Note. – These lines were impromptu ones on this happy effort of mind, and the words in St. Pancras may echo when more wonderful orations are forgotten. It was a speech showing the fraternity of age, decay, and death, and pointing to the compensations for the inequalities of Time in the heritage of a glorious eternity.

George Castleden.

The Zulu War had officially finished in July, with the British annexation of the former independent Zulu Kingdom, but the ramifications rumbled on for months.

23rd September 1879 Leighton Buzzard Observer

Our Blackamoor Wars. To the Editor of the Leighton Buzzard Observer.

Sir, - It is asked - Will the nation endorse these invasions by Civilisation and Christianity? Surely Lord Liverpool's "This is too bad" would be a suitable rebuke to wars, sans honour, sans gold, sans everything which may be urged as pleas by their originators. Truth will declare the monstrous crimes, perpetuated under the mask of "pride, pomp and circumstance of glorious war!"

When a boy I looked upon the pictured dismay of the cannibals by the humane blaze of Robinson Crusoe's gun; I little thought, in age, to see "the Zulus, not liking the Gatling gun," surprised, jumping, and falling in death under the well-aimed fire of this weapon by England's well-skilled Christian chivalry.

Really, in the destruction of life it appears almost as heroic when we coax within range a flock of sparrows, then boast the bag, as when we coax these savages into the "open," point our machines on the black wall human target, and hurt the natives by hundreds into death.

In such unequal warfare to boast of victory or renown would not go down with military men, who must think small of such an aping of European battles in which Greek meets Greek. Shades of warriors! What would you say to a battle array with brute force and ignorance against intellect, science, and trained skill? To borrow from the *Sporting World*, it would be, methinks, the long odds of "Monmouth Street to a China orange." Whig, Tory, and Radical condemn these two ominous, disastrous, and, many say, ignominious wars. We shall be pleased by an insertion.

I am, sir, your obedient servant, George Castleden

[N.B. I am aware that 'Blackamoor' is an offensive term, used here for the native people of South Africa. I include it as the original language used at that time, and to keep the transcript exact. Ed.]

Castleden's standpoint on the expansion of the British Empire, and the position of allegedly Christian soldiers using the new machine guns against tribal enemies did not go down well with local Tories, especially Mr. Franklin. A long argument ensued.

30ᵗʰ September 1879 Leighton Buzzard Observer

Mr. Castleden and our Blackamoor Wars. To the Editor of the Leighton Buzzard Observer

Sir, - Your correspondent, Mr. Castleden, says, "It is asked, will the nation endorse these invasions by Civilisation and Christianity? – This is too bad." I think as he himself once said of the late onslaught by Russia on Turkey, that it was "a just punishment for its barbarities;" but, whether so or not, it is certain it was such "an invasion by Civilisation and Christianity" on the poor Mahomedan Turk as evidently met with the hearty endorsement of my friend Mr. Castleden, who was so deeply enraptured with such an exhibition of "the pride, pomp, and circumstance of glorious war," as it would seem from his former effusions on that subject, that his "peace-at-any-price" proclivities were so far forgotten as to lead him almost to consent for England to have joined hypercritical Russia in that "holy crusade." In Mr. Castleden's fiery rage, in endeavouring to culminate that Conservative Government which has been guilty of the crime of checkmating "Holy Russia" in her selfish ambition in the East, he has fallen into the same gross inconsistencies as most of his Radical confreres, for these very same Radicals who were a short time ago condemning and abusing the Government because they refused to undertake (what was equally the duty of every Government of Europe, if a duty at all) the punishment of the Bulgarian atrocities, by the arbitrament of the sword are now condemning the very same policy which they had previously advocated, although in this case that policy has to be undertaken for the defence and permanent security of our own kith, kin and countrymen from the over-bearing acts and threats of a savage tyrant, who defies the just remonstrance of Her Majesty's Commissioner. That defiance has now met in deed and in truth with a "just retribution and punishment for its barbarities." "Truth," as interpreted by George Castleden, may declare this punishment and retribution a "monstrous crime," but "Time" will prove it to be at least an act of liberty and freedom to the late subjects of the now incarcerated King Cetywayo.

Edward Franklin, September 27th 1879.

7th October 1879 Leighton Buzzard Observer

To the Editor of the Leighton Buzzard Observer.

Sir, - Your correspondent's undisguised manner of writing commands attention, if I demur to his matter. To quote me relative to "Bulgarian atrocities" and apply words to our invasions is "too bad" also, and can only be explained by the "Russian phobia" which appears alike to afflict London's ministers and village politicians. Relative to our "checkmating Holy Russia," I used once to play chess, and, accepting the figure, it is allowable for me to say I hope the "scientific frontier" move may not turn out "a fool's mate." Wait till "hypocritical Russia" – another snap – invades. The initiative invasion by England is indeed "too bad." To manure our arid sands with the bravest of the brave, to bury millions of our gold in Oriental waste, when it is so wanted at home, and that under the fear or scare of what Russia may do, is neither to hope in man or trust in God. Defence is ours; defiance, the madness of party, may realise the heathen proverb – "Those the gods intend to destroy y=they first make mad." May this have no calamitous confirmation in Christian England. I will no further intrude on "dishonouring and destructive wars," in which this country of civilisation has been plunged, and surely, boasting of our high Christian elevation among the nations, ere we call Russia "hypercritical" and other vituperative names, pray let us look at home, and some of our hypocrites repent, if the way is not open to repair.

Your obedient servant, George Castleden, 1st October.

14th October 1879 Leighton Buzzard Observer

Our Blackamoor Wars. To the Editor of the Leighton Buzzard Observer

Sir, - In spite of the bewailing complaint of Mr. Castleden that it is "too bad" to quote his former words, which so severely condemn himself, allow me (not a London minister, but only a "village politician") to remind him that it is a poverty of argument which compels Liberals of his evidently weak calibre to resort to the undignified art of calling names; I will not therefore stoop to call Mr. Castleden a Russophil, however much he may deserve that epithet, but Turcophile as he undeservedly and unwisely assumes me to be, I certainly object to a believer in that exploded "masterly inactivity" policy which is most assuredly responsible for the gross blunder of allowing the late Ameer Shere Ali to drift into the arms of Russia. He asks me to "wait till Russia invades." Wait, indeed, till, if not a "fool's mate," we should find ourselves in a "fool's paradise," with Russia in possession, and England, including George Castleden, without – worthy objects indeed of the scorn which has been foolishly poured on that "scientific frontier" of which we have already proved the real and genuine value in the rapid march of our army to punish the outbreak at Cabul. As to the Zulu war, will your correspondent let me request him to listen to the conclusive evidence of three eminent and justly-honoured eye-witnesses. I mean Sir Evelyn Wood, and Colonels Buller and Pearson. On the same subject the Duke of Somerset (quite as good an authority I should think as G. Castleden, although of the same side in politics) says – "Observe in this Zulu war what gallant actions there had been; how many had risked and sacrificed their own lives in order to save a comrade; such deeds were an honour and glory to British troops." But "No," says Mr. Castleden, whose sympathies are only with our savage enemies, and all other enemies of his own country, whilst all the sympathy which is expressed for our countrymen and colonists who were massacred at Insandula is some feeble twaddle about "manuring the arid sands" with their bones. In fact, the murder of our envoys, and the poverty of the people, are about the only (albeit debasing) cries by which the Liberals hope to regain place, and a forlorn hope indeed it will doubtless prove to be. As Mr. Castleden seems perfectly unable to explain the glaring inconsistencies of which, in my last letter, I have shown him to be guilty, will he, on the invitation of a "village politician," kindly take the advice to himself which he is ready so spontaneously to offer to others – to look at home and see if there are "no hypocorism to repeat," whilst "the way is still open to repair." He will not afterwards he so eager to declare as "monstrous crimes" what "Time" is already proving to be judicious acts of "freedom and liberty," combined with increased security to the British Empire.

Edward Franklin, October 9th, 1879.

21st October 1879 Leighton Buzzard Observer

Our Blackamoor Wars. To the Editor of the Leighton Buzzard Observer.

Sir, - As our distinct views have been inserted in the Observer, and, as we must agree to differ, I will only trouble you with a last brief note, and then leave. Time to decide the dispute. One avowal I emphatically make: the policy of the wars we condemn; the bravery of the soldiers none will question. Now, let an opinion from a friend in Tavistock speak for itself. I read it just before Mr. Franklins letter. These words are apt, truthful, predictive, and sarcastic; and, as the Tories once "caught the Whigs bathing, and ran off with their clothes," so I hope, will call us Whigs, Liberals, or Radicals, good counsels yet may serve and save England, even worked out by Tory chiefs: - "I agree with you. Neither of these wars were just. Can anyone say when this precious Afghanistan business is to end? It seems as though we should invade and retire, invade and retire, to the end of the chapter, interposing the murder of an envoy now and then as an episode. This will soon cease to astonish. And this envoy butchered! Well, who is to follow suit! If this Ministry last a little longer they will secure the slaughter of all the distinguished diplomatists in the Indian service. The just finale would be to send Lard Salisbury himself to Cabul" My thanks are due for these words, and, being in such good company on the question, I leave it to one verse, which may both expound and defend:

We hail Wood, Lowe, yes, land brave men,
But must the Zulu war Condemn,
As needless and unjust;
Invasion form a Christian land
I dare not, cannot understand;
Denounce it then I must.

One parting caution. Wrest not words, neither strain a sentence to suit selfish views; then, "what is truth" may be argued, if not solved, without asperity, and argument may close without animosity.

George Castleden, Woburn, October 15th 1879.

4th November 1879 Leighton Buzzard Observer

Our Blackamoor Wars. To the Editor of the Leighton Buzzard Observer.

Sir, - From reading the letter of Mr. Franklin in your paper of October

14th it is certain he quite misunderstands Liberal views as to the Afghan and Zulu wars, neither does he understand Mr. Castleden. The question is not about our soldiers. No one can doubt the gallantry of General Roberts, or the bravery of our men in the way they have scattered the Afghan forces. No one can question again the gallantry of the soldiers in Zululand in conquering a race of warlike savages; but, as to the righteousness of our policy, we maintain that any nation is dishonoured when is makes paltry pretexts for the purpose of unjust aggression on its weaker neighbours. Liberals object, in the name of righteousness, to the aggression upon the people of Afghanistan. We are told it is a "spirited foreign policy." If Mr. Franklin can justify by clear argument the Zulu and Afghan wars, he certainly will be a clever village politician, and fit to be private secretary to Earl Beaconsfield. The Marquis of Tavistock said at Luton – "We want a foreign policy which will maintain the integrity of the empire, but will maintain it without annexation and aggrandisement," adding that we wanted "not a foreign policy to bolster up the Turkish Empire – an empire which he believed (and Europe believed) was doomed to destruction." Mr. Franklin must admit that the Afghan war has proved a disastrous failure. Notwithstanding the bravery of our troops and all the boasting of a spirited foreign policy, it is a wretched muddle.

I am, sir, yours, etc. A Liberal

4th November 1879 Leighton Buzzard Observer

Sir, - With your usual forbearance, and love of fair play, you will be good enough to insert these few lines, on the "last brief note" of my friend Mr. Castleden, whose "emphatic avowals" and barefaced but unproved assertions have become so far modified and qualified that he is now willing to "leave *Time* to decide the dispute." This is indeed a "far cry," we know, from such declarations as "monstrous, ominous, disastrous, and ignominious," but then we know that "discretion is the better part of valour," and, seeing my pen and ink opponent in so sorry a plight, I will be generous enough to wait with a full confidence that before even "the aged sleep well" Time will have proved the Zulu war to have been "a judicious act of freedom and liberty," not only to our own colonists, but also to the natives of Zululand. Mr. Castleden also finds it now necessary to call to his help against the "village politicians" a champion hailing from the small pocket borough of the Russell family named Tavistock, who may possibly, for aught I know, be a fellow-recipient of the bounty of that House. Let me, then, tell both the "local poet" and his Tavistock henchman that this "Afghan business" would not have been begun, nor have ever become necessary, but for the gross negligence and criminal blunders of the party of statesmen whom they unwittingly support, and, as is pretty certain that this Ministry will last more than a "little longer," we shall be able to test the accuracy of the Tavistock "prophecy," which I in turn dare prophecy will be falsified in equally an absolute a manner as have so many other Liberal predictions – the war with Russia and the fall of the Government to wit. In the meantime, Lord Salisbury will be more useful at home than at Cabul, to sweep away the misrepresentations and specious sophistry of Liberal orators by the decisive tests of actual facts, as he did last week to the enormous and enthusiastic gatherings at Manchester; in that capacity it will not be necessary nor possible for him "to run off with the clothes of the Whigs," for the very sufficient reason that they have not a vestige of such articles in the shape of a policy left wherewith to cover their nakedness. Nor will I imitate the bad taste of your correspondent, and, because he differs from me in opinion, wish him is such a position as might endanger his life. Such a wish would only be evidence of a feeling for personal and physical injury – another grave inconsistency on the part especially of a man professing Liberalism. Anything but liberty that, "to think, to utter, and act in accord therewith;" yet another contradiction of himself; and, not "to wrest," but accurately quote his words, and I have done with him, "I shun controversy," wrote Mr. Castleden on the 16th January, 1879, in the Observer for that week, yet continually since he has written in the Press on controversial subjects. Wish him at Cabul! No, never; let him rather still continue to make himself an exhibition of the weakness and conglomeration of inconsistencies which can exist in the mind of a modern town Liberal "politician," and thus become the safe and innocent butt for the thrusts of the pen of a "village politician."

Edward Franklin, Eversholt, Oct 23, 1879.

The latter two letters were intended for insertion last week, but were crowded out. We hope now to have heard the last of this controversy. Ed. L.B.O.

But they had not, and Castleden seems to have had the last word:

11ᵗʰ **November 1879** Leighton Buzzard Observer

Our Blackamoor Wars. To the Editor of the Leighton Buzzard Observer.

Sir, - My thanks are due to "Liberal" for his just remarks on these unjust wars; and for his reference to the sound constitutional speech of the Marquis of Tavistock at Luton. Let the opinion of one opposed to me in politics aptly close my side of the controversy: - "This is the question of humanity and Christianity distinct from party bias or political proclivities." An extract from the Luton speech suits this close: - "An empire, not of annexation and aggrandisement, "may by a worthy aim, but an empire gained by invasion, aggression, and injustice cannot prosper while the eternal principles of right and truth prevail.

With thanks to yourself, I am sir, yours obliged, George Castleden, Woburn, 5th November.

As an antidote to the politics and war-themed letters, Castleden had been engaged in correspondence with the name-sake town (now City) of Woburn in Massachusetts, USA. Woburn, Mass. was settled in 1640. When visitors came to England, Castleden received them and showed them around the original Woburn.

29th November 1879 The Cambridge Independent Press (see also 2nd December Leighton Buzzard Observer)

An American at Woburn. The Woburn Journal, published at the Woburn in Massachusetts, lately contained the following:-

A Day in Woburn, England. Friday, Sept 25th, 1879. We left London on the nine o'clock train of the London and North-Western Railway, and at a quarter after ten we alighted at Bletchley Junction to change cars for Woburn. A branch line connects Bletchley with Bedford and the second station from the former place is known as Woburn Sands. Arrived at this latter place we inquired for Woburn proper, and learned that it was some three miles distant. A barge, however, which runs regularly from this town to the railway station, stood in waiting, and, being desirous of gaining a little information relative to the place and people we were about to visit, we took seats with the driver. We opened the conversation with the remark that we were natives of Woburn, and asked how long he had lived thereabouts. He looked at us scrutinously, and, with a puzzled expression, said he was born in Woburn, too, but that he couldn't remember ever having seen us. In explanation we asked if he had ever heard of a Woburn, America. He believed he never had. We took pains to enlighten him upon this point, and to explain the nature of our visit. The drive was a very pleasant one, and the road led along finely cultivated fields and pleasant woods. Our companion took pains to tell us all he knew about the country and people, so that by the time we reached the town we felt quite well informed about it.

Having a letter of introduction from our townsman, Mr. Geo. M. Champney, to Geo. Castleden, a gentleman whose name has not infrequently appeared in these columns at the end of many a fraternal letter from across the waters, we made our way directly to his house.

We found Mr. Castleden surrounded by his books. His greeting was cordial; and we soon learned that, in anticipation of our visit, he had taken several important steps to render our stay a profitable and interesting one. Among other things he had written to His Grace the Duke of Bedford, requesting permission to show us the Abbey on our arrival. The latter kindly consented and said that he might do so by giving notice to the housekeeper a day or two beforehand.

Unfortunately, we had come upon Mr. Castleden wholly unannounced; and, as we wished to return to London that night, it seemed as if his plans for our entertainment would work for nought. In the dilemma we made a short call on Mr. Geo. Russell, the grandson of the Duke, and he very kindly offered to send word to the housekeeper for us directly, so that we might visit the Abbey that afternoon.

This matter having been arranged, we walked through the village a short distance and stopped into the Town Hall, where the fortnightly session was being held. The building itself is a small affair, and hardly comparable to our own Town hall before its renovation. The magistrates who were holding the court, gave us a friendly nod on being informed from whence we came, and wanted to know if Woburn, America, could boast of but one breach of the law in the course of two weeks. We acknowledged that such a thing would indeed be a novelty at home; but reminded them that our Woburn was a large manufacturing place of ten thousand inhabitants, and not a small agricultural village one-fifth as large. After this our conductor invited us to the hotel the "Bedford Arms" for lunch, and a good lunch it was too. About one o'clock Mr Geo. Russell sent a dog-cart and driver to the hotel, and informed us that they were at our disposal for the afternoon.

Previous to the introduction of railways, Woburn was a great staging centre, and in those days it was a larger and busier town than at present. By stage it was somewhat more than forty miles to London, and a good hours' ride.

Leaving the town we now took a two mile drive on this old stage road. On our left was he large brick wall, fourteen miles in circumference, which encloses the park and private grounds of the Duke. I should have said ere this that the day was an exceptionally fine one, and although it was Autumn, fields and wood appeared as green and fresh as in middle of Spring. Anyone who has seen rural England under such favouring circumstances knows what a beautiful sight it is. There appears to be a freshness and brightness to their landscapes that one seldom finds at home.

At the end of our two mile drive we reached the main entrance to the park, and were readily admitted. It is useless for me to attempt a fitting description of the beauties which met our eyes at every turn during the next hours' drive. Washington Irving has somewhere remarked that no American need visit foreign counties to see beautiful scenery; for he will find nothing more beautiful and grand than he can find at home. This is perhaps true; yet as we drove through the fine fields of the park that afternoon, with hundreds of deer quietly grazing on either side of us; next by some pretty sheets of water facing the stately Abbey itself; and then into strips of forest where pheasants, hares, and partridges started up every few feet, I could not wonder where such a similar drive could be taken in America.

We reached the grounds of the Abbey about half past two, and Mr. Castleden's presence readily gained us admittance from the silk and satined lackey who presided as gate-keeper. The Abbey itself, as viewed from the outside, is a very plain but substantial looking building of white stone. We were ushered into the drawing room, where we registered our names, and where we were soon joined by the housekeeper.

The first thing that attracted our attention on leaving the drawing room was a fine portrait of the present Duke taken in 1874. It shows a fine head and form and a commanding mien. Next came the portraits of the Duchess and her daughters, all painted by the artists of the day. But let me now attempt even an enumeration of the paintings we saw in the corridors and rooms of this palatial house. The collection consists largely of portraits of the Russell family for eight generations back, although there are several landscape paintings by Vandyke, Sir Joshua Reynolds, and other artists of repute. We were shown over almost the whole house, and the rooms are rich and beautiful beyond all description. Imagine the richest furniture and finest decorations possible, and your imagination cannot lead you into an exaggeration in regard to the splendours of Woburn Abbey. All that wealth, art, and good taste can do, seems to have been done to render the residence of the Duke of Bedford palatial in the fullest sense of the word. We had visited several royal residences in Europe, including, of course, the Queen's Castle at Windsor; but as we saw only a few of the most public rooms in these places, and as the carpets were usually up, and the furniture covered, I had never had my expectations as to what I had always conceived to be the splendours of a royal palace fully realised. Here, however, all my pre-conceived ideas on this subject were abundantly realised. Among the most interesting of the apartments shown us was the suite of rooms occupied by Queen Victoria and Prince Albert on their visit to the Duke in 1841. The bedroom was especially noteworthy.

While walking through one of the entries the bell for lunch rang, and we saw the attendants come out and open the doors for the family to go to the dining-room. I presume we were not expected to look, but I confess to throwing a glance over my shoulder to gain a sight of the Duchess and her daughters. We Americans claim to be so strongly democratic as not to care so much for titles and royalty, nor for those who bear them; but our curiosity usually gets the better of our politics, and I venture the assertion that no person will go further to see a king or lord than an American.

Having left the Abbey, we took our way to the Sculpture Gallery, which is near-by. We had but a cursory view of the works of art here shown, but I should say the collection was of rare value. We now stepped into the gardens which are on the same scale of beauty and magnificence that we witnessed elsewhere. Mr. McKay, the head gardener, here joined us and showed us the special things to be seen. A fallen tree attracting our attention, he told us that Mr. Gladstone, the ex-Premier, had felled it with his own hands when on a visit to the Duke, last October. It is his favourite method of taking out-door exercise.

We strolled down to the gardener's cottage where he showed us the hothouses and the grapery, besides entertaining us with some intelligent observations relative to English political matters. He is a Scotchman of good understanding, and I could wish our stay with him might have been lengthened. With a photograph of Gladstone from him as a remembrance, and a hearty shake of the hand, we bid him good-bye, with many thanks for his kindness to us. The grapes exhibited in the library the past week were a gift from this gentleman.

We drove back to the village hurriedly, in order to escape a threatening shower. Mr. Castleden having wearied himself in his capacity as a guide, now left us for a few moments rest, and we occupied the interval by calling upon Mr. Fisher, the bookseller and printer. We enjoyed a pleasant half hour's chat, and our good impression of Woburn people was strengthened.

Mr. Castleden again joined us and took us thought the cemetery, which is very prettily situated a short distance from the main street. After a pleasant call on the apothecary, it was time to take dinner at the hotel. Here a fresh surprise awaited us in the matter of a nice piece of venison which Mr. Geo. Russell had the kindness to send us.

The early evening was spent in calling upon the post master, Mr Sergeant, the gentleman to whom Mr Champney addressed his first letter. He is now an invalid, yet he was not too ill to give us a hearty welcome, and to render our short visit with him one of the pleasantest we had made in the town.

At eight o'clock we bid good-bye to our host, Mr. Castleden, and I'm sure we shall neither of is ever forget that we are indebted to him for one of the most enjoyable days spent in Europe, and for the better appreciation of the hospitality and good will of a true English gentleman.

Previous to my visit to Woburn, my impressions of the English were not of the best. The supercilious and almost sneering tone in which they are prone to speak of America, and Americans had disgusted me; and the ignorance they display when talking of our country and its institutions, is sufficient to stir up the blood of even the most phlegmatic. But I left Woburn feeling that I had grievously misjudged our cousins over the water and that I had either been unfortunate in my previous acquaintances, or had too hastily formed my opinion of certain English traits of character. We left the country very shortly after our Woburn visit, so that it is not strange that my present recollection of England and its peoples are of the pleasantest; and I'm sure they will always remain so whenever I call to mind the incidents of the day of which this letter is a chronicle.

C.N.

The surreal spectacle of William Gladstone chopping trees in Woburn Park would seem to be true, as it was reported in the Leighton Buzzard Observer in October 1878.

2ⁿᵈ **December 1879** Leighton Buzzard Observer

A Warning to Hale Aged Men! [After reading Mr. Gladstone's Edinburgh Speech, 25th Nov.]

Old man, beware! Mind blazes bright,
The body in decay;
Upon the save-all is the light,
It soon must melt away.

Delusive Age! it cheats the man,
He listens to its voice,
Fondly be believes in vernal youth,
And says – Young man, rejoice!

An Eastern blast, down goes the snuff,
A frost-bite gives the chill;
In vain the doctor sends the "stuff,"
In vain bestowes his skill.

Beware, great man, Death's sudden shaft
May in the snow-storm fly;
A patriot you will ever live,
A patriot you will die.

The vital strength of man is low
At three score years and ten;

GRAND ENTRANCE, WOBURN PARK.

25: The Grand Entrance to Woburn Park, as used by Queen Victoria in 1841 ...and the American visitors in 1879. An undated postcard.

'Tis labour, sorrow, fear and woe,
    Among the aged men.

    George Castleden, Woburn.

Note – Writing these lines the news told the sudden death of Mr. Serjeant Cox, another emphatic call to the healthy aged.

6th **January 1880** Leighton Buzzard Observer

Lines on the Tay Bridge Accident. Sunday, Dec. 28th

If Nature is imposed upon, be sure
Whilst sun, and moon, and stars endure,
She will assert her way.
Omnipotent, by right and might,
She hurls the offender into the night,
And laughs at his dismay.

If scientific wit will fly,
If geologic pride will pry,
Each step may lead to doom!
Nature has secrets all her own;
In seizing them death may be known,
And man may find his tomb!

The steam steed snorts, but where's the rein,
To curb, or its wild rush restrain?
Man, helpless, looks and sighs,
As plunging down the gulf of doom,
Too late his cry, "I find the tomb,"
And impotently dies.

Man knows but *little*; he may know
Too *much*, but increase may be woe!
"eat and be gods!" O man,
If pride, ambition, hate, gold, fame,
Urge thee to win a vicious name,
Homes, climes may feel the bar.

Be wise to know what wisdom is;
Peace and goodwill is honest bless,
Their home the feeling heart,
Man's brain may scale, search either pole,
But only soul can speak to soul,
Old year, as we now part.

I sow a moral from this tale –
Ye who are busy on Time's rail,
As ye speed on beware!
In life 'tis death! A moment may
Speed on the soul to Heaven's aye day
Or plunge in night's despair!

George Castleden
Woburn 31ˢᵗ Dec.

Note. – It may be said to limit science after what has been done is presumption. Let me say geologic wit may scan granite pages of creation, yet there is a limit. Scientific lore may be disastrous ignorance, geologic dictum gross impiety, and engineering skill link to calamitous folly. The pace, night, journey, cars, road, were all against the laws of Nature; the result, eternity to many souls. And on this last morn of a dying year let one solemn caution weigh – Remember that unnecessary work on the Sabbath Day is *against the laws of God*.

A violent storm had lashed the 18-month old Tay Bridge on the evening of 28ᵗʰ December, which it had not been designed to withstand. Trains were only allowed to cross one at a time, so the disaster could have been worse, but as it was, about 75 passengers and crew were killed, the exact number being unknown, as many bodies were washed away in the flood.

16ᵗʰ March 1880 Leighton Buzzard Observer

An Election Rhyme, by an Old Whig.

I hear again of civic war,
Again religious strife;
Again will sound the din and jar
Upon my closing life.

I've fought with fathers; I may tell
We fought for truth and right;
They sleep within the silent cell,
I soon may find its night!

Yet on this fray in life's last day
Let me, electors, say,
Vote all for peace, and bid its foe
To cut and run away.

Tell war's proud sons it will not pay,
Whate'er the conquest be;
Bibles and bullets, if they join,
Make gross hypocrisy.

"He bade the waters round thee flow,"
Stand on the rock of peace;
"No walls of brass could guard thee so;"
Bid all invasion cease.

Beware, wrong done will soon return
On the wrong-doers pate;
If done by climes, or Christians, mark,
This is God's righteous fate.
[Colossians 3c. 25v.]
G.C.

Note. – Doctor Watts might give our Foreign Secretary good counsel, and, if well to "keep the powder dry at home," his policy would save wanton and cruel use of it abroad.

O, Britain, praise thy mighty God,
And make His honours known abroad;
He bids the ocean round thee flow,
No walls of brass could guard thee so;
Thy children are secure and blest,
Thy shores have peace, thy cities rest;
To all the Isle His laws are shown,
His Gospel's through the nation known;
And so in nobler works and ways

He calls the Britons to His praise.
Woburn, 11th March.

Another election was on the horizon, one which the Liberals would win by a significant margin.

16th March 1880 Leighton Buzzard Observer

Whigs or Tories – Which? To the Editor of the Leighton Buzzard Observer.

Sir, - If I take words uttered, years ago, by the present Duke of Bedford, they may serve in the coming election, and may lift the dispute out of the bog of personality, and place it on the rock of principle: - "Electors of Bedfordshire – With you rests the decision, whether you choose Colonels Gilpin and Stuart, and restrictive and Conservative measures, or Colonel Higgins and myself, and expansive and liberal measures." Terse and wise, this was truth in a nutshell; and, use this sentence fairly, and the battle may be fought without personal animosity. If I read history truly, Whig principles have made us renowned wherever liberty is prized or freedom valued. Riots have marred some Whig measures, but I challenge our foes to deny that they have ever been *right* in respect of its civil liberty, and as to religious liberty, they have been in unison with the lines which seem to embody true toleration –

"Let Caesar's due be ever paid
To Caesar and his throne
But Conscience and souls were made
To be the Lord's alone."

Still in coming strife I suppose it will be, as I read when a boy – "Party is the madness of the many for the gain of the few," and again partisan insanity will prevail. Will is it that, modified by the ballot and other preventatives, an election does not mean a carnival for the constituency and ruin for the candidate. As an old Whig, I ask a brief space for these Conservative words, and mitigate neighbour and local animosity in another constitutional struggle.

I am, sir, yours obediently and obliged, George Castleden

23rd March 1880 Leighton Buzzard Observer

The Massachusetts Town of Woburn. The following lines from a correspondent, together with extract from the Woburn Journal (Mass.) may be interesting to many of our readers in Leighton Buzzard and Woburn: -

Sir, - A few weeks ago you gave an account of a pleasant visit of two

American friends to our town. Before that, a friendly interchange by two unknown friends had given to the two Woburns a relationship they had not known before, and which we hope may issue in repeated fraternal visits and offices when the original writers shall sleep, and this small seed of peace and good-will, obscurely sown, may grow into a great tree. Having posted the Observer to America, I was pleased by reception of a *Woburn Journal*, and, as a special reference is made to Leighton, a reprint of that portion may be of interest, and, locally, help the cause of fraternity between two great countries owning the same ancestry, speaking the same language, worshipping the same God. You have obliged by printing apt and good words for our election strife; add to this peaceful words by His Grace the Duke of Bedford, which, followed out, are calculated to serve the whole civilised world: -

"Friendly relations between England and the United States are so essential to the peace and well-being of the world that everyone who has contributed towards this end has done a good, a very good deed." I might refer to the good deed – the last of his valuable life – of the Prince Consort, in the Trent affair, as an illustrious proof of how the "soft answer turneth away wrath." – how an Esau and Jacob quarrel was stayed by the wise and kind counsel of this great and good Prince. Hear another: - "There remains to us at least the consolation of remembering that his last recoded act was one of inestimable service to his county and to humanity. It was an act of peace, of benediction, of good-will." Let such benign counsels and agencies prevail, and then England and America, united in amity, may speak peace to all Christendom.

I am, Sir, your obliged servant, George Castleden. Woburn, March 17th, 1880

[extract.]

"Woburn, England. - I have been favoured recently with occasional copies of the Leighton Buzzard Observer, a paper published in the town of some note of that name in Bedfordshire, England, and not far away from old Woburn. There being no daily or weekly paper printed at Woburn (it has a monthly issue in pamphlet form, containing railway tables and local notes), the Leighton Buzzard Observer having considerable circulation there, serves as the vehicle for those inclined to express their views on the politics of the day and matters of home interest. Among its writers is Mr. Castleden, the valued correspondent with our town, and the obliging forwarder of the paper. Before proceeding to the special object of this communication, it may not be amiss to fancy some person to be curious to know how such a peculiar name became attached to the town in question of Leighton Buzzard. If such a name were found as the patronymic of one of our southern or western villages, it might reasonably be inferred it was from the fact of its being infested with that scavenger bird the turkey buzzard. That such an origin has been claimed for the old English town is known form the statement, gravely made, that the sexton of the old church, in showing to visitors its ancient decorative glories, points to the brazen eagle perched above the lectern or reading-desk as the original buzzard that gave the town its name.

Whether the sexton is betied in this current story I have no means of knowing, as the young gentleman from here who visited old Woburn last autumn did not extend their researches into that neighbourhood. The name, however, proceeds from an entirely different source. It comes through one of the numerous corruptions of an earlier name which quite commonly befall those of a personal as well as those of a geographical character. Thus it is well known our neighbouring city of Boston draws its designation from a place of the same name in England, which was long ago founded as St. Botoph's town. The original of the city of York, England, was in old Saxon Eurwic. It is said the sailors of H.M.S. Bellerophon have transformed it into Billy Ruffian, and the Aeolus into Alehouse. In like manner the town of Leighton Buzzard was in the twelve century christened Leighton Beaudesert. The last part of the name is of undoubted Norman origin, signifying a fine open plain. Since the time of the Conquest, or a little later, no material change has been made in the first part of the compound, but the last has been seriously curtailed of its beauty by being transformed to the image of a vulgar bird. But while some of the things in which "time works wonders" are sorry improvements, others are wrought into forms of greater comeliness and beauty. But I am wandering farther from my purpose than I intended, which was to refer to some of the articles from Mr. Castleden's pen which have appeared in the paper on whose name I have been commenting. Particularly I wish to notice and ask you to reprint a poem from the paper last received. The articles in previous numbers on the Afghan and Zulu wars contained in brief space the most caustic criticisms on the policy of Lord Beaconsfield. More prominent writers than Mr. Castleden have given the Premier more unrest, but if he should have read these short pieces he must have felt the impolicy if not the iniquity of his course. - G. M C."

30th March 1880 Leighton Buzzard Observer
Good Friday Eve – A Regal Coincidence

Strange things do hap! Victoria, Queen
Of Britain's sea-girt isle,
Leaves home a little while,
And o'er the daughter's grave proves life's a dream!

Eugenie, once God's sceptred toy,
Embarks the same day;
Her purpose is to pay
A mother's tribute to her only boy!

So woe now joins the twain in heart,
In realms, in rule diverse;
Yet truth we tell in verse –
They each act now a mother's holy part.

God bless the twain in grief, we say,
Direct, protect, and save,
Upon the land, the wave;
Sincere the wish, the prayer we truly pray
George Castleden, Woburn.

13th April 1880 Leighton Buzzard Observer

An Election Polling Day, 1880 Compared with the Years 1826 – 1831-2. To the Editor of the Leighton Buzzard Observer.

Sir, - On a spring morn, at seventy-five, I once more recorded my vote for the Liberal candidates. Reviewing the space of nigh sixty years in the experience of county elections, I thought it a privilege in age, and at home, thus to exercise, quietly, the franchise; and in this review, comparing bygone scenes of extravagance and dissipation at the then Bedford election carnival, I could not be but grateful I had lived to see so salutary a change. As the polls indicate a Liberal majority and point to a displacement of the Tory Prime Minister, I take it for granted what can be done will be done in reversing policies inconsistent and injurious, and, in the Zulu and Afghan wars, ignominious and inhuman - policies at which England's best instincts revolt, and which her Christian principles abhor. Whether past misdeeds may be remedied, and past loses may be restored, are questions for the future. In the world of morals it is written - "The past is" - irreversible, unchangeable, enduring. These partly apply in the world of politics, but in this change I do hope a meretricious "honour" will no longer lead constitutional England on to the perilous bog of annexations, nor that a cruel hypocrisy will distinguish our Christian commonwealth among the nations of Europe. The fight has been; and all who have fairly fought for principles, and have not resorted to guile or unfair tactics, will ground arms, and, forgetting the irritation of the day, neighbourly animosity will vanish; but, as a Liberal from the earliest day, I must not close this note without paying a tribute to that "grand old man."

THE MORTUARY CHAPEL AND NEW CHURCH, WOBURN.

26: Woburn Old Church, tower and Mortuary Chapel, in 1898. Published in "In Our Own Country".

The member for Leeds and Midlothian, who by his mental giantry has so nobly wrestled for those truths which, as policies, have given us liberties at home, the envy of the other nations, and have made as a terror to the despotians abroad. May this great man be yet spared to reap some fruit of his aged labour which shall cheer and bless life's eventide! And –

"Then may his sun in smiling decline,
And bring a pleasing night."
I voted, then, 'mongst Woburn's dead,
I strolled 'neath morning's sun;
I thought of friends and farmers fled!
Their busy day all done.
Now, on their graves a mint a rhyme,
To sound, this day, the nought of hollow Time!
George Castleden, Woburn, 6th April.

13ᵗʰ April 1880 Leighton Buzzard Observer

Liberal Welcome – An enthusiastic meeting of Liberal electors took place at the Bedford Arms Hotel, on Friday, congratulative to the Marquis of Tavistock, on his return for Bedfordshire. The chairman of the committee, the Rev. J. Andrews, first read an address to the noble Marquis, which was cheered by the crowed room. The Marquis of Tavistock then replied in a speech which won repeated cheers, and, after giving good words on the great principles so long enshrined in the Russell family, sat down. Lord Charles Russell then responded to the wish of the meetings, and in a truly heart-toned speech delighted all. To both the youthful Members of Parliament his lordship spoke words of aged wisdom, and gave some good, feeling counsel. Then hearty cheers welcomed the son, Mr. George W. E. Russell, and, as he told election facts, spoke on the cause the company had met to serve, and gave humorous anecdote, one seemed to see in this scion the promise of a future political eminence, and when the aged neighbour feelingly and solemnly hoped the two young Russells might fill the place of their noble fathers, and wage successfully the conflict in behalf of civil and religious liberty so long as tyranny frowned and despotism oppressed, he had the voice of the audience with him, amid responsive cheers approval. A vote of thanks, moved by the Marquis of Tavistock, to the chairman, having been acknowledged, then a Woburn political meeting, the like of which has not been seen for years, closed. Lingering among the groups this though struck and cheered: - "While the aged may soon leave time, the younger generation, thus brought into genial communion, may, by it, be better furnished for the fight of constitutional liberty, and when we shall have "shuffled off the mortal coil," and shall sleep with our fathers, may arising sons do doughty deeds in freedom's hallowed cause.

New actors, scenes, for ever rise,
Old actors fall beneath the skies;
Yet as we fall our shout will be-
Hail to the spread of liberty!
And may the nations of the earth be free.
George Castleden.

13th April 1880 Leighton Buzzard Observer

Reception to Mr Russell. This town gave a spontaneous and hearty reception to George W. E. Russell, Esqr., on his return from Aylesbury. The bells rang merrily; neighbours and friends turned out, and, taking horses from his carriage, gladly drew the youthful M.P. to his worthy father's home. An address, on the spur of the moment, had been thought on, but years and cheers interfered with its delivery; a few congratulatory words, and a few of thanks from Mr. Russell, closed this town welcome. Afterwards, the address was received, and a happy reply has sealed this election event as a very pleasant memory; one which Woburn's boys and girls may talk of when they become England's "citizens of credit and renown." – Address – "Sir, - Please to receive the congratulations of your fellow-townsmen on your honourable return to Parliament for Aylesbury. All honour to that ancient Vale for thus nobly returning one bearing the worthy name of the historic House of Russell; and "the Woburn Whig" respected here. May you long sit in the Senate, working for the civil and religious liberties of England, and may you win renown by adding many liberal deeds to the now ample annals of the illustrious House of Russell. Receive, sir, our hearty congratulations, and may health, honour and usefulness be your portion to a long distant day, is our town to welcome to your paternal home on this auspicious return. Signed, on behalf of your fellow-townsmen - Geo. Castleden." Reply – "Woburn, April 5th, 1880 – Dear Mr Castleden: The kind congratulations of my fellow townsmen could not reach me more appropriately than through you, who are so old a friend personally, and have been a political adherent of my family for so many years. To you and to all those kind feelings you express I beg to offer my most cordial thanks. My reception by my fellow-townsmen on Saturday afternoon was one of the most unexpected and most gratifying events of my life, and I beg to make my acknowledgements to all who took part in it. My hope and constant endeavour will be that, in my public life, I may not bring discredit on the place where I have spent so many years. Believe me, dear Mr. Castleden, yours ever sincerely, George W. E. Russell.

20th April 1880 Leighton Buzzard Observer

The Elections. To the Editor of the Leighton Buzzard Observer

Sir, - Incidents, unexpected, relative to the Election, and somewhat romantic, make it a last memory with an old man. I thank you for the insertions of last week; and be so good as to print the two verses I now send, especially as by Herbert Gladstone, Esq., they have been very kindly acknowledged. Hurrah for Midlothian, Bedfordshire, Aylesbury, Worcestershire and Leeds!

Your obliged servant, George Castleden.

"On the spur of the moment," by an aged bard, on Mr Gladstone's last speech and the reference to "Three Allsops": -

Sire Gladstone won the Northern Shire,
The Son lost Middlesex;
If Leeds should send young Herbert still,
It will the Tories vex.

If Worcester should a son return,
Hurrah for Liberty;
Then England will have three good men,
To make her great and free;
Then raise the cheer for kindred – Gladstones Three!
G.C., Woburn.

In Eversholt, the Conservative-supporting Mr. Franklin quietly seethed…

27th April 1880 Leighton Buzzard Observer

Unexpected Election Incidents

To the Editor of the Leighton Buzzard Observer

Sir, - In your last, from the pen of my friend, Mr. Castleden, we find "incidents, unexpected, relative to the Election, and somewhat romantic, make it a last memory with an old man." To my surprise, we now find he and his party, as the result of a Liberal victory at the polls, assuming the once despised role of bluster, bounce, braggadocis, and even contempt of the defeated Conservative party. Here we, as another "unexpected incident," also really so drifted into the "glory business" within less than a month as to have become already "the terror of the despots and despotisms of Europe!" To quote "G.C." and "C.B.S.," whether such an "unexpected incident" is likely actually to occur under that "grand old man" (Gladstone), who is now again a Premier, may best be judged by the "terror these despots exhibited" when

Denmark was so disgracefully deserted by him, after being told so boldly she should not stand alone. Another "unexpected incident" relative to the elections which must surely "make it a last (bitter) memory to an old man" is the public confession by Mr. Morley that "in the hurry of the moment," and in his eagerness to overthrow Lord Beaconsfield, he put his politics before his religion, which reminds one of Mr. Howard's cry of agriculture before politics, to gain votes of farmers, whilst in his address at Bedford, after the poll was declared, Radical politics stood first, and agriculture stood simply nowhere. Small wonder is it either, after the correspondence made public between himself and the renowned O'Donnell, and that between Col. Sir R. T. Gilpin and the Secretary of the Farmers' Alliance, that even the great Whig Duke of Bedford is reported as being greatly annoyed at such "unexpected incidents." If a majority made up of such a fortuitous concourse of Whigs, Radicals, Home Rulers, Atheists, and Republicans, should prove to be long-lived, it would be indeed an "incident unexpected," and if it be true that "history repeats itself," it will even yet perhaps become "a last (sad) memory with "the aged bard" to realise that repetition of history – viz., the second downfall of "the People's William."

Yours obediently, Edward Franklin.

27th April 1880 Leighton Buzzard Observer

Liberal Enthusiasm

To the Editor of the Leighton Buzzard Observer.

Sir, - Having had a copy of your valuable paper sent to me in Lancashire last week, I was greatly amused by the enthusiasm of the "Woburn Poet" on the triumph of the Gladstones. Now, sir, I think it would be a pity to pass over many other signal Liberal victories, Northampton not excluded, without equal mention. Therefore, being thus actuated, I have endeavoured to pen a few lines to follow those of "G.C.'s" in your last issue:-

B is a Bradlaugh, philosophy's pet;
R is for Rathbone, left out in the wet;
A is an Adam, who wants to resign,
D is for Dilke, who for place has design.
L is for Labouchere, who leads Truth b ythe node;
A is Argyle, who'll do no great things,
U is Sir Ughtred, turned out of Hastings;
G is for Gladstone, fierce and verbose,
H his son Herbert, who now to Leeds goes.
A.M.N.

This acrostic for Bradlaugh refers to Charles Bradlaugh (1833-1891). Having won his seat in Northampton, as a committed atheist, he then refused to swear his allegiance to the Crown in the Houses of Parliament on the Bible, wishing merely to affirm his allegiance. There was no existing procedure for him to do so, and it took eight years of legal wrangles to sort out, including his imprisonment. Castleden choose to ignore this letter, but others were to come about Bradlaugh that he could not.

4ᵗʰ May 1880 Leighton Buzzard Observer

The Ballot: Protective to the Constituent, Preservative to the Candidate

To the Editor of the Leighton Buzzard Observer

Sir, - Now the battle is lost and won, a word or two on some of its tactics may be a hint, and serve on the coming Ballot Bill. Publicly, I referred to blots on it; let them be removed, and all would benefit. First, let me copy an answer on the receipt of a test paper inviting me to vote: -

"Woburn, 31 Mar., 1880. – Gentlemen – Accepting the Ballot in its integrity, I return, by post, the enclosed, and think I may say, on the part of electors, *voting is our* business on the polling day. To sanction such a paper seems to me to be an affront to common sense, an encouragement to duplicity, if not affording a cloak to positive and cowardly treachery. - I am, gentlemen, your faithful servant - George Castleden. - Messrs. Whyley and Piper."

This seems one blot. Blot 2 - canvassing. Candidates' addresses, welcome visits from them, local public meetings, are all in harmony with our improved election doings, but canvassing mars. Blot 3. "Costly election machinery" might be abolished. Candidates should be preserved from the heavy costs of retained agents, especially as the real work is often done by the worthy unpaid. Blot 4. Printed circular letters; if not verified, to be punishable. If these blots have consideration, and one of our new M.P.'s would give a first effort for their erasure, surely it would contribute to the simplicity, harmony, and integrity of England's grandest display of constitutional liberty, while it would tend to lessen personal animosity.

Having fought in our election conflicts since 1826, I might "shoulder the crutch and show how fields were won," but I would rather bring experience to bear on the present; and, if it may enlist influential Senate minds, I respectfully beg of them to make the Ballot complete, and no longer let it be "a delusion, a mockery, and a snare." I am admonished to ask your admission of this letter by words – see Eccles 9c., 10v.

I am, sir, your obedient servant, G.C., 27ᵗʰ April.

Note. - Let the above be my best notice of the limping lines signed "A.M.N." And, as Edward Franklin writes "friend," a friendly word or two

357

may best close. Ever write to serve and save, and, when age falls this "pure intent" will give supportive and salutary self-convictions of right, which none of the wrongs and thieves of time can ever rob you of or take away.

P.S. - After writing this, I received the Isle of Wight Express, 24th. A leader in it is so to the point, I wish I might copy: a short extract must serve. "Perjured constituencies. Practical lying of large numbers of Midlothian electors, who, after signing a paper, promising to support, voted on the other side," &c.

4th May 1880 Leighton Buzzard Observer

Woburn, Mass. - Geology. To the Editor of the Leighton Buzzard Observer

Sir, - Perhaps an extract from a letter received to-day may be grateful to your townsman, and be encouraging to local authors: - "I was glad to receive the lectures given at Leighton Buzzard by Mr. E. W. Lewis. I read them with much interest. They present, in a clear and brief way, the whole subject of geological formations, and give one the most exact knowledge of the different strata of your neighbourhood. I wish some one might perform a service for the region about and including our Woburn. We have one very accomplished geologist in town, but he has never given us an account of the rocks, minerals, and clays of this locality. The whole subject is an exceedingly interesting one, but to grasp it in its great principles, as well as in its details, is almost a work of life." If you can insert, I will post to my friend, and so both sides of the Atlantic may be gratified by this fraternal grasp of each other's hand.

I am, sir, your obedient servant, George Castleden, 30th April.

The election result debate had its course, and now Castleden was free to take those airy walks once more.

18th May 1880 Leighton Buzzard Observer

A May-Morn Musing in Woburn Park

A bright May-morn, wind chill and east,
Yet on the Abbey knoll
I lingered, viewed the landscape wide,
And communed with my soul.

"Nature with open volume shows
Her Maker's power abroad,"
I thought, and uttered on this scene,

All worthy of a God!

The spring green trees, the emerald sod,
The browning herd of deer,
Reclining oxen grouped abroad,
Were pictures, sunlit, clear,

In silent pleasure a lone bard
Surveyed the sylvan scene,
With thoughts his own he held regard
On life's long lengthening dream.

Yon Abbey pile reminds this May
Of Time's dark mystic flight;
Yon Abbey lawn recalls the day
Now lost in Lethe's night

Within have dwelt historic men,
The Statesmen of their day:
Earls, dukes, and lordlings, patriots then,
Now lost in long decay.

"Lord John," a name of Premier fame,
Links future, present, past;
And Woburn Russells will remain
While liberty shall last.

Hail to the scions rising still
To wage stern Freedom's fight;
Be their's ancestral wit and will,
Ancestral worth their might.

So as I stroll beneath these limes,
Muse scenes and actors gone,
I seem to scan an ever past
To present men unknown!

"Shades hunting shades!" in this Park tale
As shadows flee away!

This moral lasts for Woburn's vale,
Life is a day in May!
A glitter on yon pool, it sparkles, dies for aye.

At this instant a sudden quench of the spark startles, and confirms life's vanity, both in the home and mansion.

Note. – Finishing this Woburn Park relic, memory reviews many scenes from boyhood's cup of amber ale on the west front lawn, all through the years to 1841, July's monarch visit to the Abbey, on to the hours of age; some scenes bright, and others dim, yet all tell the time-repeating tale of the ceaseless flight of time, the changes, deaths, which in the run of seventy years have marked. Repeatedly, these home Elysian fields' shrouded their vernal scenes in deathly gloom, and proved God's Bible truth is very true – "That all is vanity beneath the sun."

George Castleden, 10th May.

His next was aimed at atheists, and, I suspect, Charles Bradlaugh, the new M.P., who had refused to swear his Oath of Allegiance, in particular. Castleden could countenance men of any faith, but not those with none.

25th **May 1880** Leighton Buzzard Observer

A Question

Sir, - In a noon on which you are eloquent at Leighton, permit an aged man's question, which, important just now, through your columns may stir thought at home, and serve the common zeal.

QUESTION FOR ATHEISTS!
Bold rebels, dare you, deny
The being of a God?
Self-pride debase, and say that I
Am nothing but a clod!

Do you reduce the god-made man,
With ken to map the sky,
To the dimensions of the pig
That snores within its stye?

Go, ask the beast upon its lair
If it desires a name?
If he will sigh for honours, fair,

Or seek for Senate fame?

Man has regrets; hopes point before;
Fears many deaths in one!
And yet you say all sense is o'er
When such a life is done.

"Abortion," then aspiring man,
Or else Creation's fool!
But pause, my pen, the Great I Am
Speaks by another school.

Where Reason is by Instinct taught,
If man a God deny,
The beast reproves, the ape retorts-
Proves man to be a lie!

Here, man, immortal, grasps at fame;
While there man fame deny!
A paradox! Here win a name
There fame ignore, decry!
The enigma solve, O man, before you die
Geo. Castleden, 19th May

Note. Yes or no settles contention. If the answer to the question be doubtful, no bigot, I leave the choice of creed; but, in behalf of man immortal, I quote apposite lines:-
    "Should all the schemes which men devise
    Assault my faith with treacherous art,
    I'd call them vanity and lies,
    And bind the Gospel to my heart."
    G. C.

1st June 1880 Leighton Buzzard Observer

Tributary Lines

On reading the following in the Daily News, 20th May: - "A letter also was read from Mr. Franklin, a well-known Liberal, who since its writing has died."

Another George has reached "the bourne"
From whence is no return;
Another friendly face and form
Has dropped in Death's dark urn.

I knew him in his youthful day –
Then ruddy, witty, keen;
And on our plain, at cricket play,
We hailed the summer sheen.

In our election fights, long past,
Companions we have been;
Now, reminiscent thought reviews
Life's varied, vanished dream!

In Woburn Park, on this May day,
I pen memoriam rhyme;
Another friend has flown away,
Another "shade" of Time!

My tribute on this Leighton son
Tones now the friendly sigh!
The younger man the goal has won,
The elder soon must die

Postscript
Nature, all sunlit, laughs around;
Is jocund, grateful, gay;
Man dies, and melts within the ground;
Moth-crushed, he flees away!

Note. The Ancients, we read, had the skull placed prominent at their banquets to remind of death! Surely, at this Leighton Liberal luncheon, it seemed as if the letter of the just deceased friend was to be a message from death, and as an echo from the grave, sounding vanity, all is vanity – that man is vanity and dust in all his flower and prime!

George Castleden

This deceased Franklin above had no connection to the local Eversholt Conservative he frequently argued with.

362

1ˢᵗ June 1880 Leighton Buzzard Observer

The Queen's Birthday

Sir, - A local bard records loyal wishes on this annual day, and, if you kindly give them circulation in your columns, they may speak for many of your readers.

> Another Monarch-birthday falls,
> And all these days I've seen;
> And this May day in loyalty,
> I sing, God save the Queen.
>
> In sixty-one birthdays now flown
> How many kings have gone!
> Yet still VICTORIA on her Throne
> Finds living homage shown.
>
> Our worthy Queen, God bless her still,
> We yet repeat this day;
> Still years of health, peace, and good-will
> Attend each coming May.
>
> This a last wish – may anger cease,
> And, on this May birthday,
> Once more I pray may smiling Peace
> Chase frowning War away.
>
> Our gracious Monarch long has seen
> Life's sad and sunny scenes;
> Help still, we say, God saves the Queen
> In life's yet darksome dreams!
>
> When this birthday shall cease in May,
> Then a fond thought may rise;
> Soul I seek the loved kindred far away –
> Reunion in the skies.
> George Castleden, Woburn, 24ᵗʰ May

Their defeat at the election had roused the local Conservative supporters to mobilise and begin planning for the next election.

8ᵗʰ June 1880 Leighton Buzzard Observer

Woburn Conservative Association. To the Editor of the Leighton Buzzard Observer

Sir, - Like our ancient friend, long asleep, I was roused by your notice, and, in a sort of dreamy doze, I said – Where am I? A club of Tories in Woburn seems a phenomenon "Rip" had never dreamed of, and at which our fathers would have gazed with the expectation of something wonderful impending! Is the lesson of this "Magpie" meet to be that the Liberals are asleep, or that our friends, not having of their own official cares, are kind enough to manage our affairs? Do they intend to *educate* the Liberals relative to the registration? If this be the benign purpose, we thank our neighbours, and join in the praiseworthy object of *serving* the constituency and saving candidates profuse and unjust expenditures. If the Woburn Conservative Club will do this good thing, perhaps they will not object to the Liberals assisting, and, mutually, making the registration lists (complete) as perfect as they can; then, without canvas, solicitation, or bribe, leave the grand issue to the ballot-box.

I am, sir, yours obediently and obliged, G. Castleden, 3ʳᵈ June.

15ᵗʰ June 1880 Leighton Buzzard Observer

The Woburn Conservative Association. To the Editor of the Leighton Buzzard Observer.

Sir, - Mr. Castleden, I see, wants to know the "lesson of this *Magpie* meet of Tories at Woburn." Let me reassure his evidently perturbed mind on this subject. What we mean is simply to give practical effect to that old but correct saying, "Sweet are the users of adversity," by forming an organisation (which the Conservatives in the county have never had before) that shall enable us to regain a representation of our conscientious opinions in the Imperial Parliament, which we have temporarily lost through lack of those united efforts which are alone attained by efficient organisation and discipline, combined with good generalship. The means by which we hope to reach this end, however, will not be to use such language as that described by some eminent persons as "polemical," whilst admitting it to be "both painful and wounding," nor by the use of such means as those for which four Liberal members have this week been justly and deservedly unseated.

Yours truly, Edward Franklin

22ⁿᵈ June 1880 Leighton Buzzard Observer

Parliamentary Elections. To the Editor of the Leighton Buzzard Observer

Sir, - Mr. Franklin refers to "four Liberals unseated." I thank him for this fact and refer him to the Canterbury Tories, &c. As I read "Election expenses," I say, "election extortions!" If a future Ballot Bill prevent not these, it will be the varies sham in Europe. Let the fact speak. Whilst thousands in the last election never thought of charging M. P.'s, yet carriages have conveyed, heavy bills have been paid, and the patriotism of some has been kept up by pouring champagne down. One last word from an old freeholder. Let the coming Ballot Bill protect the voter, and preserve the candidate from these unfair "election expenses," or else we wink at wrong, and help to perpetuate a mockery, a delusion, and a snare.

Yours obediently, G. Castleden

IMPROMPTU LINES

Five thousand pounds! A burning shame,
Methinks, to win a Senate fame;
M.P. means "I must pay."
Electors, just one word with you.
And, ere an old un says adieu,
Hear truth that he may say.

If M.P.'s pay to do your work.
They do it, sure, on *trust*;
How they recoup I cannot say,
But surely M.P.'s must
Expect return as they dub down the dust.

THE FINANCIAL PROPOSALS

Thanks, Statesmen, although income may
A penny more be called to pay
The world whirls on its axis
And while States last no doubt they must
Be still kept up by golden dust,
Which means – dub down the taxes.

The malt made free, the beer must pay;
Men need not drink, they surely may,
And if they do they pay;
So up and down out taxes go,
If Whigs or Tories, it is so;
For taxes, then, hurra!

Necessity's despotic law
Knows no appeal; 'twill sternly draw
John Bull to pay the taxes;
And, though he grumbles, still to pay
He won't refuse; and still to-day
The world whirls on its axis,
While Britons about who well can pay the taxes.
G. Castleden.

While Bradlaugh still refused to take his Parliamentary Oath, the Government seemed paralysed in how to handle the impasse.

29ᵗʰ June 1880 Leighton Buzzard Observer

The Bradlaugh Lock. To the Editor of the Leighton Buzzard Observer

"We have no right to go behind a man's oath to search out his religious views."

Sir, - These wise words of the Prime Minister seem to be the only key that can liberate from a fix which Parliament is now placed in. A civil right has been set aside by a wrongful scare; a citizen, claiming constitutional patent privileges, is to be imprisoned by a motley majority, each one of which holds his seat on the very grounds Mr. Bradlaugh contends for, and which, as law, ensures the liberty and independence of the House of Commons. I would not venture to censure the 275, but surely we may say of the 230 that they voted for the very life of representative government and in such a conflict the classical adage is despotic – "Let justice be done though the skies should fall." Without the majority mean to immortalise the man as a martyr or hero by inscribing on history this as the "Bradlaugh Parliament," surely the sooner they "hark back," to use a hunting phrase, the better. Purely as a civil question do I venture this as the honest common sense and law view of the question, without any reference to party dogma or religious creed.

I am, sir, yours obediently, George Castleden, Woburn, Midsummer Day.

6ᵗʰ July 1880 Leighton Buzzard Observer

Parliamentary Corruption and Infidelity. To the Editor of the Leighton Buzzard Observer.

Sir, - Although Mr. Castleden "refers me to the Canterbury Tories," I would ask him, through your columns, to note that up to present ten Liberals have been unseated to three Conservatives. Each of the latter received the condolences of the judges who unseated them, and whilst the proportion of Conservative who have maintained their seats on petitions is much greater than the Liberals, some of the latter, as in Macclesfield, were declared by the judges to have gained their seats, "by an organised system of bribery and corruption." Even Mr. Castleden must, I think, admit that such facts as these are strongly discreditable to the immaculate party of which he is a member - a party from whom we often have heard denunciation of the Conservatives as being the party of corruption *par excellence.* I hope therefore we shall hear less of such nonsense in the future – from them at least, till they shall have become purged from the stain of that corruption which has been so conclusively proved to exist.

Mr. Castleden's views on the "Bradlaugh lock" somewhat surprised me, but I am afraid he has only followed other eminent examples in disregarding the last sentence of his letter on this subject, and, giving preference to his own "party dogma" by wishing the 275 to "hark back." Now, that feat has been performed by the Liberal majority, and what is the unedifying spectacle presented to our view? It is certainly to be regretted that a representative of our country should be found assisting in the acts of such a drama. In the Book of al books, it is written, "The *fool* hath said in his heart there is no God;" yet it was to facilitate the entrance of the first Atheist to the British House of Commons that this Liberal majority was ready, at the sound of the Government whip, to reverse the honest judgement of the same House, pronounced without pressure only eight days previously. The late Conservative majority has been many times taunted with being a "mechanical majority"" but were they ever found voting black was black, and in eight days after declaring that the same "black" was, after all, "white?" I verily believed myself until now that it was only "the stupid Tory party" (according to the Liberal doctrine) that was possibly capable of performing such an extraordinary act as this, and would have thought, but for this, that as the Liberals are no persistently eager to represent themselves as the party who always give their votes in accordance with a honest, and not a party judgement, they would have preferred to let an honest judgement stand, "though the skies should fall," even at the risk of losing an infidel, seeking admission on doubtful grounds, to give his support to a Liberal Government, and ready to perform the farce of taking as affirmation to be loyal to that Sovereign when he openly presses to be ready to use his best endeavours to dethrone from the rule of Empire.

Yours faithfully, Edward Franklin, July 2nd 1880.

13th July 1880 Leighton Buzzard Observer

Election Corruption. To the Editor of the Leighton Buzzard Observer.

Sir, - In the unseating of Members of Parliament does it not prove the voters to be corrupt? If canvassing, conveyancing, coin, corresponding, &c., are to rule, and candidates pay, while we have got rid of rotten boroughs something in the State very rotten remains. And, if the Ballot be not conclusive, any extension of the constituency may extend election corruption. To prevent this all parties may aid and assist.

Yours obediently, George Castleden, July 7th.

3rd August 1880 Leighton Buzzard Observer

Election Corruption. To the Editor of the Leighton Buzzard Observer.

Sir, - Is the Ballot to be a snare or security? If thousands voted last election without canvassing or coin, why should not all be put on the same level? If money be used despotically, it becomes an arbitrary power. Mr. Justice Lush, on the Chester unseating, says: - "It is a very great misfortune for these gentlemen - Messrs. Dodson and Lawley - that they unhappily became implicated without any fault of their own in the acts of a large association." In a new Ballot Bill (1) prevent this peril by a penal clause; (2) protect the candidate's pocket; (3) place every voter on the same level. These P's I believe are sound. They may serve, and they might save another Chester "misfortune" which, by the agency of organisation, may slip into election culpability, and, inadvertently, perilous, criminality. My fear is that any "association" may vitiate the principle of the Ballot and jeopardise the candidate.

Yours obediently, G. Castleden

Note. – Reading *Public Opinion*, we say, either return to open voting, or do away the mask which allows

"The man to smile and smile
And be the villain still"

With all the national political upheaval, he still found time for lines on more local matters.

3rd August 1880 Leighton Buzzard Observer

Lines on hearing a Centenary Address to Sunday School Scholars – "Weeds and Flowers" – in Ridgmount Chapel, by Rev. W. Tomkins. – 18th July.

Your "weeds and flowers," O, may they teach,
To hearts all tender may they preach,
The sermon – weal and woe:
The thorn, twitch, nettle, all may say,
O, youth, beware of sin's foul way,
Root vice nor let it grow.

"Floral Apostles," in their bloom
Tint, scent, and cheer sunshine and gloom;
And, as they wither, die
In dust, all fragrant, they may say,
Like us, men fragile fades away
'Midst sorrow's saddening sigh.

Moral.
Flower tints may teach that bloom is death;
Their scent, the sweet, is dying breath,
Earth is a blighted shore!
There, *Eden*, vernal ever is,
There blooms a never-fading bliss,
There Death can kill no more.

Note. – This being an inspiration of a Sabbath, I close with a verse from Longfellow: - "The poet and his songs." I adapt it with respect and gratitude toward my American bardic brother. He has keyed in apt notes the truth relative to many a jarring song of mine: -
"For voices pursue him by day,
And haunt him by night,
And he listens, and needs must obey
When the Angel says – Write!"
George Castleden, Woburn, Beds.

17<u>th</u> <u>August</u> <u>1880</u> <u>Leighton Buzzard Observer</u>

A Thought on the Afghan Catastrophe. To the Editor of the Leighton Buzzard Observer.

Sir, - We send our crack soldiers into a jungle trap, and they are pounced upon by human leopards and tigers, and cruelly torn to pieces. We proudly send our educated chivalry to be the prey of coloured savages, and again the mad repetition of some of the best bones in England are to bleach on the burning sands and mountain passes of India. Perhaps this is righteous retribution for our wrong of invasion and annexation under the mask of a "scientific frontier." Hear an authority. "But if, as we have always maintained, interference in Afghanistan is not only useless but mischievous to this country, no words can be too strong for the criminal folly of those who have launched us upon a policy in which victory brings us no credit and defeat no compensation." – Daily News, 31st July, 1889.

Hear other opinion, and, surely, "back out," common sense enjoins and common Christianity demands. If this thought has insertion, it may serve. It may encourage solitary sowers of truth, hoping to harvest time more favoured reapers may garner fruit for the healing of the nations. Is it, in the nation as sometimes in an individual, that instead of the retrace of wrong, and the deed of reparation, there is to be proudful persistence even to ruinous reprisals? From signs, I hope the fear of being thought afraid will not hinder the doing right.

Yours obediently, George Castleden, Woburn, August 2nd, 1880

The Daily News article quoted there could have been used several times since 1880, with minor changes in language. The last letter was immediately followed by:

17th August 1880 Leighton Buzzard Observer

What is Church?

To the Editor of the Leighton Buzzard Observer

Sir, - I enter not into the dispute further than to say that it is too bad for Priest, Presbyter, or Pope to dogmatics, imprecate, or fulminate on a matter made by man so elastic that, with more clarity and less acrimony, all may agree to differ. As a solution of a knotty question, I offer the lines of the Rev. George Crabbe; and, as it is the pith of one of the Articles of the Church of England, and, as all "upper room" theologians adopt it, surely it might be accepted by the Christian world as a satisfactory settlement of the Church-dividing controversy. As a lady said, "Hear the sweet words of the bard with a sour name: -

"What is a Church? Let truth and reason speak;
They would reply – the faithful, pure, and meek;
From Christian folds the one selected race,
Of all professions, and in every place."

Read, mark, learn, and inwardly digest these good words, and flatulent intolerance will vanish, and the sour eructations of bigotry will cease.

Yours obediently, George Castleden, Woburn 12th August 1880.

A letter appeared on **24th August 1880** *from someone who signed themselves as "Nemo", commenting that all religious men should be of one purpose, and they should all study the work of Bishop Harold Browne.*

31st August 1880 Leighton Buzzard Observer

To the Editor of the Leighton Buzzard Observer.

Sir, - Avoiding controversy, I thank "Nemo" for giving, pertinently, the article I referred to. I have no doubt George Crabb, vicar of Aldborough, had it in view when he penned the pithy lines you were good enough to print; and I commend this article to all who have not "swallowed the steeple" alone, and have not imbibed deeply of Romist stimulants. With such elevated devotees of the Ceremonial Church I dare not argue; it seems as bootless, for conviction, as to attempt to persuade Toby Tosspot, "with three bottles in his head, serpentining home to bed," to join the Temperance Society. "Nemo" will kindly receive the vinous illustration as he speaks of "old wine" with an apparent smack of its "richness of flavour"

I am, sir, yours obediently, George Castleden, August 24th, 1880.

The Battle of Kandahar, on 1st September, was the last major engagement in the Second Anglo–Afghan War. British troops, having been besieged in the city, were rescued by a relief column from Kabul, led by General Roberts.

7th September 1880 Leighton Buzzard Observer

India (Afghan Wars). - Its Profits, Perils, Prospects. To the Editor of the Leighton Buzzard Observer.

Sir, - An old proverb says - "What comes under old Nick's belly swiftly goes over his back." Whether our Imperial acquisitions partake of this risk, or ban, I leave, but if I read the lives of Clive, Warren Hastings, and other Indian celebrities aright, I find truth in lines, little altered –

"All change to evade
They invasion defied, for the sword is their trade."

Win by the sword, hold by the sword, stands true for all time; whether it has paid I leave the ruins of other lands to tell; and whether India will not cost us *too much*, commercially, future history may crushingly and mournfully tell. Just now the heart is pained by the Candahar slaughters of our crack soldiers by semi-savages. Surely this looks like national retribution for going where we ought not to have gone, and doing what, if done to ourselves, had been reckoned sufficient to have made "all England a camp, and every man a soldier." In this matter I regret, as the country, polled, proclaimed against these unrighteous wars, that our Government did not endorse it by at once backing out, heedless of the howl, and careless of the sneer. Moral, political courage might have to wait for vindication, but, as sure as the God of truth and equity reigns this resolve would have won future solid fame far beyond annexing jungle grounds and burning sands, which, drenched with some of our best blood, may in history remain monumental of our folly and hypocrisy – *folly* in educating first-class soldiers to be trapped and slaughtered, pell-mell, in an Indian village; and surely sad *hypocrisy* may be charged on us, as a Christian nation, in manufacturing such hollow subterfuges as "scientific frontiers, etc.," for wars aggressive and unprovoked. Let local pathetic fact add mournful force to the above. In our pleasant lines lady and her four children find home, while the husband seeks "the bubble, reputation." The morning's paper tells us he is slain in the last slaughter? Here a home is blasted with war, in which victory wins naught, and defeats are aggravated by a sense that they follow on folly, and are the punitive consequences of sorry national hypocrisy. But I suppose this will last while peoples intoxicate themselves with prestige, and individuals get drunk with pride; no remorse, no reparation, and alike in homes and climes the poet's burning lines still be sadly realised –

"Man's inhumanity to man

Makes countless thousands mourn."

Surely peaceful policy, a pure humanity, and practical piety, prompt stern consideration of the cost and cruelty, concomitants of our sword colonies.

I am, sir, yours obediently, George Castleden. Woburn, August 26th, 1880.

5ᵗʰ October 1880 Leighton Buzzard Observer

Bread and Meat

To the Editor of the Leighton Buzzard Observer

Sir, - Man, being a granivorous and carnivorous animal, needs feeding. Warmth is also essential but, as the "Sunbeam Bottling Company, Limited," is in abeyance still, we briefly refer to bread and meat. How it is that distant bakers can bring a cheaper loaf to our parts puzzles? Might I suggest, as fair to all, that a local Assizes or that our Boards might arbitrate for each district. Surely, as guardians of the poor, the poor man's loaf claims their especial care; and surely ratepayers, when they find meat 7d. and 8d. to the "Union," and 10d. to themselves, may ask the reason why? These discrepancies in man's fodder disturb his ruminating powers, and, chewing the cud of *calculation*, he needs a simplified mode of arithmetic to solve what, mildly put, seems irregularity. An insertion may serve the public weal.

I am, sir, yours obediently, George Castleden, 30ᵗʰ Sept.

One wonders what corners were being cut to supply the poor house with meat at 70-80% of the High Street price? Before 1872, the British elections had been public, and who you voted for was published openly afterwards. This allowed landowners and employers to know who their tenants or employees had voted for, and woe betide someone who had voted against their master! The introduction of the secret ballot led some to use underhand means of securing votes…

12ᵗʰ October 1880 Leighton Buzzard Observer

Election Corruption Canvassing, &c. To the Editor of the Leighton Buzzard Observer

Sir, - Surely Canterbury, Oxford, Sandwich, and others will vouch for my heading, and surely they suggest that the Ballot, to be worked in its integrity, must be supplemented by a penal clause prohibiting personal canvassing and agent bribing. If Englishmen boast of representative distinction, and sometimes talk of its purity, don't let them wink at practices which, named truly, are lies, bribery, and mercenary shams, perpetuated under the mask of performing the highest constitutional duty of which, an Englishman, ewe boast. Any duplicity is both dishonourable and disgraceful. Canvassing and unauthorised payments, punished penally would protect the candidate and constituent; add this penalty to the Ballot, then a long farewell to the gentlemanly delinquencies, agent irregularities, and other subtle seductions which are being brought to light in the present election inquiries.

These blots remove, then, if not pure,

Elections may be more secure; -

The bribed and briber then would be

In fear of penal infamy.

Permit this line, and I remain, sir, Yours obediently, George Castleden, October 8ᵗʰ

12ᵗʰ October 1880 Leighton Buzzard Observer

Death of Mr. Chapman. - Our obituary notes the decease of one widely recognised as an old friend, Richard Chapman, for nearly forty years dispensing assistant in the surgery of Messrs Parker and Veasey at Woburn. Seldom may we meet with character more thoroughly honest and unselfish, manifesting the modern grace of true Christian charity. Few will be more missed of more deservedly claim the respect and attachment of all classes. "When may be found the like again?" - *Contributed.*

27: *An animated street scene at the corner of High Street and Park Street, Woburn. From a postcard used in 1917.*

19ᵗʰ October 1880 Leighton Buzzard Observer

A Tributary Note – Mr Chapman.

"Few will be more missed of more deservedly claim the respect and attachment of all classes." Observer, 12ᵗʰ October.

> A useful life for others done!
> He plodded on, 'neath Woburn's sun,
> He was a local friend.
> Obscure in times, to fame unknown,
> Without position, and alone
> He did to dust descend.
>
> How many of our mortal ills
> He cured by plaisters, draughts, and pills,
> In those long-flying years;
> This missing man, in merry mood,
> Would mingle words both quaint and good,
> While bottling smiles and tears.
>
> Yes, in yon corner of our town,

For forty years, with scant renown,
Poor Chapman plodded on;
He truly served the Parker race,
Had deep attachment to this place,
Tho' not a Woburn son.

He waned, he withered, passed away!
Yet when he left the other day
Thought, perhaps, he might return!
But now in Kent's rich garden soil
He rests, relieved from all Time's toil;
He sleeps within "the bourne."

Life's destiny he worked out here;
His death among his kindred there
Completes "Time's tragedy." (1)
He served, he suffered, died; what *more*
Of those who longest walk Earth's shore,
As shadows chase and fire? (2)
Nor will I in this requiem lay
Beyond my province rudely stray;
He found the common doom!
Respect, may memory honest pay
To one who served a long kind day,
Then fell in Earth's vast tomb!
One moral may approve my tribute lay
"Ready, ay, ready" (3) he whom Death shall call away.
George Castleden

Notes.
1. "Life's tragedy comes when Death enters."
2. "Fantastic chase, of shadows hunting shadows."
3. "Ready – Ay, ready, sir."
Woburn, 14th October.

Another severe famine in Ireland had led to some families being evicted by their landlords for failing to pay rent. A large number of these landlords were English. A groundswell movement took root, encouraging tenants to refuse to pay their rents, resist these evictions, and attack the land agents who represented English owners. Some in England proposed a heavy-handed invasion and use of force to tame the uprising. Others, like Castleden, suggested more peaceful solutions.

21st **December 1880** Leighton Buzzard Observer

A Thought on Ireland's Problem

Separation or Subjugation – Which? A Grave Question for our Senators

And will it come to this? The choice is, which-

The separation or the cruel sword?

Will wrong, long done, repeated oft, and yet

By fallacy misnamed State policy

Return in retribution on the heads

Of those who sanction not the primal sin?

Is party strife to rise, to roar, to vex-

Aye, plunge in deep perplexity the man

Who would the past repair, the present join

To future time, unshackled from sad wrong?

Can it be done? If Whig and Tory meet

In loyal amity, can they absolve

The wrongs of ages, and obliterate

The writings on the rock *against* the sword?

I fear no answer may afford the hope

Of cancelling the hoarded wrongs of time –

The legacy of fathers, who have made

Their sons executors; and to their deed,

Which Heaven's pure Chancery will not accept.

We sign our hand, endorse the sin, the seal

Afresh the conquest of the Isle by blood.

No; "The past is;" and Ireland stands a proof,

Among the nations, that this righteous law

Immutable, inflexible, still rules,

In sinning atoms, or delinquent isles.

Can wrong, repeated years, be blotted out?

I ask the question, moralist, of you!

We hear it said "That moral wrong may be

Politically right." A bag, a mare,

On which oft statesmen flounder, sink, are lost!

Sow with the sword, and dragons teeth will rise;

Sow with the plough, grain harvests cheer our eyes.
Let history tell, and let our colonies
Be evidence of profit and of loss.
I've done; at sunset hour I sow this thought,
As truth which, buried, may spring up to serve
In some mind – mind when I no longer wake
To right or wrong upon this earthly ball;
Or to "man's inhumanity to man"
Bear mournful testimony, sigh, and say –
When will the fiends of hatred, pride, and lust,
Be all transformed, and "men be brithers a'!"

Note – "Separation or subjugation" has been the alternative mooted by a high authority. Now, amid strife, turbulence, and crime, the problem – How to govern Ireland? Seems, in solution, to be the more difficult, inasmuch as remedial measures do not allay the burning fever of inherited discontent, bred first by conquest, and fed by various wrongs, up to a late period, by "Saxon supremacy," and something very like selfish brutality. If Mr. Gladstone's palliative measures fail, or are defeated, then a long farewell to hope!

George Castleden, Woburn, Dec. 14th

V

Letters: 1881

Ireland – War – A Hockliffe Burglar – William Hensman – Australian Flowers – The Comet – U.S. President Assassination – Steam v. Electricity – Woburn, Mass. – Bribery – Accidents

11th January 1881 Leighton Buzzard Observer

Ireland. Fame! – "Boycotting." Ireland gives no trouble just now; she has given us a new word; may I ask space for a rhyme on it?

> Men, avaricious, grasp at fame
> Above the clutch of gold;
> Crave, strive, and toil to win a name
> By all men to be told
>
> Methinks, just now, we hear a name
> Which will not be forgot;
> A fame unsought on Ireland's soil,
> Immortal sounds "Boycott."
>
> In Ireland's problem this one name
> Implies a scorn, a scare;
> "Boycotting" is neglect and pain
> To men who do and dare.
>
> A brave man's shield, it covers well,
> In wrong, from hate, neglect,
> He smiles when malice scowls farewell:
> True silence will protect.
>
> A bad man's dirk, the stab is safe
> In silence, secrecy;
> The coward 'neath the mask may smile
> In hidden infamy.

So "Boycotting" affords a theme
To tone our New Year's day –
An echo sounding in life's dream
The dreamers fled away!

One last good wish – may Ireland still
Know Freedom's blessing smile,
"Boycotting," wrong, and treason flee
The long-called "Sister Isle;"
Right, Peace, and Mercy kiss, agrees the while.
George Castleden, January 6th

Charles Boycott was a Land Agent on an estate in Ireland. The Irish Land League were campaigning for better conditions for tenant farmers, and organised the local workers to ostracise him, so he was refused service in local shops etc. The agricultural workers refused to follow his instructions, and eventually, the British Army and Royal Irish Constabulary had to be brought in to ensure the harvesting could be done by Orangemen. Boycott left Ireland soon afterwards, but his name became synonymous with a non-violent campaign to ignore and refuse to work with someone.

18th January 1881 Leighton Buzzard Observer
A Woburn Park Stroll – A Reminiscent Rhyme; 24th Dec., 1880.

Again the year has brought the day
I never may forget
Again it joins the bygone hours
Of sunshine, dark regret.

Again upon my errand, lone,
I toddled down the hill;
Looked on sunlighted evergreens
In wintery beauty still.

The third Park Office in my day
I entered, and I saw
The stewards, clerks, who now obey
The Ducal office laws.

I mused of agents long ago;
My thoughts they were my own –
Of days, friends, customs, vanished now
Unheeded and unknown.

Then in the open Park I strolled,
And, on the Abbey steep,
I looked upon pictorial scenes,
Of oxen, deer, and sheep.

I passed the Lodge, and saw within
A peacock strutting gay;
Brown, white, green, red, purple, and blue
All glinting in Sol's ray.

Then 'neath the Abbey roof I sat
And thought of Lord John's phrase;
"Rest and be thankful" suited age,
And suits remaining days.

My visit done, a friendly grasp,
Good wishes all sincere;
"May mercy, goodness, close the *old*
And welcome the *new* year.

Then homewards, as I made a call,
Saw marks of decay;
Disease had paled, but still the hope,
Death might stay long away.

So in this time of coming home,
'Midst sunlight falls the gloom;
And, mingling in life's Christmas boon,
Are weepings o'er the tomb.

And last I viewed a novel sight
In Woburn's wintery sky;
God's "bow" gave courage, cheer, and light,
And bade dark fear to fly.

George Castleden

Note. – At noon an evanescent rainbow hung over our Park Street. A thing of beauty, it passed transiently away, and now remains only a memory!

"So joys the sweetest
Oft the fleetest
As quickly flee away."
Woburn, 13th January.

25th January 1881 Leighton Buzzard Observer

A Season Rhyme

Sir, - You gave me space for a "stroll" on one of the mildest days in our mild winter; let me companion it by a rhyme in one of the severest and, perhaps, most calamitous.

On early morning's bed I lay,
And heard load Arctic howls
From Northern bears, and angry wolves,
In bitter winter growls.

On icy wings snow-flakes flew by;
I listened to the blast,
And, trembling 'neath increasing years,
Find energy is past.

The morn mind prompts; Job may express
Thoughts which may now be told –
"His ice in morsels He casts forth,
And who can stand His cold?"

O, fickle clime, as woman fair
And fickle thou can'st be!
Come, smiling skies, come, balmy air,
Come genial constancy.

On "Auld Land Syne" I muse and view
This wild and snowy storm,
By blazing fire, yet, pulses chill,
Scare keep the body warm.

The east wind bites, the atom sleet
Intrudes within my home;
A wrathful eve, a night of death
To many a waif unknown!

Lord Campbell's life in the last day
Bade me instruction reap;
Sudden he passed in age away,
And calm was his last sleep!

So let it be when duty's o'er;
Then from Time's winter day
May we, in peace, on Heaven's bright shore
Find summer bliss for aye.

P.S.
"He rides upon the storm!" yet fear
Invades the anxious breast;
"Home over there" no storm shall tear
All restlessness is rest!

George Castleden

1st **February 1881** Leighton Buzzard Observer

Lines – Chronological, Historical, Political. "First English Parliament, January 19th 1258" (Almanac.)

Six hundred years have flown, a few years more,
Since Parliament first ruled on England's shore:
Kings, Queens, and Nobles, peoples, all have fled –
As vanity and dust rest 'mongst the dead!
Homes, houses, dynasties have passed away;
Forgotten are their forms, forgot their day!
Caesars and clowns have mingled in death's sleep –
The dust of ages o'er their ashes sweep!
Successive Parliaments have vanished all,
And over most is cast oblivions pall.
Now 'neath the January Arctic sky,

I note this Serate fact. It may supply
A chronological link in History's chain,
And join an Edward's to Victoria's reign –
Connect it with our present Parliament,
Where Irishmen contest the landlord's rent;
Past wrongs array against the present hour,
And show democracy the victor's power.
The problem puzzles – What is right to do,
And can the Senate join acts kind and true?
Can Gladstone's remedies have healing away,
Or will Coercion rouse men not to obey?
"But what will be will be!" a motto sure
Hung in our street; Fate bids it to endure:
I've told a fact which joins Plantagenet
To Brunswick's House; nor will my muse forget,
While in the Senate strife may intervene,
To, loyal, shout – God Save our noble Queen.
George Castleden, Woburn, Beds. 19th Jan.

8th February 1881 Leighton Buzzard Observer
Postscript to "Lines Chronological, Historical, Political."

In 1256 Parliament first sat;
1881 M.P.'s are in full bat:
Hard hitting, in our cricket's summer phrase,
Hard sitting, sure, in winter nights and days.
Warm Irishmen get up the steam and spout,
Torrid within, and frigid all without.
While senior and juvenile M.P.'s
Find their vocation not inglorious *ease*;
Asleep, they wake and wish the Speaker power
To stop the flux of Pat's long-winded hour!

Note. – I had written this rhyme, then I read from *Punch* the "Moan of the Member." So misery makes mirth, and the two independent heads may think alike without theft.

Two "nobs" may think, without collusive guile,
The self-same thought to bid to weep or smile;

Apart, at distance far as either pole
May utter thought to bless or blast the soul.
Then grateful be if, in the study's hour,
You find your thoughts confirmed by greater power,
And with the wits of world resounding name
You think alike; 'tis solid, silent fame.
George Castleden, February 3rd, 1881.

In the **1st March 1881** *Leighton Buzzard Observer is a long letter from Edward Franklin on "The Woburn Whig", George William Erskine Russell, grandson of the 6th Duke of Bedford, who was now M.P. for Aylesbury.*

8th March 1881 Leighton Buzzard Observer

Unjust War. To the Editor of the Leighton Buzzard Observer.

Sir, - Some time ago I wrote on our "Blackamoor war." May I ask a space for a word on our Cape disasters. First, a sound question is asked – What business have we there? If the Dutch, long ago, went out into this wilderness, built their homes and cultivated, and left this inheritance to their sons, and if our lands adjoin, how much better their neighbour friendship than their fear and hate, under the terror of the sword. Statesmen may, under the charm of "annexation" and "scientific frontiering," be beguiled, but the common sense, truthful view of the question is well expressed in the pithy words of our "Woburn Whig," printed in the last Observer. He "wished to raise his voice as emphatically as he could against what he believed to be the greatest crime that a civilised nation could be guilty of – the crime of an unjust and unnecessary war." Is England's fame to be lost in the juggles of India? Perhaps the future may tell of the humanity and profit of our plough colonies, while the sad slaughter of our chivalry, and shameful squanderings of England's wealth have attended the conquest our sword colonies. May the God of our fathers mercifully help us to escape from the delusion and wickedness of these unnecessary, unnatural, and unchristian strifes, is the earnest wish of,

Yours obediently, George Castleden, Woburn, March 3, 1881.

22nd March 1881 Leighton Buzzard Observer

To the Editor of the Leighton Buzzard Observer

Sir, - Permit this supplement. Surely the Boers have right, aye religion, on their side. It is a first law of nature to defend *home*, and they have a right to say – we will negotiate, but we will resist invasion. Europe takes this view of it, and America must endorse it. In fact, was it not part of the appeal to the people at the last election? But, like a proud man, having taken a wrong step, he has neither conscience nor courage to repent or retrace, but on, on, must go, and so alike we find personal ruin and national disaster ending oftimes in ignominy and death. Oh, if men had the bravery to say, in time – "I was wrong," what personal wrecks, what seas of gore had been saved, and how Burns's lines had been limited – "Man's inhumanity to man." Who defended themselves against the threatened invasion of Bonaparte, "when all England was a camp, and every man a soldier?" Let a truthful answer be given to this question, and surely every Englishman should shun invasion, which, perpetrated by a Christian nation, may, in history, blazon it as both tyrannical and hypocritical. The bard has sung, "England, with all thy faults, I love thee still," but woe be where self so hardens the heart as to turn the human fault into demon crime. This pride will do in the individual; this *prestige* may do for a nation. May the armistice settle into peace.

Yours obediently, George Castleden, Woburn, March 11th, 1881.

Castleden's suggestion that the Boers could be right would obviously have run deeply against the national feeling in England, and found him few friends.

29th March 1881 Leighton Buzzard Observer
Original Poetry – On the Burglar at Hockliffe Grange

If Mr. Hawk had seen the pane
Between him and his prey,
Perhaps Mr. Hawk had thought again,
And flown another way.

But, self-absorbed, this Mr. Hawk
Was blind, tho' keen of eye,
And in his pounce he found a trap
Of pain and misery.

Moral
Keen-sighted man, beguiled by prey,
Is sadly blind to fate,
And, captured by his selfish sway,
He finds the trap – too late!
Woburn. G.C.

Peace!

Thanks to the Gladstone Ministry that, dazzled not by the prestige of false glory, they have won a victory for peace which justice approves, humanity will rejoice over, and mercy salute with her sweetest smile.

Hail, Gladstone, on this peace renown!
It adds a laurel to thy crown,
Long may it vernal be;
Among thy trophies chiefest shine,
Shed light on life's sun-setting time,
And gild felicity.
G.C.

Hockliffe Grange was the home of Colonel Richard Thomas Gilpin. According to the Bedfordshire Mercury, burglars entered by removing a piece of stiff wire netting from the larder window and wrenching off two iron bars. £55 worth of silver cutlery were taken, but a valuable gold 'loving cup' which had been presented to Richard Thomas Gilpin on the occasion of his eightieth birthday the previous month, was left behind. Two dishevelled men who arrived at Bletchley Station and booked tickets to London by the first train were suspected of being the culprits, but they were not stopped in time, and got clean away.

29ᵗʰ March 1881 Leighton Buzzard Observer

How to Work a School Board. To the Editor of the Leighton Buzzard Observer.

Sir, - On the *legal* aspect questions will be asked; permit two or three other questions which "reports" prompt. Would it not have been kind, aye, just, to have shown *courtesy* to the two ministers in the appointments? Is the self-nomination of Messrs. Hamilton, Crouch, and Hipwell a sign of Church despotism, or of pride – "Stand by?" With such a specimen of exclusion in Bedfordshire, what are we to expect in counties (villages) less favoured? Have we, as Nonconformists, in forsaking the voluntary education so serviceable here for sixty years – have we set up a system compulsory to our pockets, assailing to our feelings, and which, used covertly, in the future may blight and blast the very principles of Nonconformity? Ridgmount prompts these questions. The light of the Press may make intolerance blink, and prevent simple men stumbling into the dark bog of bigotry. In aid of the principles of civil and religious liberty, I hope these questions may, locally, have circulation in your paper.

I am, sir, yours abediently, [sic] George Castleden, March 22, 1881.

Of course, it would have to be a letter about education that featured a rare miss-spelling by the Observer type-setter! Also in this edition, a letter from Edward Franklin, replying to another letter writer the week before, sneeringly refers to Castleden's letter as "the prattle of our 'Local Poets'".

5th April 1881 Leighton Buzzard Observer
Original Poetry. The Press. First Printing in England, 26th March 1471. (Almanac)

Sure this March fact 1 4 7 1
May be March told 1 8 8 1,
And win a short renown;
The Census years have, many flown,
And many records are unknown –
Are lost to Woburn town.

This printing day joined shades of night;
Its inky cloud swathed rosy light;
It rose in lustrous fame.
Old England hails, in its great hour,
Her freeborn Press in giant power,
Its world-wide sounding name.

O, may the Press instruct, direct,
In right lead on, from wrong protect –
Save from dire falsehood's power.
In England's future may its voice
Resound, rebuke, restore, rejoice
Till Time's departing hour
G. Castleden, 31st March

12th April 1881 Leighton Buzzard Observer
Original Poetry. A tributary lyric on Sir Charles Reed M.P.
When long ago in old Bolt Court,*
I paid my bill to thee:
How little then was known or thought
Of life's own mystery

Our fathers, brethren, soldiers in
The Gospel chivalry;
They passed away, left pious names
In pulpit history.

Your sire will live while orphans vouch
To Death's remorseless aim;
Mine, buried here, yet lives a son
Of Mercy's loving reign.

In School Board annals now inscribed
You die, Sir Charles, in fame!
I wait in age the common doom,
And here 'twill close our name.

Once, as "M.P." I wrote to thee,
Referred to bygone scenes
It ratified the long ago,
And called up vanished dreams.

Upon your day of sepulture
I muse a last good-bye!
Good men must fade, their works endure -
This cheers sad sorrow's sigh.

The dark procession moves along
Vast London's living way;
In home I pen a requiem song
I mark thy burial day.
And on thy dust my friendly homage pay.

Woburn, George Castleden.
*Note. – In 1843 this incident in our lives occurred. In 1876-7 the last
letter interchange took place, and now Matthew 24 c. 41 v. tells the last
scene of life's varied "play in which men are actors all!"

*Sir Charles Reed FSA (1819-1881) was a British politician who
served as M.P. for Hackney and St Ives. He was also Chairman of the
London School Board, and a lay Congregationalist preacher, hence*

Castleden's interest. A week later, there was another tribute to pay:

19th April 1881 Leighton Buzzard Observer

Tribute Lines in Life or Death to The Earl of Beaconsfield.

Great man! work, work, has made thee great!
A struggle up life's hill;
Yet, manful, thou has conquered fate,
Thy power, heroic will!

We call thee great, 'gainst Senate hosts;
"I will be heard," you said;
That prophecy has been fulfilled,
Obstructions all has fled!

Uprising in your mental might
You fought, with valour, won;
Then highest rank and proudest men
Have hailed you master-son!

In politics divergent we,
My tribute is your due;
Thanks from a grateful memory
Shall tone this home adieu.

Great, kind, I here may pen, and why
Self-made you rose 'bove foes;
And, as a kind word ne'er can die,
Once more, at life's nigh close
I add my tribute thanks, repeat
Self-will achieves renown:
The moral, stern, Death soon may call
And strike Life's structures down.

Note. – These lines were penned ere I read an excellent article in the Daily News, from which I extract. "He had a profound sympathy with youth. Young men he seemed to think, at that time, were the mainspring of all that is enterprising and conquering in all the departments of the world. If a young man on either side of politics in the House of Commons gave any promise of making his mark, he was sure to receive the commendation and encouragement of Lord Beaconsfield."

George Castleden, Woburn, April.

Lord Beaconsfield was a title bestowed on Benjamin Disraeli, twice Prime Minister. Despite being of the party opposite to all of Castleden's views, he still paid credit where credit was due.

19ᵗʰ April 1881 Leighton Buzzard Observer

Woburn – The Rev. M. Castleden, of Woburn, was buried on the 11th November, 1848. He was formerly the pastor at the Independent Church at Hale Leys, Aylesbury. – *Aylesbury News* "Record of Local Occurrences."

28: *George Street, at the main Woburn crossroads. The buildings on the right have since been demolished, and the area is now grass. An undated postcard.*

26ᵗʰ April 1881 Leighton Buzzard Observer

Chronicle of Local Events. To the Editor of the Leighton Buzzard Observer.

Sir, - Your two items from the Aylesbury News moved thought. Of Philip Duncombe, Esq., in one of our pleasant lanes I met him on his last ride. Incautiously putting a tight boot on the wounded foot, this caused rapid inflammation, and ere the week was gone I was startled by hearing of that gentleman's death. Of my respected father, his own graphic words may best tell this part of a loving tale: - "I left the dark Vale (Aylesbury) behind, and found these Elysian fields, in which I have been charmed, and have breathed the air of civil and religious liberty, for forty years." For nigh forty years he lived, laboured, and loved here, then slept 'neath Woburn sky.

"Yet, being dead, he speaketh."

Your [sic] obediently, G. Castleden.

3rd May 1881 Leighton Buzzard Observer

Original Poetry. An Old Cricketer's Lines, Written on the Burial Day of Lord Beaconsfield.

> Birds wing and sing, the flowers of Spring
> Cheer, deck, this burial day;
> To the dark bourne, whence no return,
> They bear his form away;
> Rank, wealth, and wit, o'er dust their tribute pay.
>
> Thou great old man, this burial day
> I'll tell a fact of thee;
> It may remain in life's told tale
> A part of history.
>
> On to the turf, at noon or eve,
> Thy wont to stroll or sit;
> There gazing on the cricket group
> Land run, slip, catch, and hit.
>
> As on the pretty ground Age sat,
> His youth come back to sight,
> And in the modern "scout" and "bat"
> Returned a past delight.
>
> As memory, fond, recalled the hours
> Of youth and friendly glee,
> They rose on mind, like faded flowers,
> A mocking fallacy!
> Yet, cheating sense at eventide,
> They banished State affairs;
> And in this rural scene he found
> Relief from Senate cares.

So Hughenden reveals a scene
In our loved cricket game:
Now its graveyard, in life's on dream,
Will prove the smoke of fame!
One common wealth when breath has fled;
One commo9n worm for woe;
One grand democracy, the dead,
Their common hall below!

A Graphic Moral.
One of Death's "slows" has "bowled" this chief
"Hard hitting," all is done!
The "score" is cast, and men approve
The total he has won.
The umpire, stern, has shouted "Out!"
Now, at my set of sun,
A country bard may fix regard
On fame for ever done!

Note. – These lines, prompted by one of Lord Beaconsfield's home habits, may have an added interest, locally, if I tell, once an enthusiast in this summer king of games, well do I remember the late Earl Grey, amid the Reform conflict, on a visit to the Duke of Bedford, looking on us for more than an hour, perhaps beguiled, forgetting Senate strifes, and, mystically, again batting on the fields of Eton or Harrow. Add other Prime Ministers and celebrities, and the Park's beechen shaded plain may, in Woburn's annals, be famed as its historic cricket ground.

George Castleden, 26th April.

3rd May 1881 Leighton Buzzard Observer

Ridgmount School Board. To the Editor of the Leighton Buzzard Observer.

Sir, - Reading your report of the second meeting of this famed Board, the thought struck – What will the minority do? Will they endorse their own nonentity by playing dummies to intolerance, or, with "bated breath and whispered humbleness," bow down to bigotry? To leave the "committee of management" all alone in its glory seems not only the *laughable* return for such a legal dodge, but it may be the *logical* mode to prevent any repetition. One says in the report - "If there had been no contest there probably would have been no committee of management." Is bigotry and revenge thus to unite in malevolence? Surely some constitutional doctor will be found among our Liberal friends to try their skill to prevent the extension of such a malignant attack on civil and religious liberty in the reign of good Queen Victoria. I could write more; less I dare not, on this Bedfordshire report.

Yours obediently, George Castleden, Woburn, April 25th, 1881.

3rd May 1881 Leighton Buzzard Observer

Mr. Castleden's Rough Rhymes. To the Editor of the Leighton Buzzard Observer.

Sir, - We were reminded in your last issue that the Aylesbury News of the day recorded the death of Philip Duncombe, Esq., as due to an injured foot; and that, doubtless, was the cause assigned in the doctor's certificate; but, since we are told that he had the misfortune to know the "Woburn Poet," who can doubt the true case of his death? The "Poet" addressed some of his debilitating "Thoughts" to him, no doubt, and Mr. Duncombe, being already in a low way with his bad foot, could not survive it. Who could? I also observe that the census of Woburn shows a considerable decrease in population. Who can wonder at it? The Duke will have to pension the rest if he wishes to have any neighbours.

Yours truly, Dolorosus et Acerbus

N.B. ("Moral," as your bard would call it). – May I ask if all the deaths due to causes similar to Mr. Duncombe's are to be re-published and moralised on, with choulish delight, in the L.B.O.? If so, o please let it be known when, that I may, inter alia, arrange my summer trip. The poet Thompson apostrophises the fair Numidian, whose charms were so disastrous to herself and the famous Masinissa, thus: - "O, Sophonista! Sophonista, O!" Mr. Castleden will certainly not be so injurious from his charms, but, having regard to the widespread distemper occasioned by his laboured lucubrations, graceless rhymes, and lame meters, to say nothing of his "morals," I make an involuntary adaptation of Thompson's tragic ejaculation – O, Mr. Castleden! Mr. Castleden O!

10th May 1881 Leighton Buzzard Observer

Mr Castleden's Rough Rhymes. To the Editor of the Leighton Buzzard Observer.

Sir, - In my letter of last week the word "ghoulish" was printed "choulish," and the proper name "Sophonisha," "Sophonista." Now, here is a most legitimate opportunity for your bard to improve the occasion. Will Mr. Castleden address a few words to your type-setter, solemnly admonishing him on the duties of his office, and exhorting him to accuracy? I would suggest that he try a little blank verse, as rhyming has a tendency to make him somewhat obscure. And, as he will be enforcing a practical lesson on an impressionable youth, here will be his chance for a "moral;" or, if he keeps them by him, he might, perhaps, even try a couple to advantage. But if he should perversely insist upon rhyme, let him not depart from his usual good and useful practice of giving a foot-note on the subject matter, which is so necessary to the interpretation. Moreover, in doing this he is, in a manner, following the custom of the very ancient Greeks, who, when the art of painting was in its infancy (like Mr. Castleden's genius), were in the habit of labelling their productions thus:- "This is a horse;" or, "This is an ox," as the case might be, their confidence in their works, and in the ability of the public to interpret them, being about equal to your author's apparently. But let not any strictures of mine exercise too depressing an influence on Mr. Castleden's youthful ambition – (taking his productions as a true indication, Mr. Castleden's allusions to age are not to be seriously regarded) – although he should not make too much of the society of the Greeks in which he now finds himself. Let him by all means send a few stanzas to your boy.

Truly yours, Dolorosus et Acerbus, Wing, May 6th

17th May 1881 Leighton Buzzard Observer

"Rough Rhymes." – Queer Times – Sour Lines

To the Editor of the Leighton Buzzard Observer

Sir, - First, thanks to you for giving circulation to my "Rough Rhymes;" and, in words printed in the last Observer, "Allow me to inform your correspondent that my name is not hid, and, as he is (perchance) a member of some secret society," I am too old, at any rate, to fight with men "in buckram, or disguised in Kendal green;) and to all the snaky genus I say farewell in a well-known line –

"Viper, you bite the file."

Let this, a last moral, satisfy and gratify your "Wing" nameless, and be a final reply to all anonymous critics (spiteful?) from Woburn's

George Castleden

Note. – "Dolorosus." I shall be obliged if some classical friend will tell if it mean "hog, dog, or mutton." "Et" means *and*; "Acerbus" I find means "a crabbed, dogged (look) bitter fellow."

Kind words may lifelong sound –

Ay, echo from the grave.

Another Rough Rhyme – Lines on the Cartoon in Punch – January 30th, 1875.

"D-sr-li-. Sorry to lose you! I began with books; you're ending with them. Perhaps you're the wiser of the two." (The Statesmen Rivals.)

Drawn from the author path I first had chose,
I sought the Senate strife, and lost repose;
And, while in it I won a sounding name,
I found the "smoke," the vanity of fame.

24th May 1881 Leighton Buzzard Observer

Public Order. To the Editor of the Leighton Buzzard Observer.

Sir, - Public opinion is a powerful friend of civil and religious liberty. When Charles would have taxed his people without consent of Parliament, public opinion said "No!" and Sydney and Hampden remain immortal in history. And, when public opinion originated the "Exclusion Bill" against the bigot James, Duke of York, court hatred was exited, and it pursued the patriot Russell to the scaffold, and made a civil martyr of one of England's worthiest sons. And now, to descend from the lofty to lower ground, yet to link then with *now*, I could not help thinking, as I read your report of a deputation to Mr. Mundella, that a little public opinion by Bedfordshire Liberals in behalf of civil and religious liberty had showed up Ridgmount bigotry and exposed a legal dodge which seems to have struck at the very spirit of Mr. Forster's Act. A compulsory charge may be harsh and grinding; give a bigot majority in a Board rule, and we are made to support denominational despotism. This is, indeed, too bad. A few lines on public opinion may enforce the above and serve in the future: -

Public Opinion may, by tongue, Press, pen,
Achieve a conquest men will not condemn;
Invasion it may plan which peace may own,
And hail a triumph without tear or groan.
No glittering curse, no crimson-coloured crime,
To blast, stain, scar a home, a town, a clime,
Its lasting trophy is a grateful heart,
From which this conquest never will depart.
Peace smiles, and hails a bloodless victory,
While hateful war, repulsed, will scowl and flee.
Yours obediently, George Castleden.

"Mr. Forster's Act" was the Protection of Persons and Property (Ireland) Act, which allowed internment without trial of those suspected of involvement in the boycott and other protests in Ireland.

31ˢᵗ **May 1881** Leighton Buzzard Observer

Original Poetry. Memory of Her Majesty's Birthday, 24ᵗʰ May 1881

Herald Verse
Victoria, Queen, in birthday rhyme
I still link history;
And, venturing loyal homage, chime
A memory it may be
Of Woburn Abbey's July throng
It's night congratulative song,
From friends departed, shadows flown!
Then 'neath our sun *now* all unknown.

This bright May morn I sing once more,
Our Queen's birthday on Britain's shore;
This vernal day I sing.
I think alone, not sad, not lone,
Time flies in my old house at home,
While I on Fancy wing.

Yes, Fancy will delusive play
O'er vanished pleasures, forms away!
Facts tombed from mortal sight.
I look on pictures, read their tale,
Reprint, recall, to Woburn's vale,
Facts whelmed in Lethe's night.

Three pictures mark the life of one
Revered and loved 'neath England's sun,
Our mother-widow Queen:
Those pictures hang in my old room;
With books and pen I coten doom,
Now win a Royal theme

I see in one the maiden form
The features kind, which will adorn
The bloom of early youth –
Yes, musing, I in vision see
The secret of supremacy,

The lustre heart of truth.

Next with Prince Albert, see the twain
In Home's sweet love united reign,
The olive branches round;
The painter shows the parents' joy
'Tis happiness with alloy,
Exquisite bliss is found.

The sweetest yet the fleetest, lo!
Life's brightness darkened by sad woe,
Tears quench a light so pure!
Queen mother! Still thy state prevails,
In all thy grief no duty fails,
Thy sceptre sways secure.

Our gracious Queen has filled the Throne
For years alone, thank God not lone,
Her better help above!
Oft sunned by smiles, if dimmed by tears,
Have rolled the long and widowed years,
In safety, peace, and love.

The girl, wife, mother, widow, all
The palace pageant, and the pall
Have been life's varied scene!
Still bridal joy and infant glee
Have charmed the lonely mystery
Of England's worthy Queen.

One more the year has rolled away,
Once more I hail the Queen's birthday
Perhaps pen my requiem line:
Still a last wish, though sung alone,
God save, bless Queen Victoria's Throne,
In long remaining time.

Note. – The herald verse refers to the Royal visit to Woburn Abbey, 1841.
And of the pictures referred to in this lay, I briefly say, the first is a copy by
Joshua Phillimore of an early portrait hanging in Woburn Abbey; for its

home reminiscences it has been a valued picture for nigh forty years. The second is a small photograph of the Royal Family at Winterhalter. When her Majesty permitted exhibition of the Family pictures as St. James Palace, my brother got tickets, and it was a happy fraternal visit, and a sunbeam on my literary life was a brotherly commendation of a piece commemorating this London event. The third is a prized engraving, published by a public print, of the widow Queen. By these pictures I attempt to embalm home thoughts of heart gratitude and profound attachment to old England's constitutional and beloved monarch, Queen Victoria.

George Castleden.

A Last Postscript Verse – 28th May

The sixty years and more I see,

The forty fourth in history

Must on its roll remain:

This, a rhyme relique in old age

May still inscribe in our home page,

In chronologic strain,

The sunshine, shade, of Queen Victoria's reign.

The Leighton Buzzard Observer ran a report of an accident befalling a Woburnite on 31st May 1881: "Serious Accident – On Wednesday last, Mr. W. Hensman, of this town, accompanied by his son, had occasion to visit his farm at Eversholt, and drove over in a trap. While he was engaged with Mr. Ward, who lives at the farm, he let fall the reins, and his mare immediately started forward. An overhanging branch of a tree caught Mr. Hensman and knocked him violently out of the trap. He sustained severe cuts and bruises, and lies in a precarious state." Sadly, he did not recover. William Hensman's Castle Works were famous in the area. His company had exhibited at the 1851 Great Exhibition, showing a four-horse power portable steam-engine, a four-horse power patent bolting thrashing-machine, an eight-row patent cup-drill, a patent hand thrashing-machine, and two patent wrought iron ploughs.

7th June 1881 Leighton Buzzard Observer

Obituary – William Hensman

Three old inhabitants, two at eighty-five and one seventy-nine years, have passed away in the last weeks of May. William Hensman came here as a young man. He entered first as implement manufactory. His natural genius was soon perceived by Mr Salmon, one of England's pioneers in agricultural machinery. Under the inspiration of the agent, and the fostering care of Francis and John, fifth and sixth Dukes of Bedford, Woburn was the birthplace of infantine agricultural implements, which have grown into gigantic shapes, and have become world-known through the Howard factory at Bedford. In after life William Hensman became our manufacturer, and his "Castle Hill Works" had for years local celebrity. There was in his life "the tide," but denials and disadvantages prevented the floating on to "fame and fortune." He sowed, and others have reaped. I remember, in one of our neighbour chats, his referring gratefully to a transfer of a patent or two to the Messrs. Howard, and he left the impression that they had behaved kindly to him. But, naturally retiring and reserved, much of the mystery of his mechanical life remained in obscurity, and much that dwelt within is hidden now. Struggles of mind, disappointment in results; discoveries by himself, and then the profitable application of them buy others; the apparent grasp of local fame, and then its vanishing; all these and sundry other items were part of the discipline of William Hensman had to go through in the home of many joys and sorrows. An even, peaceful, unambitious life; quaint, sometimes odd inexpression; never spiteful or malevolent, holding tenaciously his own view, he was naturally kind hearted and considerate, and we record in the day of prosperity his factory was the refuge to many a waif and stray who sought work, and could turn their hand to any of its occupations, and there are those who remain who testify of kindness in its open door when other doors were shut. But now, with patrons famed, contemporaries honoured after life's fever, he sleeps! An accident extinguished life's snuff, and saying our last good-byes of "peace," we left the dying neighbour meeting the inevitable as another illustration of the poet's lines when he bids Death say to the aged man –

"This long-liv'd debt is due, and should have been paid
When first her flame began to burn:
But I have stay'd too long, I have delayed
To store my vast, my craving run.
My Patent gives me power,
Each day, each hour,
To strike the homely thatch, and shake the princely tower."

I believe the annals of agriculture give the mowing and reaping machines as the products of Bedfordshire, and when I was a boy I remember the outcry against the haymaking machine, These, and others our neighbour had to do with, and on them was his inventive genius exercised in his early day, and some of the first specimens were exhibited at the Woburn Park sheep shearings. As an aged man looking upon his quiet, obscure life, thinking upon his past; never hearing discontented of querulous complainings on passing ills or clouds, I rather think, as a long useful and peaceful neighbour townsman, verse from the "Elergy" will well express his life, and might be a truthful epitaph:

Far from the madding crowd's ignoble strife
His sober wishes never learn'd to stray:
Along the cool sequestered vale of life,
He kept the noiseless tenour of his way.
George Castleden

21st June 1881 Leighton Buzzard Observer

Lines – On the receipt of Australian Land and Sea Flowers from a Friend, not seen for 45 years.

Thou fragile thing! a thing of nought;
Over the sea thou stirrest thought
Within the chamber, bed;
At sunrise time, in hopes and fears,
An aged man looks down life's years
And communes with the dead.

Thou pretty weed! the ocean foam
No more shall crest thy tints at home;
No more its sunny breath
Will o'er this heath-born stranger sigh:
No; beautiful 'neath Woburn's sky,
Thou tallest me of death!

The death of friendship, and of those
Who died as friends - not lived as foes –
Who are remembered yet:
A weed across the trackless sea
Pulses the ebbing memory
With times it might forget.

And so, in June's bright sunny beam,
I do indulge morn's waking dream
Inspired by friendship's boom:
The pretty, tinted, lifeless flowers,
Australian weeds, call up home hours
From Time's voracious tomb.

P.S.
Go back, my weed of thought; speed thou
To friends I ne'er shall see:
Tell them dead flowers bloom out a song
Of gratitude from me,
An aged bard and friend – G.C.
George Street, Woburn

Note. – Forty-five years ago a ruddy lad companioned us on our beautiful cricket ground; then I lost sight of him. Three of four years ago some of my productions found him in the far West; he sent a pleasant response, and so Time's chasm has been bridged by heart words, over which spirits travel, and friendship telegraphs its smile and kind word."

Pure fame is this, when friends agree,
And souls are linked across the sea
By friendships bond, heart unity –
A conquest this to boast.

Go then, my song, across the sea:
Amy friend afar may welcome thee:
While age no more his smile may see,
The note shall not be lost.

What a shame this old friend is not named, or it would have been possible to track down his story.

5ᵗʰ July 1881 Leighton Buzzard Observer
Original Poetry – On the Comet, Seen 27ᵗʰ June, 1881.

Illustrious stranger! Speeding where?
I sing this wondering star,
And in our childish song I say,
"I wonder what you are?"

For size and pace faith must believe
What star-lore men essay;
Where thou hast travelled who can tell,

Ere visiting Earth's day –
Or rather night? Thy brilliant flight
Beats computation's ken;
Whence thou comest, whence thou goest
Is dark to gazing men.

Eccentric with a fiery tail,
Thy course just now is light,
But who shall track thy plunge profound
Into the stellar night?

Year roll; where, then, if wit is right,
When seventy years have fled,
Again you'll visit Woburn's night
Us Woburnites all dead?

We gaze, we wonder, and adore;
Still night's stupendous scene
Proves men are pigmies in their lore,
And life's transient dream!

Moral
If age may tell this comet's flight,
Hear truth; at its return,
Age, youth, will sleep in the grave's night -
Be dust in Time's vast urn!

Note. – A brilliant extract from Dr. Young will lighten my dark rhyme and
gem one of Nature's prodigies with the pearl of Christian truth: -

Hast thou not seen the comet's flaming flight?
Th' illustrious stranger passing terror sheds
On gazing nations, from his fiery train,
Of length enormous; takes his ample round
Thro' depths of ether; coasts unnumbered, worlds
Of more than solar glory; doubles wide
Heaven's mighty cape; and then revisits Earth,
From the long travel of a thousand years,
Thus, as the destined period, shall return.

Me, once on earth, who bids the comet blaze,
And with Him *all* our triumph o'er the tomb.
George Castleden, June 30th

I think "Illustrious Stranger" would make a far better name for the comet seen in 1881 than the official one of "C/1881 K1"! It was the first comet to be photographed, and was visible from some places around the globe until February 1882.

12th July 1881 Leighton Buzzard Observer
Original Poetry – The Attempted Assassination of the President of America.

Sad news is sped across the Atlantic wave;
Foul murder hatch'd no wit nor skill could save:
A brain diseased, or else a heart most bad
Contrives and executes a slaughter sad –
Bids Europe's nations execrate the blow
Which clouds America with crimeful woe.

Men stand aghast, but helpless seems to be
In these repeated deeds of butchery!
They see the mighty fall on Death's dread shore;
One will, one hand, one shot, and all is o'er!
Among the throng the assassin steals his way
Staunch to his purpose stalks his helpless prey,
Achieves an ignominious renown
By startling men in striking Garfield down;
He bids for fame inscribed in blood-writ shame,
And leaves on History's page a murder's name.

Poor Garfield rose, America's clear light
The sudden fell into historic night!
In sympathy we share our kinsmen's grief,
Condole, but helpless to afford relief;
But truly hope in this atrocious crime
God hides some good and veils some bright design.
George Castleden, 7th July

President James A. Garfield had been shot in the waiting room at Sixth Street Station, in Washington, by Charles Guiteau, an amateur politician, who believed Garfield was only in power due to his influence. Mortally wounded, but alive, the President was rushed back to the White House, where doctors tried to locate and remove the bullet from deep inside his body.

26th July 1881 Leighton Buzzard Observer

Original Poetry – A Tributary Tone on Dean Stanley
"Good men live after death"

Good man, kind man, man of peace,
A requiem note is mine;
I add a tributary tone
To sound in coming time.

Good men will tell thy genial worth,
Grave men will o'er the sigh;
Men kind and worthy of each Church
Will mourn such men must die

I saw thee act the Christian part
Beneath old Bedford's sky,
John Bunyan pulsed they frater heart
In holy chivalry.

Amid the throng I stood alone;
I saw they noble dame;
Again I note in my old home
The vanity of fame!*

Again I mourn the spoiler's hand
Robs us of one so pure;
But Arthur Stanley's good in life
Will through all time endure.

This wild-flower wreath from one unknown
May mix in richer bloom
And 'mongest the floral tribute shown

May deck his Abbey tomb.

George Castleden, Woburn, July 21st

"Men will mourn a staunch and affectionate friend, who, in spite of a gentleness which made the paths of peace natural to his feet, always responded with a chivalrous readiness when he was called to the championship of persecuted and deceived merit and unpopular opinion. The England of our generation has had, and has lost, many a greater man than Arthur Stanley. It has not had to say farewell to any purer and better. - Daily News.

*Note - In 187-, when the statue of the "Elstow Tinker" was given to the town by His Grace the Duke of Bedford, was unveiled by the Lady Augusta Stanley.

Together *then*, in works of love and peace.

Together *now*, in realms where strifes all cease

Arthur Penrhyn Stanley was the Dean of Westminster, and a leading liberal theologian of his time. By now, Castleden had enlarged his readership to Woburn, Mass., as well as Woburn, Beds.

26th July 1881 Leighton Buzzard Observer

Woburn, Mass.: Woburn, Beds. To the Editor of the Leighton Buzzard Observer.

Sir, - I am congratulated in having so interesting and instructive a correspondent across the Atlantic. As "special correspondents" are deservedly popular for their trouble and skill in making us acquainted with mundane affairs, I will, with your help, give a few extracts from a friendly writer whom I have never seen, but to whom, in spirit, I have been introduced, and with whom I have been in much mental talk and epistolary pleasure; and, taking high commendation for our guide - that "he who does the smallest deed to aid peaceful relations between England and America does a good, and a very good, thing" - I say, taking this as our motto relative to peace and goodwill, it is the sole impulse, while it is the great charm which has lent to our "G. C." correspondence much of its present pleasant interest, and it may give a value to it in future. Another reason for insertion is that in a letter, dated June 30th Mr. Champney writes:- "Since the letter came to hand I have received several Leighton Buzzard Observers containing your rhymed and prose contributions to that paper. It is really interesting to observe the strong desire that yet possesses you to influence your countrymen in the ways of peace and justice." Now, one more extract will evidence to the political feature of the correspondence, which I hope younger neighbours, on both shores, may, fraternally, carry on when we, the elders, drop the pen:- "I am glad to see the interest taken by your people in our American Minister, Mr. Lowell. I think he is fully worthy of it, for he is not only a poet of high grade but he is a scholar in other departments, a diplomatist, and a man of exalted personal character. It is a credit to our Administration here to send such a man to the mother country to represent its interests and nationalities. I am proud even of the distant relationship be bears to me. I trust his mission to England will promote the good feeling between the mother and daughter, and tend to make the harmony between them perpetual. It should be so; and, if our public men do their duty, no collision or mistrust will ever stain our national intercourse." By giving circulation to these excellent words you may, locally, be doing "a good and a very good thing" in the cause of peace, and, as the small seed sown now, it may thrive and grow when the sowers sleep.

I am sir, your obedient servant, George Castleden, 21st July.

2nd August 1881 Leighton Buzzard Observer

Woburn, Mass.: Woburn, Beds. (2) To the Editor of the Leighton Buzzard Observer.

Sir, - Other extracts from the letter of which you have inserted a portion may serve the cause of peace and humanity. Mr. Champney kindly writes of some sentences in the Observer: - "They ought to, and will, make an impression. Such frequent and pungent settings forth of sound and healthy principles will find soil in which to germinate and bear fruit. That it is the only way by which the world is to be reformed, and brought up to   higher standards of justice and equity. When the American colonies started out to obtain their rights, it was the persistent efforts of a few men, who put on record and reiterated their convictions of duty, that brought the people up to the point of resistance. It was Garrison and a few 'agitators' that so wrought upon the mind and heart of the same people as to convict them of the evils of slavery, and hence to abolish it amid the exciting scenes of the great civil war. And so it must be with the wars in Asia and Africa, and the intolerance that comes from some landlordism in Ireland. These must be stopped or modified by the persistent talk and sharp pens of men who are in earnest to see the world advance in the principles of peace and right, under the banner of mutual hopefulness. It was encouraging to see the Gladstone Ministry suspend the cruel war with the Boers, and retreat from the position assumed by the Tories. It is gratifying also to see the same great leader making every effort to subdue the passions and relieve some of the burdens of the Irish. I am aware it is quite impossible to make Ireland contented and happy, as long as it is ruled by home demagogues and (almost) traitors. But, as I look at it, the new Land Bill will do much to equalise the conditions of the people, and will be the entering wedge of still greater reforms in the future. We have many foolish or wicked men here who are busying themselves with English affairs, more for political effect in this country than for the redemption of the Irish at home. England may have cause to complain of this. If she does, I believe our Government will be ready to repress anything unlawful and unfraternal."

I may not send across the Atlantic a better response to Mr. Champney's letter than the magnificent endorsement of its peace and goodwill in the peroration of our great Prime Minister on the Transvaal debate. In it breathing thoughts and burning words combine to enforce those just and humane principles which have made and can only make England great, glorious, and free. Mr Gladstone says: - "We have endeavoured to do right and eschew wrong, and we have don et that in a matter involving alike the lives of thousands and the honourable character of our country. And, sir, whatever may be the sense of gentlemen opposite, we believe we are supported, not only by the general convictions of Parliament, but by those of the country. We feel that we are entitled to make that declaration, for from every great centre of opinion in Europe, from the remotest corners of Anglo-Saxon America, have come back to us the echoes of the resolution we have taken – the favouring and approving echoes, recognising in the policy of the Government in ambition higher than that which looks for military triumph of for territorial aggrandisement, but which seeks to signalise itself by walking in the plain and simple ways of right and justice, and which desires never to build up empire except in the happiness of the governed." Ever may such principles guide, guard, and bless our beloved commonwealth.

I am, sir, your obedient servant, George Castleden, July 27th.

...not that this intercontinental readership impressed the local Conservative, Edward Franklin...

16th August 1881 Leighton Buzzard Observer

To the Editor of the Leighton Buzzard Observer

Sir, - Mr. Castleden, in a recent issue, parades the opinion of some unknown person in America, "to serve the cause of peace and humanity." A great deal of cant and humbug has been uttered and written upon these words by certain persons, both great and small, of Liberal opinions, about the disgraceful Transvaal surrender. Allow me, therefore, to quote a correspondent on the spot, during the recent parade of our troops into and their immediate departure from Potchefstroom, which the present blundering Government fancy is sufficient to uphold the honour and prestige of England after the treachery of the Boers of that place: -

"In the arrival here at Potchrefstroom of the column which left Newcastle on the 28th of May the farce enacted by the home Government well nigh completes itself. How it is viewed by the English public I know not, though I trust it is with a sense of shame and humiliation; but out here the greatest contempt and disgust is exhibited, and the confidence and trust of the English colonist and Kaffir population in the honour and integrity of England has completely vanished. The baseness of it all strikes one the more forcibly from being on the spot, and the cruel wrong done to the people stands out the more apparent. Potchefstroom of all others held out the most gallantly, and under the circumstances of privation and hardship which, while the annals of glorious deeds and heroic action last, must ever be remembered. The brave defenders of the fort maintained a long and determined resistance against overwhelming odds. Not until famine at its last stage compelled them to surrender did they evince the slightest desire to capitulate, and even then this capitulation was the result of Boer treachery and dissimulation. For what good has all this been done? What is the reward for their loyalty and heroism but to see their freedom taken from them, and the land they defended, with the pluck and courage of the old English style, handed over the rule of a hated and incompetent enemy. Bitter must have been the pill which General Buller found himself compelled to swallow as he rode into Potchefstroom at the head of his column and marched through the town with all the paraphernalia of a conqueror. In silence the column wended its way along the principle street in Potchefstroom, silently it was greeted by that portion of the English population who turned out to watch the parade past, while with sneering looks and sarcastic remarks the Boers clustered together to gaze on men whom they despise and underrate. I fear the men would not have been flattered had they comprehended the various remarks passed upon them; perhaps it was just as well they did not understand; the unwelcome job set them has been as it is bad enough without adding insult to injury. To all who took part in that march and entry into Potchefstroom, to all who that day witnessed the painful scene, and who have the honour, prestige, and glory of Old England at heart, that day will be remembered as one of disgrace and shame, a black stain on the page of English honour, which has never before known disgrace. The feeling in Potchefstroom is one of bitter and undisguised hatred of Mr. Gladstone and the members of her Majesty's Home Government. Forsaken stores and empty houses tell their own sad tale of ruin and desolation. During the war property was unspared, large stores were looted and pillaged, and the loyal owners suffered grievously. The very sight of the place fills one with regret and sadness as one recalls the past, with its humiliation and infidelity. The prestige and honour of England is now but a byword amongst our brother colonists; scorn and contempt for Mr. Gladstone and his Government are hardly terms sufficiently strong to express the feeling exhibited, while the respect of the native population, its trust and belief in the power of England has vanished. Headed by the English colonists, a great native war will ere long prevail; the massacre will be terrible, for it will be a war of extermination of a hated and persecuting race. With the Bible in one hand the Boer breathes prayer and cant, while with the other he oppresses the black man and tries to behave likewise to the English colonists. Let him beware that he does not try their patience too far. Mr. Gladstone and his Government have given in to the Boers on all points, but his example will not be followed out here, and resistance will be the sole reply to persecution. What England could not or would not do the English colonists and native population will accomplish; much blood will be spilt, and the whole tragedy that must come sooner or later will be the result of the cowardly bungling of the present Government. There is very little left now to tell of English doings out here; England has forsaken her countrymen in their time of need, and many will try to forget that they are Englishmen – most are ashamed of the very name."

As for the debate upon the Transvaal question, and the majority of 109 thereon, one remark will suffice to show the real bearing of the question as to the making of England either "great, glorious, or free." Does Mr. Castleden think, or even dream, that the aim of the obstructionist Home Rulers in the present Parliament is to conduce to the attainment of either of those objects? And yet they are always to be found voting with the Government on questions such as this (Candahar to wit), where a surrender is to be made. I can only congratulate Mr. Castleden and his Liberal party on having obtained such a splendid Parliamentary majority on such an anti-national policy, which so misrepresents the nearly universal opinion outside of Parliament. I may add that the latest telegraphic accounts from the Transvaal to this date only tend to justify the worst forebodings of the correspondent in question. The native population, finding that the "great and glorious freedom" they have enjoyed under England has departed, are preparing to fight their slave-driving masters, the Boers. This will doubtless "serve the cause of peace and humanity" in the opinion of Mr. Castleden and those of his kidney, in America, who chatter so much about the "ways of right and justice;" but most common sense Englishmen will be inclined, I think, to believe that it will yet further conduce to a state of war and bitter in-humanity.

Yours sincerely, Edward Franklin.

23ʳᵈ August 1881 Leighton Buzzard Observer

Woburn, Mass., Woburn, Beds. [No.3]

Sir, - Illness has interfered with intent, or this third extract you should have had earlier. I sincerely hope Mr. Champney's sanguine words may be realised:- "I believe your agricultural season is a prosperous one. After a severe winter you will have an abundant harvest. I am sure if any set of people are deserving, it is the farmers, the producers; they generally work hard for modest pay, while many wild and reckless speculators live in extravagance and luxury. Our season in New England is unusually cool and backward, though the July and August heats may bring everything to abundant maturity. The moisture and coolness have had a lively effect upon the grass, trees, and shrubbery, all of which are rich and thrifty in growth. With such a season we almost rival England in verdure. It is said that our western grain crops will be lighter than last year, but the increase of acreage will, probably, make up any deficiency, so that we shall still be the great grain-producing nation of the world."

As education seems the grand remedy of all Governments in the civilised world, I give one extract on it, from this letter, and then close:-

"Our town schools have just closed their yearly season with great satisfaction to the people and credit to the teachers. How pleasant it would be if you could step in at some of the examinations and make some of your wise remarks to the children. We should all enjoy such a season very much."

Thanks, unknown friend: this visit, *a fact*, would beat fiction! But in memory of a revered father, forty-one years inspector of one of Old England's free schools, and twenty-one years of service myself, I might, out of this dual experience, say something amusing, if not wise, to the scholars of a New England school. At any rate, in the columns of the Observer I may send across the Atlantic three parental words which have done service in our generations:- Truth, Honesty, Punctuality.

Now, thanking for the reprint of lines in the *Woburn Journal*, July 29ᵗʰ, and hoping still for the providential restoration of the President, and trusting that his presidency will be a bright chapter in the history of the United States, and with an old man's best wishes that the amity and prosperity of "Anglo-Saxon America" – to quote from Mr. Gladstone's eloquent peroration – may serve and bless the civilised world,

I am, sir, your obliged servant, George Castleden, Woburn, Beds., Aug. 16.

30th August 1881 Leighton Buzzard Observer

Original Poetry. An Old Man's Thought on a Suspension of Life.

Life past, life present, life to come:
Life, *future*, called, must call me home!
What home? I hear a critic cry;
The answer, true, who can supply?
I muse the ages past; all die;
No echo *where* tells 'neath the sky;
And the long *present* I have seen
Is voiceless now as morning's dream.
The wit, devine, and statesman, where?
And sons of Home are vanished air!
The universal doom all feel,
But *where* the Home none may reveal!
Time is a triune vanity;
Eternity, reality!
We test the first in love and hate
And prove the last Eternal Fate!
Here man is lost, can tell no more,
His wisdom reached on earth's dark shore:
Faith views the telescopic scene
And says that life is no9t a dream;
Assures us 'tis the passage clime
To Home, eternal and divine

P.S.
Life is suspense I passed from strife,
Lost sorrow, pain and care;
I neared the bourne whence no return,
Then wake on natal air.
And yet how easy then were death;
'Twere bliss almost to die!
A mystery 'tis, reviving breath
Renews life's mystery

Note. – These lines had a peculiar application as I read of the *extinction* of life in the Earl of Gainsborough by a similar feint! With help all at hand while lone, at midnight I fell, yet, in darkness, life's snuff, preserved, relighted and still glimmers.

George Castleden

13th September 1881 Leighton Buzzard Observer

Steam v. Electricity. – The theory of science "bottling of sunbeams" has excited some humour, but, if it move thought, a point is gained. Think and do. This is a short sentence, but it is pithy. Now, I wish to ask what scientific results will follow when Queen Electricity succeeds King Steam? We are told speed silence and security will do away with dash, crash, smash, and hash. Whether the Queen's lucidity may balance the King's fervency, or the prosperity of her Majesty's reign will compensate his Majesty's shareholders, is all in the obscurity of the future; only as we read of what is doing, and what may be, we may suppose the improbable is at hand, and the impossible is not far off. And, if the winged lightning is reined, and is made the servant and messenger of man, surely sunbeams may be caught and bottled, and the superfluous snow-flakes and rain-drops may be stored and utilised. If these ink drops make others think for the service of man, my thought may not be in vain, and your columns will not be used for nought.

I am, sir, yours obediently, George Castleden

It had been August 1875 when he had written about the proposed 'Woburn Sun Beam Bottling Company'. I don't what had prompted the resurrection of the idea, but it was in 1881 that the Niagara River's first hydroelectric generating station was built, generating power from the Niagara Falls. Silent electricity replace the mighty crash of steam? Never, surely....

20th September 1881 Leighton Buzzard Observer

"Bottling of Sunbeams," &c.

To the Editor of the Leighton Buzzard Observer

Sir, - You have allowed me to ventilate some scientific fancies; permit now a coincidence. After reading in the Observer, my last, on turning to the Daily News of the same date, in a leader I find these coincident words: - "But there is another question which is quite as well deserving the attention of our scientific men, and that is what may be called the storage of heat. When we, shivering through a September that is but as ill-timed December, read of the intensely warm weather now prevailing in the United States, we may well wish that some means could be discovered by which the needless overplus on the American Continent might be drawn off to enliven and warm our colder clime," &c.

, This extract I give, gratified to find two minds, apart, without any collusion, may hit on some thought; and I can't close this brief note with a better wish for our worthy cousins than – when they have utilised "the Falls of Niagara" and made it a rival of steam – that some brother could "tap the torrid heat of Washington and turn it on to London's winter." All the benefactors, philanthropists, and philosophers of the past and present must hide or pale their diminished faces before the uprising sun of such a son of mercy for all mankind.

Our kinsfolk across the Atlantic do go in for big things; this would be the biggest, the most blessed and blessing achievement that man and science could accomplish, relative to Nature needs and her apparent superfluities. I will not weaken by superfluous words.

I am, sir, yours obediently, George Castleden.

Note. – One Napoleon has left an immortal sentence in his "inexorable logic of facts," but facts completed, accomplished.

Then when 'tis done the fact is won:
Man bottles solar beams?
Scoffers may all then loudly laud
As facts what they dubbed dreams!
All through the year "I can't" near wins;
"I'll try" may often *do*;
I will" is potent to achieve
Whate'er it may pursue;
Think, do, wait, win, four words for conquest too.

The stricken U.S. President, James Garfield, who had been shot in July, lingered on until September, then finally succumbed to his injuries.

27th September 1881 Leighton Buzzard Observer

Tributary Lines on the Death of General Garfield.

Poor Garfield! Gallant was thy strife with Death!
The fight is o'er! Still now thy struggling breath.
In lustre deep went down thy mortal sun;
Peace in thy fall, a noble victory won.
Good, just, and kind, these virtues leave a light
To gild America's sad mournful night,

While the world drops the sympathetic tear
And gives departed Worth its grief sincere.
Yet out of gloom, which shrouds our kinsmen's skies
May help and peace come forth, and light arise.
Amid the mourning homage let me tell
Our Gracious Queen's all womanly farewell.*
God bless her for kind words – words sweet to sound
O'er Sorrow's realm, and Death's dark woe-strewn ground;
And; while the curse of Sin sheds ebon night,
Love's sunshine gilds and cheers with warmth and light.

* "Words cannot express the deep sympathy I feel with you at this terrible moment. May God support and comfort you as He alone can." Queen Victoria, to Mrs. Garfield.

George Castleden, Woburn, September 24th, 1881

The press had reported that Queen Victoria, widowed by Prince Albert nearly 20 years ago, and still in mourning, had sent condolences to Garfield's widow. This touching gesture brought forth further poetry:

4th **October 1881** Leighton Buzzard Observer

The Sister Queens!

One touch of death makes nations kin!
This month has proved it so;
America and England sigh,
And weep in mutual woe.

Two Sister Queens upon this day,
Though dwelling far apart,
Bow to the destiny of death
And feel the mourner's smart

In deep-heart grief our gracious Queen
Responsive weep at home,
Yet sends the hallowed diamond tear
Across Atlantic foam.

The Sister Widow feels the grace

By queenly goodness shown;
This beam of love reflects, returns,
Gilds, cheers, each sister's home.

Our kinsmen, homes in that vast land
See friendship, peace, goodwill –
A proof, if sad, that hand in hand
Love holds in Britains still.

If Death seals amity, we win
From Sorrow's loss a gain;
Mercy a compensation gives
For Separation's pain
(25th Sept.)

Note. – "Among the flowers about the coffin was a wreath sent from the British Legation, having the inscription: - Queen Victoria, to the memory of the late President Garfield and the American nation."

Add lines written on the funeral day: -
Poor Garfield's death unites two realms apart,
And links in mourning every Briton's heart;
From Her who gems Great Britain's Royal Throne
To Greater Britain's sons, all heave the tribute tone.
George Castleden, Woburn, Beds., Michaelmas Day.

11th October 1881 Leighton Buzzard Observer

Woburn, Beds.: Woburn Mass. (4) To the Editor of the Leighton Buzzard Observer.

Sir, - By printing an extract from a letter "Woburn, Mass., Sept. 10th," you may, in a small degree, serve the cause of brotherhood, and gravity some of your readers: -

"I thank you for the kind words and good wishes expressed to me personally, and also for the pleasant feeling awakened by a perusal of the printed sheets which recalls so happily the mutual friendship between yourself and Mr Champney, and through your representations the mutual good will between the Woburns. I trust the author and sender of so many friendly messages across the Atlantic may retain his present intellectual strength for several years to come, and let

'Time as he flies increase to his truth,
And give to his mind what he takes from his youth.'

"I very seldom quote poetry, but these lines came to my mind instinctively, and express in verse what I was trying to say in "home prose." Mr. Doyle and myself frequently speak of that pleasant September day we spent with you nearly two years ago. I still recall it as one of the most profitable days which I spent in Europe, and certainly one very rich in reminiscences. Please remember me to my Woburn friends, one and all, some of whom at least I hope to see some years hence, when I hope to re-visit Woburn; and believe me, dear Mr. Castleden, yours very truly,

Edward F. Johnson."

If the copy of this friendly extract in the slightest degree promotes the future frater grasp of brethren my friend will rejoice, and in a more laudable pursuit I cannot pass life's sunsetting hour.

G. C.

Note. - Extract from the Woburn Journal, Sept 16th: - "Early Records of Woburn. - The town records of Woburn begin in the year 1640. They are in the handwriting of Edward Johnson, who was one of the seven chosen 'for erecting of a church and town.' Mr Johnson was a clerk of the committee, and afterwards clerk of the town until the year 1672 - a period of thirty-two years. * * * The writings of Edward Johnson have become part of the standing memories of New England. His 'Wonderworking Providences' is as well known as Mather's 'Magnalla,' and, if the original manuscript could be found, its money value would run into hundreds, if not, thousands of dollars. Woburn may well cherish its legacy of records in the handwriting of this famous man."

Woburn, Beds, 5th Oct., 1881.

Although it is accepted that Woburn, Mass. took their name from Woburn, Beds, I cannot discover why it was chosen or if there was a connection to the first settlers there in 1640.

25th October 1881 Leighton Buzzard Observer

Woburn - The Storm.

While Boreas was playing nine-pins among the trees in this locality this "scientific gale" toppled down the vegetable ornament in our George Street. Thousands, whom the kindness of Lord and Lady Charles Russell permitted to stroll in their beautiful garden, will hear with regret that the handsome centre cedar, sheltered as it seemed, was caught in this cyclone storm and fairly uplifted, and now in recumbent beauty it waits removal from a spot where it has stood for, perhaps, centuries, and as a tree of many memories. In looking upon this reclining, dying friend, lines graphic and solemn toned my regretful gaze:

417

Like crowded forest trees we stand,
And some are marked to fall;
Death's axe will smite at God's command
And soon will smite us all."
G.C.

29: A view out across the rooftops of Woburn to Bedford Street from the top of the Mortuary Chapel. The Magpie Inn is approximately centre, with the Crawley Road in the distance.

25th October 1881 Leighton Buzzard Observer

The Late American President

In *Harper's Weekly*, Sept. 24th, two engravings moved thought on the "last scene;" they may complete my series on this world-lamented tragedy in America.

"At the Window."

Poor Garfield! 'tis a respite in the strife!
I muse and look upon thy placid brow:
How feebly flickers the low flame of life,
And yet with thee it is hopeful now;
Good men all pray; fond kin record the vow.
Upon the ocean scene they gentle eye
Unknowing looks a last, a kind good-bye;
Thy thoughts how deep! The reminiscent sigh

O'er *hatred* nursed which bids thee prematurely die.

"In the Shroud (coffin) Flowers."
The sleep of death! A good man rests from *hate*!
Yet love still hovers o'er his calm repose,
The strife is ended in a victim's fate!
Flowers tell our tale; fresh as the morning's rose
Man flourishes, and fades ere evening close
Here manhood, hope, and love, all in full bloom,
Are withered in an hour; joy fades in woes!
The seat of honour sinks within the tomb.
And *true* ambition's vault met hatred's dastard doom.
George Castleden.

8th November 1881 Leighton Buzzard Observer

My Sonnet! *[On looking at the largest ash, blown down in Woburn Park, Oct (21st) 29th.]*
The woodman spared this tree, the thunderous gale
Has laid it low in Auburn's lovely vale.

Ash, monarch of our Park. I see thee prone;
The democratic wind has hurled thee down:
For many year they bole has braved the storm;
Still years have weakened, and in age forlorn,
On the same spot which saw thy sprouting birth,
In giant bulk I see thee stretched on earth,
No more to flourish or rise again!
A tree of note in Bedford's wide domain,*
A tree well known in boyhood's earlier time:
A tree 'neath which, monumental, marks time flown
And generations gone to men unknown!
A tree deceased a moral may supply –
As you lie low, old friend, so soon must I.

* This ash tree, I believe, is mentioned in Loudon's Encyclopaedia, for its magnitude and quantity of timber, as one of the two or three in the Isle.

P.S.
Looking on the tree all around hung

Autumn's burnished beauty of death!
Grand, gorgeous, glorious.
See all around rich giant flowers bloom,
Sunlit they blaze above vast Nature's tomb!
Springtide and Summer deck brown Autumn's bier,
Hoar Winter soon will stalk, and shroud the death-struck year.
So Time is over on the wing –
Past, present, future, three in one;
While man, on ever-dying thing,
Lives now, and lives the life to come!
Sings Earth's my lodge, Heaven is my mansion home.
George Castleden, 31ˢᵗ October.

As this may appear on a natal day, I may add a coincident closing verse: -

Birthdays speed thoughtlessly along;
Time has no present stay;
Just like a story or a song
We pass our lives away. (November.)

15ᵗʰ November 1881 Leighton Buzzard Observer

An acrostic Verse

Written after the Leeds speeches by the Right Hon. W. E. Gladstone, M.P.

G reat man, great in thy truth; great in thy mind;
L oved in thy home, and loved by liberty:
A dmired by friends, abused by foes, *daft*, blind.
D istinguished thou in present history,
S o also in thy mental mystery.
T ake then this Woburn wish by one unknown,
O n this grand day of platform chivalry;
N ow may fresh strength in age yet still be shown,
E 'en till thy fiercest foe thy patriot virtues own.

Sir, - As I have received thanks for the above, perhaps it will give pleasure to some of your readers if you print it. I don't expect to convert our Tory friends, but I may, at seventy-seven, leave it as my humble tribute to one of the most truthful, eloquent, and patriotic Statesmen of my day and generation.

I am, sir, your obedient servant, George Castleden, Woburn, 9ᵗʰ Nov.

22nd November 1881 Leighton Buzzard Observer

Woburn Mass: Woburn, Beds. – No.5. To the Editor of the Leighton Buzzard Observer.

Sir, - In the Woburn Journal, Oct. 28th, I read that which I think may serve by a reprint in the Observer.

"Woburn, England, and the President. The following poems have been sent to us by our worthy friend, Mr. Castleden. They appear in the Leighton (Eng.) Observer in two different issues. They express in forcible and sympathetic words the deep feeling aroused in England by the sad and untimely death of our President. This case of General Garfield is one of those singular instances of rapid elevation by which a man springs, as it were, with a single bound into the realm of the universal. Two years ago he was known only as an able and industrious member of Congress. To-day his name and fame are the property of the civilised world. This great achievement of securing so large a space in the eyes of mankind is partly due to the "deep damnation of his taking off," yet more to the heroic patience and endurance with which he bore the pain and suffering of his long struggle with death, but more than all to the revelation that had been made of his intellectual supremacy, his sterling honesty, his warm affection, and the innate nobleness of soul. These were brought out and intensified by the sympathies of a world that watched his bedside with the interest of a mother bending over the couch of a suffering child. In the second of the "Tributary verses," by Mr. C., it is a marvel to see how a sturdy Englishman, full of loyalty to his beloved Queen, can place beside her in his affection the simple-hearted yet noble woman who but a few months ago was the unknown companion of a man whose fame was only ion the bud. Truly he says "one touch of death makes the whole world kin." And will not this community of sorrow bind still more closely together the two great nations, who speak the same language, and in whose veins flow the same blood? – G. M. C."

Then are reprinted the "Tributary Lines on the Death of General Garfield" and "The Sister Queens" from the Observer.

So may this "hand in hand grasp across the Atlantic" long continue, and make the two Woburns representative of frater amity and national good will.

George Castleden, George Street, Woburn, 16th November, 1881.

There is a letter from Edward Franklin in the **29th November 1881** *Leighton Buzzard Observer, on the current political outlook, railing against Mr. Gladstone and Liberal M.P.'s. The "Woburn Whig" is roundly criticised, and Franklin expects "his faithful henchman, the 'Bard of Woburn' might give us a 'few lines' to adorn the tale and 'point the moral'", which Castled was, as ever, delighted to do:*

6th December 1881 Leighton Buzzard Observer

Ireland's Problem? Addressed to Whig and Tory.

To the Editor of the Leighton Buzzard Observer

Sir, - Perhaps my lines may suit many who see in Ireland the grave of Ministries. It seems a sad inheritance, and a continued perplexity. My only object in troubling you is to stay recriminatory reproaches over a national job, which, if it could be undone, might be the best solution for both great parties. But, alas! As most likely your correspondent knows, "the past is," and whether for good or evil, results are inexorable.

> A bard of Woburn tells but truth,
> He heard in Woburn in his youth.
> Then grey-heads quoted Irish song,
> In proof that *right* had been made wrong.
> From Castlereagh, who thought that be
> By "union" made the Irish free*
> Down to our Gladstone, all have found
> Green Ireland still volcanic ground!
> Clad in a creed which scorns the light,
> Beneath are ills, above is night!
> First conquered, then too long oppressed,
> What saviour can give Ireland rest?
> Or hope for that all-righteous day
> When fraud, wrong, curse, shall flee away?
> *Lament* that what is done can never be
> *Undone*; in this regret all *may agree*:
> "What can't be cured," in nations or by men,
> "Must be endured," so signs bard C...n.
> George St., 29th Nov.

* When Lord Castlereagh abrogated the Irish Parliament, Tories rejoiced and some Whigs were glad. Whether this was an added wrong, History may tell, and whether Ireland is to be another proof that they who win by the sword must hold by the sword History will also tell.

The Bribery Prosecutions

To the Editor of the Leighton Buzzard Observer

Sir, - The startling sentences on these "Agents," while severe are salutary. I fought, fifty years ago, in the battle when the Marquis of Tavistock resolved against such doings. The "Oaken bough" was our distinction, and the Marquis contributing £2,000 for a new wing to the County Infirmary remains a memorial of this wise, just, and merciful resolve and protest against the election extravagances then rife in our country. In the election of your townsman, Francis Bassett, Esq., I was surprised at items which, as a matter of course, were passed; and I turned away sorrowful from that custom authorised such an expenditure. Now, surely, with the political opinions of the candidates spoken and published, with the Ballot to secure the constituents, and with education to instruct, "agents" should be abolished; canvassers should not be wanted; and cash should be strictly confined to the official and necessary outlay. This happy consummation achieved, taken a long farewell to bribery, corruption, and treason. Then a Corrupt Practices Bill would become a dead letter, and Englishmen would never more witness the painful and humiliating spectacle of the 29th, when learned, topping, local men, snared by custom, received a sentence from our judges which thrills many a home, and which to its keen severity has the added poignancy of a prison ignominy, crushing and almost unbearable. Such a fact, supporting views on the Ballot which I have urged, while very painful, is very confirming and conclusive.

I am, sir, your obedient servant, George Castleden, Woburn. Nov.30th, 1881.

Also of this date, "An Irishman" replies to Franklin's last letter saying, "The "Woburn Bard" is fulfilling a noble duty, preaching peace and good-will on both side of the Atlantic, and, if there is a hereafter, and the mind does live after the grave, what better preparation can there be than this?".

13th December 1881 Leighton Buzzard Observer

Bribery

To the Editor of the Leighton Buzzard Observer

Sir, - In support of my letter inserted last week permit an eloquent voice to be heard from across the Atlantic. It is an extract only; but, as Englishmen both sides smarting under this monetary curse, let us invoke the powers of the Press to stay this blasting and ignominious criminality.

"Again, I charge you, next Tuesday, and between this and that, to frown upon all misuse of money for election purposes. This is a lawful use of money for the publication of tracts and documents, for the establishing of political head quarters, and maintaining them; for holding great mass meetings to present the principles which you think most important. We must admit there is a right use of money for campaign purposes, but there is also a wrong use, and he who puts a bribe into the hands of a voter, or bring mercenary or corrupt influence to bear upon him, is sinning against God, and sinning against the city, and sinning against the nation. God thunders in His Bible, "Fire shall consume the tabernacles of bribery?" Away with it from the ballot-box! If a man next Tuesday shall try to tamper with your vote, clutch him by the collar and shout 'Police!' An election that cannot be carried without bribes ought never to be carried at all... It is the appalling crime of the country, and I charge you to resist it, whether you stand in the legislative hall, or, next Tuesday, as private citizens, deposit your ballots. Frown upon bribery; it is the curse of Brooklyn; it is the curse of New York; it is the curse of the nation' (Dr. Talmage).

Now, let me add two English testimonies, and my threefold cord will be strong. Mr Russell, at Aylesbury, said – "Now those are just the necessary expenses which I am convinced it is our duty to aim at – in fact, to make impossible, and win again for the electorate of England freedom from the power of the purse and the deceitfulness of riches." – Sir Henry Verney, M.P., says – "Depend upon it the man who *bought them would sell them*. If he paid money to obtain their votes, somehow or other he would get something he wanted in compensation."

The ballot and bribery seems to me such a combination of *fooldom* and *rougedom* that, did not *fact* vouch it, all sane, honest men would say – Incredible!

I'll take your gold, says Hodge, then, with a wink,

The other gent will have my vote for a drink.

George Castleden

P.S. – Thanks to an Irishman for a truthful and kind word; also a right word on war in the Observer.

December 6th, 1881

13th December 1881 Leighton Buzzard Observer

To the Editor of the Leighton Buzzard Observer

Sir, - In your last week's issue the "Woburn Bard" says "his only object in troubling you is to stay recriminatory reproaches" over a *national job*, the results of which are inexorable. Has he, indeed, become a convert to Home Rule for Ireland? If so, he must be prepared to be condemned as a heretic, even by the Radical Minister, Mr. Chamberlain, who declares against it as a danger to the unity of the Empire of Great Britain. But he says that Ireland is a "sad inheritance and a continued perplexity," and my charge against the Government, which he can neither *meet nor deny* the truth of, is that, having been unmistakeably warned by Lord Beaconsfield of the "danger existing in Ireland, whereby results might accrue scarcely less disastrous than either pestilence or famine," they were "guilty of the criminal weakness" of trying the dangerous and disastrous "experiment" of trusting to the ordinary law, until both law and order were vanquished, and terrorism, lawlessness, murder, outrage, and disorder, became rampant, and the conflagration which at that time might have been easily and promptly distinguished has been allowed to develop into a rebellion which, on the confession of Ministers themselves, cannot be quelled by an army of soldiers larger than were required in the Crimean War, and 20,000 constabulary in addition. And, though "all may agree" in the vain regret of Mr. Castleden that "what can't be cured must be endured," yet none can deny but that "*prevention is* far better than *cure*;" and, in disregarding that truth, the Government have dug their own grave in Ireland, and the earlier they are consigned to their just doom, and thus give place to better men, who will carry out the first and paramount duty of every Government – viz. To govern – the better it will be for the future of that unhappy country.

A few words to your correspondent, "an Irishman," who complains that I should find fault with the Government for what he designates the misfortunes of Ireland. Here in the first place he is entirely mistaken. It was the *misfortune of Ireland* to have to suffer from famine three years ago. I condoled with her in that affliction, but the late Government, who nobly did their part to meet it – and that successfully I believe – *were not found fault with* because Ireland suffered that infliction; but the state of affairs which has prevailed nearly the whole time since the present Government took office is due to their own culpable blunders; and, if that is not so, let "An Irishman" disprove or defend them from the indictment above. That would be more profitable, not to say courteous, than (evidently fearing to attempt the hopeless task) to misquote me as "lamenting the blessings of peace." On the contrary, rather is it because, having never even "seen or felt a gunshot wound," I can yet feel a deep and real sympathy with those who have thus suffered, and my view of that matter is that a sham peace, like that with the Boers, is but a truce, and not a real peace; therefore it is a direct progenitor of more bloody wars, and deplorable "gun-shot wounds." Indications are unhappily not wanting that future troubles are brooding in South Africa; and, if the Government were themselves sanguine that real peace is secured in that quarter, the 2,000 troops now in Newcastle would have been ordered to England before this. Let me also tell "An Irishman" that my idea of the British Lion is not what it *seems to him* to be; and here I make another charge against the Government, at the risk of the displeasure of "An Irishman," who must defend them if he is able. I say it was a crime to set him to fight the Boers, when the terms we obtained by it might have been better secure without. If we are to suffer *dishonour*, let's have it without

the *bloodshed*. His parody would have therefore run more appropriately thus:
-

"We – the Liberals – don't want to fight, but, by Jingo if we do,
'Neath three defeats, make up sham peace, and claim its "vindication" too;
To make our Queen a Suzerain we'll meekly bear the shame
Of shredding British soldiers' lives for such a worthless aim."
And, seeing that England has now no "big allies" in Europe, and cannot keep the peace at home, she is at present unable, even if she wished, to indulge in either "big or little wars." I trust that the "peace and goodwill" recently wired may therefore continue, to the benefit of both communities. In conclusion, having disposed of the letter of your correspondent, and replied to most of his queries, I am not sufficiently egotistic to tell him who or what I am, beyond stating that *I am not* an anonymous Irishman, but an English working man, who seeks not to hide his name.

Edward Franklin, Eversholt, December, 7th 1882. [1881]

20th December 1881 Leighton Buzzard Observer
Original Poetry. Accidents by Fire and Water

Nature outraged will have revenge;
She claims it as her due:
'Tis mystery, and yet I see
Two proofs that it is true.

Vienna, London, both affirm
That Nature's laws are stern;
Abuse, a monster, may arise,
And on the abuser turn.

The fire-horse man will madly spur,
No peril will restrain;
The speed is swifter than the wing
And yet where is the *rein?*

He uses fire as children do –
Plays with explosive light;
Then, by gunpowder air is hurled
Into volcanic night.

Fire and water, elemental goods,
As servants men obey;
But, make them masters, then beware!
Where shall the ruin stay?

Yet hear a warning, saving word;
Let Nature's laws be free;
Coerce, constrain, compel, and lo –
Disruption's misery.

But who dare hear the pace is fast,
The drivers, Scrip and Co.;
Let shares but rise, be deaf, blind, dumb
To scientific woe.

And on we go! We can't return
To safer pace; 'tis slow;
Vienna's hall, and London's yell
May tell the fiercest woe;
But, Plutus science rule – on, on we go!
What Prospero can hold, what Ariel can whoa?

George Castleden, Woburn, December 1881.

The reference to Vienna is probably to the Ringtheater, a popular public venue. On December 8th, it had been destroyed in a fire that killed 449 people. The site is now the federal headquarters of the Vienna police. I am less sure about the "Accidents by Water". There had been a large storm around Berwickshire in October, causing the death of 189 fishermen, known as the Eyemouth Disaster. Perhaps it was that.

27th December 1881 Leighton Buzzard Observer
Original Poetry. Accidents (2). Air and Sky.

Dangers stand thick thro' all the ground
To push us to the tomb;
Let not crude Science lend a hand
To hurry mortals home.

Nature profound! Her secrets who
Can dive, or soar, or brave?
And yet man will presume to bind
Queen Nature as his slave!

Two other proofs before me tell
How vain is this essay;
And how the laws of Nature will,
Imposed upon, repay!

Elastic air was for the wing –
Not leaden-footed man:
Ballooning is a foolish thing,
A scientific sham

The toy is launched, and nature smiles
To see in upper air
Man, in his proud aerial skill,
The gate of Heaven will dare.

And then she blows a storm, and he
A leaf before it flies!
His pride, his skill, presumption flee,
A vanity he dies.

Ah! Hatfield House, historic name;
We hear a fact, sad, new,
That Nature's laws, if trifled with,
Exact a heavy due.

The poor man, Dimmock, give his name,
The victim, lo! He fell!
The lightning stolen from the sky
He touch'd, death rang his knell!

My verse may warn, may save from woe,
From knowledge that may be;
A tyrant which man made is, lo,

A monster misery!

George Castleden, Woburn, Dec.

Castleden liked evidence that his opinion that new-fangled science was dangerous was correct. Walter Powell, a Welsh colliery owner and Conservative politician, accompanied Captain Templer and Mr. A. Agg-Gardner, in a hot air balloon ascent from Bath. It travelled over Somerset to Exeter and then into Dorset. They tried to descend near Bridport, but struck the ground so hard that Templer was thrown out, then Agg-Gardner fell out from a height of about eight feet and broke his leg. Powell remained in the basket, and was blown out to sea. The balloon, and Powell, were never seen again. The 22-year-old William Dimmock had been a gardener in the service of the Earl of Salisbury at Hatfield House. He was killed whilst wiring up the generators for the country house to enjoy the 'new' electric lighting.

27ᵗʰ December 1881 Leighton Buzzard Observer

Ireland's Problem. To the Editor of the Leighton Buzzard Observer.

Sir, - Mr. Franklin is in such good hands, the two "Irishmen," that if such truth don't avail I cannot state it more truly. My own contention has been for years, as "a conquered country" aggravated by oppressive acts, that to both of the great parties Ireland would be a sad inheritance, and a sore perplexity; and frankly giving credit now to Whig and Tory to repair, I say, if "the past is" unredeemable, unretraceable, waste not time in recriminatory reproaches, merely to increase irritation, but rather retire on the eternal retributive doctrine that wrong done to a nation, or an individual, must have its due reward. Passing now through keen punitive penalties, as consequences, let all encourage penitential endeavours to soothe, and, if the mitigation of severities can be accomplished, prey don't het the zeal of party, merely for the gain of a few, intercept a grand rectification of a part of Ireland's wrong by that "great physician Gladstone, who has already healed as many of her wounds; may he have her safety in his charge until brighter days." To this I heartily say amen, and thank "Irishman" for the just tribute to one who, if he fails in his wise and pacificatory measures – then, farewell to hope!

Your obedient servant, G. Castleden

Note. – This brief letter was written, when a public print gave me this apt paragraph:- "The miseries of Ireland are not to be cured in a year or in two years: but the blessed progress of healing must be gradual to be efficacious; yet, so sure as the harvest follows the seed time, the date i snot far distant when the woes of that distracted country, bullied by a Strangboro', pillaged by a Strafford, and sold by a Castleraugh, will be no more than a fireside story of the past, and men will marvel as they listen to think of what their sires could be guilty." Christian Globe.

21st December.

There is also another long letter from Edward Franklin in this edition, directed against all the others who recently had argued with him in the press.

VI

Letters: 1882 - Onwards

Alfred Smith, Woburn Postman – Death of George Champney, Woburn, Mass. – Charles Bradlaugh – Assassination attempt on Queen Victoria– Acknowledgement from Buckingham Palace – Death of Richard Gilpin – Ireland – Cricket v. War – War in Egypt – Acknowledgement from Downing Street –Catholic Church – Woburn Bible Society – Death of Castleden – "Woburn Park" rediscovered.

3rd January 1882 Leighton Buzzard Observer

Ireland's Problem

To the Editor of the Leighton Buzzard Observer

Sir, - I noticed that in your last week's paper Mr. Castleden says that I am in "good hands," and I suppose, to show us his confidence in the great abilities of the "two Irishmen," he must needs join their company, and whistle to endeavour to keep up their courage in fighting a losing battle. Like the Government which he supports, however, he "has piped unto them, and they have not danced," or there would now be no cause for "recriminatory reproaches," which are both *needful and just*. I would therefore wish him joy of his Irish comrades, which love to utter their "sneers" about the "Dutch courage" of that "British Lion" which their own countrymen dare not openly meet, but where "admirable courage" shines to perfection when sneaking under a hedge and shooting down innocent victims from behind; and who – thus flatly contradicting their own bard – tell us that "Ireland's only hope is to trust to the creed of a Roman Pope." Where, then, is the need of the "great physician Gladstone," or Mr. Castleden's "Amen" in the dark? It is this "great physician" himself who has put far away those "brighter days" from a "conquered country" he has "aggravated by oppressive acts;" and Mr. Castleden and his Liberal Government may therefore appropriately "retire on the eternal 'retributive doctrine' that such wrongs done to a (conquered) nation must (and will) have its due reward."

Edward Franklin

P.S. - My "moral" - as Mr. Castleden would say - is plain. "Those who live in glass houses should be cautious how they throw their stones." How beautifully consistent is it for your rabid Radicals, who went nearly mad with the thought of outrages committed in Turkey, for which the late Government was not responsible to complain about "recriminatory reproaching" against their Government for outrages committed in Ireland, for whose good government they are deeply and directly responsible, and whose apologists have a hardihood, in this dilemma, to exclaim in despair. "What can't be cured must be endured." And then vainly speak of it as a "solution" to "Ireland's problem." Save Ireland, I say, from such miserable friendship and worthless "solutions."

10ᵗʰ January 1882 Leighton Buzzard Observer

Alfred Smith (20), Late Postman. After a short illness, this youth fell; and, in the midst of busy avocations and youthful expectations, surely such a death supplies an apt illustration of Job's words, 9c. 25v.

> The Postman falls, and verifies
> The Bible's solemn lore;
> And swifter than a comet's post
> Life passes: is no more!
>
> "Time, what an empty vapour 'tis,
> And days how swift they are:
> Swift as an Indian arrow flies,
> Or as a shooting star."
>
> So Watt's has sung, so Alfred proves,
> In the pale sleep of doom;
> His active limbs wait their remove
> Unto the parish tomb.
>
> The admonition of this death
> May loudly to us say –
> Be ready, all ye young and old,
> Be ready for Death's day.
>
> For swift and sure Time speeds along,
> Incessant is its flight;
> And on its borne we mortals all
> Drop in the grave's cold night.

An aged bard respects dirge notes
Over this postman's dust;
His days were few, his death was swift;
As he now lies – all must.

A Burial-Day P.S.
They brought him out; borne down the lane.
Kindred and neighbours mourn;
I looked and sighed o'er youthful fame;
Now in our garden bourne
He finds the home from whence is no return.
George Castleden.

On the **17th January 1882**, *there were two more letters from Franklin, raging at the writer calling himself 'Irishmen'. The LBO Editor said the correspondence on the subject should now stop.*

24th January 1882 Leighton Buzzard Observer

Sick Man's Friendly Society. – As the old name on the list, hearing our annual statement of the seventy-seventh year of this Samaritan society read, while ruminating on the drift of neighbours, friends, and relatives down the stream of time, I could not help thinking of the poet's lines, so illustrative of the past and present of this home visiting charity: -

Men speed! They come and go,
Continue *never!*
But Woburn's brook of woe
Flows on for ever.

While the groan of sorrow sounds, and the tear of death may fall, may friends still arise to mitigate and soothe. – G. C.

24th January 1882 Leighton Buzzard Observer

Obitual. – Woburn, Mass.; Woburn, Beds.

Sir, - Some of your readers will feel an interest as they read the mournful fact that Mr. G. M. Champney, my unknown, intelligent, and highly-valued correspondent, in Woburn, Massachusetts, died suddenly on the 4th. As our correspondence has been printed on both side of the Atlantic, and, as your columns have given circulation to a portion, please to give this short notice of the death of an American cousin who, in New England's Woburn, for the last eight years, has, in spirit, been the warm sympathiser with our

"Old Woburn," as he originally styled it. I cannot enter as I would, by reason of indisposition, into such a spirit separation, but I may write that in our interchange of thought, peace and good-will was its key-note, and, as brethren, we agreed that peace with England and America meant peace to the world, and, while to the last of our letters Mr. Champney held loyal allegiance to his Republican principles, he always wrote in an affectionate spirit relative to the monarchical institutions of the Mother Country. This, for the present, is all I can send, but let these words sound the heart tribute of respect and gratitude, mingling with mournful sympathy, over the dust of Mr. G. M. Champney.

I am, sir, your obedient servant, George Castleden

*Despite the plea from the Editor on the 17th, there are two more letters on the 'Irish Problem' in the **31st January 1882**, including a long one from T.B. of Aspley Guise. The Editor finally stopped correspondence on the matter.*

7th February 1882 Leighton Buzzard Observer

Obitual. Woburn, Mass.: Woburn, Beds.

To the Editor of the Leighton Buzzard Observer

Sir, - In memory of our departed friend, permit a few extracts from American papers. Their reprint in your columns will vouch to the singular epistolary interchange of thought, while telling a friendly episode of age when "nothing can harm further."

"George M. Champney, librarian at the Woburn Public Library, fell dead in the outer vestibule of the library, about two o'clock yesterday afternoon... About the time the new library was opened Mr. Champney opened a correspondence with Mr. George Castleden of Woburn, England, the whole of which has been printed in the *Woburn Journal*, and was of much interest to its readers. Mr. Champney was born at New Ipswich, N.H., March, 1812." - *Boston Daily Globe*, January 5th.

The *Woburn Advertiser* had an article of regret and respect on the loss of this worthy and esteemed townsman. The Journal says of him:- "Mr Champney was born in Ipswich, N.H., on March 6th, 1812, and educated at the Appleton Academy in that town. He was for many years a member of the firm of Champney Brothers, doing business in Boston, where he had a large circle of friends and acquaintances, who will learn with deep sorrow his sudden death and sincerely mourn his loss. He had resided in Woburn about thirty years, and during all that time no citizen of the town enjoyed a larger measure of public confidence and esteem than he. For years he was an active member of the Woburn Library Committee, and has discharged the duties of librarian with great fidelity and to the entire satisfaction of the public, having been by taste, habit, and education particularly fitted for the position. He was a gentleman of scholarly instincts and attainments; a lover of books; a pleasing writer; and an active, earnest promoter of education among the people. Mr. Champney's frequent contributions of "Library Notes." And literary correspondence with Mr Castleden, of Woburn, England, to the *Journal*, have been very interesting and valuable, and highly relished by the reading public. On the correspondence with his English friend above mentioned he had prepared an article which was to have been printed in this paper next week."

If I give an extract from a private letter, it may estimate and serve kindred spirits, under the like impulse, to leave the world in some small degree better than they found it: - "Mr. Champney will be much missed by his many Woburn friend in England, Yours was a remarkable friendship in many particulars. I, who have known you both, realise as no one else can appreciate how great a sorrow the now severance must cause the survivor. It is singular that you, the older and feebler, should have survived him, the stronger and more able-bodied."

So Mr. Edward F. Johnson writes and testifies, and with this I close at present; I may trouble you with a third when I hear again from Woburn, Mass.

This tributary note is a sympathetic offering to the memory of our friend. May his good wish for peace, and good-will among fellow-men by it, in some humble degree be perpetuated, at any rate, in the two Woburns.

I am, sir, your obliged servant, George Castleden.

Not content with his first two tributes, he then penned a third:

21st February 1882 Leighton Buzzard Observer
Woburn, Mass.; Woburn, Beds.

Sir, - Perhaps a few tributary lines will well close this Woburn, Mass., obitual fragment. Let me preface them by an extract from "George Eliot" in an instructive lecture by Mr. G. W. E. Russell, M.P., and which surely applies to my departed friend and others, on both the English shores: - "The growing good of the world is partly dependent on unhistoric acts, and that things are not so ill with you and me as they have been is half owing to the number who lived faithfully a hidden life, and rest in unvisited tombs."

Not shining brass nor gilded names
Avouch earth's noblest, worthiest fames;
The pious, useful, peaceful poor,
On Mercy's roll here all obscure,
In works that serve and last will aye endure.

In Memoriam

On Mr. George M. Champney, who died in Woburn, Mass. 4ᵗʰ January, 1882.

Friend of my soul, unknown, unseen,
A friend of mystic sway:
Thy friendship warmed life's winter scene,
And lighted darkening day.

In peace akin, our fellow-men
We wished them brithers a'-
All tyrannies we did condemn
And hoped all hates might fa'.

Two men obscure, no lust of gold
Inspired the frater pen;
Our guerdon the intent to serve
The weal of Englishmen

Each wrote for truth, Peace, Liberty.
Each in a Woburn town!
One "G. M. C." and one "G. C."
Both Georges, sans renown.

And yet kind words did cheer us on;
Kind deeds will never die;
And Russell's name inscribes a fame*
On this friend history

But he is gone! his thought no more
Will pulse responsive art;
Nor shall I more, on England's shore,
Hail his fraternal part.

Across the sea, and in my home,
I hear the kind regret
That Death has sued this Woburn son,
And early claimed the debt.

The younger gone! life's spark is fled;
Thought's wire is broke for aye!
Mind's cable-flushings are put out,
It's light has died away!

Age, dun and dim, may friendly sigh
Over this shade unknown;
His work is done, and soon may I
Be with the shadows flown. +

Ye working men, a line to you
May bid my verse endure;
Work the world's weal; yes, labour true,
Although your rank's obscure!

George Castleden

* An interesting fact has come out in the correspondence. The present talented representative of the United States, the Hon. J. Russell Lowell, bears this name in memory of the original founder of Woburn, Mass., and on my writing this fact to Mr. Champney, singular to say, he replied, "I ought to be proud, as by a material relation I can trace distant kinship with so worthy a man as Russell Lowell. And, link the kindnesses in the seven years, shown by our historic House of Russell, and surely the future will prove my line.

And Russell's name may seal a fame
On this friend history.

+ "Shades hunting shades, fantastic chase!
Man is immortal till his work is done." – Young.

P.S. One more extract I give from the *Boston Transcript*, Jan. 21ˢᵗ. The writer says of Mr. Champney: - "He loved books, and his reading took a wide range. His own efforts as a writer, illustrated in his lectures on Shakespeare, Fox and others, together with many stray poems, mark his devotion to literature, and the noble and gentle instincts of his nature. From his childhood to the day of his death he was an ardent and devoted student of Shakespeare, and collected for his own library and that of the town everything pertaining to his life and works."

Here, adieu! the poet writes:
"Friendship, alas! 'tis but a name,
A charm that lulls to sleep;
That follows honour, wealth, and fame."

Here I would rescue a Woburn friendship from this class, and, as the survivor, I close these tributary thoughts of respect with the sincere sigh of –

He's gone,

"Peace be to his memory." – Amen

Woburn, Beds., 15th Feb., 1882.

21st February 1882 Leighton Buzzard Observer

School Board Elections. To the Editor of the Leighton Buzzard Observer.

Sir, - In our town the schoolmaster seems to have been at home while school-boys abroad have scrawled matter on the parish walls neither pastoral, polite, or peaceable. As a little town rather out of neighbour joint, this provocative process does not mend the dislocation, especially when a peaceful and inexpensive mode had before served. Let not a permanent retention of parochial office be a prohibitory exclusion to other ratepayers, not let suspicion be generated that behind "honour" there may hide power, patronage, or pay, three fascinating lures for frail mortals dressed in "a little brief authority." These few words are written to promote, in the future, neighbour amity, to prevent neighbour injustice, and as a protest against needless strife and waste of money. As I read the report in the Observer I thought a little humour on this farce of "much ado about nothing" might serve and save. Who paid for the band I know not; but dropping off to sleep under the tones of "See the conquering hero comes," and then consolative notes to comfort the defeated, surely, I said, this is not the "Cotter's Saturday night;" and we close by hoping in all School Board elections they may be relieved of that which was offence, expensive, unneighbourly, and unjust in Woburn. Our own first election, and Crawley's last, remain in proof that these local conflicts may be avoided.

Yours obediently, G.C., Woburn, 8th Feb.

14th March 1882 Leighton Buzzard Observer

A Woburn Congratulation

On the preservation of our beloved Queen, 2nd March, 1882.

A madman's tube has blazed a fame
Far as our Navies sail;
Its flash precedes, on history's page
Our good Queens's coming tale

From hall and fane, 'neath many a sky,
Went up the shout and prayer –

"God bless the Queen, be ever nigh,
God save from hurt and snare."

So good from ill, thank God, may come,
In loyalty and love;
So may it be till, in Heaven's Home,
Our Queen is blest above.

There hate lives not, there treasons cease,
There madness lures no more:
There joy *is* joy, there peace *is* peace,
And love *is* evermore.

Once more an old bard prayerful sings
Grateful rejoicing strains;
Strains which responsive voices hail
Wher'er Victoria reigns.

A Last Loyal Wish
May golden fruits, and rosy flowers,
Grace, cheer our Queen's still autumn hours;
In winter's distant sunset days,
May Earth's low notes sound Heaven's loud praise.
George Castleden, Woburn, 8th March.

This assassination attempt on Queen Victoria was actually the eighth attempt on her life. Roderick McLean was a poet who had sent his work to the Palace, but only received a dismissively curt reply. He went to Windsor with a pistol, and fired at the Queen. Two passing Eton school boys then attacked him with their umbrellas, and he was soon overpowered and in custody. After a trial, he spent the rest of his days in Broadmoor Asylum. The case prompted a change in law and the introduction of the Trial of Lunatics Act 1883.

21st March 1882 Leighton Buzzard Observer

The Bradlaugh Block. To the Editor of the Leighton Buzzard Observer.

Sir, - Does not Mr Franklin look down the marrow bone of Toryism, and see in Mr. Bradlaugh only the "Radical" and "unbeliever?" Open-eyed, he would see, as Liberals see, Mr Bradlaugh the representative of Northampton.

Instead of the Tories seizing this return as a block for party purposes, I guess all Liberals would hail a method to meet the case; and, instead of aiding and abetting in an act of high treason against our prized representative system, if they would help to amend any blot, it would be creditable and serviceable. If I view it right, as the law now stands, the majority are lawless, and, as a tyrant power, would slay on the shrine of Parliament its own vital life. Without touching the religious item, I venture these few words on the civil fix Parliament is now in. I repeat, if Tories can solve it, let them; if Liberals are trying their best, let them assist, instead of using this return as a block; for, recollect, behind this party stratagem there may be, after "big words," the humiliation of being forced to "eat the leek."

Your obedient servant, George Castleden. March 17th, 1882.

Mr. Castleden's Poetical Lines of Congratulation to the Queen – The following acknowledgement has been received by the author: - "General Sir Henry F. Ponsonby has received the Queen's commands to thank Mr Castleden for his congratulation of the 8th inst. – Privy Purse Office, Buckingham Palace, S.W., 10th March, 1882"

A fairly curt reply from the Palace to a poet that had sent a poem about the Queen being shot at by a poet who had received a curt reply! Oh, the irony!

28th March 1882 Leighton Buzzard Observer
Woburn – A March Fair Rhyme

A stall-less fair, this March cold day,
Incites a reminiscent lay,
Of home, that is to say, I frame a rhyme a change in time,
And, while my verse is not sublime,
It chronicles our day.

In Time's past dream, the agent Steam
Has changed full many a scene,
And turned them into smoke!
The Rail our traffic now commands:
At Woburn Sands the station stands;
Old Woburn is a joke!

It's trade us low, yet "Banks" do show;
Some ancients tell past weal and woe;

But markets, fairs are o'er.
Inns, once, are out! Another race
Wins "siller" by a newer pace;
Old times return no more!

As on our town of past renown
I, from my door, look up and down.
Fond memory bids me say –
Adieu friends, neighbours, farmers all,
Oblivion throws its ebon pall
Over your burly day:
And but a few, in Woburn's vernal spot,
Remain to tell its fading, and its*not*!

Moral
So Time and Death change both small and great,
That dwell beneath the sky;
Old Rome, my home, both illustrate
Life is all vanity
George Castleden, 24th March 1882.

Dislike it as he may, Castleden had to see and accept that as Woburn Sands had the benefit of a railway station, it had become more important than Woburn. The Duke had wanted a station nearby the Abbey, and had backed the line through his land, but the engineers were not able to traverse the same steep inclines that had played havoc with horse-drawn carriages between Bow Brickhill, Woburn Sands and Woburn, so this was as close as the line could go.

28th March 1882 Leighton Buzzard Observer

The Bradlaugh Block. To the Editor of the Leighton Buzzard Observer.

Sir, - If your readers will, in reading Mr. Castleden's letter in your last issue, substitute the word "Cloture" for "Bradlaugh," and "Liberal" or "Radical" for "Tory," oh! what an "obitual!" Will you riddle me this riddle? Why is it that Nonconformists – Christians *par excellence* – are so in favour of the Atheism of Bradlaugh; or, if they like it better, Bradlaugh the Atheist; the name and cause of who seems to act like soothing syrup upon a fractious child, whilst any one called Ritualist, parson or layman, acts like a red rag on a mad bull?

Friday.

...and in the same edition this was from Edward Franklin:

To the Editor of the Leighton Buzzard Observer

Sir, - Mr. Castleden very wisely declines to touch the "religious item" in the Bradlaugh "fix;" if he were himself, however, "open-eyed," instead of blinded by the "marrow-bone" of *Liberalism*, through which he views that "item," he would know, like the rest of the world, that this "Radical unbeliever" and *political friend* of his himself raised the religious item," by refusing to go through the (to him) "meaningless formula" of taking that oath which it is evident, after that avowal, have been, and still would be – were it allowed – open and arrant blasphemy. The Tories did not therefore raise the "civil-fix" in which the Arch-Atheist has so very cleverly placed himself, and from which his patrons, the present Government, even by resorting to "dishonest devices," cannot release him. If the action of the majority were indeed "lawless and treasonable," and the "humiliation" of the Government so *great*, in being thus forced thrice to "eat the leek" of *defeat*, there is – thank Heaven – "a method to meet the case" which, "I guess (not) all the Liberals would hail," namely, to appeal to the nation, the "final court of appeal," for the law on the matter; we could then test the point in our own county whether our members have not - as I contend – misrepresented the majority of their constituents by voting to allow an unprincipled and infidel disloyalist to swear allegiance, *by the God he denies*, to the Sovereign on the throne of this realm, of whom his paper thus writes: -

"Our sires veil their faces in shame

For the sons who disgrace their name;

Who bow to a crowned thing

To a puppet they call a King.

Freedom's voice no longer is dumb;

To the sound of her trump we come;

We are sworn to put tyranny down,

We strike at the *Throne* and the *Crown*."

There are, sir, times when "silence becomes a crime;" let Mr. Castleden *connive* and *condone* the hypocrisy and mockery of such an oath, taken by a man who dares publish such words, if he will; but he may rest assured that no true and loyal Conservative will "aid and assist in such an act of high treason" against our prised monarchical system and Christian Constitution.

... who then continues against another correspondent, who called himself "That Irishman Again".

4th April 1882 Leighton Buzzard Observer

The Bradlaugh Block. To the Editor of the Leighton Buzzard Observer.

Sir, - My notice of Mr. Franklin's letter will be brief, and it shall be, on my part, the close of this controversy. The religious test I touch not. Constituencies, and not candidates, is the question. It is a question of legality or illegality; not orthodoxy and heterodoxy. If our fathers were at fault in making the law, amend; but an old classic adage has it "Let justice reign through skies should fall." Recollect ancestral wisdom ruled that the firm foundation of the Representative Temple must be the choice of constituencies.

I don't heed anonymous writers, but in defo ce of Nonconformists, to your scribe, "Friday," I offer a definite protest against any affinity with the atheist, or sympathy with atheism. To me the belief in no belief ids so absurd, so idiotic, that, whether asserted by a Tom Paine, Voltaire, or by living infidels, it has always struck me they must have sceptical swallows far beyond Jumbo's capacious throat, or else they must be intellectual curiosities, provoking the worthy Dominie's very just exclamation of "Prodigious!"

I am, Sir, your obedient servant, George Castleden. March 30th, 1882.

The American poet, Henry Wadsworth Longfellow, had died. Castleden was obviously a fan…

11th April 1882 Leighton Buzzard Observer

A sprig of Cypress for the Grave, from Woburn.

New England and Old England sigh,
A bard will sing no more;
Esteemed, beloved, Longfellow lives
On Britain's either shore.

A frater bard across the billowy sea
Has left crime-jarring earth; 'tis ever song
In spirit-land, and brother harmony
Old England pays respect to one whose tongue,
So musical, refused notes harsh and wrong.
Longfellow's muse charmed many a home,
If not first-class by critics placed among;
And genuine love ascends to speak and tone

The echoes of regret both sides old ocean's foam.
He, seventy-five, retires! I, seventy-seven,
Pen a fraternal tributary verse –
A spark of mystic light in gloom of even!
He thought, and wrote, to bless, and not to curse,
And kindred minds his praises will rehearse;
Unknown, the living bard may gratefully write,
Across the sea may float his tribute verse,
And age obscure may this last wish indite –
O that all bards had left, like him, their foot-prints' light*

* "Whose lives sublime
Leave guiding foot-prints on the sands of time."
Note. – "Longfellow was a man full of interest, enthusiasm and belief in England – his belief that they (the two Britains) had a common work to do, in respect of which they were bound to make any sacrifice." – (S. Morley, *Daily News*, March 28th.)
George Castleden
P.S. – I will close with an ancient saw suited to all mental workers, and which, I think, your new librarian might find an opt expression, writ 1800 years ago, of the work done by Woburn's friend, Mr. George Champney.

"He that is well employed in his study, though he may seem to do nothing, does the greatest thing of all others; he lives and the moderating of our passions, and obliges human nature, not only in the present, but in all succeeding generations." (Seneca).

Well said, old sage! this ancient saw,
Observ'd by man, and made a law,
Obliges all mankind!
Mind-sowers sow, and reapers may
The harvest gather through life's day,
Exhaustless fruitage find.

Were star quenched on high,
For ages it would light;
Still travelling downwards from the sky,
Shine on our mortal sight.

So, when a great man dies,
For years beyond our ken,

The light he leaves behind him lies
Upon the pats of men. *–Longfellow*

11th April 1882 Leighton Buzzard Observer

The Bradlaugh Block. To the Editor of the Leighton Buzzard Observer.

Sir, - Considering that some of our greatest writers in the past and in the present use a non de plume, I am surprised that Mr. Castleden should hesitate, as he states in his letter he does, to notice anonymous writers. Truly he is a great man! However, he has shirked the question altogether, nor has he riddled the riddle I sent. It is useless his trying to discover the religious aspect of this Bradlaugh question, and I apprehend none but a political dissenter would attempt so to do. But, without being a classical, some one says, "He who fights and runs away, lives to fight another day."

Friday

Another death to comment on, but this one a great deal closer to home, at Hockliffe Grange:

18th April 1882 Leighton Buzzard Observer

Obitual. Sir Richard Gilpin, Bart.; Died 8th April, in his 82nd Year.

Old man, farewell! an old man says
To thy familiar name;
For many years a useful man,
You won a worthy fame.

A boy of Bedfordshire, a man,
Of *parts* in life's strange play;
"Seven ages" yours, and in old age
Saw strength you melt away!

A Beds. M.P. for many a year;
A magistrate as well;
A gentleman in manners long –
To thee a long farewell!

I tone this Hockliffe requiem note
By one injunctioned more –
Serve, save, and help your fellow-men,

445

On earth's life-wrecking shore.

Apart in mind, akin in heart
Men, honest men, do see
'Tis "God's best work;" so Pope has sung;
With Pope we all agree.

All titles cease; Sir Richard fails,
Like Beaconsfield's last Earl!
So "vanity of vanities"
Marks Time's all-whelming whirl!

An old man's moral seals the tale;
Neighbours, companions, flee!
The Grave, the common home of all,
And then – Eternity.
George Castleden.11ᵗʰ April.

But another critic had taken a dislike to Castleden's latest…

25ᵗʰ April 1882 Leighton Buzzard Observer

To the Late Sir Richard Gilpin, Bart. To the Editor of the Leighton Buzzard Observer.

Sir, - Leighton has always had its mesmerists and its mesmeric mediums, from the time of the sturdy Hockliffe Road blacksmith onwards, and therefore I make use of one of such mediums to send you this letter. Wandering with some other Shades the other morning down to the landing stage of Charon's Ferry, to see the last comers, and to bear the news, we found that your paper contained two poetical communications with reference to the late Sir Richard Gilpin. Mr. Derbyshire's we considered rhythmical, and that it spoke well for his head and his heart; but the other, by Mr. Castleden, we did not like, nor did we like the one he wrote upon "Longfellow." He might have left him alone, as I did not know the man he referred to. I will not go into verbal criticism, but I must protest against the "Hail, fellow, well met!" sort of jocularity evidenced in his opening apostrophe – "*Old man*, farewell!" Passing on then to the fourth verse, I wish you, sir, and your readers very carefully to read it through, because it strikes me that this Bard of Woburn, posing as he does as the opponent of Romanists and Ritualists, is guilty of teaching invocation to the saints with a vengeance himself. After leaving Sir Richard dead and buried in the third verse, he suddenly breaks forth with an injunction which he lays upon the departed to help those who are left behind. To prevent misconception, I quote the lines I refer to: -

"I tone this Hockliffe requiem note

By one injunctioned more –

Serve, save, and help your fellow-men,

On earth's life-wrecking shore."

Then we come to the last verse. I certainly should have thought the Bard of Woburn, as a Christian, would have written differently of death and eternity, for it is very strange that he should tell those yet living to "flee death and eternity." Has he been so taken up with Bradlaugh and his teachings, and the Bradlaugh dead-lock, that he has imperceptibly come to believe in his disbelief? If not, what does he mean?

Seneca's Shade

P.S. - I am a firm believer in as well as afraid of ghosts, having once been very frightened by one in Sandy Lane many years ago, and hence I felt bound to send you the foregoing. Let me add that the few well-chosen words spoken by Mr. Macnamara, the Rev. Mr Ouvry, Mr. Harris, Dr. Lawford, and others, are well worthy of the late Sir Richard Gilpin, but the simple touching sermon of Mr. Gray makes one feel the full force of prayer - "Let me die the death of the righteous, and let my last end be like his " Yet, after all, no lines, prose or poetry, can equal the pathos of those grand old line - "Blessed are the dead which die in the Lord, for they rest from their labour, and their works do follow them."

…but this time it was his supporters who got first reply…

2ⁿᵈ May 1882 Leighton Buzzard Observer

"Seneca's Shade" and Mr. Castleden

To the Editor of the Leighton Buzzard Observer

Sir, - As one who has often read with much pleasure Mr. Castleden's poetical contributions to your paper, I beg you will allow me space to reply, if a reply be necessary, to the ignorant pedantry of "Seneca's Shade." His criticism, if it be one, shows beneath it a narrowness, an envy, and an ignorance that surprises. You, the editor of a paper of such long standing as this, have surely had sufficient experience to enable you to judge of the suitability or unsuitability for your columns of your correspondent's contributions; and yet "Seneca's Shade," from every sentence of whose letter misunderstandings glare, questions your and Mr. Castleden's knowledge of the simplest forms of expression. Mr. Castleden is a stranger to me; I have never seen him; but, if I may judge from his writings, he is a kindly old gentleman of whom we should be proud, for his poetry is ever pure and irreproachable in teaching. Even were it poor poetry (and I contend it is not), we should honour the man for the goodness of his motives and teachings. In the opening words of the poem, "Old man, farewell," there is nothing objectionable but much that is poetical. Who but one with a most fertile mind would say there is, about those three words, "jocularity?" To me they convey the sadness of the poet's feelings. The fourth verse "Seneca's Shade" has wholly misunderstood. Mr. Castleden there enjoins this of us who are living (and not the dead) to

"Serve, save, and help your fellow-men,
On earth's life-wrecking shore."

Further, it is but justice, the right of all (although denied Mr. Castleden by "Seneca's Shade") to quote correctly. Where, in the verse below - a *verbatim* quotation from Mr. Castleden - does he tell us to "flee death and eternity?"

"An old man's moral seals the tale;
Neighbours, companions, flee!
The Grave, the common home of all,
And then – Eternity."

The veriest schoolboy would be caned for so ignorantly construing that which is at once simple, correct, and noble. I am personally deeply indebted to Mr. Castleden for the sympathy and sweetness of his writings to your paper, which remind me of a part of one of Longfellow's apostrophes in the song Hiawatha: -

"Homely phrases, but each letter
Full of hope and yet heart-break;
Full of all the tender pathos
Of the Here and the Hereafter."

I am, sir, yours truly, W. Odell.

2<u>nd</u> May 1882 Leighton Buzzard Observer

Seneca. To the Editor of the Leighton Buzzard Observer.

Sir, - I should not have troubled myself with "Seneca's Shade," only, as he seems a coming scribe, it may assist him in future lucubrations to hear what Seneca says for the encouragement of obscure writer, who, with a good intent, write to further the amenities and *not* foment the animosities of life. Whether self-confessed ignorance may be enlightened I know not; but, to wrest words is easy to a jaundiced mind; to apply them honestly may be too hard a task for a masked one: -

"He that is well employed in his study, though he seems to do nothing, does the greatest things yet of all others; he lays down precepts for the governing of our lives, and the moderating of our passions; and obliges human nature, not only in the present, but in all succeeding generations." (*Seneca.*)

Whether the "Shade" comes up to this substance I leave with your readers. Perhaps his next visit to "Charon's Ferry" will make him older and wiser, but I, at any rate, must bid a long farewell to all anonymous "Shades," or else it may be –

"Shadows haunting Shades! fantastic chase!"

Yours obediently, George Castleden, Woburn, April 27.

P.S. – I ought to thank "Shade" for this opportunity of circulating these good words of 1800 years ago. It may be compensative good for *evil meant.*

30: *The rear of the Market Hall, Woburn, from Leighton Street. The Bank which once operated here was a Barclays branch. An undated postcard.*

9th May 1882 Leighton Buzzard Observer

"Seneca's Shade." To the Editor of the Leighton Buzzard Observer.

Sir, - In my obscure, unselfish wish to serve and please, W. Odell's letter is a trophy I shall gratefully prize. Unknown to each other, let me, by your column, thank him for the friendly, generous, and truthful exposition of my tributary lines on Sir Richard Gilpin, and for the quiet masterly consignment of "Seneca's Shade to the limbo of all such-like dunces or literary delinquents. Thanking Mr. Odell sincerely for very pertinent remarks, for a last time, I add – critics, honest, I am always glad to hear and profit by; but, where nerves malevolently are touched, or motives are imputed, common fair play and honesty demand their exclusion if the writer is ashamed of his own name. Rhyme on the "Negatives" might have explained some misrepresentations my anonymous friends have obtruded in the Observer. Perhaps lines of long ago may best close this note; and certainly in them is a stern moral on the hand-in-hand life and death just now in the palace!

"Princes, this clay must be
Your bed, in spite of all your towers."

Hear the poet: -
"How frail, men, things! how momentary, both!
Fantastic chase of shadows hunting shades!
The gay, the busy, equal, the unlike;
Equal in wisdom, differently wise!
Thro' flowery meadows, and thro' dreary wastes,
One bustling, and one dancing, into death.
There's not a day but, to the man of thought,
Betrays verse secret, throws some new reproach
On life, and makes him sick of seeing more."
Yours obediently, George Castleden, Woburn 3rd May 1882.

9th May 1882 Leighton Buzzard Observer

Seneca's Shade and Mr. Castleden. To the Editor of the Leighton Buzzard Observer.

Sir, - I yield to none in respect and esteem for Mr. Castleden, and I always read all his communications. He draws his bow at a venture, but his thought-arrows often, in my judgement, miss their way, and are marred by his mannerism. As a veteran newspaper correspondent, I am sure he will take this in good part, for neither "envy, malice, or uncharitableness" ever entered into my mind. I only pushed to extreme what might appear to a man not having the same regard for Mr. Castleden as I have. I thank him for his quotation from "Seneca,"

And only wish everyone would read L'Estrange's "Seneca's Morals." I will give him another quotation, this time from Dionysics, the comic poet, and is about all I fancy he has left behind. It is "either say something better than say nothing or say nothing." I may say he thoroughly diagnosed my health when he spoke about bile, for I have had a most dreadful bilious attack. With reference to his naughty virtuperative words are answered with a fuquaque. As to his saying I misquoted, I did nothing of the sort; it was copied for me by a reliable scribe from the original. I, equally with Mr. Odell, understood what Mr. Castleden's meaning was; still, it had been pointed out to me by another that it bore the interpretation that I put on it. I have read Mr. Odell's letter through, and I think, if he takes his copy and with his pen writes dele opposite the above-mentioned words and the padding, he will find that the skeleton left – looking at it philosophically – will hardly give him matter enough to make a good syllogism; and, if he looks at it aesthetically, I think he will find it "too utterly too too." Hard words break no bones especially in dealing with a shade.

Seneca's Shade.

16ᵗʰ May 1882 Leighton Buzzard Observer

Memory Lines.

The Bright & Black Saturday; May 6ᵗʰ, 1882.

"Light and shade attend the path we tread."

Too true this truth, this sixth of May;
At Epping loyal, grand, bright, gay;
Pleased thousands hailed our Queen:
Grandmother long, this day made *great*;
Homes joys sound sweet midst shouts of States*
Hurrah for Birth and Scene!

In Dublin Park two murders thrill –
The very world with anguish fill,
At deeds terrific, fell!
Aghast men gaze on such a scene;
Awake, it seem a horrid dream,
Turns Earth into a Hell!

With bright and black life's path is strewn;
'Tis smiles and tears to all;
In the thatched cot, on England's Throne,
The candle and Death's call
Will tell of joy, of anguish, and the pall!

Note. – All was bright and fair. It was a "Queen's day" *indeed*. Also on that day our worthy Queen became great-grand mamms. "All that's bright must fade, the brightest still the fleetest." At even the black darkness fell in an assassination which horrifies the whole civilised world.

Poor Burke, Lord Cavandish, by fate,
Fall 'neath the dark assassin's hate!
The blood of innocents cries out,

Vengeance on all the rebels rout.

George Castleden. The funeral day of Lord F. C. Cavendish.

* The Queen and Epping Forest. – An interesting incident of the Queen's visit to Epping Forest may be noted. A few moments before the Royal train left Chinford for Windsor, her Majesty beckoned the Lord Mayor to the carriage in which she was seated, and in a few kindly and gracious words expressed her pleasure in the ceremony in which she had taken part, and her extreme approval of the action of the Corporation in securing the forest for the enjoyment of the people. It needed only these few words from the lips of the Sovereign herself to give the last happy touch to the day's proceedings – *City Press*.

16th May 1882 Leighton Buzzard Observer

Seneca's Shade. To the Editor of the Leighton Buzzard Observer.

Sir, - Once more for good. I thank "Seneca's Shade" for wishing every one to read "Seneca's Morals." The very volume is before me, and from page 4 I quote another aphorism: - "There is not any man either as great or so little but he is yet capable of giving and receiving benefits." If a "benefit" shall acerne from this critique, then the "Shade," comically, does substantial good; and for the future let me recommend the "Essay on Anger," page 259, as an alternative on any return of the "Shade's" most "dreadful bilious attack." In fact, it is an essay useful to all jaundiced minds, who, caught in Anger's toils, madden themselves, and play the fool with a vengeance. Well it is when they do not perpetrate prodigious crime. Let an "Evergreen" rhyme, after reading the "Shade," close all controversy, tone any future criticism, and teach all wisdom.

16th May 1882 Leighton Buzzard Observer

On the Early Rhododendron in Woburn Park Evergreens.

My scarlet friend, again I view
Thine advent on this Spring;
Again thy tinted life I see
In it's full blossoming.

The peacock, pheasant, rabbit, hare,
Here skip, and play, and shine;
Nature is evergreen and fair;
Poor man, fades in his prime!

These flowers again recall the dead!
I muse the Ducal Three!
Agents and tenants all have fled,
Their time – eternity!

In eve's still walk I muse and talk,
And culture thought in gloom;
O, may it fruit, some soul recruit,
When thought no more may bloom –
One thinker more consigned to earth's huge tomb!
George Castleden, Woburn, May 9th, 1882.

30th May 1882 Leighton Buzzard Observer

The Political Situation. To the Editor of the Leighton Buzzard Observer.

Sir, - The late Lord Beaconsfield was a man of great penetration and clear insight, but he evidently entirely overlooked the abilities of some of our Conservative politicians in and around Leighton, or surely they would have received some well-merited distinction at his hands. Far away and before all must be noticed that patriotic and constitutional Eversholt politician Mr. Franklin, to whom we are so greatly indebted for periodically setting us right concerning the mementoes questions of the day, preserving us from imbibing any dangerous radical notions, and, above all, keeping at bay so effectually the otherwise unassailable Mr. Castleden. In fact, I very much doubt whether most of us would have any clear or definite idea as to the manner in which we are governed, or be able to form a correct judgement as to who are the proper Statesmen to rule this great empire, did not Mr. F. So kindly set us right on the subject; and I am sure every true patriot who really feels disgusted at the way in which the aforesaid great empire is now being disintegrated must feel grateful to him for the spirited way in which he dresses down those formidable adversaries, Mr. Gladstone, Mr Bradlaugh, and the Woburn Poet (sic.) Now , sir, I am not much of a politician myself; I understand holding horse outside the Bell, or carrying parcels for ladies and gentlemen, much better than I understand a Parliamentary debate; but it is with the profoundest satisfaction that I read Mr. Franklin's letters, and I quite agree with him in everything he says; and, as a result of a careful study thereupon, have come to the careful conclusion that every calamity which has happened to our country for the last two years, including the bad weather and the potato disease, is the result of disastrous Radical policy. There are a few things, however, which are still rather cloudy in my dull mind, and which I should very much like Mr. Franklin to clear up, as I have the greatest confidence he will. I only mention one or two now, as I know the time of great men is fully occupied. Amongst other things, I should like to have – firstly, an explanation of the coalition of the Conservatives and the Parnellites, as shown by the divisions in the earlier stages of the *Cloture*; secondly, a short outline (not exceeding twenty columns) of a scheme to govern Ireland satisfactorily in its present condition. [N.B. – This might serve as a basis for the Conservatives Irish policy, when they return to power.] Thirdly, the probable evil results, social and national, likely to arise through the House not adjourning as usual on the Derby day. If he will answer the above at his earliest convenience, I shall be extremely obliged, and, if quite satisfactory, I will trouble him to answer a few more at some future time.

I remain, sir, your obedient servant, Tasmetah, Barrow Path, Leighton Buzzard. May 24th, 1882.

6th June 1882 Leighton Buzzard Observer

Ireland's Problem. To the Editor of the Leighton Buzzard Observer.

Sir, - "There is not any man either as great or so little but he is yet capable of giving and receiving benefits." – (Seneca). This aphorism alike pleads, and, whether it to be the Herculean efforts of our great Prime Minister to benefit Ireland, or to the humbled essayist who scrawls his words of *peace* on village walls, alike be honour paid to the *intent*. Two murders, the most atrocious ever scribed on the page of history, of worthy men actually bearing the olive branch, speaks almost the hopelessness of any pacificatory policy to injured and revengeful Ireland. Whether Cromwell, in his Protestant zeal sinned against the law of nations and Lord Castleraugh, in his Tory zeal, completed wrong, time and truth may test; but, *now*, Ireland is the *inheritance* of parties, and pains, penalties, and liabilities must be met. In a long life I have seen this isle tomb of Ministries! Whether it will be the grave of a Gladstone Cabinet a short time may tell; and, if such a patriot, either deceived or disheartened, falls, methinks whoever succeeds may find it a volcano, eruptive and burning. *Consequences* for a *cause* for which the present is not answerable is the penalty paying for past wrong, and, mysterious as it is, it is justice eternal. On the even of Lord Cavendish's funeral, amongst home's vernal scenery, I took a stroll, and, contemplating the scene in Edensor's grave-yard, I contrasted Nature's life and harmony here with the dark crime causing the bitter mourning wail there. Joining a neighbour our converse was on Ireland's tragedy, and both of us, despondent, stood on the stile pausing on the problem, the perplexity of politicians, and wondering when and how solution may be found. Pacing our emerald fields, and looking down the avenue on to the Abbey Pile, glorious in the sunset, I thought of the great year 1688, and its peaceful revolution, in which the historic names, Cavendish and Russell, so patriotically united; and such a happy constitutional settlement has given the peace and prosperity of centuries. Long may it last. And this funeral-evening reflection was closed by thinking Sorrow heaves her saddest sigh over Death's cruellest strokes. Once more in this problem, if kindness and law may not soothe and save, force is only a remedy so long as the screw is on, the fetter manacles, and the sword shall smite. The severe measures for poor Ireland, all humane and good, I would wish to see avoided; but in her crime-stricken madness how can safety to self and others be attained? May this "heart-breaking" problem still have a merciful and just solution is, sir, the ardent wish of yours obediently, George Castleden.

Re-igniting "Ireland's Problem" quickly brought Franklin back out in counterpoint:

13ᵗʰ June 1882 Leighton Buzzard Observer

To the Editor of the Leighton Buzzard Observer.

Sir, - After perusing Mr. Castleden's last contribution on "Ireland's Problem," I am tempted to remark that "surely the times are out of joint," or we should never have found this veteran supporter and worshipper of our "Heaven sent Premier" canvassing *the probable fall* of the Cabinet over which he presides with such discredit to himself and accumulating disaster to his country. Mr. Castleden I think, however, has good cause to utter his "bewildered lamentations" at the proved inability and total failure of Mr. Gladstone to solve the "heart-breaking" problem which Mr. Castleden now admits has, under the treatment of the "Great Physician," developed itself into a chronic disorder so deep and vital that "whoever succeeds may find it a *volcano* eruptive and burning." This is "a legacy," however, which one would expect from a "jelly-fish" Cabinet, destitute of the "backbone" requisite for the government of Ireland, a country which above all things requires governing *first* and legislating for *afterwards*; and, just in proportion as the flaccid policy of the Liberal Ministry has infringed this cardinal principle, so have their difficulties deservedly increased. It is, I believe, thirteen years since Mr. Gladstone began his "new departure" in a measure of spoliation and confiscation in Ireland, and great promises of the contentment we were to witness as a *result*, we find it now a "volcano eruptive and burning." On the admission of his most faithful admirer, Mr. Castleden, who, as a Liberal elector, must take his full share of the condemnation which the mere recital of these facts show to be richly merited at the hands of a people justly indignant and avowing contempt for a "Ministry of Failure."

Yours truly, Edward Franklin, Eversholt, June 10ᵗʰ 1882.

13ᵗʰ June 1882 Leighton Buzzard Observer

Woburn. A Tribute. – "An American Leaflet: a hand-in-hand grasp across the Atlantic, by two G. C.'s" – Mr Castleden, of Woburn, Beds, and Mr. Champney, of Woburn, America – has been printed by Mr. H. G. Fisher, of this town. It is a gracefully worded expression of the "friendship, goodwill, and peace" which should govern the two great Anglo-Saxon nations.

20ᵗʰ June 1882 Leighton Buzzard Observer

On Reading the Right Hon. John Bright's Birmingham Speech.

Thanks to thee, Friend, a sage M.P.,
For wise words on all books;
As an old "Isaac," thanks to thee
For words on "Salmon"-hooks.

In age and feebleness I read
Your words, endorse them to,
Books have been friends in many a need.
Now, as I sigh adieu,

I may commend this speech to all
Who would be *useful men*;
Read, learn each day, and wit will fall,
So signs George Castleden.
Woburn, 20ᵗʰ June.

20ᵗʰ June 1882 Leighton Buzzard Observer

Ireland's Problem. To the Editor of the Leighton Buzzard Observer.

Sir, - In 1847 I wrote on Ireland's difficulty, political, moral, and social, much as I do now. Then I quoted from their great orator, Curran, and experience convinces that wrong done to a people or a person must return; hence I beg to close all controversy with Mr. Franklin and his *freves*, by giving a rhyme recipe which I fancy applies alike to an empire and a home, a Czar or a peasant serf; and, from the first Whig to the last Tory, *all* may find in its righteous *keeping* the truest Conservatism, or, in its selfish *breach*, Imperial ruin and domestic and personal wreck. I might enlarge on this theme, but age and failing powers say – No.

A low eternal, age, bears away
Over this mundane state;
'Tis mystic, all must it obey;
'Tis fickle, yet 'tis fate.

This law binds men in righteous awe-
"*Give* as ye would *receive*;"
This, Heaven's own rules worked in Earth's school,
Who then would wrong, deceive?
Seek peace, shun wrong, in truth and right believe.

Permit, in behalf of the dead, my thanks to your correspondent for the "tribute." Mr. Champney's fraternal spirit would rejoice if from our "remarkable friendship" the "leaflet should be the means of sowing one seed of peace and good-will on any soil, or any tried and tempted soul led to disobey

"What conscience *dictates* to be done."

Yours, obediently, George Castleden. George Street, June 13th, 1882.

20th June 1882 Leighton Buzzard Observer

A long letter criticising Edward Franklin and his politics, by "Chapeau Rabattu", was printed.

27th June 1882 Leighton Buzzard Observer

Ireland's Problem

Sir, - I am sorry that "age and failing powers" compel Mr. Castleden to close the controversy he raised in your issue of June 6th on "Ireland's problem" with the *lame and impotent* conclusion that "'Tis a fickle fate, all must obey," and therefore that, "Anarchy and ruin may still hold away," though these two years Liberals have had all their way. But, whilst such a veteran as Mr. C. Gives up – not unnaturally – *in despair*, the "problem" requiring its solution now in the "distressful country," and on which I give the very prevalent opinion (which has coincided with the opinion of a well-informed *staunch Liberal-* I mean the late Under-Secretary, Mr. Burke, that we have "Mr. Gladstone to thank for it all"), your correspondent "Chapeau Rabattu" with more "valour than discretion" comes forth like "an injured innocent" to (in effect) request you to *silence* my "wild and irrational splutterings" with that Brummagem invention, the "Cloture." Whether such am aim does not show, on the part particularly of a *Liberal by profession*, that he is not wanting in the possession of a "few rank weeds of malice and narrowness" of his own, no one can doubt; and I am both amply "recognised and promoted" to find that "Chapeau Rabattu," like Mr. Castleden, is in too great a despair of achieving any success in even attempting to demolish any part of that "incongruous bunch" of mine which he finds so "burdensome" to his "political palate."

One almost wonders as what "council of Radical mice" "Chapeau Rabattu" was commissioned to "Bell this Tory cat," which so persistently alarms them with its presence, "whether they will or not." I am, indeed, afraid that my anonymous opponent will find it necessary, before he silences either my noisy tongue or stops my pen, to exclaim, in expiring accents, that "Surely it were a cursed spite that ever he was born to set me right," and he will *before then* find that *I am capable* both of forming an opinion and *acting* upon it myself, whilst I am (although a Conservative) also incapable of insinuating, like your Radical correspondent, "Chapeau Rabattu," that every other person should not have the same liberty of opinion and action; and. Until he has learned to practice such a real Liberalism as well as profess it, I would advise him not to set himself the futile task of correcting those who do, and thus cease "to waste the sweetness – or sourness – of his rhetorical flowers on the desert air," unseen, unknown, and unheeded.

Yours faithfully, Edward Franklin. June 24th, 1882.

This next anonymous item in the local news columns has all the hallmarks of being by Castleden.

4th July 1882 Leighton Buzzard Observer

Missions – Again another annual sale in aid of the Church and London City Missions, under the care of Mrs. Southey, with kind helpers, was held in the Town Hall on the 27th and 28th ults. Completing the twentieth year many changes have occurred since long ago; hands and hearts which gladdened ours are gone, garden scenes have faded, and familiar forms have melted; but still hearts and hands helped, and from the stalls, well spread, and kindly served by willing workers, many friends bore their spoils away, and a double joy seemed to follow – the serving of good societies, and the pleasing of themselves. Commenced in the gardens of Lord and Lady Charles Russell, may these sales continue to aid, so pleasingly and effectually, these home and foreign missions of England's favoured land.

> Long may such help for peace be found,
> Long may kind helpers gather round;
> And midst the strifes and dins of time
> Point to the Cross, and calms divine.
> May mission love help war to cease,
> And mingle nations in an ever peace.

In August, his attention turned back to cricket, it what was to be one of the most momentous summers in the history of the sport, and one which has been celebrated ever since (if you are Australian…)

1ˢᵗ **August 1882** Leighton Buzzard Observer
England and Australia – A Ballad on Cricket and the War

To-day I scan the cricket "team,"
All named for pastoral strife,
In young Australia's sunny scene,
Its laughing winsome life.

An old man's pulses seem to swell
At this Australian hit;
In this July old age may sigh,
When in his cricket wit-
He struck the ball, and strolled the plain
With mates bowled down and fled!
Still, memories charm, and scenes remain;
Still, as I stroll the dead,
I hear their shout, I see each form;
Like shadows they have flown!
Our games in Woburn Park forgot,
And I a "bat" unknown.

Still as I read the list of men
Furnished with bat and ball,
Who in this pastoral war I deem
Obey their country's call;
I sing – Go forth, hit, scout away,
Uphold the "noble game;"
Australia's empire's youthful day
May seal your home-won fame.

May Western commerce, peace, its charm
Banish aggressive hate;
Nor may it know of wars alarms
Which noise the Mother State.
May Tylecote, peaceful, tell of Beds

At our Antipodes;
And when he bats, scouts, bowls, or runs,
Across the Western seas,
From Bedfordshire he bears his name –
With mates he'll win a cricket fame.

So on this morn, somewhat forlorn,
Age cozens time by rhyme:
A wicket scene again I dream,
Then, on the stream of Time
Where it may float I do not know:
On a memorial day
The busy brain, at work again,
A tribute note will pay
To one, whose peace and kindness done,
Passed from this home in July's sultry sun.

A contrast may my theme impress –
Our cricketers sow peace,
And frater "bats" and brither scouts
May bid wars woes decrease.
I sigh o'er what I read this morn,
News from swarth Egypt's sand;
There blood and fire and strength and wealth
Drench, roll the Eastern sand
And Englishmen are waved to death
By Honour's gory wand.

Hurrah for cricket's peaceful *ball*:
Down, down to war's red game!
Now soldiers, sailors, hasten all
To seek Egyptian fame!
Brave men! 'tis hollow; and, I say,
Avert war, Heaven, I pray;
Reign, healing Peace, assert thy sway,
Stay rapine's carnage day;
And so among past cricket men
Sincerely scores George Castleden.

George Street, Woburn 22nd July, 1882.

8th August 1882 Leighton Buzzard Observer

Reporting. To the Editor of the Leighton Buzzard Observer.

Sir, - Relative to a Woburn item in your last, give me a small space to do public service. If the higher courts allow reporting, surely the lower courts and "boards" should not object. In all public speaking, the tongue nimble, facts may be distorted, figures magnified, and, a little truth mingled, as Tennyson says, may make "the blackest of lies." A first letter forty-five years ago denounced anonymous writing; a *last* may condemn anonymous speaking, and point its remedy in healthy and honest reporting of what I said. No Englishman, or lover of fair play should object to this. With a reporter we have a sanction for truth, a security against slander and lies, and a salutary check to the tongue-assassin, who, privileged and protected, may be tempted to *stab* or *cut*, and, cowardly, say, "You canst not say I did it."

Yours faithfully, George Castleden, Woburn, 1st August, 1882

8th August 1882 Leighton Buzzard Observer

Thoughts on the War. To the Editor of the Leighton Buzzard Observer.

Sir, - In keeping company with the Turk, has it been creditable to our Christianity? And to war on a Stock-jobbing speculation is not a dignified conflict. The common mind sees in this war much *mystery*. What is it for? Is *misery* to the State, and to many a home, to be the cruel answer? As the question is, it seems the Cross by the Crescent may be beguiled. Civilisation and Christianity may be bamboozled by Oriental craft and duplicity. And will it be, at last, too late to repair – that England will commit a last fault by falling in the net of diplomatic cunning and betrayal? Will it be written that we sink wealth and worth in eastern seas and on desert sands, and then over England's Egyptian grave, it may, outlasting the Pyramids, write that by ambition lured, by honour led and mocked, war entombed the bravest of the brave? Forbid it, Heaven, in mercy! Christians must pray. These are thoughts for thought. If they are prophetic, a prophet has no honour in his country.

As one who hears war's sad proclaiming death,
I write all tremendous with bridled breath;
Sincerely pray catastrophe may fail,
And peace around its plenitude prevail;
I watch the sign, but sadden as I see
War frowns in *mystery* and *misery*.
George Castleden, Woburn, 3rd August, 1882.

461

Woburn Memories! On the Death of a Friendly Neighbour. August 1882.

The Niece has passed full soon away;
A Woburn short and useful day
Spent in her cozy home.
The names of yore in her are gone,
Names once town known, forgot, unknown,
Have now far ever flown!

Like other tenants in our street,
She vanishes, no more will greet;
Her shadow, aye, has fled,
Few now remain in Woburn town
Who knew its traffic-trade renown;
The *many* all are dead!

The actors, properties, and scenes
Have passed away; like passing dreams,
They quit the present day!
I 'shuffle on the stage' and tell
Another neighbour's long farewell;
In life's long-chequered play;
Then with them all I hie away,
And leave to future bards Time's coming day.
George Castleden

Note. – As we saw this Woburnite go into the narrow cell, and looked on kindred dust, we mused the vanity of life's hopes and boons, and, amidst our garden graveyard, the poet's lines told mourners and neighbours of their final destiny: -
"We read their monuments, we sigh, and while
We sigh, we sink, and are what we deplored;
Lamenting, or lamented, all our lot!
Is death at distance? No; he has been on thee,
And gives sure earnest of his final blow.

29th August 1882 Leighton Buzzard Observer

The County Representation. To the Editor of the Leighton Buzzard Observer.

Sir, - Remembering the political strait of 1831-2, and the after elevation of some of the sons of our nobles, I saw force in your leader, supposing the House of Lords were impracticable – that, to prevent stagnant legislation for a present emergency, without periling a future redundancy, the remedy suggested in your last words might be approved by all in such a fix; and then who more eligible than "the eldest sons of a few of the leading nobles of the Liberal party?" While rumour has been busy relative to the county, whatever may be its future, I trust in Bedfordshire progress may not give place to retrogression, nor that Liberal extension and expansion may be superseded by Conservative restrictive men and measures.

I remain, sir, yours obediently, George Castleden, August 23rd.

Following the first defeat on home soil for the English cricket team, by Australia at the Oval, the Sporting Times famously published a mock obituary, saying the body of English Cricket would be cremated and the ashes taken to Australia, and thus the Ashes Cricket Tour was born. However, the 'Sudden Death' in the following poem seems to refer to a spectator who had died during the game.

5th September 1882 Leighton Buzzard Observer

Sudden Death at The Oval. Australian and English Cricket Match, 29th of August.

The "demon bowler" at his play
Hurled down the stumps this August day.
And crushed the English score;
A great defeat in pastoral strife;
A bloodless *win* in eager life,
We hail our game once more.

We think of greens and summer flowers,
Of active limbs and zestful hours -
Of Woburn players fled!
Our village, town, and county "teams" -
A modern term – have from our scenes
Found the "elevens" dead!

A few remain, a veteran few,
Who on the green 'neath summer's blue
Spent this Olympic day;
And memory hails the pleasant dreams,
Returns our cricket phantom scenes,
Scenes sepulchred for aye.

Moral.
Death demon is of man's swift game;
He *bowls* the churl; the son of fame
Feels his resistless might;
Unerring, sure, his ball must lie
Within the vault of night.

This tournament of bat and ball
Death's signet, solemn, scribed for all;
His moral, let it tell:
George thought not as he lounged the scene
Strolled 'mongst the thousands on that green
That he had *scored* farewell?

Note. – This great brither match of cricket was marked by a sudden
death of a spectator, George; hence the rhyme memory:
Death bowled this ebon trimming ball;
His aim is sure, he levels all
Atoms and cumes before him fall.
George Castleden. Woburn, August 31st, 1882.

10th October 1882 Leighton Buzzard Observer

Egypt's War: Its Close. To the Editor of the Leighton Buzzard Observer.

Sir, - We all rejoice at the brevity of this war. It is mitigation priceless. In a
sentence I write, while the counsel is, "if possible live in peace with all men."
Yet one who has lived in some of Europe's carnage-desolating wars hopes
fervently that all future wars may be equally short, sharp, and decisive. Pray
give a corner of the good news (16th), and a note informs of a coincidence of
how minds may think alike though far apart, and it may encourage others
when I may enter no more into "the pride, pomp, and circumstance of
glorious war:"-

"If brevity's the fame of war,
Gladstones and Wolseley sound it out afar."

The War: Its Close. An Englishman's Grateful Rhyme

Short, sharp, decisive was this war;
With shouts we hail the close;
Pray that this fierce Egyptian jar
May sound a long repose.

Proud of the men whose master mind
Planned well the morning fight,
Proud of the men whose courage sealed Their valour, fame, and might.

So Egypt's strife may win renown
In annals still of peace;
The war we feared may God still crown
By liberty's increase.

I am in unlooked for company in the words short, sharp, decisive. The Speaker of the House of Commons was using them on the day I first wrote them, and this coincidence I may, in age, repeat kind words - "great minds jump together."

G. C. Woburn, 4th Oct.

The Anglo-Egyptian War had lasted from June to September this year. A Nationalist uprising was quelled, and the leader, Ahmed 'Urabi, sent into exile. This was one of the smallest wars Britain engaged in, with official British causalities being only 57 troops. Far more casualties were due to heatstroke than enemy action. However, it gave Britain a success and increased the Empire's foothold in North Africa, so was celebrated as a great victory, even locally in Woburn Sands. The Duke of Bedford presented a highly-decorated scroll to a returning hero, who lived in Aspley Guise, watched by crowds and the Mayor and Corporation of Bedford. "To Major General Drury Curson Drury Lowe, C.B. Commander of the cavalry division of the Expeditionary force in Egypt. Sir, we, the undersigned inhabitants of Woburn, Aspley Guise, Woburn Sands, Wavendon and Crawley beg leave to offer you our most cordial and respectful congratulations on your return from active service in Egypt". Castleden is among the signatures, but he had obviously not been able to get to see the presentation himself. Now into his late 70's, perhaps he was too unwell to travel far.

7th November 1882 Leighton Buzzard Observer

Woburn Sands. – Egypt. – Woburn.

Thinking of an early bed, I was cheered by a neighbour's account of the doings at Woburn Sands, and relative to the "presentation." As he told me of the kind and good words spoken by His Grace the Duke of Bedford, the grateful and feeling reply of General Drury Lowe, and apt, vigorous, and kindly speech of Lord Charles Russell of thanks to the ducal president, I felt like the old veteran who showed how former "fields were won;" and the thought struck me that I might speak the gratulations of other aged absentees from this local recognition of English bravery. I may also close this tribute line to all our Bedfordshire Egyptian soldiers, by saying, as the *brevity* of this war has been invaluable, may it be its proud distinction till the extinction of all war shall bless the nations of the earth with universal peace. Amen will many say.

G. C. November 1st, 1882.

14th November 1882 Leighton Buzzard Observer

Lines on the High Fir at Woburn, blown down by the storm, 24th Oct.

Historic tree: I sung of thee,
And told of England's history
'Neath the dark Stuart Line;
A Russell noble felt their might,
And perished by tyrannic spite;
So read in "Burnett's time."

His widowed Lady sowed this tree,
In Abbey days of misery.
In this October storm
This vegetable ensign, wide,
Of Woburn Park's great forest pride
Is toppled, lies forlorn.

A local tree: to lands around
A mark it rose; it told the ground
Of Woburn's vernal site;
Two hundred years stood storm and blast,
But the wild storm of Tuesday last

Hurled down its pole and height.

A bardic fir: but for this tree
I never might in poetry
Have won verse trophies true;
For Egypt's lay, "thanks" on this day
The post has bought; and now I say
To thee, high fir, adieu!

My Father's tree: he loved the walk
And with his friends would stroll and talk
Beneath this Russell tree;
And, looking back on darksome times,
His heart rejoiced he lived in "lines"
Of light, peace, liberty.

And so on this historic tree
A first rhyme germed, and this from me
May be a *last* Park lay;
I look upon the blown down tree,
I link it with life mystery
In a bright Autumn day.

Note. – In Woburn Park, looking upon the giant flower of autumn, I missed a long familiar fir, which, topping surrounding trees, has been a mark for many years. Over the fallen tree I have mused the *fact* that more than forty-five years ago a kind word written by the Duke of Bedford to my farther, perhaps, determined a long vocation in verse; and on this day a coincidence, as I record the past, brought a note of "thanks" from Downing Street for my last "Egypt" rhyme; and, reading Mr. Gladstone's splendid speech, I was pleased I had written almost impromptu on the glorious close of this war.

Proud of the man whose master mind
Planned well the morning fight;
Proud of the men whose courage sealed
Their valour, fame, and might.
George Castleden. 27th Oct.

I'm sure a note arriving from Downing Street would have cheered Castleden immensely.

21st November 1882 Leighton Buzzard Observer

"The Catholic or Universal Church." To the Editor of the Leighton Buzzard Observer.

Sir, - I was instructed by Mr. Gray stating that Mr. Harris had been "more ingenious that ingenuous" in the use of the "Article." Respectfully I ask the rev. gentleman to favour us with a true meaning or definition of his "Catholic or Universal Church." This happy combination I have long wished for. Will High Church proclivities hasten the "consummation devoutly to be wished?" To be ingenuous, I have heard of two extremes against the "Universal Church" - the first, "No steeple, no Church!" and when Janet, in the Highlands, said she had "No faith in the Church outside herself and her brother Jamie, and sometimes she was not vera sure of him." The Scotch dame's *limit* surely must be sufficient, and satisfactory to the most rigid and exclusive sect. It is the Catholic and Universal Church that many Nonconformists wish to see, and, living in a home where "think and let think" has ruled for many years, I seize this a last opportunity to offer to all theological disputants a recipe which may soothe, serve, and save, and point the Catholic and Universal Church -

"Let names and sect and parties fall,

And Jesus Christ be all in all."

Amen, signs on who, believing not in the establishment of the "Catholic Church" by "Pope, presbyter, and priest," sees a time - it will be *Catholic*, and may be *Universal* - when Christians however divided onminor points, still believe in the same Deity and Saviour, adopting, heart and hand, the great Master's New Commandment - "That ye love one another" (John 13c, 35v.)

I use names, therefore I remain, Sir, your obedient servant

George Castleden, Woburn, November 16th, 1882.

28th November 1882 Leighton Buzzard Observer

Woburn Bible Society, 20th November.

Some sixty years have flown away
Since started first this Bible day;
The "fathers" gathered here:
In the ivied church, Duke John, the "chair;"
"Prophets" then known – where are they, where?
The generation – where?

The grave has hidden, and old Time
Flows on, and over mark and line
Its whelming waters sweep;

It buries Empires, neighbours, names
Alike entombs all mortal fames,
And seals oblivions sleep.

Yet sons may carry on the tale;
And as I linger in home's vale,
Age may recount to men,
In Woburn still, this autumn night,
The Bible advocates cast light;
And who will dare condemn?

Instead of father's sons arise
And congregate beneath our skies;
Men urge in our Town Hall
The circulation of God's Word;
Pure, peaceful, it will life record
In death, till skies shall fall,
And Time is hid 'neath Nature's funeral pall!

Man, short his span, his service, day, soon done;
Truth that he speaks or scribes survives the sun.

Note. – This annual meeting of the Woburn Bible Society, over which
Mr. Theodore Harris presided, *proves* what a common platform is on which
all Christians may meet to circulate God's Word. Sinking minor differences
here, brethren in harmony join, and surely such union *points* a realization of
the Catholic and Universal Church all Christians desiderate.

George Castleden, Woburn, Nov. 21ˢᵗ

28ᵗʰ **November 1882** Leighton Buzzard Observer

To the Editor of the Leighton Buzzard Observer

Sir, - I should like, with your kind permission, to say a few words on the
subject of sundry letters in the Observer of last week.

And *first*, in regard to Mr. Castleden's. *He* would be a hopeful man who
would fix a date when there will be here in England an Universal Church,
meaning thereby, a Church to which all Christian believers shall belong,
seeing

That almost every year adds to the number of sects. By Catholic may not
we understand a Church that is suited to all persons, and all nations, and

all times; and he would be a strange species of Christian who is prepared to assert that the Church, as founded by Christ – the Church which dates from the Day of Pentecost – is not Catholic in that sense. The two lines –

"Let names, and sects, and parties fall,

And Jesus Christ be all in all,"

Are very good; but who can any man be said to be a disciple of Jesus Christ who ignore the acts, and words, and prayers of Jesus Christ? He founded the Church. I do not know whether any "Pope, presbyter, or priest" ever founded a Church. If they did, as a lover of our dear Lord, I venture to say, "Away with it." Our Lord prayed that His people might be *one*. Are we all acting according to the spirit of that prayer?

[Continues to address other recent letters]

Delta

P.S. – Many thanks for putting in these letters. Those of my Dissenting brethren always make me feel deeply grateful to the old Church of England, of which I have always been a member.

5ᵗʰ December 1882 Leighton Buzzard Observer

Church and Dissent. "Catholic and Universal Church". To the Editor of the Leighton Buzzard Observer.

Sir, - "Delta" criticises so kindly that I beg a small space to explain, and throw light on what I may have left obscure. When I speak of a Catholic Church, I refer to the model before Constantine turned it into a Roman Catholic hierarchy. Then "Pope, presbyter, and priest" began to rule, and, "dressed in a little brief authority, they have, through the ages, played tricks to make the angels weep." Whether the simple elements of the Universal Church may ever predominate, with "delta," I am in doubt. Pay, patronage, and power, are so fascinating with the pulpit that, whether it be in a village Bethel or in Rome's St. Peter's, the possessor holds with the keenest tenacity to his pulpit privilege to curse by bell, book, and candle; and, in the spirit of persecution –

"Deal damnation round the land

On each I deem thy foe."

Instead of an open-eyed gate upon the ruin of the world by sin, and the remedy by Christ, in the dissemination of which we might all unite, we squint down the marrowbone of sect, limit the limitless, array a dogma against the divine command of "Whosoever will let him come," and, with the Pope in the stomach, man blights and blasts many a fair field, while Imperial persecution, "doing God service," may desolate peoples. Will Christians ever return to the Church Original? I close with "Delta's" excellent words and home question to all Christians, "Our Lord prayed that his people might be one. Are we all acting according to the spirit of that power?" These are suggestive words; make them *practical*, and a long step is made toward the Catholic and Universal Church.

Yours obediently, George Castleden, Woburn, December 1st, 1882.

19th December 1882 Leighton Buzzard Observer

To the Editor of the Leighton Buzzard Observer

Sir, - In your column I asked a rev. Gentleman to ingeniously define his Catholic and Universal Church. By another clergyman Nonconformists were asked to define a State Church. I would avoid disputation, neither would I venture upon another's vocations; but, approving much of the Rev. F. A. Adam's words: - "Friendly controversy, if the aim be simply to elicit the truth, and to disentangle it from report and prejudice, is highly serviceable," I gratefully adopt these sentiments, and beg to ask what his own opinion may be of a State Church? If it to be the Apostolic, Catholic, or Universal Church, a solution will be given to one of life's problems, and, dwelling long on and among the flats of Bedfordshire, my wits will be sharpened relative to Christ's spiritual headship and man's secular supremacy. If Constantine, meaning well, turned the "Catholic" into the *Roman* Catholic Church, might not Henry VIII., with other motives, found a Protestant Church, having in it all the elements of Christ's gospel, yet, by ignoring Christ's words - "My Church is *not* of this world," place an insuperable obstacle in the way of those who think and say –

"Let Caesar's due be ever paid

To Caesar and his throne,

But conscience and souls were made

To be the Lord's alone?"

If these questions are granite nuts to crack, perhaps our best refuge may be in – "The past is!". And, while as Nonconformists we hold our own, we will be neither foes nor invaders of an Established Church's secularities, so long as her supremacies coerce not the sacred rights of conscience, or, by persecution, invade and attack our civil and religious liberty.

As a friendly Nonconformist, I am, sir, yours obediently, George Castleden. Woburn, 13th Dec. 1882.

20th February 1883 Leighton Buzzard Observer

Woburn – A Good Deed. – In 1804, by good men, was founded the "Sick Man's Friend Society." It has overcome early difficulties, and now this unsectarian, catholic society stands healthy in its funds; and, so long as "the ills to which flesh is heir," and sorrows, the heritage of humanity, afflict, so long it may be hoped friends will rise up to mitigate and help. The visitors at their monthly meeting were gratified much by the secretary announcing an anonymous gift of £5: and, in directing the return of their warm thanks, regretted that such unobtrusive generosity, according to the donor's desire, must be nameless. However, with the kindly aid of the past, given by friends departed, it is now in the fund which has administered Samaritan aid among our cottagers for many a year. And, as a last thought from the oldest name left, begun in a right spirit, the hope may be indulged that the spirit may ever govern the operations of this society in the future Woburn generations.

The row about Charles Bradlaugh M.P. refusing to take an Oath in Parliament rumbled on. A Bill was put forward to allow him to take an Affirmation instead was defeated in 1883.

20th March 1883 Leighton Buzzard Observer

To the Editor of the Leighton Buzzard Observer

Sir, - The right of petition is one of our most cherished rights. A Woburn petition against the Affirmation Bill moves thought, and surely the Press will allow the reasons of one for not signing. All my life repudiating religious tests, I could not, at sunset, sign for that which, as a religious test, debars or excludes. I say solemnly in aiding an Affirmation Bill I have no sympathy with Atheism, nor do I invade the sacredness of God. To charge this, because I would prevent legislative despotism and Parliamentary hypocrisy, is too bad. Tests our fathers were persecuted with, when the sacramental one excluded from place, power, and patronage. Our friends the Quakers knew long their injury; and, when Lord John Russell removed the last from the Jews we thought this civil injury and injustice was consigned to the limbo of intolerant things. Knowing the persecuting nature of religious tests in the past, let us have no Star Chamber attempt of smuggling in the present; and, amongst Tory denunciation and bigot accusation, let Liberals do a civil duty, heedless of a scare which assumes the features of another theological test. Northampton has chosen its representative; secure him by affirmation; and then leave them with conscience; otherwise you invite the solemn mockery which a test protects; and you may sanction a senatorial lie which an oath covers. Hear the other side.

Your obedient servant, George Castleden.

17th April 1883 Leighton Buzzard Observer

To the Editor of the Leighton Buzzard Observer

Sir, - Reading "Mr. Smith to the Right Hon. W. E. Gladstone," I give the last words of this letter, in order to add a few thoughts written *before* on parish management: - "I have been guardian for forty-five years, and have done all I could to prevent a reckless expenditure, *yet it has kept creeping on*." Sitting in our Hall at the Lady-day meeting, I was struck with the unsatisfactory results. My own view of this meeting of ratepayers was that it only put the train on the legal line, giving sole and whole control to officials for another year. When the ratepayers abdicated their vestry duty, they were relieved also of the responsibility of ordering, but the privilege was continued to them of *paying*. Perhaps this helps Mr. Smith's "creeping on." And when I heard the wail about our dust-laying cart, I said, would our fathers, in a monthly meeting, have so generously downed with the dust, say, £75? Examine this Woburn Town Hall fact, and it may echo the truth that cash is best in the hands of the ratepayers. One thing seems proved at these Lady-day meetings – namely, that officials easily operate on the pockets of payers not vastly pleased nor satisfied by the exaction. Two noble Lords – Salisbury and Rosebery – touch this topic. Would that their counsel showed to the ratepayers the policy – aye, necessity – of putting their shoulder to the wheel before invoking some Parliamentary or country Jupiter! In the relinquishing of "vestry" inquiry and inspection, neither landlords nor tenants have benefitted, and in the delegation of the duty to others, while enjoying the dance, they have the felicity of paying the piper. Perhaps this fable may teach when truth fails. This is my reason for troubling the Press on "local rates."

Yours obediently, G. Castleden, Woburn, 6th March 1883.

24th July 1883 Leighton Buzzard Observer

Ireland. - Its Troubles. To the Editor of the Leighton Buzzard Observer.

Sir, - I must not intrude between Mr. Franklin and his opponents, neither do I venture to solve the enigma of Irish politics; but after reading the Observer I read *Christian Globe*, and in an article this passage struck, and, as I should like to put Messrs. Franklin and Co. All right in the controversy, I ask you to assist by inserting the extract in your next: - "It is a changed world, and the problem which confronts us in Ireland is essentially a social one, with which politics have little or no concern. Let sophists argue as they will, it is hopeless to dream that a country can ever be truly loyal in which the mass of the people can barely support the burden of their wretched lives, and in their penury are driven to eating boiled seaweed and the very grass by the roadside. Can Mr. Parnell suggest a remedy for this?"

A loyal nation dining on seaweed,

Would prove attachment very green indeed;

To shout or bray its thanks on roadside grass
Would prove the nature of the patient ass,
And bid the United Kingdom to prepare
For angel's food, or else chameleon fare.
Your obedient servant, George Castleden. 2nd July.

...and that is the last letter I can locate from Castleden to any newspaper, fittingly on the same subject as one of his first in 1847, although that sadly shows how little had changed in that problem. Ill-health possibly prevented him from writing more, I do not know. He was now 79 years of age, quite an achievement for the time, but Edward Franklin still managed to have the last word in the Press:

31st July 1883 Leighton Buzzard Observer

Ireland. Its Troubles. To the Editor of the Leighton Buzzard Observer.

I have no wish to resist the intrusion of Mr. Castleden whatever. In the true spirit of *real Liberalism* I say at once he is entitled to hold and express his opinion on all public questions; but when such a veteran as he can make no better defence for the Gladstonian treatment of "Ireland and its Troubles" than to suggest that, after all, the Irish problem is a *social* and not a *political* question, I am justified in concluding that not only does he admit that the "Gladstonian treatment" *is a failure*, but that, in the natural order of true logic, it was doomed to failure from the fact that, where a social remedy was required the Grand Old Man, after Mr. Castleden's heart, has been persistently blundering from the first by applying "political plasters" without number. No Conservative could more fitly demonstrate the "political quackery" of a Grand Old Man, who (if Mr. Castleden's latest doctrine be correct) must indeed have proved himself, on this "Irish problem," a Grand Old Muddler. That a veteran Liberal can do no better now for Mr. Gladstone than this must, I think, sufficiently account for the absolute silence of those "lesser lights" of Liberalism in this neighbourhood whom Mr. Castleden designates as "my opponents." Like the "early cloud and morning dew," they are now nowhere to be found. But, sir, the electors of this county and country will have to pass a judgement on many other of Mr. Gladstone's "muddles." What, for instance, of his latest – the Suez Canal agreement; an agreement which even such a grand financial personage as he cannot get the country to *agree with*. Lest, however, he and his Cabinet get drowned in the water of a Suez Canal, he *drops* his agreement in haste, and makes for the shore of office, to continue to enjoy the "loaves and fishes" provided by a faithful country, whose business he thus disastrously mismanages. What "keen penetration," splendid "sagacity," and eminent "statesmanship" is here exhibited, compared especially with the "profitable bargain" made by the late Lord Beaconsfield in the Suez Canal shares.

Yours truly, Edward Franklin, July 20th, 1883.

Yet Castleden remained well enough to publish one more booklet of his poetry, in February 1884, possibly called "Sunset Rays", a fitting last title to his canon of work.

In the 22nd July 1884 Leighton Buzzard Observer, there is a long report on the 40th anniversary of the Rev. James Andrews' pastorate at Woburn Independent Chapel. There was a public tea in the newly-refurbished Town Hall, and a public collection had raised just under £200 for him. Castleden is mentioned as having received a £1. 1s. donation towards the collection from Mrs. Catherine Beard, formerly Miss Gascoyne, "...well known in this town...", who was now the wife of a clergyman. No other mention is made of Castleden as having been part of the celebrations. Was he now too frail to attend? The end was nigh.

9th September 1884 Leighton Buzzard Observer

The public will learn with regret of the death of our own old townsman, Mr. G. Castleden, in his eightieth year. The deceased will be remembered as the author of many poetical effusions. For many years Mr. Castleden took an active part in the management of the schools in connection with the Independent Chapel of this town, and Sheep Lane. His death took place on Monday last, Sept 1st, and the funeral on Friday.

16th September 1884 Leighton Buzzard Observer

The Late Mr. Castleden was buried in the Baptist Chapel on Friday, Sept. 5th. There were present Mr. Michael Castleden, nephew of the deceased; Mr. Horsham of Canterbury; Mr. and Mrs. Gooding, &c. Lord Charles Russell and Mr. George Russell, M.P., who were continual visitors on Mr. Castleden during his illness, were at the grave. There were also Miss Courtney and Miss Laws of Aspley Guise; Mr. Blundell., of Birchmoor; Mrs. Aikenhead, of Woburn Sands; Mr. Wilson, formerly of the Park Farm Office, Woburn; Mr. Sprague, steward Woburn Abbey and Mr. Mackie, of Woburn Abbey Gardens. There were a number of ladies and gentlemen of the town and locality; amongst the tradesmen were Mr. G. B. Clarke, Mr. Horton, Mr. Fisher, and others. Mr. Joseph Hill and Mr. William Hill, of Potsgrove, perhaps the oldest and most attached friends of the Castleden family, attended by invitation. The funeral was conducted by Mr. Mackay. The coffin was of

WOBURN PARK,

A FRAGMENT

IN RURAL RHYME.

"Go little book,—
I cast thee on the waters—go thy ways!"

WOBURN :

PRINTED AND PUBLISHED BY S. DODD.

1839.

31: Frontispiece from Castleden's first work, "Woburn Park", published in 1839.

polished oak, and made by Mr. George Woodstock, a friend of the deceased gentleman. The Rev. James Andrews, minister of the chapel, officiated. Mr. Castleden was the only surviving son of the Rev. Michael Castleden, who was for a long term of his life a most popular preacher and a renowned classical scholar. His pulpit is now occupied by a gentleman no less an ornament to society. Mr. George Castleden died at the same age as his father (79). In early life he was an inveterate cricketer, and when Woburn was famous for its successful eleven, Lord Charles Russell, who stood at the grave, was one of the foremost men. Mr. Castleden was the author of many little volumes of local poetry. His father was a staunch supporter of the House of Russell, and perhaps the two members of that house who stood at his son's grave are the truest representatives of the family of the past.

23rd September 1884 Leighton Buzzard Observer

George Street, Woburn - Messrs. Cumberland and Hopkins are favoured with instructions from the Executor of the late Mr. George Castleden to sell by auction on Monday 29thSeptember 1884 at Twelve o'clock, the whole of the antique and useful Household Furniture, Library of about 800 vols., and effects, consisting of a mahogany and oak dining and occasional tables; Pianoforte by Warnum; Chippendale chairs, easy ditto, in mahogany, walnut and cane; antique bureau, with book case, secret drawers, etc.; book-cases, weather glass, Brussels and other carpets, carved mahogany sofa, in hair; mahogany and other bedsteads, feather beds, mahogany pedestals and wash stands, chest of drawers, toilet glasses, oil paintings, old engravings, crockery, the usual kitchen utensils, and a miscellaneous assortment of useful and curious items. May be viewed on the morning of the sale, and catalogues had at the Bedford Arms Hotel, Woburn, at the place of sale; and of Auctioneers High Street, Leighton Buzzard.

A library of 800 books! I wonder what eclectic local treasures he had collected together? It was to be 15 years before his name appeared in local newspaper columns again.

29th December 1899 Bedfordshire Times

Local Topics - Here is another little old book, printed and published by S. Dodd, Woburn, 1839, entitled "Woburn Park, a fragment in rural rhyme." The anonymous author puts on the title page –

"Go, little book –

I cast thee on the waters – go thy ways."

After sixty years this little book reached my hands with the leaves uncut.

Such is fame! Let us look at it. There is an elaborate dedication to one, Michael Castleden, and then an address to the "Courteous Reader" who is asked to look upon this little production with a favouring eye, to examine not according to the critic's craft, and know that its composition has whiled away many an hour. On the next page appears the following "quatrain": -

My own dear Park, be thou my song!
Thy many hallowed spots
Will bloom afresh on memory's waste,
And grateful fragrance yield.

Such is the theme of Canto I. The poet is an enthusiastic cricketer and he devotes Canto II to the game. For example –

Now for our game – my muse take wing
"Arms and the men," I fain would sing!
And though the critic open his eyes
And stare with wonder and surprise,
To see I quote, on such a theme,
Old Virgil's line; and to be just,
Bestows on it supreme disgust!
Yet I proceed, and sure 'tis plain,
To attempt to play "the noble game"
Without both men and arms is vain.

Concerning these touching lines the critic would humbly observe that he humour and the rhyme are alike sublime. We will get our sporting editor to quote some more when the County Club plays in Woburn Park. Canto III sings of Woburn Abbey and its magnificence, the sculptures and the historical associations, with tributes to John Locke and Lord Erskine, Fox, Lord Holland, Lord Grey, Lord William Russell, and the noble Duke. Here, of course, the poet's swelling rapture outstrips the feeble possibilities of the English tongue. He confesses himself beaten, and says –

Unequal to the task, I feint,
Nobility like this to paint;
'Twill shine amidst heraldic blaze,
The brightest line of sculptured praise.

But at least one person still had personal memories of the Castleden family:

12ᵗʰ January 1900 Bedfordshire Times

Local Topics. An interesting note from Dr. J. Coombs throws light upon the authorship of the little old book of poetry on Woburn Park, referred to in these notes last week. Dr. Coombes says "It was written by George Castleden, a man of some literary attainments, and dedicated to his father, the Rev. Michael Castleden, congregational minister at Woburn, a man highly esteemed and a very good preacher. He had a fine and powerful voice, and once recited to me in a very impressive manner, Addison's Universal Prayer, 'Father of all in every age,' etc. I knew son and father intimately, and the latter was a frequent guest at my house half a century ago."

*In the **2nd November 1906** Bedfordshire Times, there is report of the death of Miss Florence Tyers, who had a "...brilliant reputation as a pianist of a high order, and she was also an accomplished executants on the harp." She had studied under Miss Harrison at Leighton House, Woburn, before going to the Royal Academy. Locally, she performed with her brother and father, and it mentions that her talent was eulogised by "the famous Woburn poet, George Castleden." She later taught music to the children of local well-to-do families.*

The next gap is much longer. Nearly sixty years after his death, and deep into World War Two, his description of a new, and quite unsporting (to him...), type of cricket bowling, from his first book, was found interesting enough to fill some column inches again.

6th February 1942 Bedfordshire Times

An early Victorian poet named George Castleden who recalls a happy childhood and youth under the beneficent shade of the Abbey (it appears he was afterwards employed, greatly to his pleasure, as a "Clerk of Works" there), apostrophizes cricket in his book of poems, "Woburn Park", printed and published by S. Dodd, at Woburn in 1839. In artless, pleasing couplets he celebrates the prowess of the Woburn cricketers who flourished under the ducal patronage and on the beautiful ground in the Park. His description of the game is nearly as spirited as, and considerably more faithful to detail than, Dickens's picture of the memorable match between Dingley Dell and All-Muggleton.

Alluding to the new and fearsome styles of bowling then coming into vogue, the poet observes:

"These *twisting* balls are all the go,
Our ancient sort we seldom know.
I think this cricket innovation
Produces bile and altercation
'Tis oft a question, to divine

32: *Woburn chapel is just left of centre in the distance of this postcard, used in 1909.*

33: *Woburn Market House and High Street, showing Dodd & Peeling's shopfront, printers of Castleden's early works. From Parry's book, "Woburn and its Abbey", published 1831.*

The ball that's pitched within the line
And 'stead of bowling, jerking may
Become the order of the day!"

He advises the batsmen to step aside from these insidious wide-pitching balls, to "resist temptation and not yield, and hit them not up to please the field", but,

"Tire well the bowler, then make play
And drive the 'twisters' far away!"

Out of all his books, letters and poems, I think he would have been pleased that it was the honourable game of cricket that had caused his name to appear again.

In the **Summer 1960** *Bedfordshire Magazine, H. G. Tibbutt wrote "A Woburn Story", giving the history of the Congregational Chapel and ministers at Woburn. A contemporary photo of the Chapel is included, showing it in a very dilapidated state, as it had looked the year before, but explains that since then, it had been taken on as a studio by artist Derrick Greaves, and had been made watertight again. It also mentions that the Memorial Tablet to Michael Castleden had been taken down and (it was hoped) would be transferred to Hockliffe Chapel. The Revs. Samuel Greathead and James Andrews are pictured, but I know of no pictures of Rev. Michael Castleden or George. Tibbutt connected the Woburn Castleden's to a branch of their family in Canterbury, and had, at that time, access to a family diary, which has eluded me. It recorded that George Castleden had been to Canterbury to see them in 1847 and 1848.*

The Bedfordshire Magazine of **Autumn 1967** *contains Faint Pencillings of the Bedfordshire Scene, an article by L. R. Conisbee, on Bedfordshire writers. Alas! he was not a Castleden fan, as his entry for Castleden in "A Bedfordshire Bibliography" of 1962 shows. In comparing the second edition of Castleden's "Woburn Park" with the first, he says, "the former octosyllabics are stretched to heroic measure". For his Bedfordshire Magazine article, after discussing three other local scribes, he says:*
"Much earlier than the preceding trio, flourished (if that is the right word) George Castleden of Woburn, son of the pastor at the Congregational church of that place. The last of his three little volumes, "completing the series Woburn Park and Conscience,' bears the title Retribution: Loyal Lyrics and Fugitive Pieces and was published at London in 1843 with a dedication, properly humble, to Lord and Lady Charles Russell. The rather grim titles of numbers two and three are those of 'historical' poems in the collections and have no personal bearing. Woburn Park, the best known,

exists in two versions, of 1839 and 1841. In the second the octosyllabics have been extended to pentameter couplets, probably to give more value for money. At its best Castleden's verse is sad stuff, hardly worth consideration. He found it difficult to leave the subject of 'dear Woburn Park', and the great to-do in July 1841 when Queen Victoria and the Prince Consort visited the Abbey and gave him a splendid excuse to return yet again:

'Good-bye' I've said again, but surely NOW

I e'en may break my rhyming vow,

Attune again my lyre:

Genius of song! I thee invoke,

I sweep the strings, my muse provoke,

Infuse poetic fire.

(The provoked muse of George Castleden is an awesome thing to contemplate.)

A Loyal Ode, sung at the West Front of Woburn Abbey; on the night of July 26th 1841 (before the Queen and the Prince Consort) must have convinced the most rabid republican of what Royalty has to endure in the path of duty:

Now, let the Welkin ring

While Woburn minstrels sing

Their loyal theme...

I hope that, despite the limitations and repetitions of his subject matter, you have enjoyed George Castleden's letters and poems, and do not consider them, as Conisbee did, just "...sad stuff, hardly worth consideration". His viewpoints on the news of the day, and snapshots of life in bygone Woburn and locale, are a unique record of the time.

Published Works

Castleden's first three books were printed in hardback, but his later works were softcover booklets, probably printed in very small numbers. These were of a very fragile construction, and none have survived to come up for sale in recent years. Therefore surviving works are available for consultation at a variety of archives, some of which require advance notice or membership to permit access. After each entry below is an indication of where the books can be seen. My repeated visits to the British Library to consult those available there has at least resulted in some of them being scanned and made available on Google Books!

The only trace of some titles are where they appear in the lists of his previous works advertised on the rear covers of later ones. As these lists appear to be in basic chronological order, a rough date of when they appeared can be estimated.

Woburn Park - A Fragment in Rural Rhyme, published 1839, by Stephen Dodd, Woburn.

Published anonymously, but dedicated to the author's father, Michael Castleden. This first book became part of a trilogy with the next two. A second edition was published in 1840. It is divided into three parts: *Early Days &c.*, *Cricket*, and *Woburn Abbey &c.* In the front is part of a quote from poet Robert Southey, "*Go, little book! I cast thee on the waters, go thy ways*". The "Final Note" is dated 24th December 1839. Author's copy of this book contains the rubber-stamped name "H. Pikesley", one of the well-known tradesmen of that period in Woburn Sands.

Christies of London sold a copy of the first edition of Woburn Park, in their Sporting Memorabilia sale, in November 2006. It was inscribed, "Mastr. O. Hooley, A present from his affectionate friend, K. S. Castleden, 27 Nov. 1862".

[British Library] [Google Books online]

Loyal Lyrics, Loyal Ode, & Fairy Song, c.1841. William Croft, Woburn.

Although anonymous, *Loyal Lyrics* & *Loyal Ode* would seem to be the extra verses of lyrics he wrote to 'God Save The Queen', which were sung to Queen Victoria at Woburn Abbey. *Fairy Song* was a longer poem about the same visit. Printed as souvenirs of the event, on paper or silk.

[Woburn Abbey Archives]

Conscience: An Essay in Blank Verse, 1842, Thomas Ward & Co.

Again, published anonymously, this was dedicated to "The Public". The preface is dated March 1842. In three parts, *Supporting the Conscience*, *Conscience "Excusing"* and *Conscience "Accusing"*, Castleden's blank verse covers historical, local and moral arguments. Well annotated with what his sources were, this work also contains a list of subscribers who had bought "Woburn Park", and a notice that the next volume, "Retribution", was already in production. "Orders will be gratefully received by the Author, at the Rev. M. Castleden's, or by Mr Dodd, Post Office, Woburn. The price not to exceed 4s."

[British Library] [Google Books online] [Oxford University]

Retribution, Loyal Lyrics and Fugitive Pieces, 1843, Thomas Ward & Co.

Still publishing anonymously, this volume was dedicated to Lord and Lady Charles Russell. The 98-page first part, *Retribution*, weaves together King Henry VIII and Cromwell. The second two parts, *Loyal Lyrics* and *Fugitive Pieces*, focus on Royal and local subjects, as well as quirkier pieces, such as "*Goodbye to my Office Desk*". Includes an advertisement for his first two books, with "Woburn Park" now selling for 3s. and "Conscience ..." for 2s. 6d. Authors copy of the book is inscribed from Castleden to Hannah Reynolds.

[British Library] [Cambridge University] [Google Books online]

Lays of Home, 1850-51, Partridge & Oakey.

Consisting of the following three volumes of poetry, each focusing on a different aspects of everyday Woburn life. Apparently originally published separately, the versions in the British Library collection have been bound together into one composite volume.

[British Library] [Google Books online]

Lays of Home 1 - Our "Inns" now "Out", 1850, Partridge & Oakey.

Printed by William Tyler, of Bolt Court, London. 9d. Preface dated 22nd February, 1850. Decries the closure and loss of four ancient coaching inns of Woburn (e.g. The White Bear, The Goat, The Windmill and The Cock) due to the coming of the railways and loss of passing trade. Some of the coaches coming through Woburn are listed. ('The Rocket', 'The Defiance', 'The Umpire' and 'The Courier') Castleden says that in 24 hours, 30 coaches and three mail coaches would pass through the town. Also describes the local

Book Society, founded in 1796, that operated from The Coach and Horses, Woburn. There are poems on the new electric telegraph and electric power. At the start of his next work, Castleden reprints some correspondence with "The Nonconformist" from April (1850?) after they reviewed this work and said it would amuse local readers but was the complete opposite of Goldsmith's renowned poem, "The Deserted Village", much to Castleden's indignation.

Lays of Home 2 - Our Market houses, Old and New, 1851, Partridge & Oakey.

Printed by William Tyler, Bolt Court, London. Contents are: "*Woburn's Long - Past (Birchmore) - Its Modern-Past - Our Old Market-House - "The Pitching," Chandlery, Barber's Shop, Etc., Of Bygone Time. - Its Park Street Front. - The Old and New Market - Houses. - Fair - Day Revels. - The Riders. - The "Great Room." - The "Town Hall."-Theatricals. - The Town Hall's Opening Day. - Our Town Criers. - The Late French War; Our "Rank and File." - Our Old Market-House "Behind." - The Old Pump, Cage, Etc. - Back lane; Its Long Inhabitant. - The Bull-Ring. - Closing Lines. - Notes.*" Beside the local contents of the poems, there are also long notes to the text, describing local events and people, and examples of speakers who had performed in the Market Hall, such as Charles Kean, in 1820-5 and Joseph Lancaster in 1806-7.

[National Library of Spain - Europeana online, from a copy given to Luis de Usoz y Rio, a friend of Benjamin Wiffen of Aspley Guise]

Lays of Home 3 - A Night Stroll in the Churchyard and Our Chapel, 1851, Partridge & Oakey.

Printed by William Tyler, Bolt Court. Advertised in the "London Nonconformist", on Wednesday, November 12, 1851: "Lays of Home by George Castleden Woburn, Beds. No.3 contains *Our Church, a Night stroll in the Churchyard; Our Chapel* & c. Price 6d. London Partridge and Oakley Paternoster-row". Also includes poems & prose on the Great Exhibition at Crystal Palace. Ends with an advert for two essays in progress: Poetry with illustrations from Shakespears' "Seven Ages" and another entitled "Die to live!", illustrated by biographical references.

[Cambridge University] [National Library of Scotland] [Oxford University]

A Memorial of the Woburn Exhibition, 1854, Dodd & Peeling.

Notes on the 1853 Exhibition held in Woburn, on Science, Art, Literature, Nature etc., in 46 pages. A few poetical lines included, but generally a report and description. The exhibits included: two paintings by Landseer, a paper peep show from London's Exhibition, geology, a case of coins from 800 B.C., a microscope, an electricity generator, a bust of Lord John Russell, a bible written on roll of parchment, items connected to three Queens, an ants' nest made in a music book, a chronicle of Kings of England from 1448, some Waterloo battle relics, some Pompeii pottery, a model of Woburn's buildings, a box made from Old London Bridge wood, some Star coral, & a stone brought from Babylon.

[British Library]

See illustration on page 480.

Richard Cobden and Woburn Sands Primitive Methodist Chapel, 22 April 1865, Publisher?

Single page, folded, containing two poems, "*Rhyme recited at the Woburn Sands Primitive Methodist Chapel, 26th December 1864*", mentioning the Friends Meeting House and change of village name from 'Hogstyend' to 'Woburn Sands', and "*Cobden*" about Richard Cobden, an English manufacturer and radical Liberal statesman, associated with two major Free Trade campaigns, the Anti-Corn Law League and the Cobden-Chevalier Treaty. Unknown if this has been extracted from a larger work.

[West Sussex Record Office - ref. COBDEN/279]

Work: - Death!, 1865, Fisher

Printed by H. G. Fisher, Park Street, Woburn. Principle parts are: *Robert Hall: A Prose Study, Ridgmount* [Ridgmont] *Memories: A Rhyme Study, Tributary: Sir Joseph Paxton – Lord Palmerston*; and *Historical Verses* on Pitt, Fox, Canning, & Palmerston.

[Bedfordshire Heritage Library]

Rambles, Etc., A Welwyn Memory, A Northamptonshire Rhyme, Rambler's Rhyme, Moses, Summer and Autumn, A Pleasant Dream and Word Acrostics

All eight of these titles had all appeared before 1870. Nothing further is known about them.

Drink, Music & Dancing, 1870, Fisher

Printed by H. G. Fisher, High Street, Woburn & C A Bartlett, Stationers Hall Court, London. 9d (Gilt edged 1s.) Dedicated to his father on the

100th anniversary of his birth. Prefaced with a copy of the acknowledgment received from Balmoral for receipt of his book "*Words*" which he had sent to Queen Victoria in 1869. The first treatise, an anti-alcohol prose on '*Drink*', prompted by the death of two friends, is turned into the acrostic: *D*elirium *T*remens; *R*uin; *I*niquity; *N*ight; *K*idnapping. The next essay, on music and dancing, is a celebration, with strong moral themes, starting with a note that it was 50 years since he started working at the Bedford Estate Office. Lines are included from a friend to whom he has sent 'Words No.2'. He mentions being under the spell of drink and gambling in the 1820's, and how he had sought employment in London, which he realises now would have been his undoing. Ends with poems on "*Three Notable Events in One November week*" [from 1869]: the new Blackfriars Bridge & Holborn Viaduct opened by Queen Victoria, The Marquises of Lansdowne and Blandford were both married, and the funeral of George Peabody at Westminster Abbey. A poem on birth of Prince of Wales follows, and finally one about Castleden's own 65th birthday.

[British Library]

Naaman, A Home Thought, An Unkind Summer Relic, A New Year's Memory

These four titles had all appeared between 1870-1872. Nothing further known.

A Potsgrove Tract, 1872, Fisher

Printed by H.G. Fisher, High Street, Woburn. 3d. Subtitled "Fruit from an aged tree". 24 pages. Dedicated to 'peasant friends, John Fowler and others' at Sheeplane Union Chapel. Keyed by a recent storm on 7th August 1872, he asserts that all nature's wonders can be attributed to God. The second part is a poem written whilst sat in his brother's garden in Mile End, next door to the 'Bancroft Grounds'. One of his Christmas Carols ends the book, referencing many other local poets, and the revolutionary effects that steam had had on travel.

[British Library] [Google Books online]

Swallow Song

Appeared between 1872 and 1873. Nothing further known.

Home birds and words, 1873, Fisher

Published and printed by Fisher and Sons, Machine Printer, Park Street, Woburn. 6d (or 9d with gilt edges) Poems on spring, Queen Victoria's birthday and a long series on birdlife. Then local flowers, the statue of Bunyan in Bedford, the Woburn cricket team, the Royal portraits at St James Palace, and the Woburn graveyard.

[British Library] [Google Books online]

The Fall of Paris and Woburn Easter Memory

Both had appeared between 1873 and 1875. Nothing further known.

Sunday-school relic, Sheep lane last memory, Hockliffe, Loyal lyrics, 1875, Fisher

Printed by H. G. Fisher, High Street, Woburn. 32 pages of Woburn prose and rhyme. Poems on the Sunday school, Sheep Lane, Hockliffe and educational matters. Includes this "*Sale Verse*":

I seek not lucre, yet it may
Some friend will ask, What is to pay?"
Grateful I close a last goodbye
Sixpence, an' please my "fruit" then try.

[British Library] [Google Books online]

The End and the Beginning, 1875, Fisher

Printed at H. G. Fisher, High Street, Woburn. Subtitled "A Woburn New Years Tract". 6d. Prose and scattered verse on life and mortality. Then "*An African Rhyme*", and "*A Woburn Postman's Carol, 1874*", and some lines on the graves of his parents.

[British Library] [Google Books online]

London City Mission, Woburn Leaflet and Woburn Park Leaflet

These three had all appeared between 1875 and 1878. Nothing further known.

War, Esther, Sunsetting lyrics, 1878, Fisher

Printed by H. G. Fisher, High Street, Woburn. 1s. Prose, opens with a Longfellow quote. After a study on "*Birthday Thought*", "*War*" follows in three parts. "*Studies: Esther*" is next, in two parts, then "*Sunsetting Lyrics*" about Queen Victoria and Albert's birthdays, in four parts. Ends with some extracts from the Woburn Journal, Mass. USA, a George Washington acrostic, lines on the May Flower and a poem on Woburn Park.

[British Library] [Hughenden Manor - National Trust]

A September Leaflet

Appeared between 1878-1879. Nothing further known.

Joseph; a Scripture study joining 1859-1879 & The death Princess Alice, 1879, Fisher

Printed by H. G. Fisher, High Street, Woburn. 4d. Includes birthday poem to the American Abolitionist William Lloyd Garrison, born the same year as Castleden. Then a poem on his own birthday, the notes of which refer to his first drawing wages from the Duke of Bedford's Estate at Christmas 1819. "*Joseph's Forgiveness*" is c.20-pages of prose based on Genesis 1, c.15-26. The remainder is made up of poems and letters on the late Princess Alice, including the tolling of Woburn Bell for her passing.

[British Library]

An American Leaflet: a hand-in-hand grasp across the Atlantic by two G.C.'s, 1882, Fisher

Advertised in Leighton Buzzard Observer, 13 June, 1882: "A gracefully worded expression of the 'friendship, goodwill, and peace' which should govern the two great Anglo-Saxon nations." Nothing further known.

Unknown title, ("Sunset Rays"?) 1884, publisher unknown

Poems on "*Sunset Rays*", the Woburn Market House, the Town Hall, Lord Charles Russell's speech in Luton, "*A Verse or Two at Sunset*", (six verses…) Gladstone's Birthday, Death, and the Queens Highland Journal. It ends with a short essay on his writings and his devotion to Queen Victoria, obviously aware of his impending demise. The last part is entitled "*Home.*", and ends:

Go forth my little book, perform thy part –
Inform the mind, and educate the heart;
Then from the grave sweet echoes may arise
To linger, serve, and save 'neath natal skies;
A mystic gift above the worth of gold,
A spirit boon the price can ne'er be told.
Go forth then little book to follow men,
With last good wishes from George Castleden.
George Street, Woburn. 22ⁿᵈ February, 1884.

[Bedfordshire Archives & Records Service – incomplete photocopy only, ref. CRT 130 Wob56]

Appendix 1

Rev. Michael Castleden's Letters

Letters from George's father, the Rev. M. Castleden, to the Monthly Magazine

March 1816 Monthly Magazine

To the Editor of the Monthly Magazine.

Sir, As we are, in our day, hearing a great deal on the subject of "divine right," and "legitimacy of sovereigns," – very pretty subjects, by the way, for Englishmen and the present family; so of course, as the priesthood gain ground in France, towards which there are at this moment making rapid strides, in their old way of persecution and blood, we shall hear from them also, of their divine right and legitimacy placed beyond all doubt, by, what they are pleased to denominate, "uninterrupted succession," and to which other churches, as well as Rome, wish to lay claim. Among many evidences of the futility of this famous succession of the Roman clergy, I beg leave to forward to you, that it may stand recorded in your Magazine for the benefit of your readers, the account we have of that noted lady, *Pope Joan*. What an interruption to the succession was this! What a fatal breaking of the chain is here? I extract it from the work of a celebrated clergy man of the Church of England.

I here insert, says this divine, the following extract, copied verbatim, by my own hand, from the scarce and curious old book, entitled, "The Nuremburgh Chronicle;" which was printed at Nuremburgh, 1493, in a popish city, by popish printers, and compiled by popish hands, no less than twenty-four years before the reformation by Luther.

[Latin version excluded] Translation: "John, of English descent, but said to have been born at Mentz, obtained the Popedom by sinister arts; for, she palmed herself upon the world as a man, when, in reality, she was a woman. In her youth, she accompanied a learned lover of hers to Athens; and there, by attending the lectures of the best literary professors, she made so great a progress in erudition, that, on her arrival in Rome, she had few equals, and no superiors, in all kinds of theological knowledge. By her learned lectures, and by her masterly deputations, she acquired so much esteem and authority, that, on the death of Leo, she was, by universal consent, (as

Martinius confirms,) created Pope. Some time after her elevation to the pontifical dignity, she became criminally familiar with one of her domestics, and pregnancy was the consequence. She took care, by every precaution, to conceal this circumstance, as long as possible; until, at last, as she was walking (in public procession) to the Lateran church, (in Rome,) she was seized with labour-pains, and brought forth her infant, in that part of the street which lies between the theatre and the church of St. Clement. She died on the spot; having held the Popedom two years, one month, and four days. Some writers affirm, that, to this very day, whenever the Pope walks in procession to the Lateran church, he constantly goes thither by another way, to avoid reviving the memory of the above mentioned detestable event; and that, in order to prevent a similar imposition, (that is, in order that the infallible church may not again mistake the sex of her popes,) the newly elected Pontiff is properly examined by the junior deacon, at the time of his holiness's first enthronement in St Peter's chair; the seat whereof is perforated for that purpose."

This said Mrs. Joan (who called herself John VIII.) was successor in the Popedom to Leo IV., who died A.D.855; and she, herself, was succeeded by Benedict III. Was not this pope, at least, the "whore of Babylon?"

Michael Castleden, Woburn, Dec.1, 1815.

The Rev. Castleden was not alone in believing this far-fetched story, and it was popular from the 13th to 16th centuries, but is now accepted as a fictional story.

After several earlier letters, discussing the suitability of various methods in paving London's streets, a writer, who signed himself just as "J.M.L.", wrote a long letter to the Monthly Magazine in **December 1824**, *in which he expressed the hope that the various London paving boards would not take up "...the wild scheme of McAdamizing the streets of this metropolis..."and that they should "look before they leap into so manifest an absurdity". He objected to the taking up of nice granite pavements, breaking them up, and using the pieces in the new road-making process. He pointed out that although Mr. McAdam had said it worked very well in the country, the Kingsland Road, which has already undergone the McAdamizing treatment, was now full of holes which weren't there before. J.M.L. believed the new road surface would collect water and filth in the winter and be responsible for intolerable dust in the summer. He thought the loose stones would provide ammunition for mischievous boys or unruly mobs, and that it would hinder repair to sewers and gas pipes. He did not have a single positive word for McAdams scheme. The scathing indictment of McAdam's system prompted a reply from a W. Castleden, of Woburn, Bedfordshire, certainly a misprint for M. Castleden.*

492

January 1825 Monthly Magazine

To the Editor of the Monthly Magazine.

Sir: According to your invitation in p.413 of your Magazine for this month, I cheerfully forward you my mite of contribution, on the new roadsmaking, or McAdamizing system. J.M.L.'s, echoing animadversion, on the statement of Mr. McAdam's finding the plan answer well in the country, "That he finds it answer well, there can be no doubt," I must say, understanding, as everybody must, the feeling which could dictate this repetition, that I am persuaded, whatever the little spirit of jealousy or envy may prompt to the detraction of such a man, posterity (human, and animal, if the latter could,) will unite to erect a monument to him, far more worthy of attraction than the Achilles of Hyde-park, with all the tears of the widow and fatherless which it records.

You must know, Mr. Editor, our little pleasant town of Woburn, within the last six months, has undergone the operation of McAdamizing. At first, some of my neighbours were grievously displeased that the good old large stones should be taken up and broken in pieces: stones, which one of the Dukes of Bedford, nearly a century ago, at his own expense, caused to be brought from that land of which Mr. McAdam is an ornament. On their removal, many, very many, hard words were uttered, and much clamour about "dust in summer, and mud in winter;" the only objections of any moment I have heard produced. Winter comes; and, sure enough, as it approached, we had mud in abundance, but good broad scrapers removed it to the sides, and then all was clean again. Then stages and waggons were in perpetual progress, and on the rains descending, their pressure brought up thick mud again. This being removed, another layer of the broken granite was thrown thinly on; and now, we have had no scraping, to the sides of the road, for nearly a month past: and though, so far as wet weather is concerned, we have had as much winter as we may reasonably expect, we have little more than a thin dirt on the surface, not deserving notice. All is hard and smooth, and carriages bowl along in a delightful style.

There is, Sir, one of your correspondents, whose name I am happy to see, in your pages of this month Mr. Farey. He knows Woburn, and the materials, round it, for road-making, well. To that gentleman, Woburn is much indebted for very many useful improvements, when he was steward under the late "Great Duke of Bedford." To Mr. F. we are obliged for our neat and commodious footpaths, begun and completed at no expense, I believe, but the mere labour. Not less useful is Mr. McAdam likely to be to us. May prosperity attend them both, and every improver of his country, whether he may excavate roads below, or cover them above!

And pray, Mr. Editor, can we have any roads without labour? or permanently good roads, without temporary inconvenience? You know well the metropolis, that place of my birth - what would be the condition of its streets, were it not for the constant employ of its scavengers? Now, only let us wait, and give the new system a fair trial; and I shall be much mistaken if, in all your London, as well as country streets, we have not less of dust to subdue, and mud to remove. For when, in summer, our watercarts come into action, the advantage of the new over the old roads and streets will be apparent; for as water falls on the granite dust, one of the strongest of cements, it will fill up the interstices, and bind, in one immovable mass, the small angular pieces below. Living, as I do, directly fronting the main street, being six yards across, the usual-width, I believe, of the McAdam roads in the country, I have watched its condition every day. You are aware, Sir, that Woburn is on the high-road to Manchester and Liverpool; consequently, we have great numbers of stage-coaches passing day and night - not less than twenty-four in the twenty-four hours. Now, as all these coaches, with great numbers of other carriages, have narrow wheels, it is notorious how adapted they are to cut through the hardest road, running, as they do, exactly on the same track; yet have we hardly the marks of the wheels, much less ruts, between here and Dunstable, although we had them so plentifully before.

Sincerely wishing, that, in every sense, we may all be in the practice of

34: Some coach traffic passes by Woburn Old Church, from a print published in 1844.

494

mending our ways, I am, Sir, a reader from the beginning of your useful magazine,

W. [sic] Castleden.

[The facts of this letter are valuable, as far as they go; and some obvious inferences may be drawn from them respecting the streets of London; but they do not meet all the objections of our correspondent, J.M.L. And again we invite attention to the *pro* and *con* of the *local* question. – Ed.]

1ˢᵗ **March, 1825** Monthly Magazine

To the Editor of the Monthly Magazine.

Sir: The letter inserted in your last number from Mr. Castleden, of Woburn, calls for some reply on my part; but before I come to that, I think it will be as well to state, that my letter, inserted in your Magazine published on the 1ˢᵗ of December last, and appearing to remark on one by S. W., that had been inserted in your number for November, was in fact written upwards of a year ago, and the letter which caused it, formed a part of the Monthly Magazine, published November 1, 1823. This, of course, your readers could not know; and as a change (or more than one) has taken place in the Editorship, possibly you did not know it yourself. I had, indeed, almost forgotten my letter on the Macadamizing system; and I only recur to the fact of its being written so long back, to shew that it might be very likely I should have one opinion of Macadamization in November 1823, and a very different one in November 1824. I say, it might be, for at the first period the system was little more than talked of in London, and had been adopted but in very few instances indeed. My letter was, therefore, entirely anticipatory; but it does not require any supernatural gift now, to see that the plan will not do well for the streets of London generally. Still it is something curious, that my year-old letter not only passed muster in the respectable pages of the Monthly Magazine, but, was also copied into some of the Morning papers from thence, as a letter written during the month of December last; so nearly did my presumption agree with the then state of the Macadamized streets of the metropolis.

So much for the time when my letter was written. And now, with regard to Mr. Castleden's opinion as to the feelings with which I remarked on Mr. Macadam, when I said, "That HE finds it answer well, there can be no doubt." I still think the same as to the country roads which he has made or mended; but as to some of his contracts for town streets, I fear he will eventually be a loser; for he will find them swallow up more granite than he expected. It is a trite remark to say, "Save me from my friends;" and I think Mr. Macadam may say this of Mr. Castleden: for, as he has pressed the question, I will ask any thinking man, whether the former has or has not found this thing answer well, when he knows that he had some thousands voted to him by parliament, to repay him what he had expended in posting over England, &c., for the sole purpose of looking to, and mending, our ways. If he did spend so much in posting, and I really cannot say he did not, he is certainly the most Quixotic north-country gentleman that ever travelled so far south, - and the luckiest, to have got it so repaid to him. Still I beg to assure Mr. Castleden, and all whom it may concern, that it is neither "jealousy" nor "envy," towards Mr. Macadam, that ever led me to make one remark, either on him or his plan. So far from it, that I say, in my former letter, it is excellent in the country and I even admit, that in some parts of the metropolis it may do very well.

It may not be improper here to state, that I am a commissioner of pavements, in a large and important parish of Westminster, where a considerable part of the inhabitants are not overburdened with riches, and who think themselves sufficiently loaded with rates and taxes; and I certainly did feel, when the first great "hue and cry" was raised some time back, about the wonderful Macadam and his plans, that I, as well as every other man placed in my situation, as guardians of the funds of our neighbours, raised for a particular purpose, ought not to yield to the first impulse of clamour in favour of a scheme that was sure to be very expensive in its outset, and which I then thought, and still do think, likely to be very uncertain in its result. Yet there were not wanting some at the board of which I am a member, who were for plunging into the fashion of the day, and trying the Macadamization of some of our streets, at once. I certainly opposed anything like an early adoption of it; my motto was at least a safe one, "Wait", and after having done so for one year, I still say, "Wait" for the thing, as to its succeeding in London, is by no means proved. About the time I mention, S. W's letter appeared in the Monthly, and being an occasional correspondent of that work, I ventured to throw together my loose ideas on the subject, and really, nothing has happened since to shake them materially. Still it is very far from my desire to exclude improvement, especially where it is said it can be had cheaper. I am therefore still waiting for conviction, while the roads are left for execution.

I was more than a little pleased to see, in a note, and in the postscript to Mr. Farey's valuable letter in your last number, a remark or two that bear upon the point in question; and, in my estimation, coming from a mind so capable of well appreciating this matter, these are worth more than all the clamour that there has been, or may be, about it; and, inasmuch as they uphold opinions which I have formed, and publicly expressed, are gratifying. It is also singular, that Mr. Castleden, who is angry with me for what I have said, has given us an eulogium on Mr. Farey, with every word of which I most cordially agree, though, unfortunately, that individual seems decidedly opposed to him in his views of Mr. Macadam, and his said-to-be new invention.

In my first letter I said, "The breaking of stones to form roads is no new thing" in this, Mr. Farey completely bears me out, by his forcible remark in the note above mentioned; where he says, that it has been a practice "of thirty or forty years' standing, and pursued as long by scores of roadmakers, from whom this good practice has been borrowed; yet the public mistakenly lavishes its praises and emoluments on an individual, as being its inventor. So much for its novelty; and now for Mr. Farey's other idea, that of the illegality of 'breaking up the pavements to make roads: I agree with him in thinking it illegal, and not at all within Mr. Michael Angelo Taylor's act, nor any local act that I am acquainted with; yet, in saying this, Mr. Farey must not consider it as coming from a legal man, but from one who considers plain common sense to be as able to understand such a matter as most lawyers. M. A. Taylor's act is a terribly voluminous one, but there is nothing in it, which I am aware of, capable of being construed into an empowering of commissioners to turn streets into roads; the commissioners are' empowered to pave and repair; and the only words that could in any way be strained at all towards such a meaning, are "other materials;" but which are used thus, when the pavements, &c. &c. are vested in the respective commissioners of parishes "And also, that all and every the pavements, stones, posts, and other materials, which now are, or which may be hereafter, placed in the foot or carriageways, &c." and the same words are afterwards used repeatedly, but always in the same general way. How far commissioners may be subject to indictments or criminal informations for their acts, I must leave to someone better learned in the law to decide; but I think it will be found that they are personally irresponsible, and that the parish, as a body, would have to defend them: but I do think, what Mr. Farey suggests about an appeal against the paving-rate, if so misapplied, would be very likely to succeed, at least under the general act; for it is not unlikely, that in some of the local acts it may be different; and they are all expressly excepted in M.A. Taylor's act; and in local acts certain estates are very frequently excepted, as, for instance, in that for the parish of St. Clement Danes, assed the 23d of Geo. III; Clare-market, then the property of the Duke of Newcastle; and certain approaches to wharfs, then the property of William Kitchener, Esq., progenitor of the present celebrated Dr. Kitchener, were expressly exempted from its operation, an continue to be so to this day.

In trying the few streets they have on the new plan, the corporation of the City of London have acted wisely, and it is to be hoped they will give the thing a fair trial; but one thing should not be forgotten by the managers of other laces, which is, that the commissioners tor whatever they are called) in the city, have the whole of its paving fund: at their disposal, and are not, as is the case in Westminster, confined to parochial districts; consequently, if it eventually should not succeed, the burthen will be light, in comparison of what it would be in a single parish. It is to be hoped, that very correct accounts will be kept of the expense of the tried streets for some given portion of time, say three years, so as to enable other parishes and places to avail themselves of such information; and in doing this, I trust the value of the pavement taken up and broken will not be forgotten; for at present I do not think that is much thought of, and yet it forms a large part of the expense.

As my letter has already stretched to a greater length than I at first intended it should do, and as I do not wish to give what I think a falling system a greater impetus in the present opinion of the public than it has already, some would-be wits even calling it Muckadamization, I will just conclude with remarking on Mr. Castleden's letter respecting the town of Woburn, that I think, as far as he wishes to compare the Macadainization of that place with the same thing in the metropolis, it is like a parody without parity; and really, it is impossible to help smiling, when he speaks of the enormous quantity of stage-coaches which pass through Woburn, "not less than twenty four in the twenty-four hours!" Let him stand on Blackfriars-bridge (and our metropolitan bridges are the places where I expected the system to succeed) for ten minutes, during almost any time of the day, and though he may not see twenty-four stage-coaches, he may see more than twice twenty-four carriages pass, and nearly all of them of a heavier description than stage-coaches, and many with as narrow wheels.

I am not at all surprised at Woburn being pleasanter in a Macadamized state, than with the old rumble-tumble pavement; I stated in my first letter, that it was the best plan for the country, and I here beg leave to repeat the same thing: but, after all, Mr. Editor, you are right, it is a local question, and as such it should be treated; and you act very properly in calling upon your correspondents to contribute their mites to the pro and con of it; though I must confess, that the scenes of mud we have had upon the Macadamized part of our streets, during the first part of the present winter, leave my mind, for the present, very much on the con side of the question.

Mr. Castleden appears to have some wish to erect a statue of brass to Mr. Macadam, that shall be more worthy of notice than even the celebrated Achilles, of Hyde-park notoriety. 'To this, of course, I can have no objection; but he seems to think that the animals would join in the work, if they could. Now, I rather doubt this; for if the newspapers are to be believed, very many valuable horse have been recently lamed by the sharp angles of the broken granite, but as I do not do the fact of my own knowledge, I lay no great stress on it but at the same time think it not improbable.

J. M. Lacey, January 10, 1825.

31ˢᵗ July, 1825 Monthly Magazine

To the Editor of the Monthly Magazine.

Sir, I regret that Mr. Lacey for a moment should think my remarks on his phrase "No doubt he (Mr Macadam makes a good thing of it." was written in anger to him, or anyone. No, sir: but at the time under a painful feeling of the reluctance in some minds to exceed the maxim well known and so happily expressed "Palmamquimeruitferat" [Let whoever earns the palm bear it]

I assure Mr Lacey, Mr Macadam is altogether unknown to me, save by his works. That our gentleman surveyors, as well as non-surveyors, of roads, have thought the best system for road making would be the breaking of the large stones into smaller, there can be no doubt: But, who has acted as well as thought? - Mr Macadam.

As to monies improperly voted to, or expended by, this gentleman, that is an account to be settled by Mr. M. and Mr. L. But, that Mr. Macadam was the first to act upon the new system, no one acquainted, for the last fifty years, with the metropolis and country of this great nation will hesitate to affirm. Then, "without grudging," let him have and wear his palm - and let honest John Bull, and all his family, add their generous acclamations - admiring our free country, where talent and enterprize are sure to meet encouragement and support, and to which the pages of the Monthly Magazine have amazingly contributed.

You perceive, Sir, Mr. Lacey scarcely touches one of the facts which I have communicated, through you, to the public, save and except the twenty-four stage-coaches which push the twenty four hours, heavily laden, with cutting narrow wheels, along the narrowest part of the street in Woburn. This, with a smile, affords Mr. Lacey an opportunity to "'invite me to take my stand on Blackfriars Bridge and, for ten minutes, during almost any time of the day, I may see twice twenty-four carriages pass and nearly all of them of a heavier description than stage-coaches, and many with as narrow wheels." This, I beg leave to inform Mr. Lacey, I have repeatedly done, and on Westminster Bridge too, and sincerely thank him for the recollection: for it at once makes the fact which I adduced in proof of the superiority of the Macadamizing system triumphant. I hope this truly odd way of meeting a fact will fix the attention of many, as they pass over the bridges; and they will then see, as in Woburn, and on along length of way, wherever this new mode may be adopted, in a little while broken moment and ruts, those great nuisances and impediments to comfort in travelling will be for ever done away: - to say nothing of the vast expense saved in wear and tear of carriages of all descriptions.

Your correspondent, in the 105th page, touches a string which vibrates through the whole body of commissioners of highways or byways, in and out of London; and which, if I be not-mistaken, will have a tenfold shock, when receipts and expenditure of turnpike gates, as already moved, become matters of investigation in a committee of the House of Commons. With that correspondent I cordially unite in saying, it is indeed strange, that the principles of the new system, being so plain and obvious, should meet with any opposition - But is there not a case for this opposition? We shall see.

I will remember some years ago when professional duties used to call me annually to your great city, passing frequently, in a light carriage the whole length of Holborn exclaiming "Oh! these miserable, noisy, comfort-destroying, stones! How many invalids have you shook and hastened to their tombs!" What lacerations and tortures to the most useful of animals, the horse, has the smooth and often irregular surface of Holborn-hill inflicted! No street, from top to bottom, for its width, is so well adapted for the new system.

We all remember with what the gaslight have to contend. Here and there was mounted a blazing lamp and people as they approached exclaimed "Bless me, what's that?" until by the gradual advance, prejudice and opposition fled before them as the darkness or error always flies before the light of truth, and the system becomes universally adopted.

So I would say having this luminous example before us, to Mr Macadam and everyone, who in any way, can do good, "nildesperandum!" [Do not despair.]

M. Castleden

Appendix 2

An Early Anonymous Poem, 1829

This anonymous poem was printed in the Congregational Magazine, of January 1829. Could this have been George Castleden's first published work, aged 25? It is extremely similar to his style. The other candidate is Benjamin Wiffen, brother of the noted Quaker poet, Jeremiah.

Sweet Woburn. Poetry – One of the Scenes of my Childhood.

"I ask but his, again to rove
Through scenes my youth has known before."

Though round thee, sweet Woburn, no streamlet is flowing,
By whose verdant margin the wand'rer may stray,
And forget, on his frame as cool zephyrs are blowing,
The toils and fatigues of a wearisome day:

Though by thick planted woods all thy prospects are bounded,
Where rude Nature reigns, unassisted by Art,
While by furze-cover'd heaths the deep valley's surrounded –
The sand-skirted scene is still dear to my heart.

For oft in these woods, where the larches are bending
Their slender-form'd boughs to each breathe of wind,
Whilst Nature, her softness and majesty blending,
The woodbine around the huge oak has entwin'd –

With my friend, or my book, have I joyously wander'd,
Now climbing the hill, now descending the dale,
The paths, that through beds of wild-flowers meander'd,
To catch the rich balm of the health-breathing gale.

Here, too, have I watch'd the sun's glorious dawning,
From its curtain'd pavilion of clouds in the east,
And at eve, from the spot where I stood in the morning,

Have seen its last rays as it sank in the west.

And sweet are the visions of memory now,
As I rove once again through thy fir-planted dell;
For they give a new charm to the scenes which I love,
On past deeds of my childhood as fondly they dwell.

My heart with the warmest affection is glowing,
As they paint, with a force that must speak to the soul,
Those friends, who the kindest attention bestowing,
Have smooth'd the rough path of scholastic control.

And can time ever cause the rememb'rance to cease;
Can kindness like theirs be effac'd from my heart,
Or will ever the tide of affection decrease,
For friends, who still bear in my trials a part.

No, feint when that heart's latest pulses are beating –
When the angel of death shall ov'r-shadow my bed,
As the moments of life shall be rapidly fleeting,
Their mem'ry shall share the last tear that is shed.

β.

Appendix 3

A Christmas Poem, 1871

In 2015, an 1870's Victorian scrapbook passed through an auction house in Bedford, containing this hand-written poem by George Castleden:

A Christmas Carol - Now and Then
  Now 'Jim' is gone! his postboy day
  Has posted from our sight;
  Sealed up by death, in sleep recline
  In our graveyard's cold night

  In Woburn's 'go', now long ago
  When 'Jim' was in his prime
  Then oft a scene in our town dream
  Would prompt a parish rhyme

  This Then is done; the years have run!
  'Jim' brought us weal and woe:
  At Christmas time, I wrote a rhyme
  Which won him coin also

  Now in this year of slaughters drear
  I sing again the post;
  Not the lane one which lit our Town
  But letters, quite a host!

  Now while flash, dash and crash the course
  Of Science steam and sin
  Amid it still the postboy calls
  And bids us groan or grin

  Once more the Boxing day time comes round
  And in revolving time
  Echo repeats from Stephens words –
  'Make Jim a bit of rhyme'
  I see the man of song and wit

I hear his humour still
Hamped by quaint fun our Master won
Much neighbourly good will

Our fathers liked to hear him joke
And at the cosy Sun
Midst curling smoke, he mirth awoke
Caused laughters merry din.

Hic jacet scribes his set of sun
It tells of deaths dark shore
At ninety his seed[?] life was done
He slept to wake no more!

Another Master holds the post
Post novelties arise
Delivered double cause some trouble
Bags, Hamper and cards surprise

Now with our then we link again
Wild lightning from the sky
By mystic art performs its part
And sparks talk sparkishly

A riddle now - It soundly sleeps
Anon it wakes and roars
It whispers softly down the street
And thunders on the doors?

But I must stay, this Christmas Day
All Christians should remember
For all shall never see the twain
Again in Old December

Then give a coin: Our wish for home
Health, peace, goodwill to men
May evil fly, may joy be known
So signs
George Castleden, George Street, Woburn, 14 January 1871.

A previous series of Carols from 1842 to 1855 are in existence and may someday appear.

Sources & Acknowledgements

Major sources of information:

Barwell, W. M., A Short History of the Woburn Congregational Church, Fisher & Sons, 1899.

Bates, A., Directory of Stage Coach Services of 1836, David & Charles, 1969.

Bedfordshire Archives & Records Service, Refs.: HN10/273/DUKE1-4, Z206/44-45, Z768, R3/2151, R3/2183, R3/2858, R3/2860, R3/2966, R3/3548 & R3/4147.

The British Newspapers Archives, online.

Burne, P., The Teetotaler's Companion, A Hall & Co., 1847.

Byrne, C. & Woods, S., Woburn Congregational Church Book, 1791-1837, Bedfordshire Record Office, 1983.

Calder, G. E., The History of Eggington, White Crescent Press, 1986.

The Congregational Magazine, annual, 1818 & 1819.

The Congregational Year Book, annual, 1848.

Conisbee, L. R., Faint Pencillings of the Bedfordshire Scene, Bedfordshire Magazine, Crescent Press, Aut. 1967.

Croft W., Sketch of the Life and Character of the Late John, Duke of Bedford, 1839.

Dodd, S, The Town of Woburn, its Abbey and Vicinity, Dodd, 1818.

The Evangelical Magazine, annual, 1801, 1828, & 1855.

Greaves, D., Personal recollections, e-mail to author, 2017.

House of Lords, Divorce & Matrimonial Causes Court, Trials, Litigation, etc., House of Lords, 1860.

Parry, J. D., Woburn and its Abbey, Longman, Rees, Orme, Brown & Green, 1831.

Spavins, K. & Applin, A., The Book of Woburn, Barracuda Books, 1983.

Stell, Christopher, Non-Conformist Chapels & Meeting Houses - Eastern England, English Heritage, 2002.

Tibbutt, H. G., A Woburn Story, Bedfordshire Magazine, Crescent Press, Sum. 1960.

Tibbutt, H. G., Hockliffe & Eggington Congregational Church 1809-

1959, Hockliffe Congregational Church, 1959.
   West Sussex Record Office, Ref.: COBDEN/279

I would like to thank the following institutions and individuals for their assistance in this project, for giving time, information, expertise or advice:
   Ampthillimages.com - J. Clark
   The Bedfordshire Archives & Records Service
   The Bedford Heritage Library
   The British Library
   J. Castleden
   Bryan Dunleavy - Magic Flute Publishing
   Google Books
   Hughenden Manor - The National Trust
   T. Slater
   The Woburn Abbey Archives
   The U.S. Supreme Court Library, Washington, USA
   Woburn Public Library, Massachusetts, USA
   The Archives of the University of California, Los Angeles, USA
   The West Sussex Record Office
   Dr Williams's Library of Protestant Dissent, London
   The Woburn Heritage Centre

   ... and the online British Newspapers Archives (Findmypast & British Library partnership), without whom...

Index

to George Castleden's Published Letters

From the following publications:
BL = Bell's Life in London
BM = Bedford(shire) Mercury
BD = Bedfordshire Magazine
BT = Beds Times
CC = Chelmsford Chronicle
CP = Cambridge Independent Press
DC = Dunstable Chronicle
EM = Evangelical Magazine
HM = Hertford Mercury
LB = Leighton Buzzard Observer
LN = London Nonconformist
LT = Luton Times
NH = Northampton Herald
NM = Northampton Mercury
SM = Stamford Mercury

Date	Paper	Content	Author	Format
Chapter 1				
19/07/1840	BL	Cricket match, Aspley v Biggleswade	-	News
31/07/1841	SM	Queen Victoria at Woburn	-	News
31/07/1841	BM	Queen Victoria at Woburn	-	News
21/08/1841	NH	"Woburn Park" criticism	-	News
28/08/1841	BM	Reply to criticism of "Woburn Park"	Q, but not in the corner	Letter
28/08/1841	HM	Review of "Woburn Park"	-	News
09/04/1842	NM	Advert for "Conscience"	-	Advert
01/06/1844	NM	Temperance Speech at Woburn by Dr Lees	-	News

07/02/1846	NM	Description of Woburn Church	W.A.	Letter
14/02/1846	NM	Reply to description of Woburn Church	Castleden	Letter
22/08/1846	NM	Potato Disease	Castleden	Letter
05/12/1846	NM	The People's Education	Castleden	Letter
13/02/1847	NM	Ireland No.1	Castleden	Letter
20/02/1847	NM	Ireland No.2	Castleden	Letter
27/02/1847	NM	Ireland No.3	Castleden	Letter
13/03/1847	NM	The Government Education Scheme	Castleden	Letter
10/04/1847	NM	The Government Education Scheme	Castleden	Letter
13/11/1847	NM	Note to Correspondents	Editor	Letter
03/06/1848	NM	Correcting Woburn Chartists Meeting report	Castleden	Letter
25/11/1848	CP	Burial of Rev. Michael Castleden	-	News
03/02/1849	NM	Woburn Book Society	Castleden	Letter
23/03/1850	NM	"Lays of Home" advert	Castleden	Advert
16/11/1850	NM	Committee for visit to London Grand Exhibition	-	News
26/04/1851	BM	Local cottage owners	Castleden	Letter
12/11/1851	LN	Advert for "Lays No.3"	-	Advert
15/11/1851	NM	At lecture on John Howard	-	News
21/08/1852	CP	Sheep Lane Chapel	Castleden	News
29/10/1853	BM	A Thought on the Grasp after Human Knowledge	Castleden	Poem
19/11/1853	BM	Russian succession	Castleden	Letter
24/12/1853	BM	Education systems	Castleden	Letter
24/12/1853	BM	Michael Castleden & Spirit Rapping	Castleden	Letter
31/12/1853	BM	Christmas	Castleden	Letter
28/01/1854	CP	Accounts of Woburn Chapel audited	-	News
28/01/1854	BM	Rev. Andrews book published	-	Advert
01/04/1854	BM	Partition of Turkey	Castleden	Letter
15/04/1854	BM	Russian Policy	Castleden	Letter

27/05/1854	BM	A Long walk	Castleden	Letter
22/07/1854	BM	"Woburn Exhibition" book	Castleden	Advert
05/08/1854	CP	Rebuilding of Woburn Chapel	-	News
28/10/1854	BM	Cholera outbreak	Castleden	Letter
18/11/1854	BM	Dark November Days Thought	Castleden	Poem
02/12/1854	BM	Last worship in temporary chapel in Town Hall	Castleden	News
13/01/1855	BM	Woburn Mechanics Institute	Castleden	Letter
17/02/1855	BM	What of Politics?	Castleden	Letter
24/02/1855	BM	A Night Thought	Castleden	Poem
10/03/1855	BM	Death!	Castleden	Letter
17/03/1855	BM	Russia & her spy system	Castleden	Letter
19/05/1855	BM	Tribute to Sir Robert Inglis	Castleden	Letter
30/06/1855	BM	Bedfordshire Reformatory School	Castleden	Poem
14/07/1855	BM	Education Questions	Castleden	Letter
04/08/1855	BM	Martyrs Monument, at Nunhead	Castleden	Poem
00/11/1855	EM	Biography of Michael Castleden	Castleden	Letter
03/11/1855	BM	The Lower Orders	Castleden	Letter
29/12/1855	BM	Tyndal and the English Bible	Castleden	Letter
Chapter 2				
Date	Paper	Content	Author	Format
12/01/1856	BM	An Anecdote	Castleden	Poem
22/03/1856	BM	Ruin! Delinquent bankers	Castleden	Letter
12/04/1856	BT	Castleden does Jury service	-	News
06/06/1856	CC	Gambling on trials	Castleden	Letter
12/07/1856	BM	Murderer Palmer's Last Words	Castleden	Letter
12/07/1856	BM	The Peace Rejoicings	Castleden	Poem
16/08/1856	BM	Death of Mrs Turney & depression	Castleden	News
11/10/1856	CP	Woburn Agricultural meeting	Castleden	Letter
11/04/1857	BM	Past Elections	Castleden	Letter
16/05/1857	BM	Voting and ballots	Castleden	Letter

23/05/1857	BM	Voting and ballots	Audi Alteram Partem	Letter
30/05/1857	BM	Voting and ballots	Castleden	Letter
06/06/1857	BM	Voting and ballots	Audi Alteram Partem	Letter
13/06/1857	BM	Voting and ballots	Castleden	Letter
15/08/1857	BM	Rev. Sleigh leaves Hockliffe	-	News
26/09/1857	BM	India. British Vengeance	Castleden	Letter
07/12/1857	BM	Wreck of the Dunbar	Castleden	Poem
09/01/1858	DC	Dunstable Chapel tea meeting	Castleden	News
18/01/1858	BM	Monster	Castleden	Letter
08/02/1858	BM	Death's Doings	Castleden	Letter
08/02/1858	BM	India	Castleden	Letter
22/03/1858	BM	South Sea Bubble	Castleden	Letter
17/05/1858	BM	Spurgeon preaching	Castleden	Letter
24/05/1858	BM	Spurgeon preaching	A Reading Reformer	Letter
31/05/1858	BM	Spurgeon preaching	Castleden	Letter
07/06/1858	BM	Spurgeon preaching	A Reading Reformer	Letter
19/07/1858	BM	London City Mission	Castleden	News
19/07/1858	BM	Starlings	Castleden	Poem
09/08/1858	BM	Two historic Woburn Cricket games	Castleden	Letter
13/09/1858	BM	Confusion	Castleden	Letter
30/10/1858	DC	Woburn chapel expenses	Castleden	News
22/11/1858	BM	Secret voting	Castleden	Letter
29/11/1858	LT & DC	Hockliffe Chapel	Castleden?	News
29/11/1858	BM	Secrecy of the Press	Castleden	Letter
29/11/1858	BM	Fundraising for Hockliffe Chapel	-	News
18/12/1858	DC	Sheep Lane, Potsgrove Chapel [and also 20/12/1858 BM]	Castleden	Letter
05/02/1859	DC	Poem on Burns [and also 07/02/1859 BM]	Castleden	Poem

05/03/1859	DC	Lord Palmerstone's speech on Europe [and also 07/03/1859 BM]	Castleden	Letter
04/04/1859	BM	Eggington British School	Castleden	News
11/04/1859	BM	The Reform Match	Castleden	Letter
25/04/1859	BM	Voting and ballots	Castleden	Letter
23/05/1859	BM	Voting and ballots	Castleden	Letter
28/05/1859	BT	Reply to Castleden	A Conservative	Letter
25/06/1859	DC	A day at Dunstable	Castleden	Letter
06/08/1859	DC	Woburn Chapel Holiday	Castleden	Letter
13/08/1859	DC	Hockliffe Sunday School anniversary	-	News
17/09/1895	DC	Woburn Missionary leaves	Castleden	News
05/11/1859	DC	Thoughts over the Grave of a Labouring Man, Potsgrove	Castleden	Poem
24/12/1859	DC	Eggington Sunday School	-	Advert
16/01/1860	BM	Coroners Inquests	Castleden	Letter
31/03/1860	DC	Eggington British School	Castleden	Letter
09/06/1860	DC	Dunstable Choral Society performs in Woburn	Castleden	News
26/01/1861	BM	New chapel, Queen Street, Hockliffe	-	News
19/04/1862	BM	Merrimac and the Monitor: Peace	Castleden	Letter
17/05/1862	BM	Hymn for the opening of the Exhibition	Castleden	Poem
21/06/1862	BM	Murder of the Innocents	Castleden	Letter
19/07/1862	BM	Sunday School Holiday	Castleden	News
22/11/1862	BM	The American Civil War	Castleden	Letter
10/01/1863	BM	Two Stuart Poets, Milton - Butler	Castleden	Poem
10/01/1863	BM	Juryman [and also 10/01/1863 BT]	-	News
16/03/1863	BM	Festivities for marriage of Princess Alexandra	Castleden	News
14/04/1863	LB	Tea drinking meeting at Chapel	-	News
01/08/1863	BM	Crimes committed against Poland by Europe	Castleden	Letter

Date	Paper	Content	Author	Format
29/08/1863	BM	A Rambler's Prose - A Hertfordshire Celebrity	Castleden	Letter
10/10/1863	BM	Woburn Bygones 1 - Cricket	Castleden	Letter
12/10/1863	BM	A Bedford Cemetery Visit	Castleden	Letter
07/11/1863	BM	The American Civil War	Castleden	Letter
26/12/1863	BM	Penny Readings	Castleden	News
28/12/1863	BM	A Christmas Strain	Castleden	Poem
05/11/1864	BT	New church for Woburn	-	News
08/04/1865	BM	Illiberality to Non-conformists	Castleden	Letter
06/01/1866	BM	Debt at Woburn Chapel	-	News
24/11/1866	BM	Things in America	Castleden	Letter
08/12/1866	BM	London City Mission meeting at Woburn	-	News
02/02/1867	BM	Presentation to Rev. James Andrews	-	News
27/04/1867	BM	Tea meeting at Woburn Chapel	-	News
11/09/1869	BT	Memories of a church collection in 1812	Castleden	Letter
Chapter 3				
Date	Paper	Content	Author	Format
13/12/1870	BT	Woburn Bible Society	Castleden	News
25/04/1871	LB	Local Committees & Boards	Castleden	Letter
30/12/1871	LT	Penny Readings at Woburn	Castleden	News
18/06/1872	BT	New Woburn Liberal Committee	-	News
22/06/1872	BT	Civic reception for Duke of Bedford declined	-	News
25/06/1872	LB	Liberal Committee	Castleden	Letter
29/06/1872	BM	The Rev. Brown	Castleden	Letter
02/07/1872	LB	Beds Election	Castleden	Letter
03/12/1872	LB	Papacy	Castleden	Letter
10/12/1872	LB	Papacy reply	Ryland	Letter
14/12/1872	BT	Letter not suitable	Editor	Letter
17/12/1872	LB	Papacy reply	Castleden	Letter
24/12/1872	LB	Papacy reply	A Former Resident	Letter

31/12/1872	LB	Papacy reply	A Former Resident	Letter
15/02/1873	BT	Woburn School Board	-	News
18/03/1873	LB	Penny Readings	Castleden	Letter
13/05/1873	LB	Bunyan Statue	Castleden	Poem
27/05/1873	LB	School Board new	Castleden	Letter
03/06/1873	LB	Queen Victoria's Birthday	Castleden	Poem
10/06/1873	LB	Death Toll - Prince Frederick of Hesse	Castleden	Poem
24/06/1873	LB	Woburn Park flowers	Castleden	Poem
05/07/1873	BT	Death of George Rock	-	News
29/07/1873	LB	Death of the Bishop of Winchester	Castleden	Poem
12/08/1873	LB	The Wigan Rail Crash	Castleden	Poem
12/08/1873	LB	Sunday School Holiday	Castleden	News
26/08/1873	LB	Streets of London	Castleden	Poem
09/09/1873	LB	Education - Voluntary v Compulsory	Castleden	Letter
16/09/1873	LB	Education - Voluntary v Compulsory	C. B. S	Letter
23/09/1873	LB	Education - Voluntary v Compulsory	Castleden	Letter
18/10/1873	BM	Ridgmont Chapel anniversary	Castleden	News
23/12/1873	LB	London fog	Castleden	Poem
30/12/1873	LB	Christmas	Castleden	Poem
20/01/1874	LB	West Haddon Tragedy - Inquests	Castleden	Letter
03/02/1874	LB	Duke of Edinburgh marries Grand Duchess Marie	Castleden	Poem
17/02/1874	LB	Last election	Castleden	Poem
10/03/1874	LB	Woburn meeting of London City Mission	Castleden	News
17/03/1874	LB	Home-Coming of their Royal Highnesses	Castleden	Poem
24/03/1874	LB	Elections & Ballots	Castleden	Letter
31/03/1874	LB	Beer in elections	Castleden	Letter
19/05/1874	LB	Education	Castleden	Letter
26/05/1874	LB	May	Castleden	Poem

02/06/1874	LB	Whitsun	Castleden	Poem
16/06/1874	LB	Unveiling the Bunyan Statue in Bedford	Castleden	Letter
30/06/1874	LB	Local Boards	Castleden	Letter
21/07/1874	LB	Woburn Park	Castleden	Poem
18/08/1874	LB	Betsy Leatherland of Tring	Castleden	Poem
25/08/1874	LB	Endowed Schools Bill	Castleden	Letter
08/09/1874	LB	Ballard of Old Back Lane, Woburn	Castleden	Poem
29/09/1874	LB	Goodbye to Swallows	Castleden	Poem
06/10/1874	LB	Russell speech at Woburn	Castleden	Letter
20/10/1874	LB	Places in Woburn	Castleden	Poem
27/10/1874	LB	Criticism	Censor	Letter
10/11/1874	LB	Leaves	Castleden	Poem
10/11/1874	LB	Criticism reply	Castleden	Letter
17/11/1874	LB	Science	Castleden	Poem
24/11/1874	LB	Popedom	Castleden	Letter
01/12/1874	LB	Criticism	An Awe-struck Admirer	Poem
05/01/1874	LB	Criticism	Montigopeligo Shandrigodos	Poem
12/01/1875	LB	Christmas	Castleden	Poem
12/01/1875	LB	Reply to critics	Castleden	Letter
26/01/1875	LB	Criticism	Awe-struck Admirer	Poem
26/01/1875	LB	Support	A Delighted One	
02/02/1875	LB	Criticism	H.	Poem
02/02/1875	LB	Gas-light supply at Woburn	Castleden	Letter
10/04/1875	LB	Woburn meeting for London City Mission	-	News
18/05/1875	LB	Woburn Union	Castleden	Letter
01/06/1875	LB	Leighton Exhibition	Castleden	Poem
08/06/1875	LB	Queen Victoria's Birthday	Castleden	Poem
22/06/1875	LB	Leighton Buzzard show	Castleden	Poem
29/06/1875	LB	A Woburn Week	Castleden	Letter

06/07/1875	LB	Death of Cox, of Speedwell Farm	Castleden	Poem
06/07/1875	LB	Criticism	A Bookman	Letter
20/07/1875	LB	Criticism	Eye Bright [Castleden?]	Letter
20/07/1875	LB	Woburn Sheep Shearing	Castleden	Letter
27/07/1875	LB	Reply to criticism	Castleden	Letter
27/07/1875	LB	Woburn Bazaar	Castleden	Letter
17/08/1875	LB	Memories and Science	Castleden	Poem
24/08/1875	LB	Gardening	Castleden	Poem
24/08/1875	LB	The Sun Beam Company	Castleden	Poem
07/09/1875	LB	Going to Bedford	Castleden	Poem
14/09/1875	LB	Temperance	Castleden	Poem
14/09/1875	LB	Sun's Rays	Castleden	Letter
21/09/1875	LB	To OXY	Castleden	Poem
28/09/1875	LB	Goodbye to Swallows	Castleden	Poem
05/10/1875	LB	Criticism	J. H.	Poem
12/10/1875	LB	Criticism reply	Castleden	Letter
26/10/1875	LB	October	Castleden	Poem
26/10/1875	LB	Woburn in darkness	Castleden	Letter
02/11/1875	LB	To OXY	Castleden	Poem
30/11/1875	LB	The Sun Beam Company	Castleden	Letter
21/12/1875	LB	Home & Foreign Missions	Castleden	Letter
28/12/1875	LB	Expecting Poem	Goose's Quill	Letter
Chapter 4				
Date	Paper	Content	Author	Format
11/01/1876	LB	School Board election	Castleden	Letter
18/01/1876	LB	Independent Chapel Annual Tea	Castleden	News
15/02/1876	LB	School Board election	Castleden	Letter
22/02/1876	LB	School Board Reply	A Small Ratepayer	Letter
29/02/1876	LB	School Board Reply	Castleden	Letter
02/05/1876	LB	Woburn Almshouses	Castleden	Letter
23/05/1876	LB	Death of Charles Inwood (OXY)	Castleden	Poem

23/05/1876	LB	East wind	Castleden	Poem
06/06/1876	LB	Queen's Birthday Royal Memory	Castleden	Poem
27/06/1876	LB	Death of Abdul Aziz	Castleden	Poem
04/07/1876	LB	Woburn Park	Castleden	Poem
19/09/1876	LB	Turkish atrocities	Castleden	Letter
30/09/1876	LB	Turkish atrocities [and also 03/10/1876 LB]	Castleden	News
10/10/1876	LB	Turkish atrocities	Castleden	Letter
06/03/1877	LB	Miss Russell's death	Castleden	Letter
26/06/1877	LB	Poem to L. R. S	Castleden	Poem
17/07/1877	LB	Education	Castleden	Letter
11/09/1877	LB	Lines on Death of a Leightonian Cricketer	Castleden	Poem
27/11/1877	LB	In defence of the Russells	Castleden	Letter
01/01/1878	LB	War in the East coming	Castleden	Letter
08/01/1878	LB	Supporting Castleden	J. Summerford	Letter
08/01/1878	LB	War in the East coming	Castleden	Letter
15/01/1878	LB	War in the East coming reply	Edward Franklin	Letter
22/01/1878	LB	War in the East coming reply	Castleden	Letter
29/01/1878	LB	War in the East coming reply	Edward Franklin	Letter
05/02/1878	LB	Letter from Castleden received but omitted	Editor	
16/04/1878	LB	War in the East coming reply	Englishman & then a Conservative [Franklin]	Letter
23/04/1878	LB	War in the East coming reply	Englishman & War Hater [Castleden]	Letter
07/05/1878	LB	War in the East coming reply	Edward Franklin	Letter
21/05/1878	LB	War in the East coming reply	Englishman & War Hater [Castleden]	Letter
13/08/1878	LB	Nonconformists meddling in Eastern problem	Minnie	Letter

25/01/1879	BM	Death of Mrs Buckett of Woburn	-	News
29/04/1879	LB	Gladstone	Castleden	Acrostic
13/05/1879	LB	Gladstone criticism	W	Acrostic
20/05/1879	LB	Zulu war	Castleden	Poem
07/06/1879	BM	Children's Tea provided by Castleden on his birthday	-	News
01/07/1879	LB	Bonapart	Castleden	Poem
08/07/1879	LB	Zulus	Castleden	Poem
15/07/1879	LB	Criticism	A Constant Reader	Letter
22/07/1879	LB	Napoleon	Castleden	Poem
19/08/1879	LB	Storm at Woburn on 2-3rd August	Castleden	Poem
09/09/1879	LB	Gladstone's speech at St Pancras	Castleden	Poem
23/09/1879	LB	Zulu War	Castleden	Letter
30/09/1879	LB	Zulu War reply	Edward Franklin	Letter
07/10/1879	LB	Zulu War reply	Castleden	Letter
14/10/1879	LB	Zulu War reply	Edward Franklin	Letter
21/10/1879	LB	Zulu War reply	Castleden	Letter
04/11/1879	LB	Zulu War reply	A Liberal	Letter
04/11/1879	LB	Zulu War reply	Edward Franklin	Letter
11/11/1879	LB	Zulu War reply	Castleden	Letter
29/11/1879	CIP	An American at Woburn	C. N.	Letter
02/12/1879	LB	Old Age	Castleden	Poem
06/01/1880	LB	The Tay Bridge Rail Accident	Castleden	Poem
16/03/1880	LB	Whig or Tory	Castleden	Letter
16/03/1880	LB	An Election Rhyme	Castleden	Poem
23/03/1880	LB	Woburn, Mass.	Castleden	Letter
30/03/1880	LB	Queen goes away	Castleden	Poem
13/04/1880	LB	Polling Day now and then	Castleden	Letter
13/04/1880	LB	Charles Russell returns to Woburn	Castleden	Letter
13/04/1880	LB	Charles Russell thanks	George Russell	Letter

20/04/1880	LB	Election Incidents	Castleden	Letter
27/04/1880	LB	Reply to Election Incidents	Edward Franklin	Letter
27/04/1880	LB	Bradlaugh acrostic	A. M. N,	Poem
04/05/1880	LB	Election	Castleden	Letter
04/05/1880	LB	Woburn, Mass.	Castleden	Letter
18/05/1880	LB	May Morn in Woburn Park	Castleden	Poem
25/05/1880	LB	Atheists	Castleden	Poem
01/06/1880	LB	Liberal Franklin dead	Castleden	Poem
01/06/1880	LB	Queen Victoria's Birthday	Castleden	Poem
08/06/1880	LB	Tories in Woburn	Castleden	Letter
15/06/1880	LB	Conservatives reply	Edward Franklin	Letter
22/06/1880	LB	Elections	Castleden	Poem
29/06/1880	LB	Bradlaugh Lock	Castleden	Letter
06/07/1880	LB	Bradlaugh Lock reply	Edward Franklin	Letter
13/07/1880	LB	Election Corruption	Castleden	Letter
03/08/1880	LB	Election Corruption	Castleden	Letter
03/08/1880	LB	Lines on a Centenary Address to Sunday School	Castleden	Poem
17/08/1880	LB	The Afghan War	Castleden	Letter
17/08/1880	LB	What is church?	Castleden	Letter
24/08/1880	LB	What is church reply	Nemo	Letter
31/08/1880	LB	What is church reply	Castleden	Letter
07/09/1880	LB	The Afghan War	Castleden	Letter
05/10/1880	LB	Cost of bread and meat	Castleden	Letter
12/10/1880	LB	Election corruption	Castleden	Letter
12/10/1880	LB	Mr Chapman dead	Castleden	Letter
19/10/1880	LB	Mr Chapman dead	Castleden	Poem
21/12/1880	LB	Ireland	Castleden	Poem
Chapter 5				
Date	Paper	Content	Author	Format
11/01/1881	LB	Boycotting Ireland	Castleden	Poem
18/01/1881	LB	Woburn Park	Castleden	Poem

25/01/1881	LB	Winter	Castleden	Poem
01/02/1881	LB	First English Parliament	Castleden	Poem
08/02/1881	LB	First English Parliament P.S.	Castleden	Poem
01/03/1881	LB	The Woburn Whig	Edward Franklin	Letter
08/03/1881	LB	Unjust War	Castleden	Letter
22/03/1881	LB	War	Castleden	Letter
29/03/1881	LB	Burglary at Hockliffe range	Castleden	Poem
29/03/1881	LB	School board	Castleden	Letter
05/04/1881	LB	Printing Press	Castleden	Poem
12/04/1881	LB	Tribute to Charles Read	Castleden	Poem
19/04/1881	LB	Death of Earl Beaconsfield	Castleden	Poem
19/04/1881	LB	Remembering death of Michael Castleden	-	News
26/04/1881	LB	Thoughts on News	Castleden	Letter
03/05/1881	LB	Burial of Beaconsfield	Castleden	Poem
03/05/1881	LB	Ridgmont School Board	Castleden	Letter
03/05/1881	LB	Rough Rhymes	Dolorosus et Acerbus	Letter
10/05/1881	LB	Correcting previous Rough Rhymes letter	Dolorosus et Acerbus	Letter
17/05/1881	LB	Rough Rhymes reply	Castleden	Letter
24/05/1881	LB	Public opinion	Castleden	Letter
31/05/1881	LB	Queen Victoria's Birthday	Castleden	Poem
07/06/1881	LB	William Hensmen's obituary	Castleden	News
21/06/1881	LB	Australian Flowers	Castleden	Poem
05/07/1881	LB	On the Comet	Castleden	Poem
12/07/1881	LB	Attempted assassination of U.S. President	Castleden	Poem
26/07/1881	LB	Death of Dean Stanley	Castleden	Poem
26/07/1881	LB	Woburn, Mass.	Castleden	Letter
02/08/1881	LB	Woburn, Mass.	Castleden	Letter
16/08/1881	LB	Situation in Africa	Edward Franklin	Letter
23/08/1881	LB	Woburn, Mass.	Castleden	Letter
30/08/1881	LB	Death	Castleden	Poem
13/09/1881	LB	Steam v. Electricity	Castleden	Letter

Date	Paper	Content	Author	Format
20/09/1881	LB	Bottling of Sunbeams	Castleden	Letter
27/09/1881	LB	Death of U.S. President	Castleden	Poem
04/10/1881	LB	Sister Queens	Castleden	Poem
11/10/1881	LB	Woburn, Mass.	Castleden	Letter
25/10/1881	LB	U.S. President	Castleden	Poem
25/10/1881	LB	Storm at Woburn	Castleden	Letter
08/11/1881	LB	Large Ash tree blown down at Woburn	Castleden	Poem
15/11/1881	LB	Gladstone Acrostic	Castleden	Acrostic
22/11/1881	LB	Woburn, Mass.	Castleden	Letter
29/11/1881	LB	Political Outlook	Edward Franklin	Letter
06/12/1881	LB	Ireland's Problem	Castleden	Poem
06/12/1881	LB	Bribery Prosecutions	Castleden	Letter
13/12/1881	LB	Bribery	Castleden	Letter
13/12/1881	LB	Ireland reply	Edward Franklin	Letter
20/12/1881	LB	Accidents by Fire & Water	Castleden	Poem
27/12/1881	LB	Accidents by Air and Sky	Castleden	Poem
27/12/1881	LB	Ireland reply	Castleden	Letter
Chapter 6				
Date	Paper	Content	Author	Format
03/01/1882	LB	Ireland reply	Edward Franklin	Letter
10/01/1882	LB	Death of Alfred Smith, Woburn postman	Castleden	Poem
24/01/1882	LB	Sick Man's Friendly Society meeting	Castleden	Letter
24/01/1882	LB	Death of George Champney, Woburn, Mass.	Castleden	Letter
07/02/1882	LB	Death of George Champney, Woburn, Mass.	Castleden	Letter
21/02/1882	LB	Death of George Champney, Woburn, Mass.	Castleden	Poem
21/02/1882	LB	Woburn School Board Elections	Castleden	Letter

14/03/1882	LB	Queen Victoria survives an assassination attempt	Castleden	Poem
21/03/1882	LB	The Bradlaugh Block	Castleden	Letter
21/03/1882	LB	Buckingham Palace poem acknowledgement	Castleden	Letter
28/03/1882	LB	March Fair	Castleden	Poem
28/03/1882	LB	The Bradlaugh Block	Friday	Letter
28/03/1882	LB	The Bradlaugh Block	Edward Franklin	Letter
04/04/1882	LB	The Bradlaugh Block	Castleden	Leter
11/04/1882	LB	Cypress for the grave	Castleden	Poem
11/04/1882	LB	The Bradlaugh Block	Saturday	Letter
18/04/1882	LB	Obitual for Richard Gilpin	Castleden	Poem
25/04/1882	LB	Criticism of Castleden	Seneca's Shade	Letter
02/05/1882	LB	Reply on criticism	W. Odell	Letter
02/05/1882	LB	Reply on criticism	Castleden	Letter
09/05/1882	LB	Reply on criticism	Castleden	Letter
09/05/1882	LB	Reply on criticism	Seneca's Shade	Letter
16/05/1882	LB	Memory Lines	Castleden	Poem
16/05/1882	LB	Reply on criticism	Castleden	Letter
16/05/1882	LB	Rhododendron in Woburn Park	Castleden	Poem
30/05/1882	LB	Political Situation	Tasmetah	
06/06/1882	LB	Ireland's Problem	Castleden	Letter
13/06/1882	LB	Ireland's Problem reply	Edward Franklin	Letter
13/06/1882	LB	An American Leaflet	Castleden	News
20/06/1882	LB	On reading John Bright's Birmingham Speech	Castleden	Poem
20/06/1882	LB	Ireland's Problem reply	Castleden	Letter
27/06/1882	LB	Ireland's Problem reply	Edward Franklin	Letter
04/07/1882	LB	Local Mission news	[Castleden]	News
01/08/1882	LB	England and Australia - Ballad on Cricket and War	Castleden	Poem
08/08/1882	LB	Reporting on Boards	Castleden	Letter
08/08/1882	LB	Thoughts on War	Castleden	Letter

29/08/1882	LB	Death of a Neighbour	Castleden	Poem
29/08/1882	LB	County Representation	Castleden	Letter
05/09/1882	LB	Sudden Death at the Oval - Cricket	Castleden	Poem
10/10/1882	LB	Egypt's War	Castleden	Letter
07/11/1882	LB	Presentation to Drury-Lowe	Castleden	Letter
14/11/1882	LB	High Fir blown down in Woburn	Castleden	Poem
21/11/1882	LB	Catholic or Universal Church	Castleden	Letter
28/11/1882	LB	Woburn Bible Society	Castleden	Poem
28/11/1882	LB	Catholic or Universal Church reply	Delta	Letter
05/12/1882	LB	Catholic or Universal Church reply	Castleden	Letter
19/12/1882	LB	Catholic or Universal Church reply	Castleden	Letter
20/02/1883	LB	Woburn Sick Man's Friend Society	Castleden	Letter
20/03/1883	LB	Woburn Petition against the Affirmation Bill	Castleden	Letter
17/04/1883	LB	Parish Management	Castleden	Letter
24/07/1883	LB	Ireland's Troubles	Castleden	Letter
31/07/1883	LB	Ireland's Troubles reply	Edward Franklin	Letter
22/07/1884	LB	Rev. Andrews - 40 years at Woburn	-	News
09/09/1884	LB	Castleden - death notice	-	News
16/09/1884	LB	Castleden - burial	-	News
23/09/1884	LB	Castleden - Auction of possessions	-	Advert
29/12/1899	BT	Woburn Park quoted	-	News
12/01/1900	BT	Woburn Park quoted	-	News
02/11/1906	BT	Death of Florence Tyers	-	News
06/02/1942	BT	Woburn Park quoted	-	News
Sum. 1960	BD	Article on Woburn Congregationalists	H. G. Tibbutt	News
Aut. 1967	BD	Article on Bedfordshire poets, including Castleden	L. R. Conisbee	News